European Football

A FANS' HANDBOOK

THE ROUGH GUIDE

There are more than one hundred Rough Guide titles
covering destinations from Amsterdam to Zimbabwe

Forthcoming titles include
Bangkok • Barbados • Edinburgh •
Japan • Jordan • Syria

Rough Guide Reference Series
Classical Music • The Internet • Jazz • Opera
Reggae • Rock Music • World Music

Rough Guide Phrasebooks
Czech • French • German • Greek • Hindi & Urdu • Indonesian • Italian
Mandarian Chinese • Mexican Spanish • Polish • Portuguese
Russian • Spanish • Thai • Turkish • Vietnamese

Rough Guides on the Internet
http://www.roughguides.com/
http://www.hotwired.com/rough

Commissioning editor: Jonathan Buckley
Editor: Dan Goldstein
Design and layout: Dan Goldstein
Production: Judy Pang, Susanne Hillen, Link Hall, Andy Hilliard
Rough Guides Series editor: Mark Ellingham
All photography: Empics, Nottingham, England

....

The editors would like to thank: Ben Goldstein, Mike Hammond, Neil Jensen, David
    Padbury, Colin Panter, Janice Purath, Mark Walker, Pre Press Action (Ely), Margaret
    Doyle and, above all, thanks to Marysia and Maxim for those six-o-clock alarm calls.

This first edition published September 1997 by Rough Guides Ltd, I Mercer St, London
    WC2H 9QJ.

Distributed by the Penguin Group:
Penguin Books Ltd, 27 Wrights Lane, London W8 5TZ
Penguin Books USA Inc., 375 Hudson Street, New York 10014, USA
Penguin Books Australia Ltd, 487 Maroondah Highway, PO Box 257, Ringwood, Victoria
    3134, Australia
Penguin Books Canada Ltd, 10 Alcorn Avenue, Toronto, Ontario, Canada M4V 1E4
Penguin Books (NZ) Ltd, 182–190 Wairau Road, Auckland 10, New Zealand
Typeset to an original design by Dan Goldstein.
Printed in England by Clays Ltd, St Ives PLC
624pp - Includes index
A catalogue record for this book is available from the British Library
ISBN 1-85828-256-X

....

European Football

A FANS' HANDBOOK

THE ROUGH GUIDE

Written and researched by
Peterjon Cresswell and Simon Evans

Edited by
Dan Goldstein

THE ROUGH GUIDES

Contents

Contents *continued*

Introduction

The past decade has seen an explosion of interest in European football. In today's multimedia world, fans are no longer limited to watching games from their own domestic league. The expansion of the Champions' League and other European competitions has given us more and more games between the continent's top sides. And cheaper travel has made it easier for supporters to follow their team abroad. Why sit in hours of motorway traffic, driving from one end of England to the other, when you could book a flight to Milan or a train to Paris to catch a game?

A true European away trip is much more than simply travelling to the stadium and watching the match. But, until now, there has been no resource for the new breed of European football fan.

Conventional handbooks and encyclopedias offer stats and facts, but precious little insight. Tourist guidebooks will tell you that "football is a national passion" and that you can "find a game most Sundays".

But where? And which teams? Are they any good? What's the best way to the stadium? Where can you buy a ticket? How much will it cost? Where can you enjoy a beer before the match? And where can you buy a shirt afterwards?

This book has the answers. The product of more than two years' research across the continent, *The Rough Guide to European Football* covers more than 50 football destinations in 27 European countries. It features more than 100 club histories, 300 photographs and 750 bar, club, restaurant and hotel tips. In short, it is an essential companion to the modern European game.

For each country, we've given not just a history of the domestic game, but a run-down of its habits, its strengths and its weaknesses, its rivalries, its media.

Then, for each club, there's a guide not just to the team but to the stadium, its catchment area, its fan base, its shops and its bars – and the day-to-day practicalities of how a visiting fan can get to know them, within the inevitable constraints of limited time and money.

Obviously, no book of this size could cover every aspect of European football. This guide is intended as a handbook to the football culture of the continent's major soccer-playing cities, rather than a straightforward list of all the greatest names. As well as making for a more pleasurable read, this approach has enabled us to give details of lower-division grounds in many cities – venues which, while they may lack the glamour of the new super-stadia, are essential destinations for the visitor who really wants to get inside a nation's footballing life.

During our research we have met hundreds of football people – former players, coaches, agents, journalists, commentators and critics. But the people who contributed most to the finished article were the fans themselves – each one with a tale to tell or a song to sing, for nothing more than the price of a pint. Now we want anyone who uses this book to help us update it. Times change. Bars open and close. Clubs alter their colours, their names, their identities, sometimes even their towns. Write to us c/o The Rough Guides, tell us what you've discovered, and in return, we'll credit the best contributions in the next edition.

Peterjon Cresswell & Simon Evans, 1997

Acknowledgements

Peterjon Cresswell:

Tom Popper (New York Cosmos)
Steve Carlson (The Lakers)
Malcolm Carruthers
Isys Hungary
Paul Wootton and Associates
Carolyn Smith
Col
Dave Rimmer (Newcastle)
PC
Laci (Vasas)
John Wright (South London Bohemia)
John Elliott
Austin and Mary
Annie Gallop (Manchester United)
DS (Liverpool)
Chris Proud (Blackburn Rovers)
Gwynnie, Bones, H, Bill, Ells (Millwall)
Radovan Radosevics (Vojvodina)

Simon Evans:

Adam LeBor and Chris Condon (BIPC)
Magdi Kútás
Andy Lyons ('When Saturday Comes')
Brian Sturgess ('Soccer Investor')
Krisztina Máhr
The CompuServe Soccer Forum
The Red Munichs
Paul Woodhouse and Martin Heap
Marcus Laughton and Chris Bailey
The supporters of Burnley FC and Újpesti
TE
Gabriella for understanding and care
Most of all, to my father for introducing me
to the game and doing so much to
nurture my interest in it

Further reading

The Encyclopedia of World Soccer, Richard Henshaw (New Republic, 1979)
The Guinness Book of World Soccer, Guy Oliver (Guinness, 1995)
The Secret Life of Football, Alex Fynn and Lynton Guest (Macdonald, Queen Anne Press, 1989)
Out of Time, Alex Fynn and Lynton Guest (Pocket Books, 1994)
Soccer Revolution, Willy Meisl (Sportsman Book Club, 1956)
Soccer Nemesis, Brian Glanville (Secker and Warburg, 1955)
Soccer, A Panorama, Brian Glanville (Eyre and Spottiswoode, 1969)
The Simplest Game, Paul Gardner (Collier, 1994)
Football, Violence and Social Identity, ed. Richard Giulianotti, Norman Bonney and Mike
    Hepworth (Routledge, 1994)
The Football Grounds of Europe, Simon Inglis (Collins Willow, 1990)
Football, Fussball, Voetbal, The European Game 1956-Euro '96, Colin Cameron (BBC, 1995)
Soccer The World Game, Geoffrey Green (Phoenix House, 1953)
Hockings' European Cups, Ron Hockings (Kenneth Mason, 1990)
Football Against The Enemy, Simon Kuper (Phoenix, 1994)
The European Football Yearbook, ed. Mike Hammond (Sports Projects, annual)

Austria

The Austrians played a pivotal rôle in the development of the European game. They instigated the forerunners of major club and international competitions, eagerly absorbed new tactical ideas, and embraced professionalism at a time when, across much of Europe, football was essentially the province of well-to-do amateurism.

Today they have little to show for their earlier innovation, save for an excellent stadium which, the Austrians hope, will enable them to make a successful bid to co-host the 2004 European Championship with Hungary. Austria's national side has never reached the final of a major tournament, and no Austrian club has ever won a modern European trophy. In one of Europe's most affluent countries, many football clubs manage little more than a hand-to-mouth existence, staggering from the arms of one sponsor to the next – and from one unwelcoming town to another – in the hope of finding their niche.

Austria's illustrious footballing past was initiated by the work of one man: Hugo Meisl. A Jewish bank clerk enamoured with English culture and a strange new ball game that came with it, Meisl dedicated his life not just to the development of the domestic game in Austria, but to furthering the cause of international football. English workers had founded Vienna's first two football clubs, First Vienna FC and Vienna Cricket & Football Club, at the turn of the century. Meisl became a member of the latter, then in 1911 helped to found a new branch of it, Wiener Amateure-Sportverein, known simply as Amateure and later to become FK Austria. Other clubs quickly sprang up, competing in a series of tournaments open only to teams from Vienna. (Despite early interest elsewhere, particularly in Graz, provincial clubs

Waltz on – Salzburg inspired a nation in '94

were not allowed into the Austrian league until after 1945.)

On the international front, Meisl instigated Austria's football rivalry with Hungary, helping to organise the first meeting between the two countries – and the first international match to be played in continental Europe – in 1902. Ten years later Meisl invited the English coach Jimmy Hogan to Vienna. Hogan, who would later coach the Hungarians with such devastating results, preached his short passing game to a receptive audience, creating what would become known as the Danubian style in which a team's forward line was complemented by wide half-backs and an attacking centre-half.

To these tactical niceties Meisl added the administrator's touch, introducing full-time professionalism to the Viennese game in 1924. Three years later his knack for football organisation gave birth to the Mitropa Cup and the International Cup, Central European predecessors of the European Cup and the European Championship, respectively.

By the Thirties Austria could boast the most dazzling national team in Europe. The *Wunderteam* lost only twice between 1931 and 1934, beating Germany 5–0 and 6–0, Switzerland 8–1 and Hungary 8–2. Their spirit was typified by their centre-forward, Matthias Sindelar, nicknamed 'Man of Paper' because of his slight build, but whose ball skills were fine enough to take him past the most physical marker. Sindelar scored twice to hand Austria the 1932 Interna-

Ex-national coach Happel is immortalised at the Prater

tional Cup, but that was to be the *Wunderteam*'s only honour. In a World Cup semi-final two years later, their subtle skills ran aground in the mud of Milan, and they were beaten by Italy.

Hugo Meisl died soon after Hitler's invasion of Austria, while his players went on to strengthen Germany's World Cup squad of 1938. During World War II, Austrian clubs won both the German league and cup, their bittersweet success a tribute to the flair of Hogan's Viennese school.

In the postwar era, independent Austria made a quick return to international prominence. A new generation of players, led by Ernst Happel, Gerhard Hanappi and Ernst Ocwirk, were determined to make an

impact on the modern game without betraying the Danubian tradition. Though nominally deploying the fashionable 'third-back' formation, the Austrians of the Fifties were a fluid outfit in which Ocwirk combined defensive duties with those of an old-fashioned attacking centre-half. Their finest hour was an extraordinary 7–5 defeat of hosts Switzerland at the 1954 World Cup.

By the Sixties, however, the modern European game was beginning to leave such scorelines – and Vienna's incurably romantic approach to football – behind. Neither FK Austria nor the team which had become their greatest city rivals, SK Rapid, were able to compete seriously in the UEFA-backed European club competitions. Domestically, too, their dominance was slipping. Linzer ASK became the first provincial team to win the league in 1965, and Wacker Innsbruck, captained by the fine international sweeper Bruno Pezzey, were Austria's team of the Seventies.

Rapid striker Hans Krankl led Austria to their best modern World Cup in Argentina in 1978, where they beat West Germany 3–2 at the final group stage. Four years later, however, the Austrians drew the vilification of a planet when they allowed their neighbours to beat them 1–0, eliminating Algeria to the two countries' mutual benefit.

Hopes of a revival, spurred by Rapid's run to the Cup-Winners' Cup final of 1985, were dented when Josef Hickersberger's much-hyped national team failed to make it past the first round at Italia '90. In September that year came a greater ignominy – a 1–0 defeat by the Faroe Islands in the latter's first-ever competitive international.

Austria's national side has still not fully recovered from that lapse. But the domestic game, well placed to take advantage of both the fall of Communism and the Bosman judgement, is showing signs of a genuine if patchy rebirth. Austria has fielded

Basics

EU nationals, Americans, Canadians, Australians and New Zealanders do not require a visa to enter Austria.

The Austrian unit of currency is the **Schilling** (ÖS), divided into 100 Groschen. There are coins for 2, 5, 10 and 50 Groschen and 1, 5, 10, 20 Schilling, and notes for 20, 50, 100, 500, 1000 and 5000 Schilling. There are about ÖS18 to £1. Exchange rates and commissions vary from bank to bank. **Banks** are generally open Mon–Fri 8am–3pm, Thurs until 5.30pm, with smaller branches closing for lunch. **Post offices** often charge less commission and are generally open until 6pm and early on Saturday mornings. In Vienna there are 24-hour post offices at central Fleischmarkt 19 and at the two main train stations, Südbahnhof and Westbahnhof. Cash machines are widespread and credit-card payment is common.

The **Austrian telephone system** is being digitalised and many numbers are changing – beware. To call Austria from abroad, dial 43, then 1 for Vienna, 316 for Graz, 662 for Salzburg. To call from the provinces, dial 0316 for Graz and 0662 for Salzburg, but 0222 for Vienna. To get an international line from Austria, dial 00 followed by the country code. Cheap inland and international rates are 6pm–8am weekdays and all day Sat–Sun. **Phone cards** cost ÖS48, ÖS95 and ÖS190. **Coin phones** take 1, 5, 10 and 20 Schilling pieces.

Austrian **trains** are clean and efficient; tickets are priced according to the number of kilometres covered. A 100km journey costs ÖS156. You can pay by credit card only if your ticket costs more than ÖS200, and an ÖS30 supplement will be charged for buying a ticket onboard. The abbreviations EC, IC and SC are used for international or inter-city trains serving major stations; D trains are reasonably fast; E trains are the slowest.

The **national bus network** is really only useful for gaining access to remote mountain locations, and charges ÖS130 per 100km. Vienna's main **bus station** is at Wien-Mitte, near the *Hilton* hotel's air terminal.

A cheaper way to travel is the **Mitfahrzentrale** service, which links drivers to **hitchers** who pay towards petrol costs (☎0222/715 0066, open Mon–Fri 9am–6pm, Sat 9am–1pm). Prices are fixed – Vienna to Salzburg is ÖS230. The German **City Netz** office in Vienna (☎0222/581 3393, open daily 8am–9pm) operates a similar service to destinations north of the border.

two finalists in European club competitions in the past four years, and on each occasion, the teams involved have captured the imagination of the nation. Given the right stimulus, Austria's interest in football remains fervent and sophisticated as ever.

Essential vocabulary
Hello *Grüss Gott*
Goodbye *Wiederschauen*
Yes *Ja*
No *Nein*
Two beers, please *Zwei Bier, bitte*
Thank you *Danke*

Men's *Herren*
Women's *Damen*
Where is the stadium? *Wo ist das Stadion?*
What's the score? *Wie steht's?*
Referee *Schreidsrichter*
Offside *Abseits*

Match practice
Austrian league football is fairly low-key. Apart from the Rapid-Austria *Meisterschaftsderby* in the Prater, the other ties that raise passions are Rapid's clashes with LASK and Salzburg, and the *West-Derby* between Salzburg and Innsbruck.

The Austrian season runs from the end of July until the end of November, and from the start of March until the end of May or early June. Indoor tournaments fill the winter break.

Most games are played on Saturdays at 3.30pm and Wednesdays at 7pm. Some televised first-division matches are on Friday or Saturday evenings, while some second-division clubs like to play on Friday nights or Sundays to attract bigger crowds.

The league
Austria abandoned its Swiss-style title round in 1993. Today's first division has ten teams who play each other four times during the course of the season. The bottom club changes places with the top dogs from the sixteen-team second division, while the second-bottom and second-top play-off over two legs. Three teams are relegated from the second, to find a place in one of the *Regionalligas* – Ost (east), Mitte (central) or West. The top team of each division goes up to the second.

Up for the cup
The Austrian cup begins with preliminary rounds in July, involving no fewer than 144 amateur teams. All ties up to and including the semi-final are played at the club first drawn out of the hat and are decided on one game, extra-time and penalties. The sixteen second-division clubs enter at the first round proper, while the ten first-division sides enter at the third round in September. The final takes place at Vienna's Prater stadium in May.

Tickets
Most Austrian grounds are small, with tickets divided into seats (*Sitzplätze*) and standing (*Stehplätze*), covered (*überdachte*) or uncovered (*nicht überdacht*). At bigger grounds there will be a *Gästesektor* for visiting fans. A stand (*Tribüne*) is generally named after its location, eg *West-Tribüne*, west stand. For an average first-division game you'll be paying ÖS150–250 for a prime seat, ÖS100 to stand.

Half-time
Bier, Wein und Wurst – beer, wine and sausages – are the staple diet, at about ÖS30, ÖS25 and ÖS25 each.

Action replay
The arrival of the German giant SAT1 into the Austrian market in the summer of 1996 was very much welcomed down south. SAT1's contract with the Austrian FA allowed ÖS5 million to be distributed to first-division clubs during 1996/97, helping towards improving stadium facilities.

The deal gives SAT1 the rights to show one live game each round, on Friday or Saturday evening, while Austrian state channel ÖRF1 get five live games each season. ÖRF1 also present *Fussball*, a goals and highlights show (Saturdays, 6–7.30pm). ÖRF1's Champions' League coverage is excellent, with extended highlights from all matches on any given match-night.

The back page
The main football publication is *Sportzeitung* (Tuesdays, ÖS18), an all-colour weekly, with all the main European results and tables as well as local news. The weekly *Wiener Sport am Montag* (Mondays, ÖS20) concentrates on Viennese football. Of the national daily press, *Kurier* has the most colourful sports coverage. Foreign newspapers and magazines are widely available in central Vienna.

Ultra culture
Gone are the days when Rapid and FK Austria fans would scrap it out on a regular basis; now they even drink in the same bars. Rapid's following is raucous rather than dangerous, and of the provincial teams, only LASK Linz send travelling support out in numbers. Neither the blatant commercialism of German fan culture nor the colourful festivities of the Italian *ultras* have yet become an integral part of the Austrian game.

In the net
There is no generic Austrian football website, but latest results and news (in German

only) can be found on the net version of ÖRF's teletext pages at: www.orf.at/teletext/200.htm. Results, scorers and goal times from the season so far, together with a stats archive for previous seasons and coverage of Austria's lower divisions, are available from the European domestic-league section of the RSSSF archive at: www.risc.uni-linz.ac.at/non-official/rsssf/results-eur.html.

Vienna

FK Austria *6*   SK Rapid *8*   FCN Admira *10*
First Vienna *10*   Wiener Sport-Club *11*

Graz, Innsbruck, Linz and Salzburg may all have enjoyed their fifteen minutes of fame, but if you want to get straight to the heart of Austrian soccer, Vienna is the only place to be. From the space and international-class splendour of the Prater stadium to the country-garden atmosphere of historic grounds such as the Hohe Warte, Vienna offers a unique and varied football experience, unhinted at in the tourist images of glitzy palaces, waltzing, stodgy cakes and *The Third Man*.

Vienna essentials

Wien Schwechat Airport is 19km south-east of central Vienna. Line #7 of the overland railway, the S-Bahn, makes the thirty-minute journey between Schwechat and Wien-Nord and Wien-Mitte stations. There are two trains an hour, 5am–10pm, single fare ÖS34. A bus service runs from the city air terminal at the *Hilton* hotel by Wien-Mitte every thirty minutes, 5am–midnight, with an hourly service through the night between April 1 and October 31. Another airport bus service runs hourly from each main train station, 5.40am–11.40pm. All bus services cost ÖS70 and take about thirty minutes. A taxi will cost you around ÖS350.

    Transport in Vienna is efficient if costly, consisting of trams, buses, the metro (U-Bahn) and the S-Bahn. Single tickets, valid on all forms of transport, cost ÖS17, available from newsstands and from machines at U-Bahn stations. They are valid for an hour from the time you punch them. Tickets bought onboard trams and buses cost ÖS20.

    Public transport runs 5.30am–12.30am, with an eight-route Friday and Saturday night bus service, 12.30am–4am, from Schwedenplatz for a flat ÖS25 fare. A travel pass, *Netzkarte*, costs ÖS50 for 24 hours, ÖS130 for 72 hours, valid from first stamping and available from newsstands and U-Bahn stations. The *Vienna Card*, ÖS180, is valid for 72 hours and offers reduced admission to many sights and museums.

    Taxis are rare and expensive. Depending on the time of day, the meter starts at ÖS24–25, with a subsequent ÖS11–13 per kilometre. Radio taxis (☎0222/31 300 or ☎0222/60 160) charge a supplement of ÖS12.

    Vienna's main **tourist office** at Kärntner Strasse 38 (☎0222/513 8892, open daily 9am–7pm) is cramped but well stocked with information. The Austrian Information Office at Margaretenstrasse 1 (☎0222/587 2000, open Mon–Fri 10am–5pm) can answer queries about travelling to other parts of the country.

    There are two excellent German-language **listings publications** for Vienna, both published on Fridays. *Falter* (ÖS28) has comprehensive nightclub, concert and cinema information; *City* (ÖS8) is thinner but still useful.

The thrilling fields

 FK Austria

Franz Horr-Stadion, Fischhofgasse 12
Capacity 10,500 (4500 seated)
Colours Violet shirts, white shorts
League champions 1924, 1926, 1949–50, 1953, 1961–63, 1969–70, 1976, 1978–81, 1984–86, 1991–93
Cup winners 1921, 1924–26, 1933, 1935–36, 1948–49, 1960, 1962–63, 1967, 1971, 1974, 1977, 1980, 1982, 1986, 1990, 1992, 1994

Traditionally Vienna's bourgeois club, now incongruously located next to a motorway intersection, FK Austria can trace their roots back to football's earliest days in the capital. Having initially been formed as a branch of the Vienna Cricket & Football Club, or Cricketer, who took part in the first-ever Austrian football match in 1894, they won the league as Amateure in 1924 and 1926, becoming FK Austria before the glorious Thirties. During the golden decade of Viennese football, FK Austria always lost out to First Vienna, Admira or their eternal rivals Rapid in the league, but won the Mitropa Cup in 1933 and 1936. The club had no home ground, playing either at the newly built Wiener Stadion or at Rapid's Pfarrwiese. The *Violetten* provided the leading elements of the Austrian *Wunderteam* of the 1930s, in particular the Czech-born striker Matthias Sindelar, whose premature retirement and mysterious suicide in 1939 signalled the sad end of an era.

The club enjoyed a postwar revival based on the passing skills of their attacking half-back and captain Ernst Ocwirk, winning four titles before his departure to Sampdoria in 1956, and keeping the tradition of playing the beautiful game before the financial imperatives of European competition began to loom on the horizon. Ocwirk would return as coach and win two more titles with FK Austria in 1969 and 1970.

Maintaining its links with the past, in 1973 the club absorbed 1915 champions Wiener Athletik Club and built an attractive young side which would win five titles in six years in the late Seventies and early Eighties, reaching the Cup-Winners' Cup final in 1978. Key FK Austria players such as midfielder Herbert Prohaska (now his country's national-team coach) and goalkeeper Friedl Koncilia also played for Austria at the 1978 and 1982 World Cups.

Hungary's Tibor Nyilasi starred in the three straight title wins between 1984 and 1986, which also saw a young Toni Polster embark on his stint of 120 goals in 145 games. By then the Violets were no longer playing at the Prater, having moved into the modest Franz Horr-Stadion in Sindelar's home district of Favoriten.

The goalkeeping of Franz Wohlfahrt helped FK Austria to three more straight titles from 1991, but regular early elimination from Europe, the rise of Salzburg and the revival of Rapid, have conspired to leave the Violets with little but a small, dedicated core of fans and a host of memories.

Here we go!
Take U1 to its southern terminus at Reumannplatz, then tram #67 for three stops, or U6 to Meidling then bus #7A or #15A for twelve stops. Both routes lead to the **Altes Landgut** roundabout. From there, you need to be on the other side of the A23 highway – over the pedestrian crossing, past the huge Ludwig store.

Swift half
There are plenty of bars along Favoritenstrasse towards the stadium. The **Gasthaus zum Kärntnerwirt** on the corner of Katharinengasse is friendly and close to the ground, with Kaiser beer and good home cooking. At the Franz Horr itself, the **Sport Buffet**, near the *Osttribüne* between the stadium and the training pitches, has pennants and pine furnishings inside, tables and chairs outside. There is also a *Kantine* selling Schwechater beer under the *Nordtribüne*.

The Prater

Ernst Happel-Stadion, Meiereistrasse 7
Capacity 49,000 (all-seated)

Austria's national stadium is also a UEFA favourite, regularly hosting European
finals, including Ajax's 1995 Champions' Cup win over Milan. Commonly called the
Prater after its setting in the city's main Prater park by the Danube, it was commissioned in 1928 to coincide with the tenth anniversary of the Austrian republic. Then
named the Wiener Stadion, it was completed in 1931, just in time to see the golden
years of the *Wunderteam* before Hitler's occupation and the onset of World War II.
The bomb damage was repaired by 1945, and the post-war Prater enjoyed full houses
and top-class, floodlit international football.

Despite the decline in the Austrian game, the Prater has continued to be improved.
Its vast roof was built in 1986, and during the Nineties it hosted matches in Casino
Salzburg's run to the 1994 UEFA Cup final and Rapid Vienna's surge to the Cup-
Winners' Cup final two years later – neither club could house such huge crowds at
their own grounds.

The Prater has been officially
renamed the **Ernst Happel-
Stadion**, after the great Austrian
international player and coach who
died in 1992, after bravely tough-
ing it out on the bench for two
World Cup qualifiers while fighting
cancer. **Rapid**, **FK Austria** and
Salzburg continue to use the
stadium for big domestic and
European fixtures, and indeed FK
Austria still have their offices here
in sector D.

Take a tram to Vienna's stadium in the park

Bright, lively, easily segregated
and beautifully positioned, the Prater is one of the few modern European super-
bowls capable of generating an atmosphere redolent of the past while remaining
thoroughly up-to-date. To reach it, take U1 to Praterstern or S7 to Wien-Nord, then a
fifteen-minute walk down Hauptallee past the Big Wheel, or tram #21 for eight stops
to Olympiaplatz.

The Prater park is full of stalls and bars for a quiet beer before the match. **Zur
Grüner Hütte**, Ausstellungsstrasse 196, on the #21 tram route, is popular, as is the
Schweizerhaus, Strasse des Ersten Mai 116. You'll find **Zum 11er**
buffets dotted around the ground, and a **bar/restaurant** under the museum.

Ticket offices are positioned at regular intervals around the stadium. Visiting
international fans are allocated sectors A or E. The higher or lower level
(*Oberer/Unterer Rang*) will be designated on your ticket, along with the *Sektor*. The
cheapest tickets for internationals at the Prater are behind the goals (ÖS200), the most
expensive in sectors B and E (ÖS400).

Entrance to the **football museum** in sector B (open Mon & Fri 10am–1pm,
Tues & Thurs 2pm–6pm, closed in August) is free. There are three sections of
souvenirs, many from the *Wunderteam* years, including Matthias Sindelar's regis-
tration card, signed before his unexpected retirement and suicide in 1939, and a
Hugo Meisl display.

Getting a ticket

The main **ticket office** is on the corner of the *Süd-* and *Westtribüne*. Away fans stand in the *Osttribüne*, home fans in the *Westtribüne*. The *Nordtribüne* has the most expensive seats in sectors B and C.

Publication

Die Wiener Violetten (ÖS15) is a quarterly magazine available from the ground on matchdays or from the club office in sector D of the Prater.

Ultra culture

Fanclub Austria 80 are a friendly, well-organised supporters' group who put out a free monthly newsletter, *Austria Aktuell*, and arrange social events.

A decade in violet – FK Austria striker Andy Ogris

In the net

FK Austria were the first club in the land to set up an official website, at: www.austria-wien.co.at/fak/. It offers a homepage and brief history in English, plus many more areas in German including a virtual *Fanboutique* where you can purchase all those longed-for purple football accessories.

🟢 SK Rapid

Gerhard Hanappi Stadion, Keisslergasse 6
Capacity 19,600 (all-seated)
Colours Green-and-white shirts, white shorts
League champions 1912, 1913, 1916, 1917, 1919–21, 1923, 1929–30, 1935, 1938, 1940–41, 1946, 1948, 1951–52, 1954, 1956–57, 1960, 1964, 1967–68, 1982–83, 1987–88, 1996
Cup winners 1919–20, 1927, 1946, 1961, 1968–69, 1972, 1976, 1983–85, 1987, 1995

Austria's biggest club for the best part of a century, Rapid recovered from near bankruptcy in 1994 to win their first title of the decade and a place in a European final two years later. Now collecting huge earnings from TV rights and merchandising, they have the potential to become major players on the continent's biggest footballing stages.

The club were founded as 1. Wiener Arbeiter-Fussballklub in 1898 by workers from a hat factory, who changed the name to Rapid under English influence a year later. The club, however, has never lost its working-class roots.

The most successful Austrian team prior to the Twenties, Rapid kept ahead of their Viennese rivals until the introduction of professionalism and the rise of Admira and First Vienna in the Thirties. Matches against FK Austria created the most interest, however, and the rivalry stills flourishes today. At the time all the main Viennese clubs practised the Danubian game, but coach Karl Rappan gave Rapid defensive steel to combat the finer game of their rivals. The arrival of prolific goalscorer Franz Binder should have reasserted Rapid's domination and added to their Mitropa Cup win of 1930, but the Nazi occupation of Austria intervened.

During the war Rapid clocked up German trophies and afterwards provided the impetus for Austria's swift postwar revival. Midfielders Ernst Happel and Gerhard Hanappi would set up wave after wave of attacks, their uncompromising style taking the Austrian league by storm and allowing Rapid to beat both AC Milan and Real Madrid in the home legs of European ties.

With the onset of the Sixties, Rapid's decline mirrored that of the Austrian game in general. But in the early Seventies Rapid commissioned Hanappi, who had become an architect after hanging up his boots, to design a new stadium near their beloved but outdated Pfarrwiese. Opened in 1977, the Weststadion was to be the perfect stage for the emerging power of striker Hans Krankl, who would lead Rapid back to the top, with championships in 1982 and 1983 and a first European final – in the Cup-Winners' Cup against Everton – in 1985. Hanappi died in 1981 and the stadium he designed was renamed after him.

Rapid were floated on the Vienna stock exchange in 1991, but lack of investment by a string of institutional shareholders ended in near-bankruptcy in 1994. A consortium of new sponsors was quickly found, and after an Austrian Cup win in 1995, coach Ernst Dokupil was able to make a string of new signings including midfielder Peter Stöger and Bulgarian defender Trifon Ivanov.

The new-look squad reached the final of the Cup-Winners' Cup, their surprising European adventure coinciding with a first Austrian title for eight years, sealed with a 2–0 win over Sturm Graz in front of 48,000 at the Prater.

Rapid lost their European final 1–0 to Paris St Germain and performed modestly

in the 1996 Champions' League. But TV revenue and an excited new generation of fans should provide a solid base from which club president Günther Kaltenbrunner, a former Rapid player-turned-banker, can mastermind the next stage of development.

Here we go!

The stadium is right by the U4 western terminus at **Hütteldorf**, where S-Bahn lines S3, S45 and S50 also stop.

Swift half

At Bahnhofstrasse 3, behind the popular *Westtribüne*, you'll find **Zum Schwarzen Peter**, a lively, smoky Balkan-run beer hall. At the other end of the stadium, behind the *Osttribüne* in Deutschordenstrasse, a less partisan element frequent the cramped **Café Corner** by Keisslergasse and the large **Stüberl zum Weststadion** at #14 opposite. Inside the ground are buffet stands dotted around the upper tiers of the *Nord-* and *Südtribune*.

Getting a ticket

The main **ticket offices** are on the corner of the *Süd-* and *Westtribüne*, and underneath the *Südtribüne*. The ground's four sections are colour-coded – blue for the visitors' *Osttribüne*, red for the most expensive seats in the *Südtribüne*, green for the *Westtribüne*.

Publication

The full-colour *Rapid Magazin* (ÖS20, monthly) is available at the ground and at most newsstands in the city.

Club shop

A **souvenir van** is open on matchdays at the corner of Keisslergasse and Bahnhofstrasse, and sells a selection of Rapid scarves and caps, along with replica shirts at ÖS700–800. The **Rapid Fanboutique** (open Mon–Fri 12.30–6pm and on matchdays) is on the corner of the *Süd-* and *Westtribüne* and generally has a bit more in stock. Neither operation takes credit cards.

Ultra culture

Rapid have the largest and most boisterous fan base in Austria. This has been known to boil over but, while there is a racist element, at home in the all-seated 'Hütteldorf' the atmosphere is mostly party-like. The **Green Bulls** and other elements start proceedings with a wall of scarves fifteen minutes before kick-off, when the Rapid club song starts up over the PA. A bad miss at this end by the visiting side leads to a chorus of *The Blue Danube* in mockery.

In the net

There is no official Rapid site, but Florian Koerner runs a no-nonsense unofficial one at: www.wu.wien.ac.at/usr/h93/h9350244/rapid.html. There are homepages in German, English and Spanish, plenty of stats and team information, plus the chance to join an electronic mailing list.

A more ambitious alternative site resides at: www.atnet.at/club/moses/rapid/rapid.htm. Among many other things this offers the full lyrics (in German) of Rapid's club hymn, plus audio interviews with players to download in WAV format. If you want to know how 'Wolfman' Ivanov feels ten minutes after being sent-off in Rapid's last game, this is the place to go.

Groundhopping

Vienna's ambivalent attitude to football – adulatory one moment, apathetic the next – is summed up by the fate of the city's minor clubs. Many either folded or were absorbed by bigger teams during the Sixties and Seventies. Of those that remain, Admira-Wacker – themselves the result of an unhappy merger – appear to have deserted Vienna altogether, while First Vienna and Wiener Sport-Club still cling stubbornly, and perhaps foolishly, to their dream of one day rejoining the country's footballing élite.

SCN Admira-Wacker

Bundesstadion Südstadt, Johann-Steinböck-Strasse 1, Maria Enzersdorf
Capacity 10,000
Colours Lilac shirts, white shorts
League champions 1927–28, 1932, 1934, 1936–37, 1939, 1947, 1966
Cup winners 1928, 1932, 1934, 1964, 1966

Slowly sinking into oblivion, Admira-Wacker should be remembered for two reasons – first, for the classic Admira Wien team which, under Hugo Meisl's guidance, won a string of titles during the *Wunderteam* years; and second, for their rôle as extras in Wim Wenders' cult film, *The Goalkeeper's Fear of the Penalty*.

Admira merged with Wacker Wien in 1971. Though it has been immortalized on celluloid, their Südstadt ground saw little league action in 1996/97. No longer able to attract fans to the far south of the city, in 1996 the club renamed themselves SC Niederösterreich Admira-Wacker, in the hope of spreading their fan base to the whole of Lower Austria. This meant playing in lilac (as opposed to their traditional all-black) as trailer before the main feature at second-division St Pölten. Attendances barely touched four figures, but the experiment looks set to continue in 1997/98, when Admira will play at **Krems** and **St Pölten**. Both towns are around 50km west of Vienna and accessible by train from the city's **Westbahnhof**. When you get there, however, you may feel the club could still do with some of Wenders' extras.

First Vienna

Hohe Warte, Klabundgasse
Capacity 12,000
Colours Yellow shirts, blue shorts
League champions 1931, 1933, 1942–44, 1955
Cup winners 1929–30, 1937, 1943

Hard to believe now, but before the Prater was built, First Vienna's Hohe Warte was

Austria's national stadium. As their name suggests, First Vienna were the city's first football-only club, formed by English gardeners on Baron Rothschild's estate. Adopting the Baron's horse-racing colours of blue and yellow, they took part in the first official match ever to be played in Austria, against Cricketer in 1894.

Built against a hillside adjacent to the Rothschild estate, the Hohe Warte hosted all Austria's earliest internationals until a mudslide during a match against Italy in 1923. After the gardeners had helped repair the

Fashion victim – Admira's fetching all-black kit is a thing of the past

damage, First Vienna hit peak form in the early Thirties, winning the league twice, the Austrian cup three times and the Mitropa Cup in 1931.

By then the Prater had been built, and First Vienna eventually found their natural place floating between the first and second divisions. In 1997, as a second-division side, they beat both FK Austria and Salzburg on their way to a cup final defeat by Sturm Graz.

For an afternoon of gentle football in one of Europe's greenest football grounds, take U4, S40 or S45 to **Heiligenstadt**, then walk straight across 12 Februar Platz, left down Heiligenstadter Strasse, and turn first right up Puchlgasse. Hohe Warte is right above you, up the sharp incline to your right as you turn into Klabundgasse.

After a climb like that you'll need a drink – the **buffet** under the main stand opens an hour before kick-off and offers Goldfassl beer, *Wurst* and hot dogs.

Wiener Sport-Club

Sport-Club Platz, Hernalser Hauptstrasse 214
Capacity 9,000
Colours Black-and-white shirts, white shorts
League champions 1922, 1958–59
Cup winners 1923

Another Viennese club fallen on hard times, Wiener Sport-Club are floundering in the *Regionalliga Ost*, despite a neat, compact stadium in the Hernals district within easy reach of the centre of town. Although not a patch on the late Fifties team that won back-to-back titles and beat Juventus 7–0 in the 1958/59 European Cup, WSC were holding their own in the first division until a financial scandal broke in 1994. Club president Herbert Rosenauer was arrested on charges of fraud, and the players went without pay for months.

Now it's Sunday morning football for the boys in white and black, although a

Rapid return – Konsel, Heraf and Stumpf celebrate victory over Feyenoord, April 1996

modest cup run in 1996/97 offered some hope for the future.

If you can get up early enough after a Saturday night in Vienna, take S45 over to **Hernals,** then a five-minute walk up Hernalshauptstrasse away from town. The **Schweiger** on the corner of Kainzgasse and Hernalshauptstrasse boasts billiards and 123 types of beer, but doesn't open until 4pm. Wait instead inside the friendly **Café Weinhold**, Hernalshauptstrasse 210, which opens at 9am on matchdays. There are **buffets** at diagonally opposite corners inside the ground.

Eat, drink, sleep...

Bars and clubs

Vienna offers three main types of drinking venue. A **Kaffeehaus** or a **Konditorei** is for daytime entertainment, offering coffee at around ÖS25 (*Schwarzer* is black, *Melange* with a drop of milk), cakes, the day's papers and, in a Kaffeehaus, billiards and alcohol. A **Beisl** is a neighbourhood pub or restaurant, serving draught (*vom Fass*) beer in half-litre (*Krügel*) or third-litre (*Seidel*) glasses at about ÖS35 and ÖS25 respectively. Wine is sold by the *Viertel*, quarter-litre, for about ÖS25 in a **Heuriger**, or wine tavern – these are summer haunts often located just outside town – the Grinzing area is popular with tourists; Stammersdorf is for the Viennese.

Nightlife in Vienna is concentrated on the narrow streets packed with late bars in the Bermuda Triangle (*Dreieck*) area by the Danube Canal near U-Bahn Schwedenplatz. Many bars in the 6th, 7th and 8th districts stay open until 4am or later at weekends, and in summer there are regular parties on the Danube island.

Sadly for football romantics, nothing remains of the classic Viennese haunts of the Thirties. Neither the Wiener Ring-Café, venue for Hugo Meisl's friendly gatherings, nor Matthias Sindelar's retirement gift to his wife, the Annahof Café, still stand...

Arena, Baumgasse 80/Ecke Franzosengraben. Concert and party venue in an old slaughterhouse, with an outdoor stage for big-name acts in summer. ÖS80–120 cover charge for techno nights, which are indoors. U3 to Erdberg.

Café Wembley, Lindengasse 47. The only football bar in town, near U3 Neubaugasse, owned by former FK Austria goalkeeper Franz Wohlfahrt. Not unpretentious, decorated with English football pennants and photos from Wohlfahrt's career. Open 9am–midnight Mon–Fri, Sat 5pm–midnight.

Hawelka, Dorotheergasse 6. The least pretentious of Vienna's famous coffee houses, open 8am–2am, from 4pm on Sundays but closed on Tuesdays. Between the Hofburg and Stefansplatz.

Krah Krah, Rabensteig 8. Popular bar in the Bermuda-Dreieck area offering a huge range of beers and occasional live jazz. Open until 2am. The **Roter Engel** opposite is open later and always has live music, for a ÖS30–60 cover charge.

Molly Darcy's, Schreyvogelgasse 1. Lively Irish pub near the university, with friendly atmosphere and unusually (for Vienna) down-to-earth staff.

Restaurants

Austrian cuisine is either heavy or sweet, or both. The classic main dish is *Wiener Schnitzel*, cutlet in breadcrumbs. This is followed by a variety of gooey cakes for dessert; *Strudel*, baked dough with various fruit fillings, is a lighter alternative to these, but not much.

Eating out can be expensive. Vienna has a variety of Chinese, Arab and Balkan eateries which tend to be cheaper than restaurants specialising in local cuisine, although a set menu (*Tagesmenu*) in a Beisl should cost no more than ÖS60 for two courses. **Mensas** – cheap, self-service restaurants for students – are generally

open to the public in term-time, and any **Würstel stand** will serve up cheap sausages and frankfurters accompanied by various sauces.

Afro-Asiatisches Institut, Türkenstrasse 3. Probably the best of the student Mensas, with a wide variety of food and plenty of posters and flyers publicising reggae and African music events in the Volksgarten. Near Rooseveltplatz.

Gasthaus Reinthaler, Gluckgasse 5. Reasonably priced, no-frills Austrian cooking, right by the Hofburg, with lunchtime specials.

Griechenbeisl, Fleischmarkt 1. Classic Viennese Beisl near the Bermuda-Dreieck area where Schubert and Beethoven wined and dined. Garden tables, ÖS200–300 all-in. Most credit cards.

Schweizerhaus, Strasse des Ersten Mai 116. Vast slabs of roast pork served up on terrace tables in the Prater park – ideal summer evening fare. ÖS100–130 should easily feed two people.

Tunnel, Floriangasse 39. Student club/café in the university area by Rathausplatz, with cheap set meals and a cellar for discos and concerts.

Accommodation

Vienna is an expensive place to stay, although the worst time for finding a room in the city is the non-football period of June–September. The **tourist office** at Kärntner Strasse 38 (open daily 9am–7pm, ☎0222/513 8892) charge ÖS40 commission for booking a room, as do branches at the airport arrivals hall and at the West- and Südbahnhof. **Mitwohnzentrale**, Laudongasse 7 (open Mon–Fri 10am–2pm and 3–6pm, ☎0222/402 6061), charge ÖS160+ for a private room, taking their commission from the tariff – their minimum stay is three days.

Myrthengasse, Myrthengasse 7 (☎0222/523 6316) and Neustiftsgasse 85 (☎0222/523 7462). Neighbouring hostels, under the same ownership, a 15min walk from Westbahnhof or 5min (or three #48A bus stops) from U6 Burggasse. Open all year round, 1am curfew, laundry facilities. ÖS140 a bed.

Hotel Orient, Tiefer Graben 30-32 (☎022/533 7307, fax 022/535 0340). Central one-star hotel near Concordiaplatz with stylish furnishings, where some of *The Third Man* was filmed. ÖS600–1000 for a single, ÖS450 without a shower, breakfast included. Most major credit cards.

Praterstern, Mayergasse 6 (☎022/214 0123, fax 022/214 7880). One-star hotel in the Prater park with satellite TV and a pleasant back garden. ÖS350–400 a single room with shower, ÖS250

without, though you may be charged for using the one in the corridor. Doubles around ÖS500–ÖS600, with breakfast. Most credit cards.

Pension Wild, Lange Gasse 10 (☎022/406 5174, fax 022/402 2168). Near the Ring, behind the university, a pleasant pension with satellite TV, sauna and solarium. Kitchen facilities. ÖS450 for a single without a shower, ÖS550 with, ÖS600 or ÖS700 for doubles, with breakfast.

Hostel Zöhrer, Skodagasse 26 (☎022/430 730). Open all year round, kitchen facilities, no curfew. ÖS170 for a dorm bed, ÖS460 for a double with bunk beds and private shower. Near U6 Alserstrasse.

As close as Austrian football gets to a living legend – Toni Polster

Belgium

Pioneers of the Continental game at the end of the nineteenth century, hosts of the European Championship at the start of the next, the Belgians are struggling to lift their game to the same level as their Dutch, French and German neighbours. Success at international level has not been achieved for nearly a decade. The Belgian league, formerly a hotbed of rivalry between the country's French- and Flemish-speaking populations, has become increasingly parochial as clubs from French-speaking Wallonia have declined in influence – either fading gracefully, like Standard Liège, or disappearing altogether, in the case of Seraing and RC Liégeois.

Today's Belgian game appears clean and cosy, but its recent history is tainted with corruption. Two pillars of Belgian football, coach Raymond Goethals and former national captain Eric Gerets, were implicated in the bribery scandal that swept Standard after their 1982 championship. Anderlecht's 3–0 UEFA Cup win over Nottingham Forest in April 1984 was aided by compliant refereeing – though it wasn't until 1997 that club president Constant Vanden Stock revealed he'd been paying off blackmailers who held *de facto* proof of the Brussels team's attempt to rig the match. UEFA's corruption investigators are still looking into allegations surrounding Club Bruges' 1–0 defeat by Marseille in the 1993 Champions' League.

Moreover, the two words most associated with Belgian football in the modern era, Bosman and Heysel, are not pleasant ones for local fans to hear. Administrative negligence undoubtedly contributed to the Heysel stadium disaster of 1985 and cast serious doubt on the country's ability to host major events – something

Penalty? The Germans fell Josip Weber, 1994

which will be tested to the full by Euro 2000, which the Belgians are hosting jointly with the Dutch. Jean-Marc Bosman's contractual dispute with RC Liégeois ended in victory for the player at the European Court of Justice in 1995, opening the floodgates of international player trade and, domestically, perhaps signalling the demise of some of the modest semi-pro clubs which lend the Belgian game such charm.

Football first developed in Belgium in the 1860s. English schools in Brussels and expatriate workers in Antwerp and Liège introduced both football and rugby to the country, and a handful of clubs were established by the early 1890s. Racing Club de Bruxelles and FC Liégeois dominated the early years of the national championship, inaugurated in 1896, before the rise of another Brussels side, Union Saint-Gilloise.

World War I saw Union's power diminish and their mantle taken by Beerschot, the Antwerp club led by the brilliant striker Raymond Braine.

Off the pitch, the Belgians were prime movers behind the setting up of FIFA, a fact which compelled them to take part in the first World Cup in Uruguay in 1930. Up until then, the only experience gained by the 'Red Devils' (*Rode Duivels/Diables Rouges*) had been in friendlies against France and the old enemy, Holland, although they did win a soccer gold medal at the Antwerp Olympics of 1920 – after the Czech team walked off the field in the final. On the ten-day boat journey to Montevideo, Belgium's star forward, Bernard Voorhoof, drank so much beer he put on eight kilos in weight. The Devils lost both their games and failed to score a goal, but Belgium were represented in the final by referee Jean Langenus – cap, plus fours and all. Argentina's defeat led to the Belgians' hotel being attacked by travelling supporters after the game.

Domestically, the post-World War II era belonged to Anderlecht. English coach Bill Gormlie took control of the club and the national side, and Jef Mermans starred upfront for him in both teams. Under another British coach, David Livingstone, Belgium put up a creditable performance at the 1954 World Cup, drawing 4–4 with England. Meanwhile, the domestic game improved with the introduction of semi-professionalism. With Paul van Himst and Jef Jurion in attack, Anderlecht won five titles in a row in the Sixties, and knocked Real Madrid out of the European Cup in 1962. But it wasn't until the Seventies that either the club or Belgium's national side made a sustained impact abroad. Anderlecht won the Cup-Winners' Cup in 1976, the year Guy Thys took charge of the national side. Four years later, his team were the surprise package of the 1980 European Championship in Italy. In the final, a late Horst Hrubesch goal for West Germany beat a Belgian side which contained Jean-Marie Pfaff in goal, Jan Ceulemans upfront and the ageing but wily Wilfried van Moer in midfield.

With Enzo Scifo replacing van Moer, much the same side sprang an even greater

British brawn, Belgian brains – Butcher is outflanked by Ceulemans, Bologna, 1990

surprise at the 1986 World Cup, beating the Soviet Union and Spain before falling to a brilliant Maradona goal in the semi-final – the team's eventual fourth place remains Belgium's best achievement at a major international tournament.

As the national team thrived, so the domestic game bounded along with it. Steel millionaire Paul Henrard pumped serious money into Standard Liège in the early Eighties. With industrial dust in the air, Michel Preud'homme in goal and Gerets at the back, Standard were a difficult side to beat. They won consecutive league titles and made the Cup-Winners' Cup final of 1982. In the following two years Anderlecht won and lost consecutive UEFA Cup finals, while Preud'homme left Standard to star in the rise of another provincial club, Mechelen, backed by wealthy chairman John Cordier. They had an easy run to the Cup-Winners' Cup final of 1988, where they beat Ajax 1–0, an historic triumph which remains Belgium's last victory in a European club competition.

Guy Thys was still in charge of the Red Devils when they fell to a last-minute goal by England's David Platt in the second round of Italia '90. At the same stage four years later, inept refereeing by Switzerland's Kurt Röthlisberger – later sent home by FIFA – refused the Belgians an obvious penalty which, if converted, would have caused Germany problems in extra time. The evergreen Preud'homme had proved himself the goalkeeper of the tournament, not least with his stupendous performance in Belgium's emotional group-stage win over Holland.

Three years on, and the picture could not be more different. Two of Belgium's greatest footballing heroes, Paul van Himst and Wilfried van Moer, have been humiliated out of the post of national coach within a matter of months, signalling the end of the managerial continuity which has served the Red Devils so well. The domestic game's brightest prospect, forward Gilles de Bilde, was banned from Anderlecht for life for nearly blinding an opponent during a game in 1996. A glut of cheap players from Eastern Europe and Africa, the lack of a coherent youth policy and the country's industrial decline have all contributed to a malaise which has seen Belgium lose its position as among the top eight footballing nations in Europe. While the bigger teams struggle to regain their former European status, a proposal for a sixteen-team Dutch-Belgian superleague frightens the smaller clubs, who survive on visits by Anderlecht and Club Bruges.

Yet there remains much that is oddly attractive about Belgian football. Away from the executive splendour of Anderlecht, most clubs have a homely, almost amateur feel about them, and the fans' hype-free, beer-heavy approach to the game is refreshingly different from that of the French or the Dutch.

Essential vocabulary
Flemish
Hello *Hallo*
Goodbye *Tot ziens*
Yes *Ja*
No *Nee*
Two beers, please *Twee bier alstublieft*
Thank you *Dank u*
Men's *Mannen*
Women's *Vrouwen*
Where is the stadium? *Hoe kom ik in de stadion?*
What is the score? *Wat is de stand?*
Referee *Scheidsrechter*
Offside *Buitenspel*

French
Hello *Bonjour*
Goodbye *Au revoir*
Yes *Oui*
No *Non*
Two beers, please *Deux demis, s'il vous plaît*
Thank you *Merci*
Men's *Hommes*
Women's *Dames*
Where is the stadium? *Où est le stade?*
What is the score? *Où en sommes-nous?*
Referee *L'arbitre*
Offside *Hors jeu*

Basics

If Belgian football is a game of two halves, Belgian society is a culture of **two tongues**. **French** is the language of Brussels and Wallonia, **Flemish** (Dutch, basically) that of Flanders. Speaking French to a Bruges barman is like adopting a plummy, shire counties accent to a Glaswegian. In Flanders, if in doubt – speak English.

EU nationals and those of the US, Canada, Australia and New Zealand require only a **passport** to enter the country.

The currency is the **Belgian franc** (BF), divided into 100 centimes. There are about 50BF to £1. There are coins for 50 centimes, 1, 5, 20 and 50BF. Notes come in denominations of 100, 200, 500, 1000, 2000, 5000 and 10,000BF. Keep a supply of 20BF coins ready for using the toilet in bars and restaurants. You may be given Luxembourg francs in your change – they are legal but unpopular tender here. Banks are the best places to **change money**, open Mon–Fri 9am–noon & 2–4pm. They charge a 450BF fee for cashing Eurocheques. Note that **credit-card payment** is not as commonplace as elsewhere in Western Europe.

From outside the country, the **telephone code** for Belgium is 32 – for Brussels add a 2 and for Bruges 51. Belgian coin phones take 5, 20 or 50BF pieces, but you can only direct-dial internationally from phones marked with European flags. For these you'll need an Intouch International non-insertable **phonecard**, available from newsagents and currency exchange offices (200BF for 20 units, 1000BF for 105). Scratch the number off the back, then dial it into the phone after calling the Intouch number. A voice will tell you in English how many units you have before you dial. Cheap rates are Mon–Sat 8pm–8am, all day Sundays and holidays.

Train travel in Belgium is quick, reliable and cheap at 300BF for a 100km journey. Return tickets at 40 percent discount are available from Friday evening to Sunday evening. There are two trains an hour between Brussels and Bruges, journey time one hour. **Buses** are generally used for short distances in and around towns. **Brussels Taxistop** (☎02/223 2231, fax 02/223 2232, open Mon–Fri 10.30am–6pm) is a shared lift service for Belgium and Europe, charging 200BF plus 1.30BF per km.

Hotel accommodation in Belgium is expensive – minimum 1000BF for a double room. The Tourism Centre in Brussels, rue Marché aux Herbes 63 (open June–Sept daily 9am–7pm, Oct–May Mon–Sat 9am–6pm & Sun 1–5pm, ☎02/504 0390, fax 02/504 0270) can make free hotel reservations anywhere in Belgium except Brussels.

Food is more important to the Belgians than it is to the Dutch, although the northern half of the country serves plainer food than the French-influenced south. Buckets of **steamed mussels** in various sauces are a staple diet everywhere. *Waterzooi*, a fish or chicken stew, is a Flanders favourite from Ghent. A **main course** will be around 500BF, but look out for *plats du jour* at perhaps 300BF. If you're on a budget, Belgium is the **home of the chip**, and proud of it.

If Belgians took their football as seriously as their **beer**, Brazil wouldn't get a look-in come World Cup time. A glass of standard **lager** – ordered as a *pintje/chope* – will probably be Stella, Maes or Jupiler, and weigh in at 40–50BF. For twice this, you can usually order any of at least twenty **speciality beers**, often many more. These may be fruit-flavoured; Trappist (such as Chimay, which comes in three different strengths); or *lambic* (aired and matured in production). Wheat beer (*witbier/bière blanche*) is a refreshing option, often served with a slice of lemon – Hoegaarden is a popular brand.

Belgian bar **opening hours** are generous, and clubbing is not nearly as popular as pubbing. Bear in mind that Belgians order in rounds. If you want to leave a club and come back later, tip the doorman 40BF.

Match practice

Although Belgian football is often seen as the poor relation of its Dutch neighbour, it is more accessible and its clubs offer much more variety. Belgium is very much an industrial society and the football club plays a valuable rôle in any town's community. Players are expected to meet regularly with fans, and local pride is paramount.

The season runs from early August to late May, with a couple of rounds clear at the end of December and beginning of January. Most games are played on Saturdays at 8pm, with a couple on Sundays at 3pm. Plum fixtures are shown live on Canal Plus and kick-off is on Fridays at 8pm.

The league

The Belgian first division has eighteen teams, the bottom two of which are relegated automatically to the semi-professional second division, which also has eighteen sides. Only the top team goes up automatically, since for the second promotion place, Belgium operates a similar complicated play-off system to Holland – the season is divided into three periods, and each period champion goes into end-of-season play-offs with the overall second-placed team. For this section (*Endronde/Tour Finale*), each team plays each other home and away, and the group winner is promoted to the first. Divisions III A and B, also permanent home of the first division's reserve teams, work on a similar basis.

Up for the cup

The domestic cup competition (*De Beker/La Coupe*) excites little interest. For more than thirty years (1928–53 and 1957–63) it wasn't played at all, but the lure of European competition revived interest.

Now, every August, some 120 teams enter the first round, including those from divisions III and IV, and the best from the previous season's provincial cup competitions. First-division sides don't enter until the last 32. Early games are decided on ninety minutes, extra time and penalties.

A famous Belgian – Jean-Marc Bosman

The semi-finals in April are played over two legs, the final on a single game, usually on the last Sunday in May at the Stade Roi Baudouin. It is preceded by the ladies' final, and tickets are available on the day.

Tickets

Sellouts are rarely a problem in Belgium, and tickets are always affordable, even though prices rise for the most attractive fixtures (*Verhoogd/Matches de Gala*). If it's a rainy afternoon, then a spot under cover (*Overdektenplaatsen/Places Couvertes*) will keep you sheltered. Most grounds still offer a choice between a seat (*Zitplaatsen/Assises*) and a place on the terraces (*Staanplaatsen/Places Debout*). A standing ticket (in the cheap *Volksplaats/Populaires*) will cost 300–400BF. The cheapest seats will be in the 400–600BF range, while the most expensive (in the *Eretribune/Tribune d'Honneur*) may run up to 1000BF.

Half-time

Matches are as much about beer and chips as football. Beer sales are essential to the financial survival of many Belgian clubs and the stadium bar will be busy before, during and after the game. Chip vans (*frituur/friterie*) surround every stadium, while grounds in Brussels and Wallonia also sell snails (*escargots*). A surprising number of club bars dispense hot Oxo.

Action replay

Belgium has five Flemish and two French channels, while stations from France, Germany, Luxembourg, Holland and England (including the BBC) are all widely available. The live Friday evening game is on Canal Plus at 8pm, with highlights on terrestial Flemish VTM at 11pm. The Saturday round-ups are *Goal!* on VTM and *Match 1* on French-language RTBF1, both at 10.30pm. Their Sunday equivalents are *Stadion Sport* (VTM) and *Sport* (RTBF1), both around 7pm. Flemish station VT4 has English Premiership action the same day at 6.30pm.

The back page

There are no daily sports papers in Belgium. Specialist soccer coverage comes from the weekly magazine *Sport Voetbal Magazine/Sport Foot* (Thursdays, 75BF), along with its monthly companion *Voetbal België/Football Belgique* (95BF), both published in two separate language editions.

In Brussels, the French-language paper *La Dernière Heure* (daily, 28BF) offers authoritative sports coverage, particularly in its weekend editions. You'll find excellent international coverage as well as domestic news and scores.

If you want to follow the Belgian game from Britain, the quarterly English-language fanzine *Diable Rouge* (£1) is heartfelt and informative. Copies are available from PO Box 10141, London N14 6SY.

Ultra culture

Belgium suffers little of the kind of organised hooliganism that afflicts neighbouring Holland. While the local police are keen to show off their riot shields and water cannons, it isn't always clear what they are there for. Some fan groups make drunken nuisances of themselves on away trips – Anderlecht's *O-section*, Standard's *Hellside*, anyone from Antwerp with a beer inside them – but overall the atmosphere is more rowdy than risky.

In the net

The excellent Belgian Soccer Archive has been alive and kicking on the Web since February 1995. Stats are the strong point, with coverage extending right down to the Brussels neighbourhood Saturday league (well, *somebody* must be interested). Everything is in a choice of French, Flemish and English, and the site includes a constantly updated – and handily colour-coded – Belgian club links page. The homepage is at: www.tornado.be/~marc.alcide/bsa/belgiansoccer.htm.

Brussels

Brussels' position in European football went down several notches following the Heysel disaster. Not only was the city's reputation in tatters – it lost its popularity as a venue for European finals (it had previously hosted eight, including the European Championship of 1972). Even the home club who played in the stadium complex, Racing Jet Brussels, moved out to Wavre, 30km away, in 1988. A lower-league Turkish team, Atlas Bruxelles, now play there.

Whether the Stade Roi Baudouin that was built in Heysel's place will stage as many big matches is open

Mine's a large one – Albert, Nilis and the Belgian cup, 1994

to question. The 1996 Cup-Winners' Cup final between Paris Saint-Germain and Rapid Vienna, with its potentially explosive mix of fans, passed off without a hitch, and the authorities hope the same can be said of the city's European Championship matches in the year 2000.

In terms of league football Brussels has always been dominated by one club – Union Saint-Gilloise before World War II, Anderlecht after it. The others have either folded, migrated or merged to help form the city's poor relations, Racing White Daring Molenbeek.

Anderlecht's facilities and resources put all other Belgian clubs in the shade, but this difference is all the more marked in Brussels. When the *Mauves* were formed in 1908, the city had four other clubs in the first division: Daring, Racing Club, Excelsior Léopold and Union Saint-Gilloise. Now only Union survive intact, and only just, eking out a bare existence on the edge of

the forested Duden park, the other side of the Charleroi canal from Anderlecht. RWDM are slightly further north, attracting a few thousand thanks mainly to the utterly marvellous fanfare band that plays all through their matches.

RWDM are a mix of four old clubs: Royal Racing Club de Bruxelles (formed 1891) and Royal White Star AC (1909) merged to become Royal Racing-White Bruxelles in 1963, who in turn merged with Royal Daring Club de Molenbeek in 1973. Racing and Daring won eleven titles between them and both teams made brief appearances in Europe. The classic derby before the war was Union against Daring, a fixture later staged at the Heysel. Until their relegation in 1973, Union were *the* Brussels club, with an identifiable neighbourhood feel and that sardonic *Bruxelleois* humour in the club bar. The few fans who still shuffle up rue du Stade do so out of a sense of duty to the club's great name.

The bars and restaurants at Anderlecht have the same executive feel as their plush stadium in the Parc Astrid. It's a pleasant place to see a game of football, but the fact is that many who do so come from out of town. Like Juventus, Manchester United and Real Madrid, the *Mauves* have fan clubs all over the country, and one of many accusations hurled at the club from the provinces is that they do not serve the city they reside in. In Flanders, Anderlecht are loathed because they are rich, can buy the best, propose Dutch-Belgian superleagues and, most of all, because they are French, and snobbish with it.

Ironically, the area of Anderlecht itself is run-down and full of poor Belgian families, whereas Saint-Gilles is mainly residential, boasting some of the city's most beautiful *art nouveau* buildings. Molenbeek is a mixture of both.

RWDM's title win in 1975 could not have been sweeter, coming as it did with a 1–0 victory over Anderlecht. The rôles and scoreline were reversed for Anderlecht's championship victory in 1991.

In Belgium, a 'Royal' tag is given to a club after 25 years' existence, but sponsorship (from Sony, in RWDM's case) does more to keep a team afloat financially, as do outgoing transfers. The sale of young prospect Johan Walem to Anderlecht in 1986 was doubly humiliating, in that Anderlecht met some of RWDM's unpaid bills as part of the deal. It is said they also wanted to buy the fanfare band, but were told they weren't for sale at any price. Some things, even in Brussels, money just can't buy.

Brussels essentials

Brussels **airport** is at Zaventem, 14km north-east of town, connected by the Airport City Express train (85BF, every 20 minutes, 5.30am–11.30pm, journey time 20 minutes) to all three main train stations. Buy your ticket at the office beforehand as the inspector will ask for a hefty surcharge onboard. A taxi will cost 1300–1600BF.

Domestic mainline **trains** all call at Gare du Nord, Gare Centrale and Gare du Midi, but the **Eurostar service** from London's Waterloo International (seven departures a day, just over three hours' journey time) serves Gare du Midi only. The main **bus station** is by Gare du Nord, from where you can also catch an airport bus (70BF, hourly, journey time 35 minutes).

City **transport** is made up of three **Métro lines** – 1A, 1B (both red) and 2 (orange) – which all cross at Arts-Loi. There is also a blue **Pre-Métro** line connecting Gare du Nord and Gare du Midi; the Bourse stop is the most central, serving the city's showpiece Grand Place. A tram system also runs underground, and a network of buses overground. The whole service runs 5.30am–midnight. There is no night transport.

A single **ticket** costs 50BF, a five-journey ticket 240BF and a ten-journey one 320BF – all available from bus or tram drivers, Métro kiosks and STIB offices. A 24-hour pass is 130BF. You're trusted to validate tickets as you enter the Métro stop or bus. To enter some trams, touch the felt strip dividing the two door halves.

Taxis are rarely hailed. Pick one up outside the main train stations or order one by phone – call Taxis Verts on ☎02/ 349 4646 or Taxi Orange on ☎02/511 2288. The minimum charge is 95BF (plus 75BF night tariff), plus 38BF per km inside the city's nineteen districts (*communes*), 76BF outside.

The TIB **tourist office** in the Grand Place (open daily 9am–6pm, ☎02/513 8940, fax 02/514 4538) is cramped and over-crowded.

Some English-language listings are published by *The Bulletin* (weekly, 85BF), including film and TV information. For club and concert details, get a copy of the French-language *Kiosque* (monthly, 60BF) or the slightly inferior *Bruxelscope* (monthly, 28BF).

Purple reign – Constant Vanden Stock celebrates twenty years of having his cake and eating it

The thrilling fields

 Anderlecht

Stade Constant Vanden Stock, avenue Théo Verbeeck 2
Capacity 28,000
Colours All white with purple trim
League champions 1947, 1949–51, 1954–56, 1959, 1962, 1964–68, 1972, 1974, 1981, 1985–87, 1991, 1993–95
Cup winners 1965, 1972–73, 1975–76, 1988–89, 1994
Cup-Winners' Cup winners 1976, 1978
UEFA Cup winners 1983

Anderlecht is a one-man empire built by booze. In the fifteen years that he was club president before handing over the post to his son Roger in 1996, brewery boss Constant Vanden Stock turned Belgium's most successful club into a professional operation boasting one of the best medium-sized stadia in Europe. That he was being blackmailed by players' agent Jean Elst for much

of this time is a matter which came to light too late for Elst's information – concerning Anderlecht's bribing of referees – to come under the jurisdiction of Belgian law.

All of Anderlecht's three European successes came during the late Seventies and early Eighties, the club's golden period. After that, the money needed to convert the Parc Astrid stadium, as it is known, and to keep Elst quiet, meant that there was less to go round on players. The *Mauves* have thus under-achieved in Europe for most of the Nineties.

Founded in 1908, Anderlecht moved to the Parc Astrid ten years later but did not grace it with first-division football until 1935, by which time a modest stadium, Stade Versé, had been built. Vanden Stock himself joined the club as a boy, but injury cut short his playing career. He became involved in management and would go on to coach the national team for a decade. The 1942 signing of striker Jef Mermans helped Anderlecht win their first title five years later. Two years after that, an English ex-goalkeeper by the name of Bill Gormlie was appointed first-team coach, ushering in a decade of seven titles that established Anderlecht as the country's biggest club. Europe remained out of reach: during the Fifties, the team lost 7–2 on aggregate to Rangers and 10–0 in a single match to Manchester United, underlining the fact that theirs was still very much a semi-pro outfit relying on local talent.

As Mermans and Gormlie bowed out, however, two inside-forwards came through the ranks to push Anderlecht to greater heights: Paul van Himst and Jef Jurion. Van Himst became the greatest Belgian player of all time, and his class and understanding with Jurion sent shockwaves across Europe.

In the early Sixties Real Madrid, CDNA Sofia and Bologna were all beaten, while at home Anderlecht won five titles in a row. In 1964, the Belgian team that beat Holland 1–0 was composed entirely of Anderlecht players.

In 1970 the *Mauves* beat Newcastle and Internazionale on their way to the Fairs' Cup final, where giving away a late consolation goal to Arsenal in the home leg proved costly, as the Gunners matched Anderlecht's three goals in the second game.

Van Himst retired the year before Anderlecht's greatest triumph – their Cup-Winners' Cup victory of 1976. A new hero had replaced him, the Dutch forward Rob Rensenbrink, fast and supremely gifted. Provided for by François van der Elst and Arie Haan in midfield, Rensenbrink was unstoppable in the final against West Ham, scoring two goals in a powerful 4–2 win. Anderlecht made the final of the same trophy the following year, losing to two late Hamburg goals, then got their revenge by beating the Germans in the second round of the same competition the year after that; they went on to reach a third consecutive final, thrashing Austria Vienna 4–0, with Rensenbrink again scoring twice. Liverpool were duly beaten in the European Super Cup a few months later.

Vanden Stock's arrival as president at the start of the Eighties signalled a new era for the club. He brought in van Himst as coach and began the development of the Parc Astrid. Anderlecht unluckily went out to a single goal against Aston Villa in a 1982 European Cup semi-final. But there was to be no mistake in the UEFA Cup a year later, when a team boasting Frankie Vercauteren

Winter's tale – Anderlecht have prospered playing European ties in icy Belgian Decembers

Heysel

Stade du Roi Baudouin,
avenue du Marathon
Capacity 41,000
(all-seated)

Heysel, Heysel. Memories
of the **1985 tragedy** have
not gone away but, officially
at least, the stadium has.
Ten years after the event,
the Stade du Roi Baudouin
('King Baudouin stadium')
was opened with a friendly
match between Belgium and

Today – new stands dwarf the original Heysel entrance

Germany. This time police were quick to stamp out loutish behaviour on the part of a
group of German fans whose sense of occasion was warped, to put it mildly.

A decade earlier it had all been very different. The build-up to the Juventus–
Liverpool **European Cup final** of 1985 saw Liverpool fans, many drunk, joined in
Brussels by neo-Nazi elements with no interest in football whatsoever. Segregation was
poor, local policing disorganised. Parts of the stadium were falling to bits.

Shortly before kick-off, a group of English fans stampeded through the supposedly
neutral block Z, and 39 (mainly Italian) supporters were crushed to death when the
sector wall collapsed. To avert the risk of further deaths, a match was somehow played
out, which Juventus won. English clubs were banned from Europe for five years.

For a time Heysel, which had been built in 1930 in the Parc des Expositions in
north-west Brussels, was closed. Then, after much haggling over who should foot the
bill for refurbishment, the Belgian FA decided to build the Stade Roi Baudouin in its
place – though some parts of the original ground remain. The first part of the renovation
was completed in 1996. The next won't be ready
until 1998, two years before the ground is due to
host the **opening match** of Euro 2000, by
which time the capacity will be 50,000.

Heysel is the terminus of **Métro line 1A**,
twenty minutes from Gare du Midi. **La
Coupole**, at avenue Houba de Strooper 264, is
the best of the bars – all of which are best
accessed by getting off the Métro **one stop
before Heysel** – and a Molenbeek one at that.
La Couronne, The large restaurant just up the
road at Strooper 286, has a great variety of stuff
on the menu and a billiard hall at the back.

The stadium **ticket office**, clearly marked
Kartenverkoop/Vente Tickets, is by Tribune #1,
along avenue du Marathon, the other side of the
Heysel Métro stop. The four stands are **colour-
coded**: #1 (yellow) is the most expensive seats,
#2 (green) and #4 (blue) are behind the goals,
and #3 (orange) is along avenue des Athletes by
the Métro stop.

Yesterday – the carnage of May 1985

and Erwin Vandenbergh swept past Porto, Valencia and Bohemians Prague before beating Benfica in the final.

By 1984, a precocious Enzo Scifo was on the scene. But a 2–0 semi-final first leg defeat by Nottingham Forest caused panic in the Anderlecht boardroom. With so much money invested in the stadium – the first in continental Europe to have executive boxes – the team simply had to reach the final. The referee for the second leg, Spain's Emilio Guruceta, has since died in a car crash, so we will never know to what extent Vanden Stock exerted a financial influence over proceedings. At any rate, 3–0 to Anderlecht was the final score, after Forest had had a penalty appeal turned down and a goal disallowed. In the final, Spurs equalled Anderlecht's 1–1 home scoreline and won the resulting penalty shoot-out – but the Brussels boxes had been filled one more lucrative time.

A European Cup semi-final defeat by Steaua Bucharest in 1986 and a Cup Winners' Cup final loss to Sampdoria in 1990 have been the club's European highlights since – although quite how Anderlecht contrived to let slip a three-goal lead with twenty minutes remaining at Werder Bremen in the 1993 Champions' League, nobody will ever know.

Anderlecht's coach at that time, Johan Boskamp, was still on the bench come the end of the 1996/97 season. In between times his *Mauves* won the title three times, including a classic double in 1993/94 when the side could boast a commanding Philippe Albert at the back, and a strikeforce of Luc Nilis, Marc Degryse and Johnny Bosman that bagged over fifty goals between them.

Boskamp quit for Morocco in 1995, only to return again the same year after Vanden Stock had experimented disastrously (and uncharacteristically) with three coaches in as many months. Since then Anderlecht have not won a thing. Out of the title running for the past two seasons, they led little Germinal Ekeren 2–0 in the 1997 cup final but eventually lost 4–2 after extra time. It was a sad way for Boskamp

to bid his farewell to the club, but the stars who graced his team during the early Nineties are all long gone, and most fans accept it is time for a change.

The return of Scifo, after more than a decade away, coupled with the arrival from across town of René Vandereycken as coach, may just stir the lumbering giant out of its stupor.

Here we go!

Take **Métro line 1B** to Saint Guidon, then a five-minute walk – around the circular Métro station, with the tower of the church of Saint Pierre et Guidon ahead of you, then left into rue Saint Guidon.

Swift half

Place de Linde, between the Métro station and the stadium, is full of bars – the *Café Half-Time* has more character than the larger *La Ruche*. *Au Cheval Blanc*, where the square meets rue Saint Guidon, can serve a decent meal at 300BF.

Past the stadium, *La Coupe* at avenue Théo Verbeeck 57 is a modern football bar embellished with team photos and a wonderful multi-coloured league ladder behind the bar. *Champions,* at rue Emile Versé 3, and the more run-down *La Caravelle,* opposite, are also fair options.

In the stadium, the small bar by sector V is less pretentious than the *Restaurant Saint Guidon* nearby. Eighties Anderlecht star Ludo Coeck, who died in a car crash, is honoured in the *Belle-Vue Club* bar by sector E4.

Getting a ticket

The main ticket office is along avenue Théo Verbeeck. The home end is in Tribune #4, access by entrance #4 or #5. Away fans are opposite in Tribune #1, entrance through gate #1 (it's marked *Bezoekers/Visiteurs*). Neutrals can go along the side of the pitch in Tribune #3 (entrances #5 and #6) or in the flashier and more expensive Tribune #1. For the time being, the cheapest places are standing ones at either end or in Tribune #1.

Publication

Anderlecht Sports is the club's bimonthly mauve-and-white publication, cost 50BF.

Club shop

The **RSCA Fan-Shop** is at the ground (open Mon–Fri 10am–6pm & Sat 10am–5pm) and acts as a showcase for the club's attempts to turn their purple badge into a modern, global sportswear brand. Be warned.

Ultra culture

The atmosphere in the Parc Astrid is intimate without being intimidating, although the visit of Newcastle for a pre-season friendly in 1996 provoked 'The Purple Vultures' into some seriously pejorative chanting for ninety minutes.

In the net

The official Anderlecht website is at: www.rsca.be. Like a lot of club-sponsored sites, it's slick and commercial but strangely uninviting – you can download a RealAudio version of the club hymn, but that's about it for user interactivity. More like it is the unofficial site run from Austria at: unet.univie.ac.at/~a9502375/index.htm. The homepage is absurdly large, but your patience will be rewarded – this is one of those rare football sites that actually makes all the new software work, including Java Applet news tickers and RealAudio interviews. Alongside this sort of content, the usual stats archives and picture galleries seem positively dull – though it's all here if you want it. The site is updated daily and all pages are in English.

Groundhopping

Some of the grand old names of Brussels football may have fled town or faded away altogether, but there's still some soccer to be seen out there in suburbia. You may be pleasantly surprised by the warmth of the welcome, but possibly not by the standard of football.

◐ RWD Molenbeek

Stade Edmond Machtens, rue Charles Malis 61
Capacity 15,000
Colours White shirts with red and black trim, black shorts
League champions 1975

Are-Vay-Day-Emm started at the top and have been in gentle decline ever since. Behind their formation was Jean Baptiste L'Ecluse, whose own building business has seen a similar slide to that of the club he poured so much money into during the Seventies.

A former chairman of Daring, L'Ecluse persuaded Racing White to merge with his club in 1973, thus ensuring immediate European football through Racing White's final league position of third that year. RWDM duly beat Español of Barcelona before bowing out to Portugal's Vitória Setúbal on away goals.

Racing and daring – RWDM's Steve Laeremans

Better was to follow in 1975, when a goal from international Jacques Teugels against Anderlecht won the club their first and only title. Key player Johan Boskamp became a local hero – until his move to Anderlecht. Though they were unable to keep their title, the team remained in the top six, and in 1977 they were only an away goal away from a UEFA Cup final against Juventus.

The club have done little since, though coach René Vandereycken did take them back into Europe for 1996/97. His departure (to Anderlecht – where else?) may test the tunefulness of RWDM's brass band in the months and years to come.

To reach the ground, take Métro 1A/B to Beekkant, then bus #85 or a ten-minute walk down rue Jules Vieujant, followed by a left down rue Osseghem.

The *Bar Sport* at rue Osseghem 208 and *Bar à L'Ecu* on the other side of the crossroads are full of football talk and memorabilia. The *Café du Stade* at the other end of the stadium, Boulevard Louis Mettéwie, is sadly closed for evening matches but perfect in the afternoon.

☻ Union Saint-Gilloise

Stade Joseph Marien, chaussée de Bruxelles 223
Capacity 12,000
Colours Yellow shirts, blue shorts
League champions 1904–7, 1909, 1910, 1913, 1923, 1933–35
Cup winners 1913–14

A more romantic ground-hop would be hard to imagine. The Stade Joseph Marien, named after a former club president, is bordered by the forest of Parc Duden on one side and by a wonderful old club bar on the other.

People crowded up the hillside in their thousands to see Union in their golden prewar days, when they were the biggest club in Belgium. The last decent Union side, that of the late Fifties and early Sixties, made occasional forays into the Fairs' Cup, beating Roma and Olympique Marseille.

Union were too proud to agree to any of the mergers that swallowed up the lesser Brussels clubs in the Seventies. The club celebrated their centenary in 1997 by being relegated to the third division. With amateur football and possibly worse looming, the forest is ghostly silent.

To reach the trees, take the Pré-Métro to Horta then tram #18, getting off at Van Haelen. From there, the stadium is a five-minute walk up rue des Glands. *La Brasserie des Sports* at rue des Glands 80 is a classic old bar, with the clicking of backgammon counters behind the hum of football talk. *Union's Tavern* on the corner of rue du Stade and chaussée de Bruxelles is another goodie. But the jewel of Saint Gilles is the stadium clubhouse itself. The barman is a friendly Anglophile (hence the Whitbread pub sign) who will happily explain at length the story behind the plaque inside, dedicated to Jef

Going down – Godtbil tries to keep the Gilloise flag flying

Valise. An eternal *Unioniste*, 'Geoff Suitcase' (real name Van Caelen) used to carry his uncle Jacques' kit bag to home games and has followed the yellow-and-blues through thick and much thin ever since.

Toone VII, impasse Schuddeveld 6. Unusual bar now firmly on the beaten tourist track, but worth a look-in all the same. Attached to the Toone puppet theatre, whose models hang from the ceilings. Just off petite rue des Bouchers. Métro to Bourse.

Eat, drink, sleep…

Bars and clubs

Brussels has neither the hip cachet of Amsterdam nor the fashionable trappings of Paris, but in a lot of ways it is **more fun** than either. For a start, there is more variety to both the beer and the bars serving it, many of which **open late**.

Unpretentious places full of locals abound – just five minutes' walk from the tourist bright lights of Grand Place, down rue du Marché du Charbon or rue du Midi, or west the other side of boulevard Anspach.

The classic *Bruxelleois* beer is **Gueuze**, which packs a hangover like a drop-kick from local lad Jean-Claude van Damme. The local spirit is a juniper gin, *pèkèt*, of which there is a famous *Van Damme* brand.

À la Mort Subite, rue Montagne aux Herbes Potagères 7. Possibly the most famous bar in Brussels, offering 'Sudden Death', which gave its name to the beer sold all over town. Smoky and atmospheric, this place has hardly changed since the Twenties. Métro to De Brouckère.

Kafka, rue de la Vierge Noire 6. Surprisingly unpretentious bar offering a choice of fifty beers, eighteen different vodkas, or a cup of hot Oxo. Métro to De Brouckère.

L'Archiduc, rue Antoine Dansaert 6. Done out like a Fred Astaire movie, with live jazz and a great mellow atmosphere. Civil opening hours of 4pm–4am. Métro to Bourse.

The Fuse, rue Blaes 208. First and easily the best techno club in town, with top-name DJs spinning. Open Saturdays only, until 7.30am. Admission 300BF. Métro to Porte de Hal.

Restaurants

The cosmopolitan mix of the city's inhabitants and the demands of the international business community mean that Brussels offers a whole world of **different cuisines.** 'Wide range' simply doesn't do it justice. A lot of places are overpriced, living off their clients' expense accounts, but you can find good-value Portuguese, Greek and North African restaurants around the Gare du Midi.

The touristy restaurants around the Ilôt Sacré, east of Grand Place, advertised by all sorts of lobsters and shellfish outside, are often a disappointment once you tuck in; a *plat du jour* around Place Sainte Cathérine will be a better bet.

Aux Armes de Bruxelles, rue des Bouchers 13. A far better fish restaurant than the many dotted around the same street, divided into a formal restaurant and a bistro. Great buckets of mussels in various sauces. Main seafood courses around 1000BF. *Plat du jour* at 495BF. Closed Mondays. Most credit cards. Métro to Bourse.

Chez Léon, rue des Bouchers 18. As touristy as it gets, but deservedly packs them in with cheap portions of mussels and swift service. Menu at 395BF. Most credit cards. Métro to Bourse, and another branch up at Heysel.

In t'Spinnekopke, place au Jardin aux Fleurs 1. Homely period building with several low-ceilinged rooms. Belgian specialities cooked in beer – the owner has published his own book of beer recipes. Main courses around 800–1000BF. Most major credit cards. Métro to Bourse.

Le Falstaff, rue Henri Maus 19–25. Famous *art nouveau* café-restaurant serving large portions of main courses until 3am Mon–Fri, 5am Sat–Sun.

Plats du jour at 350BF. Covered terrace facing the Bourse. Most credit cards. Métro to Bourse.

Le Pré Salé, rue de Flandre 16. Around the corner from the flashier establishments of place Sainte Cathérine, a neighbourhood diner serving fish and local dishes at very reasonable prices. The plats du jour here are an excellent deal. No credit cards. Métro to Sainte Cathérine.

Accommodation

Brussels hotels tend to cater for the business community and its Monday–Friday schedule, so always check for bargain weekend rates.

If you're arriving at the airport, the **Destination Belgium** information desk (open daily 6.30am–9.30pm, ☎02/720 5161) has a free hotel reservation service – pay a deposit upfront and have the amount deducted from your hotel bill. The **Acotra Travel Agency** at rue de la Madelaine 51 (open Mon–Sat 10am–5pm, ☎02/512 7078) books youth hostel accommodation. The cheap hotels around Gare du Midi and Gare du Nord can be pretty seedy.

Centre Vincent van Gogh, rue Traversière 8 (☎02/217 0158, fax 02/219 7995). Youth hostel with no curfew and single rooms available at 620BF. Doubles 510BF a head, dorm beds 380BF. All with breakfast included. Obligatory 100BF for sheets. Free lockers. Great late-night North African bars opposite. Most major credit cards. Métro to Botanique.

Fouquets, rue de la Bourse 6 (☎02/512 0020, fax 02/51 9357). Perfectly located pension with singles at 1400–1700BF, doubles 1850–2250BF, breakfast 150BF. Most major credit cards. Métro to Bourse.

George V, rue t'Kint 23 (☎02/513 5093, fax 02/513 4493). Period neighbourhood hotel with ornate balconies overlooking a whole mess of bars down below. Singles at 2000BF, doubles 2500BF. All rooms with cable TV, bar downstairs. Visa and Mastercard accepted. Métro to Bourse.

Sleep Well, rue du Daimier 23 (☎02/218 5050, fax 02/219 1313). Quality youth hostel with a bar, cable TV, and currency exchange downstairs. Double rooms at 640BF per person, quads 510BF. Near Gare du Nord. Métro to Rogier.

Come on down – even the tourist traps of the Grand Place are worth having a swiftie in

Bruges

Belgium's leading tourist city plays host to its second biggest football team, Club Bruges, and their groundshare neighbours Cercle. 'Club', as they are known to all, represent the pride of Flanders, working class and Flemish-speaking, and gain support from all over the region.

Throughout Belgium, Club are very much the neutrals' favourite, famed for their team spirit and honest endeavour. In Bruges itself, support for the two teams is divided fifty-fifty, but any cross-town rivalry pales next to the mutual hatred of Anderlecht – any chance of Flanders getting one over on the fat cats from Brussels is more important than the local derby match. With Bruges being such a small town – population around a quarter of a million – players of both sides mix socially, and the local football community is tight-knit and friendly.

Football was first played in Bruges at the English College in the district of Sint-Andries west of town, where the Olympiastadion is now sited. Both clubs were founded in the 1890s, Cercle's players being mainly upper-class Dutch and Englishmen, later local, academic Catholics.

In the early days Cercle had the better of things but it wasn't until the rise of Club in the late Sixties that Bruges as a city put itself on the football map. The groundshare between the two teams began in 1975. Until then, Club had been playing at the atmospheric De Klokke on Torhoutse Steenweg, while Cercle were at the Edgard Desmedt stadium on nearby Magdalenstraat, both just south of Sint-Andries.

With both clubs experiencing serious financial difficulties, the then mayor of Bruges, Van Maele, had a municipal stadium built at the end of Olympialaan – the Olympiastadion.

It was ready just in time to catch Club's purple patch under Austrian coach Ernst Happel, which included two major runs in Europe – both of them, curiously, ended

That Fleming feeling – Verheyen and Staelens

by Liverpool in the final. Cercle, meanwhile, could only watch and slide.

The teams have met in two Belgian cup finals – the first, in 1986, being the only one ever played at the Olympiastadion. Club won that game, and ten years later they repeated the triumph, at Brussels' newly refurbished Stade du Roi Baudouin, and thus achieved the domestic double; their previous title win meant that both clubs had already qualified for Europe before a ball was kicked on final day.

Neither final was a classic, but plenty of league derbies have been. In 1990/91 Club beat Cercle 10–0, with the Australian Frank Farina scoring four. A year later there were another ten goals – though any comfort Cercle drew from the 5–5 scoreline was tempered by the fact that Club's ninth title was already in the bag at the time.

Cercle's relegation in 1997 has put the dampers on derby day for the foreseeable future. Unless they can scramble back up sharpish, the next big football event in town will be Euro 2000.

A family affair – Club players celebrate their 1996 Belgian cup final win over Cercle

The thrilling fields

Club Bruges

Olympiastadion, see p.34
Colours Blue-and-black striped shirts, black shorts
League champions 1920, 1973, 1976–78, 1980, 1988, 1990, 1992, 1996
Cup winners 1968, 1970, 1977, 1986, 1991, 1996

Belgium's most successful provincial side, Club Bruges need to repeat the European form of yesteryear if they are to stay up with the big boys on course for the Dutch-Belgian superleague. The departure of two key players – Australian sweeper Paul Okon and Croat striker Mario Stanić – for Italy resulted in an inconsistent campaign in 1996/97. With the evergreen Franky van der Elst now nearer 40 than 30, the likes of Lorenzo Staelens and Gert Verheyen also showing their age, and offers coming in for the team's other goal-hungry Croat, Robert

Spehar, incoming coach Eric Gerets is going to have to redeploy a new set of troops if Club are to repeat their double success of 1996. Ironically, they were denied a second consecutive title in 1997 by Gerets himself, whose Lierse team pipped Club by two points.

It is now five years since Club made a European final, five since they were in a semi. Domestic success in a league as weak as Belgium's is not enough to keep the top names in the medieval beauty of Bruges.

Although one of the earliest Belgian clubs to be founded (in 1891), the *Blauw-Zwart* ('blue-and-blacks') didn't really come into the frame until around eighty years later, when future Anderlecht president Constant Vanden Stock oversaw the rise of Raoul Lambert and the arrival of Rob Rensenbrink from DWS Amsterdam. The team managed cup wins in 1968 and 1970, and regular, if unsuccessful, European action generated a real buzz around De Klokke. After finishing runners-up five years in six, Club eventually won their first modern title in 1973 and hired wily coach Ernst Happel a year later.

During Happel's four-year reign, the *Blauw-Zwart* became Belgium's top club. The team moved to the Olympiastadion and seemed immediately inspired by their new, modern surroundings. Suddenly, Club were beating European teams of the highest pedigree – AC Milan, Juventus, Real and Atlético Madrid, Roma, Hamburg.

Twice they made a European final, twice they were slightly unlucky to be beaten by Liverpool. In the 1976 UEFA Cup, Club got two goals in the first quarter of an hour in the first leg at Anfield, then conceded three in the space of six second-half minutes; a 1–1 draw was not enough at the Olympia-stadion. Two years later Club made the European Cup final for the first and only time, and had to play Liverpool on what was virtually their second ground – Wembley stadium. The Belgians approached the game suffering an injury crisis, and a Kenny Dalglish goal settled a poor final. Future national coach Georges Leekens played at the back for Club in both ties.

At home, the team's three consecutive titles embraced a league and cup double in 1977. By the time Happel left in 1978, Club had firmly taken their place among a Belgian 'big three', alongside Anderlecht and Standard Liège. With big local hero Jan Ceulemans coming through as the best forward talent since Lambert, the side couldn't match the form of Happel's team in Europe but remained consistent at home, at times featuring the odd foreign star such as Frank Farina and France's Jean-Pierre Papin. With Franky van der Elst solid in midfield, Club twice made further European semi-finals, losing to Español in the 1988 UEFA Cup, and Werder Bremen in the Cup-Winners' Cup four years later.

In the mid-Nineties, under coach Hugo Broos (another good old boy who was in the side against Liverpool at Wembley) and with Staelens picking up Ceulemans' mantle, Club continued to succeed at home and frustrate in Europe. The ease of their 1996 double win, which featured twenty league goals from Stanić and only thirty conceded by loyal goalkeeper Dany Verlinden, perhaps said more about the problems at Anderlecht than the quality of the rest of the Belgian league.

In 1996/97, Steaua Bucharest knocked Club out of the qualifying round of the Champions' League, before Schalke 04 did the same in the UEFA Cup.

Swift half

The **Clubhuis** by blocks 10/11 is a spacious Club bar at the stadium – pay your money at the till before handing your receipt over the counter and picking up your pint.

Publication

Blauw-Zwart Magazine (monthly, 60BF) is Club's official organ, and has been for over fifty years. One of its main contributors

Bruges essentials

Bruges' **bus and train stations** are south of the town centre, fifteen minutes' walk straight up Oostmeers. The city's transport comprises a network of **buses**. Much of the town centre is pedestrianised – most buses stop by Biekorf near the central Markt square.

Buses run 6am–11pm. They're 40BF a ride (tickets available onboard), or 270BF for ten rides, 105BF for a day ticket – all available from the **De Lijn kiosk** on Stationsplein. There is no night transport. To call for a **taxi**, dial ☎050/333 881 or ☎050/334 455.

The main **tourist office** is by the Markt at Burg 11 (open April–Sept Mon–Fri 9.30am–6.30pm, Sat–Sun 10am–noon & 2–6.30pm; Oct–March Mon–Fri 9.30am–5pm, Sat 9.30am–1.15pm & 2–5.30pm, ☎050/448 686, fax 050/448 600). There's a smaller branch inside the train station. At either office you can pick up a copy of the comprehensive, free, Flemish-language listings monthly, *Exit*.

The Olympiastadion

Olympialaan 74, Sint-Andries
Capacity 18,000 (16,000 seated)

The Olympiastadion is Belgium's
only major **groundshare**, and a
successful one at that. Club and
Cercle have an equal share of the
facilities, and each has their own
club bar and office, either side of
the VIP/press entrance in the main
west stand. Naturally, Club's beer is
slightly cheaper than that of their
posher neighbours.

Big in Bruges – but there's nothing Olympic about it

Each club pays an equal share of
their takings at the gate to the local council, who built the ground in 1975. However,
with Cercle's relegation in 1997, this sum is barely likely to cover the administration
costs of keeping the club here.

For most of their two decades together, Club have come out on top. Cercle didn't
manage to win a derby match here until 1988, by which time Club had won five titles
away from their old De Klokke ground.

The Olympiastadion feels both functional and lived in, an atmosphere which may
change when **ground improvements** commence in 1998. The current capacity of
18,000, including room for 2000 standing customers, will rise to an all-seated 30,000.
The name may even be changed to **Flandriastadion** – but only if they can get this past
Brussels.

On derby day Cercle fans occupy the north *Kirk* (church) end, Club's the south *Bad*
(swimming pool) end, but north *blok* #19 is favoured by both for most of the season.
Cercle normally play on Saturdays, Club traditionally Sundays – although TV and
European commitments can complicate the issue.

On matchdays, **special buses** are laid on from Stationsplein, in front of the train
station to the ground, ten minutes' drive away, for the usual 40BF ticket. The buses
then wait at the end of Olympialaan until after the game. If you'd prefer to have a little
more time on your side, bus #5 or #15 from the station to Sint-Andrieskerk will drop
you right by the best bars on Gistelsesteenweg, near the stadium. Allow fifteen minutes
for the journey.

Former Club Bruges, Anderlecht and Sheffield Wednesday striker **Marc Degryse**
has a stake in *Los Amigos* at Gistelsesteenweg 471, a lads' pub with disco lights and a
games room. *De Platse*, on the other side at #536, is more ornate, ideal for the older
generation of fans. The perfect mix is at *De Chalet*, #530, full of friendly local character
and host to the FC Sint-Andries pub team.

The main **ticket offices** are at diagonally opposite corners of the stadium, one
between entrances D and E, the other between A and B. The best (and dearest) seats
are in the *blok* #2 of the west stand, though anywhere in *bloks* #0–1 and #3–9 in the
west or east stands will give you a decent view from along the sides of the pitch.

Behind the goals, *blok* #19, running all along the church end, is where you'll find
the cheapest seats.

For the time being there are **standing places** available through entrances A, C and
F. **Visitors** are usually allocated *blok* #15, at the far side of the south end, entrance E.

for most of that period, Roger Pollet, son of Armand who won a championship medal with the team in 1920, was a much-loved local figure who died in 1996.

Club shop
A new **Clubshop** is being opened for the 1997/98 season, in a freshly built, brown-brick building at the end of Olympialaan. It's not certain if the small store under the *Clubhuis* will stay open as well.

Ultra culture
Club fans like a beer and a sing-song, and provided nobody mentions the word 'Anderlecht', everyone's happy. They share an affinity with Feyenoord's faithful, and drinking sessions when the two sets meet are the stuff of legend.

In the net
A couple of Club websites have recently disappeared, but Michel Britte's unofficial site continues undaunted at: www.inconnect.com/~mbritte/club/index.htm. Everything's kept nice and simple, and while it's clearly not going to set cyberspace on fire, all the news, stats and picture galleries are kept scrupulously up-to-date.

 ## Cercle Bruges

Olympiastadion, see p.34
Colours Green, white and black striped shirts, black shorts
League champions 1911, 1927, 1930
Cup winners 1927, 1985

The *Groen-Wit-Zwart* ('green-white-and-blacks') are Bruges' second club whose books have seen players from all around the globe, but who have never recovered the form they showed before World War II.

Formed by former students of the Sint-Franciscus Xavelus Institut in 1899, Cercle were the first club from Flanders to win the Belgian championship, in 1911. With

regular international Florimond van Halme playing at centre-half, Cercle went on to win the double in 1927 and the title for the last time in 1930, before van Halme retired.

Much of the next four decades were spent flitting between divisions, before the club's move to the Olympiastadion in the Seventies attracted a better class of foreigner. Former Danish international captain Morten Olsen spent a couple of seasons here, but the team's only modern honour has been a cup win in 1985, Cercle beating Beveren on penalties in the final.

Cercle's hero of the early Nineties was Josip Weber, a Croat-born striker who became a naturalised Belgian to play for

Ilie Stan – one of Cercle's many Romanians

the Red Devils at the 1994 World Cup. He scored 130 goals in six league seasons before moving to Anderlecht in 1994/95.

Cercle have continued to make the most of cheap East European talent, but in 1996 Romanian internationals Dorinel Munteanu and Tibor Selymes both left, for Cologne and Anderlecht respectively. The departure of the club's top scorer of 1996/97, Hungarian Gábor Torma, to Roda JC Kerkrade of Holland, coincided with relegation.

Swift half

The **Cercle Pub** in *blok* #12 of the stadium is a friendly bar which is open on Monday, Wednesday and Friday evenings as well as on matchdays. The modest **club shop** is downstairs – open only on matchdays, credit cards politely refused.

'Let's all meet up in the year 2000...'

In the year 2000, for the first time in football history, the finals of a major international tournament are being staged by **two countries**. Two years before Japan and South Korea try to outdo each other in extravagance over the hosting of the World Cup of 2002, **Holland and Belgium** will stage **Euro 2000**.

The competition format will be much the same as at Euro '96 in England. Sixteen teams will be divided into four groups of four, with the top two going through to play out quarter-finals, semi-finals and a final – making 31 matches in all. The Belgians and Dutch will be **kept apart** in groups A and D, and both will play their matches on home territory. The **opening match** will be at Brussels' Stade du Roi Baudouin on June 10, the final either at the Amsterdam Arena or Rotterdam's De Kuip on July 2.

Six other stadia are down to stage the remaining matches: Arnhem's Gelderland and Eindhoven's Philips stadium in Holland; Bruges' Olympiastadion, Anderlecht's Parc Astrid, Charleroi's Mambour, and Liège's Sclessin in Belgium.

Arnhem's Gelderland 'Eurodrome' has been under construction since 1996. When complete, towards the end of 1997, it will have a movable floor and roof, allowing it to adapt to host a wide range of events, sporting and otherwise. In contrast, the Belgian grounds are old and still in need of **major works**. Even the Parc Astrid does not yet measure up to UEFA's requirements of 30,000 seats. Charleroi's current ground holds only 19,000 (9000 of them standing), while Standard's Sclessin has 12,000 seats – renovation and expansion of the *Tribune Terril* are on the drawing board to increase this.

Bearing in mind Heysel, the Ajax-Feyenoord ultra violence of 1997, the availability of cheap booze on cross-Channel ferries and the long-running feud between Holland and Germany, **security** will be of paramount importance. Although some of the football was disappointing at Euro '96, the security arrangements made for an almost totally incident-free tournament. This was doubly impressive considering that it was the first European Championship to feature sixteen teams.

The reality is that only five European countries can reasonably stage a sixteen-team tournament, and of these, **Spain** is the prime candidate to host Euro 2004. The other four have all hosted the event since 1980, which means that further shared hosting (Austria and Hungary have also applied for 2004) will surely be upon us.

As for the football, the **qualifying draw** for Euro 2000 will take place in December 1997. The summer of 1999 will see a six-team tournament played in several of the newly converted stadia, featuring Belgium, Holland, France, Germany, Japan and South Korea.

And the year 2000? Lars Ricken, David Beckham, Raúl, Christian Vieri and Patrick Vieira should all be established internationals by then; the challenge facing the Low Countries is to provide a stage worthy of their high talent.

In the net

Cercle promise an official club website soon, but in the meantime there are a number of fan-run alternatives. Perhaps the best is Wim van Lancker's effort at: users.skynet.be/sky43760/. It's a straightforward site featuring regularly updated news and stats, and English-language pages are under construction.

Eat, drink, sleep...

Bars and clubs

Bruges is one of those small tourist towns where the nightlife, such as it is, is best **during the week**. At weekends the cafés around the Markt are packed with coachloads of people from out of town, and 't Zand square, nearer the train station, is a more bearable option. Locals prefer the **typical Flemish bars** tucked away down side-streets.

't Brugs Beertje, Kemelstraat 5. Friendly pub famed for its huge selection of beers, nearly two hundred in all. Open 4pm–1am, closed Wednesdays. Between 't Zand and Markt. All buses to Markt.

Cactus Club, Stint-Jakobsstraat 33. The town's major venue for live acts and DJs, entrance around 150BF for a local band, 300BF for a foreign one. The club organises an open-air festival at Minnewaterpark in July. All buses to Biekorf.

De Hobbit, Kemelstraat 8. Popular, studenty bar/club with occasional live music and a full menu. Open late (for Bruges). Closed Mondays and Tuesdays. Between 't Zand and Markt. All buses to Markt.

Straffe Hendrik-Huisbrouwerij, Walplein 26. Straffe Hendrik, the most famous Bruges brew, pale in colour and sharp in taste, is the only beer sold here, at the brewery and museum of the same name. Ten-minute walk from either 't Zand or the station, or if you're feeling lazy, it's on the circular #1 bus route.

Man with a plan – new Club coach Eric Gerets

The Top, Sint-Salvatorskerkhof 5. Perhaps the best bar in town, run by a genial East Londoner, attracting the Cercle fraternity and anyone else interested in listening to some decent sounds until late on. All buses to Sint-Salvatorskerk.

Restaurants

Like everything else in Bruges, restaurants are geared to the **tourist market**, but that doesn't mean you have to spend a fortune to eat well. If money is really tight, check out the *Bauhaus* or *Passage* hostels, whose restaurants do cheap deals, or the fish stalls by the Vismarkt. Beware that many Bruges kitchens close early, generally around 9pm; Zuidzandstraat, off 't Zand, has a couple of later options.

Bruges Bistro, Noordzandstraat 58. Local café/restaurant off 't Zand, selling reasonably priced main courses cooked in Bruges beers, all for far less than you'd pay on the square itself. Closed Sundays. No credit cards. All buses to Sint-Salvatorskerk.

Le Chagall, Sint-Amandsstraat 40. Laid-back restaurant with a terrace just off the Markt, also selling snacks. Eel, mussels and shellfish are the specialities. Main courses around 500BF, most major credit cards. All buses to Biekorf.

't Paardje, Langestraat 20. Unpretentious place east of the town centre, serving tasty eel and mussels dishes at around 500–700BF. Closed Monday and Tuesday evenings. No credit cards. Ten minutes' walk from the Markt, bus #6 or #16 from the train station.

De Sneeuwberg, Hallestraat 2. Just off the Markt, with a terrace and all the trimmings, but the mussels, North Sea fish and *waterzooi* are palatable and affordable. Most major credit cards. All buses to Biekorf.

Verdi, Vlemingstraat 5. Classy-looking but reasonably priced diner where Bruges steak and salmon are the specialities. Closed Tuesdays. Most major credit cards. All buses to Biekorf.

Accommodation

Central Bruges has bundles of hotels, though none is particularly cheap. Both tourist offices offer an **accommodation service**, whereby they charge 400BF to book you a room, which is then deducted from your hotel bill. The city has a handful of youth hostels, and the slightly cheaper hotels are to be found just north of the Markt around the Spiegelrei canal.

Bauhaus International Youth Hostel, Langestraat 135–137 (☎050/341 093, fax 050/334 180). Relaxed youth hostel with dorm beds at 300BF; singles, doubles and triples and quads also available. Cheap restaurant downstairs open until midnight. Most major credit cards. Bus #6 or #16 from the station.

Hotel Jacobs, Baliestraat 1 (☎050/339 831, fax 050/335 694). Friendly, comfortable three-star hotel north of the centre, ten minutes' walk from the Markt. Double rooms, nearly all with bath/shower, at around 2000BF. No singles. Most credit cards. Bus #4 or #8 from the station.

The Passage, Dweerstraat 26 (☎050/340 232, fax 050/340 140). Just east of 't Zand, a clean and comfortable hostel with a bed-and-breakfast option next door. B&B doubles at 1200BF, dorm beds around 350BF, breakfast included. No lockout or curfew. The restaurant downstairs is a bargain for Bruges – main courses at 250–400BF. Bar open until 3am. Most major credit cards. All buses to Sint-Salvatorskerk.

Le Singe d'Or, 't Zand 18 (☎050/334 848, fax 050/346 628). Clean, simple, centrally located hotel that was a meeting place for Club Bruges players just before and just after World War II. Singles at 1000BF, doubles 1500–2400BF, bathroom facilities in the corridor. Most credit cards. All buses to 't Zand.

Snuffel's Traveller's Inn, Ezelstraat 47–49 (☎050/333 133, fax 050/333 250). Hostel with dorm beds at 325BF; doubles at 450BF per person, breakfast included. No lock-out or curfew. Decent café downstairs. No credit cards. Bus #3 or #13 from the station.

Bulgaria

Neutrals and supporters of the underdog everywhere were delighted when Bulgaria knocked Germany out of the 1994 World Cup and earned themselves fourth place overall in the tournament. Sadly, success has not bred success.

Bulgarian football is in a mess. While the country emerges slowly from the clutches of a desperate economic crisis, the national team's progress has been hindered by a rift between star players and the Bulgarian FA. Hristo Stoichkov, Bulgaria's greatest player of all time, snubbed the opening qualifying games for the 1998 World Cup, in which Bulgaria lost 2–1 in Israel and beat Cyprus 3–1. (Even the latter match has since been clouded by controversy, since it emerged that Cypriot players placed huge bets on a final score of...3–1 to Bulgaria.)

Crying wolf – Trifon Ivanov points the finger, Euro '96

Meanwhile, domestic first-division matches are postponed because the visiting team cannot afford the petrol money. The nation's most popular club, Levski Sofia, have stopped charging the token pittance for tickets because fans simply don't have it. No wonder Bulgaria's top players set up a bank in 1995 as a way of protecting their income.

In football terms, the country was a late developer. Bulgarian students returning home from Istanbul formed the first team in 1909, and the two oldest surviving clubs, Sofia's Slavia and Levski, were founded shortly afterwards. The Black Sea port of Varna and southern city of Plovdiv also took to the game during what were, in the Balkans as elsewhere in Europe, years of war and turbulence.

When the situation was calmer, regional leagues were established, followed by a national championship in 1937. Meanwhile, international games were mainly confined to 'friendlies' against neighbouring states.

With the arrival of Communism in 1945, Bulgarian football remained insular while acquiring a new, rigid domestic structure. From then on teams represented state bodies. The populist Levski became an arm of the interior ministry, and an army team was established, to be called CSKA; over the coming decades they were to receive the lion's share of players and funding, while the traditionally bourgeois Slavia, champions in 1941 and 1943, fell out of favour and lost their best players.

Naturally CSKA dominated the league, winning nine titles in a row in the Fifties – a record they share with just three other European clubs, Celtic, Rangers and MTK Budapest. Yet in all this time, the only player of world class they produced was inside-forward Ivan Kolev, who starred in Bulgaria's first appearance in the World

Cup finals in 1962; the team managed a goalless draw with England but were eliminated without winning a match.

As the Sixties wore on, the army slowly lost its all-powerful grip on the game, and Levski, with centre-forward Georgi Asparoukhov in his prime, began to pick up the occasional title. Asparoukhov was the finest Bulgarian player of his day, but injury prevented him from showing his best at Bulgaria's next two World Cup appearances, in 1966 and 1970. He died in a car crash in 1971.

For the time being, international success was confined to the Olympics, in a soccer tournament dominated by Eastern bloc 'amateur' sides; Bulgaria won bronze in 1956 and silver twelve years later.

There were to be no more World Cup adventures until 1986 when, in the opening game of the tournament, Nasko Sirakov stooped low to head home a late equaliser against the champions, Italy. It was a false dawn – the Bulgars again went home without a World Cup win. But Sirakov's header would prove a strange pre-echo of events in the 1994 finals.

Throughout the postwar era, Bulgaria had been the Soviets' closest East European ally. In keeping with strict Communist doctrines, Bulgarian players were forbidden from going abroad to earn a living and that, as much as anything, contributed to the national team's poor World Cup showings. One English journalist described the 1986 side as "a disgrace to football", such was their apathy.

Even then, the cracks were beginning to show. Rival fans from CSKA and Levski became engaged in decidedly non-Soviet bouts of crowd violence. In 1985, fighting between the two sets of players stopped the domestic cup final; in the aftermath, the authorities forced both clubs to dissolve and reform as Sredets (CSKA) and Vitosha (Levski), while banning several players, including Levski's Sirakov and a young CSKA striker by the name of Hristo Stoichkov, for life.

Neither ban lasted more than a year. Bulgaria's political and sporting climate was thawing. Sirakov was allowed to become one of the first internationals to move abroad, and went to play for Real Zaragoza. Stoichkov, a headstrong teenager who could sprint 100m in eleven seconds, went on to become top scorer in both the Bulgarian league and the Cup-Winners' Cup in 1988/89. The latter campaign included three goals for CSKA against Barcelona,

Stooping to conquer – Lechkov gets in front of Hässler, and the rest is history, New York, 1994

Basics

Since the summer of 1996 Bulgaria has been in deep **economic crisis**, a situation which intensified in the spring of 1997, when the local currency's value fell tenfold against the dollar. Although things improved slightly after the election of a new government, intending travellers should check with the Foreign Office or equivalent authority for an update before booking their journey.

All EU citizens, Canadians, Australians and New Zealanders need a **tourist visa** to enter Bulgaria. This costs $56 from your Bulgarian embassy. In Britain this is at 184-186 Queens Gate, London, SW7 5HL (☎0171/584 9400, fax 0171/584 4948, allow one week for processing). An on-the-spot **entry visa** costs $95, while a transit visa, valid for thirty hours, is $62. American citizens need only their passport.

On arrival in Bulgaria, you will also be obliged to fill out a 'statistical' card, handed out on the plane or available from customs guards. This must be stamped at your hotel or accommodation agency. If you're staying with friends, you'll have to ask them to stamp it at the local police station. A **$100 fine** will be imposed if you cannot return it to customs on departure.

The Bulgarian currency is the **lev**. There are hundreds of private **exchange offices** all over Sofia, with rates clearly marked and no commission charged. Credit cards are not widely accepted, and it's wise to bring a certain quantity of US dollars or Deutschmarks in small-denomination notes.

Buses were once the best way of getting around the country, but a 1996/97 petrol crisis made many services subject to change or **last-minute cancellation**. If in doubt, take a **train**, and hope that the line has been electrified.

Public **payphones** are rare, but if you do chance to stumble across one, it'll take 20 or 50 stotinki (0.20 or 0.50 lev) coins. BETKOM **cardphones** are in main hotels and post offices, where cards are on sale for $1.50, $3 and $5.

A call to non-Balkan Europe costs $0.90 a minute. To call abroad from Bulgaria, dial ☎00, followed by the country code. Remember that Bulgaria is one hour ahead of Central European time. From outside the country, the international access code for Bulgaria is ☎359, followed by 2 for Sofia, 32 for Plovdiv.

whose coach Johann Cruyff immediately took out an option to sign him – exercised a year later, after Stoichkov had hit 38 goals for CSKA to earn himself Europe's 'golden boot' as the continent's top scorer. Stoichkov's goals helped the Catalans to four consecutive Spanish titles – though injury and suspension ruled him out of the finals of the 1991 Cup-Winners' Cup and 1992 European Cup.

If he was influential in Barcelona, his impact at international level would change Bulgaria's status in the eyes of the world forever. Even after Emil Kostadinov's last-minute goal in Paris had booked the Bulgarians their ticket to USA '94, the team had history against them. This, after all, was the nation that had never won a match

in the World Cup finals. When Nigeria took them to the cleaners in their opening game, it looked like being the same old story. But suddenly, after beating Greece, Argentina and Mexico (with Stoichkov on target against each), Bulgaria were on a roll.

In the quarter-finals, they were 1–0 down against Germany when a Stoichkov free-kick levelled the scores. Three minutes later the bald head of midfielder Yordan Lechkov met a swift cross, just as Sirakov's had done eight years earlier, and the world champions were beaten. Sofia went wild. Players' values soared overnight.

Disappointing performances against Italy and Sweden left Bulgaria in fourth place. But Stoichkov, Lechkov, Kostadinov and co bounced back to beat Germany again in a

European Championship qualifier in Sofia in 1995. Now we saw a different Stoichkov – a true leader of men, not just a muscular striker with a swagger in his stride and an attitude in his head.

He scored all three Bulgarian goals at Euro '96, but it wasn't enough. The heroes of 1994 looked past their sell-by date, and when coach Dimitar Penev, Stoichkov's old buddy, was sacked, the striker vowed never to play for his country again.

There may yet, however, be a final twist to the tale. In the summer of 1997, Stoichkov made his peace with new coach Hristo Bonev, turning up at the latter's house in Plovdiv (also Stoichkov's hometown) with a bouquet of flowers; two days later he was back playing for his country again, and scoring again, in a World Cup qualifier against Luxembourg.

So Bulgaria's football legend goes on – at least until the time comes to find a new Hristo Stoichkov.

Essential vocabulary
Hello *Zdravei*
Goodbye *Dovizhdane*
Yes *Da*
No *Ne*
Two beers, please *Molya, dva bira*
Thank you *Blagodarya*
Men's *M'zhe* (МЬЖЕ)
Women's *Zheni* (ЖЕНУ)
Where is the stadium *Kude e stadion?*
What's the score? *Kak e igra?*
Referee *Sadiya*
Offside *Zasada*
Most of all, remember that Bulgarians shake their heads for yes and nod for no.

Match practice
Bulgarian league football is a cheap if uncomfortable way of spending a Saturday afternoon. Facilities are poor, crowds low, refereeing decisions often questionable.

The big games are Levski-CSKA and any game involving Sofia clubs against those from Plovdiv – particularly Botev.

The season runs from mid-August to early December and from February to June,

with most matches on Saturday afternoons. Some fixtures in the capital are played on Friday night or Sunday afternoon. Kick-off times get gradually earlier as winter creeps in, with games at 6pm until September, 5pm until October, then 3pm and 2pm; in the spring season the trend reverses.

The league
The Bulgarian league has three main divisions. At the top, the *'A' Grupa* has sixteen teams, with the bottom three changing places with the top three of the twenty-team second division, the *'B' Grupa*. The third division, *'V' Grupa*, is regionalised into four separate sections, with group winners changing places with the bottom four of the second.

Up for the cup
Bulgaria has two cup competitions – the *Kupa Na Balgariya* and the *Profi-Liga Kupa*. The latter is much the longer established and until 1991 was known as the Soviet Army Cup. It is effectively a league cup, involving teams from the top two divisions who are divided in four groups of four at the quarter-final stage. The group winners play two-leg semi-finals for a place in the May final at the Vasil Levski stadium, and entry into the Intertoto Cup.

The early rounds of the main cup tournament, which was inaugurated in 1981, are played over one leg, with first-division teams entering at the last-32 stage, at which point matches start to be played on a two-leg system until the one-match final at the Vasil Levski in June.

In both cup tournaments, away goals count double in the case of level aggregate scores, with the 'golden goal' and penalty rule applying if teams are still tied.

Tickets
Although your ticket might indicate a row (*red*, HTL) and a place (*myasto*, V Z O J), this invariably means any spot you like on a peeling, splintered wooden bench. Wherever you go, you'll be paying a nominal fee if anything at all. There are no matchday

Even immortals need a drink from time to time – Hristo Stoichkov and team-mates, USA '94

programmes at league games, but the Bulgarian FA can normally be relied upon to produce a money-spinning, glossy souvenir for internationals against Western teams.

Half-time
Sunflower seeds are sold in newspaper cones outside grounds. Snacks are otherwise pretty minimal and you'll see no great rush to whatever poor buffet facilities may be on offer.

Action replay
All domestic football is shown on State channels Kanal 1 and Efir 2. Kanal 1 shows the prestige games, European matches and Bulgarian internationals. *Sportna Sabota* on Saturday afternoons on Efir 2 shows line-ups from league matches and changes to the scorelines as they happen.

There are two main highlights shows, Kanal 1's *Sportna Mrezha* ('Sports Network'), at around 11pm on Saturdays, and Channel 2's 'The Third Half', which is shown on Sunday lunchtimes, then repeated, with more analysis, on Monday nights at 11pm. The private TV station *Novay Televiziya* shows German *Bundesliga* action on Sunday afternoons. Eurosport

and DSF are popular, and pirate decoders for Sky are widespread.

The back page
The economic crisis of 1996 decimated the emerging sports press which had sprung up in 1994/95 to clip the heels of the Communist daily monolith, *Sport*. Only two dailies now remain, *Meridian Match* and 7 *Dni Sport*, both with fine foreign coverage and full Premiership results. In Sofia, Western press is available at the newsstand of the Sheraton hotel on pl Sveta Nedelya.

Ultra culture
Although rivalry is fierce between Levski and CSKA, there is no organised ultra culture as such – simply the usual flags, scarves and insults. Violence is rare these days.

In the net
The best one-stop source for Bulgar soccer information on the Web is run by the Bulgarian FA themselves, at: bfu.online.bg/. The excellent homepage is updated daily, and deeper into the site you'll find such gems as lists of referees and officials, plus still photographs of national-team and European club action, courtesy of Reuters.

Sofia

🔵 CSKA 44   🔵 Levski 46
🔵 Slavia 48   🔵 Lokomotiv 48

Sofia is not Bulgaria's only major footballing city. Plovdiv boasts particularly fervent support and at any one time may have three clubs in the top flight, while the Black Sea port of Burgas has recently rallied around its major team, Neftokhimik; when Bulgaria played Luxembourg in the town in the spring of 1997, 30,000 turned up to watch – 8000 more than the ground's official capacity. In terms of football heritage, however, you can't beat Sofia, not least because all but one of the last ten league titles has been won by a club from the capital.

In Stoichkov's shoes – CSKA striker Nankov

The thrilling fields

🔵 CSKA

Stadion Balgarska Armia, bulevard Dragan Tzankov 3
Capacity 30,000 (all-seated)
Colours All red with white trim
League champions 1948, 1951–52, 1954–62, 1966, 1969, 1971–73, 1975–76, 1980–83, 1987, 1989–90, 1992, 1997
Cup winners 1981, 1983, 1985, 1987–89, 1993, 1997

The most titled team in Bulgarian football history are not the most popular. Nicknamed the *Chorberi* ('soup-eaters') by fans of rivals Levski, CSKA were formed during post-war Communist restructuring as the sports club of the Bulgarian army. The authorities were keen that Septemvri, as they were originally known, should have the country's best players and facilities, and the team duly won the league on a play-off basis in their first season and, as CDNA, went on to win a remarkable twelve titles in thirteen years between 1951 and 1962. Forwards Dimitar Milanov and Ivan Kolev were the big names of the Fifties, Petar Jekov and Dimitar Yakimov those of later years. In 1957 the club had their own ground built next to the Vasil Levski Stadium, and in 1964 they became CSKA.

The name change heralded the end of the club's all-powerful position. But the more challenging domestic scene made CSKA more competitive in the European club tournaments which were emerging.

On three occasions CSKA knocked the holders out of the European Cup – Ajax in 1973, Liverpool in 1980, and Nottingham Forest in 1982. They also reached a European Cup semi-final (against Inter) in 1967, and a Cup-Winners' Cup semi (against Barcelona) in 1989.

Sofia essentials

Bus #84 runs every twenty minutes between Sofia's **airport**, 12km east of town, and central Orlov Most, near the Vasil Levski stadium in Na Svobodata park. A taxi should cost around $10 but bargain with your driver first.

Sofia **city transport** consists of buses (5am–midnight), trolleybuses and trams (both 5am–1am). Single tickets cost $0.15 and can be purchased at ticket offices and newsstands; they should be validated onboard. A day ticket is $0.50 and a five-day pass is $2 – both must be date-stamped on purchase.

Flagging **taxis** down in town is easy, but be sure to establish the fare to your destination before you mvoe off. To call a cab, dial *Okay* on ☎02/2121 or *Softaxi* on ☎02/1284.

Sofia's main **train station** is the Tsentralna Gara, just north of the centre of town by trams #1, #7 or #15. Buying a train ticket is slightly complicated. Windows 1–8, upstairs at street level, are for destinations in the northern half of the country, while downstairs is for southern cities. There are ten trains a day to Plovdiv, taking just over two hours and costing about $2 first class. Also downstairs is the Rila office, where you can make (compulsory) advance bookings for **international journeys**. You will need your passport and no little patience.

The main **tourist office** is the English-speaking *Balkantourist*, 1 bulevard Vitosha (open Mon–Fri 8am–3pm, Sat 8.30am–1.30pm, ☎02/875 192). The town's only English-language **listings guide** is the monthly brochure *Sofia City*, free at major hotels, with restaurant and cinema information plus some useful telephone numbers.

In Sofia the club remained unpopular, but out in the provinces, a generation of fans was raised on these televised European games. What else was there to get excited about in Gabrovo or Dimitrovgrad? When these new fans came up to the capital, they were invariably faced with a blue wall of Levski support, and the Seventies and Eighties were marked by some serious face-offs on derby day.

Some players thrived on the tension. Hristo Stoichkov was in the thick of the 1985 cup final brawl, which resulted in the club being forced to play under the name of Sredets until 1990. By then Stoichkov had left for Barcelona – for his last match he came out wearing a #4 shirt in recognition of the four goals he had scored against Levski the week before.

Bulgaria's Communists lost power in 1991, and the withdrawal of army influence made the mid-Nineties fallow years for CSKA. Today, however, the club are attached to Multigroup, a vast new enterprise created from the ashes of former state concerns, and have won back some of their political favour. Former Levski boss Georgi Vasilev coached them to a league and cup double in 1997, giving CSKA the chance to raise their European profile once more.

Here we go!

The Balgarska Armia stadium is 200 metres from the Vasil Levski in Borisova Gradina, formerly the Park na Svobodata. The same transport information applies – see p.47.

Swift half

You can get a drink at any of the kiosks in the Borisova Gradina park – or try the **Amerika 94** buffet inside the Vasil Levski stadium, next door to CSKA's ground.

In the net

There's a smart, smooth-running unofficial CSKA website at: www.belloweb.se/cska/. The text is available in four languages, incuding English, and is particularly strong on history – links take you to sites of some of the clubs the team has eliminated from Europe down the years, including Ajax, Liverpool, Barcelona and Juventus...

Awkward squad – Levski knock Rangers out of Europe, 1993

 Levski

Office ulitsa Todorini Kukli 47
Stadium Vasil Levski – see panel opposite
Colours All blue with yellow trim
League champions 1933, 1937, 1942, 1946–47,
1949–50, 1953, 1965, 1968, 1970, 1974, 1977,
1979, 1984–85, 1988, 1993–95
Cup winners 1942, 1982, 1984, 1986, 1991–92,
1994

Levski, formed by a group of young enthu-
siasts in 1914, have always been the team of
the people. From their base around the
Levski and Podujane districts of north-east
Sofia, site of the club's old home ground,
Levski still rule the capital – though in the
provinces, support is divided with CSKA.

Levski's best team is often said to be
the one which won four titles immediately
after World War II, playing on the site of

what is now the Vasil Levski stadium. Aware of Levski's popularity,
the Communist authorities
attached the club to the interior
ministry in an attempt to identify
the team with government – then
made the mistake of changing the
club's name to Dynamo Levski.
Meanwhile, the favours granted to
army club CSKA further angered
Levski's support, and set up the
Bulgar game's fiercest inter-club
rivalry.

After a decade of CSKA domination, and with their old name
back, Levski picked up again in the
Sixties. They had a new stadium,
the Gerena, later to be renamed
after the hero of the day, centre-
forward Georgi Asparoukhov. His
goals helped Levski to three titles
between 1965 and 1970, the last
after the club's amalgamation with
Spartak Sofia.

As 'Levski-Spartak' the club
enjoyed a halcyon period in the
mid- to late-Seventies, ironically
after Asparoukhov's death, winning
three domestic championships and knocking Ajax out of the UEFA Cup.

Derby games with CSKA became more
and more tense – Levski's punishment for
their part in the 1985 cup final furore was
to be disbanded and reconstituted as
Vitosha. After the slow disintegration of
Communism, however, the club won their
old name back and suddenly appeared well-
placed to take advantage of the new market
economy, breaking away from the interior
ministry and attracting the cream of the
new local sponsors.

With a team boasting most of the Bulgarian internationals who had not already
left for Western clubs – including Emil Kre-
menliev, Daniel Borimirov and Petar
Houbchev – Levski won three titles by
large margins between 1993 and 1995.
Increasing support meant that all home
league games were now taking place in the
Vasil Levski, and in 1993 the team were

unlucky not to qualify for the Champions' League after beating Rangers and losing narrowly to Werder Bremen.

Bulgaria's poor UEFA ranking deprived Levski of a place in the same competition for a further two years, and the subsequent loss of income led to a sell-off of key players, including all the aforementioned internationals and the veteran goalscorer Nasko Sirakov.

As CSKA's star rose and the local economy crumbled, Levski president Thomas Laftchis took the unprecedented step of granting free entry to all home games for the 1997 spring season, while behind the scenes, a return to the Gerena in 1997/98, at least for non-derby games, was also being discussed.

Here we go!

See box below.

Swift half

The **Siniya Bar**, an innocuous-looking restaurant on ul 11 Avgust also known as the **Blue Bar**, is for Levski fans. It's near the #9 trolleybus stop on Rakovski between Dondoukov and Slivnica boulevards. From here it's a ten-minute walk to the national (Vasil Levski) stadium. Some fans still have a traditional pre-match beer by the old Gerena stadium in Podujane.

Publication

Levski is a monthly newspaper ($0.20) whose main strength is large photo features on star players and classic matches.

The Vasil Levski stadium

Bulevard Evlogi Georgiev 38
Capacity 70,000 (all-seated)

Bulgaria's **national stadium** was built on the site of a much more modest pitch where Levski played until just after World War II. As well as internationals, the stadium plays host to Levski Sofia's home games but, confusingly, is not actually their home ground.

Named after a 19th century national hero, the Vasil Levski has an ornate entrance which gives out onto a large bowl of a stadium whose interior is covered in rust and graffiti. Apart from a single roof covering the directors' seats, the ground is **open to the elements** – pleasant on a summer evening, bitter in February.

The **view is excellent**, if a little distant from the action across the running track. For club matches the atmosphere is a little one-sided, except for local derbies with CSKA, whose supporters have a reputation for scuttling home quickly from the north end after the final whistle.

The stadium is by bul Balgaria on the city side of Borisova Gradina, formerly the Park na Svobodata. This is a pleasant **fifteen-minute walk** south-east from the city centre, but you could take tram #2, #12, #14 or #19 down Graf Ignatiev to the inner ring road. Bus #84 from the airport stops at Orlov Most on the other corner of the park.

There are a couple of **bars** in the underpass just before the park, the Excalibur probably the best of them. Facilities in the Vasil Levski leave a lot to be desired but there are two **buffets** – the incongruously flashy *Amerika 94* by sector #7, and there a less gaudy bar/restaurant at sector #26.

The **ticket office** is by the main entrance. Assuming that a nominal fee will one day be charged for matches once more, a ticket in sector B (south side) will put you with the Levski fans for club matches. Sectors A and V are reserved for **away fans** at international matches.

Also by the main entrance is the **Museum of Physical Culture and Sports** (open Tue–Sat 10am–6pm). It has a few football souvenirs among the cycling and gymnastics photographs, and some documentation in English, including a free leaflet.

In the net

The *Blue Avalanche* unofficial Levski site is at: members.aol.com/Serdica/levski.html. Stats and links are the strong point, along with some English-language news – though you may find the site as a whole a tad heavy on the graphics.

Groundhopping

Postwar amalgamations have taken their toll on Sofia's minor clubs, but two outfits remain to give the visitor a chance of viewing first-division football away from the windswept bowls of CSKA and Levski.

✪ Slavia

Slavia stadium, ulitsa Koloman I
Capacity 32,000
Colours All white with black trim
League champions 1928, 1930, 1936, 1939, 1941, 1943, 1996
Cup winners 1996

Slavia are the oldest Bulgarian club still in existence. Founded in 1913 and built with money from the city's new rich, they are nicknamed the Royals because of their early connections.

With a fan base in the west of town, around Ovcha Kupel, Slavia were Sofia's leading club side before the Communist reorganisation of sport that followed World War II. At that point Slavia became Strojtel, the team of the construction union, then Udarnik, before reverting to their original name in 1958. Throughout this period they were regular top-three finishers but rarely challenged the hegemony of CSKA and Levski. Their only major European run was to the semi-finals of the 1967 Cup-Winners' Cup, where they were beaten by Rangers.

In 1995, the arrival of veteran goalscorer Nasko Sirakov, from Levski via

Botev Plovdiv, helped the Royals to their first league championship in more than fifty years. They won the cup that season, too, in bizarre fashion. Slavia were a goal up against Levski with fourteen minutes left to play in the final, when Levski president Thomas Slavchis summoned his team from the pitch. They did not return (Slavchis claimed his gesture was meant as a stand against corruption), and Slavia were awarded the match 4–0.

The club's 1996 UEFA Cup appearance was brief, but a third-place league finish in 1996/97 granted them another bite at the European cherry.

To get to Slavia, take tram #5 or #19 from the Ruski Pametnik, south-west from the centre of town, for ten minutes down bul Deveti Septemvri. The stadium is on the right-hand side, just before the Ovcha Kupel marketplace.

There are a couple of small bars between the tram stop and the stadium – *Za 2 Leva* is as good as any.

✪ Lokomotiv

Lokomotiv stadium, bul Rojen 23
Capacity 25,000
Colours Red-and-black striped shirts, white shorts
League champions 1940, 1945, 1964, 1978

Very much Sofia's fourth club, Lokomotiv actually went out of existence for two seasons while they were merged with Slavia in 1969. The Railwaymen, with international Atanas Mihailov scoring the goals, bounced back with a league title in 1978 and a UEFA Cup run two years later, in which they beat Ferencváros, Monaco and Dynamo Kiev before losing in the quarter-finals to VfB Stuttgart.

Their stadium, with two stands but no floodlights, was rebuilt soon afterwards but has seen little European action since. It lies north of the centre, five #12 tram stops from the main train station along bul Alexei Tolstoy. There is a whole row of open-air

Snow joke – volunteers help soldiers clear the pitch for Bulgaria's Euro '96 qualifier with Wales

stand-up bars along the boulevard, none of them favoured by fans any more than the others.

Eat, drink, sleep...

Bars and clubs

Bulgarians are great drinkers of **wine**, even cheaper here than it is in your local Tesco. *Melnik* and *Gamza* are reliable reds (*cherveno vino*), *Misket* and *Euxinovgrad* tasty whites (*byalo vino*). A local beer (*bira*), *Zagorka* or the sweeter *Astika*, will cost around $0.75, while a foreign brew might be twice that. *Rakiya* is the local spirit.

Always look your drinking companion in the eye when you **clink glasses**. If you're alone in a bar and befriended by Bulgarians, it is not unknown for someone to slip something into your glass and rob you of your belongings while you sleep.

On and around Sofia's main bulevard Vitosha you'll find privately run Western-

style **bars** and the occasional *mekhana*, or traditional taverna.

Alcohol is also sold from people's basement flats – you'll see a regular **vodka trade** down at street level. **Nightclubs** usually charge an entrance fee of $2–3 which includes your first beer.

Art Club, Ivan Asen 6. Popular underground venue refurbished in 1996, with live music and buzzing atmosphere until closing time at midnight. Tram #4 or #10 to Orlov Most.

Club Chaos, pl Varazhdane. By the corner of bul Stambuliiski and bul Hristo Botev, a late-night, two-floor dive in a converted chapel featuring loud music and serious drinking.

Football café, Alabin 50. Actually a nameless bar on the second floor of the offices of the Sofia District Football Assocation, featuring soccer chat and memorabilia. Open until 8pm weekdays. The restaurant on the first floor is a hangout for journalists and players' agents. Also check out the **Bar Ajax** next door. Tram #5 or #19 to bul Vitosha.

Swinging Hall, Dragan Tsankov 8. Probably the best live music venue in town. Large bar, pool room at the back, jazz souvenirs on the walls. $2 admission includes a beer. Short walk from the Vasil Levski stadium. Tram #2, #12, #14 or #19.

Restaurants

Bulgarian **cuisine** is heavily reliant on grilled skewered meats (*kebapcheta*) and pork (*svinsko*). Meat stews slowly cooked with vegetables (*gyuvech* or *kavarma*) can be an interesting alternative. Salads are generally simple, fresh and tasty. A **main course** should not set you back more than $5. **Street food** is widespread and cheap, and stalls sell sweets as well as savouries – *baklava* and *banitsa* are among the local pastries. None of the restaurants listed below takes credit cards.

Brux, pl Varazhdane. This small spot by the corner of bul Stambuliiski and bul Hristo Botev is a classic cheap late-night eaterie, which just happens to be opposite Club Chaos. Grilled meats and wine until the early hours.

Budapest, Rakovski 145. Elegance at half the price you'd pay by the Danube, with Central European décor and Hungarian musicians. Expect to pay about $5–8 for a main course. Open daily 10am–11.30pm. Centrally located. Tram #9.

Kashtata, ulitsa Verila 4. Atmospheric old two-storey *mekhana* serving typical Bulgarian cuisine at about $3–5 a throw. Some tables outside. Open daily noon–midnight. In a small street opposite the palace of culture.

Krim, ulitsa Slavianska 17. Russian cuisine in stylish surroundings for $5–8 a main dish. Garden open in summer. Open Mon–Sat noon–3pm & 6pm–11pm. Tram #1, #2 or #7 to inner ring road, then a short walk towards town.

Tom's New York Deli, ulitsa Karnigradska 14. Perfect spot for breakfast in a narrow street off Vitosha, opposite the Bulgarian FA office. Thick sandwiches, salads, coffee and beer. Open 8am–midnight. For deliveries call ☎02/805 232.

Accommodation

For decades Bulgarian hotels were filled by pre-booked package tours and prices are still not geared to the independent traveller. The local **star-rating system** is hopelessly optimistic and you won't find many comfortable budget hotels in town.

Most tourist accommodation is at the foot of Mount Vitosha, in villages like Dragalevtsi – forty minutes by public transport (tram #9 or bus #64) or a $7–10 taxi ride.

The best urban alternative is **private accommodation**, which costs around $15–18 for a room, normally with two beds. Prices vary slightly according to location and facilities. Rooms can be booked at *Balkantourist*, bulevard Stamboliiksi 27 (open daily 8am–6pm, 8pm in summer, ☎02/884 430), or at their desk in the arrivals lobby at the airport – though you will still need to collect your key from their office in town. Both offices can also book hotel rooms.

Hemus, bul Cherni Vrah 31 (☎02/639 51, fax 02/661 318). Tower block hotel near the palace of culture. All rooms with bath, some with views of Mount Vitosha. $50 single, $70 double, including breakfast. Most major credit cards. Tram #6 or #9 from Hristo Botev.

Serdika, bulevard Janko Sakazov 2 (☎02/443 411). It's worth booking ahead through *Balkantourist* for this well-kept hotel near Orlov Most. All rooms with bath. $50 a single, $70 a double, breakfast included. Most credit cards. Tram #3 or #4 from Vitosha, then head for pl Vasil Levski.

Slavianksa Beseda, ulitsa Slavianska 1 (☎02/880 441). Privatised but nevertheless gloomy hotel in the centre of town. Still, it's clean and all rooms have a bath. $40 a single, $50 a double. No credit cards. Tram #12 from the train station.

Sun, bulevard Maria Luiza 89 (☎02/833 670, fax 02/835 389). Small, comfortable Twenties hotel refurbished in the early Nineties. All rooms have bath and television. Singles $80, doubles $100, including breakfast. Amex accepted. Centrally located. Tram #1, #7 or #15 from the station.

Croatia

Having struggled for half a century to find its footballing identity, the former Yugoslav republic of Croatia now needs to assert it. The Croats still have the gifted generation of players who took their newly independent nation to the finals of a major tournament at the first attempt. But a disappointing Euro '96 may turn out to have been the last chance for some of those ageing, exiled stars to shine.

On the face of it, it's hard to see how Croatia is going to produce another wave of players like the *zlatna generacija*, the Golden Generation, of 1987. Midfielders Zvonimir Boban and Robert Prosinečki, defenders Robert Jarni and Igor Štimac, and star striker Davor Šuker won the World Youth Cup representing Yugoslavia in Chile in 1987. They were a rare crop, the best since Diego Maradona's Argentine winners of 1979, perhaps better. But even then, the country they represented was starting to fall apart.

Boban's story says it all. At 17 he had already made Dinamo Zagreb's first team. At 18 he was captain. At 21 he was the chief protagonist in a series of incidents whose notoriety will live on for generations – in May 1990, fighting between Dinamo and Red Star Belgrade fans at Zagreb's Maksimir stadium forced the local (mainly Serb) police to act. In the ensuing mayhem, Boban kicked a policeman in the head. Although he was later proved to be defending himself and the young fans around him, Boban fled and was banned from competing in the World Cup, Yugoslavia's last, that June. His compatriots Šuker and Alen Bokšić spent the tournament on the bench, though Jarni and Prosinečki both played in the side that reached the quarter-finals before losing to Maradona's Argentina on penalties.

Friends and countrymen – Šuker and Boban

When war between Croatia and Serbia broke out in 1991, the stars fled into exile. Boban went on to a long and successful stint as a squad player with Milan. Alen Bokšić, absent in Chile but the scorer of the goal that won the Yugoslav cup for Croatia's Hajduk against Serbia's Red Star Belgrade at the end of the 1990/91 season, earned his fame with Marseille, then Lazio and Juventus. Prosinečki had an up-and-down time with Real Madrid, Oviedo and Barcelona. Šuker scored hatfuls of goals with Sevilla and Real Madrid.

In truth, Croatia, like the other former Yugoslav republics, has always exported its best talents, both players and coaches. Four key Croat members of the Yugoslav side which entertainingly featured in the three World Cups of the Fifties – Bernard Vukas, Vladimir Beara, Zlatko Čajkovski and Branko Zebec – all played abroad. Josip

Skoblar won the Golden Boot with Marseille in 1971, while the Vujović twins, Zlatko and Zoran, were part of the great Bordeaux side of the Eighties.

On the bench, Čajkovski and Zebec both had spells in charge of Bayern Munich in the late Sixties. Tomislav Ivić coached Ajax, Porto and Fenerbahçe. Otto Barić transformed Salzburg in the Nineties. Čiro Blažević earned so much money from his successes in Switzerland, he could go home and *buy* Croatia Zagreb, leading club in the new country's capital city.

Before they could get the chance to impress would-be foreign buyers, however, Croat players had to do battle in a Yugoslav league in which the odds were always stacked – by fair means or foul – in favour of Belgrade. Croat teams had held the upper hand before World War II, Zagreb's Gradjanski winning the first and last pre-Tito Yugoslav titles in 1923 and 1940. Split provided 12 of the 24-man squad who took

Yugoslavia to the 1930 World Cup semi-finals. And the team representing the Nazi puppet state of Croatia gave a good account of themselves in wartime friendlies against other Axis powers.

Yet once power shifted to Belgrade in Yugoslavia's postwar, centralised economy, Croatian teams had to make do with little victories, the biggest being Dinamo Zagreb's Fairs' Cup win of 1967 – the only European trophy for a Yugoslav club during the Tito era.

Croatia had four regular representatives in the old Yugoslav first Division – Dinamo, Hajduk, Rijeka and Osijek. In the absence of a national team, Dinamo became the symbol for Croatians to rally round, and their title win of 1982 made a national hero of coach Blažević.

When Croatia became independent, these nationalist feelings were duly exploited by President Franjo Tudjman, a lifelong football fan and former chairman

Floored – Alen Bokšić dances around his marker in a symbolic World Cup qualifier with Bosnia

of Partizan Belgrade. A league was quickly set up, chickens were cleared from some of the smaller pitches, and Dinamo (later 'Croatia') Zagreb were assured as much favour as politically possible.

A monument stands where the first football match was played in Croatia, in the small town of Županje, Eastern Slavonia, in 1880. If Croatian football is to grow, it needs a strong grassroots infrastructure to do it. Otherwise, the next golden generation will be basketball players.

Essential vocabulary
Hello *Bok!*
Goodbye *Do vidjenja*
Yes *Da*
No *Ne*
Two beers, please *Dva piva, molim*
Thank you *Hvala*
Men's *Muški*
Women's *Ženski*
Where is the stadium? *Gdje je stadion?*
What's the score? *Koji je rezultat?*
Referee *Sudac*
Offside *Ofsajd*

Match practice
With the exception of most matches at Hajduk, some at Croatia Zagreb and those featuring either team as visitors at Rijeka or Osijek, Croatian league football is low-key. Average crowds are less than 5000, mainly because people have more to worry about than football. There are no real derbies – younger fans have no sense of what it's like to hate Red Star Belgrade and be able to express that sentiment across a stadium at fever pitch.

The season runs from August to mid-December, then again from March until early June. Sunday is the traditional match-day. A couple of clubs, such as Inker Zaprešić and Varteks Varaždin, play home games on Saturdays. Not all grounds have floodlights, so games kick off at 5pm in August, then half-an-hour earlier each month until December, when kick-off can be as early as 1pm. This trend is reversed through the spring.

The league
The structure of the league is always a thorny question in Croatia. Most people want a reduction in size of the *Prva A HNL*, in order to raise standards. But in the past, small-town mayors often promised their constituents first-division football, and used all their political connections to get it. A mediocre league is what everyone got.

At the end of the 1996/97 season, however, the authorities finally took the plunge and reduced the size of the *Prva A HNL* (or *1.A liga*) from sixteen to twelve teams. The semi-professional second division, the *1.B liga*, is also due a shake-up and could be divided into as many as five regional leagues. And there is also the possibility that the Croats may repeat their experiment of 1995/96, and introduce Swiss-style promotion and relegation.

If none of this happens in 1997/98 – blame the man from the town hall.

Up for the cup
The Croatian Cup (*Hrvatski Nogometini Kup*) begins in August with 32 second- and third-division clubs playing a two-legged qualifying round for sixteen berths in the first round proper. The sixteen first-division clubs join at this stage, for the first of five two-legged rounds (away goals deciding if necessary) running up to the final in May. If the final involves two provincial clubs, then there is one game at Zagreb's Maksimir stadium. If one team is from Zagreb, then the final is played over two legs. In 1997, however, the final was a city derby between Croatia and NK Zagreb, resulting in a single match at the Maksimir.

Tickets
The only time you'll have trouble getting a ticket is for the bigger matches in Split. Otherwise head straight for the ticket office (*blagajna*), where prices are usually displayed prominently. The stand (*tribina*) will generally be described by its geographical location – *zapad* (west), *istok* (east), *jug* (south) or *sjever* (north). Standing room is denoted as *stajanje*, a seat as

sjedenje. A reasonable seat for an average league game should cost no more than 20–30kn, the best in the house about 50kn. For big games, prices tend to be raised about twenty percent. There are no programmes, but bigger clubs publish their own monthly magazines.

Half-time

Beer and *čevapi*, Turkish-style thick grilled meat stuffed into bread, are the order of the day – 25kn will cover both. Before and during the game, vendors pass among the crowd with baskets of pistachios, roasted peanuts, pumpkin seeds and popcorn.

Basics

It cannot be stressed enough that the vast majority of Croatia is **safe** and, though you may not credit it, **fun**. It will be at least five years before the tourist trade picks up again properly after the war; in the meantime, **enjoy the place** before thousands follow in your footsteps.

EU citizens need only a **valid passport** to enter Croatia. Americans, Canadians, Australians and New Zealanders need a **visa**, issued free at the border. Keep your passport on you at all times as there are often random checks.

The Croatian currency is the **kuna** (kn), divided into 100 lipa. There are notes for 5, 10, 20, 50, 100, 200, 500 and 1000 kuna and coins for 1 and 5 kuna, 1, 2, 5, 10, 20 and 50 lipa. There are about 9kn to £1. Banks are generally open Mon–Fri 8am–6pm, often with a two-hour break around noon, and 8am–noon on Saturdays. Credit-card payment is widespread in the main towns. For cash advances, most machines take Mastercard, while Splitska Banka's take Visa. Many services, such as hotels, calculate payment in **Deutschmarks**, which will always be gratefully accepted as payment.

Phone cards (*telefonske kartice*) are available at newsstands (marked *Vjesnik* or *Tisak*) or post offices, marked *HPT*. The cards come in 25-unit (10kn), 50-unit (18.23kn) and 100-unit (28.46kn) varieties. To dial abroad from Croatia hit 99, followed by your country code. There are no cheap international rates. **Post offices** have booths (*kabina*) for international calls – pay for the amount used as you leave.

From outside the country, the **code for Croatia** is 385, followed by 1 for Zagreb or 21 for Split. To call within Croatia, simply add a 0 to the city code in the normal fashion. For local calls, use 1 kuna pieces in payphones.

Buses are the best way to get around the country – efficient and comfortable, with journeys costing around 3kn per kilometre. **Trains** are slower and less frequent, but cheaper. The line between Zagreb and Split, which runs through the formerly Serb-held region of Krajina, is running normally again. There's one train a day and two at night, taking nine hours and costing around 100kn. By day it is one of the most spectacular train journeys in Europe; at night, police patrol the corridors so safety is assured.

Croatia suffers a general lack of reasonably priced **accommodation**. While many hostels are filled with war refugees, hotels cater for the business community, leaving precious little in between. One way round this is to arrange a **private room** with a family, which should cost no more than 100–130kn per person per night. Bargain for a discount if you're staying for more than three nights or paying in Deutschmarks.

The war savaged Croatia's once-thriving **restaurant trade**, and eating out is considered a luxury. A decent spread of delicious Croatian specialities (especially fish and seafood) will set you back at least 70kn. One exception to this is the commonplace pizzeria, where an excellent home-baked pizza and a beer can often be had for 30–40kn. Takeaway snacks like *burek* (thick pastry with cheese or meat) make for an alternative cheap filler, available from street stalls or holes in the wall.

Draught **beer** (*pivo*), either light (*svijetlo*) or dark (*tamno*), is around 10kn a half-litre. *Ožujsko* and *Karlovačko* are the acceptable local brews, but Slovenian Union is better. Local red or white **wine** (*crno* or *bijelo vino*) is excellent and cheap.

Light the blue touch paper – Hajduk Split's *Torcida* welcome their heroes onto the pitch

Action replay

Many Croats blame the malaise inherent in the domestic game on the lack of interest shown by national television. State channels HRT1 and 2 hardly touch sport, leaving domestic football, and much else besides, to HRT3. Their coverage includes a Sunday afternoon sport show, *Sport Nedjeljom*, which may contain a live league match, or perhaps half of one. This is followed by a highlights show, *Top Sport*, at 10pm. The channel's most popular programme is *Petica* (Mondays, 9pm), which features highlights from around Europe. HRT3 also shows a live English Premiership match on Saturdays at 4pm, a live Spanish game at 8.30pm the same day, and the repeat of an Italian one around 11pm on a Sunday. HRT2 shows Croatia's internationals live.

The back page

Like most ex-Communist East European countries, Croatia has a classic, newsprint-heavy sports daily, *Sportske Novosti* (3.50kn), with a thicker *Vikend* edition. It offers reasonable coverage of foreign leagues, and also publishes a fortnightly colour magazine, *Super Sport* (13kn).

Ultra culture

"They think they invented it," complains one Serbian fan, reflecting on Croatia's contribution to ultra culture. But, in a sense, they did. In the Fifties, fans from Split followed Hajduk all over Yugoslavia, making more noise and creating more colour than any in Europe. Their style was seized upon by the Italians who, in turn, sold a more sophisticated version back to Yugoslavia in the Eighties. As ethnic tensions began to simmer, matches between Dinamo or Hajduk on the one hand and Belgrade's Red Star or Partizan on the other became ever more ferociously supported, until the infamous Dinamo-Red Star clash of May 1990. After several years of separation, however, both sets of fans would grudgingly admit that they miss each other.

At national level, post-independence solidarity has broken down, with rival factions from Split and Zagreb more concerned with insulting each other than with the events on the pitch during big internationals.

The Croatian ultra scene is documented each month in the glossy magazine *Navijačka Tribina* (15kn), which also organises supporters' trips abroad.

In the net

The Croatian FA host one of the best federation-run websites in Europe at: www.tel.hr/ns/hns/. Well structured and with just the right amount of graphic content to keep you interested without slowing your computer to a crawl, the site offers a comprehensive history in English (with archive photos of key players), club information and up-to-date stats from both domestic and international competitions. If it's news you're after, then Tomislav Djerek's Croatian Sports Server will deliver at: sport.cro.net/soccer/index.html. This is an efficiently run, businesslike site, the highlight of which is a regularly updated, English-language news wire covering basketball, tennis and other popular Croatian sports – and with no soccer stone left unturned.

Zagreb

Croatia Zagreb 57
NK Zagreb 60

Zagreb was one of the former Yugoslavia's three main footballing centres and regularly played host to key internationals, including two games in the European Championship finals of 1976. A city of a million people, its modern footballing reputation has been built on the back of one team, Dinamo, themselves constructed from the ruins of the two leading prewar clubs and currently (perhaps only temporarily) playing under the name 'Croatia'.

Zagreb's first club were HAŠK, formed by students and intellectuals in 1903. The city's *Sokol* movement – popular in countries under the Habsburg yoke and dedicated to uplifting the national spirit – helped found smaller clubs soon afterwards. In 1912 Zagreb became home of the football branch of the newly formed Croatian athletics federation. The three

Zagreb essentials

Zagreb's **airport** is near the village of Plesso, nearly 20km from town. **Buses** (15kn) run roughly every hour, 7am–8pm, to the city's main bus station on Držićeva, to the south-east of the centre. The main **train station** is nearer town, a ten-minute walk straight up Praška as you come out. Tram #6 runs from the bus station to the train station and from there into town.

Central Zagreb is criss-crossed by a comprehensive network of **trams** – buses run between the centre and the suburbs. Transport runs 5am–midnight, and specially numbered night trams run regularly along the lines to and from the main square, Trg Bana Jelačića. Tram tickets cost 3.70kn from a newsstand, 4kn from the driver. Validate them in the ticket punchers onboard. A single ticket is valid for ninety minutes, no matter how many transfers you make. A **day ticket** (*dnevna karta*) costs 11kn and is valid until 4am the next day, no matter when you buy it.

Taxis are ruinously expensive, with a 40kn start-up charge, after which it's 6kn per kilometre, plus a twenty-percent surcharge 10pm–5am and all day Sundays. There'll always be a couple outside the train station, but to call one dial ☎970.

The main **tourist information office** is in one corner of the main square at Trg Bana Jelačića 11 (open Mon–Fri 8.30am–8pm, Sat 10am–6pm, Sun 10am–2pm, ☎01/272 530, fax 01/274 083).

English-language **listings information** is confined to a free monthly brochure, *Zagreb Events and Performances*, available at the tourist office. Locals find out what's on in the daily paper *Večernji List*, or in the free monthly *Moj Zagreb*.

main clubs of the day, HAŠK, Gradjanski
and Concordia Zagreb, played friendlies in
Maksimir park, then took eight of the seventeen Yugoslav league titles between the
wars, Gradjanski winning five. While most
of the Yugoslav national team were provided by Split, inner-city rivalry kept
interest in football high, and the *Zagreb*
café on Zrinjević became a vibrant meeting place for fans and players alike.

With World War II came a brief period
of Croatian 'independence' under a Nazi
puppet regime. Three national titles were
competed for, and Gradjanski won two of
them, before merging with HAŠK to form
Dinamo under the Communists in 1945.

Although Communist Yugoslavia's President Tito was said to be a Dinamo fan,
the balance of power was definitely in Belgrade's favour for most of the postwar era.
Such was the importance of Dinamo to
the Croatian people, under what they saw
as Serb domination, that few other clubs
could gather support in the city.

The thrilling fields

 ### Croatia Zagreb

Croatia's 1996/97 double winner – Otto Barić

Maksimir stadium, Maksimirska 128
Capacity 57,000 (all-seated)
Colours All blue
League champions (Yugoslavia) 1948, 1954,
1958, 1982
Cup winners (Yugoslavia) 1951, 1960, 1963,
1965, 1969, 1980, 1983
League champions (Croatia) 1993, 1996–97
Cup winners (Croatia) 1994, 1996–97
Fairs' Cup winners 1967

The richest and most favoured team in
Croatia have lost valuable ground in their
bid to dominate the domestic game and
advance on Europe. Three domestic titles
in six years seems scant reward for a club
with such obvious built-in advantages as
this, and in three years of European football

(one season was missed as the result of a
ban for previous crowd trouble), they have
won just two ties in five, against teams from
Albania and the Faroe Islands. Moreover,
having been used as a pawn in a series of
political games since national independence
in 1992, the team have lost the mainstream
support of the nation they all but represented in Tito's Yugoslavia. As Dinamo, they
had almost the whole country behind them
when they took on the big boys from Belgrade in the postwar era.

Dinamo's early successes – three league
titles and one cup in the decade after 1945
– were all the more remarkable considering that the Yugoslav army side, Partizan
Belgrade, had taken three key international

players, Branko Zebec, Stjepan Bobek and Zlatko Čajkovski.

It was the Sixties, and a series of classic European clashes, that set Dinamo's spacious stadium, the Maksimir, buzzing. A Fairs' Cup run in 1963/64, when the team beat Bayern Munich and Ferencváros before finishing as runners-up to Valencia, was no more than a prelude to eventual triumph in the same tournament in 1967, when a Dinamo team without stars beat Juventus and Eintracht Frankfurt before overcoming a full-strength Leeds United in the final.

The club entered something of a decline in the Seventies, when Hajduk took over the mantle of Croatia's flag-bearers in the Yugoslav league. It took the return of mercurial coach Čiro Blažević, after a successful exile in Switzerland, to rejuvenate the club. With the goals of Zlatko Kranjčar and sound defending from centre-back Velimir Zajec and goalkeeper Tomislav Ivković, Dinamo won the Yugoslav league by five points in 1982. Doves were released

over the Maksimir, Zagreb went bananas and Blažević was near-deified.

The stadium underwent major improvements for the hosting of the World Student Games in 1987 and, with stars from Yugoslavia's World Youth Cup triumph of the same year, the stage was set for another Dinamo revival as the Nineties approached. It wasn't to be. Before the shine had worn off the medal he'd won as Player of the Tournament in Chile in '87, playmaker Robert Prosinečki was poached by Red Star Belgrade. A second comeback by Blažević turned out to be a pale shadow of the first. And Davor Šuker's arrival from Osijek served only to unite the provincial town against the capital – within months he was on his way to Spain.

It was another Osijek goalscorer, Goran Vlaović, who was persuaded to move to Dinamo and help them win their first Croatian league title in 1993. In the meantime, Čiro had returned for a third time, at the behest of Croatian president Franjo Tudjman. Blažević headed a consortium which

Blue boy – the goals of Goran Vlaović helped Croatia Zagreb to their first post-independence title

bought Dinamo – then called HAŠK-Grad-janski – and, assured by Tudjman of as much state support as necessary, took over coaching duties as well. The coach reduced his involvement, active and financial, when he took charge of Croatia's national team in early 1994.

By then, a huge rift was emerging between management (under pressure from Tudjman and his henchmen) and fans over the club's name. The dispute upset team morale, and this in turn allowed Haj-duk to steal the domestic limelight.

But Croatia Zagreb it is for the time being, and they have the goals of Australian international Mark Viduka to thank for their double-winning run in 1997. With wily old Otto Barić in charge, the team had been playing as well as at any time since Croat independence. And though the coach has since departed for Fenerbahçe, the scouting network he left behind has been scouring the country for talent before a serious attempt on Europe in 1997/98.

Getting a ticket

The former club kiosk on Kvaternikov trg is awaiting relocation after a McDonald's was built in its place. For the time being, with the Maksimir rarely full, buy your tickets at the ground. The booths are to the right of the stadium as you approach from the tram stop by the park. *Tribina Zapad*, the impressive, renovated west stand, has the most expensive seats, facing the 'Bad Blue Boys' opposite. Home fans also gather under the scoreboard, while away fans will be at the park end.

Here we go!

Take tram #4 from the train station (seven stops, allow fifteen minutes) or tram #11 or #12 from Trg Bana Jelačića (seven stops, ten minutes) to the stop named **Buko-vačka**. The stadium is to your right.

Swift half

Bars line Maksimirska cesta on the way to the stadium. The **HAŠK Café** (at #111) and the **GOL Bufet** (#106, opposite) are the most popular, five minutes' walk away. At the ground, the **Domagoj** restaurant by the ticket office (entrance by the side door inside the stadium gates) has some great old photos of Dinamo's finest moments – waiter service, so at half-time you're best off queuing at its buffet/grill counter outside.

Publication

The monthly magazine *Croatia Zagreb* (8kn) is available at the ground and at newsstands across the city.

Club shop

Although souvenirs are available from the club office at the stadium, there is no shop there as such. **Valentino Sport**, Mak-simirska cesta 43 (open Mon–Fri 10am–7pm, Sat 9am–2pm, no credit cards), ten minutes' walk into town, has a decent selection of shirts and souvenirs of both Croatia Zagreb and the Croatian national team. Credit cards are accepted at their similar store in town, **Valentino Moda**, on the corner of Trg Bana Jelačić and Ilica (open Mon–Fri 8am–8pm, Sat 8am–3pm).

Ultra culture

Whereas Hajduk's *Torcida* is a very Mediter-ranean experience, Dinamo's **'Bad Blue Boys'** have copied much of their style from England. Many of the BBB have short-cropped hair, and a few actually look mean. Synthetic drugs help in this process, and the lower part of the *Tribina Istok* is awash with chemicals and booze. Once Dinamo get their old name back and the fuss has died down, the BBB will probably move onto other things.

In the net

The Bad Blue Boys won a crucial battle in the propaganda war over the club's name when they set up their own website before management had a chance to instigate an official one. A large but strangely unthreat-ening bulldog scowls at you from their homepage, flanked by a pair of old-style Dinamo badges (the phrase 'Croatia

Zagreb' is nowhere to be seen). The news section, in Croatian only, is laden with talk of politics and fan violence rather than events on the pitch, but it's still worth having a peek at: public.srce.hr/~dspahija. For the official party line, head for: www.nkcroatia.hr. Like the BBB site, the club version has no English, but the pages are regularly updated and informative enough.

Groundhopping

Croatia Zagreb dominate the city's footballing life. The town's second team, **NK Zagreb**, maintain a discreet presence in the Croatian first division but have never won a thing, while down in the depths of the *Središte* (central) region of the amateur third division you'll find what remains of **Trešnjevka Zagreb**, another of the city's old historic clubs.

These days, though, a new team are challenging the hegemony of Dinamo/Croatia – **Hrvatski Dragovoljac**, or Croatian Volunteers. Formed three years ago for the benefit of civil-war veterans and their families, the club have an ambitious and eccentric president, Stjepan Spajić, who hopes to relocate the team somewhere in the vast expanse of urban housing estates that is Novi Zagreb. (In 1996/97 the team played the first half of the season near the Bosnian border, the second in the southern Zagreb suburb of Velika Gorica.)

If Spajić succeeds, he'll not only improve life in entertainment-starved Novi Zagreb – he'll also bring some much-needed football competition to Croatia's capital.

◖ NK Zagreb

Stadion NK Zagreb, Kranjčevićeva 4
Capacity 18,000 (10,000 seated)
Colours All white

NK are very much Zagreb's second club. Tucked away in the west of the city, they

spent decades yo-yoing between the top two divisions of the old Yugoslav league. In the weaker Croatian league, they have regularly finished in the top three without threatening the domination of Croatia Zagreb and Hajduk, or widening their fan base beyond the same shuffling old locals who have been watching them since Tito's day, together with a small huddle of ultras known as the 'White Angels'.

Their ground, with its impressive main stand, narrow terrace opposite and cycling track ramps behind the goals, is a pleasant venue for a gentle afternoon's football. The atmosphere is relaxed, the nationalist sentiment refreshingly muted – over the past few years the team have fielded a variety of ethnic Bosnians, Albanians and Italians as well as Croats.

To see them in action, take tram #3 or #9 from the train station, or tram #12 from Trg Bana Jelačića, to **Tehnički Muzej**. The stadium is on your right.

The **Ozalj** on the corner of Kranjčevićeva and Tratinska is the best pre-match choice for a swift half. The bars behind the terrace, particularly the **Boćar**, are also worth a look-in. Inside the ground, the **Zagrebački Bijeli** restaurant on the far side of the main stand has a café area by the main doors.

Eat, drink, sleep...

Bars and clubs

Civil war broke out just as Zagreb was really sinking its teeth into the first fruits of freedom. Western bands had always played Zagreb regularly, but the summer of 1989 buzzed with a frenzy of club and concert activity. Nowadays the scene is still good – possibly the best and most accessible east of Vienna – but it needs a shot in the arm from somewhere.

By the market, off Zagreb's main Trg Jelačić, are two parallel streets jam-packed with bars, Opatovina and Tkalčićeva. There are six in a row down Opatovina, of which

Kvazar is the main hangout. A couple stay open until 2am.

Fanatic, Ribnjak 20–22. A short walk around Zagreb cathedral from Trg Jelačić, the *Fanatic* has a hip clientèle, wacky decor and excellent sounds. Opposite, in the park, is the *Ribnjak*, which has an unhip clientèle, terrible decor and poor sounds, but always seems to be the last bar open as dawn greets Zagreb.

Jabuka, Jabukovac 28. 'The Apple' offers a decent night's drinking and indie noise. Open until 2am Thurs–Sat. Bus #102 from Britanski Trg.

Klub Z, Tkalčićeva 16. Large, pleasant bar with a pub feel run by ex-Dinamo star Velimir Zajec. Football on TV, Stella Artois on draught.

Pivnica Medvidgrad, Savska 56. Simply the most popular bar in town, vast and always

Name of the game – Dinamo and the 'BBB'

Few fans in Europe have experienced a decade as extreme as Dinamo Zagreb's **'Bad Blue Boys'**. Formed in 1986, the BBB were one of several Italian-style ultra groups in former Yugoslavia whose activities became more overt – and extreme – as nationalist tensions rose. Their rivalry with Red Star Belgrade's *Delije* spilled over during the infamous Dinamo–Red Star clash of May 1990, when the BBB rained **broken chairs** down onto their foes. In less than two years, some of those fans would be facing each other on the battlefield.

By 1992, however, the BBB found themselves up against a more **insidious enemy**. In the masterplan devised by independent Croatia's first head of state, President Franjo Tudjman, Dinamo would dominate the new Croatian league and represent the nation in Europe every year. Europe, according to Tudjman, should not assume Dinamo were still a club of the old **Communist system**. He called for a new name – HAŠK-Gradjanski, after the two clubs which originally merged to form Dinamo. The fans couldn't chant it. He thought again. Dinamo had always represented the aspirations of the Croatian people, so why not call them Croatia? **Croatia Zagreb!**

Having persuaded coach Čiro Blažević to buy the club, Tudjman now had a football team to operate in the national interest. The BBB didn't see it his way. Dinamo were the side their fathers followed in the Sixties. Dinamo put one over Belgrade by winning the

'Silent complicity' – Blažević

Yugoslav title in 1982. Dinamo's shirts were stained with blood that May afternoon in 1990... So the ultras continued to chant **'Dinamo!'** at matches. Tudjman refused to budge. The BBB responded by burning down his podium. The credibility of Blažević sank as his silent complicity continued. The BBB became a rallying point for opposition to Tudjman's regime, as well as attracting every right-wing bonehead in the city.

In 1996, management introduced a **new club badge** incorporating the former emblems of HAŠK, Gradjanski and Dinamo. The team were drawn to play Spartak Moscow in the UEFA Cup, but management would only allocate tickets for the away leg if fans agreed to wear scarves and shirts bearing the new badge. They refused. The 1997 spring season opened with a visit to Šibenik, where Zlatko Canjuga, a Tudjman ally, was attacked by members of the BBB while he sat in a café.

When good sense prevails, Dinamo, rather than the Bad Blue Boys, will be the ones making a name for themselves across Europe.

crowded. Serves its own beer brewed on the premises, plus a range of barbecued meats. Tram #14 or #17.

Restaurants

Although Zagreb suffers the ills afflicting many Croatian restaurants – overpriced and empty – it offers a reasonable amount of cheap takeaway options. The **Bonita** 24-hour snack bar (Cesarčeva ulica 3, on the corner of Trg Jelačić) and the **Pingvin** (Nicolae Tesle 7, one minute's walk south of Trg Jelačić) are good spots to know. The latter, above the *BP Jazz Club*, does huge sandwiches until 2am daily, 3am Fri–Sat. The row of snack bars between Trg Jelačić and the market are a sound lunch option.

Kaptolska Klet, Kaptol 5. Croatian national dishes in a spacious, elegant restaurant opposite the cathedral. Elevenses at 19kn. Terrace open in summer. Open until midnight daily. Most major credit cards.

Nokturno, Skalinska 5. Good standard pizzeria slap between the two main bar streets of Opatovina and Tkalčićeva, with plenty of variety and good salads. Around 20–30kn a pizza. Open until midnight daily. Most major credit cards.

Phoenix, Jurišićeva 19. Recently opened Mexican restaurant, five minutes' walk from Trg Jelačić with decent burritos and chilli. Cocktails available. Around 40–50kn a meal. Open until midnight Mon–Sat, closed Sundays. Most major credit cards.

Pivnica Tomislav, Ul baruna Trenka 2. Its address belies its prime spot on Tomislav Trg, a minute's walk from the train station. This wonderful, cheap, friendly cellar bar has a separate restaurant area serving reasonably priced local cuisine. Open until 11pm daily. Mastercard accepted.

Split, Ilica 19. Possibly the best fish restaurant in town for the price, centrally located, only a short walk from Trg Jelačić. The day's specialities are posted up on a board in the courtyard.

Open until midnight Mon–Sat, closed Sundays. Most major credit cards.

Accommodation

The advice is simple – book ahead, either through the tourist office (☎01/272 530) or your local Croatian tourist board. For **private rooms**, try the **Staza** office at Heinzelova 3 (☎01/213 082, open Mon–Fri 9am–6pm, Sat 9am–1pm). They charge around 150kn a night for a single, 250kn for a double. All the hotels listed take major credit cards and normally charge in Deutschmarks.

Astoria, Petrinjska 71 (☎01/430 444, fax 01/434 956). Centrally located two-star hotel between Trg Jelačić and the train station. Ask for a room with a television. Laundry facilities. Chinese restaurant downstairs. Around DM100 a single, DM150 a double.

Dubrovnik, Gajeva 1 (☎01/455 5155, fax 01/424 451). Overlooking Trg Jelačić, a two-star hotel with TV in each room, air conditioning, laundry facilities and summer terrace café. Around DM120 a single, DM160 a double.

Hotel Laguna, Kranjčevićeva 29 (☎01/333 533, fax 01/334 185). Handily situated right by NK Zagreb's stadium, a large hotel with gym and sauna. Each room has air conditioning, bath and satellite TV. DM110 a single, DM140 a double. Tram #3 or #9 from the train station to Badalićeva.

Omladinski Hostel, Petrinjska 77 (☎01/434 964). The only youth hostel in town that's open all year round, so often full. Five minutes' walk from the train station, no curfew. Clean and comfortable, showers in the corridor. DM25 per person in a twin room, DM20 in a triple, including tax. No credit cards.

Studentski Centar, Savska 25 (☎01/274 674). Open from mid-July to September, the best hostel in town in the main student complex. Dorm beds at DM20. Tram #4 from the train station. No credit cards.

Split

Split is the South America of Europe, a footballing Rio in miniature. Its crumbling, graffitied city walls play host to endless games of street football. Its fans, their matchday parades, their torch-bearing, even their very name – *Torcida* – have been borrowed from Brazil. Its stadium, the Poljud, is Croatia's soccer cauldron, a tempestuous bowl of passion and colour, barely a firework's throw from the calm, clear blue of the Adriatic. No wonder the Croats prefer to play their big international matches here.

The footballing life of the city revolves around a small area where the old Hajduk stadium once stood, halfway between the ruined palace of the Roman emperor Diocletian and the Poljud. Although the pitch is still intact – used for youth games – the stands have long gone. Not the spirit,

though. The Stari Plac, or *Plinada* ('Gasworks'), where the main road leading to the Poljud, Zrinjsko-Frankopanska, meets Matoševa, is a hive of activity on matchdays. From this small square, home of the *Torcida*, their bar and several others, the Split anthem *Ništa Kontra Splita!* ('Don't Dis Split!') thunders out towards the stadium half a kilometre away.

As kick-off time approaches, a huge gathering of supporters sets out on the gentle incline up to the Poljud, along which they are joined by hardcore followers from the nearby Skalice area, and the stadium slowly fills with a drunken revelry which will later spill out over the waterfront and onto dawn. These days, however, the performance of the team has caused these fans to drink more out of desperation than of celebration...

Seaside folly – Hajduk's Poljud stadium looks and sounds fantastic, but costs serious cash to keep

Split essentials

Croatia Airlines run a bus service (20kn) between the **airport** at Trogir, 23km from Split, and their main office on Obala Hrvatskog Narodnog Preporoda (known as the Riva) an hour and a half before and after each flight.

The Riva is Split's main drag, stretching along the bay from Diocletian's Palace to Trg Republike. On arrival, as you face the Adriatic from the train or (adjacent) bus station, turn right and the Riva is three minutes' walk away.

Most of central Split is **easily accessible on foot**. A bus network covers the rest of the city in four zones – zone 1 is adequate for most visitors' needs. Tickets are sold at newsstands (6kn for a double, simply stamp one end when you get on) or onboard (8kn). Buses run 5am–11pm and there is no night transport.

Taxis are generally parked outside the train station or on Trg Republike; they charge 15kn plus 7kn per kilometre. To phone for one, dial ☎021/47 777.

The **tourist office** is on the Riva, at Obala HNP 12 (open Oct–Easter Mon–Fri 9am–3pm, Sat 8am–1pm; Easter–Sept daily 7.30am–8pm; ☎021/342 142). The office produces a monthly **listings guide** in English, *Split City Guide*, available here or at most travel bureaux in town. Club and concert information is included, with the unfortunate omission of any addresses.

Foreign newspapers are on sale at the International Bookstore, Obala HNP 10.

The thrilling fields

Hajduk Split

Stadion Poljud, Poljudsko šetalište
Capacity 50,000 (all-seated)
Colours White shirts, blue shorts
League champions (Yugoslavia) 1927, 1929, 1950, 1952, 1955, 1971, 1974–75, 1979
Cup winners (Yugoslavia) 1967, 1972–74, 1976–77, 1984, 1987, 1991
League champions (Croatia) 1992, 1994, 1995
Cup winners (Croatia) 1993, 1995

The oldest Croatian club still in operation, thanks to a loyal, passionate fan base and a constant stream of local talent, Hajduk Split have overcome severe difficulties of finance and logistics to establish their position in modern-day Croatia.

The financial burden of maintaining a stadium as magnificent as the Poljud – with its complicated, earthquake-proof roof – is awesome, especially considering the average league crowd in Croatia and the lack of substantial television rights. Hajduk enjoyed a fair run in the 1994/95 Champions'

League, finishing as runners-up to Benfica in the group stage and holding the eventual winners Ajax at home before losing in Amsterdam. But it is the sale of players that keeps Hajduk afloat. Five key members of the current national squad were raised here: Aljoša Asanović, Slaven Bilić, Alen Bokšić, Robert Jarni and Igor Štimac.

This export trade is nothing new. Hajduk won three Yugoslav titles in six years in the early Fifties, before goalkeeper Vladimir Beara and forward Bernard Vukas went abroad. The best-ever Hajduk side of the Seventies was actually several sides, the squad rebuilt each year as the stars of the previous season were sold to foreign clubs, among them Zlatko and Zoran Vujović (Bordeaux), Ivica Šurjak (Udinese), Iko Buljan (Hamburg) and Ivan Katalinić (Southampton), the last returning to coach the side in the early Nineties.

Each time Hajduk rebuilt, their fans, the *Torcida*, urged for more. Twice Hajduk reached a European semi-final, twice they lost to an English club by narrowest margin – to Leeds by the only goal in the 1973 Cup-Winners' Cup, to Spurs on away goals in the 1984 UEFA Cup. Hajduk's sales policy cost them that final push at the highest level, and it has continued to work against them in the latter half of the Nineties, as the better-funded Croatia Zagreb have usurped the Dalmatian club's position at the top of the domestic tree.

The club were formed by expatriate students in Prague who, after seeing Sparta and Slavia, wanted to see the same in their home town of Split. On returning home, they gathered in the Troccoli café and worked out the finer details of their idea, but the team still needed a name. Eventually Hajduk, the name given to the ferocious Dalmatian bandits at the time of the Ottoman occupation, was decided on by one of their professors.

Hajduk played friendlies at the military training ground of Kraljeva Njiva and were founder members of the Yugoslav league in 1923. That same year, the team toured North Africa, beating Marseille 3–2 while they were there, and thousands gathered at the port to welcome them home. Football had become an integral part of city life. By 1930 Hajduk had won two titles, had had

an operetta (*Kraljica Baluna*, 'The Queen of Football') written in their honour, and nearly all their team had appeared at international level for Yugoslavia, not least at the inaugural World Cup.

Today Hajduk retain all their traditional assets – a vast Dalmatian catchment area, exemplary youth development and insane local support, but their idealistic approach to football is in danger of being overtaken by the modern world.

Getting a ticket

For a big game at the Poljud, hustling for tickets is the prime talking point all week. For an average league game, you will easily be able to get tickets on the day.

In the former case, the **Torcida Shop**, Obala HNP 15 (open Mon–Fri 9am–noon, 5–7pm, Sat 9am–noon), near the main tourist office, should be your first port of call in the hunt for tickets. Travel agents often sell them as well, so keep your eyes peeled. At the ground, there are small concrete ticket huts along the Kaštelanska side

As war loomed, Hajduk played their last European tie as a Yugoslav club in Austria – against Spurs

Finest hour – Asanović eludes his Anderlecht shadow in Hajduk's 1994 Champions' League run

of the ground, the left turn from Zrinjsko-Frankopanska towards the sea.

Your ticket will indicate a *sektor*, a row (*red*) and a seat (*sjedalo*). The *Torcida* occupy the cheaper north side, while away fans are allocated sector A, in the south-west of the ground. The *Tribina Zapad* (west) has the most expensive seats, along with press and VIP boxes.

Here we go!
Most fans either walk or rev up their mopeds along Zrinjsko-Frankopanska to the Poljud, a kilometre from town. If it's raining, take bus #3 or #17 from the train station.

Swift half
The *Torcida* bar, **Club Navijača Torcida**, is on the first floor at Stari Plac 17 – turn to the stairs immediately to your right as you enter. Open 5–11pm, with a side TV room draped in scarves overlooking the

old pitch, it is not only cheap (6kn a beer) and friendly, it is the perfect introduction to one of Europe's most genuine and overt football cultures. Downstairs, the **Café Rossi** begins to party from mid-morning on matchdays. Further towards the ground along Zrinjsko-Frankopanska, the **Bar Tim**, near the corner with Lučićeva, is popular for a last call. The **Caffe Bar Hajduk**, under gate F, is your best bet inside the stadium.

Ultra culture
Many claim that Hajduk Split's *Torcida* were Europe's first ultras. Looking at the superb photo collection in their bar, you'd be hard-pressed to correlate those eager, dapper Dalmatians in trilby hats with the choreographed groups of modern-day Italy. But back in the Fifties the *Torcida* were the first fans to carry torches, the first to construct large banners, the first to co-ordinate songs – and certainly the first to organise away

trips across the land. They took their lead from South America. Before the main feature, cinemas across Yugoslavia showed newsreel footage of the 1950 World Cup in Brazil, with frequent shots of the crowd. Despite the disappointment of seeing their heroes lose to the host nation, back home fans were so impressed by the atmosphere generated at the Maracaná stadium that they endeavoured to create their own.

A group of Split students based in Zagreb decided to turn a match against Red Star Belgrade into such an event. Two trainloads came down to Split, partying outside the *Park Hotel* to keep Red Star players awake the night before the game. The next day, October 28, 1950, they sparked off wild support at the Stari Plac, encouraging Hajduk to come back from a goal down, Bernard Vukas scoring the winner in the 87th minute. At the final whistle, the newly named *Torcida* rushed onto the pitch and carried the goalscorer from the stadium into town. A movement was born.

In the net

Like a vast metallic flying saucer surrounded by mountains on one side and the sea on the other, the Poljud stadium shines out from the official Hajduk Split homepage. It is not the only memory-hungry slice of graphics on the site, but be patient – there's some great content here, including an illustrated, English-language history of the *Torcida* and updates on former Hajduk stars now playing abroad. Like the club which sponsor it, this site is brimming with pride and innovation, but will be even better when all the rough edges have been smoothed off. Point your browser at: www.hajduk.com/.

Eat, drink, sleep…

Bars and clubs

By day the cafés along the Riva bustle with custom. By night the narrow maze of alleyways of Diocletian's Palace nearby are like

a giant floodlit game of snakes and ladders, everyone tumbling into square after square, each one full of bars. Square one is Mihovilova Širina, the palace entrance, thronging with groups of people eager to set off for the night in any given direction.

It's easy to get lost inside the palace, but it is well-lit, which is probably just as well – Split is Croatia's drug capital, with a serious heroin problem, so keep your money safe. The city is also the capital of Croatian pop, and music is always blaring out from any given bar or window.

Bili As, corner of Narodni Trg/Kraj Sv Marije. Pleasant corner football bar owned by former Hajduk captain Dragan Holcer, with black-and-white photographs and other souvenirs from his career. Two minutes' walk from Mihovilova Širina up Marulićeva.

Dioklecijan, Alešijeva 3. Enter the palace at Mihovilova Širina, turn immediately right into Dosud and at the end you'll find this small, local bar with its charmingly rundown terrace and perfect view over the Adriatic. Open daily, 7am–10pm.

Klub Zanatlija, Krešimirova 7. Large cellar bar in the darkest depths of the palace, buzzing with football talk the night before a big match. Enter the palace at Ispod Ure, the far side of Narodni Trg, and walk straight ahead down Krešimirova.

Puls Kavarna, Buvinova 1. Just off Mihovilova Širina, the hippest designer bar in the palace, with a cool crowd and decent sounds. Open daily until 1am.

Shakespeare, Uvala Zente 3. Down by the marina, a brash and mindless three-level club with a terrace for starlit groping. Bus #10 from Tržnica, or a taxi ride from the train station.

Restaurants

Dalmatian cuisine is the best in Croatia, a delicious mix of local seafood, fresh vegetables and olive oil. *Dalmat brodet* is a typical dish, but there are many variations.

Competition won't bring prices down until the tourist trade picks up again, but you can still eat much more cheaply in Split than in Zagreb.

Central, Narodni Trg 1. Attached to the *Hotel Central*, a large restaurant with tables outside on the square. Daily specials at 20–25kn for a main course. Open until 10pm, most credit cards.

Pizzeria Galija, Tončićeva 12. Reasonably priced, centrally located pizzeria serving a variety of pizza and pasta dishes. Separate bar area, air conditioned. Open Sundays, no credit cards. A five-minute walk from Trg Republike up Marmontova.

Plava Peka, Poljudsko šetalište 9. Pricey but polished eaterie near the Poljud stadium, specialising in shellfish, grilled meat and local dishes. Bread baked on the premises. Open until 1am, most credit cards. Bus #17 from Tržnica.

Star Rock Café, Tončićeva 6. American-style diner with walls decorated with mock souvenirs from the music business – tacky and popular with players on international duty. Five-minute walk from Trg Republike up Marmontova.

Zlatna Ribica, Kraj Sv. Marije 12. Small, friendly, family-run diner by the fish market selling plates of *lignje* (scampi) and other freshly caught delights for 20–30kn. Closed Sundays. A minute's walk from Trg Republike.

Accommodation

Lack of competition will keep hotel prices high in Split until the tourists come back in numbers. A private room is probably the best option, arranged through the tourist office (☎021/342 142). Rates are set at 98kn for a single and 156kn for a double including tax. Pay the whole amount to the English-speaking staff, who will then give you a receipt and point you in the right direction. All hotels listed take most major credit cards.

Hotel Bellevue, Bana Jelačića 2 (☎021/585 701, fax 021/362 383). Perfectly located by central Trg Republike and the bay, a three-star hotel with TV in every room and a restaurant downstairs. DM100 for a single, DM140 a double. Ten-minute walk from the train/bus stations.

Hotel Jadran Koteks, Sustjepanski put 23 (☎021/361 599, fax 021/361 381). Four-star hotel on the far side of the bay by Uvale Baluni, with an outdoor pool and gym. TV and air conditioning in every room. DM110 a single, DM160 a double. Bus #8 from the station.

Hotel Marjan, Obala Branimira 8 (☎021/302 111, fax 021/342 930). A huge hotel overlooking the bay. Outdoor swimming pool, discotheque, restaurant, rooms with air conditioning. Out of season DM110 a single, DM150 a double. Bus #8 from the station.

Park Hotel, Hatzeov Perivoj 3 (☎021/515 411, fax 021/591 247). Pleasant, air-conditioned four-star hotel near the beach with a palm-lined terrace, shower and TV in each room, plus a decent restaurant. Out of season DM130 for a single, DM180 for a double. Bus #3, #5, #8 or #17 from the station.

Prenocišste Slavija, Buvinova 2 (☎021/47 053, fax 021/343 567) Slap in the heart of Diocletian's Palace, a comfortable if noisy pension close to the nightlife action. DM80 a single, DM120 a double. A ten-minute walk from the station, entering the palace via Mihovilova Širina.

Czech Republic

The day after the end of Euro '96, hungover workmen cleared the empty bottles from the sticky paving stones of Prague's main Wenceslas Square. The party for the Czechs' surprising final appearance had gone on all night, despite the flukey 'golden goal' defeat by Germany in extra time. Fans and players alike had enjoyed a month of beer and football. The Czech Republic was on the map.

Though the team's subsequent failure to qualify for the 1998 World Cup has cast a retrospective shadow over it, Euro '96 was a turning point for the Czech game. The national side were making their début in international competition after the division of Czechoslovakia in 1993. Their success sold players all over Europe – top agent Pavel Paska was negotiating the deals within hours of the Wembley final – and focused the hearts and wallets of the new Czech business class, who had previously favoured investing in tennis and ice-hockey.

In 1976, it was with a core of Slovak players that Czechoslovakia pipped England to qualify for the knockout stage of the European Championship in Yugoslavia. Having beaten Holland after extra time in the semi-finals, the Czechoslovak team were leading world champions West Germany 2–1 until the last minute, then showed immense character in winning a penalty shoot-out with the scores at 2–2.

In 1996, under stern-faced coach Dušan Uhrin, it was a purely Czech team in the spotlight. President Václav Havel, a crusading dissident playwright twenty years earlier, was now seen commiserating with his team in their Wembley dressing room.

For much of the Nineties Czech football, still a predominantly working-class pursuit, suffered the familiar post-Communist ills of underfunding and low crowds.

Last gasp – Šmicer equalises against Russia

The country's two main clubs, Sparta and Slavia Prague, missed Slovak rivalry after the Czech and Slovak leagues divided in 1993; financially fragile, they both lost out at the hands of shaky entrepreneurs. League champions and UEFA Cup semi-finalists in 1996, Slavia were forced to sell four key players to finance the rebuilding of their run-down Eden stadium.

Yet Slavia's title win confirmed the political changes of the new republic. For the five long decades since their last championship in pre-totalitarian 1947, Slavia had suffered under the state manipulation of domestic football. Generations of Slavia stars were lost to the army side, Dukla, and in the early Nineties their eternal rivals Sparta were perceived to be the team of the government. Even at the last minute, older Slavia fans were still expecting state intervention to rob them of their title.

Their celebrations had a sad edge. Slavia stalwart and national hero František Plánička stayed alive just long enough to be told the news of the team's championship win, and Euro hero Karel Poborský delayed the signing of his transfer from Slavia to Manchester United so as not to coincide with Plánička's funeral.

Poborský's sharp, quirky talents typify all that's been good about the Czech game since its development at the start of the century. His inventive lob which knocked Portugal out of the Euro '96 quarter-finals echoed the audacious, chipped penalty with which Antonín Panenka beat West Germany in 1976, and even further back to Prague's prewar footballing heyday.

In those days, many Czechs learned their quick-thinking skills from *České ulice* – street football in which beating the man was paramount. Those skills, coupled with a brisk, short-passing style (common throughout the Danube basin but intro-duced, in fact, by English and Scottish coaches), made Czech sides formidable opposition at both club and international level. Slavia and Sparta, who between them took every prewar domestic title but one, also mustered three wins in the Mitropa Cup. Goalkeeping captain Plánička, with seven Slavia team-mates, led the Czech national team to the 1934 World Cup final. They came within eight minutes of winning it. Winger Antonín Puč put them ahead with twenty minutes remaining against the hosts and favourites Italy, who had the woodwork to thank for not going further behind before Plánička misjudged Raimondo Orsi's cross-cum-shot and the sides were level again. Italy won 2–1 in extra time and Plánička would always blame himself for the defeat.

It was much the same story when Czechoslovakia met Brazil in the 1962 World Cup final, as another hapless goalie, Viliam Schrojf, effectively lost the game for

Chip and tuck – Karel Poborský's stroke of genius claims another scalp for the Czechs at Euro '96

Basics

Americans and EU nationals need only a **passport** to enter the Czech Republic. Australian, New Zealand and Canadian citizens require a **visa**, available at their Czech embassy, at Austrian or German border crossings, or at Prague's Ruzyně airport.

The Czech currency is the **crown**, or koruna, usually indicated Kč and divided into 100 haléřů. Crown coins come in denominations of 1, 2, 5, 10, 20 and 50, with 20, 50, 100, 200, 500, 1000 and 5000 crown notes. There are just over 50Kč to £1. The crown is convertible in the West, but you'll get a far better rate changing back unused crowns in the Czech Republic.

The centre of Prague is littered with **exchange offices** which generally offer poor rates. Banks (usually open Mon–Fri 8am–5pm) are a better bet. Most major towns have credit-card cash machines, but outside Prague, shops and restaurants are generally cash-only. In Prague there are a handful of 24-hour exchange offices – one at Staroměstské náměstí 21, another at the airport.

The Czech **telephone system** still leaves much to be desired. From outside the country, the telephone code for the Czech Republic is 420. Dial 00 to call abroad once inside the country. There are no cheap rates for international destinations – a call to the United Kingdom will cost 31Kč a minute, anytime. Internally, the cheap rates are Mon–Fri 4–7pm and all day weekends. City codes are as follows – Prague ☎2, Brno ☎5, Ostrava ☎69 and Olomouc ☎68.

Most telephone boxes now take phone cards (*telecarty*), available at newsstands and post offices for 100Kč, 200Kč or 300Kč. There are some coin phones, for which you'll need 2Kč or 5Kč pieces.

Travel around the Czech Republic is cheap, if slow. There are three kinds of **train**. The slower they go, the cheaper they are. The fastest are express (*expresný*); then fast (*rychlík*); and finally ordinary (*osobný*). International through trains require a seat reservation (*místenka*).

Prague has two main train stations – Hlavní nádraží for trains from the west, Holešovice for the service between Berlin and Budapest. Both are on red metro line C, although Hlavní nádraží is only a five-minute walk from Wenceslas Square.

Czech **buses** are even cheaper than trains, and many castles and popular village destinations can only be reached by road. From Prague, most long-distance buses leave from the station by Florenc metro stop (yellow line B or red line C).

a different kind of Czech team. Their star was Josef Masopust, midfield leader of the defence-minded army side, Dukla Prague, who would dominate the postwar Czechoslovak championship.

Under Communism, Dukla had first pick of the country's best players. By the time their power began to wane in the Seventies, Slovak teams such as Spartak Trnava and Slovan Bratislava had the country's real strength in-depth, although Dukla still provided two key players for the 1976 European Championship team – goalkeeper Ivo Viktor and midfielder Zdenek Nehoda.

Dukla were doomed to obscurity, at least temporarily, by the fall of Communism. Sparta's domination of the Eighties looked set to keep the team at the top of the new Czech-Moravian league in the Nineties, but when they hit a cash crisis in 1995/96, the door was left open for Slavia and a handful of provincial sides.

Sparta revived sufficiently quickly to regain their title in 1997. But it was a close-run thing, and Slovan Liberec, Petra Drnovice, Baník Ostrava and Sigma Olomouc may all be regular challengers by the end of the millennium. Leading the way for the out-of-towners could be Boby Brno, the focal point of fervent Moravian regional passions, who often draw five times the Czech league's average attendance of 5000.

Essential vocabulary

Hello *Ahoj*
Goodbye *Na shledanou*
Yes *Ano*
No *Ne*
Two beers, please *Dvě piva, prosím*
Thank You *Děkuju*
Men's *Muži*
Women's *Ženy*
Where is the stadium? *Kde je stadíon?*
What's the score? *Jaky je?*
Referee *Rozhodčí*
Offside *Mimo hru*

Match practice

In this age of golden goals and rich agents, most Czechs still get by on the simple pleasures of beer, sausages and *kopaná* – football. Here the game is a cheap, basic form of entertainment, short on modern facilities. Crowds are small, but then, so are most grounds. Only Sparta's renovated, all-seater Letná currently meets international standards.

The Czechs enjoy a season of two halves, running from early August to late November and late February to early June.

Although Sunday is the traditional day for football (Saturday is for ice-hockey), some lesser Prague clubs play early on Saturday afternoons. One live television game is scheduled for 4.30pm on Fridays. For the first and last few rounds of the season, most other weekend games also kick-off at 4.30pm, but the closer you get to winter, the earlier this becomes. Expect 1.30pm kick-offs in November and February.

The league

The *Českomoravského liga* (Czech-Moravian league) came into being for the 1993/94 season after Slovakia left the old Czechoslovak federation.

At the time, officialdom's insistence on retaining a sixteen-team first division came in for criticism by sages who predicted it would lead to falling standards. However, the rise of provincial sides previously denied access to top-flight football by the presence of Slovak clubs has inspired a surge of interest in soccer right across the new republic, even if not all the football is exactly world-class.

At the end of each season, the two bottom-placed sides from the top flight, the *I. fotbalová liga*, change places with the top two from the *II. fotbalová liga*. The semi-professional third division is divided into two groups, one eighteen-team Czech (ČFL) and one sixteen-team Moravian (MSFL). Slavia and Sparta's 'B' teams play in the ČFL, Ostrava's, Olomouc's and Brno's in the MSFL – but none of them can be promoted. Otherwise the winners of each section swap places with the bottom two of the second division. The fourth is similarly divided into five *divize*, A-C Czech, D-E Moravian.

Up for the cup

After a *předkolo* ('preliminary round') for the minnows in late July and a first round in August, the *Pohár ČMFS* starts in earnest when the first-division clubs join at a seeded, second-round stage. Ties are decided over one game, including the quarter- and semi-finals in April. The final takes place at the Strahov in May. After what happened to them at Euro '96, the Czechs seemed unlikely candidates to adopt the controversial 'golden goal' rule – yet their 1997 cup final between Slavia and Dukla was decided in precisely that way.

Tickets

Prices vary according to the standard of stadium and level of interest. A seat for a big league match at Sparta's comfortable Letná could set you back 100Kč; to see a lesser team visiting Bohemians or Slavia should only cost 30Kč. At most grounds you should be able to get your ticket at the ground a few minutes before kick-off.

Places will be divided into seated (*k sezení*), generally a spot on a bench, and standing (*k stání*). Stands will be open (*krytá*) or covered (*nekrytá*). For the Letná and the Strahov, your ticket will indicate a sector (*sektor*), a row (*řada*) and a seat (*místo* or *sedadlo*). Most clubs issue a programme, on sale at the ticket office, for 10–30Kč. At many games you'll come across a variety of vendors offering an array of old football badges, often very cheaply.

Half-time
Beer (*pivo*) and sausages (*klobása*) or frankfurters (*párek*) keep most fans going of a Sunday. Beer is always within range of the average fan's pocket, rarely more than 15Kč, while sausages are 20Kč with bread and mustard. Service can be painfully slow, so get in line well before half-time.

Action replay
Privately owned broadcasters TV Nova, who blew the Czech market wide open with decent coverage of live league football in 1994, had the carpet swept from under them when a multi-million dollar deal was announced between the league and Dutch satellite TV company NetHold in 1996.

Although the five-year deal began in August 1997, the new arrangement overlaps with Nova's for one season and the Czech-Moravian FA have decided to allot each company the rights to half the plum Friday afternoon fixtures for 1997/98.

A century-old rivalry – Slavia clash with Sparta

NetHold's other plans are not yet known, but TV Nova will still show its Saturday lunchtime preview, *Sportžurnál*, and round-ups on Sunday (*Minipenalta*, 20 minutes of highlights at 9.30pm) and Monday (*Penalta*, an hour of highlights and analysis at 5pm).

State TV had its fingers burned when Nova launched a successful legal action to ban its pirate league coverage, but still holds the rights to the Champions' League and to international matches.

German, Austrian, Slovak and Polish channels are easily available throughout the Czech Republic.

The back page
Fans' staple diet is the daily *Sport* (6Kč, no issue on Sundays) – classic, print-heavy, advert-free fare which has changed little since Communist days. Monday's edition (an extra 50 haléřů!) has a good league round-up along with Premiership results and goalscorers. The weekly *Gól* (Thursdays, 10Kč) gives equal space to football and ice-hockey, whereas the glossy monthly *Fotbal Sport* (19Kč) is all soccer features and news. The back page of the English-language weekly *Prague Post* (Wednesdays, 40Kč) offers easily comprehensible football coverage.

Newsstands on Wenceslas Square sell a large range of foreign newspapers, including that day's *International Guardian*.

Ultra culture

Unless there's a big game at Sparta or Slavia, crowds in Prague are so low that trouble is minimal. Certainly, you'll find little of the pseudo-Italian posing you might see in Poland, Hungary or the former Yugoslavia.

The Sparta–Slavia clash (*derby obou 'S'*) is one of the oldest of its kind in continental Europe, but for half a century it was more a point for discussion than an excuse for the venting of bitter partisan feelings. The ironic rivalry between the two clubs began with the first match in 1896, the result of which has still not been agreed. Some say 0–0, others 1–0 to Sparta after a disputed goal. The debate goes on to this day and, while it may not always be pursued at such a cerebral level, the rivalry has rarely been something worth wrecking a train over.

Sparta are the only Prague club with a following in the modern sense, but the lads are more rude than rowdy. In the provinces, you might find tension in the air when Sparta travel, or when Boby Brno play at home. The pride of the capital of Moravia, Brno attract a large nationalist following and a hardcore section of fans. Derby games with either of their two big Moravian rivals, Baník Ostrava and Svit Zlín, have been known to boil over.

In the net

Libor Laubacher maintains an excellent generic Czech football site at: users.czn.cz/~laubache/fotbal/main.htm. Everything's in English, the latest top-flight results skim along the bottom of the screen and there's an excellent player database into the bargain.

For a complete Czech stats overload, head for: ulita.ms.mff.cuni.cz/~zavora/football/. You'll find the result of every Czech international ever played, a huge domestic-league archive and the latest women's football scores at both club and international level. There's also a news feed from local press agency ČTK but, unlike the statistics, the stories are Czech-language only.

Comic but canny – Czechs financed their extended stay in England by betting against their team

Prague

Sparta 75 Slavia 78 Bohemians 80
Viktoria Žižkov 81 Dukla 82

While the provinces are home to some of the Czech Republic's up-and-coming sides, it is in the capital that the heart of the country's football beats loudest. Eccentric, romantic, anachronistic but above all an essential part of everyday city life, soccer in Prague is unique and unforgettable, if not always for the most obvious reasons.

The thrilling fields

Sparta Prague

Stadión Letná, Milady Horákové 98
Capacity 22,000 (all-seated)
Colours Claret shirts, white shorts
League champions 1912, 1919–23, 1925–27, 1932, 1936, 1938–39, 1944, 1946, 1948, 1952, 1954, 1965, 1967, 1984–85, 1987–91, 1993–95, 1997
Cup winners 1964, 1972, 1976, 1980, 1984, 1988–89, 1992

Record title winners, AC Sparta are the biggest club in the Czech Republic. Their huge support has kept them at the top for the best part of a century, the only low point coming with relegation in the Slovak-dominated mid-Seventies, after which the club bounced back to take ten titles between 1984 and 1995. They were first in line for regular and lucrative participation in the Champions' League, and seemed a shining example to the rest of Eastern Europe on how to succeed in a post-Communist world.

Things started to go wrong when former car mechanic Petr Mach picked up Sparta for a song in 1992. Mismanagement over the expensive modernisation of the club's superb Letná stadium caused near bankruptcy in the winter of 1995/96, forcing a quick sell-off of players and allowing

eternal rivals Slavia to take the title in May 1996. That same month, Slovak steelworks VSŽ Košice bought the club and its huge debts. The new owners, who are also sponsors of the ambitious Slovak club 1.FC Košice, have successfully exported cheap Slovak players to Prague, and pulled off a masterstroke when they appointed former club captain Josef Chovanec to the post of first-team coach midway through the 1996/97 season; under Chovanec, Sparta surged up the table to reclaim the championship they had lost the previous year to Slavia.

Thanks to the dilapidated state of the Strahov stadium, Sparta are now also earning revenue from hosting national team games. Yet they still have some serious reorganising to do if they again want to challenge for European riches.

Sparta's first golden era was in the Twenties. Founded as Athletic Club Královske Vonobrady – literally 'King's Vineyard' – in 1893 and becoming Athletic Club Sparta the following year, they played their first derby against Slavia on the Letná playing fields in 1896.

Sparta attracted working-class support, earning the nickname železná ('iron') Sparta. They won the first Czech league in 1912, seven more titles in the 1920s and the inaugural Mitropa Cup – an embryonic international competition open to Central European clubs – in 1927.

Their prewar star was inside-forward Oldřich Nejedlý, top goalscorer at the 1934 World Cup, but a player whose domestic era was dominated by Slavia. A second Mitropa Cup win in 1935 coincided with the rebuilding of the Letná stadium after it was gutted by fire. (A much later redesign, in 1973, turned it into a perfectly formed, compact ground, converted to an all-seater in the mid-Nineties.)

Although the club were forced into a series of name changes, Communist

Czechoslovakia was kind to Sparta. In contrast to sorry old Slavia, Sparta received some state support, pinching a title every few years from Dukla.

Today, for fans and politicians alike, the club are more than a name at the top of the league table – and how 'Iron Sparta' progress with their Slovak steel bosses is of crucial importance to the modern development of Czech domestic football.

Here we go!

Take green metro line A to **Hradčanská**, then a five-minute walk along Milady

Man in tights – veteran Sparta striker Horst Siegl

Horákové. A slower route – red metro line A to **Vltavská**, then tram #1, #8, #25 or #26 – offers a better selection of bars.

Swift half

If you're coming via Vltavská, the **Na Staré Kovarné** on Kamenická is a perfect, run-down, smoky beer hall. If it's too full, take your pick from several options along Veletržni. Opposite Hradčanská metro, on Dejvická, there's the **restaurace Dejvická** at #2, and the **Bruska** bar at #18. Inside the ground, the **Občertsvenó** has two slow-moving queues shuffling towards buffets selling Samson beer and sandwiches.

Publications

Spartăn Letenský is the A4-sized programme, sold around the ground at 25Kč.

Club shops

There are two stores opposite each other by the ticket office on the Milady Horákové side of the ground. The **Sparta Shop** (Mon–Fri 9am–6pm, Sat 9am–noon & on matchdays, no credit cards) has a small selection of cups, spoons and glasses. **Fans Club Praha** at #98 (Mon–Fri 9am–6pm, Sat 10am–2pm, Sun 1–5pm, no credit cards) has more to choose from, including old videos and some classic Czech three-coloured horns (*tralalák*) at 70Kč.

In town, the **AC Sparta Praha** shop at Betlemské náměstí 7 (Mon–Thurs 10am–5pm, Fri 10am–4pm, no credit cards) deals in Sparta (and Slavia!) souvenirs, match tickets, money changing and gambling.

Ultra culture

Sparta's younger following gather behind one goal, in sections D3,

B4, E1 and C4, waving a few flags and setting off the occasional firework.

Sparta's club song, played before kick-off
and after every goal, is unpopular and uninspiring. Away fans are behind the opposite
goal, in sections I, K, H and J. Neutrals are
best placed in sections D1, D2 or D6, near
the bar.

In the net

A huge Czech-only site can be found at:
omega.vsz.cz/student/xvondrak/start.html.
The latest news and results are here if you
can decipher the accents, while a stats
archive includes an entire page devoted to
the Sparta-Slavia derby; surprisingly, that
first game in 1896 is shown as a draw.

Prague essentials

An express bus runs every twenty minutes from Prague **airport** into town, first stopping at Dejvická metro stop, the terminus of green metro line A, then into town by the
Czech airline office on Revoluční, five minutes' walk from Náměstí Republiky metro
stop on yellow line B. The service runs 7.30am–7.30pm, and costs 15Kč for the 20-
minute journey to Dejvická, 30Kč for the 35-minute run into town. Pay the driver.

Three local buses also run every twenty minutes, 5am–midnight: #119 from
Dejvická, #108 from Hradčanská (green line A) and #179 from Nové Butovice (yellow
line B). These cost the price of a local transport ticket, 10Kč, which is valid for at least
an hour from when you first stamp the ticket's arrow end on boarding at the airport.

There are two kinds of **transport tickets**, both valid for Prague's metro, trams and
buses. For one ride of up to fifteen minutes, or up to four stops on a metro line, buy a
6Kč ticket. Alternatively, a 10Kč ticket lasts for sixty minutes at peak times, ninety at
evenings and weekends.

The orange ticket-dispensing machines can be tricky: choose the ticket type, press
'*výdej*' for as many tickets as you want, then insert your coins. Change will be given. It's
probably easier to buy a handful from newsstands or *DP* windows at metro stations.
There you can also buy a 24-hour pass for 50Kč, a three-day one for 130Kč or a weekly
for 190Kč, valid from the time of first stamping. Your full name and date of birth must
be filled out on the back.

The **metro**, clean and fast, has three colour-coded lines: green line A, yellow line B
and red line C. Transfers (*přestup*) are possible at Muzeum (A and C), Můstek (A and B)
and Florenc (B and C).

The city's transport system runs 5am–midnight. There are a night bus and tram
routes, running every forty minutes between midnight and 4.30am. Trams stop at
Lazarská crossroads on Spálená near Národní třída, most buses at the top of Wenceslas
Square near Muzeum metro.

Prague's **taxi drivers** have earned their grim reputation. The cabs standing in
Wenceslas Square are there to rip you off. Try to hail a moving one in the street. Once it
stops, make sure it is clearly marked as a taxi, with fares prominently displayed and a
black-and-white chequered stripe along the side. Ensure the driver does not turn on the
meter, set to 1, until you get in. You should be charged an initial fare of 10Kč, then no
more than 16Kč per kilometre. The least disreputable companies are *AAA* (☎02/3399)
and *ProfiTaxi* (☎02/1035). These firms should charge no more than 300–400Kč for the
journey to the airport.

The main **tourist information office** in Prague is the central, English-speaking
PIS, Na příkopě 20 (☎02/544 444, Mon–Fri 9am–6pm, Sat 9am–3pm), with other
branches in the Old Town square and in the Hlavní nádraží. None of these, however,
can help with accommodation enquiries.

Prague is woefully short of English-language **nightlife information**. The weekly
Prague Post (Wednesdays, 40Kč) is a decent, if staid, source.

Angry young man – Patrik Berger at Slavia

🌑 Slavia Prague

Edenu, Vladivostocka 1460/2
Capacity 16,000 (5000 seated)
Colours Red-and-white halved shirts, white shorts
League champions 1913, 1924–25, 1929–31, 1933–35, 1937, 1940–43, 1947, 1996
Cup winners 1997

"Slavia, do toho!" shout the club's fans, pleading for their team to hit the back of the net. Slavia's goal was finally reached on an emotional afternoon in May 1996, when the country's oldest and most revered club won the title after fifty years of gerrymandering and downright oppression.

Formed in the late nineteenth century as a Czech-language literary and debating society, and viewed with deep suspicion by

the ruling, German-speaking Habsburg authorities, Slavia attracted rebellious young members of Prague's intelligentsia.

A sports branch was set up, and the football section opened for business in 1892, taking its colours of red-and-white with a red star after what was then the independent Czech flag.

Slavia first met Sparta in 1896, and the two clubs took it in turns to win the Czech title until the arrival of hardcore Communism in 1948. By then two generations of fans had been raised to root for either Slavia or Sparta, Slavia attracting the university-educated, Sparta the working-class support.

Former Scottish international John Madden guided Slavia through the glory years in the professional era of the Thirties, when the team won six titles and provided eight of Czechoslovakia's World Cup runners-up team in 1934. Goalkeeper František Plánička was the hero of the day, Slavia through and through, while winger Antonín Puč will go down in history as the all-time top scorer for Czechoslovakia.

Slavia won the Mitropa Cup in 1938, by which time prolific forward Pepi Bican had arrived from Vienna. With Bican leading the line, Slavia dominated the Czech-Moravian wartime championship and took the Czechoslovak title in 1947. Within a year, however, state president (and former Slavia player) Edvard Beneš had resigned to hand full power to the Communists, and Madden had died while still in the Slavia coaching job – and still preaching the short-passing game.

In the total restructuring of Czech football which ensued, Slavia were renamed Sokol Praha 7 and lost half their squad to the newly formed army side, then called ATK. An ageing Bican moved to Vítkovicé. The devastation was completed at the start of the Fifties when the club, then Dynamo Slavia, were forced from the newly rebuilt Letná to a working-class area of tower blocks, railway sidings and a large cemetery – 'Eden'. Slavia slumped to the second division but fought back in the mid-Sixties,

The Strahov

Stadión Evžen Rošicky, Olympijska
Capacity 19,600 (all-seated)

The Czech Republic's national football stadium, officially named after a well-known victim of Nazi terror, Evžen Rošicky, is commonly called the Strahov after the four-arena sports complex there and the monastery nearby. High up over Prague, the Strahov has the perfect setting for major events but its tatty condition has persuaded the authorities to move Czech national games to the Letná.

Athletics are now the Strahov's main *raîson d'être*, but cup finals are still played here, and the stadium also hosted the later rounds of Slavia's 1996 UEFA Cup run, when **AS Roma** and **Bordeaux** were among the visitors, and there was a genuine buzz in the air.

To get there, take bus #371 from Anděl or #176 from Karlovo náměstí. For major events, bus #35 also runs from Anděl.

The **Snack Bar Strahov** by gate A3, open until 9pm on weekdays, is worth a look-in for its two walls of black-and-white photos of Czech football heroes, and its 12Kč Gambrinus beer.

The **Wepo** restaurant nearby is the classic cheap Czech lunchtime *bufet*, with bendy aluminium cutlery, 9Kč Staropramen and a terrace view of the complex.

winning back their name and their status and clocking up a handful of European appearances. Twenty years later, Slavia players marked the student demonstrations of November 1989 with a pre-match show of support.

After the fall of Communism, the club found itself in the unaccustomed position of having an exciting crop of young players it could actually keep. But Slavia still had a run-down wooden stadium and the club's new owner, a millionaire Czech-American by the name of Boris Korbel, expected instant results and left after a series of boardroom disputes in 1994.

In the absence of Korbel's cash, key players such as Patrik Berger were sold to balance the books. But Jan Suchopárek, Radek Bejbl and Vladimír Šmicer stayed, to be joined by Karel Poborský from Viktoria Žižkov, and these players were the engine that powered Slavia to their thrilling UEFA Cup run – when Roma were among their victims – and title win in 1996.

All four went west (for a total of 350 million crowns) after Euro '96, and a weakened Slavia squandered the chance of further riches when they were crushed by

Grasshopper Zürich in the Champions' League qualifying round that summer. Nonetheless, the team made a decent stab of their title defence in 1996/97, finishing only four points shy of a much better-resourced Sparta.

In 1997 Slavia also won the Czech-Moravian cup for the first time in their history, beating born-again Dukla with a 'golden goal' ten minutes into sudden-death extra time.

The club's prime concern now, however, is the renovation of Eden – Grasshoppers' coach was not the first to mistake the stadium for Slavia's training ground...

Here we go!

There are three ways of finding Eden. Take green metro line A to Náměstí Míru, then tram #4 or #22; red metro line C to I P Pavlova, then tram #4; or red line C to Vyšehrad, then tram #7.

Swift half

The Eden restaurant once attached to the stadium is long gone, replaced by a kitsch Seventies-style leisure centre – the rather

The kangaroo stands proud outside Bohemians – but his latest hop has been down, not up

disappointing **Eden restaurace** is on the first floor, with dishwater beer and desperately slow service.

Outside the ground, your best bet is the **Pivnice U Stadión**, on the corner of Vršovická and Čeljabinská – cheap, simple and unpretentious.

Inside the stadium, the **Krušovicky Klub Slavia** terrace bar under the main stand is a joy, with the club's history displayed across its walls. It's open to the public during the week but on matchdays you'll have to convince the doorman that you're an important visitor from abroad.

In the net

In addition to his generic Czech footie site, Libor Laubacher somehow finds time to maintain an unofficial Slavia site at users.czn.cz/~laubache/slavia/slavia.htm. Compared with some one-club sites it's a little thin, but Libor is promising a major reconstruction soon.

Groundhopping

Few European cities offer minor grounds as atmospheric as Prague, and the lesser clubs' preference for playing on a Saturday means weekend visitors can often see a match at one of them as a prelude to the main event the following day.

Bohemians

V D'oličku, Vršovická 31
Capacity 17,000 (3000 seated)
Colours Green-and-white shirts, green shorts
League champions 1983

Bohemka, also nicknamed the Kangaroos after a tour of Australia in 1926, are a short hop from neighbours Slavia and have suffered a similarly blighted history. They were originally AFK Vršovice, named after the working-class district of Prague in which they play. Their humble ground, D'oliček ('the Dimple'), saw hard times and several name changes under Communism. At one time the Kangaroos were even known as Spartak Stalingrad.

Under coach Tomáš Pospíchal, the club hit a purple patch in the Eighties, making the UEFA Cup semi-final in 1983, the year they won their first league title. They came within minutes of another in 1985. According to Pospíchal's book *Fotbal nemá logiků* ('Football Has No Logic'), published a decade later, there were forces at work preventing further success. Fraud investigators, perhaps tipped off by inscrutable Sparta and Dukla, arrested a club official and Bohemians' good name has been tainted ever since.

In more recent times the club, relegated and then promoted by default in 1996, have only themselves to blame for failing to consolidate their top-flight status – they were relegated again in 1997.

To reach the Dimple, take red metro line C to I P Pavlova or green metro line A to Náměstí Míru, then tram #4 or #22 to Vršovické náměstí.

The **U tří soudků**, on the corner of Sportovní and Vršovická, is a classic old football haunt, its back room swamped in pennants, its bar serving Louny beer at 9Kč and cheap food.

🌑 Viktoria Žižkov

Na Žižkov, Seifertova třída
Capacity 8000 (1500 seated)
Colours Red-and-white striped shirts, red shorts
League champions 1928
Cup winners 1994

Ah, Žižkov! Elsewhere in Prague, fan loyalty may depend on your father's persuasion, but Žižkov's is one born of the Prague 3 district, with its run-down bars and staunch Communist loyalties. After decades in the doldrums, the club was rescued in the spring of 1992 by multi-millionaire Vratislav

Čekan, who saw it as his mission to rejuvenate his beloved *Viktorka*. Leasing the stadium from the Prague 3 district council, Čekan raised the club from the bottom of the third to the first division in two years, his influence peaking with a Czech cup triumph in 1994.

The bubble burst when the local sports authority realised they had a similar municipal contract signed the year before. Protracted Czech bureaucracy then caused Čekan to pull out in the summer of 1996. Although the team have lost faith, a visit to Žižkov, with its piped chants and flat caps, is like a taste of milltown England in the 1890s.

To get to Žižkov, take tram #5, #9 or #26 from the Hlavní nádraží train station. It's about a ten-minute ride.

Once in the vicinity of the ground, the bars of Žižkov are your oyster. If you get tired of gloom and grime, the **Pod Viktorkou**, Seifertova 55, opposite the ground, has discovered the delights of tablecloths and wallpaper. Inside the

Bred by Žižkov – Slovak striker Tibor Jancula

ground, the **restaurace** behind the home goal doesn't sell beer, but a stall round the corner serves Velkopopovický Kozel at 12Kč.

☾ Dukla

Na Julisce, Postovni schránka 59
Capacity 28,000 (11,000 seated)
Colours All yellow with claret trim
League champions 1953, 1956, 1958, 1961–64, 1966, 1977, 1979, 1982
Cup winners 1961, 1965–66, 1969, 1981, 1983, 1985, 1990

Let's face it – visitors don't come to Dukla Prague for the football. They come because this classic old Communist outfit were featured on Liverpool underground band Half Man Half Biscuit's song, *All I Want For Christmas Is A Dukla Prague Away Kit*. Not that the band ever spent much time in drab Dejvice, with the huge Socialist-Realist Hotel International towering over it.

Few former Eastern Bloc army clubs sank as low as Dukla in the summer of 1994. Having been relegated from the first division after one win all season, the club couldn't afford the professional licence fee to stay in the second division, and Dukla's management reluctantly volunteered to send their team into the amateur third.

In line with the Communist restructuring of the game, the Czechoslovak army was given its own team, ATK, in 1948. They became Dukla in 1956. The club could call up any player they liked by simply drafting him into the army, and the generals had wise advisors. Josef Masopust, European Footballer of the Year in 1962, led the team to five national titles in the Sixties, along with a European Cup semi-final, against Celtic in 1967.

Of future generations, goalkeeper Ivo Viktor and Zdeněk Nehoda, the most-capped Czech player of all time, starred in Czechoslovakia's European Championship-winning side of 1976. With Nehoda and Ladislav Vízek, Dukla had a fairly successful

time of it in the Eighties, and even won the cup – on penalties – as recently as 1990.

But by then there were new forces in charge – market ones – and the army withdrew its support in January 1994. Since then, Dukla have slowly pulled themselves up by the bootstraps under the enterprising leadership of a new owner, Bohumir Duričko. In 1995/96 Duričko bought another Czech side, second-division FC Pribram, and subsumed them into Dukla, who then assumed Pribram's position in the higher division.

Then, as if in synchronicity with Half Man Half Biscuit's comeback album, the team came back up to the top flight in May 1997, the same month they reached the cup final for the first time since 1990.

Crowds at Dukla rarely averaged more than 1500 even in the Seventies, so don't expect to see hordes of fans in replica shirts as you make your way to a game at their Juliska stadium. Take green metro line A to terminus Dejvická, then tram #20 or #25 to the end of the line at Podbabská. The stadium will be in sight, but it's still a steep walk up Pod Juliskou on your left. Allow plenty of time.

Before your climb to the stadium, grab a cheap Gambrinus beer in the basic but friendly **Pod Juliskou**, on the corner of Pod Juliskou and Koulova. Once in the stadium, the club need your custom at their **Občerstvení Vlajka** in the main building.

Just inside the main doors, by the Občerstvení, you'll find a whole list of souvenirs beautifully displayed in the club shop, including *that* away shirt at 580Kč. The shop is open on matchdays and occasional mornings, credit cards unheard of.

Eat, drink, sleep...

Bars and clubs

Czech beer is the best and the cheapest in the world. In tourist traps near to Prague's major attractions, you may be stung for 50Kč a beer, but otherwise you

All I want for Christmas is a series of ground improvements... Duka's bleak Juliska stadium

should be paying 15–25Kč for a half-litre of the stuff. **Beer** (*pivo*) is either light (*světlé*) or dark (*tmávé*). Waiters will come round and serve you with half-litres of *světlé* until you indicate otherwise or place your beermat over your empty glass to get the bill. The **classic brews** are Plzeňský prazdroj (known as Pilsner Urquell in export markets) and Budvar (the original Budweiser). Beers local to Prague include Staropramen, Krušovice, Měšťan and Radegast. The best commonly available **dark beers** are Braník and Purkmistr.

The average beer hall (*pivnice*) will close around 10–11pm. A wine bar (*vinarná*) will tend to close later. The local spirit is *becherovka*, a strong liqueur. Watch out for sanity-stealing absinthe bars.

Nightclubbing is as good as you'll find anywhere in Eastern Europe. Entry is either free or around 30–50Kč, depending on whether there is live music. Drinks are generally more expensive than in beer halls, but not prohibitively so, and most places stay open until at least 3am. There is no main nightlife area in Prague, although Wenceslas Square is home to some tacky discos.

Bunkr, Lodecká 2. The city's main alternative club, a little dated and overpriced. Open 8pm–5am. Náměstí Republiky metro.

Evropa Café, Václavské náměstí 25. Elegant if overpriced spot for breakfast on Wenceslas Square, below the *art nouveau* hotel of the same name. Open from 7am.

Malostranská beseda, Malostranské náměstí 21. Modest but welcoming live venue, generally for jazz or blues acts. Open until 1am. By Malostranská metro.

Radost Fx, Bělehradská 120. Large, bright and reliable nightspot near I P Pavlova metro stop, with a trendy café on ground level. Both are open until 5am.

Sport Bar Praha, Ve Smečkách 30. American-style operation with several giant television screens displaying live soccer action. Two large bar areas, pool tables, extensive if pricey menu. Five minutes' walk from Wenceslas, open until 2am Sun–Thurs, 4am Fri & Sat.

U Zlatého tygra, Husova 17. Classic busy beer hall in central Nové Město, favourite haunt of writer and football nut Bohumil Hrabal before his death in 1997. His seat under the huge poster of Antonín Panenka will probably be revered longer than the framed photo of Bill Clinton's visit. Doesn't open until 3pm.

Restaurants

Most beer halls serve hefty portions of pork, dumplings and sauerkraut, mainstays of the Czech high-calorie diet. A restaurants (restaurace) will have a slightly more adventurous menu, although the clientèle will probably still be tucking into goulash or **beef in cream sauce** (svíčková). Fish also features on most menus. **Lunch** is the main meal of the day, and most restaurants close by 10pm. Expect to pay 100–200Kč for a full spread and surly service. If you're on a budget, an old stand-up bufet can provide a main course for under 40Kč.

Krušovicka, Široká 20. Friendly pub/restaurant five minutes from Old Town square, offering main courses at under 60Kč and namesake beers aplenty. No credit cards.

Pravěk, Budečská 6. Decent range of dishes ranging from seafood to poultry and game, served in an imaginative setting. Around 200–250Kč for a main course. Most major credit cards. Náměstí Míru metro.

U Mecenáše, Malostranské náměstí 10. Perfect setting for the big blowout, with a patio and gorgeous medieval interior. Adventurous menu, with main dishes around 350–500Kč. Kitchen open until 11.30pm, most major credit cards. Malostranská metro.

U supa, Celetná 22. 'The Vulture' is a fourteenth-century pub/restaurant off the Old Town square selling dark Braník beer and light Krušovice, with a courtyard open in summer. Popular with the more upmarket football fan. No credit cards.

Vltava, near Rašinovo nábřeží. Down by the river near Palacký bridge, a quiet fish restaurant serving huge portions of carp and trout in dozens of ways for less than 150Kč a dish. No credit cards.

Accommodation

Finding a centrally located budget hotel in Prague in high season can be a huge problem. The best option may be a hostel bed or a private room arranged through one of the accommodation agencies – two are listed below. Make sure your room can provide **decent transport** into town – Prague is a big place and you could be stuck way out in the suburbs.

Ave, Hlavní nádraží (☎02/2422 3521). Accommodation office in the main train station, conveniently open daily 6am–11pm in summer, 6am–4pm in winter. Limited choice of private rooms but cheaper than most. Singles for under 200Kč, doubles for under 400Kč.

Hello, Senovážné náměstí 3 (☎02/2421 2741). Five minutes' walk from Hlavní nádraží station, this agency offers private rooms for 400–800 Kč. Open daily 9am–10pm.

Hotel Evropa, Václavské náměstí 25 (☎02/2422 8117). Cut-price luxury at the most beautiful hotel in town, bang in Wenceslas Square. Reserve a room well in advance – they're a bargain at 1500–2000Kč a single, 2000–2800Kč a double; the higher rates are for suites with period furniture. No credit cards.

Kafka, Cimburkova 24 (☎02/273 101). Slightly out of the centre, but freshly renovated, comfortable, clean and a short walk from Viktoria Žižkov's ground. Singles up to 900Kč, doubles no more than 1300Kč. Tram #5, #9 or #26 from the main train station. Most major credit cards.

Libra-Q, Senovážné náměstí 21 (☎02/2410 2536). Best hostel deal in town, centrally located and without a curfew. Singles with a bathroom at 750Kč, without 450Kč; doubles 1100Kč and 700Kč respectively; 200Kč for a share of a four-bed dorm.

U krále Jiřího, Liliova 10 (☎02/2422 2013). Tiny pension in the Old Town above the James Joyce pub, with attic rooms and its own bar. 1000Kč a single, 1800–2000Kč a double, most major credit cards.

Denmark

'We have won the revolution," says one club director, remarking on the radical changes that Danish football has undergone in the past decade. Within the space of a few years, the domestic Danish game has been transformed from an amateur curiosity into a thriving, professional league.

Although paid players were belatedly allowed into the national team in 1976, it wasn't until 1991 that Denmark embraced fully fledged professionalism with the creation of the *Superliga*. Since then crowds have soared, sponsors are competing to be associated with the big clubs, and media companies are battling for broadcasting rights. Those who sat down in 1990 to chart out the future development of football in Denmark must be feeling rather pleased with themselves.

Like all revolutionaries, the progressives in Danish football had to fight hard to bring about change. There was the conservative sport establishment to convince but, more importantly, there was also an ideological opposition, in what is a deeply social-democratic country, to the commercialisation, competitiveness and personality cults of modern soccer.

Yet the national team's surprise success in winning the 1992 European Championship took the sting out of opposition to the new approach. When the Danes beat Germany 2–0 to be crowned kings of Europe, the sons and daughters of those stern egalitarians were dancing in the streets, their faces painted red and white.

Latecomers to the modern business of football they may have been, but the Danes were one of the first continental nations to take up the game. Københavns Boldklub (KB) were founded in 1876, long before most of the big English clubs had had their

Great Dane – Schmeichel at Euro '92
....

foundation meetings in the local pub. With this head start Denmark performed well in the early Olympic competitions. In London in 1908 they won the silver medal, losing to England in the final after beating France 17–1 in their opening match – a game in which Sophus Nielsen scored ten goals, setting an international record which has not been broken since. (One of Nielsen's team-mates, Niels Bohr, went on to win the Nobel prize for physics.)

Four years later, in Stockholm, the Danes were again Olympic runners-up. But by the Twenties, the Danish game was in decline and it wasn't until 1948 that they made any further impression, winning bronze at the London games.

As in Sweden, strict amateurism forced many of Denmark's best players to leave the country. The first Dane to make an impression abroad was Nils Middleboe, who played at Chelsea between 1913 and 1921. Three members of the 1948 Olympic bronze-medal winning side, Karl Præst and Karl and John Hansen, moved to Juventus, and by the Sixties Danes were popping up all over Europe – St James' Park veterans may recall one Preben Arentoft scoring a crucial goal for Newcastle in the 1969 Fairs' Cup final.

The Danish league was dominated by a dozen or so small teams from Copenhagen until the Sixties, when Århus and Esbjerg began to make an impact. Meanwhile a Copenhagen Select XI, comprising players from KB, B93, Frem and AB and known as the *Stævnet*, competed without distinction in the Fairs' Cup.

After a silver medal performance at the 1960 Rome Olympics, the Danish national team failed to qualify for the final stages of either the World Cup or the European

Championship for more than two decades. But the seeds of change were planted in 1976, when the Danish FA finally bowed to pressure to include professionals in the side. The man who forced their hand was Allan Simonsen, European Footballer of the Year in 1977, who set a continent alight in the colours of Borussia Mönchengladbach and Barcelona, before ending his career with a bizarre move to Charlton Athletic of the English second division.

Simonsen was to be a rôle model for a whole generation of Danish players in the Eighties, when the likes of John Sivabæk, Jesper Olsen, Peter Schmeichel and Jan Mølby all moved to England. Liverpool midfielder Mølby, with his perfectly developed Scouse accent and Sunday League beer belly, was the most popular; 'keeper Schmeichel the most successful – a giant rock of a man upon whom Manchester United were to build their Nineties legend.

It wasn't just English football which witnessed an influx of talented Danes. Michael Laudrup, probably the best player Denmark has ever produced, enjoyed a glittering career with Lazio, Juventus, Barcelona and Real Madrid. And Flemming Povlsen was a consistent goalscorer with Cologne, PSV and Borussia Dortmund before injury forced him into premature retirement in 1995.

Perhaps appropriately, it was a non-Dane, German-born Sepp Piontek, who was to bring the country's scattered exiles together and mould them into a world-class national team. It was his Denmark side which beat England at Wembley in 1983 to qualify for the European Championship finals for the first time.

It was to be an impressive début. After losing to France in their opening game, the Danes qualified from their group thanks to a 5–0 hammering of Yugoslavia

The prodigal son returns – Michael Laudrup, Euro '96

Basics

Citizens of the EU, America, Canada, Australia and New Zealand require only a **passport** to enter Denmark.

The Danish currency is the **krone** (plural kroner) and there are around 9kr to the pound. Change money at banks – there is a **fixed commission charge** of 25kr regardless of the amount. Banking hours are Mon–Fri 9.30am–4.30pm. You'll find plenty of cash machines accepting all major international cards.

You can buy **stamps** at newsagents as well as post offices, most of which are open Mon–Fri 9am–4.30pm. There are two kinds of **public telephones**: coin phones (minimum 2x1kr for a local call, 5kr for an international one) and yellow card phones; cards cost 20kr, 50kr or 100kr and are available in newsagents. The international access code for Denmark is 45 and there are no individual city codes. To get an international line from inside the country, dial 009.

Denmark has an excellent domestic **train network** run by DSB, the Danish state railways. Tickets are heavily subsidised – the longest single journey will cost you no more than 230kr. Seat reservations are compulsory and tickets cannot be bought on trains. Also, be aware that there is no discount on return tickets and that prices are around twenty percent higher at weekends.

Only trips to outlying areas will require you to become acquainted with Danish **buses**, but this is a country with a huge number of islands and you may well find yourself wanting to make use of the odd **ferry**. The cost of this will be included in your train fare if it is part of a DSB service. Otherwise, as a foot passenger you'll pay around 40kr for a short crossing – just turn up and pay at the terminal.

and a thrilling 3–2 victory over Belgium. In the semi-finals they played most of the football against Spain but lost on penalties.

The Spaniards crushed Danish hopes again at the Mexico World Cup two years later. As in France, Piontek's Danes impressed in their group games, defeating Scotland, Uruguay and West Germany. But they were destroyed 5–1 by Spain in the second round.

After losing all three group games at Euro '88 and failing to qualify for Italia '90, Denmark looked a fading force. But their greatest moment was yet to come.

Having apparently missed the boat to Euro '92, the Danes were handed a last-minute lifeline when Yugoslavia, the team which had topped their qualifying section, were squeezed out of the tournament by the pressure of international sanctions. The Danish squad would be without Michael Laudrup, who wasn't seeing eye-to-eye with coach Richard Møller Nielsen. But other stalwarts such as Schmeichel, Povlsen and Michael's younger brother Brian were happy to cancel their summer holidays in order to represent their country.

Even so, the team were badly underprepared – and looked it after a dull goalless draw with England and a 1–0 defeat by hosts Sweden in their opening games. But an unexpected victory over France earned the Danes a semi-final against the holders Holland which they won on penalties, and suddenly Møller Nielsen's men found themselves in the final against newly united Germany. There, a stunning goal from John Jensen, which was to earn him an ill-fated move to Arsenal, and a late clincher from Kim Vilfort saw the gate-crashers run away with the prize. Nobody – Danes included – could quite believe it.

Although Denmark failed to qualify for USA '94 and failed to impress at Euro '96, the national team are being usefully reshaped by a Swedish-born coach, Bo Johansson, while the Danish game now enjoys a level of respect in international circles which would have been undreamt of a generation ago.

Essential vocabulary
Hello *God dag*
Goodbye *Farvel*
Yes *Ja*
No *Ny*
Two beers, please *To øl, tak*
Thank you *Tak!*
Men's *Herrer*
Women's *Damer*
Where is the stadium? *Hvor er stadion?*
What's the score? *Hvad er stillengen?*
Referee *Dommer*
Offside *Offside*

Match practice
Danish fans are justly famed for their sense of humour. Ask a local to translate the chants, or at least those which aren't sung in English – many Danish terrace ditties are lifted straight from Old Trafford. Denmark's newly emerging football culture is heavily influenced by the English scene. Most Premiership teams have Danish supporters' clubs, and many Danes follow an English team as well as a local one.

Unlike the Swedes, however, the Danes have generally avoided copying Eighties-style English hooliganism. The national team's fans have dubbed themselves the 'Rooligans' and pride themselves on being easygoing. A quiet afternoon at a Danish game is a taste of how small-country football should be.

Games are usually played on Sunday afternoons at 3pm, although there are occasional midweek rounds during the spring, and live TV matches are normally on Friday nights.

The league
The season starts in late July and there are eighteen *Superliga* rounds before the end of November. Denmark's winter break is one of Europe's most generous, lasting until early March. A major fixture pile-up before the season finishes towards the end of May is the rule.

The *Superliga* was originally an eight-team competition with sides meeting each other four times. In 1995, the league was expanded to twelve clubs, playing each other three times in the course of a season. After each team has played all the others home and away, the top six clubs are given home advantage for the third encounter.

The *Superliga* is sponsored by brewers and soft-drink manufacturers Faxe, and is officially called *Faxe Kondi Ligaen*.

The bottom two teams in the *Superliga* are relegated and replaced by the top two from the first division. The second division is split into East and West, and below these come the *Danmark Serie* – regional leagues.

Up for the cup
Currently the Compaq Cup, Denmark's main knockout competition, begins in July and finishes the following May. The cup final is always played at the national stadium, the Parken in Copenhagen, and is a one-legged affair with extra-time and penalties if need be.

Tickets
Ticket prices are around 50–70kr for standing and upwards of 80kr for seating. Sellouts are rarely a problem unless there's a big European game on, so just turn up and buy your ticket as you go in. A seat in the stand will be denoted as a *siddeplads* while a chunk of concrete on the terraces is a *ståplads*.

Half-time
Sausages (*pølser*) are a national institution and are available from stands in most grounds. They come either as a hot dog, with fried and raw onions and a choice of mild or stronger French mustard, or served on a piece of card with bread and mustard. If hunger strikes after the final whistle, don't panic – you won't have to walk far to find a *pølser* wagon parked on a street corner outside the ground. Beer, usually an excellent local brew such as Carlsberg, Faxe or Tuborg, is available outside most stadia and inside the bigger ones. Most grounds have clubhouses or fully blown restaurants, and these are always popular – arrive early if you want a pre-match meal.

Kiss and make up – Danish supporters pioneered the modern footie fashion for face-painting

Action replay
A new Danish sports channel has won the rights to broadcast *Superliga* matches for the 1997/98 season, so state TV's tradition of a live game every Friday night and highlights packages on Sunday evening is subject to change. The satellite channel Super Sport broadcasts live matches as well as highlights from all the major European leagues, while the TV3 satellite channel has Champions' League rights.

The back page
The Danish quality press traditionally gave little coverage to football, but the rise of the national team and increasing popularity of the *Superliga* have brought a surge of serious football writing in papers such as *Berlingske Tidende*, *Ekstra Bladet* and *Aktuelt*. An increasing number of books have been written on the game from a new generation of writers such as Jakob Kvist, whose work – an inside look at the 1992 side and *The Ambassador*, a biography of Michael Laudrup – has won praise from Denmark's famously precious literary scene as well as making the bestsellers' lists.

As its name suggests, *Tipsbladet* (Fridays, 8kr) began life as a betting guide, but it has developed into an informative weekly football tabloid with results and news on the game from all over the continent – you'll find two pages on English football with news from the Nationwide League as well as the Premiership.

Ultra culture
Danish fans invented the fashion for face-painting and costumes with their red-and-white make-up and outrageous, self-mocking Viking outfits. Supporters' clubs are well organised and tend to enjoy close contact with club management. Away support, previously non-existent, is on the rise and, apart from occasional incidents involving Brøndby and FCK fans, hooliganism is rare.

In the net
The Scandinavian Infoweb company runs an extensive Danish-language site at: www.infoweb.dk/superliga/danmark.htm. Updated daily, it's a fine source of news and results, and covers major European leagues as well as the *Superliga*. Stats freaks may prefer Jesper Lauridsen's archive at: www.daimi.aau.dk/~rorschak/sl/dmtur.html. This covers all levels of the Danish game and offers an embarrassment of links to stats sites worldwide.

Copenhagen

Brøndby 90   FCK 92   Akademisk 94
Hvidovre 94   Lyngby 95

One of the keys to the *Superliga*'s success has been the extent to which teams from the provinces have challenged for top spot. Be that as it may, Copenhagen remains both the heart and the soul of Danish football, a city of soccer contrasts between modern, professional clubs and smaller, traditional teams where the attitude and atmosphere are so old-fashioned, you feel like buying a newspaper to check that it really is the Nineties.

The thrilling fields

 Brøndby IF

Brøndby Stadion, Park Allé, Glostrup
Capacity 22,000
Colours Yellow shirts, blue shorts
League champions 1985, 1987–88, 1990–91, 1996–97
Cup winners 1989, 1994

In a city full of teams with long histories and proud traditions, it is the youngest club which has made the biggest impression in the professional era. *Brøndbyernes Idrætsförening* were founded in 1964 as a local league club based in the industrial outskirts of the capital. After eighteen years in the lower divisions, the club were promoted to the old first division and turned semi-professional. In 1985 they lifted their first Danish championship and took the decision to become the country's first fully professional club.

The bulk of Denmark's 1992 European Championship-winning side had been with Brøndby in the mid-Eighties – most notably John Jensen, Peter Schmeichel and Brian Laudrup. And it was the Laudrup family who were at the heart of Brøndby's irresistible rise. Brian's and Michael's father,

Finn, was a leading player with the historic amateur club KB in the Seventies and had a spell in Austria with Wiener SC. At the end of the decade Brøndby – then in the third division – invited Finn to join them. He surprised everyone when he accepted the invitation and helped plant the first seeds of professionalism at the club before returning for a brief spell at KB. In 1981, at the age of 36, he came back to Brøndby to lead them up to the top flight.

Finn's most important decision was to encourage his son Michael to leave KB as a schoolboy for the more professional (but then second-division) Brøndby. The move revealed the bankruptcy of KB's amateur approach and indicated the growing status of Brøndby. In 1982, Finn retired and his No.10 shirt was taken by Michael. When Michael left after a season and a half, Brian stepped into his shoes.

Finn Laudrup is rightly credited for introducing real scouting, training and overall professionalism to Brøndby, but his pioneering work was so nearly destroyed. In 1991 the club's ambitious directors, flush with cash from the heavy exporting of talent, decided to purchase a major Danish bank, Interbank. The move was a disaster: Interbank quickly went into receivership, leaving the club saddled with huge debts. Ground development plans were put on hold and Brøndby had no choice but to continue selling players.

Happily, the business failure had little effect on the club's growth. On the field, Brøndby enjoyed a run to the semi-finals of the UEFA Cup in 1991, becoming the first Danish team to beat Italian opposition when they scored a 1–0 first-leg victory over Roma. In 1995, they dumped Liverpool out of the Cup-Winners' Cup.

Yet it was off the field where Brøndby proved themselves to be at the vanguard. As well as *ad hoc* improvements that have increased their stadium capacity, there has been the rapid growth of a large and well-organised fan base across the country.

The formation of FC København in 1991 completed the picture – now Brøndby fans had someone to hate as well as love. Brøndby's view of FCK's support as rootless and middle-class has helped shape their own perception of themselves as genuine, working-class fans following a genuinely professional club.

Here we go!
Take S-tog Bx, B or B+00 to **Glostrup** station, then bus #131 to the stadium. Give yourself at least half an hour for the whole journey.

Swift half
Hovsa, Seminarievej 1, is just five minutes' walk from the ground and has a fine pennant collection, satellite TV and a summer beer garden. Fight your way through the yellow-and-blue shirts ordering glasses of draught Tuborg. Everyone knows this as the pre- and post-match bar so it is always crowded on matchdays, but this is one place in Copenhagen where they don't mind you drinking on the street outside.

Publications
A bog-standard match programme is produced for all home games and costs 10kr.

Club shop
Souvenir booths are at all corners of the ground, the biggest by Gate C at the south end terrace, where the team's most boisterous fans stand.

Ultra culture
At the end of 1993 the official fan club, **Brøndby Support**, had barely a thousand members; today it has close to ten times that number, with separate sections all over the country. With their combination of Latin-style flames and flags and British-influenced chants, this lot are the most passionate supporters in Denmark. You will struggle to find a higher replica-shirts-per-fan ratio anywhere in Europe.

In the net
You'll do well to find a more adventurous single-club website than Brøndby Support's

Time warp – Brøndby mix it with past and future player John Jensen

chunk of web space at www.bif.support.dk/. There's a section in English and a comprehensive multimedia area which offers JPEG images of Brøndby action (including Dan Eggen's winner at Anfield in 1995), WAV audio files of player interviews, and a virtual songbook. As is so often the case, though, the English-language news is not updated as frequently as its vernacular equivalent.

FC København

Idrætsparken, P H Lings Allé 4
Capacity 40,000
Colours All white with blue trim
League champions 1993
Cup winners 1995, 1997

When the *Superliga* was launched, debate began as to how Copenhagen's established amateur clubs might be able to compete with the pros of Brøndby and go-ahead provincial clubs like Aalborg, Århus and Odense. The answer was they couldn't.

B1903 may have finished second in 1992 but KB were nowhere – they had won their last title in 1980 and had been relegated a season later. The two clubs that had dominated prewar Danish football and won titles regularly until the Eighties were becoming museum pieces.

B1903 had players and money but no support. KB had the fans but neither cash nor talent. Harald Nielsen, an ex-B1903 star who had played with Bologna in the late Fifties, led a group of businessmen and former players who had reached the same conclusion – merge the two to create a credible Copenhagen club. The result was FC København.

The new club had lofty ambitions from the start. First they signed a deal to play home games at the Parken, the national stadium in the centre of town. Second, they spent a small fortune on bringing in some of the top players from the provinces as well as a couple of signings from Brøndby.

The ambition quickly bore fruit. In their first *Superliga* season, 1992/93, FCK won the championship. But the instant glory and

---

Copenhagen essentials

Air travellers will arrive at **Kastrup** airport, 8km from the centre of Copenhagen. Scandinavian Airlines (SAS) provide a bus to the central train station (Hovedbane Gård) which leaves every 15 minutes and costs 35kr. The service runs daily 5.45am–9.45pm and the journey takes around 20 minutes. City bus #250S costs 13kr, leaves every 20–25 minutes and takes about half an hour to do the same journey.

Ferries from Norway and Sweden dock at Nyhavn, just a ten-minute walk from the heart of the city centre, while **international trains** arrive at Hovedbane Gård, opposite the Tivoli gardens and just a few minutes' walk from the main pedestrian shopping street, Strøget. **North Sea ferries** from Hull and Newcastle arrive at the port of Esbjerg on the Danish mainland – a 270km train ride from Copenhagen.

Public transport in the capital is made up of buses and S-tog suburban trains. Services run 5am–12.30am, after which there are **night buses**. The *Copenhagen Card* costs 140kr and allows free use of the city transport system for 24 hours, plus entry to most museums; a 48-hour version costs 230kr, a 72-hour one 295kr. If you aren't going to visit museums, 24-hour travel cards are available on a zone basis: a central-zone ticket costs 65kr, a two-zone one is 70kr, while a three-zone *Rabatkort* is 85kr. The *Rabatkort* is a strip of ten tickets which you can share by double-stamping. For a single journey buy a *grundbillet* (10kr), valid for an hour within two zones.

The main **tourist office** is adjacent to the train station at Bernstorffsgarde 1 (Mon–Fri 9am–5pm, Sat 9am–2pm, ☎111 325).

media attention failed to create a firm fan base. Crowds remained well below half Brøndby's average of 12,000, leaving most of the Parken empty and without atmosphere.

The cosier Østerbro stadium next-door, currently home to lower-division B93, would be a more suitable venue but to move there would be an acceptance of the club's failure to attract grassroots support.

Cup wins in 1995 and 1997 have maintained the team's momentum, but as a club, FCK remain a dream that has yet to be fully realised.

Here we go!
Take any S-tog to Døsterport, then bus #1 or #6. Allow twenty minutes from the main train station.

Swift half
Although the Parken houses a pool hall and the glitzy Parken Sports Café with its busts of great Danish sportsmen and women, FCK fans meet at the **Søhesten** ('Seahorse'), Sølvegade 103. It's a straightforward pub with large draught Tuborgs at 25kr.

Publications
A decent programme is produced for all home matches and costs 10kr.

A survivor from KB days – FCK's Christian Lønstrup

Club shops
The **FCK Shop** behind the north stand has all manner of trinkets decorated in the white of B1903 and the blue of KB. **Planet Football**, on the corner of the south and west stands, has foreign footie gear.

Ultra culture
Brøndby fans just laugh at the **'Cooligans'** – FCK's attempt at a fan group. Perhaps as a result of the club's well-heeled location, supporters are overwhelmingly middle-class and dominated by Copenhagen's media crowd. It's rumoured that the Cooligans' first demand of club officials was that press passes be accepted outside the press

box, so that TV presenters and DJs could stand together in the east stand. As one Danish journalist puts it – "they are trying so hard to be fans".

In the net
FCK themselves host an impressive bilingual website at: www.united.dk/fck/. It includes an unusually honest history of the club, but has a tendency to worthiness. Livelier, but in Danish only, is an unofficial site at www.proactive.dk/fckfan/. If you want to meet the infamous Cooligans in their virtual bar, head straight for: inet. uni-c.dk/~rachlin/cooligan.htm.

Groundhopping

At the last count, Copenhagen boasted some sixteen clubs playing in the *Danmark Serie* or above. At any one time there are bound to be at least two or three in the

Gazza gab – a typical pre-season visitor pokes fun at Hvidovre

Superliga, plus a handful in the first division. The atmosphere will be anything but highly charged, but many of these clubs are steeped in history and are worth ninety minutes of anyone's time.

Akademisk Boldklub

Gladsaxe Idrætspark, Skovdiget 1, Bagsværd
Capacity 10,000
Colours Green shirts, white shorts
League champions 1919, 1921, 1937, 1943, 1945, 1947, 1951–52, 1967

AB are a relic of the old amateur days. In the past they played at Fælled Park in the city centre and membership was restricted to university students and professors. In the early Sixties they moved out to the Gladsaxe stadium in the suburb of Bagsværd and the old boys stopped coming. AB have lifted nine titles but their last win was in 1967 and today they rarely attract more than 400 souls to their windswept athletics stadium. The club enjoyed a mini-revival in the early Nineties, fighting their way from the *Danmark Serie* up to the dizzy heights of the *Superliga*, but their top-drawer status may not last long. Gladsaxe is a 25-minute ride on bus #250S from Hovedbane Gåde.

Hvidovre

Hvidovre Stadion, Sollentuna Allé 1–3, Hvidovre
Capacity 15,000
Colours Red-and-white shirts, blue shorts
League champions 1966, 1973, 1981
Cup winners 1980

Hvidovre are the local rivals to Brøndby, their star having fallen as Brøndby's rose. Many of the club's youth products, such as Peter Schmeichel, have been snapped up by their wealthier neighbours, and the

He's fat, he's round, his motor's in the pound...

Never mind Peter Schmeichel or the Laudrups – to many English fans, **Jan Mølby** is the first Danish footballer who springs to mind. Robust and rotund, he was a fixture in the great Liverpool side of the late Eighties – strolling around the middle of the park, whacking huge cross-field passes and launching rocket free-kicks.

But while his impeccable scouse accent won the hearts of the Merseysiders and greatly amused the rest of England, in his homeland Mølby was far from a major star.

A scouser and a gentleman – Jan Mølby in defeat

Part of the reason for his obscurity was that Mølby never played top-class football in Denmark. He began his career with his local team Kolding IF, a second-division club in Jutland. He left for **Ajax** at the age of 19, spending two seasons in Amsterdam before moving to Anfield for £575,000 in August 1984.

Mølby was part of the 'red-and-white dynamite' generation but was far from being a regular starter for Denmark, sitting out a string of internationals on the bench. By contrast, in more than ten years at Anfield only injury ever kept him out of the side.

As Mølby's waistline grew, so the area of the field he covered shrank in proportion. By the end of his Liverpool career he was rarely seen outside the centre circle, though he was no less effective for that.

Jan Mølby comes from a long line of Danish players who make no secret about their fondness for a pint or two. Incarcerated for drunk-driving early on in his Liverpool career, he was the inspiration for the Kop's now-infamous terrace taunt: "He's fat, he's round, his motor's in the pound…"

In early 1996, Mølby moved to South Wales to become player-manager of **Swansea City**, confirming what many in Denmark had long believed – that he would never return home as a player. Clearly upset at the way his team lost the 1997 third-division play-off final to Northampton Town – by a twice-taken free-kick in the last minute – Mølby still made sure he shook the hand of all the officials and Northampton players before leading his men from the Wembley pitch. No doubt he got the beers in, too.

---

trend shows every sign of continuing. Still, the team are popular opponents for English clubs seeking pre-season friendlies, and the stadium restaurant is decorated with old advertisements for games against QPR, Wolves and Liverpool. To get to Hvidovre, take S-tog A towards **Hundige** and get off at **Friheden**, five minutes' walk from the ground. The official fan club, the **Red Blacksmiths**, meet at **Johnny's Bodega**, Hvidovre vej 256. Sink a beer here, against a backdrop of photos of the championship sides of 1966, 1973 and 1981.

Lyngby

Lyngby Stadion, Lundtoftevej 61, Lyngby
Capacity 15,000
Colours Blue shirts, white shorts
League champions 1983, 1992
Cup winners 1984, 1985, 1990

After two league titles and three cup wins in the days immediately prior to professionalism, Lyngby FC are struggling to adjust to Denmark's brave new footballing world. The club's financial problems have

Park life – the Parken stadium comes alive for internationals but few turn up to watch FCK

prompted rumours that they may become the third team to be incorporated into the FCK family. If so, you may not have long to visit the Lyngby Stadion, a tiny, homely venue surrounded by neatly trimmed hedges. Take S-tog B or B+ towards Holte, get off at **Jogersborg**, and from there take a second train towards Nærum, one stop to **Lyngby Lokal**.

The family feel of the club is evident in the **Stadion Restaurant**, where members of the **Blue Vikings** fan club chat over a beer with club directors and assorted ex-players.

Eat, drink, sleep...

Bars and clubs

The Danes love their beer, and for good reason – it's some of the cleanest-tasting and most drinkable in Europe. Many bars closely resemble English pubs. Prices are higher, but rarely reach the exorbitant levels of Sweden or Norway. In fact, many people from elsewhere in Scandinavia come to Copenhagen for a cheap weekend away. The Danish attitude to licensing laws is refreshingly lax – no matter what time of day or night it is, you'll always find somewhere to get a drink.

Bananrepublikken, Nørrebrogade 13. Hip, three-level bar with ethnic sounds, multi-cultural crowd and decent food. Tuborg on draught. Located in fashionable Nørrebro, Copenhagen's answer to Soho with scores of bars and restaurants, trendy clientèle and party atmosphere.

Café Osborne, Elmegade 23. Expat without being overbearingly so. Sky TV, Irish motif and beer at 25kr a pint. Fixture list posted outside. In Nørrebro.

Café Stadion, Norre Allé 27. Traditional Danish bar, a ten-minute stroll from the Parken. Pool, TV and cheap daily menu.

Café Zeze, Ny Østergade 20. A wide selection of bottled beers and excellent filter coffee make it worth hunching your shoulders to squeeze into this tiny, atmospheric city-centre bar.

Peder Hvitfeldt, Peder Hvitfeldtsstræsse 15. A straightforward, central drinkers' bar that's always busy with a young, lively crowd.

Restaurants

Eating out in Copenhagen needn't require an extended overdraft. Look for restaurants serving a *Dan Menu* – a two-course lunch of Danish cooking for around 80kr. If you tire of fish and potatoes, the city has plenty of ethnic options, among the cheapest of which are the many *schawarma* bars on Nørrebrogade. Bear in mind that in many restaurants, dinner is much more expensive than lunch, so stoke up early and stick to *pølser* at night.

Kashmir, Nørrebrogade 35. Cheap and spicy specialities from the disputed territory. In trendy Nørrebro.

Peder Oxe, Gråbrødertorv 11. Fair-priced restaurant with an excellent salad bar. Good lunchtime deals, centrally located.

Quattro Fontane, Guldbergsgade 3. An excellent, mid-priced Italian in a Nørrebro street full of reasonably priced restaurants.

Rust, Guldbergsgade 8. Named after the young German who flew a private plane into Red Square in the Eighties, the restaurant boasts a fine international menu while the building also houses a decent bar and weekend disco.

Accommodation

Finding somewhere to stay shouldn't present too many problems – paying for it is another matter. Look on the bright side, though: accommodation is cheaper in Denmark than elsewhere in Scandinavia, hostels and 'sleep-ins' are all clean and comfortable, and hotels, though not cheap, usually include a superb, eat-as-much-as-you-like breakfast as part of the package.

Absalon Hotel, Helgolandsgade 19 (☎242 211). Simple, modern, central hotel, 300–400kr.

City Public Hostel, Absalonsgade 8 (☎312 070). Just ten minutes' walk from the main train station. The ground floor is a huge 60-bed dorm, and there are smaller options on other floors. Beds for 80–150kr.

Missionhotellet, Nebo Istedgade 6 (☎211 217). Mid-priced hotel in a central location, friendly English-speaking owners. Around 350kr.

Sophie Amalie, Skt Annæ Plads 21 (☎133 400). Luxury upmarket hotel next to the harbour. You'll pay upwards of 500kr, but it's worth it.

England

After a decade of declining attendances, crowd violence and enforced exile from Europe – English football is back. The country which pioneered professional football and sent missionaries around the world to promote the game is once again leading the way. This time it isn't distinguished gentlemen in blazers and players with long, baggy shorts who are showing the world how soccer is played – it is slick marketing men, stockbrokers and businessmen who are leading a revolution in how the sport is packaged, presented and sold.

While many fans have found the rapid changes to the game hard to stomach, few would deny that something had to be done. By the Eighties, English clubs were banned from European competition because of the thuggery of their fans. Thirty-nine Juventus fans died at the 1985 European Cup final at Brussels' Heysel stadium, as a result of the hooliganism of Liverpool supporters. It was by no means an isolated incident – throughout the Seventies and Eighties, English fans had wreaked havoc across the continent and at home.

Ageing English stadia were also a source of concern, particularly after the deaths of 45 fans in a fire at the Valley Parade ground of Bradford City in 1985, and the Hillsborough tragedy of 1989, when 95 people were crushed to death at an FA Cup semifinal between Nottingham Forest and Liverpool. The inquiry into that day's events produced the Taylor Report, the implementation of which has resulted in dramatic changes to grounds across the country. Famous old terraces such as Liverpool's Kop and Manchester United's Stretford End have gone forever – to be replaced by modern, all-seated stands.

What the Taylor Report did for the game's structures, television has done for

The tears of a clown – Turin, July 4, 1990

the structure of the game. Tired of sharing television income with lower-division clubs, the top English teams broke away from the Football League at the start of the Nineties and, together with the Football Association, created the Premier League – a new élite of clubs independent from the lower divisions. With a free hand, in 1992 they signed a £300 million deal which gave live TV rights to the satellite station BSkyB,

Some photographers are on the pitch, they know it's all over – Moore and Rimet, Wembley, 1966

and highlights packages to the nation's state terrestrial broadcaster, the BBC. The deal dramatically increased the income of the top clubs, while Sky's high-octane marketing helped raise interest in the domestic game to levels not seen since the Sixties.

The clubs took full advantage, bumping up ticket prices and signing lucrative sponsorship deals. Some, such as Tottenham Hotspur and Manchester United, were floated on the stock exchange, giving them access to new sources of capital and setting a trend for others to follow as the Nineties went on. Meanwhile, the Bosman ruling gave English clubs – with their new-found ability to pay huge salaries to players – the chance to compete at the highest level of the European transfer market, perhaps for the first time.

Today the FA Carling Premiership, to give it its proper, sponsor-friendly title, has become the soccer equivalent of the NBA. While the faces of its stars loom large on the country's poster sites, its logo can be found on everything from pencil cases to packets of crisps.

Not everyone is happy with the way this revolution has turned out. The Taylor Report was supposed to be about forcing clubs to give fans better value for their money. Yet one of its consequences has been to price many fans out of the game altogether. At some clubs, such as Newcastle, it is almost impossible to see a game without coughing up for a season ticket in the summer. Of those that can still afford to go to games, many complain that the new all-seater stadia lack the kind of atmosphere once generated from the terraces. Lower-division clubs, despite having subsequently signed a TV deal of their own, are struggling under the dual burden of having to pay inflated wages while being deprived (by Bosman) of much of their previous transfer income.

And although England may be leading the way on the business front, it still has a way to go to reclaim its place as the Continent's leading nation on the field. Since the return of English clubs to European competition in 1990/91, their performances have been largely disappointing. In the Champions' League, especially, England's standard-bearers have been found wanting, prompting claims that clubs have fallen behind the rest of Europe in both skill and tactics – claims only partially answered by Manchester United's run to the semi-finals of the competition in 1996/97.

The response has been a full-scale attempt to 'Europeanise' English football. The sweeper system is in vogue, European players and coaches are hunted after, the long ball is frowned upon. Again, opinion is divided on the issue. Some, notably the body representing England's professional players, the PFA, suggest that the influx of cheap foreign imports will ultimately damage the country's ability to nurture fresh, indigenous footballing talent. Others argue that this new, cosmopolitan era amounts to a welcome if overdue acknowledgement that the English game does not have all the answers.

Prior to the Fifties, the idea that England could be anything other than the best in the world was unthinkable to most fans. After all, this was the home of football.

The rules of the game were adopted by the Football Association upon its foundation in 1863. (To this day, the FA remains the only federation in the world not to have the name of its country in its title.) In 1871, the world's first cup competition – the Football Association Challenge Cup, known as the FA Cup – was introduced. The early competitions were dominated by southern teams drawn from public schools and amateur gentlemen's clubs. But the game was spreading fast in the north of England, particularly in Lancashire. Here players were drawn from working-class backgrounds, and many sought – and received – a wage for their efforts.

In 1883, Blackburn Olympic won the FA Cup, defeating Old Etonians in the final. It was a symbolic result – the victors were a workers' team from a mill town, the vanquished a group of former students from one of the country's leading privately-run schools. There was no turning back.

In 1885 professionalism was legalised, and three years later the Football League was founded. Although the founding meeting took place in London's Fleet Street, the capital, and the south of England in general, had little to do with the world's first professional soccer league. The twelve founding members were all from the north and the Midlands. Lancashire made up half the league, with Preston North End, Blackburn Rovers, Accrington Stanley, Bolton

Call me Alf – the man in the blue tracksuit

Basics

Visitors arriving in England from the continent often remark that they feel they have **left Europe**. It's not just that cars drive on the left-hand side of the road or that the policemen wear strange helmets; in many important cultural ways, England differs from mainland Europe.

However, this is part of the United Kingdom and, by extension, part of the European Union – so although **passport controls remain** for EU citizens, there are no visa requirements. Visitors from other countries should check with their local British Embassy before travelling. Non-EU residents travelling into the UK are asked to fill out an **entry form**, or landing form if they are flying.

The currency is the **pound sterling**, abbreviated as '£' and divided into 100 pence. Coins come in denominations of 1p, 2p, 5p, 10p, 20p, 50p and £1; notes in £5, £10, £20 and £50. Most banks are open Mon–Fri 9.30am–3.30pm, though some stay open later and are also open for a few hours on Saturday morning. **Cash machines** can be found throughout all towns and cities, and **credit-card payment** is more widespread here than anywhere in mainland Europe.

From outside the country, the international telephone code for the UK is ☎44. Some of the major English **city codes** are: inner London ☎171, outer London ☎181, Birmingham ☎121, Manchester ☎161, Liverpool ☎151 and Newcastle ☎191. Public phone boxes take coins of 10p upwards, although many are now for card use only – **phonecards** are available from post offices and newsagents at £2, £5 or £10. There is a reduced rate for international calls between 8pm and 8am weekdays, and also all weekend. For an international line dial ☎00; for the operator dial ☎100. A growing number of public phones take credit cards as well as phonecards.

The local **train network** is certainly not up to European standards, and tickets are expensive to boot. The cheapest way to travel is to book a week or two weeks in advance and buy an *Apex* or *SuperApex* ticket. If you can't do this, then *saver* and *super-saver* returns are the cheap options. If you plan to travel around the country by train you can buy weekly or monthly *Britrail* passes before coming to the UK – contact your local rail company for details. Inside the country, if you are aged under 24 you can buy a *Young Persons' Railcard* (£16), which gives a 30 percent discount on fares.

National Express provides express **bus and coach services** between all major towns. The services are much cheaper than their rail equivalents, and popular routes can get booked solid; if you can, reserve in advance.

England is not famed for its cuisine but there are some tasty **traditional dishes**. 'Fish and chips' is unpredictable, generally better in the north of the country (though this is contested by southerners) and on the coasts. Traditional English **casseroles** and **stews** can be delicious in good restaurants and family-owned pubs. The **English breakfast** – a vast fry-up of bacon, egg, sausage, mushrooms and tomato, served with either toast or fried bread – may be a shock to the system of those used to starting the day with a coffee and a croissant, but such is its popularity that many cafés and pubs offer 'all-day breakfast', giving the visitor a chance to try it at lunch.

The **English pub** has been exported around the globe and while many of the imitations may get the design right, few manage to re-create the atmosphere. Some of the best are in isolated villages, but in cities, every suburb has its 'local' – often a community centre with sports clubs and quizzes, as well as food and drink. And speaking of drink, don't expect your **pint of bitter** to be chilled – the natives like it lukewarm.

In many city centres, pubs are being replaced with hideous **theme bars** or trendy cafés which try to imitate the design and atmosphere of a European café – some of the latter are worth a peek inside, most are not.

Wanderers, Everton and Burnley among the county's representatives. Professional clubs were springing up all over the north, strengthened by imports from Scotland. To this day, the north and Midlands remain the dominant regions in English football – the title has only been in southern hands sixteen times in more than a century of competition, and ten of those titles have been won by Arsenal.

In 1892 the League expanded to two divisions, and by 1923 two regional third divisions had been added. That structure remained untouched until 1958, when the bottom two divisions became national. Today England remains the only country in Europe with four fully professional, national tiers of clubs.

'Go on, you have the rest of the caps' – Clemmo and Shilts, 1979

The English also pioneered international competition – of a sort. The 1872 goalless draw between England and Scotland in Glasgow was the first-ever game between two footballing nations. However, while they were quite content to arrange games against other British sides in the so-called 'home internationals', the FA were reluctant to participate in the international competitions that emerged in the decade before World War II. England had toured the continent as early as 1908, playing Austria, Bohemia and Hungary – but they consistently declined to compete in the World Cup until 1950, when they went to the finals in Brazil.

They needn't have bothered. Defeats by Spain and (embarrassingly) the USA led to a rapid, first-round exit. While they were clearly beatable overseas, England remained impregnable at home – until Puskás' Hungary came to Wembley and won 6–3 in 1953. The defeat did more than shatter a record; it finally alerted the English to the fact that the game was now progressing in Europe much more quickly than in its homeland. When England failed to win a game at the 1958 World Cup in Sweden, coaches began to look to the continent for ideas. England reached the quarter-finals of the same event in Chile four years later, but were still some way short of the finished article when Alf Ramsey, their team manager, began preparations for the World Cup England would host in 1966.

It was Ramsey who introduced the 4–4–2 formation to the English game at international level. The press were sceptical of a formation which ignored wingers and inside-forwards (traditionally two areas of English strength), and Ramsey's side were labelled "The Wingless Wonders". With the exception of the classy West Ham pair of centre-half Bobby Moore and midfielder Martin Peters, Ramsey's side contained few stars. His system was based on hard work and versatility.

Within days of the 1966 World Cup kicking-off, the critics had been forced to eat their words. Mexico, France and Argentina were all arrogantly despatched, setting up a semi-final with Eusébio's Portugal. Bobby Charlton (who, in the absence of the out-of-favour Jimmy Greaves, was

England's main flair player) then scored twice in a 2–1 win which was as close as the scoreline suggests.

In the final England met West Germany, against whom – odd though it may seem today – they had never lost. The game was to be a topsy-turvy affair. Haller gave the Germans the lead on twelve minutes. Six minutes later, Hurst headed an equaliser. In the 78th minute Peters looked to have wrapped the game up for England, but in the last minute Weber scored to take the game to extra-time.

Ten minutes in, a shot from Hurst bounced down off the crossbar. Roger Hunt, following up, was so confident the ball had crossed the line that he pointedly failed to do the obvious and knock it into the net. The Swiss referee, after consulting with his Russian linesman, duly gave a goal. But the Germans were furious, and TV evidence later added some ammunition to their argument.

In the last minute, with the opposition gambling everything, Hurst put the game beyond doubt with his third goal, and the World Cup was England's.

Four years later, in Mexico, the Germans would have their revenge – though it seemed unlikely when the quarter-final in Guadalajara stood at 2–0 to England with an hour gone. The fatigue of the English full-backs – wilting under the heat, the altitude and Ramsey's insistence on sticking with 4–4–2 – allowed West Germany back into the game, and they eventually won 3–2 after extra-time.

For the national side, worse was to come. England failed to qualify for the 1974 or 1978 World Cups, leaving the Scots as Britain's sole ambassadors at the game's highest level. English clubs, however, had seized on the post-1966 euphoria – and on Ramsey's tactical innovations – and were finally making their mark in Europe.

Prior to 1966, no English club had made the final of the European Cup. The only glory had been in the Cup-Winners' Cup, with Tottenham lifting the trophy in 1963 and their fellow Londoners West Ham winning it in 1965. But, just two years after the World Cup victory, Manchester United

They don't like it up 'em – Bryan Robson hauls down West Germany's Hans-Peter Briegel, 1982

beat Benfica to become the first English side to win the European Cup. In the same year Leeds United won the Fairs' Cup, starting a sequence in which that competition would be won six seasons in a row by English clubs.

Between 1977 and 1982, the European Cup never left England, Liverpool (three times), Brian Clough's Nottingham Forest (twice) and Aston Villa all winning the competition. Had it not been for Heysel and the subsequent ban on English participation in Europe, the hegemony would surely have continued.

It was in 1982, under Ron Greenwood, that England returned to World Cup action. But the squad that travelled to Spain contained two key players, Kevin Keegan and Trevor Brooking, who had sustained long-term injuries. Neither played any part until fifteen minutes from the end of the team's second-round match against the hosts (who, thanks to an absurdly top-heavy competition structure, had already been eliminated). England needed a goal to stay in the tournament; Keegan, twice Europe's footballer of the year, missed it.

Four years later, with Bobby Robson now at the helm, England had the goals of a young Gary Lineker to thank for taking them to a quarter-final against Argentina – in which they were beaten by both 'The Hand of God' and, for Maradona's second goal in a 2–1 defeat, the Feet of God.

At the 1988 European Championship in West Germany, in which England lost all three of their matches, to Ireland, Holland and the USSR, it seemed that the enforced absence from continental club action was already having a detrimental effect. But the emergence of Paul Gascoigne to act as Lineker's main supply line coincided with Italia '90 – Robson's swansong as manager, and a World Cup which will forever be associated, at least in English minds, with one man and his tears.

In the early Nineties, Graham Taylor's spell as England boss was characterised by tactical ineptitude (taking off Lineker against Sweden at Euro '92) and the odd slab of bad luck (Ronald Koeman's ability to stay on the pitch to win a World Cup qualifier for Holland in Rotterdam). Terry Venables would be the new broom to sweep away such irrelevances as Taylor's flirtation with the long ball, and had it not been for Gareth Southgate's penalty miss at Wembley, Euro '96 might have been for El Tel what the 1966 World Cup was for Sir Alf – not just football coming home, but turning up on the doorstep with some silverware tucked under its arm.

As the memory of yet another crucial defeat by the Germans fades, the tournament's lasting legacy becomes clearer. Venables' side, with their four-goal win over Holland in particular, had won English football the respect of Europe once again. So, too, had English fans – Euro '96 was the most relaxed, trouble-free major tournament to be held in Europe for a generation.

As the marketeers, the money men and, conceivably, Glenn Hoddle will testify, not since Bobby Moore raised the Jules Rimet trophy has English football been in a healthier all-round state.

Match practice
The days of turning up ten minutes before kick-off, paying at the turnstiles and grabbing a pie and a pint on the way to the terraces are over. For Premiership football, at least, you need to plan in advance – tickets for big games are a rare commodity and you will pay accordingly. In return you will be treated to some of the best facilities in European football. As well as modern all-seater stands offering unobstructed views of the action, you will find fast food outlets, on-site bookmakers, restaurants and a huge selection of club merchandise.

While the cold pies and smelly toilets have gone, some of the old English match-day traditions remain. For many fans, Saturday wouldn't be Saturday without a visit to the pub before the game. And with the advent of Sky Sports, the pub has assumed another rôle – as a venue for watching the game. Rather than pay out for the satellite equipment and subscrip-

Swing low – Houghton leaves Hoddle trailing, 1988

Association and the Premier League. The bottom three clubs are relegated and replaced by the top two from the first division of the Football ('Nationwide') League, plus the winners of a series of play-offs.

The same system operates for promotion and relegation between the three divisions of the Football League. The bottom side in the third division are replaced by the champions of the Conference, a national semi-professional league, providing the latter have a stadium which meets League regulations.

Up for the cup

The FA Cup is the oldest national cup competition in the world. Unlike in most European countries, the cup has serious status and attendances are as high as, if not higher than, those at league games.

Around 500 non-league clubs begin the competition in August, fighting to earn a place in the first round proper in November, when they are joined by the second- and third-division clubs. Premiership and first-division sides don't join in until the third round in early January.

Ties are played on Saturdays with the exception of live televised games and replays. The format for all rounds is one-leg games, with a replay in the case of drawn matches. In the past there was no limit to the number of replays that could be used to decide a tie, but these days there is only one replay after which the game goes to extra-time and penalties if necessary. The semi-finals are held at neutral venues and the final takes place at Wembley in May.

A second knockout competition, the Football League Cup, was begun in 1961 and is currently sponsored by Coca-Cola. The cup is open only to clubs competing in the Football League and the Premiership, and until the semi-finals all rounds are played midweek. The first two rounds and semi-finals are two-legged affairs.

tion, large numbers of fans pop down to their local to watch the top clashes, reviving the fortunes of many ailing pubs and clubs, and creating a new form of support.

Although stadium developments have taken place in the lower divisions as well, at Nationwide League grounds you will find much more of the old scene. Terracing remains, tickets are cheaper and easier to find, and though crowds are much smaller, there is arguably more intensity to the occasion – these fans are truly committed to the teams they are watching.

The season begins in mid-August and ends in mid-May, with no winter breaks. There are, however, 'blank' weekends prior to England international matches.

Saturday league games kick-off at 3pm. Midweek fixtures – of which there are more in England than anywhere in Europe – traditionally take place on Tuesday or Wednesday nights at 7.30pm or 7.45pm. Kick-off times for live TV matches vary, but Sunday games usually kick-off at 4pm, while those on Mondays start at 8pm.

The league

The twenty-team Premiership is administered jointly between the Football

In recent years, the top clubs have shown less and less interest in the League Cup, with some sides such as Manchester United fielding virtual reserve teams. With constant complaints from managers and players over the heavy fixture programme and (from 1997/98) the loss of a UEFA Cup place for the winners, the future of the tournament is in jeopardy.

Tickets

For Premiership games you should contact clubs in advance to enquire about availability. All clubs have 'ticketline' numbers dedicated solely to providing information, and in most cases you can book your seat over the phone with a credit card and pick the ticket up at the stadium on matchday.

Ticket prices for Premiership matches range from £15 to around £50. Most clubs offer reduced-price admission for children and pensioners.

Half-time

An English football ground is one of the few places in the world where you can eat a boiled hamburger – avoid them at all costs. That aside, the food and drink on offer inside grounds varies enormously. Some clubs serve draught beer before a game, others don't. Some clubs offer decent hot pies, others stodgy cold ones. In recent years, fast-food outlets offering more varied choice have popped up inside newly redeveloped stands.

But the best bet remains to do your eating and drinking down the road, before and after the game. You'll find a pub on the corner of almost all English grounds except for some of the new, out-of-town stadia. In the north of England, the traditional drink is a pint of bitter or ale. Fans in the south tend to drink 'lager' which is a fizzy, chemical-riddden version of European beer. Other alternatives include Irish stout (such as Guinness or Murphy's) which can be found all over the UK, while more and more pubs are stocking major brands of bottled European and American beers.

Those too young or too old to go to the pub, or those who just never got out of the habit, suck on boiled sweets or chew on toffees throughout a game. There is usually a newsagents close to a football ground where you will find traditional favourites such as Everton mints and humbugs. Sucked properly, one of these can last almost an entire 45 minutes.

For more substantial football food, there is always the 'chippy'. Wherever you go, you'll see fish and chips or pies being consumed with remarkable pace, both

Swing lower – Taylor and Lineker sit at opposite ends of the bench in Stockholm, 1992

before and after a match. Traditional town-centre grounds will have a chippy close at hand, and these are a far better bet than the hamburger and hot-dog stands which line the streets around the stadium.

The back page

Strangely, for a country with a huge interest in football and sport in general, England does not have a daily sports paper – or a weekly one, for that matter. Visiting foreign fans have been known to pick up a copy of the *Daily Sport*, mistakenly assuming it to be a sports paper. It is in fact a soft-porn and scandal sheet, with perhaps the odd topless blonde in a Chelsea shirt.

One of the reasons for the lack of a dedicated sports paper is the excellent coverage afforded to football by the general dailies, all of which boast large sports sections. Of the broadsheet papers, the *Daily Telegraph* is hard to beat for the sheer scale and weight of reporting, while the *Times* has cornered the market in eye-catching graphics and the *Guardian* boasts the most accomplished columnists.

The mass-market tabloids – the *Mirror, Sun* and *Daily Star* – are much more sensationalist but are often the first papers to break transfer stories and other rumours. The mid-market tabloids – the *Daily Mail* and *Express* – are an accessible compromise between sophistication and sleaze.

On Sundays and (increasingly) Mondays, all papers offer pull-out sports or football sections with full match reports and results from around the country.

The newsstands also boast an ever-growing number of magazines devoted exclusively to football. Once upon a time there were only the weeklies *Shoot!* and *Match*, both of which were (and still are) aimed squarely at kids. Their dominance was challenged at the start of the Nineties by a more mature weekly, *90 Minutes*, but this sadly closed in 1997 under pressure from a clutch of monthlies its success had spawned – among them the heavyweight *FourFourTwo, Goal* and the less reverential *Total Football*.

Still very much alive and kicking is another monthly, *When Saturday Comes*, which began life as a monthly national fanzine but has developed into a professionally laid-out magazine with articles by journalists as well as fans.

There is barely a professional ground in the country where you won't see a locally produced fanzine on sale, offering healthy competition to the (usually bland) matchday programmes and official club magazines, which are also swelling in number. While some fanzines have 'gone glossy' during the Nineties, there are plenty of others which are still photocopied and stapled together by a group of mates and have the appearance of *samizdat* pamphlets.

Finally, *World Soccer* is a reliable monthly round-up of the game across the globe, while *Football Europe* offers more detailed coverage of the European scene.

Action replay

For decades, football on television in England meant *Match of the Day* – a Saturday night highlights package on BBC 1 which has become a national institution.

The show usually has lengthy highlights from two featured games, with goals from all the other Premiership clashes and analysis from studio guests. The man fans in England love to hate is Jimmy Hill – a mediocre player in the early Sixties whose deliberately provocative opinions still raise living-room tempers, even after more than twenty years on the screen. The show is fronted by the likeable Des Lynam, who has no background in the game but is a more relaxed and effective presenter because of that.

Although *Match of the Day* remains the most-watched football show, for those with cable connections or satellite dishes, football on TV means Sky Sports. With three channels devoted to sport, Sky has the rights to live Premiership games, the Nationwide League, the League Cup and most England internationals.

The main live Premiership action is on Sunday afternoon and Monday evening, although there is a game of some kind on Sky almost every night, as well as chat shows, magazines and highlights packages.

It's not only Sky's volume of programming. The channel's presentation, similar to that of SAT 1 in Germany, is radically different from that which was offered up in the days when the BBC and its commercial terrestrial rival, ITV, enjoyed a duopoly. Viewers are treated to a staggering range of camera angles, replays, opinions and on-the-spot interviews, while analysis is provided by former Scottish international striker Andy Gray, who is just as quick and courageous with his opinions as he was inside the penalty area. Gray's use of on-screen 'drawings',

Don't worry, Gareth, you'll still get a TV ad – Wembley, 1996

along with other gimmicks borrowed from US sports coverage, at first provoked amusement. But they highlight the fact that, unlike so many pundits, the man not only has a keen tactical awareness but is also willing to share it with his audience.

While their schedules prevent them from matching Sky for depth or detail, ITV still have a decent-sized armoury of football programming, with live Champions' League games (followed by a highlights round-up of all the other night's games) and, from 1997/98, exclusive live coverage of the FA Cup, featuring another affable old pro, commentator Brian Moore.

Another commercial station, Channel 4, has a live Italian game on Sunday afternoons, along with an excellent Saturday morning magazine show, *Gazzetta Football Italia*, which has interviews, highlights and previews of the Sunday game.

Sky shows live Spanish football on Saturday or Sunday nights, and features occasional live Scottish games, as well as highlights from the Scottish league.

Cable and satellite viewers in England can also pick up German football on SAT 1, as well as highlights packages on Eurosport, DSF and other European channels.

Ultra culture

While hooligans across Europe may still regard England as their rôle model, the 'English disease' has largely been cured in its homeland. True, there is still a nasty element who occasionally travel with the national team, as the violence which resulted in the halting of a game against Ireland in Dublin in 1995 highlighted. But fans no longer travel to games expecting trouble; parents no longer fear their kids may return home from the game with a stab wound; and supporters of all persuasions happily wear their replica shirts to matches, making the loudest possible statement of their allegiance – and spawning an entire industry in the process.

Much of the credit for the suppression of hooliganism has gone to the police, to closed-circuit TV cameras and to all-seater stadia. But there has also been a dramatic change in the attitude of fans. The Eighties saw independent supporters' clubs springing up all over the country and attempting to present fans' viewpoints to the club owners. The fanzine movement also did its bit by channelling traditional rivalries in a more constructive way. Today the nationwide Football Supporters' Association brings these disparate groups

Alright on the night – Alan Shearer hails an England goal before collapsing with another injury

together and lobbies the authorities on issues affecting fans.

In the face of Bradford, Heysel, Hillsborough and Graham Taylor, the English football fan turned the other cheek and decided to have a laugh – inventing a range of new terrace tunes (*Blue Moon* at Manchester City, *Always Look on the Bright Side of Life* at Sheffield Wednesday), pulling on fancy dress, and coming to matches with inflatable bananas, fish and canaries, rather than Stanley knives.

In the past few years, however, many fans have become concerned that the pendulum is swinging too far in the other direction, turning football from a rootsy, honest pastime into sanitised, 'family' entertainment. Inside grounds, most of the organising is now done by private security firms rather than club employees. As well as ejecting people from the stadium for threatening behaviour or obscene language, the security men have also clamped down on fans standing up to watch the game. After several incidents at Premiership grounds where fans were thrown out for refusing to sit down, there have been mass

stand-ups within stands. The Manchester United chant *"Stand up for the Champions"* is a typical accompaniment to this act of mass defiance.

There are also signs that English football may be becoming a little too quiet for its own good. With the country's old 'singing ends' demolished, there is no one area in most stadia were noise can be generated, no community to create new chants. Fans who used to stand together are now dispersed around the ground, in numbered seats assigned by the box-office computer.

In the net

The best of many generic sites is run by the *Daily Mail* at: www.soccernet.com. Each Premiership and Nationwide League club has its own mini-homepage, and the news and match reports archives – taken from the paper – are second to none. For rolling news, the punter's favourite *Sporting Life* has a new football site at: www.sporting-life.com. There's an online 'vidiprinter' for news, results and action graphics, and as you might expect, there are plenty of opportunities to place that bet.

London

Like Paris or Rome, London's importance as a football city bears little relation to the number of national championships its clubs have mustered. Few European cities have as much regular representation in their country's top division – often five or six teams – but these clubs share just thirteen titles between them, and Arsenal have won ten of them.

In terms of its prestigious position as an international venue, only Paris can challenge London, The capital is the seat of the Football Association, the stuffy body of ex-public schoolboys who ran the game until the Football League was founded, and who have been responsible for internationals and the FA Cup ever since. The FA was formed in 1863 in the Freemasons'

In Ruud health – Gullit at Wembley, May 1997

Tavern in Great Queen Street, where a group of genteel public schoolmasters met to draft a set of rules for the game. Firmly amateur, invariably upper class, the game in London and the south-east centred around an annual Challenge Cup played for by teams from the country's highest institutions. Its first final was at Kennington Oval, now a cricket ground. Its first winners were The Wanderers, a team composed of old Harrovians originally based in Snaresbrook, near Epping Forest. Ever since then, London has traditionally performed well in the glamorous cup competitions, but poorly in the long, gruelling league championship.

Arsenal and Tottenham Hotspur form the city's big rivalry, the clubs being three miles apart in the north of the city. Attracting different communities – Arsenal Irish and Greek, Spurs traditionally Jewish – they have famously loathed each other from the day in 1913 when Arsenal moved across the Thames from Plumstead to Highbury.

Spurs opposed the move, and ne'er the twain have met. Like the big north London pair, Chelsea attract a following from across the Home Counties as well as in the capital. West Ham are firmly rooted in the East End, home of London's famous Cockneys, while further south-east, Millwall and Charlton attract a similarly strong local partisanship. QPR, Wimbledon and Crystal Palace draw varying degrees of support, depending on league position and the weather, from the west, south-west and south-east respectively, the latter two now based at Palace's Selhurst Park.

Soccer in London was perhaps at its best in the Sixties and Seventies, when the city's status as the 'Swinging' capital of the world's music and fashion industry seemed to rub off on its football clubs. Spurs and Arsenal won the double, Chelsea and West Ham the FA Cup and European honours. Even QPR and little Fulham drew big crowds, the latter by dint of hiring Bobby Moore and George Best to play for them.

It was a great time to be young, free, single and football-supporting – although by the late Sixties, the cross-town rivalries were spilling into ugly violence.

After the dark ages of the Eighties, today London can again be regarded as a kind of Socceropolis. But while football's version of Swinging London was essentially inward-looking, today the capital is a cosmopolitan centre whose style, services and amusements attract contemporary stars like Gianfranco Zola and Jürgen Klinsmann, while Pelé, Puskás and Maradona occasionally pass through town for some event or other, and the city is packed every weekend with young, footie-loving Europeans on spending sprees.

The bubble may yet burst, but until it does, the view from inside is as appealing as any in Europe.

The thrilling fields

 ## Arsenal

Highbury stadium, Avenell Road, N5
Capacity 38,500
Colours Red shirts with white sleeves, white shorts
League champions 1931, 1933–35, 1938, 1948, 1953, 1971, 1989, 1991
Cup winners 1930, 1936, 1950, 1971, 1979, 1993
Cup-Winners' Cup winners 1994
Fairs' (UEFA) Cup winners 1970

As one English football writer once put it, Arsenal were not put on this Earth to be loved. They are at once Boring Arsenal, Lucky Arsenal, and by far London's most successful club. Prior to the rise of Manchester United, they were England's best-known club overseas, their name evoking a feeling of gravitas and tradition. In fact, Arsenal brought the name across with them when they moved over the Thames from the Royal Arsenal Armaments Factory in Woolwich, in the depths of south-east London.

Formed as Dial Square FC in 1886, the team were at first composed mainly of Scots employed at the munitions works. They borrowed a set of red shirts from Nottingham Forest, and the club have worn red ever since. They soon changed their name to Royal Arsenal FC, and were quick to adopt professionalism in 1891. They were promoted to the first division in 1904, but ran into financial difficulties and were relegated nine years later.

Arsenal's owner, Henry Norris, had the idea of moving the club to a part of London that had a greater potential catchment area, with easy access from King's Cross – a site was chosen next to Gillespie Road station in Highbury, north London. Royal Arsenal became simply Arsenal FC and, thanks to Norris' influence, they were admitted to an extended first division after World War I – at the expense of Tottenham.

Arsenal have never been relegated since. Herbert Chapman arrived at the club as manager in 1925, and in his nine-year stint, he not only turned a rootless club without honours into the most feared in the land – he altered the game almost beyond recognition. Chapman and his right-hand man, forward Charlie Buchan, drew up a new tactical strategy in which the team's centre-half became a third-back – stifling the opposing centre-forward now favoured with a change in the offside law. This evolved into the 'WM' formation, soon successfully used across Europe.

Chapman's Arsenal was diverse and quick. With prolific goalscorers Joe Hulme and Cliff Bastin on the wings, and Alex James and David Jack at inside-forward, Arsenal were the kings of the counter-attack and the breakaway goal. Their 'Lucky' tag was thus earned.

After beating Chapman's old side Huddersfield to lift the FA Cup and their first honour in 1930, Arsenal then won the title three years in a row. Chapman's untimely death in 1934 prevented him from seeing out Arsenal's treble. Radio commentator George Allison took his place, and with newcomer Ted Drake breaking all scoring records, Arsenal retained their superiority.

The postwar period began successfully with two league titles and another FA Cup win. But before long Arsenal hit a trough of mediocrity that was to last until the late Sixties, when a little-known manager by the name of Bertie Mee dragged the team into the modern era. Its spine was again Scots, with internationals Bob Wilson in goal, Frank McLintock at centre-half and George Graham as the midfield mechanic. Upfront was Charlie George, a young, long-haired prodigy and the hero of Highbury's North Bank. His extra-time goal which beat Liverpool in the 1971 Cup Final became a legendary strike, and Arsenal were to win the double days later with a victory at (of all places) Tottenham. The success followed a storming Fairs' Cup final win over Anderlecht the previous season, which saw the Gunners pull back a 3–1 deficit to forge a 4–3 aggregate win in the second leg.

Lone Gooner – Liam Brady waits for his team-mates to catch up

The double-winning side did not go on to dominate the English game, as many predicted they would. Instead, Arsenal ticked over quietly through the Seventies until a crop of Irishmen breathed new life into the side. Liam Brady was a midfield player with a left boot of precision and elegance, Frank Stapleton a classic centre-forward, David O'Leary a solid centre-half, and Pat Jennings a goalkeeper of immense ability whose shock move from Tottenham all but ripped the heart out of White Hart Lane.

Although this side won neither a league title nor a European honour (the closest they came to the latter was a penalty shoot-out defeat by Valencia in the 1980 Cup-Winners' Cup final), they appeared in three consecutive FA Cup finals, winning the 1979 'five-minute final' against Manchester United at the very death.

The appointment of George Graham as manager in 1986 ushered in Arsenal's most successful modern period. Under Graham, the Gunners were never less than tight at the back – the sight of captain Tony Adams forever appealing for offside earning them the 'Boring' tag they have struggled so long to be rid of. But they were also a team of fighters, their spirit never better demonstrated than in the last-minute Michael Thomas goal that beat Liverpool at Anfield in 1989, to win Arsenal their first championship since 1971.

The title was won again in 1991, with a side that conceded just eighteen goals. The club put the development of Highbury top of its priority list (above the acquisition of new players), but still the honours kept coming – two domestic cups in 1993, followed by the European Cup-Winners' Cup, secured with a 1–0 win over Parma in Copenhagen in 1994. Graham prized the European honour above all others, and the team did not let it go until the 120th minute of the following year's final against

Real Zaragoza, when the Gunners' big 'keeper David Seaman was left stranded by a remarkable lob from Nayim, a former Tottenham star.

The Graham era ended in scandal when he was forced to resign following the revelation that he had taken cash from the Norwegian players' agent, Rune Hauge. Both Adams and striker Paul Merson then hit the headlines for their abuse of alcohol and drugs. And the team as a whole was mired in disciplinary problems, both on and off the pitch.

The surprise hiring of French coach Arsène Wenger in the summer of 1996 signalled a sea-change in the club's thinking, however. With the Dutch star Dennis Bergkamp and stalwart Ian Wright upfront, Arsenal quickly won back their lost credibility – not to mention a place in Europe for the 1997/98 season.

Here we go!

Piccadilly line Tube to **Arsenal** (zone 2), the former Gillespie Road station which Herbert Chapman persuaded London Transport to rename after the club.

Swift half

Arsenal's ground is surrounded by pubs. The most obvious one to head for is **The Gunners**, 204 Blackstock Road – a ten-minute walk from the ground. It is packed with framed programmes, pictures and shirts, and has a pool room at the back. The **Plimsoll Arms**, 52 St Thomas' Road, is closer to the ground and is more popular with fans despite (or maybe because of) its plain interior. The **stadium bar** underneath the North Bank is better than most in London, with a live band and two counters serving beer.

Tickets

Tickets for non-members go on sale a month before the game, with postal and telephone applications only for the matches with Spurs, Chelsea, Liverpool, Manchester United and Newcastle. Personal callers otherwise should go to the **main ticket office** behind the East Stand in Avenell Road. Matchday tickets for non-plum fixtures are available from the Clock End turnstiles. Seats in the luxurious North Bank are £12–22, the Clock End £13, and

It ain't over... Michael Thomas completes the greatest championship finale in history, Anfield, 1989

London essentials

Of London's two main **airports**, Heathrow (25km west of central London) is the world's busiest, while Gatwick (50km south) is mainly for charter flights. **Heathrow** has four terminals; 1–3 are for British Airways domestic and European flights (except Amsterdam, Athens, Moscow and Paris) and all other major airlines, while terminal 4 is for BA intercontinental and KLM. **Gatwick** is divided into north and south terminals, with a monorail service running in between.

From Heathrow, an underground train to the centre costs £3.20. The service runs daily, 5.30am–11.30pm, and takes around an hour. Terminals 1–3 and Terminal 4 have separate stations on the same line. Alternatively, **Airbuses A1** and **A2** (daily 5.30am–8.45pm, every 20–30 minutes, journey time one hour, £6) go via Hyde Park Corner and Victoria coach station; and Baker Street, Notting Hill Gate and Euston station respectively.

Although further out from the centre, Gatwick is actually better-served by public transport. The **Gatwick Express** overground train takes just thirty minutes to do the journey to Victoria (24 hours, every fifteen minutes daytime, hourly 1am–4am, £8.50).

Forget the idea of getting a **taxi** to or from either airport. In addition to being ruinously expensive, a cab can easily get caught in the city's monstrous traffic – even on a Sunday.

The famous colour-coded **London Underground** ('the Tube', 5.30am–midnight, from 7am Sundays) is dirty, infrequent, overcrowded and overpriced. Security alerts, suicides, maintenance and all manner of other horrors may delay you, so always leave yourself as much time as possible. That said, when it is working well, the Tube is still the best way of moving around the city. The **main train stations** (Paddington, Euston, King's Cross, Waterloo and Victoria) all have Tube stops of the same name. The network is divided into six zones: central zone 1 and neighbouring zone 2 are ample for most needs, except for trips to Wembley (zone 4), and Tottenham and West Ham (zone 3). Tickets are bought at Tube stations – a single fare in zone 1 is £1.20, rising to £3.20 for an all-zone single. A carnet of ten zone 1 tickets is £10.

The red London **bus network** is part of the city's charm. A journey of a couple of stops costs 60p – tell the conductor or driver your desination. The city boasts a big network of **night buses,** most of which pass through or leave from Trafalgar Square.

If you are venturing south of the Thames to clubs such as Crystal Palace, Millwall or Charlton, you will have to use London's suburban **overground train network**; services are less frequent than the Tube, but the ride is usually more pleasant.

A *One-Day Travelcard* for Tube, bus and train, valid Mon–Fri from 9.30am and all day Sat–Sun, is £3.20 for zones 1–2, or £4 for all zones. The cards are sold at stations and newsagents, but are not valid on night buses.

London's **black taxi cabs** are luxuriously roomy, but come at a price. Hail one with the yellow-lit flag showing. The minimum fare is £1, for around 1km, the metre clicking thereafter at 20p intervals; there are surcharges for extra passengers, travel after 8pm and at weekends. If you need to call a cab, dial ☎0171/272 0272 – the minimum call-out charge is £2.

Minicabs, whose drivers may not be as knowledgeable as their famous competitors, are at least cheaper, and don't baulk at going south of the river. *Addison Lee* (☎0171/387 8888) are as reliable as any.

The main **tourist offices** are at the Heathrow Tube station concourse (daily 8.30am–6pm), Victoria station forecourt (daily 8am–7pm), and the *Eurostar* arrivals hall at Waterloo station – where you will be deposited if you come by train from the continent. The best **listings information** guide is *Time Out* (Wednesdays, £1.70).

Gallic Gunners – Wenger brings another Frenchman to N5

the West Stand £13.50–28. For all ticket enquiries, call ☎0171/704 4040, or the dial-a-seat number: ☎0171/413 3366.

Publications

The matchday programme is £1.50, while the official club magazine is *Gunners* (monthly, £2.50); both have colourful features about the club, but are nothing special. The most widely-read fanzine is *The Gooner* (£1.50), although *Up The Arse* (£1) is also popular.

Club shop

Your first port of call should be the spacious **Arsenal World of Sport** (open Mon–Sat 9.30am–6pm and on matchdays, most credit cards), next-door to Finsbury Park Tube and train station. For those not travelling via Finsbury Park, there is the smaller **Gunners' Shop** (open Mon–Fri 9.30am–5pm and on matchdays, Visa and Mastercard only) along Avenell Road behind the East Stand.

Club museum

Many leading European clubs are satisfied with showing visitors a trophy room full of undocumented plunder. The **Arsenal Museum** (open Fridays only, 9.30am–4pm, £2) is a refreshing change, with interactive displays and a twenty-minute film in the video lounge. As well as accommodating

tour parties, it is also open to North Bank ticket holders on matchdays, an hour or so before kick-off.

Ultra culture

The first-rate facilities of the North Bank stand are a classic example of the gentrification of English club football. Gone are the days when Spurs and Chelsea fans would regularly invade it for pitch battles on derby day. Today the clientèle are well-heeled and well-behaved. It remains the end towards which the players prefer to attack, however, and for good reason.

In the net

The official website cuts no corners and resides at: www.arsenal.co.uk. You'll find superb graphics, up-to-date 'Gunformation' and a stats database which has to be seen to be believed. Arsenal can even act as your Internet Service Provider through *AFCi Connect*. As an antidote to all this slickness, try the unofficial *Arseweb* site at: www.netlink.co.uk/users/arseweb. It's fun, witty and irreverent – all the things, in fact, which Arsenal and their fans are not supposed to be.

Chelsea

Stamford Bridge, Fulham Road, SW6
Capacity 28,000 (all-seated)
Colours All blue with white trim
League champions 1955
Cup winners 1970, 1997
Cup-Winners' Cup winners 1971

Chelsea are London's rootless cosmopolitans. Their stadium was built before the club was formed and their glitzy following is famously drawn from the transient world of stage and screen. The club's location, close to the trendy boutiques and art galleries of the King's Road, was the fashionable place to be in the late Sixties, and Chelsea had a team of swingers to match. The FA Cup win of 1970 was the high point in the club's history, but 1997's repeat performance, after near bankruptcy and much second-division football, has come at another high-water mark.

By 1998 Stamford Bridge will be transformed into a stadium fit for the millennium, with the completion of the Chelsea Village in the South Stand. This will contain a three-star hotel with penthouse suites, 34 flats, shops, offices, restaurants, a sports bar, a leisure centre and a football museum. A train station will be built next door. All this is the brainchild of controversial chairman Ken Bates, who wrested control of the club from the Mears family in 1982.

It was H A (Gus) Mears who had the stadium built in 1904, with a view to offering it to nearby Fulham. When they refused, a club had to be formed to play in it. Chelsea FC were founded in 1905. Players were hired, including the famous 22-stone goalkeeper Bill 'Fatty' Foulke, from Sheffield United.

Stamford Bridge, with its oval shape and running track, was one of the finest grounds of its day. But it wasn't until former Arsenal star Ted Drake came in as manager in the early Fifties that Chelsea actually won anything. A Peter Sillett penalty beat Wolves in the deciding game to win the championship in 1955. It remains Chelsea's only title to date – and one that would have brought an appearance in the inaugural European Cup that September, had the Football League not viewed the fledgling competition as a joke.

Chelsea's golden era began when Tommy Docherty replaced Drake as manager in 1962. The club had just won the FA Youth Cup for the second year in a row, with a team which included goalkeeper Peter Bonetti, midfielders Terry Venables and John Hollins, and forwards Peter Osgood and Bobby Tambling. With the first team floundering in the second division,

Docherty chucked the boys in at the deep end. They won promotion immediately. Docherty then bought the mercurial Scots winger Charlie Cooke to send over crosses for the prolific Tambling and Osgood. These were exciting times. London had become the pop and fashion capital of the world. Film stars, hairdressers, restaurateurs – all would hang around the club, accompanying the players to nightspots after matches.

Docherty got Chelsea as far as the Fairs' Cup semi-final of 1966. He was replaced by Dave Sexton, a graduate of the West Ham academy, who brought in a bargain basement forward, Ian Hutchinson, nurtured the precocious midfielder Alan Hudson, and added some steel to the line-up in the form of Dave Webb and Ron 'Chopper' Harris.

The team's star turn came in the 1970 Cup final with Leeds – a game that pitted chic flamboyance against a sixty-game-a-

Chelsea chic – 'Chopper' Harris leads the way

season mean machine. After four hours of football – a muddy draw at Wembley followed by a gruelling replay at Old Trafford – flamboyance triumphed. It would do so again a year later, when Chelsea beat Real Madrid, after another replayed final, to lift the 1971 Cup Winners' Cup.

On the back of this success, the club began to build a huge East Stand at vast expense. Its completion coincided with relegation. Nearly bankrupt, they sold their main asset, young midfielder Ray Wilkins, and the team spent much of the Eighties shifting uneasily between the top two divisions. With creditors knocking on the door and an evil racist following in the Shed end, few outside the club would have mourned its demise. But Ken Bates, an outspoken businessman, took it upon himself to save Chelsea from liquidation. He spent ten years making more headlines than the team itself, but made a wise investment in hiring Glenn Hoddle as player-coach in 1993. Under Hoddle, Chelsea made the Cup final and Europe the following year.

Meanwhile, the club's leading shareholder Matthew Harding, though an outspoken critic of Bates, provided the fortune needed to finance the chairman's master plan for Stamford Bridge's redevelopment. Harding's obvious love of the game brought a human face to the much-maligned club leadership and helped to lure Ruud Gullit to Chelsea, first as a player and then, after Hoddle was named England coach in 1996, as manager.

Gullit brought in Italian stars Gianfranco Zola, Roberto di Matteo and Gianluca Vialli, plus a host of other exotic foreign imports. Harding's death in a helicopter crash heralded a brief pause in the club's extravagant progress, but ultimately there was no stopping them – Zola, di Matteo and veteran striker Mark Hughes were the stars of an easy 2–0 win over relegated Middlesbrough in the 1997 FA Cup final.

Here we go!
District line Tube to **Fulham Broadway**, then turn left out of the station – the

ground is about a ten-minute walk away, on your left.

Swift half
The classic Chelsea drinking holes are in the King's Road, at the other end of Holmead Road and parallel streets. The extravagant **Imperial Arms** (577 King's Road) was a favourite of Matthew Harding's; **Come The Revolution** (#541) is more funky and laid back. The **Stamford Bridge** at 466 Fulham Road, near the tube station, is a favourite for cheap eats. At the bars around the ground, beer is served until about twenty minutes before kick-off.

Tickets
The main **ticket office** is near the main entrance behind the South Stand-to-be (open Mon–Fri 9am–5pm, matchdays from 9am). Away fans are allocated space in the lower tiers of the East Stand (access gate #8). Non-members can buy tickets in the lower section of the Matthew Harding Stand (£20), the East Upper (£25) or the East Middle (£40). For advance credit card bookings, call ☎0171/386 7799.

Publications
The Chelsea matchday programme is thick but pricy at £2, while the club's official monthly magazine (£2.95) is better than its title – *Chelsea* – suggests. Among the fanzines worth picking up are *The Chelsea Independent* (£1) and *The Cockney Rebel* (£0.30).

Club shop
The newly opened **Chelsea Megastore** (open Mon–Sat 9am–5pm and matchday Sundays, most credit cards) will sell you anything from the latest replica shirt to an Italjet scooter in Chelsea blue.

Ultra culture
Chelsea's 'Headhunters' were one of England's most notorious fan groups during the Seventies and Eighties, growing more and more fanatical as Chelsea's football got worse and worse. The Shed, where they

gathered, was an uneasy place to be of a Saturday afternoon, a meeting point for violent and racist elements from all over the south-east. The fact that it has since been knocked down to make room for the multi-purpose South Stand is indicative of the wind of change blowing through Chelsea – though whether all the Shed-heads have made the transition to cool cosmopolitans remains to be seen.

In the net

The official site is at: www.chelseafc.co.uk. It's pretty good, but forces you to register before you can get beyond the opening page. Head instead for an unofficial site run from Norway at: home.sol.no.roaaune. Proudly proclaiming itself to be frame-, java- and audio-free, it's refreshingly simple but still utterly comprehensive.

Glory days – Greaves in his irrepressible prime

Tottenham Hotspur

White Hart Lane, 748 High Road, N17
Capacity 27,000 (all-seated)
Colours White shirts, navy-blue shorts
League champions 1951, 1961
Cup Winners 1901, 1921, 1961–62, 1967, 1981–82, 1991
Cup-Winners' Cup winners 1963
UEFA Cup winners 1972, 1984

Glory, Glory, Tottenham Hotspur, runs the song, but the Lilywhites have been off the glory trail for too long now. The first British club to win a European trophy, always renowned for their adventurous football, they have had a mediocre time of it since their last FA Cup win in 1991.

That summer saw electronics million-aire Alan Sugar assume the club's vast debt and attempt to transform Tottenham into an American-style sports operation. After a bitter courtroom dispute with former Spurs manager Terry Venables, Sugar seems comfortable keeping the club ticking over in mid-table, as just another branch of his leisure and communications empire.

Although White Hart Lane is being rebuilt to give it an overall capacity of 38,000 by 1999, whether all those extra fans will bother to turn up is a moot point.

Tottenham Hotspur Football Club were started by a group of bookish schoolboys who met under a lamp-post near the current ground. They took the name Hotspur from the Shakespearean character Harry Hotspur, nickname of Henry Percy of the Northumberland family whose ancestral home was near Tottenham marshes.

The club moved from Northumberland Park to White Hart Lane in 1899. They won the amateur Southern League in 1900 and became the last non-league club to win the FA Cup the following year. At an official dinner afterwards, the local mayoress tied blue-and-white ribbons to the Cup, insti-gating a tradition that has endured to this day. With Football League status assured in 1909, a new stand was built with a cop-per cockerel perched on top – the club's future motif. Spurs flitted between divi-sions between the wars, winning the Cup in 1921 with the inventive Jimmy Seed run-ning the show against Wolves.

The arrival as manager of Arthur Rowe, a former Spurs player whose career had been cut short through injury, saw the team rise quickly to the top in the early Fifties. Playing a style called push-and-run, in which short passing and quick movement were paramount, Spurs won the second and first divisions in consecutive years. In the team were future England manager Alf Ramsey at full-back, and wing-halves Bill Nicholson and Eddie Baily, soon to become the coaching duo who would lead the club into their most successful era.

Two more wing-halves would be crucial to Nicholson's and Baily's plans: Danny Blanchflower, all anticipation and positional sense, and Dave Mackay, tough tackling and inspirational. With inside-forward John White picking up Blanchflower's precise passes, Spurs began an unbeaten league run in 1960 that culminated in their securing the century's first league and cup double the following spring.

As 1961 drew to a close, the signing of Jimmy Greaves from AC Milan made the team perfectly poised to become English pioneers in Europe. Though they were pipped by the odd goal in seven by Benfica in the 1962 European Cup semi-final, Spurs

successfully defended the FA Cup, then destroyed Atlético Madrid, 5–1, in the Cup-Winners' Cup final of 1963. England's first European club trophy was in the bag, and it had Tottenham's blue-and-white ribbons draped around it.

The retirement of Blanchflower, injuries to Mackay and death of White – struck by lightning on a golf course – saw a slight dip in the club's fortunes. But Terry Venables' arrival from Chelsea helped Spurs to an FA Cup final win over his old club in 1967. And the goalkeeping prowess of record Northern Ireland cap Pat Jennings was becoming another feature of the side – as it would remain until his surprise move to Arsenal in 1977.

The Nicholson era had as its swansong three UEFA Cup runs – one of them, in 1972, victorious. Upfront, the wily Scot Alan Gilzean was joined by England internationals Martin Peters and Alan Chivers, while young Steve Perryman showed a cool head as midfield anchor. Between them they had the edge over Wolves in a fiercely contested, all-English final.

Nicholson's surprise resignation in 1974, after nearly forty years with the club, left a gap which Tottenham struggled to fill. In 1977 the team were relegated, and though they bounced straight back up again, the old Spurs fire was barely flickering.

There were some bright spots, however – the breakthrough of the precocious midfield talent of Glenn Hoddle, and the pioneering signing (at a time when foreign players were a novelty in English football) of Argentines Osvaldo Ardiles and Ricardo Villa after they had starred in the 1978 World Cup. Under the dour but decent managership of Keith Burkinshaw, Spurs kept playing entertaining football, and eventually it paid off with two FA Cup final wins – the first, in 1981, featuring a classic dribble and goal from Villa.

Although Tottenham again won the UEFA Cup, on penalties at home

Eye on the ball – Reeves and Perryman, Wembley, 1981

Wembley

Wembley stadium, Empire
Way, Wembley, Middlesex
Capacity 80,000 (all-seated)

England's most famous and
most maligned football landmark is to be knocked down
and rebuilt before the century
is out. The stadium's **twin
towers** will be all that remain
of a place which has been an
institution since its grand
opening in 1923. Although
there is no doubting the awe in

To be continued – the twin peaks of Metroland

which Wembley is held abroad, too many regulars at England internationals have had
enough of its limited toilet, catering, parking and transport facilities, let alone the fact
that too many seats have a restricted view.

The Wembley plans are ambitious. The twin towers will be repositioned, and the
whole stadium will be **turned ninety degrees**, with the outside walls forming a
sweeping curve. This will allow for them to act as a projection screen, showing the
action to viewers gathered in a broad piazza outside. The roof will have retractable pan-
els. The capacity will stay at 80,000 but the **sightlines and leg room** will be
improved. A new Wembley Stadium train station will connect directly with Eurostar,
Heathrow and Intercity services.

All this should be in place by the year 2000, in time for England's bid to host the
World Cup in 2006. During the two-year hiatus needed to build it, England, under contract to play their home games at Wembley until 2002, will play around the country.
Many fans think this should have happened long ago. England's Wembley residency
has not always been a popular one – though the psychological advantage it gives over
their opponents is undeniable. England are the only nation to have won the World Cup
playing **every game at the same stadium**, an achievement that would have been
echoed thirty years later at Euro '96, but for a shoot-out defeat by Germany.

In addition to internationals, Wembley is also associated with the FA Cup final, and
couldn't have received better promotion than its inaugural match on April 28, 1923.
Barely completed four days earlier, it was swamped by an estimated **200,000 people**
for the Bolton-West Ham 'White Horse Final', so named because PC George Scorey, on
his big white horse Billie, helped clear the crowd from the pitch.

To follow in all those footsteps, take the Metropolitan Tube line (much quicker than
the Jubilee, which runs parallel) from town to **Wembley Park** (zone 4, £3.60 return).
Allow thirty minutes. The stadium is across the road down Wembley Way.

The Globe pub opposite Baker Street Tube station is ideal for a jar before the journey up to Wembley. Once there, the best place for a quiet beer is the **Green Man** at
64–70 Dagmar Avenue, opposite the Hilton Hotel. In fine weather there is a beer garden and barbecue, while the large interior is bonehead-free and the car parking space
for customers is cheaper than Wembley's. There are also some **hotel rooms** to rent.

Advance **tickets** should be bought directly from the Wembley office, clearly
marked at the end of Wembley Way, near turnstile J (☎0181/900 1234, open Mon–Sat
9.30am–9pm, Sun 10am–6pm, most credit cards). Seat prices for internationals range
from £15 to £45.

Drive on the left – Ginola's first game at the Lane

Here we go!

Victoria Tube line to **Seven Sisters** (zone 3), then change there for an overground train to **White Hart Lane**; alternatively, you can take the latter direct from Liverpool Street. Allow thirty minutes for the whole journey from town. Walk right down White Hart Lane, then turn right at the T-junction with Tottenham High Road. The stadium is two minutes away. Buses #149, #259 and #279 run up the High Road.

Swift Half

The former **White Hart** pub is now a nightclub, while the **Corner Pin**, on the corner of Park Lane and Tottenham High Road, is members only. **The Park**, 220 Park Lane, by Northumberland Park station, and **The Victoria**, 34 Scotland Green, are pubs the club recommends to supporters coming without colours. **The Bank**, on the corner of White Hart Lane and Tottenham High Road, is a trendy bar with big-screen football – doormen screen the clientèle on matchdays. For food, the **Hotspur Restaurant,** 759 Tottenham High Road, does everything with chips. Alcohol is served at the small bars dotted around the ground (as are bagels), but there's no booze at half-time.

to Anderlecht in 1984, financial problems overshadowed most of the Eighties. The big-money signings of Chris Waddle and Paul Gascoigne from Newcastle, the refurbishment of the East Stand and the reorganisation of the club as a publicly quoted company nearly conspired to drive Spurs out of business in 1991. After a stunning Gazza free-kick in the semi against Arsenal, and despite the same player's self-inflicted injury in the final against Nottingham Forest, Tottenham won their eighth FA Cup that year.

After Venables had departed in acrimony, the unpopular Sugar invited Jürgen Klinsmann onto his yacht in Monte Carlo and offered him the chance to become part of a brave new Tottenham, alongside Romanians Gica Popescu and Ilie Dumitrescu, and coach Ardiles. Klinsmann jumped at the chance, but within a year the rest of the cast had been thrown overboard, and the German decided to follow of his own volition in the summer of 1995.

Since then Ardiles' replacement, the former England captain Gerry Francis, has stuck, like his chairman, to a safety-first policy. The fans, meanwhile, have taken to singing "Are you Arsenal in disguise?" at their own players...

Tickets

Non-members can go to the East, West or South Stands. The last, built in 1995, is steep-sloping behind one goal and offers a great view – a corner section is allocated to away fans, turnstile entrance on Park Lane. The North (Paxton Road) Stand opposite is being rebuilt in the same style. The main **ticket office** is on the corner of Park Lane and Tottenham High Road (Mon–Fri 10am–6pm). When the Paxton Road end is re-opened there is a matchday ticket office there. Prices range from £17 in the South

Stand to £33 in the West. The Tottenham Ticketline number is: ☎0181/396 4567.

Publications

The Spurs matchday programme is £1.80, while the monthly colour glossy magazine, one of the better of its type, costs £2.50. Among the fanzines are *Spur of the Moment* (£1) and *Cock A Doddle Doo* (£2).

Club shop

There are stores at either end of the ground, open Mon–Sat 9.30am–5.30pm, and on Sunday matchdays.

Ultra culture

These are the calmest of the main London clubs' fans, especially since seating conversion removed The Shelf, the standing area along one touchline. As a pressure group, however, the **Independent Tottenham Supporters' Club** have been important in adding their voice to the financial debates, throwing their weight behind Terry Venables during his dispute with Sugar.

In the net

Tottenham's official site is essentially a merchandising operation: www.spurs.co.uk. To the club's credit, however, it does offer a link to an unofficial site at: www. sys.uea.ac.uk/Recreation/Sport/thfc.html. Replica shirts or shirty match reports – the choice is yours.

West Ham United

Boleyn Ground, Green Street, E13
Capacity 26,000
Colours Claret shirts with sky-blue sleeves, white shorts
Cup winners 1964, 1975, 1980
Cup-Winners' Cup winners 1965

West Ham is best known for being home to the so-called 'Academy of Football' whose rigorously technical approach produced a trio of World Cup winners in the mid-Sixties. But although they have won two FA Cups since, United's stance is traditionally that of the underdog, fighting relegation battles with spirit and guile.

The club were originally the company team of the Thames Ironworks, founded in 1895 – hence their nicknames 'The Hammers' or 'The Irons'. They became independent and joined the Southern League in 1900, moving to their present ground four years later. Like any East End family, West Ham kept a tight grip on the purse strings, and the club's youth policy has always been important.

Apart from losing the 'White Horse Final' to Bolton as a second-division side in 1923, West Ham's story starts in earnest in the mid-Fifties. Members of their young squad including Malcolm Allison, Noel Cantwell, John Bond, Dave Sexton and Frank O'Farrell (all of whom would later coach top clubs) would meet after training and discuss tactics. The local game was going through an identity crisis after England's 6–3 thrashing by Hungary in 1953. Jogging endless laps in training wasn't delivering the goods – so what to do instead? Sitting for hours in Cassetari's Café near the ground, the young Hammers would plan out moves using salt cellars and vinegar bottles – moves which would culminate in a second-division title in 1958, after years in the doldrums.

With Ron Greenwood in charge (West Ham changed managers every ten years or so, keeping the job in the family), the lessons at Cassetari's paid off. Three class youngsters, half-back Bobby Moore, inside-forward Martin Peters and centre-forward Geoff Hurst, were the stars of the show. West Ham won the Cup in 1964, then the European Cup Winners' Cup at the same Wembley stadium a year later, 2–0 over TSV Munich 1860. A year after that the trio were back to pick up the World Cup for England, Moore as captain, Hurst and Peters as the goalscorers.

In the Seventies, Peters left for Spurs and Trevor Brooking came through the ranks, an Academy player if there ever was one. Billy Bonds was the stalwart in front of the defence, Brooking the provider of the destroying pass. West Ham won the Cup twice more, then lost the Cup-Winners' Cup final to Anderlecht in 1976.

After that the Hammers began to yo-yo unpredictably between divisions. When they reached Wembley again, for an FA Cup final against Arsenal in 1980, they were a second-division side. As the Eighties went on they were forced to sell the family silver to survive – Tony Cottee and Paul Ince going to Everton and Manchester United, respectively. Transfer fees still wouldn't meet the expense of making Upton Park all-seater, however, so the board tried to instigate a bond scheme, requiring fans to pay £500 for a lifetime's use of a seat. The proposal saw mass protests, and the

scheme was eventually dropped. In the end, Sky's TV money helped towards the impressive renovation in 1995 of the North and Bobby Moore Stands.

Here we go!
District line Tube to **Upton Park**; turn right out of the station, then take a five-minute stroll down Green Street.

Swift half
The classic West Ham pub is the **Boleyn Tavern**, down Green Street from the Tube and past the stadium on your left-hand side. It's a large pub with a wooden interior and two spacious bar areas. For food and a slice of history, **Cassetari's Café** is round the corner at 25 Barking Road. In the ground you'll find bars dotted all around, such as the Trevor Brooking and Geoff Hurst bars in the main West Stand, serving beer up to fifteen minutes before kick-off.

Tickets
Upton Park, as the Boleyn Ground is almost always known, is up close and personal. The **ticket office** in the West Stand on Green Street is open Mon–Fri 9am–5pm and on matchdays from 9am. Away fans are allocated a block in the North Stand, with turnstile access from Green Street, just before the ticket office. Home fans are based in the lower tier of the East Stand, the former 'Chicken Run' (seats £22–26) and in the Bobby Moore Stand (£17–25). Neutrals are best placed in the West Stand (£23–30). The club's dial-a-seat service can be reached on: ☎0181/548 2700.

Publications
The matchday programme is £2. West Ham don't issue an official club magazine, but there are

I didn't get many with me 'ead – Brooking at Wembley, 1980

plenty of unofficial glossies. The main fanzines are *On a Mission* (£1.50), *Over Land and Sea* (£1) and *The Water in Majorca* (£0.50).

Club shop

There's a new, spacious shop (open Mon–Fri 9.30am–5pm, Sat 9.30am–1pm, later on matchdays, most credit cards) at 39–41 Barking Road, round the corner from the ground past the *Boleyn* pub.

Ultra culture

The conversion of Upton Park to an all-seater ground disbanded the Chicken Run, the standing area in the East Stand and soapbox for so much East London banter. These days you'll hear regular choruses of *I'm Forever Blowing Bubbles* coming from the Bobby Moore Stand, but the atmosphere is rather more sedate than in the Seventies. The infamous **ICF**, West Ham's often dangerous travelling support, have also calmed down. The Bond Scheme dispute galvanised independent support against the club management, channelling all that aggression into a common and worthy cause.

In the net

The official site can be found at: www.westhamunited.co.uk. It's graphics-heavy but very approachable, for all that. For a quirkier view of Hammers life, check out North Bank Norman's unofficial site at: www.ironworks.com/westham.htm.

Groundhopping

At the last count, London boasted thirteen teams playing in England's top four divisions. Of these, Premiership clubs Crystal Palace and Wimbledon operate England's only successful (if grudging) ground-share at Selhurst Park. Palace's former tenants there, Charlton Athletic, moved back to The Valley in 1991, and now play first-division football, along with Queen's Park Rangers, whose home is at Loftus Road in Shepherd's Bush, west of town.

Crystal Palace

Selhurst Park, Park Road, Norwood, SE25
Capacity 30,000 (all-seated)
Colours Red-and-blue striped shirts, white shorts

Palace are a team of misconceptions. There has been a Crystal Palace club since 1861, but the current one wasn't formed until 1905, by staff who worked at the Palace. The ground they first played on also hosted England internationals and the FA Cup final before World War I. Today there is no Crystal Palace in the area of south London known by that name (it burned down in 1936) and no football club there, either, the team having moved to Selhurst Park in 1924. Take a bus marked 'Crystal Palace' from central London and you face a stiff 45-minute walk to Selhurst.

The FA originally opposed Palace's formation in case the team reached the Cup final and played it as a home game. They needn't have worried. Palace achieved nothing whatsoever until the arrival of outspoken manager Bert Head in the Sixties. With the help of some Chelsea cast-offs including Bobby Tambling, Head took Palace into the top flight for the first time in 1969. Three years later Malcolm Allison took charge and changed the club's colours from claret and sky-blue to red-and-blue stripes, saying he wanted them to look like Barcelona – Palace were relegated twice in the next two seasons.

Allison redeemed himself when he and his fedora hat took Palace to an FA Cup semi-final in 1976, but it wasn't until his assistant, Terry Venables, took over the managerial reins that things really started to happen. In this, his first coaching job, Venables led the club back to the first division in 1979, and for a brief week or two Palace were top of the league. Then star full-back Kenny Sansom was sold to Arsenal, Venables quit, and the 'Team of the Eighties' were relegated in 1981.

A former chairman of Wimbledon, Ron Noades, took control of the club, and in

Palace are back in the Prem – but for how long?

the late Eighties he appointed a young Steve Coppell as manager. Coppell's collection of lower-division finds and park players, including Ian Wright, Mark Bright and John Salako, clawed their way into the top drawer in 1989, and a year later beat Liverpool 4–3 to set up that long-awaited Cup final appearance, against Manchester United. Palace drew the first game 3–3, then lost the replay 1–0. A year later they made third place in the first division, their best finish to date. But losing a their UEFA Cup place to Liverpool on an administrative ruling was a bitter blow to an ambitious young squad, and relegation was followed by Coppell's resignation in 1993.

Since then Palace have been up and down again, while Coppell has returned as manager – twice. Having missed out on promotion in 1996, thanks to a last-minute Leicester goal in the play-off final, Palace dealt a similar blow to Sheffield United in the 1997 version, to make it five changes of status in nine years.

While Chelsea attract London's media types and new political class, Palace are a magnet for comedians and anyone in the capital with a sense of humour. To join them for a laugh, take an overground train from Victoria or London Bridge to **Norwood Junction**, about a twenty-minute ride. Out of the station, walk up to the crossroads ahead, turn left down Selhurst Road, and the stadium is on your right. **The Cherry Tree**, 32 Sta-

tion Road, between Norwood Junction and the stadium, is the traditional pre-match watering hole – get there early for a seat.

⬤ Wimbledon

Selhurst Park, see p.125
Colours All blue with yellow trim
Cup winners 1988

Ever since Wimbledon's original ground at Plough Lane proved too expensive to redevelop, popular club owner Sam Hammam has been weighing up his options – including a possible move to Dublin. But still the Dons stay at Selhurst Park, attracting a few thousand faithful, and now with the promise of a cash injection from a consortium of Norwegian businessmen.

After a famous Cup run as a Southern League side in 1975, Wimbledon gained entry to the fourth division in 1977, and climbed steadily up the ladder. Perennial goalscorer Alan Cork stayed with them all the way until they made the first in 1986.

This was the era of the Crazy Gang, personified by the impish Dennis Wise and hardman Vinnie Jones. They played a fairly ugly brand of football, but their pub-team humour and collective spirit took them to an FA Cup final win over Liverpool in 1988. England's European ban prevented the club from taking their rightful place in the Cup-Winners' Cup.

Nine years later the team were again denied a European spot – this time, playing a more attractive game under the careful guidance of manager Joe Kinnear, by chronic fixture congestion and the increasingly unplayable Selhurst Park pitch.

If you want to watch the Dons among their own supporters, note that while Palace fans are happiest at the Holmesdale Road end of Selhurst, Wimbledon's prefer the Whitehorse Lane stand, in front of Sainsbury's. If you miss them, you might catch a few for a post-match chat at the cook-chill counter.

Eat, drink, sleep…

Bars and clubs

For all the city's reputation as a wild, party town, most London pubs are subject to the same Draconian licensing laws of 11pm closing. The exception is Soho, especially around Old Compton Street (Tube to Leicester Square) where you can get a drink in any number of **continental-style bars** until 1am at least.

Many pubs now have **big screens** for televised football, but be aware that wearing football colours on matchday may make it hard to get served in the West End.

As for the **beer**, the Guinness in north London is the best you'll probably get outside Ireland, and draught Czech lager is becoming justly commonplace – but you could be paying £2.50 a pint for either. Northerners complain about the quality of the **bitter** down south, but there are often good deals on cheap pints of it.

When it comes to clubs and concerts, London really excels – there are literally hundreds of events to choose from every night, but beware that top dance clubs charge up to £15 admission, and snotty doormen won't let you in wearing trainers.

Football Football, 57–60 Haymarket. The first of its kind to open in town, before Euro '96, this themed bar/restaurant is run by two ex-players who give a percentage of their profits to the Professional Footballers' Association. The mementoes on display are impressive even if some of the life-size models are a little tacky. The bar area is light and pleasant, while the large restaurant is reached down a tunnel designed like Wembley's. Pricy, but worth a visit. Souvenir shop by the main entrance. Open daily noon–11.30pm. Most major credit cards. Tube to Piccadilly.

Loughborough Hotel, corner of Loughborough Road and Evandale Road. Two floors of a big old hotel with a pub downstairs, offering various kinds of dance music in different rooms, and often a live African band playing. £5 entrance, reasonable bar prices. Lots of other clubs nearby. Tube to Brixton.

A bit of a long shop – London's soccer stores

The boom surrounding the Premiership and Euro '96 saw several football-related stores open in the capital. On Saturday afternoons these and their longer-established rivals are choc-full of fans eager for shirts, scarves, fanzines, and anything else that might seem vaguely hip or interesting. Below is a selection of the best places, all of which take most major credit cards.

House of Football, 11 The Island, Charing Cross Road. Modest but colourful store on the traffic island near the National Portrait Gallery. Open Mon–Sat 10.30am–6.30pm, Sun 11am–6pm. Tube to Charing Cross.

Soccer Scene, 30/31 Great Marlborough Street. One of three neighbouring stores under the same management that were the first in the capital to stock a selection of foreign football shirts. The other two stores, at 17 and 23–27 Fouberts Place, are rather cramped, but the latter does mail order. Open Mon–Sat 9.30am–7pm, Sun 11am–5pm. Tube to Oxford Circus.

Sportspages, Caxton Walk, 94–96 Charing Cross Road. Established sports book store which stocks a huge selection of fanzines, videos and football literature. Open Mon–Sat 9.30am–7pm. Tube to Leicester Square.

World of Football, 119–121 Oxford Street. Two floors of soccer shirts and souvenirs, with boots downstairs, but the shop is a little soulless. Open daily 10am–7pm, Sun noon–6pm. Tube to Oxford Circus.

Sports Café, 80 Haymarket. Three American-style sports bars in one, with a restaurant, a dancefloor and hundreds of satellite TV channels. Autographed Pelé shirt hidden among the boxing gloves and racing cars. Open until 3am Fri–Sat. Most credit cards. Tube to Piccadilly.

Terry Neill's Sports Bar and Brasserie, Bath House, 53 Holborn Viaduct A good spot if you're after a more down-to-earth pub feel than the tackier sports bars in the West End. Run (and often frequented by) the former Spurs, Arsenal and Northern Ireland manager Neill, whose mementoes cover the walls. Tube to Blackfriars.

Velvet Underground, 143 Charing Cross Road. Popular, friendly club decked out in primary colours. Decent sounds, admission around £5–7 most nights. Open 10pm–3am, closed Sun & Tue. Tube to Tottenham Court Road.

Restaurants

No-one goes to England for the food, but London can at least provide as big a variety of **international cuisine** as you'll get anywhere outside New York. The West End is the best stomping ground, Soho in particular being full of cheap Chinese and not-so-cheap Italian restaurants. Brick Lane and Westbourne Grove are full of curry houses, though wherever you are, there's bound to be 'an Indian' nearby.

Nazrul, 130 Brick Lane. One of many low-priced Bangladeshi diners in the area, the Nazrul offers huge portions of top-notch, authentic food, with little profit margin for the owners to improve the décor or furniture. Open until midnight Sun–Thur, 1am Fri–Sat. Bring your own wine. No credit cards. Tube to Aldgate East.

Pollo, 20 Old Compton Street. Classic budget Italian diner, always busy despite there being two floors of tables. Incredibly cheap, open past midnight. Tube to Leicester Square.

Sea Shell Fish Restaurant, 49–51 Lisson Grove. The most famous fish-and-chip place in town, so you may have to wait to get seated. All kinds of fish, grilled or fried, with assorted side dishes. Far more expensive than you'd pay at your corner chippy, but worth it. Most major credit cards. Closes 10.30pm. Tube to Marylebone.

Ye Olde Cheshire Cheese, 145 Fleet Street. Nine bar and restaurant areas in this atmospheric 17th century building, with a menu featuring 'traditional' English fare such as roast beef and Yorkshire pudding. About £10 for a main course. Most major credit cards. Tube to Blackfriars.

Accommodation

London is an **expensive city** to stay in. It's virtually impossible to pay less than £50 for a double room, and you could easily be charged twice that, even in a moderate hotel. **Bed-and-breakfasts** might be a better option – you'll find them grouped around the main train stations, but check your room first. There are eight official **youth hostels** in town, for which an IYHF or YHA card is required. Foreign guests can buy an *International Guest Pass* (£1.50) to stay at hostel rates. The YHA central reservations number in London is ☎0171/248 6547 (daily 6.45am–11.30pm).

Edward Lear Hotel, 28–30 Seymour Street (☎0171/402 5401, fax 0171/706 3766). Former home of the famous limerick writer, a pleasant, central B&B which welcomes children. Singles £40–50, doubles £55–85 with breakfast. Visa and Mastercard accepted. Tube to Marble Arch.

Luna and Simone Hotel, 47–49 Belgrave Road (☎0171/834 5897). One of dozens of places along Belgrave Road, a serious walk or #24 bus ride from Victoria, but worth it for comfortable rooms with a colour television, some with bath. Decent breakfasts. Singles £25, doubles £35. Visa and Mastercard accepted.

Oxford House, 92–94 Cambridge Street (☎0171/834 6467, fax 0171/834 0225). Cosy B&B near Victoria coach station, with spacious rooms and a TV lounge. Singles £30, doubles £40. Triples and quads also available. Visa and Mastercard accepted (with surcharge). Tube to Victoria.

Birmingham

England's second city in terms of size and population, Birmingham cannot claim to wield the footballing influence of either London or the north-west, but it is proud of its importance in the development of the game. In addition to Aston Villa, the region's major club, and nearby Coventry City, the West Midlands conurbation boasts a number of England's 'sleeping giants' – Birmingham City and, in the adjacent Black Country, Wolverhampton Wanderers and West Bromwich Albion.

All these last three are currently playing Nationwide League football, underlining both the area's potential footballing strength and the extent to which the mod-era era has, so far at least, passed much of the region by.

My friend Stan – Villa's goalscoring saviour?

Aston Villa

Villa Park, Trinity Road, Birmingham B6
Capacity 40,300
Colours Claret shirts with sky-blue sleeves, white shorts
League champions 1894, 1896–97, 1899, 1900, 1910, 1981
Cup winners 1887, 1895, 1897, 1905, 1913, 1920, 1957
European Cup winners 1982

Aston Villa entered the century as the best side in English football and they will leave it as a major club. But for most of the past hundred years they have consistently failed to live up to the high standards set by their Victorian-era successes.

Villa were the first giants of English football. It was no surprise that they were founder members of the Football League – they had won the FA Cup the year prior to the League's inception and one of the leading members of the club, William McGregor, was the man who proposed the founding of the League and became its first chairman. With Scottish-born George Ramsay a vital influence both on and off the field, Villa dominated in the Victorian era. Their distinctive claret shirts with blue sleeves were copied by Burnley and West Ham United, as clubs in all parts of the country tried to imitate the success of the Birmingham side.

In 1897, Villa became the first team to do the League and FA Cup double, and the trophies continued to roll in until World War I. After it, though Villa remained a force in the first division thanks largely to the goals of prolific striker Harry Hampton and later 'Pongo' Waring, they were no longer the mighty power they had once been. Relegation in 1936 seemed an epoch-shattering disaster; in reality it was only a foretaste of what was to come after World War II. Once again Villa found themselves struggling to rebuild after hostilities and, two years after an FA Cup final win over Manchester United in 1957, they were again relegated to the second division. Wily manager Joe Mercer brought them back immediately, and a year later Villa won the inaugural League Cup. But Mercer's promising side, which included England international forward Gerry Hitchens, failed to develop. Mercer took his coaching skills to Manchester City, Hitchens went to Inter Milan, and Villa were relegated again in 1967.

In 1970 the unthinkable happened – the club sank into the old third division. For two years Villa Park, one of the premier grounds in the country, played host to small-town football, while across town, Birmingham City were preparing for a flamboyant assault on the top flight. It wasn't until 1975 that Villa won back their first-class status, under the management of Ron Saunders. Saunders was a stern figure, but his strict discipline and eye for talent helped breathe new life into Villa. They won the League Cup by beating Norwich at Wembley in 1975, and won it again two years later, after a third replay against Everton. In 1981, with Saunders still very much in charge, Villa won their first title for seventy years, finishing four points ahead of a highly fancied Ipswich Town.

If few had expected a title, even fewer could quite believe it when Villa won the European Cup the following season. Anderlecht were beaten in the semi-finals and in the final against Bayern Munich, Breitner, Rummenigge and all were defeated by a goal from Villa's bulky, bearded target man, Peter Withe. The victory was made all the more remarkable by the fact that first-team 'keeper Jimmy Rimmer was injured and had to be substituted by a completely untried youngster, Nigel Spink.

The Villa side of the day had few stars, but Saunders and his successor, Tony Barton, had struck just the right balance of youth and experience, flair and grit. There was the tough Scottish midfielder Des Bremner, the talented young playmaker Gordon Cowans, flying wingers Tony Morley and Mark Walters, and the burly central-defensive pairing of Ken McNaught and Allan Evans. Above all there was Withe, a man who could make even a tap-in look clumsy – as he did in Rotterdam against Bayern – but whose presence was enough to strike fear into any central defence in Europe.

As Barton was succeeded by Graham Turner and then by Billy McNeill, Villa failed to replace the older players in the side, and were relegated again in 1987. They bounced back within a season under the former Watford manager Graham Taylor,

Birmingham essentials

The main terminal of Birmingham **airport**, 12km east of town, is connected to Birmingham International **train station** by a courtesy bus that serves each incoming flight from the arrivals hall. Four trains an hour run from Birmingham International to **New Street station**, journey time fifteen minutes, single fare £2. New Street, which serves mainline trains to London and Manchester, is in the city centre.

The main **bus station** is at Digbeth, a ten-minute walk from New Street. The main city bus company, *Centro*, operates a two-tier fare system, in which off-peak travel (Mon–Fri 9.30am–3.30pm & 6pm–11.30pm, Sat–Sun all day) costs just 80p for any journey. A limited night service is run through Friday night/Saturday morning and Saturday night/Sunday morning, between 1am and 4am. Pay your fare to the driver, who can also issue **day passes** at £2.30. For a **black cab**, call *TOA* on ☎0121/427 8888.

Tourist information is available at two offices, equidistant from New Street: at 2 City Arcade, off New Street (open Mon–Sat 9.30am–5.30pm, ☎0121/643 2514,); and at the Central Library, Chamberlain Square (open Mon–Fri 9am–8pm, Sat 9am–5pm, ☎0121/236 5622). The offices issue a free fortnightly listings magazine, *What's On*, also available in major clubs and venues.

who set about building a younger team that included some of the most exciting players seen at Villa for years – among them the skilful winger Tony Daley and a masterful midfield signing from Crewe by the name of David Platt. After they finished second in the league in 1990, much was expected of Taylor's side. But then the boss made the worst decision of his career – he left his promising young team for the England manager's job.

Since then, the most widely supported club in the Midlands and their chairman, Doug Ellis, have provided no shortage of cash to invest on players. Ron Atkinson took over from the ill-starred Slovak Josef Venglos as manager in 1991, and under Big Ron, Villa spent heavily and progressed steadily, becoming regular title and European contenders. Atkinson's replacement, Brian Little, a hero of the triple-replay League Cup final of 1977, has continued to spend millions in the transfer market and kept Villa among the top five clubs in England.

And after all the trials of this century, Mr McGregor would surely have settled for that.

Withe or without you – Peter directs a killer lay-off

Here we go!
The nearest train station is **Witton**, three stops from New Street and two minutes' walk from the ground. From Birmingham city centre you can take **bus #7** to the ground – allow fifteen minutes.

Swift half
Villa Park is out by a motorway junction, surrounded by warehouses and garages, and a fair walk from the pubs and shops of Aston. Nearest pubs for a pre-match beer are **The Harriers**, at the junction of Broadway and Davey Road, and **The Witton Arms** by the train station. The spacious Harriers has table football, pool and plenty of sport on TV; the Witton is shabbier but convenient for fans coming by train.

Tickets
The view from anywhere inside Villa Park is excellent. Home fans sit in the huge Holte End or the nearest section of the Doug Ellis Stand to it. Neutrals are best off in the Trinity Road Stand, while away fans are allocated adjacent corners of the Doug Ellis Stand and North Stand, blocks Q and R, through the turnstiles on Witton Lane. Tickets can be ordered by credit card on ☎0121/327 7373.

Publications
Villa's matchday programme (£1.20) is glossy but has plenty of substance to back up the photography – a rarity in England.

Club shop
The official store (open Mon–Fri and matchdays 9.30am–5pm) is between the North Stand and the Trinity Road Stand.

In the net
An official website is promised for sometime during the 1997/98 season. Until then, check out the unofficial version at: www. villan.demon.co.uk/villa/. It's a businesslike, likeable site, dominated graphically by the grand red-brick frontage of Villa Park.

Clap hands – Sullivan and Brady salute St Andrews' finest

Groundhopping

☕ Birmingham City

St Andrews, St Andrews Street, Birmingham B9
Capacity 24,796
Colours Blue shirts, white shorts

Despite a strong support base, Birmingham have not a single major honour to their name, and have spent most of their life bobbing up and down between the top two divisions – with notably less upward movement in recent years.

The club joined the Football League in 1892, after spending seventeen years playing in regional competitions. It wasn't until the Twenties that they showed any signs of potential with a sustained spell in the top flight. In 1931 they reached their first FA Cup final, losing to local rivals West Bromwich Albion.

After a quiet decade or three, the Blues were surprisingly selected as England's representatives in the Inter-City Fairs' Cup – the forerunner of today's UEFA Cup. They reached the final in 1960 and 1961, losing to Barcelona and Roma. Four years later, they were back in the second division.

The Seventies saw Birmingham at their best. From 1972 to 1979 they competed in the top flight, with the likes of Trevor Francis and Bob Latchford wowing the crowds, dressed in a now immortal shirt of blue with a single, white centre stripe. Francis was sold to Nottingham Forest in 1979, becoming England's first £1 million player. City were relegated.

They slumped into the third division in 1989, and though promoted in 1992 they have only recently begun to look like a club with serious ambition once more. In 1994 club chairman David Sullivan, owner of the *Daily Sport* newspaper, and his colourful CEO Karren Brady gave an open chequebook to manager Barry Fry. After using a League record 46 players in 1995/96, City had a massive staff but showed little in the way of progress. Trevor Francis returned to the club as manager in 1996, but it remains to be seen whether he will have the same impact on St Andrews that he did as a player two decades ago.

St Andrews is about a mile east of **New Street station**, a twenty-minute walk (follow signs for Small Heath), or take bus #15, #17, #96 or #97. A taxi from the station will cost £3–4.

A pre-match pint is best supped near New Street station. **The Trocadero**, 19 Temple Street, is a spacious pub that serves decent food and welcomes neutral fans.

Eat, drink, sleep...

Bars and clubs
Birmingham's nightlife is widely dispersed. Many congregate in trendy pubs and clubs in central Broad Street and Brindley Place, the student area of Moseley can be lively of a weekend, and there are a few popular Irish pubs in the Digbeth area.

Bakers, 163 Broad Street. City-centre club with cheap student nights on Tuesdays and, on Saturdays, Republica for more populist dance music.

Bonds, Hampton Street, Hockley. On a Saturday night Miss Moneypenny's features house and rare grooves for £7–10 admission with occasional visits from big-name DJs. Bus #74 from town.

The Dubliner, 57 Digbeth. Probably the best Irish bar of the many in the area, near the city's main coach station, with decent pub grub and live bands most nights.

Ronnie Scott's, 258 Broad Street. Centrally located live music venue, with jazz, blues and world music plus a separate tapas bar.

Restaurants

Centrally located places cater to the business crowd, but you can find good ethnic eateries in the Chinese quarter at the top of Hurst Street, and in the southern suburbs of Balsall Heath and Sparkhill, home of curry houses serving Balti – a tasty, cheap kashmiri stew, served with nan bread.

Calabash, 32–38 Coventry Road, Digbeth. Large West Indian restaurant near the coach station, with tropical décor and fine cocktails. Open Tue–Thur 7pm–10.30pm, Fri–Sat 7pm–11pm, and Sunday lunchtimes. Most major credit cards.

Celebrity Balti, 44 Broad Street. Centrally located Balti house near the International Convention Centre. A little pricy, but the food is great. Most major credit cards.

Leftbank, 79 Broad Street. Elegantly converted Victorian banking hall serving first-rate *nouvelle cuisine* at around £15 a head. Set menus at £10 and £12.50. The fish soup is particularly recommended. Open Mon–Sat until 10pm. Most major credit cards.

Maharaja, 23–25 Hurst Street. Incongruously located in Birmingham's Chinatown, near the Hippodrome, this place serves North Indian and Mughal cuisine in a cosy, agreeable atmosphere.

Main courses around £6–8. Most major credit cards.

San Carlo, 4 Temple Street. Near St Philip's Cathedral, this is a better bet than the branches of Italian chain restaurants in nearby New Street, if for no other reason than that it serves fresh produce cooked by real Italian chefs. Main courses £7–10. Most major credit cards.

Accommodation

The B&Bs and cheaper hotels are to be found two miles west of town along Hagley Road (buses #9, #19, #120, #126, #192, #193 and #292) and at Acocks Green, four miles south-east of the centre (buses #1, #11, #37 and #38). The International Convention Centre **tourist office** in Centenary Square offers cut-price weekend deals on business-class hotels.

Ashdale House Hotel, 39 Broad Road, Acocks Green (☎0121/707 2324, fax 0121/706 3598). Cosy place with TV in every room. Singles £20–25, doubles £32–38. Visa and Mastercard accepted.

Bridge House Hotel, 49 Sherbourne Road, Acocks Green (☎0121/706 5900, fax 0121/624 5900). Clean, comfortable B&B with a shower/bath and TV in each room. Single rooms £33, doubles £47, most major credit cards.

Kennedy Guest House, 38 York Road (☎0121/454 1284). Downbeat but comfortable B&B just off the Hagley Road stretch of similar establishments. Singles around £25–30, doubles £40–50, most major credit cards.

Robin Hood Lounge Hotel, 142 Robin Hood Lane, Hall Green (☎0121/778 5307, fax 0121/604 8686). Guesthouse five miles from the city centre. All rooms with a television, some with bath/shower. Singles at £25–30, doubles at £40–50. Most major credit cards.

Youth Hostel, Cambrian Hall, Brindley Drive (☎0121/233 3044). Single rooms with bath/shower, dorms with kitchen facilities. £10–12 per person, but only open July 12–Sep 17.

Manchester

Manchester United *135*
Manchester City *139*

While there is no doubt that the north-west is the stronghold of English football, the two major cities of the region, Manchester and Liverpool, continue to compete for the right to be the capital. After being overshadowed by Liverpool and Everton in the Seventies and Eighties, Manchester – or, more accurately, Manchester United – have dominated English football in the Nineties.

The wider Greater Manchester region, which as part of the old county of Lancashire was the engine behind the growth of professional football, is enjoying a boom. In 1996/97, all four of England's professional divisions were won by teams from the region. But while the area is packed with small-town sides scrapping for a piece of the pie, only the Manchester clubs have had the resources to succeed in the modern era of sky-high salaries and corporate sponsorship.

Both Manchester sides, City and United, have enjoyed periods of ascendancy since World War II. But in the Nineties their fates have been very different. United, under Alex Ferguson's coaching and Martin Edwards' business leadership, have re-emerged as the dominant club in the English game. Throughout their barren years in the Seventies and Eighties, they maintained a large support base which spread far beyond the boundaries of the city. Today no club in the country, and quite possibly the planet, matches them for marketing and commercial acumen. City, meanwhile, are struggling in the Nationwide League, their recent history scarred by boardroom acrimony, inept coaching and other man-made disasters.

In many senses the two clubs sum up the two sides to the city. United epitomise the industry and wealth which made Manchester the world's first industrial town. City, based in the Moss Side district, an area blighted with social problems, attract a young support which identifies with 'Madchester', the capital of the UK indie music scene, drugs culture and 'baggy' fashion.

The two clubs' souvenir shops reflect the dichotomy perfectly. United's *Megastore* sells mass-produced tack to visitors from all over the world. City's little hut sells designer gear modelled on the look and attitude of two of the club's current celebrity fans, the Gallagher brothers of Britpop band Oasis. Yet however much United's loyal support (much of which, contrary to opinion, does come from Manchester) feels embarrassed about the

Manchester essentials

Manchester's **airport** is the biggest in the UK outside London and lies 16km south of the city centre. Trains leave the airport every fifteen minutes (5.15am–10.10pm, with occasional service through the night) for **Piccadilly train station** in the centre of town. Journey time is around 25 minutes.

Most Intercity trains from around Britain also come into Piccadilly, but those from the north-east and some minor regional trains roll up at **Manchester Victoria**. The two stations are connected by the *Metrolink* – a **modern tramway** which has reduced the traffic congestion which once plagued the city. *Metrolink* runs from Bury, 16km north of the centre, to Altrincham 15km miles to the south. Tickets are purchased from automatic machines at stations, of which there are eight in the city centre. The main **bus station** for services to other cities is at Chorlton Street, close to Piccadilly.

The **tourist office** (open Mon & Sat 10am–5pm, Tue–Fri 9am–5pm) is at the town hall, in St Peter's Square. Best source for **listings** is *City Life* (fortnightly, £1.40).

crass commercialism, they know that the Japanese tourists buying *Red Devil* teddy bears are helping to pay for the stars their club are able to attract and, more importantly, keep and develop. And most of the City faithful, still turning out in impressive numbers even when their heroes have been at the wrong end of the first division, would happily trade some style for silverware.

The thrilling fields

 ## Manchester United

Old Trafford, Sir Matt Busby Way, Manchester
Capacity 55,300 (all-seated)
Colours Red shirts, white shorts
League champions 1908, 1911, 1952, 1956–57, 1965, 1967, 1993–94, 1996–97
Cup winners 1909, 1948, 1963, 1977, 1983, 1985, 1990, 1994, 1996
European Cup winners 1968
Cup-Winners' Cup winners 1991

The brand played on – unofficial United garb

As any Mancunian who has travelled will tell you, to the outside world, United *is* Manchester. How many pidgin English conversations have begun with the words 'Manchester United', quickly followed by the name 'Bobby Charlton'?

Which begs another question – why is the world so besotted with Manchester United? For a start, because they were the first English club to make an impression in Europe, with a talented, young Fifties side playing attractive, attacking football. When that side was tragically destroyed by the Munich air disaster, the sympathy of the world was with the club. And those sympathisers were delighted when, ten years later, United lifted the European Cup. They were the first English side to do so and won the hearts of uncommitted fans across the country, thanks in part to the presence of some of the brightest stars to illuminate modern English football – Bobby Charlton, George Best and Denis Law.

Like other European clubs with nationwide support, such as Bayern Munich and Juventus, United are also one of the most disliked clubs in the country. Every committed fan in the land recalls the kid in the playground who, rather than support his local team, wore a red-and-white shirt and dreamed of one day actually seeing a match at Old Trafford.

Founded as a railway workers' team, under the name Newton Heath Lancashire and Yorkshire Cricket and Football Club, in 1878, in their early years the club were rarely on a stable financial footing. Newton Heath joined the Football League in 1892 but went bankrupt ten years later, swiftly re-emerging as Manchester United – despite a strong lobby who preferred the name Manchester Celtic. Between the wars, United were firmly fixed in the shadows of a more popular and more successful Manchester City. Old Trafford was destroyed by bombing in World War II, and there were many who felt the club might not get off the ground in peacetime.

Simply the Best – Georgie before he became a Porgie

Bill Shankly wandered past the ground and saw the wreckage. "I thought that's it – this is the end," he recalled.

But United survived, playing their games at City's Maine Road for three seasons while Old Trafford was rebuilt. While at Maine Road they took on a former City and Liverpool right-half by the name of Matt Busby as manager. Just as his fellow Scot Shankly would do at Liverpool, Busby set about building a team that played modern football with style. Initially his personnel were pre-war players, including Jack Rowley, Stan Pearson and skipper Johnny Carey, who led United to the 1948 FA Cup and then the league title in 1952.

Off the field, however, Busby was setting up a matchless scouting system and youth scheme. As his side aged, he plugged the gaps with locally produced youngsters. The policy was so successful that between 1953 and 1957, United did not sign a single player from another club.

The young side which picked up two titles in 1956 and 1957 was dubbed the 'Busby Babes'. Among the many talented young players, the one who stood out was Duncan Edwards, who made his début for United aged just sixteen, and who went on to become the youngest man ever to play for England. Although he played most of his games in the centre of defence, Edwards was ahead of his time in that he could, and did, play in most positions on the park. With Edwards bossing the defence, Bobby Charlton at inside-left, Tommy Taylor at centre-forward and Eddie Coleman the playmaker in midfield, United became the first English team to enter the European Cup in 1956. The Football League was sceptical, but it was another sign of Busby's vision that he saw the importance of European competition and pressured the FA into backing United's adventure 'abroad'. In the first game, Belgian champions Anderlecht were crushed 10–0 in Manchester, then Borsussia Dortmund and Athletic Bilbao were disposed of, before United were stopped by Real Madrid.

United's second European campaign ended in tragedy. Following a quarter-final, second-leg draw in Belgrade against Red Star, the team plane crashed after attempting to take off from Munich airport. Among the dead were eight United players – Edwards (who fought for his life for fifteen days), Taylor, Coleman, Roger Byrne, David Pegg, Mark Jones, Geoff Bent and Billy Whelan. To this day the clock outside the club offices at Old Trafford remains set at 3.04 – the time the plane crashed.

Busby survived to begin the whole process again, but it was four years before the new United took shape. The new side, which won the FA Cup in 1963 and the title two years later, still featured Bobby Charlton, but by then Busby had switched him to a more central rôle. Charlton's place on the left flank was filled by a young Irishman, George Best, who acted as the provider for Denis Law, a former Manchester City striker who had been brought back from a miserable year with Torino for a British record fee of £115,000.

In the European Cup quarter-final of 1966, United defeated Benfica 5–1 in the

Stadium of Light, but went out to Partizan Belgrade in the semi-finals.

United won another title in 1966/67, when they remained unbeaten at home, and this time there was no stopping them 'abroad'. After coming back from 3–1 down in the last twenty minutes at Real Madrid in the semis, United faced Benfica again, this time in front of 100,000 at Wembley. The game stood at 1–1 and had gone into extra-time when 'keeper Alex Stepney sent an aimless punt upfield and Best ran on to it, danced through, and slotted the ball past Henrique. Young forward Brian Kidd and Charlton then struck twice within six minutes – and ten years after Munich, United had become the first English team to win the European Cup.

A year later Busby moved 'upstairs' to become general manager, but his successors, Wilf McGuiness and Frank O'Farrell, could not sustain the momentum. Charlton retired, Best went to seed, Law went back to City. United were relegated in 1974, their final nail a backheeled goal from Law in the Manchester derby. (Law was devastated and was substituted immediately, but as other results came through he was slightly comforted by the knowledge that United would have gone down anyway, even without his goal.)

United bounced back to the top flight straight away, but for the next two decades they would rarely look like championship material. Tommy Docherty's brash mid-Seventies youngsters, with Lou Macari upfront and Steve Coppell on the wing, were FA Cup specialists. So were Ron Atkinson's dynamic Eighties side, with England skipper Bryan Robson in midfield, the diminutive Scot Gordon Strachan alongside him and the peerless Irishman Paul McGrath in the centre of defence. In between, former Chelsea manager Dave Sexton kept "feeling good about the future" but never delivered jam today.

In 1986, when nearly twenty years had elapsed since United's last title, the club turned to a winner, and another Scot, Alex Ferguson. He had led Aberdeen to the European Cup-Winners' Cup in 1983 and, although his job appeared to be on the line on several occasions, his gritty determination finally brought the results United chairman Martin Edwards demanded. In 1990 the team won the FA Cup, and the following season defeated Barcelona to win the Cup-Winners' Cup – England's first European honour since Heysel.

The prize Old Trafford wanted more than any was the championship, and Ferguson duly delivered it in 1992/93, after making what one critic called "the deal of the decade" to buy Eric Cantona for a pittance from holders Leeds.

Cantona's United did the double in 1994, missed out by a point to Blackburn a year later, then became the first English team to win the double twice in 1996.

Like Busby before him, Ferguson has pinned great faith in youth. The results have been stunning to watch, but they have also made United less dependent on big-money transfers than their rivals. With Welsh winger Ryan Giggs, David Beckham, the Neville brothers, Paul Scholes and Nicky Butt all coming through the ranks to take their place in the Theatre of Dreams, who needs Brazilians and Italians?

All that remains now is for United to claim Europe's top prize – an immensely more difficult task than it was in 1968, but not something that seems beyond the club in its majestic, modern incarnation.

Here we go!

Take the *Metrolink* **tram** heading for Altrincham from any city-centre station. Get off at **Old Trafford** and walk down Warwick Road, past the Lancashire cricket ground, and keep heading straight on until you reach Sir Matt Busby Way and the stadium. Your *Metrolink* ticket costs £1.30 return.

Swift half

There are a couple of pubs by the crossroads of Chester Road and Warwick Road which you will pass on your way from the tram station. **The Trafford** is packed out on matchdays, but further down Chester

Road, the **Gorse Hill Hotel** is actually a decent traditional pub with a big-screen TV which attracts those unable to strike a deal with the touts outside the ground. Another option is to get off the *Metrolink* a stop earlier at Trafford Bar – facing you as you leave the station is the **Tollgate Inn** on Seymour Road, where you may actually get served and still meet up with some Old Trafford regulars.

At the ground itself is the **Red Café** in the North Stand which, like the stadium, is booked up in advance for all games. You'll get in during the week (the Café is open 12 noon–11pm daily), but don't bother unless you're turned on by the idea of eating burgers while surrounded by videos of Bryan Robson injuring himself.

Tickets

With more than 130,000 members, United could fill a stadium twice the size of Old Trafford for most major games. Season-ticket holders take up most of the seats and spare tickets are rare. In the circum-stances, visiting neutrals are best placed in the away fans' section, but there are only 3000 seats and advance booking is essential. Call the ticket office direct on ☎0161/872 0199.

Club shop

The large **Superstore** at the corner of the East and South Stands and the even bigger **Megastore** behind the Stretford End (now officially renamed the West End) sell everything from the very latest yellow/green/blue/white/grey away shirt to United all-over body spray. Prices are high, but there was a big sale of Cantona products when the great man hung up his boots in the summer of 1997. Both shops are open Mon–Sat 9am–5pm, Sun 10am–4pm.

Club museum

The excellent Manchester United Museum is behind the East Stand and incorporates the trophy cabinet and a small theatre where you can watch films of games past. £2.95 gets you past the door.

Ooh-aah – Fergie, Sir Matt and the Cup-Winners' Cup

Publications

United Review (£1.50) is the matchday programme, notable for a great cover based on the original Sixties design. The official monthly magazine is *United* (£1.95); the most entertaining page is the letters section with its unedited contributions from 14-year-old Malaysians – "when I cannot doing my mathematics homework, I look up at my United posters and the problem is solved." Of the fanzines, *Red News* and *United We Stand* (both £1) are a refreshing antidote to the marketing hype.

Ultra culture

The Stretford End is no more than another feature in United's museum but, as the Champions' League campaign of 1996/97 showed, Old Trafford can still create atmosphere. The East Stand makes plenty of noise and the West (still the Stretford End to most) is competing hard. United fans have played a major part in the revival of the English football song – the *Marseilleaise* was popular during the Cantona era, as was the Gap Band 'Ooh-Ah!' chant since adopted across the country but originally used here, for defender Paul McGrath.

In the net

The official United site is run by Sky Sports at: www.sky.co.uk/sports/manu. There are a few titbits of news and chat, but the site's target audience is kids – hence the amount of fairly inconsequential multi-media content. For a bit more substance, head for Jørgen Trankjær's unofficial Danish site at: home4.inet.tele.dk/trankjar/united.

 **Manchester City**

Maine Road, Moss Side, Manchester
Capacity 32,000
Colours Sky-blue shirts, white shorts
League champions 1937, 1968
Cup winners 1904, 1934, 1956, 1969
Cup-Winners' Cup winners 1970

An Atlético Madrid, Torino or Munich 1860 fan would understand. Life is hard when your team are constantly in the shadows of more successful city rivals. It gets harder still when the media begin to talk as if there is only one club in town. And as for your heroes being relegated in the same season as 'that lot' are doing the double, well...

At least, when United were drawing all the accolades in the Sixties, City were able to spoil the party by winning some silverware of their own. This time around, United's glory has coincided with the worst spell in City's history. A lethal cocktail of boardroom disputes and embarrassing managerial musical chairs culminated in the despair of relegation from the Premiership in 1996. City became the laughing stock of English football, and it hurt.

But visit Maine Road and you'll find an impressive stadium, a loyal, knowledgeable

crowd, and a resilient sense of humour. There may be plenty of people laughing at City, but down at Maine Road, they can take a joke.

The club certainly have history on their side. City were the first team from Manchester to win the FA Cup when they beat Bolton Wanderers in 1904. They spent part of the Twenties in the second division, won the Cup again in 1934 and the title in 1937, then got themselves relegated just prior to the outbreak of World War II.

In the Fifties, City manager Les McDowall based his team's tactics on those of the great Hungarian side of the era, with Don Revie, later to become a successful manager with Leeds, playing the deep-lying centre-forward's rôle of Nandor Hidegkuti. Just as England couldn't understand what Hidegkuti was doing inside his own half at Wembley in 1953, so English sides couldn't work out why Revie, with a #9 on his back, was wandering deep into midfield.

In 1956 the strategy brought City an FA Cup final win over Birmingham – though the game is better remembered for the part played by City's goalkeeper, Bert Trautmann. Trautmann, popular with local fans despite having fought for Germany in the war, discovered after the game that he had played the final minutes with a broken neck.

A fallow decade then followed until 1965, when City appointed Joe Mercer as manager and Malcolm Allison as his assistant. Within a year they had built a completely new team around winger Mike Summerbee (whose son Nicky was to play for City thirty years later), midfielder Colin Bell and striker Francis Lee. In 1968, just two years after winning back their first-division status, City won the title. The campaign ended in dramatic style. City were being chased to the wire by United and needed to win their last game away to Newcastle – they just managed it, 4–3, with two goals from striker Neil Young. With United winning the European Cup that season, City fans boasted that their idols were not only English champions but *de facto* the best team in Europe.

A year later City beat Leicester 1–0 in the FA Cup final, but it gave the club a crack at Europe in the Cup-Winners' Cup the following season. City seized their moment, beating Athletic Bilbao and Schalke 04 on the way to the final against Górnik Zabrze of Poland in Vienna. City won, more easily than the 2–1 scoreline suggests, with goals from their on-song strike pairing of Lee and Young.

It looked as though City would win another title in 1972. But in March of that year, with the team sitting pretty at the top of the table, Allison persuaded Mercer to sign Rodney Marsh from QPR. Mercer's team had succeeded by playing simple, fluid, passing football. Now Marsh, a fancy-dan crowd pleaser, typical of the period, disrupted the rhythm of the side. In the end, City didn't even make the top three.

Mercer left that summer and Allison took charge for part of the next season. There were two other managers before former player Tony Book took charge in 1974 and led the side to a League Cup win over Newcastle, memorable only for Denis Tueart's unlikely bicycle-kick goal. Under Book, City were prospering. But at the end of the Seventies, the decline set in.

Allison returned as manager in 1979, in a strange arrangement whereby he shared coaching duties with Book. The idea was that of City chairman Peter Swales, a wealthy local businessman who'd decided City needed a dose of glamour if they were to progress. Swales had money to spend and Allison certainly spent it – his £1.5 million purchase of the uncapped Steve Daley from Wolves is still rated by many as the worst piece of transfer business in English football history. At the same time, Allison sold two of City's best young players – midfielder Gary Owen and the talented England international winger Peter Barnes.

Allison was fired in 1980, but City's long-running comedy act was only just getting into its stride. Tommy Hutchison scored for both teams when City drew 1–1 with Tottenham in the 1981 FA Cup final – and the Londoners went on to win the replay. In 1983 City were seven minutes from first-division safety when they allowed Luton's Yugoslav super-sub, Raddy Antić, to score from outside the box. They spent two separate spells in the second division before Howard Kendall dragged them up by their boot-straps at the end of the Eighties – but the club then let Kendall go back to his beloved Everton.

When Francis Lee finally rode in on a white horse to oust the hated Swales in 1995, he brought in an old friend, Alan Ball, as manager. Ball, a member of England's 1966 World Cup-winning side had a poor track record as a manager, and sure enough, despite the presence of Georgian midfielder Georgi Kinklazde and German striker Uwe Rösler, City were relegated on the last game of the 1995/96 season.

There is a theory that says the Premiership is heading in the direction of American sports, with major cities having only one 'franchise' – and the recent problems at Maine Road (and Everton) seem to support that view. City are surely too big a club to suffer such a fate. Chairman Lee is considering a move to the new Manchester stadium being built for the Commonwealth Games in 2002, and if his money runs out before then, there's always Liam Gallagher. First, though, City need to win promotion – and fast.

Here We Go

Bus #99 from Piccadilly stops on Lloyd Street, about five minutes' walk from the ground.

Swift half

One of the most popular pre-match spots is **The Claremont** at 112 Claremont Road. It's a spartan bar, full of fans on matchdays, but can be a bit rough during the week. The **Sherwood Inn** at #417 on the same street is smarter.

Tickets

Although City have maintained high levels of support outside the Premiership, getting tickets is not a problem at Maine Road.

The **ticket office** at the ground is open prior to games and during the week, 10am–4pm. The club's ticket information number is: ☎0161/226 2224.

Club shop

The **hippest club shop** in England is on the corner of Maine Road and Claremont Road, by the Supporters' Club building, and is open Mon–Sat 9.30pm–5.00pm, later for midweek home games. The **Soccer Shop** opposite sells unofficial gear including the controversial 'Uwe's Dad Bombed Old Trafford' T- shirts.

'And he's taking them all on' – Kinkladze gets in the derby mood

Publications

The matchday programme (£1.70) is not a bad read, which is more than can be said of the official monthly magazine, *City* (£1.95). Heavy sarcasm and anti-United gags are the stock in trade of the fanzines *King of the Kippax* and *Bert Trautmann's Helmet*.

Ultra culture

Blue Moon may have given way to *Wonderwall* but nobody sings – or laughs – like the **lads on the Kippax**.

City's travelling support is, if anything, even sillier. Once a fairly rough contingent with a reputation for trouble, they invented the Eighties fad for inflatables with their rubber bananas, and remain innovative – how many other sets of fans would react to a drubbing at Grimsby by doing the conga?

In the net

City's official homepage comes replete with Oasis-style signage and ambitious – if not always successful – graphics. Content-wise it's hard to fault, so go straight to: www.mcfc.co.uk. For a peek into the weird world of being a City fan, try the *Blue View* email message centre at: homepages.enterprise.net/dbennett.blueview.html.

Eat, drink, sleep…

Bars and clubs

Manchester nightlife is among the best in the UK. The **music clubs** pride themselves on being at the cutting edge and as well as traditional **pubs**, the city also boasts many **café-bars** that are packed out at weekends. The scene is rapidly changing – listed here are some of the more established venues.

Barça, Catalan Square, Arches 8–9. Owned by Simply Red frontman Mick Hucknall, this spacious café bar has a terrace overlooking a Spanish-style plaza. Look out for David Beckham and Posh Spice among the clientèle.

J W Johnson's, 78 Deansgate. Flashy cocktail bar with a wide range of bottled beers for those who don't fancy a *Multiple Screaming Orgasm*. Operates as a tea and coffee bar during the day.

Sankey's Soap, Beehive Mill, Jersey Street. Dance club with techno on Friday nights and more mainstream sounds on Saturdays; the latter are smart dress only.

The Haçienda, 11–13 Whitworth Street West. Like many of Manchester's venues, the Haçienda was created out of unlikely premises – in this case an old yacht showroom. Once home to New Order and the Factory Records crowd, it struggled in the early Nineties before returning to form as a top dance venue.

The Old Wellington Inn, Shambles Square. The oldest pub in Manchester opened in 1378 and has been serving up fine pints of bitter ever since. Very central.

Restaurants

Manchester is the best English city outside London for tasting **ethnic food**. Chinatown is in the centre of the city close to Piccadilly, while the Rusholme district is packed with curry houses, as is Wilmslow Road, close to the Manchester City ground – the latter area is cheaper.

Armenian Tavern, 3–5 Princess Street. Albert Square. Famed for its lavish banquets and its *baklava*, this place also does set menu dishes for a very reasonable £5. With a bit of luck you might even bump into an Ararat Yerevan fan.

Café Istanbul, 79–81 Bridge Street. Extremely popular, well-established Turkish restaurant which for more than seventeen years has been proving that Hakan Sükür lives on much more than kebabs. Genuine Turkish breads and terrific fresh salads.

Henry J Bean's, 42 Blackfrairs Street. Busy with office workers getting tucked into Tex-Mex nosh at lunchtime, and taking advantage of happy hour on cocktails in the evening (5.30–8pm). Chilli, steaks, spare ribs and burgers.

Jewel in the Crown, 109 Wilmslow Road. Unlike many of the Indians in the area, this one is licensed and has a small bar. The Lamb Raan is highly recommended.

Prague Five, 40 Chorlton Street. Wide selection of European beers, with the emphasis on those preferred by Sparta and Slavia fans. The broad menu features interpretations of classic Central European dishes.

Accommodation

Like many English cities, Manchester has plenty of accommodation for business people and any number of cheap B&Bs, but not much in between.

Burton Arms Hotel, 31 Swan Street (☎0161/834 3455). A traditional B&B above a pub. Close to the city centre but with only eight rooms, you should definitely call in advance.

The Crown Inn, 321 Deansgate (☎0161/834 1930). Very central B&B accommodation above a traditional pub.

Gardens Hotel, 55 Piccadilly (☎0161/236 5155). Right on Piccadilly Gardens, doesn't suffer too much from the noise. This accommodating three-star place has a bathroom and TV in each room.

YHA Manchester, Potato Warf, Castlefield (☎0161/839 9960). Youth hostel with singles, two-, four- and six-bedded rooms, all en suite. Full catering, 24-hour access, optional breakfast.

Style file – the king on the catwalk

Liverpool

Liverpool *143*
Everton *146*

Liverpudlians are a proud lot. No other city in England matches Merseyside for local patriotism. And though the city has faced some of the worst social and economic problems over the past two decades, it has also had much to be proud of in the record of its two football teams, Liverpool and Everton.

Yet, curiously, neither club has had much to shout about in the Nineties, save for the odd victory in cup competitions. And in any case, football on Merseyside is recovering from more than just a slump in form. Heysel and Hillsborough had reverberations far beyond Anfield Road, but the feelings remain strongest among those directly affected by the tragedies.

As a city, Liverpool offers little for the tourist. Sure, there's the Beatles Museum, and the Albert Dock by the River Mersey has been spruced up to offer a façade of modernity and affluence, but beneath the surface Liverpool remains a city with plenty of problems, not least crime.

Catch an older scouser in a good mood in a pub, however, get him talking about football, and you're in for a good night. This is a city whose supporters have seen the best in Europe – and seen their own boys reign supreme over them.

All it wants now is for the good old days, like the Beatles, to come rolling back.

The thrilling fields

Liverpool

Anfield Stadium, Anfield Road, Liverpool
Capacity 41,500 (all-seated)
Colours All red
League champions 1901, 1906, 1922–23, 1947, 1964, 1966, 1973, 1976–77, 1979, 1980, 1982–84, 1986, 1988, 1990
Cup winners 1965, 1974, 1986, 1989, 1992
European Cup winners 1977, 1978, 1981, 1984
UEFA Cup winners 1973, 1976

No club in England has ever been able to sustain domestic success for such a long period as Liverpool. And no club in England has a better record in European football.

Ever since Bill Shankly took over the reins at Anfield in 1959, Liverpool have been an example of all that is best about British football. The sides managed by Shankly, Paisley, Fagan and Dalglish may have contained fewer stars than many of their rivals, but they all played by the Liverpool passing method, as taught by the legendary 'bootroom' where coaching staff met to discuss selection and tactics.

Liverpool essentials

Liverpool's airport at Speke is chronically under-used and served by few flights, international or domestic. You will probably arrive by train, at **Lime Street station,** which is in the centre of the city. Buses and coaches pull into the station on **Islington Street,** close by. All local public transport is provided by **buses** – the main service runs until around 11.30pm, with a limited night service on some routes after that. For the latest on **fares** and other information, call the 24-hour enquiry service on: ☎0151/708 8838.

There are two major sources for **tourist information.** The *Merseyside Welcome Centre* at the Clayton Square Shopping Centre (open Mon–Sat 9.30am–5.30pm) and the *Tourist Information Centre* in the Atlantic Pavilion at the Albert Dock complex (open daily 10.00am–5.30pm).

The club were founded by John Houlding, the owner of the Anfield ground. Prior to 1892, Everton had been the only professional club in the city and had played at Houlding's ground. But the landlord fell out with his tenants and set up his own team, originally under the name of Everton; on March 15, 1892 he changed the club's name to Liverpool and the team won admission to the League the next year. The club won two titles before World War II and two more between the wars.

In the first post-war championship, Liverpool won the title by a single point from Manchester United. The star of the side was Scottish striker Billy Liddell, but high expectations for the coming decade were not realised, and in 1954 the club were relegated. They spent eight years in the second division, before Bill Shankly's young team climbed back to the top flight in 1962.

Shankly had an astute grasp of the psychology of sport, imbuing his side with a self-confidence that became the hallmark of Liverpool sides down the years. The sign "this is Anfield" that greets players as they go down the tunnel to the field is a symbol of the man's method and his scouse arrogance – though Shankly, like Matt Busby up the road at Old Trafford, was a Scotsman.

Within two years of taking the club back to the first division, Shankly had delivered the title. The next season Liverpool won the FA Cup and in 1966 they won the league again and made it to the final of the Cup-Winners' Cup, which they lost to Borussia Dortmund. Shankly's side included a strike partnership of England's Roger Hunt and Scottish international Ian St John. Ron Yeats was the hard man in defence and young Ian Callaghan was the creator in midfield.

By 1973, Shankly's boys of the Sixties had obviously aged, but the new generation were, if anything, even hungrier for success, particularly in Europe. In the UEFA Cup that season, they defeated AEK Athens, Dynamo Berlin and Tottenham to set up a final with Borussia Mönchengladbach. Liverpool won the first leg 3–0 with two goals from Kevin Keegan. In the second leg the Germans led 2–0 at half-time but the Reds hung on to claim their first European honour.

Shankly retired a year later, confident that his new side was capable of going on to greater things under his replacement, and former assistant, Bob Paisley. The optimism was well-placed. In Paisley's nine years in charge Liverpool won six league titles, three European Cups and one UEFA Cup. Like his predecessor, Paisley had an exceptional eye for young talent. Some came through the ranks of the youth system, but many were bought. However, Liverpool rarely bought established players from rival clubs, preferring to bring in promising youngsters from lower down the ladder. Keegan and goalkeeper Ray Clemence came from lowly Scunthorpe United, while classy Scottish centre-half Alan Hansen was spotted at Partick Thistle.

When Keegan left for Hamburg in 1977 (after Liverpool had again beaten Mönchengladbach to win their first European Cup), Paisley brought in Kenny Dalglish to wear Keegan's #7 shirt. Dalglish was the perfect replacement – an effortless edge-of-the-box predator who crowned his first season by scoring the only goal of the European Cup final against Club Bruges at Wembley.

Paisley retired in 1983, and two years later Dalglish took over as player-manager. In his first season in charge, Liverpool did the double. Dalglish's sides were perhaps the most exciting of all the Liverpool championship teams. Ian Rush was the goalgetter, Peter Beardsley his impish, irrepressible assistant, John Barnes the flamboyant provider from the wing.

But while on the field Liverpool were enjoying the final years of their incredible run of success, away from the action the club had been shaken by two tragedies – Heysel and Hillsborough. The first was the result of hooliganism at the 1985 European Cup final against Juventus, which left 38 dead and 454 injured when a wall collapsed after a charge by Liverpool fans – fourteen of whom were later sent to prison by a Belgian court.

On April 15, 1989, 95 Liverpool fans died and 170 were injured at an FA Cup semi-final against Nottingham Forest at Sheffield Wednesday's Hillsborough stadium. Prior to the game, a gate was opened admitting Liverpool supporters into the packed Leppings Lane end of the ground. Supporters at the front of the enclosure were suffocated in the crush. In the days following the tragedy, Anfield was covered in scarves and floral tributes, among the most poignant of which was a wreath from Juventus. Players and club officials attended the funerals of the victims, and the city closed ranks.

Fighting for the right – Souness and Bonhof, 1977

It was perhaps the stress resulting from those tragedies that led Dalglish to quit in 1991. He was replaced by his former team-mate Graeme Souness, whose only achievement in a disappointing three years in charge was an FA Cup win in 1992. Souness left the club with a host of expensive players who were failing to live up to Anfield's expectations, and the club returned to the bootroom in search of stability, appointing Roy Evans as manager.

Evans put the emphasis back on youth, bringing in Steve McManaman, Robbie Fowler and Jamie Redknapp. While their consistency and commitment have been questioned, at their best the new Liverpool are at least reminiscent of the Anfield sides of old. The football is back on track – now it's time for some silverware.

Here we go

From Lime Street train station take **bus #17, #26, #27** or **#217** to **Anfield Road**. Allow twenty minutes.

Swift half

The Arkles at 27 Anfield Road is the most popular of the many pubs in the area around the ground. It's busy both before and after the game – when fans crowd in to check out the day's other results on the big-screen TV.

Tickets

Anfield has always been tricky to get into, and since the demolition of the Kop reduced the capacity of the ground, it has become even tougher. Big games will be sold out in advance, but for other games, the **booking line** is: ☎0151/260 8680. Visiting supporters are normally allocated an area of the Anfield Road Stand.

Club shop

There is a shop by the **Shankly Gates** at the corner of the Anfield Road Stand and the Main Stand, and another behind the Kop. Both are weekdays 10am–4.30pm, and on matchdays.

Publications

The **matchday programme** (£1.50) is regarded as one of the best in the Premiership. Liverpool publish a wide range of official magazines, from kids' posters to quality monthlies, while the major fanzines are *When Sunday Comes, All Day and All of the Night* and *Red All Over The Land*.

Ultra culture

The Kop, a "seething mass of humanity", as one critic described it, is no more and Anfield's atmosphere has suffered as a result. Gone is the surge of fans, running

What a strike – Fowler backs the dockers

 Everton

Goodison Park, Goodison Road, Liverpool
Capacity 40,500
Colours Royal blue shirts, white shorts
League champions 1891, 1915, 1928, 1932, 1939, 1963, 1970, 1985, 1987
Cup winners 1906, 1933, 1966, 1984, 1995
Cup-Winners' Cup winners 1985

Everton were the first professional club in Liverpool and were founder members of the Football League. In 1892, after a rent row with the landlord of their Anfield Road ground, they moved across Stanley Park to Goodison Road, their home ever since.

Around the corner from the stadium in those early days was a sweet shop whose owner used to promote his wares by throwing toffees to the crowd before the game – hence the club picked up their nickname, 'The Toffeemen'. The sweet shop has long since gone but the tradition of throwing toffees remains. There is even a black-and-white sweet known as an 'Everton mint', whose origins date back to the days when the side wore black shirts with a white sash and were known as the 'Black Watch'.

It was in those colours that Everton won their first title in 1891. The team switched to royal blue and white ten years later, and in 1905 they won the FA Cup. Another league title was added in 1914, but World War I put paid to hopes of a prolonged spell of success.

In 1925, the club signed William Ralph Dean from their near neighbours Tranmere Rovers. 'Dixie' Dean, as he quickly became known, scored sixty league goals in the 1927/28 season as Everton won the championship. His record still stands today and is unlikely ever to be beaten.

Although Everton were relegated in 1930, they bounced back swiftly, winning the second-division title in 1931 and taking the championship in their first season back. Another title was added in 1939, with a new star in the #9 shirt – Tommy Lawton. Although only nineteen, Lawton was an

down the terraces after each goal or near miss. Gone is the mass choir that turned Merseybeat hits like *You'll Never Walk Alone* into world-famous football anthems.

On the plus side, a trip to Anfield is no longer something for away supporters to lose sleep over – violence around the stadium is rare and Liverpool's travelling supporters, once among the worst-behaved in the country are angels compared to their predecessors.

In the net

The official Liverpool site is currently under construction. Until it surfaces, try the excellent unofficial homepage that resides at: anfield.merseyworld.com. In addition to the usual news and stats, the site has a welcome campaigning edge with its *Justice For The 96* (Hillsborough victims) area. You can also buy bits of stone from the old Kop – all proceeds to charity, naturally.

England international who had been signed from Burnley. When he arrived at Lime Street station, Dean was there to greet him and make a symbolic handover of power. But Lawton's hopes – and those of Everton – were again to be dashed by gunfire. After the end of World War II, neither Lawton nor Everton would enjoy the same level of success. In fact, it was to be more than a decade before Everton were challenging for top honours again.

In 1961, Harry Catterick began a twelve-year stint in the Goodison dugout. In 1963 Everton won the championship with a side inspired by Scottish midfielder Alex Young, who Catterick labelled 'The Golden Vision'. After Everton won the FA Cup and England the World Cup in 1966, Catterick bought England's young midfielder Alan Ball and teamed him up with Colin Harvey and Howard Kendall in the centre of the park; from there they provided the ammunition for striker Joe Royle. Another FA Cup win followed in 1968 and the league was won with style in 1970.

It was Kendall who was behind Everton's next spell of success, taking over as manager at the start of the Eighties, and winning the Cup for Goodison in 1984, when the Scottish strike pair of Graeme Sharp and Andy Gray were on the mark in a 2–0 win over Watford at Wembley.

Both men were to play a key rôle in Everton's success the following season, when the Blues won the title by a massive thirteen points and also gained the first European honour in the club's history. After knocking out Inter Bratislava, Fortuna Sittard and Bayern Munich, Everton defeated Rapid Vienna 3–1 in Rotterdam to clinch the Cup-Winners' Cup.

There was no weak point in the side, which played fast, passing football married with aggression. Welsh international 'keeper Neville Southall had the sound central defensive partnership of Kevin Ratcliffe and Derek Mountfield in front of him. Peter Reid, a bargain buy from Bolton, was a true general in the centre of the park, feeding

Irishman Kevin Sheedy on the left flank and Trevor Steven on the right. But the team was not infallible. Three days after winning in Europe, they faced Manchester United in the FA Cup final with a unique treble in their sights – and lost 1–0.

With cash rolling in, the club signed Gary Lineker from Leicester City for the next season. Although few complained about the quality of the football, it was a painful year for Evertonians, as Liverpool pipped them by two points to the title, then defeated them 3–1 in the first all-Merseyside FA Cup final. Still, another title followed in 1987, before Kendall stunned the club by leaving for Athletic Bilbao.

Kendall's assistant Colin Harvey took over, and in 1989, in the emotional aftermath of Hillsborough, the side lost another FA Cup final to Liverpool, 3–2.

Rearguard reinforcement – new boy Bilić

Kendall returned in 1990 but his second spell in charge was trophyless. He was succeeded by Mike Walker, who spent a fortune in vain. Joe Royle took over in November 1994, and at the end of that season Everton beat Manchester United 1–0 in the FA Cup final.

Royle resigned in March 1997, paving the way for a second return by his former team-mate Kendall. In the close season club chairman Peter Johnson offered fans a referendum on whether to leave Goodison and move to a new 60,000 all-seater stadium. To the surprise of many, the fans voted for the move.

But while they might be happy to say goodbye to the old ground, whose tight location made it difficult to renovate, the faithful at the Gwladys Street end want more than a state-of-the-art stadium.

Home end – Goodison may soon shut for good

Here we go!

Take **bus #F9** or **#19** from Sir Thomas Street, close to Lime Street train station. Get off at Walton Lane, then just stroll down Goodison Road.

Swift half

You've plenty of choice. The **Winslow Hotel** at 31 Goodison Road is the nearest pub to the ground, straight across from the main stand, but a better bet is **The Abbey**, which is popular with away supporters as well as the locals.

Tickets

With the exception of games against Liverpool and Manchester United, getting a ticket at Goodison should not cause too many headaches. Credit-card **bookings** can be made on: ☎0151/525 1231.

Publications

As well as the fairly predictable **match-day programme**, there are two well-established fanzines, *Gwladys Sings The Blues* (£0.80) and *When Skies Are Grey* (£1).

Ultra culture

Goodison is a tight ground whose Main Stand leans so close over the edge of the pitch that, before the days of fences, goalscorers were in danger of disappearing into it in mid-celebration.

The **Gwladys Street boys** never were a match for the Kop in the singing department, but this crowd is as passionate and as fiercely partisan as any in England – and the hecklers will have you in stitches with their one-liners.

In the net

There is no official site either current or planned, and several unofficial homepages have recently closed their doors. Luckily, Robert Newton keeps the royal-blue flag flying with *Bluenet* at: www.geocities. com/Colosseum/1268.efc.html. It's a very comprehensive site – and Everton addicts get the chance to join a separate *ToffeeNet WebRing* news group.

Eat, drink, sleep…

Bars and clubs

Liverpool may no longer be the epicentre of British pop, but it boasts some of the top **dance clubs** in the north and the city centre has a fine mix of traditional pubs and newer café-bars.

Baa Bar, 43–45 Fleet Street. Close to Cream (see below) in the Palace complex, this designer bar attracts a hip pre-club crowd. Reduced prices in the day, resident DJs in the evening.

Cavern Pub, Matthew Street. Although most locals are sick of Beatles exploitation, tourists enjoy this theme pub crammed with photos of the Fab Four and the lesser-known Merseybeat bands. Next door is a re-creation of the Cavern Club where Lennon and McCartney débuted.

Cream, Wolstenholme Square. The best of the Mersey club scene, this huge venue attracts bus-loads of ravers from across the UK. The three separate dance areas can pack in over 2000 guests. Top UK and European DJs perform here regularly. Dress is informal but the doormen can be selective and will not admit anyone in trainers.

The Philharmonic Dining Rooms, Hope Street. Don't be put off by the name – this is a genuine Victorian-era pub with all the trappings. Wide range of cask ales and bottled beers.

Restaurants

The **Albert Dock** shopping area has plenty of eateries including Italian, French, German and Indonesian and most of the city-centre pubs serve snacks or bar meals. Liverpool had a Chinese community long before most of the UK and this is reflected in a wide choice of **Chinese restaurants** and take-aways.

El Macho, 23 Hope Street. In one of the better eating and drinking areas of the city, this is a quality Mexican restaurant serving all the favourites, plus one or two more unusual items.

Everyman Bistro, 9–11 Hope Street. Popular with students from the nearby University, the Everyman offers a broad range of dishes at very reasonable prices, including hearty soups and tasty stews.

Mayflower, 48 Duke Street. Broad-ranging menu featuring Cantonese, Peking, seafood and vegetarian dishes. Busy, central and mid-priced.

Harry Ramsden's, Brunswick Way, Sefton Street. After starting life in Yorkshire, Ramsden's chain of fish-and-chip restaurants are all over the UK now. The idea is that the traditional English meal need not be served in newspaper and eaten while sitting on a park bench. In typical Yorkshire fashion, however, there is only one thing on the menu and you'll eat that, lad!

Accommodation

Liverpool is not geared up to house vast numbers of tourists but, like all ports, has a history of accommodating a large transient population. The result is a high concentration of **cheap B&Bs** and budget hotels, of admittedly variable quality. If you're turning up on spec, both **tourist offices** (see p.143) will book a room for you without charging commission.

Aachen, 89–91 Mount Pleasant (☎0151/709 3477). Small hotel with rooms in the £25–35 range. Centrally located, and with an eat-as-much-as-you-like breakfast.

Britannia Adelphi, Raneleigh Place (☎0151/709 7200). A famous hotel in the centre of the city with rooms in the £35–70 range. Full comfort at reasonable prices.

Feathers, 117–125 Mount Pleasant (☎0151/709 9655). In a street full of B&Bs and small hotels, *Feathers* has double rooms from £35 and a bar and restaurant. Excellent value, central location.

YMCA, 56 Mount Pleasant (☎0151/709 9516). The most central of the city's youth hostels and up to the usual YMCA standards of cleanliness. Dormitory beds from £12.50 a night.

Geordie heaven – Newcastle's Nineties renaissance

No region in England has produced as many top players as **the north-east**. Almost every school and boys' club in the area has a famous son who has gone on to play for his country and coach at the highest level – the Charlton brothers, Bryan Robson, Bobby Robson and so on.

St James' joy – Newcastle fans hail another goal

Yet until five years ago the area lacked a club capable of taking the modern game by the horns. Now its biggest club, **Newcastle United**, are enjoying an unprecedented renaissance, sparked by the commercial know-how of chairman Sir John Hall and the motivational skills of former manager Kevin Keegan.

If ever there were a club ripe for a multi-millionaire to take over, Newcastle were it. Forget the smaller teams who had no chance once the maximum wage was abolished. Here was a city with a **massive pool of support**, a great tradition of producing quality footballers – but a team that hadn't won a title since 1927. When Hall took over the club in 1991, Newcastle were struggling in the second division and seemed to have a better-than-evens chance of dropping into the third. Hall and Keegan didn't just save the club from the scrapheap – they propelled Newcastle into Europe and created one of the new generation of **Premiership super-teams**.

Once Keegan had saved a young Newcastle side from oblivion, he set about steering them back into the top flight in 1993. Even from there it seemed there was a huge chasm between the Magpies and the Premiership élite, but Hall's re-constituted board provided the cash for the manager to go shopping – bringing the likes of David Ginola, Philippe Albert, Les Ferdinand and Tino Asprilla to the club. In 1995/96 Newcastle **led the Premiership table** for most of the season, but a loss of concentration in the run-in gifted the title to Manchester United.

Geordie disappointment turned almost immediately to joy, however, when it was announced, that summer, that Newcastle had bought **Alan Shearer** for £15 million. It wasn't just the status of the player or the world-record transfer fee that got the city excited. Shearer was **a local lad**. Throughout their history the club had bred talented local youngsters, only to be forced to sell them – everyone from Len Shackleton to Peter Beardsley, Chris Waddle and Paul Gascoigne. (Only Jackie Millburn, 'Wor Jackie', remained loyal to the club through thick and thin.) Now, with Shearer's arrival on Tyneside, the era of Geordies starring everywhere except in their hometown was over.

Six months later Keegan stunned Newcastle by quitting, within weeks of his team putting five past Manchester United and seven past Tottenham at St James' Park. His replacement, **Kenny Dalglish**, has since had to deal with some of the boardroom tension (Newcastle became a publicly quoted company in 1997) which is said to have prompted Keegan's departure. More pressingly, he has also faced a long-term injury to Shearer, before a ball of the 1997/98 season was kicked. And still, for all the euphoria, for all the crowds, for all the noise, for all the cash, the **trophy cabinet is bare**.

None of it matters. To describe what has happened at St James' Park in the last five years as a revival would be an under-statement – Newcastle have been **born again**.

Finland

But for a few colourful names, football would be a dead duck in Finland. Ice hockey is by far the country's most popular team sport, and football culture is a fairly recent concept. Two things have happened, though, to help put soccer on the nation's sporting map – Jazz and Jari.

FC Jazz have given the moribund domestic game a rare taste of the exotic over the last four years. Based in the western coastal town of Pori, famed for its annual summer jazz festival, FC Jazz were formed from the local post-office team in 1992. With their Brazilian imports, including top scorer Luís António, they won the title the very next year and again in 1996.

The other star name in Finnish football is striker Jari Litmanen, whose goals for Ajax – since he moved there to replace his hero Dennis Bergkamp in 1993 – have provided the Finnish game with its first representation at top European level.

Today Finland has become a popular destination for English Premiership clubs seeking some pre-season friendly action, and for football fans wanting a summer break, it is significantly cheaper than neighbouring Sweden or Norway.

Historically, though, the Finns are footballing makeweights. The national team has not reached the finals of any major competition since losing the semis of the 1912 Olympic soccer tournament, and Finnish clubs have rarely made an impact in Europe.

The first national championship was held in 1908 and the event was dominated by teams from Helsinki until World War II. Postwar, provincial teams came to the fore, especially TPS Turku, Reipas Lahti, KuPS Kuopio and Haka Valkeaköski. Interest was generated by the regular visits of top continental sides in the early rounds of European club competitions. All-time

Jari Litmanen – Finnish football superstar

top league goalscorer Kai Pahlman became a folk hero for his stunning goal for HJK against Manchester United in the first round of the European Cup in 1965. That same year, he was the main attraction in the HJK-Haka fixture which drew more than 17,000 to Helsinki's Olympic stadium.

During the Eighties the game gradually became semi-professional. As standards rose, so the league's top players began to drift abroad, mainly to Scandinavian countries – although Ari Hjelm, Finland's most capped player and highest goalscorer, and Mixu Paatelainen became popular figures in Germany and Britain, respectively.

Despite one legendary win by TPS Turku over Internazionale at the San Siro in

FINLAND

1987 – Mika Aaltonen's goal earning him a brief contract with Bologna – the domestic game attracted scant national attention until the Nineties, when the rise of FinnPa, an ambitious club to rival HJK in Helsinki, breathed new life into football.

There is a theory that the Finns will always struggle at international level, but the appointment as coach of Richard Møller-Nielsen, who led Denmark to the 1992 European Championship, may yet unlock some hidden potential.

Essential vocabulary
Hello *Hei*
Goodbye *Näkemiin*
Yes *Joo*
No *Ei*
Two beers, please *Kaksi kaljaa, kiitos*
Thank you *Kiitti*
Men's *Miehet*
Women's *Naiset*
What's the score? *Mikä on tilanne?*
Where is the stadium? *Missä on stadion?*

Referee *Erotuomari*
Offside *Paitsio*

Match practice
If you're looking for real stadium atmosphere in Finland, you'll find it at the ice-hockey rink. Few football fans travel, so there is little rivalry between supporters, and this is reflected in the mood of calm which descends on most matches. During the game, the loudest noise you'll hear will probably be the players shouting to each other.

Finland's long, harsh winter means football has to be played over a short season. The first games begin in mid-April and champions are celebrating in mid-October.

Given the short campaign, there are often two rounds in a single week, and games are usually played on Thursdays and Sundays.

At either end of the season, kick-off time is 3pm, but this is the land of the Midnight Sun, and during the middle of the

Ibrox export – international goalkeeper Antti Niemi makes himself comfortable at Rangers

Basics

EU, US, Canadian, Australian and New Zealand citizens need only a valid **passport** to enter Finland for up to three months.

The Finnish **currency** is the markka, indicated as FM and divided into 100 penniä. There are coins for 5p, 10p, 20p, 50p, FM1 and FM5, and notes for FM10, FM50, FM100, FM500 and FM 1000. There are around FM9 to £1. On arrival in Helsinki, money can be **exchanged** at the airport (open daily 6.30am–11pm), at Katajanokka harbour (open daily 9am–1pm & 3.45–6pm), and at the main train station (open daily 8am–9pm). Ordinary banks are open Mon–Fri 9.15am–4.15pm, and charge around FM15 commission for exchanges. Money can be also changed in most hotels, but at a poorer rate. **Credit-card payment** is widely used in major towns, and even in Helsinki taxis.

Finland is connected north–south as far as the **Arctic Circle** by a reliable if expensive **train service**. A journey between Helsinki and Tampere takes two hours and costs about FM80. Journeys east-west, and travelling in the north of the country, are best accomplished by **bus**. Services are run by private companies sharing a common ticket system, with fares calculated according to distance (roughly FM50 per 100km). Return tickets on long-haul journeys work out 10% cheaper. *Radio City* (96.2MHz FM) operates a phone-in shared lift service each Thursday (☎09/694 1366) with English-speaking staff.

If you fancy catching some **Estonian football**, which like Finland has a summer season, note that visas are no longer required for EU nationals travelling on the **hydrofoil service** between Helsinki and Tallinn. A return ticket costs FM180. For more details, call the Helsinki office of *Estonian New Line* on ☎09/680 2499.

Telephones – look for the word *puhelin* on the dilapidated booths – take FM1 or FM5 coins or phonecards; the latter come in FM30, FM50 and FM100 sizes and can be bought from *R-kioski* stands. From outside the country, the **dialling code** for Finland is ☎358, followed by a ☎9 for Helsinki. To get an international line inside Finland, dial ☎990 followed by the required country code. Cheap rates apply Mon–Fri 10pm–8am and all weekend.

Remember that for most of the year, Finland is **one hour ahead** of Central European Time, two hours ahead of GMT.

campaign, kick-off can be as late as 6.30pm, no floodlights necessary.

The league

Finnish football dispensed with its complicated 'league of two halves' structure in 1997. Now the Finnish premier division, or *Veikkausliiga*, has been reduced to ten clubs. Teams plays each other three times for a 27-game season. If the top two clubs are level on points, a two-leg play-off decides the winner.

The bottom-placed team is relegated to the first division, *Ykkönen*. This is divided into two ten-team sections, southern (*etelälohko*) and northern (*pohjoislohko*).

Midway through the season, the top five in each go into a nine-game play-off league (*ylempi loppusarja*), the winners of which are promoted to the premier division automatically. The second-placed team then plays off over two legs with the ninth-placed *Veikkausliiga* side.

Up for the cup

The *Suomen Cup* was first contested in 1955 and has not been able to raise much interest in its forty-year history – though as always there is the prospect of European football for the winners. The first-division teams enter at the sixth-round stage, *Veikkausliiga* sides in the seventh.

Finnish line: Liverpool are untroubled by tiny MyPa, 1996

The cup final is traditionally the last game of the season, played in October at the Olympic stadium in Helsinki.

Tickets

Tickets are sold at the turnstiles – simply ask for *"yksi lippu"* ("one ticket"), and you're in. Should the heavens be threatening to open, you might want to make sure your seat is covered or *katettu*. Uncovered places will be marked *ei-katettu*.

A ticket for a domestic fixture shouldn't set you back more than FM40–60. Both of Helsinki's two football venues, the Olympic stadium and the Pallokenttä, are all-seated.

If you want to book in advance for a big game without going to the stadium, there are several offices in Helsinki city centre which sell tickets, among them *Lippupavelu* at Mannerheimintie 5.

Half-time

At half-time people rush to the beer tents, where a half-litre costs about FM15 and a grilled sausage (*makkara*) with mustard and ketchup around FM6.

Action replay

One live league game is shown by the *YLE* network every other Sunday, on either channel 1 or 2 depending on the whim of the schedulers. *YLE 1*'s sports news show, *Urheiluruutu* (Sundays, 8.30–9pm) offers highlights of the day's action. Finland's newly launched *Channel 4* also has the rights to show two plum league ties live, to be decided in the course of the season.

English football is popular here and in the course of the Premiership season, around fifteen games will be shown live on state *TV2* (Saturdays, 5pm).

The cable channel *SuperSport* offers Sky's Sunday afternoon and Monday night Premiership games live.

The back page

Finland's biggest sports paper is the weekly *Veikkaaja* (Mondays, FM10), which offers coverage of British and European football as well as the domestic game. For the latest news and results, there is no daily sports press but the general newspaper *Helsingin Sanomat* has stats and other bits and bobs in the *Tulokset* section of the *Urheilu*, or sports pages.

In Helsinki, foreign newspapers can be found, on the day of issue, at the *Academic Bookstore*, Pohjoiseplanadi 39.

In the net

Riku Suoinen runs a comprehensive stats service at: www.dmi.tut.fi/riku/soccer-html/fin.html. It's part of a wide-ranging European stats site, always accurate and lovingly updated.

Helsinki

For decades, football in the Finnish capital was dominated by one club – HJK. The country's most illustrious side had HPS and the long-established HIFK as early rivals, when the domestic championship was only nominally 'national', effectively being contested by teams from Helsinki and around.

Modern-day opposition did not arrive until the airline-sponsored team FinnPa began to challenge for honours in the Nineties. Affluent and ambitious, FinnPa nakedly poached key players from their city rivals and successfully dented their support

base in town. Today derby games between the two sides can draw crowds of up to 10,000, three times the league average.

In Helsinki, only two stadia host football matches: the Olympic stadium and the Pallokenttä, opposite each other in the north of town. The Olympic is used for internationals, the cup final and some big league fixtures, but most games take place at the smaller Pallokenttä (literally – 'ball pitch').

The Pallokenttä has been greatly refurbished in recent years, having had its surface relaid and floodlights installed.

Helsinki essentials

Helsinki's airport, **Vantaa**, is 20km north of town and served by frequent airport buses (5am–midnight, journey time thirty minutes, FM24). Buses make several request stops before terminating at the main **train station**. A **taxi** will be quicker but cost around FM150.

The ferry lines *Viking* and *Silja* have their terminals on opposite sides of the South Harbour (docks known respectively as *Katajanokka* and *Olympic*), a walk of less than a kilometre to town. The train station is in the city centre, next door to one of the two city **bus terminals**. All **trams** stop immediately outside or around the corner on Mannerheimintie. Just across Mannerheimintie and a short way up Simonkatu is the second city bus terminal and the long-distance coach station.

Helsinki is hemmed in on three sides by **water** and all the places you'll want to go are either within walking distance or a few minutes apart by an integrated transport network of buses, trams and metro. A **single journey** on any of these costs FM9 and unlimited transfers are allowed within one hour. A multi-trip ticket gives ten rides for FM75. A *Helsinki Tourist* ticket, available in one- (FM25), three- (FM50) or five-day (FM75) versions, allows travel on all buses and trams.

Single tickets can be bought onboard, others from the bus station, *R-kioski* stands or tourist offices. Enter buses at the front; trams, front or back – don't forget to stamp your ticket in the machine. Tram line #3T tours the city in a **fifty-minute round trip**, and there are brochures available in English describing the route. Metro tickets can be bought from machines in the stations. Public transport runs 5am–1am and there is no night service.

Taxis levy a basic charge of FM12, with a further FM7 per km, plus a FM7 evening surcharge after 6pm, and a FM13 surcharge from 10pm Saturday until 6am Sunday. Phone for one on ☎09/700 700.

The main **tourist office** is at Pohjoisesplanadi 19 (May–Sept Mon–Fri 8.30am–6pm, Sat–Sun 10am-3pm; Oct–April Mon–Fri 8.30am–4pm, Tues–Fri 8.30am–4pm; ☎09/169 3757, fax 09/169 3839). It dishes out free street and transport maps, along with the useful free tourist magazine *Helsinki This Week*.

The free fortnightly paper *City-lehti* can be picked up in record shops, restaurants and metro stations, and has concert and club **listings**, with a section in English.

The Olympic stadium

Olympiastadion,
Mannerheimintie
Capacity 50,000

Built for the 1940
Olympics, which it even-
tually hosted twelve years
later, Finland's national
stadium is a pleasant all-
seater tucked between
Sibelius park and an area
of **lakes and woodland**
some 2km north of the
city centre. Normally
used for athletics meet-
ings and rock concerts,
the Olympiastadion also
stages a **handful of**

Tower of power – the ground hosts footie as well as athletics

football games every year. These include HJK's top fixtures, most of Finland's international matches – though there have been recent moves to stage some of these at
smaller provincial stadia in Tampere and Turku – and the domestic cup final.

Football crowds barely touch a quarter of its capacity, which is a shame as the
ground is one of Europe's most convivial. Its main feature is a large white tower behind
the main stand, which offers a stunning view of Helsinki and beyond to Finland's
southern coast. If there's nothing going on at the ground, the **tower is open** to visitors,
Mon–Fri 9am–8pm, Sat–Sun 9am–6pm, admission FM5.

To reach both tower and ground from central Helsinki – from the huge *Stockmann*
department store or the *Forum* shopping centre – take tram #4, #7 or #10 north up the
main avenue, Mannerheimintie, for ten minutes. Alternatively, you can **walk it** from
the main train station in around twenty minutes. A taxi will cost FM40–50.

There are several bars near the Olympic stadium, equally handy for games at the
Pallokenttä next door. The **William K**, Mannerheimintie 72, is a cosy local which specialises in beer from around the world. The **City Marathon** (nicknamed *Pääty*),
Mannerheimintie 17, has a more sporting feel, as do the **Paitsio** ('Offside',
Mannerheimintie 104) and the **Sporticafé**, Savilankatu 1B – this last being the most
convenient for the Pallokenttä. There is also a café within the Olympic stadium itself,
to the right as you come in via the main entrance.

When it comes to buying a ticket for domestic games at the Olympic, simply pay
your money at the turnstiles. For internationals, the **ticket office** is open for advance
sales in block A, under the main stand. This is where the most expensive seats are, at
around FM200, with prices falling to FM100 in block D, and FM70 in blocks B, C, E
and F around the ground.

It is assumed that **visiting supporters** at internationals have already bought their
tickets from their home associations. Anyhow, as so few tend to come, no permanent
away sector is allocated to them.

At one end of the main stand you'll find the **Sport Museum** (open Mon–Fri
11am–5pm, Thur until 7pm, Sat–Sun noon–4pm, admission FM10). The bulk of the
large collection is dedicated to Finland's famous long-distance runners, but there are
some soccer souvenirs, including some natty Finnish kits from the Fifties.

Groundhopping

● HJK

Pallokenttä, Mannerheimintie
Capacity 10,000
Colours Blue-and-white striped shirts, blue shorts
League champions 1911–12, 1917–19, 1923, 1925, 1936, 1938, 1964, 1973, 1978, 1981, 1985, 1987–88, 1990, 1992
Cup winners 1966, 1981, 1984, 1993

The relaxed, improvised atmosphere of Finnish football was never better illustrated than in the legend that surrounds the founding of Helsingin Jalkapalloklubi. Apparently the club's founding president, Fredrik Wathen, a former world champion speed-skater, was having a quiet ice-cream when he decided it would be a good idea to set up a football club.

Other teams, notably, HIFK, were already established in the Finnish capital, but it wasn't long after their formation in 1907 that Klubi became top dogs, not just in Helsinki but across Finland.

That status has paled slightly over the last five years. With Jazz Pori hogging the limelight nationally and the upstarts of FinnPa trying to pull the rug out from underneath their older city rivals, HJK approached their ninetieth year at their lowest ebb since the late Sixties.

The team haven't won the title since 1992, and in 1996 they suffered the indignity of playing-off to stay in the premier division.

Despite this, HJK still attract the biggest crowds, their loyal support having been raised on six titles between 1981 and 1992, and European home wins over Liverpool and Porto. Key players in that era included Jari 'Jallu' Rantanen, who later scored five goals for IFK Gothenburg on their run to the UEFA Cup in 1987, before moving on to Leicester City – and then defecting to the dreaded FinnPa...

● FinnPa

Pallokenttä, see HJK
Colours All white with blue and red trim

Though they have yet to really break through nationally, FinnPa are the first modern club to challenge HJK in Helsinki. Named after the state airline Finnair, who sponsor the club, Finnairin Palloilijat rose from the lower divisions to achieve premier division status in 1993.

In 1965, when the club was founded, the airline was called Aero Oy and the team Aeron Palloilijat. In those days it was just a team of airline workers playing in the local leagues for fun. But after Aero Oy became Finnair in 1969, the team – as FinnPa – suddenly found its wings, climbing through the ranks as never before. As perks for players became more attractive, so a better quality of football was achieved.

With stunning originality, the team are nicknamed 'The Flyers'. In the mid-Nineties they have won over neutrals and players alike with an open, attractive brand of football. Former HJK stalwarts Markku Kanerva, Jallo Rantanen and Tommi Paavola have all gone across to FinnPa in the last couple of years, and there's no sign of any air traffic flying in the opposite direction.

Eat, drink, sleep...

Bars and clubs

Although alcohol is by no means cheaper, at least the drinking laws in Finland are more liberal than in Sweden or Norway.

Beer (*olut*) is sold in two main categories: *III-Olut*, available in shops and cafés, and the stronger *IV-Olut*, which can only be bought in *ALKO* stores, restaurants and nightclubs.

The *ALKO* stores (open Mon–Thurs 10am–5pm, Fri 10am–6pm, Sat 9am–2pm) offer local strong brews like *Karjala* and *Lapin Kulta Export* at around FM8 a bottle.

Vodka is the most popular spirit, particularly *Finlandia*. Keep an eye out for *Koskenkorva-Viina* (or *Kossu*), a 38 percent vodka distilled from wheat.

In bars, ask for a *tuoppi*, a half-litre of draught beer, and be prepared to part with about FM25. Licensed restaurants and pubs usually close around midnight or 1am, clubs at 3–4am. Admission for the latter will be around FM20–30. None of the venues listed below is more than a short walk from the train station.

Berlin, Töölönkatu 3. All-purpose club – depending on the night, you'll find acid and hip-hop sounds, heavy rock, or mainstream dance.

Kannas, Eerikinkatu 43. The fights and drunken sailors that made this bar a Helsinki legend for fifty years have given way to new management attempting to create a Sixties Americana look, complete with pool table and movie-poster tablecloths (and rarely any fights).

Kappeli, Esplanadi park. An elegant glasshouse with vast windows overlooking Esplanadi and the harbour, with live entertainment during the summer. The cellar, **Kappelin Olutkellari**, is a good spot for a late drink. Open daily 9am–4am.

Molly Malone's, Kaisaniemenkatu 1C. A popular bar with Finns, for whom Irish 'pubs' are a novelty. Usual Irish trappings and plenty of sports talk. Open daily.

Vanhan Kahvila, Mannerheimintie 3. Comparatively cheap self-service bar. Fills quickly, so try to arrive early for a seat on the balcony. Downstairs, the **Vanhan Kellari,** erstwhile home of Helsinki's beat poets, is cosy and smoky.

Restaurants
Eating in Helsinki, as in the rest of the country, isn't cheap, but there is plenty of choice. Fish (*kala*), reindeer (*poro*) and elk (*hirvenliha*) are the mainstays and you'll also find a lot of Russian dishes.

At a typical **pizzeria** you'll pay around FM60 for dinner, providing you don't drink

alcohol with your meal. Finnish restaurants and those serving Russian specialities can be expensive – expect to spend at least FM150 per person. Restaurants are usually open daily until around 1am, though the kitchens often close at 11pm. If you're watching the pennies, many places offer a fixed-price menu at lunchtime, some for under FM40.

Until early evening you can get a reasonable dish – and the weakest beer, *I-Olut* – in *baari*, which serve straightforward Finnish dishes for FM35–50.

Kannu, Punavuorenkatu 12. Much of the original interior, designed by Alvar Aalto, remains in this locals' haunt, where the staff dish up stodgy, down-to-earth Finnish food. Tram #3T or #3B.

La Havanna, Uudenmenkatu 9–11. Pioneering Cuban eaterie doing great things with seafood. Calm at lunchtime, at night it's packed with boozers and Latin American music fills the air. Short walk from the train station.

Ravintola Lappi, Annankatu 22. A fine, though not cheap, restaurant specialising in real Finnish food like pea soup and oven pancakes, as well as Lappish specialities of smoked reindeer and warm cloudberries. Short walk from the train station.

Saslik, Neitsytpolku 12. Highly rated for its Russian food, served amid lush, Tsarist-period furnishings and accompanied by live music. Closes midnight. Tram #3T or #3B.

Zetor, Kaivokatu 10. Popular restaurant done up Country & Western style, with tractors, straw, the works. Short walk from the train station.

Accommodation
Finnish hotels offer sauna, swimming pool and enormous breakfasts, but at high prices – more than FM500 for a double room. At weekends and in summer (which is when the football's on, remember), **prices often fall**, sometimes to as low as FM300 for a double. Always phone well in advance to get the best bargain.

Tourist hotels (*matkustajakoti*) are more basic, but clean and comfortable, with doubles around FM200. Again, always book ahead, particularly in summer.

In Helsinki, you can book a room for a FM12 fee through the **Hotel Booking Centre** at the train station near the left-luggage office (mid-May to mid-Sept Mon–Fri 9am–9pm, Sat 9am–7pm, Sun 10am–6pm; rest of year Mon–Fri 9am–6pm; ☎09/171 133, fax 09/175 524).

Academica, Hietaniemenkatu 14 (☎09/402 0206, fax 09/441 201). A well-placed summer hotel with morning sauna and pool. Around FM300 for a double. Hostel-type accommodation is available in another section on production of an IYHF or student card, June–Aug only, for around FM100 per person. Bus #18 or tram #3T, or a ten-minute walk from the train station down Salomonkatou.

Euro Hostel, Linnankatu 9 (☎09/622 0470, fax 09/655 044). Comfortable place in a clean modern building with free morning sauna and twin beds (not bunks). Open all year. FM115–175 per person. Single and double rooms also available. No credit cards. Close to the *Viking Line* arrival point; take tram #4.

Matkakoti Margarita, Itäinen Teatterikuja 3 (☎09/669 707). Fairly basic place with a Russian atmosphere, set in a quiet street close to the train and bus stations, and quite adequate for a night's rest. It also rents rooms cheaply by the day for those arriving in the city early and leaving later the same day. Around FM300 a double. Close to train station.

Finland expects – national coach Møller Nielsen

Omapohja Gasthaus, Teatterikuja 3 (☎09/666 211). Downstairs from Matkakoti Margarita, this place has four rooms each with en-suite facilities, colour TVs and a microwave oven. Around FM300 a double. Close to the train station.

Satakuntalo, Lapinrinne 1 (☎09/695 851, fax 09/694 2226). Handily located summer hotel which doubles as student accommodation. Shared bathrooms. About FM180 for a single, FM230 for a double, FM80 for a dorm bed. Self-service laundry. Ten-minute walk from the train station.

Stadionin Retkeilymaja, Olympiastadion (☎09/496 071, fax 09/496 466). From a football point of view, the youth hostel with the best location in Europe, with an entrance on the far side of the Olympic stadium complex. FM60–135 per person. Own café on site. Open all year. No credit cards. Trams #3T, #4, #7A and #10.

France

The French, founding fathers of international football, are now also the face of its future. Just outside Paris, the new Stade de France will stage the 1998 World Cup final. Inside the capital, Paris Saint-Germain have achieved European success untainted by corruption and backed by a pay-per-view subscription TV company. Stadium, football club and television channel are all products of the modern era.

The soccer-loving neutral should be delighted. For decades the French have played a stylish, attacking game, particularly at international level. Yet their rewards have been relatively few.

After fruitlessly chasing European trophies while home crowds dwindled, French clubs are on the up. PSG's Cup-Winners' Cup win of 1996 coincided with Bordeaux's brave twenty-game drive to the UEFA Cup final; both teams showed that French players can not only woo, they can win. TV money from Canal Plus has seen most of the major clubs climb a mountain of debt.

The French domestic game, with no inner-city rivalries, still attracts only modest crowds. Many French stars play abroad and the most consistently successful club, Monaco, are little but a royal pastime.

Yet Auxerre, from a town of 40,000 people, are an example of what can be achieved. The club's adventurous youth policy, which produced Eric Cantona in the Eighties, resulted in a league and cup double in 1996.

Now the country's biggest club, Olympique Marseille, are building a training centre at their ground, the Vélodrome – which, together with nine other stadia, is being overhauled for 1998.

These grounds last saw World Cup action in 1938, when the French were chosen as hosts in honour of their contribution

Is it a bird? 'Fraid so – the France '98 mascot

to the structure of the world game. After overcoming early problems of oval-ball domination at home and English intransigence abroad, Robert Guérin co-founded world football's governing body, FIFA, in 1904. Another Frenchman, the organisation's president for more than thirty years, Jules Rimet, was behind the introduction of football's greatest trophy, the World Cup, in 1930.

Europe's major trophies were also French inventions, Gabriel Hanot founding the European Cup in the late Fifties, Henri Delaunay the European Championship not

Mad in Marseille – Michel Platini scores in the last minute of extra time against Portugal, 1984

long after. Today, the man following in the footsteps of these great historical figures is Michel Platini – the nation's chosen ambassador for the 1998 World Cup. Platini might seem a romantic choice for such a high-profile, businesslike rôle. But it is not hard to understand why the French have put their faith in him. Before Platini's arrival as a player, the French had won none of the trophies their administrators had given the world.

Between the Fifties and the Seventies, only provincial clubs Stade de Reims and Saint-Étienne came close to lifting a European trophy. Reims lost the first-ever European Cup final to Real Madrid in 1956, then lost the same fixture to the same team three years later. In between, the side provided the core of a high-scoring French national team that gained third place at the 1958 World Cup, thanks to thirteen goals – still an all-time tournament record – from Just Fontaine and the vision of Raymond Kopa, the greatest French player of his day.

Saint-Étienne, French champions seven times between 1967 and 1976, featured in some classic European ties, the most memorable a 3–1 quarter-final defeat at Liverpool in the 1977 European Cup, a year after the French side had lost the final of the same tournament to Bayern Munich.

Saint-Étienne – *Les Verts* – were the first French club to engender a modern fan following. Just as significantly, in the late Seventies they provided a home for the emerging vision of Michel Platini – a vision that would shine not just in French club football, but in three World Cups and one stunning European Championship.

First spotted playing for his hometown team AS Nancy-Lorraine in 1975, Platini scored three goals in four qualifying games to take France to their first modern World Cup finals in 1978. There they were unlucky to be drawn in a tough group alongside Italy and the host nation, Argentina; the French lost to both by the narrowest of margins, and went home.

Misfortune would strike again in Spain in 1982. Coach Michel Hidalgo, a veteran of Reims in the Fifties, had built a midfield of rare talent, with Platini, Alain Giresse and Jean Tigana. Even more than in Argentina, France were a joy to watch. They were 3–1 up in extra-time of an electric World Cup semi-final with West Germany and, despite having lost defender Patrick Battiston to a wild and unpunished challenge by German 'keeper Toni Schumacher, they continued to attack. The strategy was naïve – leaving gaps at the back, the French allowed the Germans to score twice, then lost the game on penalties.

It seemed the French could not win and entertain at the same time. But two years later, in the European Championship on home soil, they did precisely that. Their midfield now given bite by Jean Fernandez, France were outstanding. Platini scored seven goals in three group games to line up another epic semi-final, this one in Marseille against Portugal. An enthralling game was tied at 2–2 and heading for penalties when Tigana went on a desperate surge down the park in the last minute of extra-time – he got to the byline, crossed low, and there was Platini to sweep the ball home. Delirium at the Vélodrome, a firework atmosphere that Paris couldn't match when France duly won the title in a dour final against Spain four days later.

Platini's last hurrah was at the 1986 World Cup in Mexico. With Luis Fernandez now the dominant midfield force, the French knocked holders Italy out in the second round, setting up a quarter-final against Brazil which featured attacking football of the highest quality; it was to end in another penalty decider, this time in France's favour.

In the semi-final the opponents were West Germany again, but by this time French creativity had dried up – Platini played bravely on through injury, but an early German goal obliged France to settle for an eventual third place.

Throughout this buoyant period on the international stage, many French clubs were in a poor state. Bound by a law of 1901, they were not allowed to make a profit or pay high transfer fees. Propped up by local councils, many set up slush funds and secret bank accounts.

Things began to change in the mid-Eighties, when Bordeaux president Claude Bez rejuvenated the club thanks not only to vast municipal loans but also to lucrative deals with the new Canal Plus TV channel. Though the experiment was to end in disgrace and financial ruin, Bordeaux were France's first glimpse of how a football club could be run in the multimedia era.

Bez opened avenues for his great rival, Olympique Marseille's Bernard Tapie. The archetypal Eighties wheeler-dealer, Tapie pushed l'OM to new heights; the team won five straight titles before making history in 1993 by becoming the first French side to win the European Cup. Days after Marseille's 1–0 win over Milan in Munich, however, news broke of the club's domestic match-fixing. Stripped of their fifth league title, l'OM were also denied the right to defend their European trophy.

One of the great Marseille stars of the era, striker Jean-Pierre Papin, had become a linchpin of the national side, now coached by Platini. The attacking combination of Papin and Cantona made France one of the favourites to win the 1992 European Championship in Sweden. Yet fans saw only glimpses of them – Platini, so adventurous as a player, preached caution as a coach. The ploy backfired, and after France failed to win a match in Sweden, he resigned.

Within eighteen months Platini's successor, Gérard Houllier, had also quit. Needing only a point from their remaining two qualifying games to book their tickets to the 1994 World Cup, Houllier's French threw away a 2–1 lead against Israel to lose their penultimate match 3–2. Then, with only a few minutes of their last match against Bulgaria left and the game standing at 1–1, Houllier brought on David Ginola as a replacement for Papin. Ginola gave the ball carelessly away deep in Bulgarian territory, and Emil Kostadinov raced away to score a winning goal that would signal not only Houllier's downfall, but the end of the international road for Papin, Ginola and Cantona.

Houllier's replacement, Aimé Jacquet, has eschewed individual flair and put the emphasis firmly on the group. And what a group it is – Youri Djorkaeff, Christophe Dugarry, Zinedine Zidane and Didier Deschamps all starred in the French side that reached the semi-finals of Euro '96, and since then they have been augmented by new talents nurtured in a model youth programme run by, of all people, Houllier – Thierry Henry, Nicolas Anelka and the Senegalese-born Ibrahim Ba among them.

Basics

EU nationals and those of the US, Canada, and New Zealand require only a **passport** to enter France. Australians require a visa, but this will be valid not only for France but for all the countries belonging to the so-called Schengen agreement on frontier controls.

The French currency is the **franc** (F), divided into 100 centimes. There are F1, F2, F5, F10 and F20 coins, and notes for F20, F50, F100, F200 and F500. There are around F10 to £1. Cash machines for credit cards are widespread, the most popular card being the *Carte Bleu* Visa.

To call France from abroad, the international **dialling code** is 33 – 331 for Paris. Coin phones (taking F1 or F2 pieces) can be found in some bars, but French public phone boxes take only **phonecards** (*télécartes*), available at most tobacco stalls (*tabacs*) and newsagents, in units of F46 and F96. **International calls** from within France are cheaper between 9.30pm and 8am weekdays, from 2pm Saturdays and all day Sundays – dial 19, then the country code. For long-distance calls within France, *except* those to or from Paris, simply dial the nine-digit number, which includes the area code. For calls from Paris to the provinces, dial 16, followed by the customer number; from the provinces to Paris, dial 16, then 1, then the customer number.

The French **transport system** is centralised around Paris, and with an excellent rail network run by the state operator SNCF. Travelling to and from the capital is quick and comfortable on high-speed **TGV trains**, which serve most major towns and for which you will be charged a modest F20 supplement. A TGV journey to Marseille takes just over four hours and costs F400. Normal SNCF express services are slower but still reliable – Bordeaux to Nantes takes four hours and costs about F220. Remember to validate your ticket before boarding.

Buses are to be avoided unless there is no other choice, but **hitching** is a possibility if money is tight; large cities have an *Âllo-Stop* office, matching drivers willing to share petrol costs with hitchers. The Paris office is at 84 passage Brady (☎0142 46 00 66).

Accommodation is generally clean, plentiful and affordable; you'll pay around F130–160 for a basic single room, a little more in Paris.

French **cuisine** is excellent if rarely cheap. Watch out for *prix fixe* lunchtime bargains, posted outside the restaurant – three-course meals can cost as little as F50.

In bars, there are generally three price ranges: one for standing at the bar (*au comptoir*), one for being waited on (*á table*) and one for drinking after 10pm (*tarif de nuit*). The cheap option is **wine**, almost always drinkable. Draught **beer** (*pression*) is sold by the 33cl glass (*demi*), at about F12–15. Light (*blondes*) and dark (*brunes*) beers are available, and sometimes the bitter *rousse*. French beers offer little regional variation, but there are often Belgian or Dutch options. The national **spirit**, particularly popular in the south, is the aniseed-flavoured *pastis*, served with a small jug of water. Many bars hum to the sound of table football (*baby-foot*) – a serious teenage pastime.

Entrance to French **nightclubs** is expensive but usually includes your first drink (*consommation*).

Ooh, aah, Cantona – but Eric has nowhere to run against Sweden at Euro '92

In the absence of a single player to capture the imagination as Platini did, the statistics tell France's mid-Nineties story: after defeat by Bulgaria in November 1993, *Les Bleus* did not lose another game at home until England beat them in the 1997 World Cup dress rehearsal, *Le Tournoi de France*.

Domestically, Tapie's downfall has led to a review of clubs' accountability, while new federation rules and tax regulations have been drafted to make it easier for French clubs to keep their talented youngsters from the clutches of foreign predators – at least until after the World Cup and all the hype it brings with it.

Essential vocabulary
Hello *Bonjour*
Goodbye *Au revoir*
Yes *Oui*
No *Non*
Two beers, please *Deux demis, s'il vous plaît*
Thank you *Merci*

Men's *Hommes*
Women's *Dames*
Where is the stadium? *Où est le stade?*
What's the score? *Où en sommes-nous?*
Referee *L'arbitre*
Offside *Hors jeu*

Match practice
Although they will be in prime condition for the 1998 World Cup, the lack of crosstown competition means that French stadia are rarely full for club matches. Only the big two, Paris Saint-Germain and Olympique Marseille, boast large followings, but most games in the south will generate a decent noise and atmosphere.

The season runs from late July until early May, with a short winter break between mid-December and mid-January. Games normally take place on a Saturday at 8pm, but clubs involved in European competition often bring their games forward to Friday evening and, as in England, there are some midweek rounds. Live games for

Canal Plus are played either side of the main matchday, generally at 8.30pm.

The league

La Ligue Nationale has two professional divisions. After pressure from UEFA, *Division 1* (often known simply as *D1*) was reduced to eighteen teams for the 1997/98 season. At the end of each season, the bottom three clubs change places with the promoted trio from the 22-club *Division 2*.

Out of Africa – 'French' winger Ibrahim Ba

The lower divisions have also been restructured for 1997/98. The former *National 1* semi-professional third tier, which comprised two groups of eighteen teams, is now a single twenty-club division known as the *National Open*. Below this, the former *National 2* and *National 3* tiers have been replaced by the four-group *Championnat de France Amateurs 1* and the eight-group *CFA 2*, respectively. Both *CFA* tiers have their groups organised on a regional basis.

Up for the cup

France has two cups. *La Coupe de France* is the oldest and best-loved domestic cup tournament in continental Europe, and has no fewer than fourteen rounds including the final. To encourage unpredictability, all rounds are decided on a single game, then extra time and penalties. Progress by modest village teams is common, although mainland visits by teams from former French island colonies like Martinique and Guadeloupe rarely last more than ninety minutes. First-division clubs enter at the ninth-round stage. The final has traditionally taken place in May at the Parc des Princes, but will be moved to the Stade de France in 1998. The winners qualify for the Cup-Winners' Cup.

The recently introduced *Coupe de la Ligue* is for first and second clubs, and is also decided by one-game rounds and a final at the Parc – the latter will become two-legged in 1998 so as not to steal the thunder of the established competition. Unlike the English, the French have retained a UEFA Cup place for their League cup winners – their reward for adopting an eighteen-team top division.

Tickets

Most French clubs operate a three-level pricing system, with a *match de gala* (against PSG, Marseille, or European opposition) being the dearest.

In general the *virages* behind the goal, which are often standing (*debout*) areas, are for hardcore support; a spot here will cost around F50–60. The *tribunes populaires* also have faithful followers, often from the older generation, happy with their regular spot in the cheap seats, high up over the action, at around F40–60. The side stands (*tribunes latérales*) are almost always seated (*assis*) and tickets here will vary in price according to the view, from F50 to F200.

For big European games, contact the host club well in advance for tickets as many are given out *en masse* to sponsors and their commercial affiliates.

Half-time

As crowds aren't a problem in France, nor is queueing for refreshment at the interval. At most grounds you can buy beer and sausages (*saucisses*). At northern grounds you'll find chips (*frites*), dished up in the Belgian fashion with mayonnaise, while southern clubs will have *merguez*, North African blood sausage. Note that alcohol is banned from certain grounds.

Action replay

Canal Plus rules the roost. The subscription channel whose money transformed French league football has now gone the whole hog in a five-year deal which includes Europe's first football pay-per-view system, for which the company has a dedicated channel, CanalSatellite. A wipe of a credit card in the decoder terminal gets you a single game (F50), or the whole round of matches (F75).

For its usual four million (non-pay-per-view) subscribers, Canal Plus still screens its live league match, *Jour de Foot*, every weekend, plus a Sunday evening round-up, *L'Équipe du Dimanche*, at around 10.30pm.

Canal Plus may have all the angles but cannot boast the commentary of terrestrial TF1's Thierry Roland and Jean-Michel Larqué. This popular duo present the French cup, most international matches, certain European ties and France's best-loved football show, *Téléfoot*, at around 11am on Sundays.

Major Italian, Spanish and German channels are easily available in France.

The back page

France has the world's finest football press. Ever since the pioneering days when Henri Desgrange, chief of the prestigious sports daily *L'Auto*, instigated cycling's Tour de France, the press has taken an active rôle in sports development. *L'Auto* gave way to the classic all-sport daily *L'Équipe*, whose football editor Gabriel Hanot brooded for twenty years on the idea of introducing a trophy for European champion clubs.

When the popular English press proclaimed Wolves 'Champions of Europe' for beating Honvéd of Hungary in a meaningless muddy friendly in 1954, Hanot got to work. Gathering club presidents in the *Hotel Ambassador* on Boulevard Haussmann in April 1955, Hanot and his team hammered out immediate plans for a European Cup, to be introduced four months later. At a stroke, European football had been dragged out of the dark ages – and in an age of Cold War inertia – to be transformed into the lucrative midweek circus we know today. A year later *L'Équipe*'s sister weekly, *France Football*, introduced the European Football of the Year award.

Both papers have produced outstanding sports writers – Jacques de Ryswick and Jean Eskenazy among them – and both are still essential reading. *France Football* (Tuesdays, F12) offers international coverage second to none, while *L'Équipe* (daily F4.90, Mondays F6) has a more domestic focus. Both have had to move with the times, *L'Équipe* with its colour supplement at weekends (F11.50), *France Football* with its new design and extra Friday edition (F8).

The leading monthly is *Guadalajara* (F20), irreverent but dedicated, with excellent in-depth interviews. Younger fans decorate their walls with posters from the other monthlies, *Onze Mondial* (F27) and *Planète Foot* (F25). Watch out for the monthly *Afrique Football* (F18), which offers fine coverage of the game in Africa.

Ultra culture

The average Frenchfan watches a game of football through a love of the sport rather than partisan interest. With notable exceptions – Metz, Marseille, Bastia, Lens – the older generation of supporters have not handed down a singular passion for younger fans to take up and interpret in the modern custom. It was only when the great Saint-Étienne and Olympique Marseille teams were riding high in Europe that France saw genuine outbreaks of mass fan culture, fireworks and all.

This was picked up by followers of Paris Saint-Germain, a club often criticised in France as manufactured, but whose 1996 Cup-Winners' Cup triumph brought thousands spontaneously onto the streets of the capital.

Crowd violence is rare, but Marseille ultra groups are a law unto themselves – as flash and as organised as any in Italy. The Vélodrome's reduction in capacity for reconstruction during 1996/97 caused a number of inter-group face-offs.

The friendliest ambience is at Lens' Stade Félix-Bollært, voted best ground in a poll of 100 French first-division players in 1996. An hour out of Paris, and a World Cup '98 venue, it's worth the trip.

Significantly, football support is also becoming fashionable, a trend which will surely gather momentum as the World Cup draws near. Throughout the spring of 1996 Hollywood's favourite Frenchman, Gérard Depardieu, could be seen, often tired and emotional, hanging around the Auxerre changing room during the team's title run-in.

In the net

Until such time as *France Football* acquires a presence in cyberspace, the French may lack a good generic site for their game. A fair few independently run servers have been and gone, but Armand Penverne is still around with his *Football Français* site at: w3.teaser.fr/~ypenverne/foot.index.htm. It's a simple affair essentially comprising just a stats archive and a selection of links, but it is reliably updated.

A substantial part of the Canal Plus website is devoted to football and can be found at: www.cplus.fr/html/sports/foot/foot.htm. Strong on graphics and handy if you want to keep up with the company's broadcasting schedule, it is woefully short on decent content. More esoterically, Erik Chaillan runs a French football prediction league at: www.insat.com/~chaillan/htm/football. And *Les Bleus*, the French national side, have a superb site dedicated to them at: myweb.worldnet.fr/~cantona/france.shtml.

I thought you looked familiar – Platini and Tigana come face-to-face in the build-up to France '98

Paris

A footballing embarrassment no longer, by the year 2000 Paris hopes to have two top club sides playing in world-class stadia, one in a revamped Parc des Princes and the other in le Stade de France. One is Paris Saint-Germain; the identity of the other is a bone of contention.

In 1990 Paris barely had a club at all. Happily, Canal Plus stepped in when Paris Saint-Germain, threatened with relegation, looked like going the way of all other major postwar teams in the French capital. Both Racing Club and Stade Français had gone under, while Red Star and Paris FC were playing to three-figure crowds in lower leagues. Even international matches were being moved to the provinces, such was the Parisian antipathy towards football.

Yet the Canal Plus gamble paid off. PSG clambered back up the ladder to attain domestic success, embellished by serious inroads into Europe. Support grew, particularly in the city's suburbs. Suddenly PSG were no longer a boardroom creation – they were an identifiable way for a suburban kid to get back at those flashy wheeler-dealers from the south.

The climax came in 1996, with PSG's Cup-Winners' Cup triumph sparking wild celebrations in the Champs-Élysées. A combination of money, luck and ambition had created a team out of nothing and thrust them into the European élite.

Perhaps PSG are not alone. Paris is a huge city, after all. Could it support more than one club capable of challenging the best in Europe? Maybe it could – but only if the Parisians themselves could agree which club.

While moves are afoot to move little Saint-Leu-Saint-Denis into the vast Stade de France in 1998, entrepreneur Alain Afflelou has other plans. He reckons Racing Club, his boyhood heroes, could be raised from football's seabed and merged

The Saint-Germain samba – Leonardo, 1997

with his sleepy, suburban US Créteil side, to form another superteam. If he succeeds where Matra Racing failed in the Eighties, history would be brought full circle.

It was in Paris that the game first took root in France. Amateur clubs from the capital won the first six French cups after World War I. Racing Club de France were the most prestigious, a multi-sport club whose soccer section became an autonomous professional outfit, Racing Club de Paris, in 1932. The team went on to become a prewar legend, boasting a multi-national group of players.

Racing's home, Colombes, hosted five World Cup games in 1938. Today it is little more than a ghostly echo of Paris' former status as football's capital – though it still enjoys some involvement in the game, which may increase with a cash injection from local government.

The game's great leap forward earlier this century had two main venues in Paris. These days, neither shows any sign of history having been made.

The former French FA office at 229 rue Saint-Honoré, in whose backroom FIFA's original members first met in May 1904, is now a house like any other in the 1st

Paris essentials

Paris has two **airports**, Roissy-Charles de Gaulle to the north, Orly to the south. A free shuttle bus takes you from Roissy to the last stop on the RER (express rail) B line, from where a F43 ticket takes you into town. Journey time is about 45 minutes. From Orly, a ten-minute high-speed shuttle (also F43) takes you to Antony on the RER B line. Alternatively, a free five-minute shuttle takes you to Pont de Rungis on RER line C. Air France run buses between the city and both airports, but take account of heavy traffic *en route*. For English-speaking information, call ☎01 48 62 22 80 for Roissy (24 hours) or ☎01 49 75 15 15 for Orly (daily 6am–11.30pm).

An increasingly popular alternative to flying is the **Eurostar** high-speed train service from London's Waterloo International. There are eight trains a day and the service takes three hours to reach Paris Gare du Nord, which is on RER lines B and D and the *métro*.

Be warned – not all *métro* signs are this pretty

The Paris **transport system** is among Europe's best, with 13 *métro* lines intersecting with four RER ones, all running 5.30am–12.30am. Free maps are given out at most stations. Lines are colour-coded, and at transfer stations they are further identified by their end stops. A single ticket, valid for one journey within central zone 1 (change lines with your validated ticket), costs F8, so a *carnet* of ten is a bargain at F46. A one-day *Formule 1* ticket, covering travel outside the central zone, costs about F30, or F90 to include both airports.

Paris also has a comprehensive network of **buses**, on which tickets are valid according to a complicated zonal system – any journey worth its salt requires two tickets. Three tickets are required on any of the ten *Noctambus* routes which operate from Châtelet during the night.

Paris has 15,000 **taxis** but finding an empty one in rush hour is nigh impossible. At night, watch out for the white light glowing on the taxi roof. Even on a night tariff, a journey in town shouldn't cost more than F50. To phone for one, dial ☎01 42 41 50 50 or ☎01 45 85 85 85.

For **tourist information**, there are four branches of the *Office du Tourisme* at the Eiffel Tower, the Gare du Nord, the Gare du Lyon and the main one at 127 avenue des Champs-Élysées (☎01 49 52 53 54). All are open daily, 9am–8pm.

The best **listings information** can be found in the weekly *Pariscope* (F3), which has an eight-page English-language pull-out.

arrondissement. After decades at 10 rue du Faubourg-Montmartre, where the European Cup was dreamed up, the editorial team of *L'Équipe* and *France Football* have moved (with great reluctance) outside town to Issy-les-Moulineaux. The old building is now a modern office block, while the shop downstairs which used to sell fading prewar sports papers is a kebab stall.

For those keen on seeing some football history, it's worth visiting the Musée National du Sport at the Parc des Princes, near the Stade Jean Bouin (open Mon–Fri 9.30am–12.30pm & 2–5pm; Sun 10.30am–12.30pm & 2–6pm, admission F20). Here you'll find two floors of souvenirs from several sports, including French captain Jean Vincent's shirt from the 1958 World Cup and a programme from the France-Italy World Cup quarter-final of 1938. The French FA at 60 bis, avenue d'Iéna, keeps a small display of mementos, including a postcard section serious collectors would kill for (open Mon–Fri 9am–6pm, admission free).

The thrilling fields

 ## Paris Saint-Germain

Euro hero – Djorkaeff in Brussels, 1996

Parc des Princes, 24 rue du Commandant Guilbaud
Capacity 49,000 (all-seated)
Colours Blue shirts with red centre stripe, blue shorts
League champions 1986, 1994
Cup winners 1982–83, 1993, 1995
Cup-Winners' Cup winners 1996

If Paris Saint-Germain didn't exist, it would have been necessary to invent them, After Racing Club's demise in the Sixties, 20,000 football-starved Parisian donors founded Football Club Paris in 1970; they would soon join forces with Saint-Germain-En-Laye to climb the league ladder as Paris Saint-Germain.

The move coincided with the complete reconstruction of the Parc des Princes, former home to Racing's football team and the *Tour de France* finale. Rebuilt with only football and international rugby in mind, the Parc seemed the perfect home for the first serious soccer team in the capital for twenty years.

And so it was. With a team starring Luis Fernandez and expensive imports like Osvaldo Ardiles and Kees Kist, PSG won domestic honours in the Eighties – albeit without generating a real fan base or ever challenging in Europe.

By the time Olympique Marseille were ruling the French roost, PSG were starting to flounder. Having turned down a deal in 1988, Canal Plus stepped in three years later, bailing PSG out to the tune of F30 million a year. The club, although still receiving financial support from city hall, became a limited company, able to wheel and deal.

With the decline of *l'OM*, fans across the country looked to PSG to fly the French flag in Europe. They weren't disappointed. Between 1993 and 1995 the team made consecutive semi-finals in three different European competitions, while solidly picking up silverware at home. Key players such as David Ginola became nationwide stars. In the Parc des Princes itself, an ultra culture developed, some of it distasteful – Liberian striker George Weah, whose goals had taken PSG to within a sniff of the European Cup final, had to endure a thoroughly unpleasant send-off to Milan, though his signing to the Italian club on the eve of playing against them for PSG hardly helped. Meanwhile, the cruder banners and mob gestures were not always appreciated by the image-conscious Canal Plus management (nor, curiously, were they picked up by the company's camera teams).

The return of former player Luis Fernandez as coach in 1994 gave the side steel to go with its style. While Ginola left for Newcastle, Fernandez became the first French coach to win a European trophy, when PSG beat Rapid Vienna 1–0 in the 1996 Cup-Winners' Cup final. While Paris celebrated in style, the players were flown back from Brussels to be fêted in the Canal Plus offices.

Fernandez's departure to Athletic Bilbao soon afterwards – and his replacement by another former player, the Brazilian Ricardo – led to the realisation that in football, maintaining success is more difficult than achieving it. PSG trailed Monaco in the league, were knocked out of the cup by fourth-division Clermont, and were whitewashed 6–1 at home by Juventus in the European SuperCup. While Ricardo kept his job, club president Michel Denisot launched an unprecedented purge of senior management. Too late, it seemed, for PSG'S bold attempt to make history by becoming the first club ever to retain the Cup-Winners' Cup also ended in failure, after Ronaldo's penalty had given Barcelona victory in Rotterdam. Brazilians Raí and Leonardo had been the only highlights of a disappointing season – and the latter was quickly poached by Milan.

If the squad is due for some serious rebuilding, then PSG's loyal support is being

The real thing – after years of playing before half-hearted crowds, PSG now have a solid fan base

Le Grand Stade

Le Stade de France, Cornillon Nord, La Plaine Saint-Denis
Capacity 80,000 (all-seated)

Rising up over a former gasworks and dominating the depressed suburb of Saint-Denis is the venue for football's sixteenth World Cup final. A mere transport zone away from central Paris, le Stade de France (or le Grand Stade, as it is popularly known) is France's **new national stadium,** with nearly twice the capacity of the last one, the Parc des Princes. It is being inaugurated with a France–Spain friendly on January 31, 1998, just over four months before hosting the World Cup opening ceremony on June 10.

Le Stade has eight levels with four tiers of stands, the lower one retractable with a 25,000 capacity. The roof, made of filtered glass and providing sound and lighting, is suspended over the lot on eighteen steel needles. The stadium's elliptical shape is said to give a perfect view for all 80,000 spectators – none more so than diners in the panoramic restaurant high up in the west stand. Everyone else will have to make do with le Stade's fifty bars and buffets.

Construction has been funded partly by a private consortium and partly by the state – both have chipped in the equivalent of **more than £100 million.** A vast commercial centre is being built next door, including a huge sports shop and an international football museum.

These are the facts. What is being debated is who will move in once the party's over. Canal Plus would dearly love for Paris Saint-Germain to assume the mantle. But the club are contractually obliged to stay at the Parc until the year 2000, and have planned major ground improvements accordingly. Local pride and modest crowds prevent both the natural and geographical candidates, Red Star and Aubervilliers, from uprooting. So in the summer of 1996, an amalgamation was formed of local club Saint-Denis and Saint-Leu-la-Forêt, 20km away.

Playing in the old northern *National 1* in 1996/97, **Saint-Leu-Saint-Denis** were ambitiously hoping to make the first division in five years. Local rivals US Créteil were even moved to the southern group to keep the new boys in the spotlight. All to no avail. While US Créteil enjoyed a giant-killing run to the quarter-finals of the French cup in 1997, Saint-Denis-Saint-Leu went **out by default,** having failed to enter their official papers on time.

For the moment, it seems residents of this forgotten working-class suburb will have to be happy with the much-needed custom le Stade will bring; successful club football may have to come later.

To **reach the stadium,** take RER line B to La Plaine Voyageurs, one stop from the Gare du Nord. The RER D line and *métro* line #13 are also being extended here and will be ready by 1998. From the station, the ground is a short walk up avenue du Président Wilson and a right turn at rue Francis de Pressensé.

You can get a beer and a taste of the area at **La Nouvelle Plaine,** 251 avenue du Président Wilson, a small, friendly Arab bar quite unprepared for the approaching tidal wave. For **lunch,** try **Le Pressensé** opposite at #258.

For those who wish to visit le Stade before its opening in January 1998, there are **tour parties** organised weekdays, 8am–5pm. Phone in advance (☎01 49 46 39 46 or 01 49 46 38 28) to arrange an English-language version. Entrance is a steep F100.

In the reception area, **Le Pavillon** (open Mon–Fri 9am–6pm, credit cards accepted) has a video display, a huge model of the stadium, a pictorial history of the construction, and the first stone encased in glass and cloaked in football memorabilia. You can also buy le Stade official **merchandise** (T-shirts, caps and the like) here.

rewarded with the renovation of the much-maligned Parc. With le Grand Stade to assume most international responsibilities – and cash injections from their European runs – the club are looking to turn the Parc into a genuine home ground.

The stadium is perfectly suited to a successful club team, with a perfect view for all 49,000 spectators, no running track, and an atmosphere easy to generate. Having chosen the Parc over le Grand Stade, PSG are keen that it does not suffer in comparison. As well as new lighting and seating for the 1998 World Cup, a supporters' centre, a panoramic restaurant and a sports superstore are all due to be built by the year 2000.

Here we go!
Take *métro* line #9 to Porte de Saint Cloud, coming out at the Côté Boulogne exit.

Swift half
Les Trois Obus, 120 rue Michel-Ange, is run by club management. Advance tickets, reasonably priced meals and pitchers of wine are on sale, under the watchful gaze of a huge mirror design of the Parc, but like many bars around Place de Saint Cloud, it's a little soulless. **Café aux Deux Stades**, 41 avenue Général Sarrail, nearer the stadium, is more like it. Although airbrushed portraits of PSG stars have replaced classic Fifties sports newspaper covers, the place still buzzes with frantic smoking, *baby-foot* action and teenage romance. The bar area is dominated by dozens of club pennants – and by a friendly landlord. Closes at 8pm, though.

Getting a ticket
Unless you're in town for a major European tie or a game against Marseille, getting in isn't a problem at the Parc des Princes. There are ticket offices dotted all round the ground.

The Parc is divided into colour-coded tiers – red, blue and yellow. The red tier is the cheapest and nearest the pitch. PSG fans go to either end, and the hardcore mob are to be found in the Boulogne red section. The blue and yellow sections are less hectic, particularly the seats in the *Tribune Paris* (G, H, I, J and K), which are accessed from avenue du Parc des Princes. For international games, away fans are allocated a corner in red *Tribune* F, accessed from rue Claude Farrere.

Publications
The Paris edition of the weekly *Journal du Dimanche* (F6.50) carries a sixteen-page PSG supplement which is then handed out at the ground the following weekend. The club publishes a colour monthly magazine, *Paris Go!* (F20).

Club shops
There are two **Boutiques du PSG** selling a full range of merchandise (including the PSG 25th anniversary CD-ROM!) and match tickets. One is just to the left of the stadium as you walk up from the *métro* (30 avenue du Parc des Princes, open Mon–Fri 9am–5pm and on matchdays), the other at 25 avenue Franklin-Roosevelt (Tues–Sat 10am–6pm). Both take credit cards. Also near the Parc is **la Boutique des Supporters**, 31 avenue du Parc des Princes (open Mon–Fri 9am–noon & 2–7pm, Sat 9am–noon), which stocks gear from all over France.

Ultra culture
Ten years ago PSG had a crowd but few supporters. Now the club has two sets of committed fans, at the Boulogne and Auteuil ends. The longest-established crew are the 'Boulogne Boys', the most fun are the *Hoolicools* and the most colourful are the *Supras* in the Auteuil end.

In the net
There's a fine unofficial PSG website at: www.cgc.ntu.ac.sg:8000/~att/ – though be warned that it may move shortly. You'll find plenty of stats in English, plus a lively French-only news section lifted from the pages of *l'Équipe*. For 1997/98, the club promise an official site at: www.psg.tm.fr/.

Groundhopping

☾ Red Star 93

Stade Bauer, 92 rue du Docteur Bauer,
Saint-Ouen
Capacity 12,000
Colours All white with green trim

Red Star 93 were formed by Jules
Rimet in 1897 – he took the reasoning
behind their Anglicised name to his
grave. Having dominated the French
cup after World War I, the club have
had a rough time of it ever since
World War II.

Currently a second-division club,
in 1997 Red Star celebrated their centenary by gathering together a
thousand current and former players
onto the Stade Bauer pitch. Between
them they had seen years of potential
mergers, liquidation and lower-league
football – but at least Red Star have
their roots in the French capital.

The pride of the Seine-Saint-Denis
department (postal district 93 – hence
the other part of the name), the club
shunned a move to the Grand Stade
in favour of a much-needed, munici-
pally funded F200 million renovation
to their tatty ground. The removal
of fences from the terraces in the
spring of 1997 might set a precedent for
other smaller clubs to follow – it has certainly increased the family atmosphere at
the Bauer.

Take *métro* line #13 to Mairie de Saint-
Ouen or, if you want to catch the last
pickings at Europe's biggest flea market,
line #4 to Porte de Clignancourt.

At half-time there's a **bar and grill**
behind the main stand, opposite the club
shop. *L'Olympic*, 105 rue Docteur Bauer,
opposite the main entrance, is a friendly
bar full of Red Star souvenirs – expec-
tant talk before the game, Gallic shrugs
thereafter.

All roads lead to le Grand Stade – well, some anyway

☾ Racing Club

Stade Colombes, 12 rue du Manoir, Colombes
Capacity 30,000
Colours Sky blue-and-white hooped shirts, white
shorts

Along with Wembley, the Maracaná and
the Azteca, Racing Club's Colombes has
staged a World Cup final – in 1938. The
stadium also played host to decades of cup
finals and internationals. Before World War
II, Racing Club de France attracted both
high society and top-class international

stars to their exclusive grounds north-west of Paris. Buenos Aires' Rácing, who also play in sky blue and white, are still known as 'The Academy'.

The football section, Racing Club de Paris, was separated when the French league turned professional in 1932. For thirty years Racing remained part of French football's élite, winning the double in 1936 with the help of Austrian *Wunderteam* goalkeeper Rudi Hiden.

Racing were dissolved in 1966. But Pierre Littbarski, Enzo Francescoli and Luis Fernandez all starred in a disastrous attempt to revive the club twenty years later, as Matra Racing. When the sponsors' money dried up, the stars fled and the club soon floundered in the lower leagues.

The latest reincarnation of the football team, Racing 92, nearly went under in 1995. But Colombes is now enjoying a F5 million facelift thanks to the regional council. Meanwhile, millionaire Alain Afflelou is trying to recapture past glories through a possible merger with his US Créteil club.

To reach Colombes, take an **SNCF train** four stops from Gare Saint-Lazare to Le Stade, then a ten-minute walk.

The fabulously tatty **RCF buffet** by gate #1 is a must, but closed on Mondays and Tuesdays. The **Café du Stade**, 67 rue Nouvelle, opposite, does reasonable food.

🌀 Paris FC

Stade de la Porte de Montreuil, 36 rue des Docteurs Déjerine
Capacity 5,000
Colours All sky blue

The very embodiment of the dishevelled 20th *arrondissement* in the east of the capital, Paris FC are run by the Bariani brothers, high up in local government. The club have the usual history of adoption and mergers. Their ground, with its two stands, is satisfyingly homely and shambolic. This is French third-division football at its muddiest – but none the worse for that.

To see the Barianis, take *métro* line #9 to Porte de Montreuil, then a short walk down rue des Docteurs Déjerine.

A **buffet** behind the goal dispenses beer and sausages all game. Towards the *métro* station, *l'Aurore*, 8 avenue de la Porte Montreuil, is for serious gamblers and pinball players.

Eat, drink, sleep…

Bars and clubs
The large, well-lit and archetypally Parisian **cafés** on the main boulevards tend to charge outrageous prices for drinking outside. Parisian **districts** quickly fall in and out of fashion, but bar-hopping is still hot around Bastille, Pigalle and Ménilmontant. **Clubbing** is an expensive habit, but worth it when the classier world music and jazz acts pass through town.

Bar Bastide, 18 rue de Lappe. Classic Bastille bar, a former Arab haunt which now attracts an alternative crowd. Métro Bastille.

Café L'Éspoir, 189 rue des Pyrénées. Invigorating North African football bar crowded with exiles from Oran, on whose ASMO side they model their own l'USMO bar team. Check out the photograph of the boss with Algerian World Cup star Lakhdar Belloumi. Métro Gambetta.

Cyrano, 3 rue Biot. Best football bar in town. The boss, Jacky, a disillusioned Saint-Étienne man, has regular visits from fans all over the world, hence the vast collection of pennants. Métro Place de Clichy.

Java, 105 rue du Faubourg du Temple. Weekend salsa joint in the Brixton of Paris, Belleville. Former regulars Edith Piaf and Maurice Chevalier would have approved. Métro Belleville.

Kitty O'Shea's, 10 rue des Capucines. One of Paris' many expat haunts, an Irish bar offering authentic décor, good food and satellite TV. Métro Opéra.

La Fléche d'Or, 102 bis rue du Bagnolet. A former railway stop on the *petite ceinture* route which now serves up pitchers of beer to a lively clientèle. Unpretentious. Métro Alexandre Dumas.

La Locomotive, 90 Boulevard de Clichy. A three-level club which had seen better days until the F Communication people stepped in. Check out DJ Laurent Garnier's regular spots. Métro Blanche.

Restaurants

No other city in Europe has a **range of cuisine** like Paris. It can cost a fortune to enjoy it – especially the local variety – but shop around; the city boasts many long-established cheap haunts, and North African, Chinese and Vietnamese food is almost always reasonably priced. All the places listed below take most major credit cards.

The Bowler, 13 rue d'Artois. English-style pub opened in 1996 with a cricketing theme, curries, roast dinners and the daily papers from Blighty. Métro Saint-Philippe du Roule.

Chartier, 7 rue du Faubourg Montmartre. Everyone's favourite cheapie, always packed, always filling. Shared tables. Closes 9.30pm. Métro rue Montmartre.

Chez Mustapha, 46 rue Volta. Friendly, family-run couscous restaurant with mystic décor. Métro Arts et Métiers.

Le Gambrinus, 62 rue des Lombards. Hearty portions of favourite French dishes at reasonable prices, right in the Châtelet area. Open until 6am. Métro Châtelet.

Le Maquis, 69 rue Caulaincourt. Excellent, cheap lunches in the heart of Montmartre with a summer terrace. Métro Lamarck Caulaincourt.

Accommodation

Even in high season (when there isn't much football on, anyway) it isn't difficult finding a reasonably priced room in central Paris. The main **tourist office** at 127 avenue des Champs-Élysées (open daily 9am–8pm, ☎01 49 52 53 54) charges a varying commission for reserving a room, depending on the hotel category.

The gasworks was prettier – but le Grand Stade will soon be one of Europe's premier football venues

If you're on a budget, then an **AJF office** will find you a room in a hostel for a 10F commission, or a bed for no extra charge. Their head office is opposite the Pompidou Centre at 119 rue Saint-Martin (open Mon–Sat 9.30am–7pm, ☎01 42 77 87 80), with branches at the Gare du Nord, the Hôtel de Ville and at 139 boulevard Saint-Michel. If you're arriving on spec, the area around the Gare du Nord will have something, though it may be a little seedy.

The following hotels all charge around F200–300 for a double room.

Henri IV, 25 Place Dauphine (☎01 43 54 44 53). Perennial classic budget lodgings with a fine view on the Île de la Cité. Book at least a month in advance. Most credit cards. Métro Pont-Neuf.

Hôtel des Academies, 15 rue de la Grande Chaumiére (☎01 43 26 66 44). Cheap, clean one-star hotel in the Montparnasse area. No credit cards. Métro Vavin.

Hôtel de Nesle, 7 rue de Nesle (☎01 43 54 62 41). Quiet place with a pleasant back garden in the Saint-Michel area. No credit cards. Métro Saint-Michel.

Idéal, 3 rue des Trois Fréres (☎01 46 06 63 63). Comfortable and friendly joint around Montmartre. No credit cards. Métro Abbesses.

Pratic, 20 rue de l'Ingénieur-Keller (☎01 45 77 70 58). If you wake up craving the Eiffel Tower, this is the place for you. No credit cards. Métro Charles-Michels.

France '98 – a nation prepares

"I want 1998 to reflect my vision of football," World Cup organising chief Michel Platini has declared. Where else but France could such a romantic figure be put in charge of such an earth-shattering event?

The 1994 World Cup in America was successful in terms of organisation, revenue and full stadia. In footballing terms, however, the last really satisfying World Cup was in 1970. Platini and his team now have to find the perfect combination for France '98. They will be burdened with a 32-team, 66-match tournament, the biggest ever. But they will also be aided by a first-rate transport system between venue cities, all of which are served by TGV train and have international airports.

Platini's organising committee are aiming to sell **2.5 million tickets**, providing 40 percent of all revenue, in ten stadia, most far smaller than those used four years previously in the States. More than half a million of these will be on sale for less than F150 – less than you'd pay to see an ordinary game in the Premiership.

In a break with tradition, teams will play their group matches in **three different venues**, thus giving the regional public a chance to see a range of different styles of football. Five- and six-match venue passes sold out within weeks of going on sale in the spring of 1997.

Tickets for the quarter- and semi-finals, final and opening match go on sale in November 1997, and are **limited to two per person**. In the likely event of demand exceeding supply, a draw will take place. Remaining single tickets for group matches go on sale in February 1998.

Prices are categorised in three bands (four at the Stade de France), depending on the view. A single category 2 seat costs F250 for a group match, F490 for a quarter-final and F1150 for a semi. Prices for that magic final ticket range from F350 to F950 for an ordinary seat, and from F1750 to F2950 for the VIP treatment. FIFA have reserved **20 percent of tickets** for sale through **national federations**.

For further information, write to: France '98, BP 1998, 75201 Paris Cedex 16, France, or telephone Paris ☎01 36 68 22 24.

Nantes

Thanks to forward thinking, faith in youth and, ultimately, good football, the sleepy city of Nantes has remained at the forefront of the French game for thirty years.

Its team, *les Canaris*, may not have enjoyed the same kind of resources, fan base or European runs as other brasher, provincial outfits, but the FC Nantes Atlantique training school has continued to produce outstanding talent.

It seldom stays long. Trying to compete with the big boys, with only rare lucrative forays into the later stages of European competition, has entailed a constant flow of major players from the Loire estuary. Of the side that won the club's last French title in 1995, Patrice Loko, Nicolas Ouédec and Reynald Pedros had all found alternative employment within two years.

Nevertheless, Nantes always seem to finish in the top six, picking up a title every five years or so, and three decades of entertaining, top-flight football have made local fans knowledgeable as well as partisan.

The team's entertainers were given the perfect stage in 1984, when a boldly designed new stadium was built in time for the European Championship. The construction of the futuristic Beaujoire, set in parkland on the opposite side of the river Erdre from the training school at La Jonelière, has since firmly established Nantes as part of the fabric of modern French football.

Although comfortable and spacious, and a popular venue for international rugby, the Beaujoire has been underused by the national football team. It was full to the brim for Platini's hat-trick in France's 5–0 thrashing of Belgium in 1984, but then had to wait more than a decade before the next appearance of *Les Bleus*, when David Ginola was the first French name on the scoresheet in a 4–0 win over Slovakia.

Driving the midfield that day were Didier Deschamps and Marcel Desailly, a

Mad about the boy – Loko at La Beaujoire

pair of former Nantes team-mates who first met when they were young lads at the training school. They were the star duo of an exceptional crop of players raised at Nantes, finding their feet not just on the pitch but also on the dancefloor at the city's New Way nightclub.

Like so many others, both would be sold on, to star together in Marseille's European Cup win of 1993, then in victories in the same competition for Milan and Juventus, respectively. Pleasing the Beaujoire crowd with France in 1998 would surely give the pair equal satisfaction – and repay a debt to the old school.

The thrilling fields

FC Nantes Atlantique

La Beaujoire, route de Saint-Joseph
Capacity 40,000 (all-seated)
Colours Yellow-and-green striped shirts, yellow shorts
League champions 1965–66, 1973, 1977, 1980, 1983, 1995
Cup winners 1979

Nantes are the third most successful league team in France, with the most modern-looking stadium and an adventurous youth policy second only to Auxerre's.

This is remarkable considering that they had not tasted top-flight football before 1963. Indeed, Football Club Nantes had been founded only twenty years before, as an amalgamation of five local clubs: Saint-Pierre, Mellenet, Loire, ASO Nantes and Stade Nantes. Straight away they won *le Championnat de l'Ouest* and *la Coupe de l'Ouest*, entering the second division in 1945.

Promotion to the first in 1963 allowed for modernisation of the club's Marcel Saupin stadium, which saw the winning of six league titles beginning in 1965. By the time Nantes had made the European Cup-Winners' Cup semi-final in 1980, it was obvious that the Marcel Saupin, now home to youth and reserve-team games, was too cramped for requirements.

The first team, quietly but effectively bossed by new coach Jean-Claude Suaudeau, had great potential, and the prospect of hosting regular European football, together with the imminent 1984 European Championship, provided a perfect opportunity for stadium architect Berdje Agopyan to try something radical. He certainly achieved it – from above, La Beaujoire looks like a particularly testing Scalextric track, with its curving roofs on either side. Inside, there is a tremendous sense of light and space.

Eight years after the Beaujoire was built, the club found themselves with debts of F60 million. They were rescued by biscuit billionaire Guy Scherrer, who gave Suaudeau the opportunity to build the team up over three years to win the title again in 1995.

Despite revenue from a run to the semi-finals of the Champions' League the following season, another sell-off followed, coupled with more boardroom disputes; Scherrer eventually quit in November 1996.

Nantes essentials

From the modest Nantes-Atlantique **airport**, an hourly TANAIR bus (F36, journey time 25 minutes) takes you to the railway stop at Gare Sud, then on to the main Place du Commerce in the centre of town.

There are **trains** almost hourly between Nantes and Paris Montparnasse, journey time just over two hours. Of the train station's two exits, Nord gives out to the stop on the green tramway line #1. The other tramway, red line #2, crosses at Commerce. Tram **tickets** (F7 each, F30 for a *mini-carnet* of five, F52 for ten) are not sold onboard but at major stops and *tabacs*. The same tickets are also valid on the city's extensive **bus network**. A day ticket (*journalier*) covering everything is F19.

Bus and tram services run 5am–midnight. **Taxis** can usually be found at Commerce, but to phone one, dial ☎02 40 69 22 22.

The main **tourist office** is also at Place du Commerce (open Mon–Fri 9am–7pm, Sat–Sun 10am–6pm). Neither *Nantes Poche* nor *Nantes des Jours et des Nuits*, given out at the tourist board, are particularly strong listings publications. There have been several attempts to launch one; the latest, *Talents 44*, is a monthly and, assuming it survives, could do with a little more low-brow coverage.

Futuristic but short on fireworks – La Beaujoire awaits key improvements for the 1998 World Cup

After a calamitous start to their 1996/97 campaign, Nantes went thirty games unbeaten and, with the goals of Chad international Japhet N'Doram, claimed their now customary place in Europe. The long-serving Suaudeau then handed over the reins to youth coach Reynald Denoueix, though the former will remain at La Beaujoire for at least another year. Denoueix's first task is to find a replacement for N'Doram, sold to Monaco for £3 million in the summer of 1997.

It has to be said that the constant sell-off has proved a constant turn-off for many fans. Nantes have rarely engendered the kind of passion inherent in working-class French towns like Lens or Saint-Étienne, and the club can draw on neither a large catchment area nor much support elsewhere in the country.

Always big on comfort and convenience (an average one parking space for every two spectators), but often short on fever, the Beaujoire is being renovated for the 1998 World Cup. Among the improvements will be the moving of the *virages* closer to the pitch – which might just provide the atmosphere to keep the latest crop of youngsters from straying too far.

Here we go!

Take tramway green line #1 to its Beaujoire terminus – allow fifteen minutes from the main train station.

Swift half

Down by the train station you'll find **Les Canaris**, 9 boulevard de Stalingrad, where a number of supporters gather before getting the tramway up to the Beaujoire.

On the way to the stadium, near Haluchère tramway stop, there's **le Café de la Gare** on chemin du Ranzay and **Bar la Beaujoire**, 1 rue de la Petite Baratte. Outside the stadium by the main ticket office there's a row of **stand-up bars** selling beer, wine and sausages. **Chez Jean-Louis** and **Le Domino** attract the largest clientèle.

Getting a ticket

The main **ticket offices** are facing you as you walk from the tramway stop. Sell-outs are rarely a problem. For the neutral, the *Tribune Jules Verne* (named after Nantes' most famous son) is the best option. Away fans are generally placed in the *Virage Océan*. For advance tickets, write to the club at: BP 1124, 44311, Nantes Cedex 03, France.

Career canary – long-serving coach Jean-Claude Suaudeau

porters' club, *Allez Nantes Canaris*, have an office at rue Regnard (open Mon–Fri 3–7pm). The club were formed in 1945 and can boast nearly a thousand members. Their office has the usual souvenirs on sale, including a copy of the team's pop classic, *La Canari Mania* (F26).

In the net
Unless you're a Norwich City supporter, you may find the orgy of green-and-yellow graphics on the main Nantes website hard to stomach. Fear not, though – this ambitious, multi-framed affair is actually not a bad site, with plenty of stats, news and gossip, and everything in English as well as French. For the future, webmaster Christophe Boulangé promises downloadable canary-coloured desktop backgrounds and screen-savers. Hold your breath and head for: services.worldnet.fr./cboulang/Soccer/Football.shtml.

Publication
Sportmania (F20) is the club's bright colour fortnightly magazine. Of the two local dailies, *Presse-Océan,* which also happens to be a club sponsor, offers more comprehensive coverage than *Ouest France.*

Club shop
Planète FCNA, 56 boulevard de la Beaujoire (open Mon–Sat 9am–noon & 2–7pm, until 11pm on matchdays, most major credit cards), is the club's spacious store near the stadium. On matchdays, on the concourse by the ticket offices, you'll find two yellow vans marked *Allez Nantes,* selling a range of souvenirs.

Ultra culture
The 1995 title win and subsequent Champions' League action motivated the 'Young Boys' in the *Tribune Loire* into noisy action. The 'Urban Service' in the *Tribune Océane* are the only mob who make the local papers, but it's pretty tame stuff. 'Yellow Flight 49', in the *Stand BN-Erdre,* produce their own fanzine, *L'Envol Jaune,* on sale at the ground. The mainstream Nantes sup-

Eat, drink, sleep...

Bars and clubs
There is a large concentration of **bars** around la Place du Commerce, but few are particularly inspiring. A little exploration might not produce anything as colourful as a night in Marseille, but will at least create a few ripples in the millpond of Nantes nightlife.

Bar de L'Adagio, 6 rue Sainte-Catherine. Elegant, pricey but fun cocktail bar featuring Jean-Yves Morinière, France's barman of the year in 1995. Near Place du Commerce.

Black Mint, 4 rue Lebrun. Hugely successful techno/rave bar/club with acceptable dance music, happy hour for those in a hurry, and large games of chess for those not. Bus #21 or #23 to Place Foch.

Café des Acacias, 6 rue des Carmelites. Delightfully friendly bikers' bar, with liberal music policy and a clientèle *au courant* with what's going on in town. Short walk from the castle.

La Belle Équipe, 10 quai de la Jonelière. Fine sports bar with a terrace looking out onto the river Erdre near the FCNA training centre. Run by ex-Nantes player Vincent Brascigliano, it is decked out in framed sports comic covers from the Fifties, with a huge window dedicated to the *Tour de France*. Full menu. Closed Mondays and Sunday and Tuesday evenings. Bus #51 from Médiathèque, or a pleasant walk from red tramway stop Recteur Schmitt.

Le Maltais, 8 rue Grande-Biesse. Classic Nantes R&R club with a wayward crowd. Reasonable prices. Sadly redecorated of late. Red tramway to Vincent Gâche.

Le Virgil, 33 rue de Verdun. Centrally located bar owned by Marcel Desailly, whose picture (in Milan colours, mind) greets the visitor. Three TV sets plus a further huge screen for Canal Plus broadcasts. Modern and spacious. Short walk from the castle.

Restaurants

There may not be much **regional cuisine** in Nantes, but at least you'll find plentiful seafood and the usual range of Chinese, Vietnamese and African eateries.

La Cigale, 4 place Graslin. Elegant brasserie inaugurated on April Fools' Day 1895. Specialities include oysters, *fruits de mer* and a variety of fish prepared according to local tradition, but it's the murals and fin-de-siècle décor that grab the attention. Bus #11 or #24.

La Cour Talensac, 14bis rue Talensac. Although suffering a*nimations musicales* at weekends, La Cour is expansive enough for you to find quiet karaoke-free corners. Open until 4am on Fridays and Saturdays. Red tramway to 50 Otages.

Le Djerba, 3 rue Lekain. Amiable diner offering North African dishes, including couscous at F57.

Near Place Graslin on the #24, #51, #54 and #55 bus routes.

L'Étoile d'Orient, 3 rue Maréchal De Lattre de Tassigny. Friendly two-floor Vietnamese restaurant with cheap menu deals. Green tramway to Médiathèque.

La Poissonerie, 4 rue Léon-Maître. Seafood delights at reasonable prices. Considering the quality of the food, the lunchtime menu at F70 cannot be bettered. Green tramway to Bouffay.

Accommodation

For a sleepy French town of less than half a million people, Nantes has a decent number of cheap rooms. A list is available at the **tourist office** in Place du Commerce.

Beaujoire Hôtel, 15 rue des Pays de Loire (☎02 40 93 00 01). Two-star hotel by the stadium, cheaper and more modest than the *Otelinn* below. Visiting teams generally stay here when necessary. Most major credit cards. Green tramway to Beaujoire.

Centre Jean Macé, 88 rue du Préfet Bonnefoy (☎02 40 74 55 74). Centrally located youth hostel catering to individuals or groups for stays of up to two weeks. Bus #22.

Hôtel de l'Océan, 11 rue du Maréchal De Lattre de Tassigny (☎02 40 69 73 51). Clean one-star hotel as cheap as you'll find anywhere in town. Green tramway to Médiathèque.

Hôtel Duquesne, 12 allée Duquesne, Cours des 50 Otages (☎02 40 47 57 24). The family-run Duquesne offers affordable luxury, with quiet rooms in the centre of town at around F200–250 a double. Canal Plus in every room. Red tramway to 50 Otages.

Otelinn, 45 Boulevard des batignolles (☎02 40 50 07 07, fax 02 40 49 41 40). Two-star business hotel/restaurant by the Beaujoire stadium. Sixty rooms, each with a Minitel point and Canal Plus. Most major credit cards. Green tramway to Beaujoire.

Bordeaux

Bordeaux is a city of immediate contrasts. Guidebooks indicate a quiet, *bourgeois* rugby-playing wine town, but your nose quickly guides you to fading riverside bars where the talk is all football.

Lying between the quaint farmhouse territory of the Dordogne and the political powderkeg of the Basque country, Bordeaux has known several spells of soccer fever. The latest came in the spring of 1996, when its club, the Girondins, capped an epic twenty-game run from the Intertoto Cup by reaching the UEFA Cup final. Defender Bixente Lizarazu celebrated victories at the Parc Lescure by parading the Basque flag; ten years before, he'd been singing with the ultras in the Parc's *Virage Sud*. The local paper, *Sud Ouest*, sold three times more copies after Bordeaux's win over Milan than it did after the death of François Mitterrand.

The club attract followers from both ends of Aquitaine society. As the sole soccer representatives of south-west France, the Girondins have always received official favour from regional government. In the Eighties, millionaire businessman Claude Bez made use of these connections to revive the club – but his under-the-counter deals were to cost everyone dear.

For the home leg of the 1996 UEFA Cup semi-final against Slavia Prague, the Bordeaux management tested the loyalty of fans by filling the Parc Lescure with sponsors and season-ticket holders, leaving just 1000 tickets for the ultras. Yet despite this and the exodus of stars that followed the 1996 UEFA Cup final, all is not lost. The aristocrats are pleased that the delightful Parc Lescure, a listed building inaugurated for the 1938 World Cup, has had a F50 million spruce-up for the 1998 version. The ultras, meanwhile, revel in the fact that a new crop of youngsters not only lifted Bordeaux to another UEFA Cup spot in 1996/97, but did it in the club's revived colours of marine blue with a white chevron.

The thrilling fields

Girondins de Bordeaux

Parc Lescure, 347 boulevard Wilson
Capacity 36,500 (all-seated)
Colours All marine blue with white chevron
League champions 1950, 1984–85, 1987
Cup winners 1941, 1986–87

Sixty years span the Parc Lescure's opening and its renovation for the 1998 World Cup. In 1938, the stadium had the feel of a grand ocean liner, embellished with a vast concrete arch, a pseudo-classical courtyard and two Olympic towers – but it lacked a football team. For all but fifteen of those years, the Lescure served rugby and cycling fans, with football as a side issue. It stood unused for the 1984 European Championship, even though the Girondins had by then acquired an ambitious club president and a star-studded side which, with Jean Tigana, Alain Giresse, Marius Trésor, Patrick Battiston and Bernard Lacombe, had just won the title under eventual national-team coach Aimé Jacquet.

Club president Claude Bez revamped the Parc Lescure in 1986, nearly doubling its capacity with the removal of the cycle track. European success was surely only just around the corner; in the previous year, 2–0 up after the first leg, Bordeaux had lost 3–0 to Juventus in the European Cup semi-finals (and thus missed out on a date with Liverpool at Heysel). Two years later they lost to Lokomotiv Leipzig on penalties in a Cup-Winners' Cup semi-final.

In anticipation of further progress, Bez made two significant business deals: one, with Canal Plus TV, was tied in with European coverage; the other was the building of an impressive team headquarters in a château, out of town at Le Haillan. The

Endgame – Lizarazu greets Matthäus before the 1996 UEFA Cup final second leg at the Lescure

potential gains of the TV contract would inspire Bez's great rival, Bernard Tapie, to bigger things at Marseille; the second deal would prove Bez's undoing, involving as it did the opening of secret bank accounts and the misuse of public money.

By the time his various frauds had been uncovered, Bez was too ill to stand trial. But the club could not escape unpunished. The Girondins were forcibly relegated in 1991, and though they quickly bounced back, they were still saddled with a F25 million debt bequeathed to them by Bez.

Enter another megalomaniac president, Alain Afflelou. Keen to extract support from the region's wealthy winemakers, he turned the team's shirts from marine blue to claret red. The vineyards didn't want to know. The ultras weren't happy either, as their patch in the *Virage Sud* became all-seated for the 1998 World Cup.

All parties, not least the players, were surprised by the 1995/96 UEFA Cup run. Only 3000 turned up to watch Bordeaux beat Vardar Skopje in the UEFA Cup first round in September 1995. By December there were 18,000 to see Real Betis vanquished in the third round. A 2–0 defeat at AC Milan in the quarter-final first leg appeared to signal the end of the road. It was anything but – the Girondins' 3–0 win in the return was voted 1996 match of the year by *France Football*, and would earn transfers to Italy for Zinedine Zidane and Christophe Dugarry.

Could Bordeaux repeat the feat against Bayern Munich in the final? Alas, they could not – and, despite a city's adulation, the club wasn't big enough to keep its stars; Afflelou followed them out of the door in the summer of 1996.

While many expected the club's fortunes to wane in 1996/97, the goalscoring of summer signing Jean-Pierre Papin and the quick maturity of young international Ibrahim Ba kept Bordeaux in the top six – and whetted fans' appetite for World Cup action in 1998.

Bordeaux essentials

Buses between the city's Mérignac **airport** and Saint-Jean **train station** run every 45 minutes and cost F33. Trains run hourly between Paris and Bordeaux, taking around three hours.

From the Saint-Jean, bus #7 or #8 will take you to Place Gambetta in town, while bus #1 runs along the waterfront to the Esplanade des Quinconces. **Bus tickets**, available onboard for F7.50 and valid for thirty minutes, also come in *carnets* of ten (F52) from *tabacs*. A day ticket is F22, and there are no night buses.

You should find a **taxi** around Quinconces. If not, phone *Taxi Blues* (☎05 56 51 39 94) or *Sud Ouest Taxi* (☎05 56 39 70 30).

The main **tourist office** is at 12 cours du XXX-juillet (open Mon–Sat 9am–8pm, Sun 9am–7pm, ☎05 56 00 66 00). Here you'll find a free copy of the excellent fortnightly listings publication, *Clubs et Concerts*. Two music shops, *Doc Rock* at 5 rue Duffour-Dubergier and *Noir et Blanc* at 19 rue des Retaillons, have up-to-date info on the local music scene.

Here we go!

Take bus #9 from Saint-Jean station to Stade Municipal, or bus #12 or #93 to Barriére d'Ornano from Pey Berland in town.

Swift half

The *buvettes* in the Parc Lescure sell only **alcohol-free** Buckler beer at F15. The best bet nearest the ground is **Le Rond de Point**, on the corner of avenue du Parc de Lescure and boulevard Maréchal Leclerc. Its bar is lined with pennants from various European campaigns, the scores lovingly written above the names of each team, serving as a reminder that Bordeaux have played more foreign cup ties than any other French club. A better bar, nevertheless, is **le Bar des Sports**, five minutes away on the corner of boulevard Leclerc and rue Léo Saignat. On offer here are couscous, paella, Amstel beer, darts and football talk until match time.

Tickets

The two main **ticket offices** are near the corner of boulevard Leclerc and rue Albert Thomas, under the giant hoop. Neutrals will find themselves in the *Virage Nord*, in blocks H–L, segregated from both home and visiting support. Blocks A–G and S–M have more expensive seats in the *tribunes latéralles* alongside the touchline. Credit cards are accepted at the ticket office.

For **advance tickets**, recommended for games against Marseille and Paris Saint-Germain, contact the club at: BP 33, 33186 Le Haillan, France (☎05 56 16 11 11, fax 05 56 57 54 46). The office is way out of town, accessible by bus #18 from Jean-Jaurès.

Publications

Le Scapulaire (F20) is a 32-page colour magazine published by the club for home games. The monthly *Foot Gironde* (also F20) is an independently produced colour monthly which also covers the quaint football scene in the Aquitaine region.

Club shop

Although Bordeaux have no shop at the stadium or in town, they do sell merchandise from their **headquarters** far out at Le Haillan, and there are stalls set out around the Lescure on matchdays. At the **secondhand bookstore** *Johnny B Foot*, 20 rue des Menuts (open Tues–Fri 10.30am–1pm & 2.30–7pm), you'll find collections of old French sports papers, postcards and other memorabilia.

Ultra culture

Le Collectif Virage Sud are a combination of two groups, *Ultras Bordeaux* and *Devils Bordeaux*, and are a colourful, likeable bunch; they at last had something to shout about during Bordeaux's UEFA Cup run of 1996.

They're also far hipper than any other ultra group in France – although the competition, to be fair, isn't that strong.

In the net

The Girondins were the first French club to have a website dedicated to them and retain a powerful presence, with a variety of sites, all of them fan-run. Perhaps the best is at: www.cs.umu.se/~kenth/gb.html. It's a straightforward site visually, but those rather bland-looking pages conceal great strength in depth, with excellent stats, GIF images of players and the Parc Lescure, a RealAudio version of the club's Wit FM radio station, and a rolling news service. The last is in French only but much of the rest of the site carries an English option.

Eat, drink, sleep…

Bars and clubs

Bordeaux has a **lively nightlife**, generally unaffected by the visitors who come here for expensive vineyard excursions. The main action is down by the *quais* alongside the river, particularly le quai de Paludate. For six months of the year, the terraces around the neoclassical centre of town are humming with tourists, but with a little luck you can wade through the tack and pick up on Bordeaux's techno, garage, punk or reggae scene.

Hôtel des Salinières, rue de la Fusterie/cours Victor Hugo. Unmissable for incurable football romantics, this tatty, peeling place features obscure pennants and trophies, and a *Wanted* poster with a price on Alain Afflelou's head. Open late, full menu. Near Pont de Pierre. Bus #1.

La Peniche, 7 Quai de la Monnaie. A *quai* bar that really stands out, with African clientèle, music and late drinking habits. A table outside allows a view of the lights along the Pont de Pierre. Bus #1.

La Sardane, 19 cours de l'Argonne. Probably the least pretentious of the bars in the Latin Quarter south of Place de la Victoire. It may get heated during televised football matches, but equally can be cooling during the long, hot *Bordelais* summer. Bus #20 or #21.

Le Jimmy, 68 rue de Madrid. Main rock venue in town that gives equal licence to name bands and local ones trying to make it in the Big Grape. Near the Parc Lescure on bus #9.

Lollapalooza, 48/49 quai de Paludate. Large nightclub playing mainly acid-jazz and other danceable solutions. Plus point – free entry. Minus point – over-vigilant bouncers. Bus #1.

Nulle parts Ailleurs, 19 cours du Maréchal Foch. Before leaving for Milan in the summer of 1996, striker Christophe Dugarry was putting

New player, old kit – Papin at the Parc Lescure, 1997

the finishing touches to his nest egg in Bordeaux, this large, pleasant bar behind Quinconces. If developed in his absence (he's now moved on to Barcelona), it may become the first real sports bar in town. On fifteen major bus routes.

Restaurants

Bordeaux has a rich **variety of food** on offer, largely on account of its proximity to Spain and the Basque country. Local fish and seafood dishes are well worth trying. The cheapest joints are down in the area by Saint-Jean train station, but life here can get a little seedy after dark.

Café des Arts, 138 cours Victor Hugo. *The* big meeting place in town – an institution ever since its inauguration in 1933. *Plats du jour* at F43, with house specialities of rabbit and *coq au vin*. Most major credit cards accepted. Bus #3, #4, #5 or #6.

Casa Sansa, 21 rue Maucoudinat. With all the usual trimmings – like huge hocks of ham hanging from the ceiling – this is a decent Spanish restaurant specialising in Catalan dishes. Two-course menus begin at F48. Off cours d'Alsace. Bus #3, #4, #5 or #6.

Chez Georges, 53 rue des Faures. The cheapest place in town for local cuisine. With a friendly smile, the owner dishes out a soup, a main course and a glass of wine, all for F35. His profit margin matches his décor. Between Saint-Michel and cours Victor Hugo. Bus #3, #4, #5 or #6.

Etchecopar, 351 avenue du Maréchal de Lattre de Tassigny à Caudéran. Large portions of genuine Basque cuisine with a range of *prix fixe* menu options starting at F59. Closed Saturdays, kitchen closes at 2pm and 10pm. Bus #18 ast Parc Bordelais.

La Papaye, 14 rue Fernand-Phillipart. *Antillaise* dishes, plus other exotic options from places such as Tahiti and Madagascar. Open every evening except Sunday. Visa cards accepted. Near place de la Bourse. Bus #22, #23 or #28.

Accommodation

The best part of town for **cheap rooms** is opposite Saint-Jean train station. Although guidebooks warn people away from this red light area, the hotels are generally safe, clean and friendly. The small **tourist office**, located to the right of the main entrance at Saint-Jean (open daily 9am–noon & 12.45–7pm, Sun 10am–noon & 12.45–6pm), can provide hotel information, as can the main office in town at 12 cours du XXX-juillet.

Bristol, 4 rue Bouffard (☎05 56 81 85 01/fax 05 56 51 24 06). Every European city has a *Hotel Bristol*. This is Bordeaux's, and it's the cheapest place in town with Canal Plus. Cheapest rooms at F175–230. Most major credit cards. Near place Gambetta. Bus #19, #20 or #21.

De La Boëtie, 4 rue de la Boëtie (☎05 56 81 76 68/fax 05 56 81 24 72). Near the Mairie, a smart but still reasonably priced place whose satellite dish can pick up a host of foreign channels. Visa and Mastercard accepted. Bus #26.

Dijon, 22 rue Charles-Domercq (☎05 59 91 76 65). A low-budget but perfectly reasonable hotel opposite Saint-Jean station, with optional shower facilities and a bar downstairs. Most major credit cards.

Maison des Étudiants, 50 rue Ligier (☎05 56 96 48 30). Just west of the Spanish quarter, this student hostel is open for guests of both sexes from July to September (allowing you to catch the first month of the French football season), otherwise it's women only. Bus #7 or #8 from the station to cours de la Libération. The **FUAJ hostel** (☎05 56 91 59 51), five minutes' walk from the station up cours de la Marne to 22 cours Barbey, has an 11pm curfew.

San Michel, 32 rue Charles-Domercq (☎05 56 91 62 48). Amiable one-star hotel opposite Saint-Jean station with a bar/restaurant downstairs, F140 a room without a shower, a little extra with. Coded door-lock for sneaking in round the side late at night. Most major credit cards.

The football club as royal plaything – AS Monaco

Europe's **smallest country** is home to the most consistently successful yet unpopular team in French football. Monaco is a cliff-top principality overlooking the Cote d'Azur, a 3km-square piece of prize real estate whose banks, casinos and hotels form the familiar backdrop for the annual *Grand Prix*. Of its 30,000 population, only one in five possesses Monaco citizenship, and few care about the local football team.

The king of Monte Carlo – Glenn Hoddle, 1988

Champions of France for the sixth time in 1997, AS Monaco receive an annual F50 million subsidy from the national council, whose president, Jean-Louis Campora, holds the same position at the football club. The money invested in the club is seen as good for the principality's image, and the 18,000-capacity Louis II stadium is one of France's finest.

The team's most famous supporter is **Prince Albert**, and the whole royal family, along with other tax-exile regulars like Boris Becker, turn out for big occasions such as the UEFA Cup run in 1997, which saw Monaco beat Newcastle before going out to Inter Milan in the semi-finals.

The club were founded in 1924, turning professional after World War II and making the top flight in 1953. Prince Rainier poured in enough money for Monaco to strike a winning formula in the early Sixties, with a team that starred future French national-team coach **Michel Hidalgo**. The red-and-whites won the league and cup twice each, then had to wait twenty years before two of the stars of Hidalgo's national team, Manuel Amoros and Bruno Bellone, helped them to a third title in 1982.

The arrival of a young **Arsène Wenger** as coach from Nancy and of Glenn Hoddle and Mark Hateley from England prompted perhaps the club's finest season in 1987/88. Wenger's team was brash and adventurous, with Hoddle in midfield playing the best football of his career. Wenger would stay at Monaco for seven seasons, taking the club to a Cup-Winners' Cup final in 1992.

Monaco's fortunes then dipped slightly before the midfield anchor from Hidalgo's France, **Jean Tigana**, took over as coach for 1995/96. That season Brazilian Sonny Anderson was the league's top scorer, eighteen-year-old winger Thierry Henry the best newcomer. By 1996/97, with Scotland international John Collins in midfield and Nigerian Victor Ikpeba back from winning Olympic football gold in Atlanta, Monaco were worthy title winners. Victory was celebrated in true Monaco style – 2000 invited schoolchildren joining 5000 paying customers in the cathedral silence of the Louis II.

For the players, motivation in such a tame atmosphere is not the only problem. The Louis II pitch, laid over a car park and a swimming pool, is in poor shape. Media attention is scant, and few fans congregate around the *Beach Plaza* hotel where the players encamp before each match.

Neither is custom particularly brisk near the ground at the *Ship and Castle*, where Newcastle souvenirs and Brown Ale are still on sale after the bar's grand opening before the UEFA Cup quarter-final in March 1997…

Marseille

Olympique de Marseille *191*
SC Endoume *193*

The only club to hold France in its grip, Olympique Marseille are as essential to this bubbling, maritime melting-pot of a city as fish to the local *bouillabaisse* stew. Halfway between Barcelona and Genoa as the firework flies, Marseille enjoys as much excess, colour and passion as any football city in Spain or Italy.

Unfortunately, it also suffers as much corruption. The shadow of one man still darkens those rose sunsets over the hills of Provence: Bernard Tapie. A former club president, boss of Adidas and socialist MP, among other things, Tapie used secret bank accounts, shady political connections and a small fortune fraudulently diverted from his business empire to push *l'OM* to four league titles, and a European Cup in 1993. He is currently serving an eight-month jail term at Paris' Santé prison for match-fixing, with further punishment likely if he is found guilty of other corruption charges.

The south-east corner of France has always been a small footballing enclave in the morass of rugby south of France's Massif Central. In the first 28 editions of the French cup, from its introduction after World War I to the end of World War II,

l'OM, as they are known, won six. To accommodate the crowds inspired by this success, and to coincide with France's hosting of the 1938 World Cup, the city's Stade Vélodrome was built. This intimidating arena has since seen some of football's greatest moments, from the Italy–Brazil World Cup semi-final of 1938, to the exhilarating France–Portugal European Championship semi of 1984, which nearly cost the BBC's John Motson his voice.

Olympique Marseille's own European nights here were as much about festival as football – the local crowd celebrating in a way the French public had previously seen only secondhand on Italian or Spanish TV.

The game has always been part of the city's street culture, in the town and back into the hills beyond. Eric Cantona learned his chops with his brothers on the high plain of Les Caillols, Jean Tigana at Grandes Bastides nearby. That *l'OM* had to buy both stars from other teams says much about the way the club used to be run.

It is only now, with a training centre being built behind the Vélodrome, that Marseille are actively involved in raising stars, rather than simply buying them.

Marseille essentials

There are **twelve trains a day** from Paris to Marseille. The main train station, Gare Saint-Charles, is walking distance from the centre of town and the Vieux Port, and is also the hub of the city's transport system. **Airport buses** (F42) leave every twenty minutes for the 25-minute journey to Saint-Charles, and the city's two *métro* lines, blue (#1) and red (#2), cross there. Buses and the *métro* run only until 9pm, after which *Fluobuses* run every fifteen minutes until 12.30am. Tickets for all cost F8 (F41 for a *carnet* of six) and are valid for any one journey up to seventy minutes.

A solitary **tram line** runs from Noailles to Saint-Pierre. For a **taxi**, call either *Tupp Taxis* (☎04 91 05 80 80) or *Eurotaxis* (☎04 91 97 12 12).

The **tourist office** is on the city's main drag at La Canebière 4 (open daily July–Sept 8.30am–8pm; Oct–June Mon–Sat 9am–7.15pm, Sun 10am–5pm; ☎04 91 13 89 00). The office can book accommodation and provide you with the area's weekly listings brochures, *Semaine des Spectacles* and *L'Officiel des Loisirs*. For more lively listings information, the *Virgin Megastore* at 75 rue Saint-Ferréol has a noticeboard with concert information and flyers.

The thrilling fields

 Olympique Marseille

Stade Vélodrome, boulevard Michelet
Capacity 60,000 (all-seated)
Colours All white with sky-blue trim
League champions 1937, 1948, 1971–72,
1989–92
Cup winners 1924, 1926–27, 1935, 1938, 1943,
1969, 1972, 1976, 1989
European Cup winners 1993

Their motto may be *Droit au But* ('straight for goal'), but Olympique Marseille's path to success, like that of true love, has rarely run straight at all. On the contrary, the club's recent history is strewn with controversy, honour and disgrace, in about equal measure.

The club have always been first to the ball, competing in the first French cup, the first national amateur championship, and the first professional league. In those pre-war days, fans crammed into the modest Huveaune stadium until, with France's hosting of the 1938 World Cup, a new stadium was built nearby. However, the Stade Vélodrome, with the bright cycling track that gave the ground its name, saw little post-war glory until Marcel Leclerc took over the club in 1965.

Leclerc revamped both the club and their stadium, brought in stars from the 1970 World Cup like Brazil's Jairzinho, and led *l'OM* to a league and cup double in 1972. It wasn't to last. By 1980 Marseille were nearly bankrupt and, worse, relegated.

Inspired by both Leclerc and by Claude Bez at Bordeaux, in 1985 new club president Bernard Tapie began the multi-million franc rollercoaster ride that scaled heights and plunged depths never before experienced in French football. Amid all the fireworks of four league titles and three epic European runs, Tapie was near deified. But one prize still eluded him, and the French nation: the European Cup.

Hand of Wad – the 'crazy dribbler', 1991

Between Marseille and the trophy lay the weight of history. A sleight of hand (an unpunished penalty-box handball by Benfica's Vata) cost them the 1990 semi-final. A sleight of foot (Red Star Belgrade uncharacteristically playing for penalties) cost them the 1991 final. Each time, Tapie swept out one load of stars for another. Jean-Pierre Papin came and went, as did Chris Waddle – *'Waddle Reviens!'* graffiti is still daubed over the stadium, begging him to return. Eventually, in the 1993 final, Tapie's Marseille faced Berlusconi's Milan and squeaked it, 1–0. The city erupted.

Only 24 hours later, news broke that the team's previous league match against Valenciennes had been fixed. The scandal dragged on for three years, in the courts and through every newspaper in the land. Tapie's dozens of corrupt dealings, using a whole network of agents and middlemen, came to light. Doubt was cast on other European results, against AEK Athens in 1989, Spartak Moscow in 1991 and Club Bruges in 1993.

Yet, in the recession-hit port, many *Marseillais* blamed Paris for plotting his downfall. Even after he'd almost dragged the club down with him, Tapie remained a popular figure in Marseille, and former Vélodrome stars such as Alen Bokšić came to visit him in jail.

Stripped of the 1993 league title and of any right to defend their European one, Marseille were relegated and eventually placed in receivership. Insolvency denied the club a rightful place in the first division in 1995, but they at last claimed promotion a year later, thanks to the help of top goalscorer Tony Cascarino. Still with the largest fan base in France, and now formed as a limited company with backing from (ironically enough) Adidas, l'OM are looking for a straight and narrow path to glory.

Here we go!

Take red *métro* line #2 to Rond Pont du Prado, leaving by the boulevard Michelet exit.

Swift half

No alcohol is on sale in the stadium. Behind it, though, by the tennis courts, is **Le Sporting** bar with a summer terrace and reasonably priced menu. The friendly **Chevalier Rose** is just past the stadium at 99 boulevard Michelet.

Tickets

Season 1997/98 should be an easier one for the football fan visiting Marseille. The previous year, the Vélodrome was under construction and admission was by season-ticket only. Now, with the new *Tribune Michelet*, the Vélodrome comfortably holds 60,000, making it the biggest in France after le Grand Stade. The **ticket offices** are at the main entrance on boulevard Michelet. The best, and most expensive, seats for neutrals are in the *Tribunes Jean Bouin*, while away fans are placed in the *Nord Populaire*, underneath the radio tower. For advance tickets, contact the club office at: 441 avenue du Prado, 13257 Marseille, France (☎04 91 76 56 09, fax 04 91 76 07 77).

Publication

A free four-page hand-out has team news on matchdays, when you can also buy a

Drawing the line – Tony Cascarino and Joël Cantona are among the 'stars' in Marseille's D2

number of fanzines from ultra groups. *L'OM Plus* (F25) is a colour bi-monthly. There is a general mistrust of any Parisian media. To earn kudos with your barman, read *Le Provençal* – particularly its Monday sports supplement – over your morning *pastis*.

Club shop

La Boutique de l'OM, 156 la Canebiére (open Mon–Sat 9am–12.30pm & 2–7pm, most major credit cards) is well stocked and has a friendly manager who'll talk about his mate Chris Waddle all day long.

Ultra culture

No fan culture in France comes close to Marseille's. Even Paris Saint-Germain refused to fill *l'OM*'s shoes in the 1993/94 European Cup for fear of fan reprisals.

The renovations to the Vélodrome in 1996/97 caused friction between groups, who were obliged to encroach on each other's territory. Riot police had to be called in to prevent serious damage at the home game with Nantes in October 1996.

The most significant group are the *Commando Ultras 84*, who boast nearly 2000 members. Their position in the *Virage Sud* is slowly being usurped, however, by the 'South Winners', while the *Virage Nord* can boast the 'Yankees', the 'Fanatics', the 'Dodgers' and the 'Thunderbirds'.

The *Club des Ultras* run a small shop, *Le Magasin Virage Sud*, opposite the Vélodrome at 46 boulevard Michelet (open Mon–Sat 9.30am–noon & 2–6.30pm and on matchdays, no credit cards).

In the net

At the last count there were more than fifteen Marseille websites, none of them run with official backing. Navigating your way around them all would be a thankless task, so Eric Durand has thoughtfully gathered them together on his site at: www.mit.edu/people/durand/OM/OM.html. Eric's own content includes a quirky stats section and a chat area, and there are links for such things as news and graphics from other sites.

Groundhopping

☕ SC Endoume

Stade Tellene, boulevard Tellene
Capacity 5,000
Colours Red shirts, black shorts

No club could wish for a finer situation than SC Endoume. Their modest ground lies at the foot of Notre Dame de la Garde, the vast basilica, 150m high, whose glittering golden Virgin Mary protects fishermen in the bay spread out below. There is no finer vantage point in all Marseille.

Unfortunately, Endoume are also in the position of sharing a city with the nation's most popular club. In truth, their paths rarely cross. When they did, for a French cup game in 1996, even the Endoume coach seemed reluctant to halt another *l'OM* cup run.

For a welcome breather from the hectic life of the city, take bus #55 from the Vieux Port to Esplanade. The next stop, Escalier, followed by a steep climb up the steps to the basilica, allows a perfect view of the action against the big blue of the Mediterranean.

Rue d'Endoume is full of small gambling bars. *Bar de l'Avenir* at #47 is the best, with card, pinball and *baby-foot* action.

Eat, drink, sleep…

Bars and clubs

Bars in Marseille are far more **down-to-earth** than their Parisian counterparts. There are plenty of bars with folk happy to provide football tales, delivered Chico Marx-style in that Marseille accent.

In the Arab quarter east of la Canebière the atmosphere gets a little seedier – unaccompanied women would be wise to head for a quieter part of town. During the day, any bar down by the Vieux Port is as good as any other. In clubs, live music is varied and there's usually something interesting going on.

À l'Artistic, 6 cours Joseph Thierry. Gambling and sports bar in the centre of town with a lively clientèle and accents to die for.

Bar des Allées, 45 allée Léon Gambatta. Base for the Marseille fan club, where away trips are organised for any of the 6000 members. Fortunately there is a long counter, plenty of bar space and a terrace. Between Saint-Charles and Réformés-Canebière *métro* stops.

Bar Les Flots Bleus, 82 corniche Kennedy. The most picturesque footie bar in all Marseille, with a huge mural of *that* night in 1993, colourful scarves and a terrace kissing the Mediterranean. Bus #83 from the Vieux Port.

Espace Julien, 39 cours Julien. The city's main music venue, with a café in the same complex, and playing host to the best jazz and African acts. Métro Cours Julien.

Le Corsaire, 1 quai de Rive Neuve. The best after-hours bar around the Vieux Port. Next door is the **New Orleans** jazz club where they give be-bop lessons before the swinging starts.

Le Talgo, 7 rue du 141ème RIA. Café/restaurant behind Saint-Charles station open daytime in the week, evenings at weekends, with internet facilities and free jazz concerts.

Restaurants

Marseille's ethnic mix is never better reflected than in its food. As well as an abundance of **all kinds of stalls** for eating on the hoof, you'll find wonderful fish and seafood restaurants and the best couscous this side of the Mediterranean.

Le Maître, 10 rue Le Maître. Wonderfully friendly North African restaurant with great couscous and a menu at F49. Closed Saturdays. Between Saint-Charles and Réformés-Canebière *métro* stops.

Le Marseillais, 2 quai de Rive Neuve. Lunchtime favourite by the Vieux Port, with seafood specialities and *bouillabaisse*. Midday menu at F59.

Le Mas, 4 rue Lulli. Nighthawks' diner near the Opéra, open until 6am. Short walk from the Vieux Port.

Le Resto Provençal, 64 cours Julien. Local dishes in the centre of town at affordable lunchtime prices, with a menu at F60. Métro Cours Julien.

Planète, 90 boulevard Rabatau. Slightly pricey African and Caribbean joint with an adjoining disco free to diners on Friday and Saturday nights. Métro Sainte-Marguerite Dromel.

Accommodation

Cheap rooms all year round can usually be found opposite Saint-Charles station — those by the Vieux Port might provide **more than just a bed** for the night. The tourist office at La Canebière 4 has a free accommodation **booking service**. Unless stated, the following should not cost more than F150–200 a double, most major credit cards accepted.

Hôtel Beaulieu Glaris, 1–3 place des Marseillais (☎04 91 90 70 59, fax 04 91 56 14 04). Right opposite Saint-Charles station. Clean and friendly.

Hôtel Gambetta, 49 allée Léon Gambetta (☎04 91 62 07 88, fax 04 91 64 81 54). Next to Olympique Marseille's supporters' club bar. Each room has a toilet and bath/shower. Between Saint-Charles and Réformés-Canebière *métro* stops.

Hôtel Montgrand, 50 rue Montgrand (☎04 91 33 33 81, fax 04 91 33 75 89). Quiet place near le Palais de Justice. Each room has private facilities. Métro Estrangin-Préfecture.

Hôtel Sud, 18 rue Beauvau (☎04 91 54 38 50, fax 04 91 54 75 62). A slightly more pricey establishment by the Vieux Port (double rooms at around F300), but with that priceless commodity in Marseille – air conditioning.

Germany

Three World Cups and three European Championships – the record speaks for itself. No football power has a better postwar success rate than the Germans. Their club sides may no longer dominate Europe in the way they did in the Seventies (though 1997 wasn't a bad year, all in all). Their league may not attract the galaxy of stars boasted by *Serie A, La Primera Liga* or the Premiership. But when it comes to the ultimate test of a nation's footballing ability, the Germans deliver.

They end the century stronger than ever. Reunification in 1990 created a wider pool of players to choose from, the *Bundesliga* is well-supported and well-organised, the major clubs are financially stable, and few of the country's top home-grown players feel the need to hawk their talents abroad.

Critics of German football claim that the game here is all about organisation, workrate and teamwork. And while there is no doubt that these are strong points of the German game, the stereotype is unfair. Germany has produced some of Europe's greatest individuals – Jürgen Klinsmann, Gerd Müller, Uwe Seeler, Pierre Littbarski, Lothar Matthäus, Karl-Heinz Rummenigge, and the peerless Franz Beckenbauer. Sure, they were all members of great teams; they were also great players in their own right.

German football has never been characterised by the fluidity of Holland or France, but nor has it been blighted by the negativity of Italy, or the crude simplicity of the Scandinavians. As in so many other walks of life, the Germans get their football

Looks familiar – Matthäus, Littbarski and the World Cup

balance right – effort married with creativity, tactical sophistication allied to physical durability.

The national team's latest honour, the 1996 European Championship, was the first title claimed by a united Germany. Before World War II, Germany's best performance was finishing third at the 1934 World Cup, when the limitations of their solid, muscular game were exposed by Czechoslovakia in the semi-finals.

All the postwar honours went to West Germany, with the East Germans (or 'German Democratic Republic') failing to make the same impression on football that they left on other areas of international sport.

The West Germans were unable to compete in the 1950 World Cup, having only been re-admitted to FIFA that year. They went into the 1954 competition with a side which combined ageing players from before the war with inexperienced youngsters. They were destroyed by Hungary 8–3 in the first round, but on closer inspection it became clear that the German coach, Sepp Herberger, had fielded a deliberately below-strength side for that match, knowing that his full team would easily beat Turkey in their next game and assure themselves of qualification with minimum effort. He was right – and the Germans went marching on, past a strong Yugoslavia in the quarter-finals and an outclassed Austria in the semis, to set up a rematch with Hungary in the final.

The 'Mighty Magyars' were unbeaten since 1950 and few gave West Germany a chance. Yet the Hungarians had been drained by difficult games against Brazil and Uruguay, and several of their players, including the legendary Puskás, were carrying injuries. The favourites raced into a two-goal lead within eight minutes, but the West Germans pulled level before half-time, and seven minutes from the end, Helmut Rahn scored his second goal of the game to give his team a shock win.

At the 1958 World Cup, the Germans finished third after losing to hosts Sweden in the semi-finals. Four years later they made it to the quarter-finals but lost out to a late Yugoslav goal.

Two years before the 1966 World Cup in England, Herberger was replaced as national coach by Helmut Schön. The Germans favoured continuity in coaching at all levels – Herberger had been in the job since before World War II. But now it was time for change, not just internationally but at club level, too.

Until 1963, West German football was unusual in having no national league structure. Domestic competition was based around four regional leagues, with a play-off between the champions determining the overall *Deutschemeister*. In addition, most West German clubs were semi-professional and unable to compete at European level

Divided we stand – West and East Germany prepare to meet for the first and only time, 1974

with the cash-rich teams from Madrid, Lisbon and Milan.

The formation of the *Bundesliga* in 1963 changed all that. Two years after the new league was founded, Munich 1860 reached the final of the Cup-Winners' Cup, and a year after that Borussia Dortmund went one better and lifted the trophy, becoming their country's first European winners.

At the 1966 World Cup, Schön profited from his players' new-found pro-

Lucky thirteen – Müller celebrates a World Cup-winning goal

fessionalism and European experience. His team rode their luck on their way to the final – both their quarter-final and semi-final opponents, Uruguay and the USSR, were reduced to nine men before bowing out. Yet the Germans genuinely were the stronger team in both games, with Beckenbauer and Helmut Haller in midfield doing the prompting for the clinical Seeler and Wolfgang Overath upfront.

Neither German nor English fan needs reminding of the thrilling Wembley final that followed, of the disputed Geoff Hurst goal in extra-time (still argued over on German television to this day), or of the 4–2 final score which, in truth, rather flattered the home side. But while England celebrated their success, the Germans would have plenty of opportunities to gain their revenge in years to come – not least at the 1970 World Cup in Mexico.

By 1970 West Germany's domestic game had become dominated by Bayern Munich, and the club provided the national team not just with Beckenbauer but with their colourful young goalkeeper, Sepp Maier, and the man who was arguably Europe's best striker of the decade, Gerd Müller – *Der Bomber*.

Müller's ten goals made him top scorer in Mexico. In the quarter-finals, after the Germans had pulled back from 2–0 down

against England in Guadalajara, it was Müller who supplied the powerful volley which won the game in extra-time. In the semi against Italy, Müller gave his side a 2–1 lead five minutes into extra time. The Italians then scored twice before Müller brought the scores level again, only to see Rivera score the winner a minute later. So another German attempt to regain the World Cup had ended in glorious failure – though the result might have been different had Beckenbauer not been forced to play much of the second half with his arm in a sling.

It wasn't long before Müller and his team-mates were to get the reward their free-flowing, athletic football deserved. A massive match-fixing scandal, involving five clubs and more than fifty players, rocked the *Bundesliga* in 1971. But the national side was relatively unaffected, since the corruption mainly involved teams seeking to avoid relegation. In the quarter-finals of the 1972 European Championship, then called the Nations' Cup, West Germany were once again drawn to play England, this time in a two-leg quarter-final. The tie was effectively over after the first leg at Wembley, where England appeared to take the field believing that the Germans would sit back, allowing Beckenbauer and the brilliant Borussia Mönchengladbach winger, Günther Netzer, to run the midfield. Netzer,

Basics

Citizens of the EU, the USA, Canada, Australia and New Zealand need only their **passport** to enter Germany.

The German currency is the **Deutschmark**, divided into 100 Pfennig. There are coins of 2, 5, 10 and 50 Pfennig, and for DM1, 2 and 5; and notes for DM10, 20, 50, 100, 200, 500 and 1000. Basic **banking hours** are Mon–Fri 9.30am–noon & 1.30–3.30pm, although in major cities some banks stay open an hour or two later. There are usually small bank offices in train stations which are open seven days a week, until 9pm or 10pm. You can change money at almost all banks, and they offer a better rate than commercial exchange offices (*Wechselstuben*).

Cash machines are widespread but the use of **credit cards** is not as prevalent as you might expect. Germany has a much less highly developed retail culture than the UK – be aware that if you want to do some last-minute souvenir shopping, most city-centre stores are closed on **Saturday afternoons**.

If you are travelling on from Germany to other countries, particularly to **Eastern Europe**, then it's worth keeping hold of any leftover Deutschmarks – you'll get good rates of exchange or discounted prices when using the German currency.

From outside the country, the **international access code** for Germany is ☎49. You can call abroad from all telephone boxes in the country except for those marked *National*. Coin phones take DM1 and DM5 coins, and credit-card phones are becoming more widespread. Alternatively, all main post offices have booths from which you can make an international call, then pay the charge at the desk afterwards. For national calls, commonly used **city codes** are: Berlin ☎30, Cologne ☎221, Dortmund ☎231, Hamburg ☎40 and Munich ☎89.

Getting around inside Germany, you can't avoid the excellent **rail service**, provided by *Deutsche Bahn* (*DB*). Fares are around DM25 per 100 km, second class, but there are cheaper deals for travel after 7pm. You'll pay a supplement for the 250kph *ICE* trains, and also for *IC* and *EC* services.

An alternative way to travel across the country is to use a **paid-hitching system**. Journeys work out much cheaper than by train, and the absence of *Autobahn* speed limits means they can be almost as quick. The best service is provided by *ADM*, who have offices in all the major cities. Their telephone number is the same in all locations – ☎19440; if you are outside a city, then simply add the city dialling code.

All major cities have **tourist information offices** who will book accommodation for a nominal booking fee. As well as upmarket hotels, you will usually have a choice of B&B in a *Pension* or *Gasthöf*, though these are not necessarily any cheaper than small hotels. German **youth hostels** are good value and graded, like hotels, by a star system.

Germany is a **beer-lover's paradise**. All locally produced brews have to comply with a 450-year-old purity law which prevents the use of chemical substitutes, and there are some superb regional variations in addition to the ubiquitous *pilsener*. Draught beer (*vom Fass*) is poured very slowly, so order a round in advance.

There's more to the **local wine** than *Liebfraumilch*. *Riesling* and *Gewürztraminer* are more interesting whites, and German red wine is also better than you might think.

A football fan can't visit Germany without tasting the sausage (*Wurst*), which comes in a bewildering array of regional varieties. If the somewhat **stodgy local cooking** gets you down, most major cities offer a wide choice of Turkish, Chinese, Italian and 'Balkan' (usually Serbian or Croatian) restaurants.

German rock music is the world's worst, but in recent years the country has produced some innovative dance sounds, and this is reflected in the popularity of the growing number of **techno clubs** in big cities.

Müller and the Bayern man's club-mate Uli Hoeness were all on target as West Germany won 3–1.

In the final stages of the tournament, Müller scored both goals in a semi-final win over hosts Belgium, then two more in the 3–0 win over the USSR which made West Germany champions of Europe.

Two years later, playing the World Cup finals on home soil, the West Germans were favourites to win but faced stiff competition from their fellow practitioners of 'Total Football', Holland. They also had to recover from the trauma of losing 1–0 to the GDR in an opening-round group game – the first and only time the two German sides would meet on the football field.

Taking the game – Klaus Allofs, Germany's engine of the Eighties

After the defeat by East Germany, the hosts reshaped their side. Netzer had been dropped before the tournament after a collapse in his club form. Now another Mönchengladbach midfielder, Rainer Bonhof, came into the side to add a bit of drive.

The team duly powered past Yugoslavia, Poland and Sweden in the second-round group stage, setting up a final against Holland in Munich. The Dutch took the lead with a first-minute penalty, but Müller, though slightly less impressive now, was still there when it mattered, equalising from the spot, then scoring the first-half winner which crowned West Germany champions of the world for the second time.

Coach Helmut Schön had seen his ten years' labour come to fruition. After the final he embraced Müller and Beckenbauer – concealing earlier differences he had had with the latter about tactics.

Müller et al had got the taste for glory. With Bayern they lifted the European Cup three years in a row from 1974. Borussia Mönchengladbach's record was even more remarkable – a historically tiny club, they won the Bundesliga five times in eight years, and the UEFA Cup twice, in the Seventies.

By 1979, West German football had become so strong that three out of four UEFA Cup quarter-finalists that year hailed from the Bundesliga. A year later, the Germans provided all four.

Yet in the second half of the Seventies, all was not quite well with the national side. West Germany played their part in the magnificent European Championship finals of 1976, but lost the final to Czechoslovakia on penalties.

By the time the 1978 World Cup in Argentina came around, Beckenbauer, Hoeness and Müller had all hung up their international boots. Despite the presence of a youthful Karl-Heinz Rummenigge, the team lacked bite and were eliminated after Austria beat them 3–2 in the second-round group stage.

The Eighties started better. Sepp Derwall's side lacked the panache of Schön's, but with a youthful midfield pairing of Bernd Schuster and Hans-Peter Briegel (the former playing his first and last major finals), and Klaus Allofs and Horst Hrubesch alongside Rummenigge upfront, they won the European Championship in 1980.

Two years later West Germany were back in the World Cup final, this time against Italy in Madrid. Their path there had been littered with controversy. Having lost their opening match, 2–1 to Algeria, the Germans contrived to 'beat' Austria 1–0 to avoid elimination, though it was clear to a TV audience of millions that the Austrians, who had already qualified for the second stage, had agreed beforehand not to stand in West Germany's way. In the semi-finals, German 'keeper Harald 'Toni' Schumacher broke the jaw of Frenchman Patrick Battiston, in what was probably the worst unpunished foul of all time, and France, leading 3–1 in extra-time, were overhauled and beaten on penalties.

There was to be no such good fortune for the Germans in the final where, with Rummenigge playing bravely through injury, they were well beaten by Paolo Rossi's Italy.

Winning ways – Bayern are champions – 1997

An early exit at the hands of Spain in the 1984 European Championship finals led to Derwall being replaced by Franz Beckenbauer as national-team coach. A novice in the dugout at this level – he did not actually have a German coach's licence – Beckenbauer was fortunate to inherit a crop of richly talented young players, including Andreas Brehme at left-back, Lothar Matthäus in midfield and Rudi Völler in attack. In Mexico in 1986, the Germans lost the World Cup final, 3–2 to Argentina. They had been two down with four minutes left, pulled it back to 2–2, then conceded a sucker-punch goal just before the final whistle. It was an uncharacteristic lapse of concentration, but in truth, had Matthäus not been so preoccupied with Maradona and had Rummenigge not been carrying yet another injury, West Germany would surely have made a better game of it.

In 1988 the Germans hosted the European Championship, but in contrast to the World Cup fourteen years earlier, they were unable to conquer the Dutch – Marco van Basten's outstanding winner two minutes from full-time deservedly winning the semi-final.

Beckenbauer refused to panic. The young Stuttgart striker Jürgen Klinsmann had joined the side for Euro '88, and with Matthäus and company in better form than ever, West Germany approached the 1990 World Cup in confident mood. They tore through the opening group stage, gained revenge over the Dutch in a bad-tempered second-round game in Milan, then edged out the Czechs to set up a semi-final with England in Turin. Like every other meeting between the countries, the game produced memorable images – not least Gascoigne's tears after Thomas Berthold had dived acrobatically to get him his second yellow card of the tournament, not least the ruthlessness with which the Germans despatched their penalties after extra-time had finished with the score at 1–1.

One of those penalty takers, Brehme, would again make no mistake when West Germany were awarded a spot-kick against

Argentina in Rome – scoring the only goal of what was indisputably the most dismal World Cup final ever played.

Beckenbauer went into the history books as the only man to captain and coach World Cup-winning sides. His replacement, the former Mönchengladbach full-back Berti Vogts, initially found it hard to follow in his footsteps. The departure of Klinsmann, Matthäus, Kohler and others to Italian clubs had weakened the *Bundesliga* and made it hard for the new coach to keep tabs on his squad. The addition of former East German players into the reckoning seemed only to complicate the issue. The Germans were well beaten by Denmark in the Euro '92 final, and two years later they again under-estimated their opponents when Bulgaria knocked them out of the World Cup quarter-finals.

Vogts survived calls for his resignation and by the time Euro '96 came around, the exiles had returned home and the *Bundesliga* was booming again. While the Germans were by no means the most attractive side on view in England, the goals of Klinsmann and the inspirational leadership of sweeper Matthias Sammer, a former GDR international, powered them to the final via a lucky quarter-final victory against Croatia and yet another shoot-out win over the English.

Against the Czech Republic in the final, the Germans were outplayed for long periods but came from behind to win, 2–1. Oliver Bierhoff made history by becoming the first player to win a competitive international with a 'golden goal', while Vogts avoided making a piece of unwanted history himself – as the only postwar German national coach not to win a trophy.

The national team's latest success has added further shine to the domestic game. For five years in a row in the Nineties the German title was decided on the last day of the season, and while the last two campaigns haven't quite managed that, the success of Bayern Munich, Borussia Dortmund and Schalke in winning European club competitions has thrown the *Bundesliga*

straight back into the élite of European leagues. Crowds are up, TV, merchandising and sponsorship money on the rise, higher-quality imports are being attracted.

But German clubs are too sensible to try to compete with the huge money being thrown around by English, Spanish and Italian clubs. And as long as the national team continue to be such a strong force, nobody in Germany will bemoan the absence of foreign stars.

Essential vocabulary

Hello *Guten Tag*
Goodbye *Auf wiedersehen*
Yes *Ja*
No *Nein*
Two beers, please *Zwei Bier, bitte*
Thank you *Danke*
Men's *Herren*
Women's *Damen*
Where is the stadium? *Wo ist das Stadion?*
What's the score? *Wie steht's?*
Referee *Schreidsrichter*
Offside *Abseits*

Match practice

After what was effectively a product relaunch in the early Nineties, Germany's *Bundesliga* is now continental Europe's most commercially successful league.

As in England, lucrative new TV contracts, the increased commercial awareness of clubs and intense media and marketing activity have propelled the domestic game into an era of unprecedented wealth and influence. Unlike England, however, Germany also had a range of modern, world-class stadia in which the revolution could unfold – the product of massive construction programmes for the 1974 World Cup and 1988 European Championship.

There has been no Taylor Report here, and no need for one. Many grounds still have standing areas, assisting in the creation of big-match atmosphere which might otherwise be reduced by the common placement of running tracks between stands and action. While many of these stadia are out of town, the transport links

Extra mustard, please – the best soccer sausages in Europe

Most league games take place on Saturday at 3.30pm. Live TV games are on Friday nights at 8pm, while there are also some Sunday games at 6pm. There are a handful of midweek rounds during the season, with games being played on Tuesday or Wednesday at 7.30pm.

The league

The *Bundesliga* consists of two divisions, with eighteen teams in each. All clubs in the top two divisions must be granted a professional licence from the German FA, the *DFB*. Clubs suffering from financial irregularities or insufficient funds can have their licence withdrawn and be consigned to the amateur leagues – this happened to Dynamo Dresden in 1995 and to TSV Munich 1860 in the Eighties.

It's a straightforward three-up, three down between the top two divisions. The bottom four from the second tier are relegated to one of four *Regionalligen* which make up the third tier. This level includes some small semi-professional clubs, amateur sides and the reserve teams of the bigger *Bundesliga* sides which, although called *Amateure*, include many paid young players. Promotion from the *Regionalligen* is achieved via play-offs.

co them are invariably excellent and, once inside the ground, you'll find facilities are second to none.

Prior to games, expect an American approach with a local radio personality taking the field, mike in hand, warming up the crowd with a mixture of team news and naff pop music. When the team sheet becomes available, only the first name of the home-team players is read out – the crowd bellows out each surname. This tradition is also followed for announcements of substitutes and goalscorers – and will also be applied to away teams if there is substantial travelling support.

The *Bundesliga* kicks-off in mid-August and takes a break from early December to late February. The season doesn't end until mid-June – two weeks earlier if there is a major international tournament in the summer. Many prominent figures in the game, including national coach Berti Vogts, are unhappy that the long winter break makes it necessary to bring players back to full fitness from a standing start twice a year. With UEFA also angling for Germany to shorten its rest period in order to accommodate Champions' League expansion, change may not be far away.

Up for the cup

Unlike many domestic cup competitions, the *DFB Pokal* is organised to maximise the possible embarrassment of top clubs. All matches are single-leg affairs, with penalty shoot-outs deciding the outcome if the scores are level after extra-time.

The seeded first round is drawn so that no two teams from the same division play each other, and the lower-division side is always given home advantage, providing for plenty of upsets and swelling the game's coffers at grassroots level. Bayern Munich have twice been beaten by village sides at this stage during the Nineties.

The first round takes place in the second week in August, followed by three more rounds until the quarter-finals in November. The semi-finals are in April, and the final is played at Berlin's Olympic stadium on the second weekend in June – a fixture which has become a real showpiece event to rival Wembley's FA Cup final.

Interest in the *Pokal* is high – a 1996 tie between two *Regionalliga* sides, Nuremburg and Greuther Fürth, drew a sellout crowd of 45,000.

Tickets

There are no officially designated all-ticket matches in Germany. If the stadium is not sold out in advance, you can buy tickets at the stadium on matchdays. At Dortmund and Freiburg almost every match is sold out, but most other grounds are big enough to accommodate fans arriving on-spec, unless there's a big derby on.

Tickets are divided into seats (*Sitzplätze*) and standing (*Stehplätze*). Look out for signs showing a *Gästesektor* for visiting fans. The areas behind each goal are *Kürve*, while each stand (*Tribüne*) is normally named according its location – *Süd-Tribüne* is the south stand, and so on. In smaller grounds there will be a *Seitentribüne*, with seats close to the edge of the pitch.

Ticket prices are very reasonable. Adult standing spaces are DM12–16, while seats can be had for as little as DM25 – though you'll pay twice that for the best seats in the house in the *Haupttribüne*. Most clubs operate a ticket hotline for information and credit-card bookings.

Half-time

Although a number of clubs have banned alcohol inside their grounds, beer is an essential part of the German football experience. At large, out-of town stadia there are scores of beer stands, with the local sausage (*wurst*) speciality sizzling nearby. At smaller, town-centre grounds, local

bars will be packed before kick-off. On any long trip by U-Bahn or S-Bahn out to a stadium, you'll see fans swigging back cans on the way. Naturally all this results in a fair amount of drunkenness on the terraces, but remember that police and/or stadium security have the right to refuse admission.

If there is a beer festival, fairground or *Volks Fest* of any kind going on in town, it will be flooded by fans after the match and terrace chants will roar on into the night.

Action replay

The subscription satellite channel *Premiere* has the rights to live league games, which are shown Fridays at 8.00pm and Saturdays at 3.30pm. You need a decoder and card to view *Premiere*, so if there's a game on that you're particularly keen to catch, head for a suitably equipped bar.

As in England, the football authorities have ensured that the game retains maximum exposure by insisting that the pay TV

Still standing – flags and sponsorship on the terraces

boys share highlights packages with a terrestrial channel – in this case *SAT 1*. Fronted by the showman of German soccer, Reinhold Beckmann, *SAT 1*'s output is lively, colourful and, even if you speak not a word of German, compelling viewing. The main highlights show is *Ran* (Fridays, 10.15 pm & Saturdays, 6pm). It features a studio audience of fans, live satellite link-ups around the grounds and interviews, as well as extended highlights of all games played that day. *SAT 1* also show four Sunday games each season, 'as live', on *Ranissimo* (7.15pm). For all other match rounds, *Ranissimo* becomes a highlights show with a similar format to *Ran*.

Domestic cup matches are shown across all the terrestrial channels – *ARD, ZDF, RTL* and *SAT 1*. *RTL* has the rights to the Champions' League, while *SAT 1* and *ARD* compete for UEFA Cup and Cup-Winners' Cup games. German international matches are normally shown by either *ARD* or *ZDF*.

Germany's dedicated subscription sports channel, *Deutsche Sport Rundfunk* (*DSF*) has failed to get much of a grip on domestic football. The station has a live second-division game on Monday nights at 8pm, plus live Spanish league action (Saturdays, 8pm) and a live Italian game (Sundays, 8.15pm) – this last being followed by highlights of the weekend's top-flight *Bundesliga* action.

The back page

The longest-established and most respected football magazine in Germany is *Kicker*. The brainchild of one of German football's founding fathers, schoolteacher Walter Bensemann, it first appeared in 1920 and has been the staple diet of fans ever since.

Kicker has two weekly editions. Monday's issue (DM3) carries interviews and main features in colour, with weekend results and reports in a black-and-white supplement, which also contains results from the major European leagues. The mid-

Wembley, 1996 – Bierhoff spins his shot towards Kouba, and Germany are European champions

week edition (DM2.30) is a thinner, black-and-white only affair featuring a wrap-up of any midweek action, plus news and previews of the weekend games.

For all its thoroughness, *Kicker* can be a bit on the serious side. For a more frivolous read, try the newcomer *Hattrick* (monthly, DM4) with its colour features and irreverent style, or the weekly *Sport Bild*, a tabloid connected to the daily *Bild*, Germany's answer to *The Sun*. Be aware, though, that *Sport Bild* covers more than football and at any one time can be full to the brim with tennis, golf or motor racing.

At the start of the season you'll see special editions which serve as a guide to the new campaign, with all the stats and player info you need. Kicker's *Bundesliga Sonderheft* (DM9) is the best of these but *Fussball Sport Extra* (DM6.90) is also worth a look.

British-based fans of the German game have their own fanzine, *Elfmeter* (£1). It's published every other month, has a witty and approachable style, and is available from: 16 Mallory Road, Perton, Staffs, WV6 7XN, UK.

Ultra culture

Nowhere is the German attitude to football as a pastime better illustrated than in clubs' relationship with their supporters. With one eye on their social responsibilities to the communities they serve and another on public relations, most big German clubs have a *Fan Projekt* – a coalition of supporters' groups and local authority-funded youth organisations. Club directors hold regular meetings with their *Projekt*, which usually runs alongside the traditional, officially sanctioned supporters' clubs.

The *Fan Projekt* idea arose as a way of involving fans at grassroots level and cutting out the cancer of hooliganism. But the latter is still a problem in the former GDR, and with extreme right-wing followers of the national team.

On a less serious note, there is a distinctly Seventies look on the terraces, with the most loyal young fans keen to show their commitment with an array of sew-on patches and pin badges stuck to sleeveless denim jackets, layers of scarves tied around the wrist, and *Kiss Me Quick Deutschland* party hats. Some fans have tried to create a more latin feel, but stadium authorities rarely permit smoke bombs or flares.

The terrace tunes will be achingly familiar to a British visitor, but most clubs also have their own rock anthem; it says a lot about German football culture that these are actually quite popular with fans.

There is another side to the fanaticism of German fans. Just as England has the *92 Club*, so Germany has its *Groundhoppers*. Unlike their English counterparts, they do not restrict themselves to their own national boundaries. Armed with that essential accessory, the international train schedule, they travel across Europe and beyond – most serious *Groundhoppers* have attended games at more than 200 stadia.

If you hear German being spoken at a ground somewhere in Europe, there are probably *Groundhoppers* about. Forget your pre-conceptions and approach them for a chat – these people do their research and will invariably know of any other games taking place later that day. Chances are, they will have visited your home ground and sunk a pint in your local, too.

In the net

Old Walter Bensemann would have been proud of *Kicker Online*, Germany's best generic football website, accessible at: www.kicker.de/. Easy to navigate with its smart, innovative graphics, the site is a treasure trove of news, stats, interviews and features – no substitute for the paper itself, but an excellent site all the same. *SAT 1*'s equivalent, *Ran Online*, is at: www.ran.de. It's less comprehensive than its *Kicker* rival, and the graphics are a bit too glitzy for their own good. Bernd Timmerman, the doyen of German soccer stattoes, runs an extraordinary online stats archive at: www.informatik.uni-oldenburg.de/~bernd/soccer.e.html.

Munich

The southern German region of Bavaria has enjoyed more footballing success than any other in the country. Yet the game in this famously independent-minded area got off to a slow start. Local *Turn* (gymnastics) associations took a dim view of soccer and managed to get the game banned in local schools for a period before World War I.

Between the wars, the region's football giants were Nuremburg, who won six championships. But the modern era has been less kind to the team often known simply as *Der Club* – they've won nothing since their last *Bundesliga* title in 1968, and are currently playing third-division football in the *Regionalliga Süd*.

A year after Nuremburg celebrated their last title, Bayern Munich were winning their first. Bayern quickly replaced TSV 1860 as the most important team in the region's capital city, and have since gone on to beat Nuremberg's record nine titles to become the *Rekordmeister* and the undisputed number one club, both in Bavaria and in Germany as a whole.

Today there is no love lost between the two Munich clubs. TSV 1860, named after the year that the *Turn und Sport Verein* ('Gymanastics and Sport Association') were formed, had been the equal of Bayern until the mid-Sixties. It was 1860, not Bayern, who were founder members of the *Bundesliga*. But it was Bayern who thrived in the era of full-time professionalism, and their superior organisation, scouting and coaching network left their neighbours standing.

The two clubs shared the same ground – the Grünwalder stadium in the Geising district of the city – until the opening of the Olympic stadium in 1972. Both initially played in the new arena, but 1860's declining team couldn't attract enough support to justify the high rent, and they returned to their original home a few years later. To the anger of 1860 fans, the club abandoned

the Grünwalder for a second time in 1994 and the 35,000-capacity stadium today hosts only the two clubs' *Amateure* games.

There is no doubt that Bayern enjoy greater support, but as 1860 fans are only too eager to point out, much of it consists of casual fans from outside the city. While 1860 claim to enjoy a bigger following in the city of Munich itself, not all Bayern fans are happy with the nationwide popularity of their team, the loyal hardcore arguing that the presence of so many day-trippers, with their freshly bought scarves and hats, adversely affects the atmosphere.

To the outsider, such squabbling might seem strange. The city approaches the millennium with both its football clubs in fine fettle – Bayern having ended a three-year title drought, and 1860 having returned to Europe after an absence of decades.

The thrilling fields

 FC Bayern

Olympiastadion, see p.211
Office Säbener Strasse 51
Colours All red with black trim
League champions 1932, 1969, 1972–74, 1980–81, 1985–87, 1989–90, 1994, 1997
Cup winners 1957, 1966–67, 1969, 1971, 1982, 1984, 1986
European Cup winners 1974–76
Cup-Winners' Cup winners 1967
UEFA Cup winners 1996

Although FC Bayern München (the name means 'Bavaria Munich') were formed in 1900, it was to be sixty years before they made a lasting impression on German football. Since then, there has been no club to match them.

The club song is *Forever Number One*, and while things may not always have gone according to plan on the field in recent years, the club's organisation and commercial flair ensure that 'Forever' is not just an idle wish.

Before World War II, Bayern defeated Eintracht Frankfurt to win the national championship in 1932, but didn't win another trophy for 25 years. The club did not gain admittance to the first season of the *Bundesliga*; the *DFB* were keen to have only one representative from each city, and chose TSV 1860 as Munich's side.

But within two years Bayern had gained promotion to the top drawer, and they finished their first season in it, 1965/66, with another domestic cup win. A year later they retained that trophy and, more significantly, also won their first European honour – the 1967 Cup-Winners' Cup. The final of that competition against Rangers drew plenty of local support, as the pre-selected venue was Bavaria's second city, Nuremburg. An extra-time winner from Franz 'Bulle' Roth made for a beery train journey home for the fans.

The European win made the rest of West Germany sit up and take notice of Bayern, who until now had been regarded as no more than a middle-ranking club. The cup-winning sides of the Sixties were dominated by three gifted youngsters – goalkeeper Sepp Maier, anchorman Franz Beckenbauer and striker Gerd Müller. Under their Yugoslav coach, Tschik Ćajkovski, Bayern played fast, adventurous and free-flowing football, with a team spirit second to none in the *Bundesliga*.

When Ćajkovski was replaced by his fellow countryman Branko Zebec in 1968, the team became better disciplined and, as a consequence, much harder to beat. They

All smiles – skipper Matthäus takes the *Bundesliga* 'salad dish', 1997

dominated the 1968/69 league campaign from the start, won the title by eight points, then completed a domestic double with a cup final win over Schalke.

In March 1970, Zebec was replaced by a former assistant coach to the West German national team, Udo Lattek. His arrival coincided with the start of an unbeaten home record which would stretch for more than four years and 73 matches. During that period, Bayern would win three titles in a row from 1972.

By 1973 Bayern were supplying no fewer than six regulars to the West German national side – Maier, Beckenbauer, Müller, defenders Paul Breitner and Georg Schwarzenbeck, and midfielder Uli Hoeness. For both his club and his country, Beckenbauer had withdrawn from midfield into a sweeper's rôle – though his interpretation of that position was so liberal that he could sometimes be the furthest Bayern player forward.

Beckenbauer had been influenced by the 'Total Football' of the Ajax side of the early Seventies, and it was the Amsterdam club that stood between Bayern and the

European domination Lattek craved. In 1973, the Germans were thrashed 4–0 in Amsterdam in a European Cup quarter-final – a defeat which prompted 'keeper Maier to throw his gloves out of his hotel window. But a year later, with Ajax eliminated, Bayern met Atlético Madrid in the final and, after an equaliser from Schwarzenbeck in the last minute of extra-time earned them a replay, they demolished the Spanish champions, 4–0.

Bayern had become the first German club to win Europe's premier club competition, and while their position of pre-eminence in the league was usurped by Borussia Mönchengladbach, the club had been bitten by the European bug. They retained their crown with a 2–0 win over Don Revie's Leeds in Paris, and in 1976

they followed Real Madrid and Ajax into the record books, becoming the third club to win three consecutive European Cups when they beat Saint-Étienne in Glasgow.

One by one, the Beckenbauer generation left Bayern. One of the last to quit was Maier, his career ended prematurely by a horrific car crash in 1979. His departure from the scene signalled the end of an era – and the start of a new one. Under the flamboyant Hungarian coach Pal Csernai, who insisted that his team approach every fixture with the same game-plan, no matter what the opponents, Bayern won the title in 1980.

They retained it a year later, with Karl-Heinz Rummenigge in irrepressible form, and in 1982 they reached two cup finals, winning the domestic version against

Munich essentials

Munich's new **Franz Josef Strauss airport** is at the terminal of S-Bahn line #8, 30km from the central train station (Hauptbahnhof). The train terminal is under the airport's arrival and departure lounges. Trains leave every twenty minutes for the centre, the journey taking forty minutes. A single ticket is DM10.

From Munich Hauptbahnhof there are twenty **trains** a day to Hamburg (journey time seven hours), 25 to Berlin (nine-and-a-half hours) and 37 to Cologne (six-and-a-half hours). From the Hauptbahnhof it's a five-minute walk to central Karlsplatz and another ten minutes to the city's main square, Marienplatz.

City transport consists of S-Bahn trains, the U-Bahn metro, trams and buses. All U-Bahn lines run through the three central stations of Marienplatz, Karlsplatz and Hauptbahnhof. **Tickets** can be bought from the blue machines at stops and stations, or from tram or bus drivers. The **fare** you pay depends on the number of zones you cross. Providing you are travelling in the same direction within the zones for which your ticket is valid, you can change as many times as you like within four hours. A one-zone single journey (*Einzelfahrtenkarte*) is DM3.30, a two-zone DM6.60, and so on. A short journey of up to four stops (*Kurzstrecke*) is DM1.70. An inner-zone day ticket (*Tages-Karte*) is good value at DM8; an all-zone version is DM16, and both are valid from the time of stamping until 6am the next day.

Transport runs Sun–Thur 5am–12.30am, Fri & Sat 5am–1.30am. There is no night transport at present but the city plans to launch an hourly night-bus service in the future. **Taxis** (☎089/21610) charge DM3, then DM2.50 per km.

The two main **tourist offices** are at Sendlingerstrasse 1, (open Mon–Thur 8.30am–3pm, Fri 8.30am–2pm, ☎089/239 11); and at the Hauptbahnhof (open Mon-Sat 8am–10pm, Sun 11am–7pm, ☎089/239 1256). There's a smaller branch at the airport (open Mon–Sat 8.30am–10pm, Sun 1–9pm, ☎089/97 59 28 15).

Prinz (monthly, DM5) is the best **listings magazine**, but the evening paper *Abendzeitung* issues a comprehensive free entertainment supplement, *münchen alive*, every Friday.

Nuremburg, but losing in the European Cup to Aston Villa. In 1984 Rümmenigge was sold to Inter Milan. His replacement was a young Mönchengladbach forward by the name of Lothar Matthäus. With Lattek back in the dugout and Matthäus adding some much-needed creativity to the team, Bayern won the title in 1985 – the first of five championships in six seasons. They also reached the 1987 European Cup final, where they lost to two late FC Porto goals.

The Nineties have proved to be a more frustrating time for Bayern. The once famous youth policy has failed to produce the talent fans had come to expect, and the club has looked to the international transfer market to fill the gaps, with rather mixed success.

A taste of Franz – Beckenbauer brings it out from the back

A returning Beckenbauer took over the coaching reins and led Bayern to the title in 1994. The following year, the club's first-ever Champions' League campaign ended with a semi-final demolition by Ajax in Amsterdam – an unwelcome echo of times past. By this time, Beckenbauer had been elected club president and appointed the Italian-born Giovanni Trapattoni as coach. 'Trap' made two big-name signings, Jean-Pierre Papin and Emil Kostadinov, who spent most of their time on the bench. In the league, Bayern finished sixth.

After Trapattoni had departed, Otto Rehhagel was lured away from his beloved Werder Bremen for the 1995/96 season. Rehhagel inherited a squad with several malcontents and an ongoing public row between his two most senior players – Matthaus and Jürgen Klinsmann. Beckenbauer, though clearly preferring his dual rôle as club president and TV pundit, ousted Rehagel before the end of the season and took personal control with just a handful of games left in the title race. It was a gamble which didn't pay off. Bayern lost to Bremen and Schalke; and Dortmund

ran off with the title. Beckenbauer later admitted he'd made an error – either he should have sacked Rehhagel earlier, or let him see the season out.

Bayern's consolation was a superb UEFA Cup run, culminating in a two-leg final win over Bordeaux. The competition was a personal triumph for Klinsmann, who scored in every round, and the victory also got the club into the record books again – as a member of the select group of teams to have won all three European trophies.

Beckenbauer moved back upstairs in the summer of 1996, then made the extraordinary decision to recall Trapattoni. It was to prove one of the *Kaiser's* more inspired decisions. While he could not stop the feuding at what the local papers called 'Hollywood City' because of its rumours, gossip and tantrums, Trap at least took time out to learn some German and engaged the support of most of the players. An early UEFA Cup exit proved a blessing in disguise, allowing Bayern to concentrate on the *Bundesliga* which, in the end, they won with something to spare.

Off the field, too, Bayern are still number one. Their worst season on the pitch for years, in 1994/95, was their best-ever financially. They signed a shirt sponsorship deal with *Opel* worth almost DM6 million a season, pulled in TV revenue from the Champions' League and announced record-breaking income from merchandising. The hype, rather than the football, saw average crowds soar to more than 54,000 – far higher than they ever got in the glory days of the early Seventies or late Eighties.

Bayern Munich are riding the *Bundesliga* boom as high as any club in Germany. Now they must continue to live up to the hype.

Tickets

The sheer size of the Olympiastadion means you stand a fair chance of getting

Brazilian bend – Elber models the 1997/98 kit

into a run-of-the-mill league clash simply by turning up and buying a ticket at the door. For big games, however, you should check availability in advance. The Bayern-Dortmund clash in 1996 attracted half a million ticket enquiries.

For such a business-oriented club, admission prices are surprisingly low. For instance, season-ticket holders (of whom Bayern would like to have more) can enjoy all home games for as little as DM90 a year.

On the day, terrace tickets go for DM10–15, uncovered seats are available from DM 15 upwards, while covered seats in the main stand cost up to DM50. The *Nordkürve* is allocated to away fans. The club operates a credit-card booking line on: ☎089/699 31 333.

Even for games which are technically sold out, Bayern fans are notorious for 'looking for the weather'; in other words, black-market tickets are cheaper when it's raining, and you may be pleasantly surprised by how far you can haggle the touts down. The bridge from the U-Bahn station is the place for wheeler-dealing.

Publication

The matchday *Bayern-Magazin* (DM2.50) is crammed with stats and information as well as the usual glossy posters and ads for the extraordinary range of Bayern products. Fanzines (all DM3) to watch for include *Sauerlandecho*, *Red News* and *Grabfelder*.

Club shop

'FC Bayern' is a registered trademark and former player Uli Hoeness, now the club's general manager, aims to have a Bayern store in every town, selling basic groceries like cheese and yoghurt with the club logo on them.

Until Hoeness' dream becomes reality, the **Bayern Boutique** (open Mon–Fri 9am–noon & 1–5pm, Sat 9am–2pm, match-days until 6pm, most credit cards) inside the club headquarters at Säbener Strasse 51, sells jars of mustard, bottles of champagne, sets of playing cards and even the odd football shirt, should you be perverse

The Olympic stadium

Olympiastadion, Olympiapark
Capacity 63,000

Bayern fans complain that too many people
watch their team. Munich 1860 supporters
want their side to play somewhere more in
keeping with their small crowds. But while the
wrangling goes on, the Olympiastadion
remains as indubitably one of Europe's classic
sports arenas.

Built for the **1972 Olympic games**, the
ground is best known for its extraordinary,
tent-like grass roof – actually best seen from
the top of the Olympic tower, which is part of
the same complex. Unlike more recent
designs, the roof covers only a percentage of
the seating, but while the wind and rain take
their toll in cool weather, the design at least
ensures that everybody has an excellent view.

Glass act – Munich's majestic marquee

After the Olympics, the stadium was the
venue for West Germany's **World Cup win**
two years later, and the scene of **Holland's
victory** over the Soviet Union in the 1988
European Championship final. **Trevor Francis** will never forget his diving header
which won the European Cup for Nottingham Forest against Malmö in 1979 – he ended
up face down on the concrete shot-throwing area, just to the side of one goal. Despite
such failings, the stadium has remained **a UEFA favourite**, hosting Marseille's
European Cup final win over Milan in 1993 and, most recently, Dortmund's unlikely
victory over Juventus in the 1997 edition of the same competition.

The **German national team** are regular visitors here, too, and the ground is playing a pivotal rôle in the country's bid to host the **2006 World Cup**.

To reach the Olympiapark, take **U3 to Olympiazentrum**, a ten-minute ride from
town, then a pleasant ten-minute walk down Lillian-Board-Weg, across the park.

There are the usual **stands serving beer** and food around the stadium. At the foot
of the TV tower, you'll find a bar and restaurant which is a popular meeting place for
fans. You don't have to pay the entrance fee for the tower to enter the bar.

enough to want one. While here you can
also pick up the club's 52-page merchandise catalogue, *Trends Für Fans*. To reach
the store, take U1/U2 to Silberhornstrasse,
then bus #15 or #25 to Grödner Strasse.

Downtown there is a smaller **club
shop** at Orlandostrasse 1 (open Mon–Fri
10am–6.30pm, Sat 10am–2pm).

Ultra culture
Bayern have a staggering 1250 registered
supporters' associations with well over

50,000 paid-up members between them.
As well as hundreds in Germany, there are
official Bayern Clubs in Japan, Kenya,
Venezuela and Ireland.

While the club happily mail copies of
the *Trends Für Fans* to all these places, local
fans are less impressed, particularly by the
diluted atmosphere that the so-called 'terrace tourists' bring to the Olympiastadion.

Bayern's number one fan group are the
'Red Munichs' – a likeable collection of a
hundred or so hardcore fans who even

travel away to watch the club's women's and amateur teams. Surrounded by terrace tourists in silly hats, wondering which one might be Matthäus, the Red Munichs try to sneak fireworks past the fun-loathing security staff and do their darndest to create something approaching a genuine atmosphere, in what at times can seem like the Disneyland of European football.

The Munichs travelled *en masse* to friendlies with Celtic and Raith Rovers in 1997, and won rave reviews from the Scottish press for their bare-chested singing – on a freezing January night in Glasgow.

The club grudgingly tolerate them as they rarely cause trouble. But then again, they probably don't buy much Bayern yogurt, either.

In the net

Bayern's official website has been at the planning stage for what seems an eternity. Until it appears, one of the best unofficial sites resides at: www.hoexter.netsurf.de/homepages/cheeky/. The history and news sections are great if you can read German, while a multitude of links will take you to other unofficial sites and those of officially sanctioned 'Fan Clubs'.

🔵 Munich 1860

Olympiastadion, see p.211
Office Grünwalderstrasse 114
Colours Blue-and-white striped shirts, white shorts
League champions 1966
Cup winners 1942, 1964

TSV 1860 München are everything Bayern are not. Bayern have won the European Cup three times; 1860 have only ever entered it once. Bayern have supporters the length and breadth of Germany; 1860 cling to a loyal, local fan base. Bayern are sponsored by *Opel*, German wing of the multi-national *General Motors* corporation; 1860 wear the logo of a local brewery,

Löwenbräu. The commercial tie-up is appropriate because 1860 are nicknamed *Löwen* ('Lions'). The trouble is, they only seem to roar every few decades or so.

They might claim more local support than Bayern, but on the field, there is no longer any doubt that Munich 1860 are the city's second team. While the club are proud of their heritage, only recently have the team begun to show any sign of living up to it, having emerged from a decade of gloom in Bavarian regional leagues.

Before World War II, 1860 competed (not very successfully) with Nuremburg for dominance in the south of Germany. When the *Bundesliga* kicked off in 1964, they were given a place in the first division. They justified that decision by winning the West German Cup in 1964.

In the following season's Cup-Winners' Cup, and helped by the goals of striker Rudi Brunnenmaier, 1860 powered their way past Porto and Legia Warsaw in the early rounds, before meeting Torino in the semi-finals. The Germans lost 2–0 in Turin, then won a thrilling second leg 3–1. In those days away goals did not count double and games level on aggregate went to a replay – which the Lions duly won 2–0.

In the final, 1860 were at an obvious disadvantage as the venue had been pre-selected as Wembley, at that time almost a home from home for some members of the opposing side, West Ham United. Two goals from Alan Sealey gave the Hammers the silverware.

If the club were dispirited by that loss, they didn't show it. They began the 1965/66 season with a 1–0 derby win over Bayern, and finished it three points clear of Dortmund at the top of the *Bundesliga* table. The championship, which remains 1860's only league win, was a tribute to the attacking 4–2–4 formation favoured by their coach, Max Merkel. Prior to the start of the season he had poached striker Timo Konietzka from Dortmund to partner Brunnenmaier in attack, and that year 1860 scored eighty goals. But the real hero worship was reserved for the team's Yugoslav

Party pooper – Borimirov poaches another late winner for 1860

goalkeeper, Petar Radenković. *Radi* had arrived in Germany with no job, nowhere to live and two suitcases carrying all his worldly goods – but convinced he could become a professional footballer. He was quickly signed by 1860 and stayed with them until 1970, going on some legendary excursions outside his penalty area, and even cutting his own top-ten single.

With Bayern winning the cup in the same year as 1860 won the league, Munich looked as if it might defy the 'one city, one team' logic of the *Bundesliga* and sustain two top-class sides. It wasn't to be. By Christmas 1966, Merkel had resigned after falling out with some of his key players, and the club never recovered.

The Seventies were a decade of utter mediocrity. The Eighties were worse. In 1981 they were relegated from the first division. A year later the club had its professional licence revoked due to financial instability, and the team were relegated again. Among the players to desert the sinking ship was a young Rudi Völler. Nine grim years in the amateur ranks followed.

In 1991, the club won back their professional licence and, under coach Werner Lorant, gained promotion to the second division. With businessman Karl-Heinz Wildmoser providing the cash, the team had clawed all the way back to the top flight by 1994.

The club's years in the wilderness had altered the character of their support. The German amateur leagues have always attracted fans who are turned off by the commercialism and impersonal nature of the big clubs, and 1860 attracted many fans with an alternative view of life. Punks and ravers took their seats next to older *Münchener* who could remember the days of Wembley and Radenković.

Today these fans have a hot-and-cold relationship with president Wildmoser. When his money talked and 1860 won promotion back to the big time, he was the hero. But he quickly turned villain he uprooted the club from their old Grünwalder ground to the Olympiastadion – repeating a similar move which had backfired spectacularly two decades earlier.

Fans who had stood on the terraces at the Grünwalder throughout the dark years were up in arms, but Wildmoser argued that if the club was to progress, it needed a bigger venue to accommodate the huge travelling support of the big boys.

The more militant supporters organised protests and strikes, but in the past couple of seasons, the fire has gone out of the clash. Wildmoser's cash has built a side that can more than hold its own in the *Bundesliga*, while Lorant has developed a happy knack of making clever signings from the international bargain basement, buying players such as Polish anchorman Piotr Nowak, Ghana's Abédi Pelé and Bulgarian striker Daniel Borimirov.

In 1997, the club seemed to have lost its chance of getting back into Europe. But cup triumphs for Dortmund and VfB Stuttgart, both of whom had finished above 1860 in the *Bundesliga* table, got the *Löwen* into the UEFA Cup by the back door.

Second best and 'away from home' they may be, but as president Wildmoser would tell you, being in Europe is a lot better than being in the *Regionalliga*.

Tickets

All standing tickets cost DM15, while seats are DM25–50. Tickets can be bought in advance at the Olympiastadion, or at the old Grünwalder from the **ticket booths** by the main road. The 1860 ticket hotline number is: ☎089/64 27 85 44.

Swift half

Fans disgruntled by the move to the Olympiastadion still meet by the old stadium in Geising before the match. **Wirtschaftswunder**, Tegernseer Landstrasse 139, is a popular *Kneipe* whose name translates as 'Economic Miracle'. The **Sängerheim Gaststätte**, a few doors down, has a framed picture of the side that won the *Bundesliga* in 1966, plus one of this season's line-up. The bar has a Serbian owner, hence the Red Star posters. Both places are a short walk from Silberhornstrasse on U-Bahn lines U1 and U2.

Publication

Löwen-Express (DM2) is the official matchday magazine and, at forty pages, can hardly be accused of offering poor value.

Club shop

There is an official club shop in the centre of town (**Fan-Shop Innenstadt**, Orlandostrasse 8) and another at the old stadium, Grünwalderstrasse 114. Both are open Mon–Fri 9.30am–5pm, Sat 9am–2pm, matchdays until 4pm.

Ultra culture

The revival of the team has been accompanied by a rapid growth in supporters' organisations. There are now more than 300 organised fan groups with over 12,000 members. As the fans are keen to point out, most of these groups are based in Munich and surrounding districts, as opposed to Ireland or Venezuela.

In the net

There's no official TSV1860 site, and several of the many unofficial ones you may see advertised play hard to get. If all else fails, head for: homepages.passau.netsurf.de/matthias.dick/. An unambitious, German-only site, it is at least reliable.

Groundhopping

⚽ SpVgg Unterhaching

Sportparkstadion, Am Sportpark 1
Capacity 10,000
Colours All red with blue trim

Hidden away in Munich's quiet suburbia are Spielvereinigung Unterhaching, a lower division club founded in 1925 and currently enjoying a spell in the second division of the *Bundesliga*.

With two top-flight teams in the city, the club struggle to pull in the crowds, relying on local residents to make up their average gate of around 3000 – easily the worst in the *Zweite Bundesliga.* Kick-off times are often switched to allow as many Bayern or 1860 fans as possible to make the S-Bahn trip out to the ground.

Like most purpose built lower-division grounds, the Sportparkstadion is rather dull. But the **Sportsadl** bar in the clubhouse pulls in a fair trade on matchdays, has Guinness on draught for DM9, and offers a fine view of the action. You'll find no silly talk of rising further here. The club seem content to produce players for the reserve teams of Bayern and 1860 – while at the same time picking up their cast-offs to help delay the inevitable return to the regional leagues.

To catch Haching before they fall, take S2 to Fasanenpark, then a ten-minute walk through the underpass and on to the stadium in the distance.

Brushed aside – another Unterhaching cup run comes to grief

Eat, drink, sleep...

Bars and clubs

Bavaria is synonymous with beer. Munich alone has six labels, including *Augustiner, Hacker-Pschorr* and *Löwenbräu* (the last sponsors of both 1860 and Unterhaching), and all have their own **beer halls** – large, noisy affairs which close around midnight. A large litre-glass is called a *Mass* (around DM10), a half-litre a *Halbmass* (DM6). Strong wheat beer, called *Weizenbier* in the rest of Germany, is called *Weissbier* here and is extremely refreshing.

The big booze-up is, of course, the *Oktoberfest,* which runs from the last Saturday in September to the first Sunday in October, at the Theresienwiese fairground (U4/U5 Theresienwiese).

The main area for nightlife is **Schwabing** (U3/U6 Münchener Freiheit), with its flash, glitzy discos. Further south, behind the university (between U2 Königsplatz and U3/U6 Odeonsplatz) you'll find things cheaper and less overbearing. The alternative district is across the river towards the Ostbahnhof in **Haidhausen** (most lines to Rosenheimer Platz).

55 Bar, Schillerstrasse 19. Classic cellar bar near the train station, a favourite with fans because of its 55 kinds of beer (only three on draught) and its buxom barmaids. Football graffiti over the walls, scarves over the bar. Open until 3am. All lines to Hauptbahnhof.

Café Schiller, Schillerstrasse 3. Big, comfortable sports bar near the main train station, with boxing memorabilia and framed autographed shirts of German football heroes. Extensive jukebox, hot meals served 7pm–1am. Open until 4am. All lines to Hauptbahnhof.

Hofbräuhaus, Am Platzl 9. The most famous beer hall in Munich, always packed before and after matches. Full of cartoon Bavarians, quoffing from customised *Steins* and tapping them on the table to the honking of oompah bands. The place has its own post office and cash machines, just in case you get caught out. Open until midnight. All lines to Marienplatz.

Nachtcafé, Maximiliansplatz 5. Great all-night haunt with live jazz, blues and funk bands after midnight, small glasses of beer at DM7, breakfast served after 3am. No cover charge, but you have to pass the bouncer test. Open until 5am. All lines to Karlsplatz.

Nachtwerk-Club, Landsberger Strasse 185. Huge warehouse disco playing house, funk or trance, depending on the night. DM10 entrance, half-litre beers at DM7, open until late. All lines to Donnersberger Brücke.

Tempel, Domagkstrasse 33. A fair way from the centre of town, the city's most popular if not most imaginative techno club DM10-15 entrance. Ten-minute walk from U6 Alte Heide.

Ultraschall, Töginger Landstrasse 400. For serious techno heads, this place is in the cafeteria of the old airport (U6 Riem). Odd venue, great sounds.

Restaurants

Bavarian cuisine is designed for Bavarians – big, straightforward and **hearty**. Munich's *Gaststätten* serve honest regional fare, generally large portions of roast pork and dumplings to go with your beer, at around DM30–40. The local delicacy is *Weisswurst*, a white sausage made from veal and herbs, whose discovery is marked by a plaque on Marienplatz; don't eat the skin. Bavarian meatloaf (*Leberkäs*) is also popular.

For lunch, the *Viktualienmarkt* by Marienplatz has dozens of **stand-up options**. In the evening, the area around Amalienstrasse and Türkenstrasse (just north of U3/U6 Odeonsplatz) has reasonably cheap **diners**.

Bayern Restaurant, Säbener Strasse 51. If your shopping trip to the *Bayern Boutique* has left you hungry, this spacious restaurant is part of the same headquarters complex and looks out onto the training ground. Food served 11am–11pm, DM20-25 for a main course. Signed photos of

Hats off to the champions – Bayern's 'terrace tourists' keep their eye on the weather

Matthäus, Beckenbauer and Müller with various members of staff, and a *Wall of Fame* at the back with blow-up team shots from down the ages. Most major credit cards. U1/U2 Silberhornstrasse, then bus #15 or #25 to Grödner Strasse.

Gaststätte Engelsburg, corner of Türkenstrasse and Schellingstrasse. Reasonably priced Bavarian dishes, including daily three-course lunchtime specials at around DM12–16. Open until 1am. No credit cards. U2 Theresienstrasse.

Hundskugel, Hotterstrasse 18 (☎089/264 272). The oldest tavern in Munich dates back to the fifteenth century and is as Bavarian as it could possibly get. Reservations recommended. No credit cards. Open daily 10am–midnight. All lines to Marienplatz.

Münchner Suppenküche. There are five branches of this Munich institution – a soup kitchen where huge bowls of authentic hearty broths are dished out in large ladlefuls. The most central branches are at the Viktualienmarkt, at Schäfflerstrasse 7 (both all lines to Marienplatz), and at Schellingstrasse 24 (U3/U6 Universität). No credit cards. Open Mon–Thur until 6pm, Sat until 2pm.

Straubinger Hof, Blumenstrasse 5. Opposite the Viktualienmarkt, a famous old tavern with a beer garden where, following the tradition of eating it only before noon, the *Weisswurst* is served from 9am. Closed Sat eve, all day Sunday. No credit cards.

Accommodation

Munich can be a pig of a city to find a cheap room in. Always book weeks before you travel, and for *Oktoberfest*, months in advance. The cheapest **pensions** are to be found near the Hauptbahnhof, but make sure you're looking around in daylight. The **tourist office** opposite platform 11 at the station will book you a room for DM6, plus

DM3 deposit. The *EurAide* desk nearby (open daily 7.30am–11.30am & 1–6pm) provides a similar service. Be aware that Bavarian IYHF **youth hostels** do not accept any guests over the age of 26.

CVJM Jugendgästehaus, Landwehrstrasse 13 (☎089/552 1410). Near the station, a hostel run by Young Christians incongruously plonked in an area of seedy bars. Clean, basic rooms, singles DM50, doubles DM80, triples DM110. Over-26s allowed but charged 15 percent extra. Breakfast included, curfew 12.30am. No credit cards. All lines to Hauptbahnhof.

Haus International, Elisabethstrasse 87 (☎089/120 060, fax 089/12 00 62 51). Youth hostel with a disco, cafeteria and swimming pool on site. Singles DM55, with shower DM80, doubles DM100/135, larger rooms also available. Over-26s allowed. No credit cards. Five-minute walk from U2 Hohenzollernplatz.

Hotel-Pension am Markt, Heiliggeeiststrasse 6 (☎089/225 014). With a perfect location by Heiliggeistkirche near Viktualienmarkt, this old pension has fading photos of celebrity guests and a grand piano in the lobby. Singles DM65, DM90 with shower, doubles DM115/150. Reserve at least two months in advance. No credit cards. All lines to Marienplatz.

Pension Agnes, Agnesstrasse 58 (☎089/12 93 061, fax 089/129 1764). Basic pension with spacious double rooms and shoebox singles. DM50–60 for a single, DM85–90 a double, breakfast not included. No credit cards. U2 Hohenzollernplatz.

Pension Frank, Schellingstrasse 24 (☎089/281 451). Come-as-you-are pension which charges DM45 per person to share a double, DM60 for a single and DM85–90 for a double, showers and breakfast included. No credit cards. U3/U6 Universität.

Cologne

Perched picturesquely on the river Rhine, Cologne is a major industrial centre which happens to have spawned some of the most successful and effective teams to have graced the *Bundesliga*. The town's big club, I.FC Cologne (in German 'I.FC Köln', meaning 'the first football club of Cologne') won the first-ever *Bundesliga* title and have been there or thereabouts ever since.

In recent years, though, the club have sunk into the mid-table mire, seeing their position as the region's major player usurped by others – notably Leverkusen, a ten-minute train ride to the north-west, whose backing from the chemicals giant Bayer allows them to spend more freely in the transfer market than their more illustrious neighbours. There is also a strong traditional rivalry with nearby Borussia Mönchengladbach.

Next to these threats, the presence of little Fortuna, a classic yo-yo team currently in the second division, in the city itself scarcely troubles I.FC Cologne and their long-suffering fans.

The thrilling fields

I.FC Cologne

Müngersdorfer Stadion, Müngersdorf
Capacity 54,000
Colours All red with white trim
League champions 1962, 1964, 1978
Cup winners 1968, 1977–78, 1983

I.FC Cologne are a product of postwar reconstruction. Just as the devastation of their major cities allowed the Germans to rebuild their infrastructure in a logical way, so the re-organisation of football gave Cologne a chance to create a team worthy of one of the nation's major cities.

Before World War II, Cologne had two major teams: Kölner Ballspiel-Club (KBC) and Sülz 07. Neither of them had made it to the final of a German championship or cup. Sülz had a strong tradition in a number of sports, while KBC were well-organised and had stronger finances. The city already had an excellent stadium – the Müngersdorfer, built as part of a huge sports complex in 1923 – so a merger to create a team worthy of such facilities made sense.

I.FC Cologne were born on February 13, 1948, and took the field four months later in the *Oberliga West*. It didn't take long for the new club to make an impact. There was a place in the final of the West German cup in 1954, and after competing in the latter stages of the qualifiers for the national title, Cologne made their first championship play-off in 1960, losing 3–2 to Hamburg. In 1962, they went one better, beating Nuremburg 4–0 in the Olympic stadium, Berlin, with a team inspired by the international full-back Karl-Heinz Schnellinger.

The club sold Schnellinger to AS Roma a year later, but there was no question that they would be founding members of the *Bundesliga*. They began the inaugural, 1963/64 season as favourites and lived up to expectations, winning the title by six points, thanks largely to the influence of Wolfgang Overath. A hard-grafting midfielder with tremendous shooting power, Overath was to stay with the club throughout his career, during which he clocked up 81 caps for West Germany.

The title gave Cologne their second tilt at the European Cup. In their first appearance in 1962/63, they'd suffered a humiliating defeat by Dundee, losing 8–1 in Scotland. In 1965 they fared better, reaching a semi-final against Liverpool. A pair of goalless draws against England's champions typified Cologne's gutsy, fighting spirit; they lost the replay 2–0.

A domestic cup win in 1968 ended Cologne's run of success, and it wasn't until the late Seventies that the fans at the Müngersdorfer had cause to celebrate once more. In 1977, with Hennes Weisweiler, architect of the great Mönchengladbach side of the early Seventies, in charge, and with Overath playing his last season, they won the cup. The following year they won it again, and also lifted the title to become only the third West German team to do the double (Schalke in 1937 and Bayern in 1969 were the other two). The last round of the *Bundesliga* title race was nothing if not bizarre – Cologne were level on points with 'Gladbach, but their goal difference was so massively superior that if they won, Weisweiler's men knew their rivals would have to score twelve to overhaul them. 'Gladbach duly beat a strangely under-strength Dortmund side by exactly 12–0, but Cologne were not to be denied – they beat St Pauli 5–0 on the same day.

Arsenal in disguise? Wolfgang Overath, 1973

Weisweiler's side, skippered by West German international Heinz Flohe and with the prodigious Dieter Müller upfront, reached the European Cup semi-finals in 1979, where they lost to eventual winners Nottingham Forest. In the Forest side that faced them was England international striker Tony Woodcock. The tall striker must have made quite an impression as the following season he moved to Cologne, where he enjoyed three seasons before being sold to Arsenal. Woodcock returned to the city to play and later coach Fortuna Köln, and still lives in the area.

Cologne's best run in Europe came in 1986, when they made it all the way to a UEFA Cup final against Real Madrid. After taking the lead in the first leg at the Bernabéu, the Germans went down 5–1 and could not recover. Supporters, however, often cite this team as the most attractive seen at the Müngersdorfer, with the wayward but magical talents of Klaus Allofs and Pierre Littbarski in the final third.

There have been no honours since. Cologne finished as *Bundesliga* runners-up in 1989 and 1990, but more recently they have drifted dangerously in mid-table. The club's leadership are far from popular with the fans, who have become frustrated with what they see as a lack of ambition – exemplified by an absence of adventure in the transfer market. The 1995/96 season saw two coaches fired as the team slipped close to the drop zone, before recovering to finish twelfth. The following campaign was little better, the club surviving in tenth place off the meagre pickings delivered by their ageing strikeforce of Bruno Labbadia and Toni Polster.

1.FC Cologne have never been out of the top flight of the *Bundesliga,* but with another modest-looking side taking the field for 1997/98, the warning bells are starting to ring.

Here we go!

From the Hauptbahnhof, take **S-Bahn line S1** to Junkersdorf/Stadion. The journey takes around twenty minutes. From the S-Bahn station, turn left and walk across the park towards the stadium.

Cologne essentials

Cologne's **airport** is 14km south-west of the city centre. Airport bus #170 leaves every twenty minutes to make the half-hour journey into town, pulling into the central bus station, just behind the main **train station**, Köln Hauptbahnhof.

An alternative to flying is to take the *Eurostar* train from London's Waterloo International to **Brussels**, and change there for Köln Hauptbahnhof. Connections and frequency of service have recently been improved, and going via the Channel Tunnel will certainly be a lot cheaper than catching a plane.

Conveniently, the Hauptbahnhof is right next door to the **Gothic cathedral** (*Dom*) which dominates the centre of the city. The Hauptbahnhof is also the central point for the S-Bahn, U-Bahn and tram networks which, as ever in Germany, make travelling around the city easy. City transport runs until around midnight, after which there is a limited **night bus** service.

Single transport **tickets** are bought from machines at major stops, the price varying according to the length of the journey. A **24-hour pass**, valid within the city boundaries, is good value at DM9.50; a three-day pass is DM19.

The main **tourist information office** is opposite the Hauptbahnhof at Unter Fettenhennen 19 (open Mon–Sat 8am–9pm, Sun 9.30am–7pm, ☎0221/221 3345). They charge DM5 commission for booking you a room, but it's worth it – they can often get discounted prices. The office also publishes a monthly guide to entertainment and cultural events. The local **listings magazine** is *Prinz* (DM4.50), which is a good source of non-sports information.

Swift Half

In fine weather the beer garden of the **Landhaus Kuckuck** restaurant in the park comes into its own. It's five minutes' walk from the stadium – as you approach from the S-Bahn station, turn left at the main entrance. Otherwise there are the usual **stands** dotted around the perimeter of the ground, pizza slices and kebabs offering a change from the sausage routine.

Tickets

Prices are very reasonable at the Müngersdorfer, with a standing ticket behind the goal costing DM14 and a side-view terrace spot DM18. You can sit at one end for DM29, while the most expensive seats, in the central, upper-deck *Oberrang Mitte,* cost DM52. Sellouts are rare, but tickets can be bought prior to kick-off at the stadium, or you can call the **ticket office** on: ☎0221/94 36 430.

Publications

Geissbockecho (DM2) is the official and rather dull match programme. The most popular fanzine is named after a former coach, *Hennes*, and copies are usually on sale outside the entrance to the *Südtribune*.

Ultra Culture

The *Südtribune* is home to the most enthusiastic and noisiest of the local support, particularly the bottom tier. The fans have a friendship with supporters of St Pauli which dates back to 1978, when Cologne won the title in Hamburg and spent the night partying around the Reeperbahn with the Pauli crowd.

You may also see a group parading a banner declaring 'Arsenal Cologne'. Although the origins of this bizarre sect are not clear, it's believed they may originally have been a Tony Woodcock fan club who continued to follow the permed one after his move to Highbury.

The biggest rivalry is with relatively distant Schalke 04 – historic foes from the pre-*Bundesliga* days when Cologne used to do battle with them for the *Westdeutsche* title and the right to represent the region in the championship play-offs.

In the net

There's no official website, but check out the London 1.FC Cologne supporters' club homepage at: village.vossnet.co.uk/t/toles. You'll find news and results in English, plus the chance to join 'FC Goats International' – a Cologne internet fan club.

Groundhopping

🐐 Fortuna Cologne

Südstadion, Am Vorgebirgstor
Capacity 15,000
Colours All white with red trim

Like 1.FC Cologne, Fortuna were formed in 1948. Like 1.FC Cologne, Fortuna came about from the amalgamation of prewar clubs – in their case Victoria, Bayenthaler and SV Köln. But there the similarity ends.

Fortuna have had just one season in the top flight – 1973/74, with Irish international Noel Cantwell in the side. But the season was spoilt for many loyal fans by the fact that the team had to groundshare with 1.FC Cologne.

Two years later the club left their old Radrennbahn ground behind for good, and moved to the newly built Südstadion. The ground was upgraded in the summer of 1994 when the north end was redeveloped, but the stadium is a disappointment – a characterless arena typical of the cheap Seventies mini-bowls that can be found across western Germany and Austria.

The club's finest hour came in 1983, when they made the final of the West German cup. Even then, 1.FC Cologne were there to steal the limelight,

defeating the 'southsiders' 1–0 with a goal from Littbarski.

Today crowds rarely pass the 4000 mark for the team's second-division games, but Fortuna can boast a loyal band of colourful and loud supporters. The 'Fortuna Eagles' are the main fan group, and they can be found singing away in the *Stehplatz Mitte* – the terracing opposite the main stand.

If you fancy singing along with them, take **tram #12** from the Hauptbahnhof to Pohligstrasse. The trip takes around twenty minutes, and the ground is on your left as you get off the tram.

Next door to the club offices at Am Vorgebirgstor 1, just down the road from the stadium, is **Bacchus**, a friendly pub/restaurant owned by the club. Dark and smoky inside, it sports a few reminders of its owners but holds off from being a Fortuna theme-bar. During the week, it

Cologne's adopted son – England striker Tony Woodcock

Mad in the Müngersdorfer – Littbarski and Kuntz, Cologne and Kaiserslautern, 1993

even does a fair trade serving business lunches. On matchdays, however, it fills up early with young Eagles preparing to fly.

Eat, drink, sleep...

Bars and clubs

Packed with bars and restaurants of all varieties and boasting an exceptionally varied nightlife, Cologne won't make you look far in your search for a pint and a bite.

The traditional local beer is *Kölsch* – a light but bitter ale which is served in a tall, thin *Stange* glass. The locals love it but the rest of Germany considers it to be the equivalent of **drinking shandy**.

The traditional setting for sipping a glass of *Kölsch is* the *Brauhaus* – a large bar or beer hall owned by a local brewery, which will often also be an ideal place to try out some local cooking at a reasonable price. There are scores of *Brauhäuser* dotted all

over the city, but some of them are a little tacky and touristy.

Cologne has a strong local **live music scene** and in the summer is host to any number of festivals, including what must be Europe's last remaining punk festival.

There is no one central nightlife zone, but the **Altstadt** (old town) area has plenty of club choices.

42 dp, Hohenstaufenring 25 The city's top dance music club, attracting DJs from across the land and with the emphasis on underground and trance. Young crowd, cover charges upwards of DM10, depending on the status of the DJ.

Brauhaus Früh am Dom, Am Hof 12–14. Can get crowded with tourists in summer, but during the football season this is an ideal, central location for tasting the local brew and nosh. Right next to the *Dom*, yet the prices are fair.

E-Werk, Schanzenstrasse 28, Mühlheim. The top venue for live music is also home to a bar, a restaurant and a café. Attracts top national and international acts as well as local talent. The *Dynamo Lounge* has an excellent restaurant with reasonably priced Italian and French dishes.

Hallmackenreuther, Brüsseler Platz 9. This is a fine example of what Germans call a 'scene bar' – a pre-party meeting point and informal nightlife information centre. Wide variety of beer and energy drinks, plus DJ action at weekends.

Joe Champs, Hohenzollerning 101. One of several American sports bars in the city and the most likely to have its TV screens tuned to football, as opposed to men in baseball caps or crash helmets. Huge steaks, usual Tex-Mex menu, American and German beer.

Restaurants

Tired with their reputation for stodgy meat, cabbage and dumpling dishes, German chefs and restaurant owners are busy trying to reconstruct the *Deutsche Küche*. The result is *Neudeutsch*. a **lighter, modern German cuisine**, and Cologne is one of the best places to try it.

Alt-Köln, Trankgasse 7–9. A central *Brauhaus* with a reputation for good, solid, local food, served in large portions and to be washed down with freshly poured beer. Not quite *Neudeutsch* but a good winter warmer. Open Mon–Sat 12 noon–12 midnight, Sun until 11pm.

Chicago Meatpackers, Hahnenstrasse 37. Don't come here unless you're hungry. Monster-sized (even by German standards) burgers and steaks, piles of chips, great fresh salads, chilli – and loads of footie on TV. Open daily 12 noon–11pm.

Lesar, Mozart Strasse 39. A friendly little tavern serving fine *Neudeutsch* dishes. Also does an excellent breakfast buffet. Open until 1am Mon–Sat, 10pm Sun.

Der Löwenbräu, Frankenwerft 21. Just in case pork, cabbage and dumplings was actually what you were hoping to eat in Cologne – this Bavarian restaurant has all the trimmings, with plenty of fresh Bavarian beer, *Weisswurst* and the rest. Just what Frau Matthäus has waiting for Lothar when he comes home from training. Open daily 12 noon–11pm.

Trattoria Tiziano, Lindenthnalgürtel Strasse. Not far from the Müngersdorfer stadium, so a good spot for a post-match supper, this is a quiet little Italian on a street with plenty of bars and restaurants. A full-sized pizza costs a reasonable DM10. Open Mon–Sat 11.30am–11.30pm, Sun until 10.30pm

Accommodation

Cologne gets plenty of tourists in summer but most of its hotels are geared towards the business community – the city has a vast *Messe* trade show centre. Many of these business hotels offer **cheap weekend deals**, but they can be a good way out from the city centre.

The resumption of the German football season in early spring often coincides with **Carnival time** in Cologne, when spare rooms fill up quickly.

Hotel Cristall, Ursulaplatz 9–11 (☎0221/163 00). Small, fairly upmarket hotel, five minutes from the central train station and the *Dom*; 85 new rooms, hotel bar. Doubles from DM160.

Hotel Rheingold, Engelsbertstrasse 33–35 (☎0221/924 090). Good value at DM65 per person in a double room, with en-suite bath/shower and colour TV. Central location.

Im Kupferkessel, Probsteigasse 6 (☎0221/135 338). Central, unpretentious place with doubles from DM50; location ideal if you are planning on clubbing.

Jügendherbergen Deutz, Siegestrasse (☎0221/814 711). Just over the river, this is a basic youth hostel, with surly and unhelpful staff who must have been trained in the GDR. Still, it's only ten minutes by U-Bahn from the centre, has clean rooms and offers a decent continental buffet breakfast Dorm rooms from DM15.

Boom-time in Berlin...

Berlin, united Germany's capital to be, is a football orphan. Unlike Paris, it has had no superteam
artificially thrust upon it to win titles and summon
Europe's best. Unlike Paris, no national team
games are regularly played here.

But, unlike Paris, there is a genuine dormant
football culture in the city, which needs only
more national exposure and half-decent club football in order to flower. Both could be provided by
Hertha Berlin, who attracted the 1996/97 season's record crowd, 75,000, to their
Olympiastadion for a second-division game
against Kaiserslautern. Hertha won both the
match and, shortly afterwards, promotion.

Behind the revival is **Rolf Schmidt-Holz**,
head of *UFA Films*, the audio-visual branch of the
Bertelsmann press empire. *UFA* were the prewar
German film studio responsible for the kind of
classic images of Berlin that still attract millions
of tourists every year. Schmidt-Holz sees Berlin as
a potential Paris and *UFA* as a potential *Canal
Plus*, and is ready to invest DM30 million in the

Hertha new boy – Bryan Roy

club in 1997/98. The Olympiastadion itself is seen as a key venue for Germany's bid to
host the 2006 World Cup, and the federal government is prepared to pump DM400 million into its renovation.

The Olympiastadion is a totalitarian triumph in granite. It's also **falling to bits**.
Aside from West German cup finals and the odd international, it has barely been used
in decades.

Berlin had been quick to take to the game in the 1870s, but Hertha's title of 1931
was the city's last. The building of Hitler's **76,000-seater Olympiastadion** kept
Berlin in the football spotlight for a while, but when Germany beat Bulgaria there in a
Euro '96 qualifier in November 1995, it was the stadium's first international game for
seven years. "The crowd," said Berliner Thomas Hässler, "was our twelfth man".

The last four Berliner clubs to play in the *Bundesliga* – **Hertha, Blau-Weiss,
Tennis Borussia** and **Tasmania** – were all quickly relegated, Tasmania's effort in
1965/66 being the worst in the league's history. Hertha were brought down to earth by
the bribery scandal of 1971, and the club have rarely been able to attract decent
crowds. But in the early Sixties they enjoyed East German support as their ground,
nicknamed the *Plumpe*, was enticingly near the Wall. When Hertha moved to the
Olympiastadion, losing their Western fan base from the working-class Wedding area,
their results were passionately followed in the East.

On the other side of the Wall, **Dynamo** Berlin's ten-year stay at the top of the East
German *Oberliga* was helped by their chief patron Erich Mielke's position as head of
the Communist state secret police, the *Stasi*. **Union** Berlin attracted genuine working-
class support, Dynamo were despised. Soon after the fall of the Wall, a Hertha-Union
friendly at the Olympiastadion attracted a crowd of 35,000.

Hertha's promotion to the *Bundesliga* might just put Berlin back on the map. If not,
the local leagues, which produced Hässler and Pierre Littbarski among others, are as
colourful and competitive as any in Germany.

Dortmund

Borussia Dortmund 226

The Ruhr is Germany's industrial heartland and in many respects it is the hotbed of the nation's football scene – the Teutonic equivalent of the north-west of England. There are top-drawer clubs scattered across the area, among them Schalke 04, VfL Bochum, MSV Duisburg and Borussia Mönchengladbach. All have had their moments – Schalke in the years before World War II, 'Gladbach under Hennes Weisweiler in the Seventies.

But in recent years it is Borussia Dortmund who have emerged as the major force. Their two *Bundesliga* titles in the mid-Nineties earned them successive places in the Champions' League, and their 1997 victory in that competition has cemented their reputation as Germany's team to beat. Dortmund have ridden the *Bundesliga* boom as well as anybody, and today only Bayern can get close to matching them for on-the-field talent and off-the-field commercial success. If the Champions' League is producing an élite of European superclubs, then Borussia Dortmund are without doubt one of them.

The fortunes of the football club have risen as those of the region as a whole have declined – the Ruhr is suffering a string of post-industrial problems, and the cliché that the team has put the city 'on the map' certainly rings true for Dortmund. Visitors come here for one thing only – a game at the Westfalen stadium – and rarely go home disappointed by what they see.

The Westfalen is proof that a state-of-the-art stadium can still provoke a pounding atmosphere, and that attracting wealthier fans and families need not mean alienating traditional working-class support. While the team's distinctive fluorescent shirts have become a consumer fashion accessory, the club recently backed striking steelworkers by offering them free seats in the ground and allowing players to take part in street demonstrations.

May 1997 – Andy Möller lifts the big one

Dortmund's 1997 European Cup final triumph over Juventus was greeted with bemusement by many. But Schalke's UEFA Cup final victory over Inter Milan, just seven days earlier, gave Dortmund all the impetus they needed – the rivalry between the two clubs (Schalke are based in Gelsenkirchen, just a few kilometres away) is one of the most intense in Germany, and derby games between the two are an unforgettable occasion.

The thrilling fields

Borussia Dortmund

Westfalen-Stadion, Westfalenpark
Capacity 48,000
Colours Fluorescent yellow shirts, black shorts
League champions 1956–57, 1963, 1995–96
Cup winners 1965, 1989
European Cup winners 1997
Cup-Winners' Cup winners 1966

BVB ('Ballspiel Verein Borussia') Dortmund were formed out of a merger of several local clubs. The original players were a 'rebel group' who left the sports club Trinity in 1909, after constant rows with Chaplain Derwald, the head of the club. They teamed up with members of two other clubs, Rhenania and Brittania, to compete as BVB in the regional leagues.

August Lenz was one of the players who came through from the ranks of the then popular street football competitions to become Borussia's first international. In 1936, Lenz led the side into the competitive *Gauliga* which covered the region, and

where their derby rivalry with Schalke 04 began to take off. Yet before World War II, it was Schalke who dominated, winning six German championships. The very presence of Schalke in the region ruled out any chance of Dortmund making the national play-offs.

In the post-war era, it was all change. In 1947 Borussia defeated Schalke 3–2 to become Westphalian champions for the first time and enter the national play-offs. Two years later they made the finals but lost out to VfR Mannheim. They finally got their first national title in 1956, when they defeated Karlsruhe 4–2. The team, coached by Helmut Schneider, retained their title a year later with a 4–1 win over Hamburg.

A few years later, Dortmund looked well set to make an impact in the new *Bundesliga*. They won the last title to be decided by the play-off system, in 1963, then in 1965 finished third in the league and won the West German cup.

While a *Bundesliga* title eluded them, Dortmund concentrated on the 1965/66 European Cup-Winners' Cup. CSKA Sofia and Atlético Madrid were defeated on the way to the semi-finals, where they met holders West Ham United. The other

May 1993 – same teams, same level, different outcome...and Möller wins the UEFA Cup for Juve

Dortmund essentials

Dortmund's **airport** is close to the city centre but is served mainly by domestic flights. Your best bet is to fly to **Düsseldorf** or **Cologne**, and catch a train from there. Alternatively, take the *Eurostar* train from London's Waterloo International and change at Brussels for Dortmund.

The compact city centre is well laid out and easily covered by foot. Dortmund's main train sation (Hauptbahnhof) is right in the middle of it, and as well as inter-city trains it acts as the terminal for the local **S-Bahn** and **U-Bahn** networks, which go well beyond the boundaries of the city to cover neighbouring towns such as Bochum.

A **one-day pass** for journeys within Dortmund costs DM9.50, or DM13.50 if you plan to leave the city boundaries. Single U-Bahn tickets are bought from machines, cost variable depending on distance. A ticket to the stadium costs DM2.80. The service runs until around midnight, after which there are occasional night buses. The main **taxi rank** is right outside the Hauptbahnhof.

The city's **tourist information centre** (*Dortmunder Verkehrsverein*) is at Königswall 20 (open Mon–Fri 9am–6pm, Sat 9am–1pm, ☎0231/14 03 41, fax 0231/16 35 93). The staff are exceptionally helpful, and this is the most **football-friendly** tourist office in Europe, offering special deals for visitors heading to the game. Among these offers is **accommodation** at up to 40 percent off the normal room rate, at some seventy participating hotels. Contact the office **in advance** on the above numbers.

---

semi-final saw Liverpool meet Celtic and the British press were licking their lips at the prospect of an all-British final. But West Ham were defeated 2–1 at Upton Park and 3–1 at the Westfalen – Dortmund were in the final, against Liverpool.

Dortmund's side included four players who would be part of West Germany's squad in that summer's World Cup – Tilkowski, Held, Emmerich and Paul. The Germans took the lead through Held on 62 minutes, but Roger Hunt levelled the game six minutes later. Then, in extra-time, midfielder Reinhard 'Stan' Libuda got the winner.

It was the first time a German side had won a European competition. More significantly, Dortmund's victory demonstrated that, just three years after its foundation, the *Bundesliga* was producing a standard of club football that was just as high that of the West German national team.

The triumph should also have heralded the arrival of Dortmund as a major power in West German and European football. Instead BVB faded, finishing third in the league in 1969, but not getting their hands on any more silverware for thirty years.

In 1972 they were relegated from the first division, and did not return there until 1976. For a decade Dortmund struggled to escape from mid-table, and in 1986 they needed an epic three-game play-off with Fortuna Cologne to avoid the drop again.

Tortuous though it was, the relegation scare provoked large-scale reorganisation of the club's off-the-field activities and a renewed effort to improve its finances. For the 1986/87 season the club signed a sponsorship deal with Dortmund-based insurance company *Die Continentale,* and visionary new club president Gerd Niebaum appointed a full-time commercial manager – then something of a novelty in the German game. Two seasons later, BVB lifted the West German cup and were back in Europe.

The Nineties saw Niebaum's Dortmund revival plan finally come to full fruition, with consecutive *Bundesliga* titles under Ottmar Hitzfeld's coaching in 1995 and 1996. The team's success was based on a series of players bought from Juventus. In 1992, German international defender Stefan Reuter was brought back to his homeland from Turin. Twelve months later, a Juve side

nationals who had fled the *Bundesliga* for Italy in the early Nineties. Kohler and Reuter had both been expected to return to Bayern when their Italian contracts were up – Dortmund's coup in signing them signalled a shift in the balance of *Bundesliga* power from Bavaria to the Ruhr.

Hitzfeld's *coup de grâce* was delivered at the Olympic stadium in Munich in May 1997. Four years after watching his team taken to the cleaners by Juventus in the UEFA Cup final, he now fielded many of those former Juve stars in Dortmund yellow. They did not let him down. Riedle scored twice in the first half, and teenager Lars Ricken added a spectacular third in the second period, just as the Italians were beginning to look dangerous – 3–1 to BVB, and Europe's highest footballing accolade was theirs.

The European Cup win has given further impetus to the club's already impressive merchandising operation – in 1995, half a million of those fluorescent yellow shirts were sold across Germany – the dazzling journey to the game is proof.

But the cash from sponsorship and merchandising has not all been paid to Juventus. The Westfalen stadium, built for the 1974 World Cup (the club's pre-1974 ground, Rote Erde, is still functioning and is right next door), has been gradually upgraded since 1986. New tiers have been added to the west and east stands, and the north stand, which contains the visitors' section is also to get another deck – the expected final capacity will be over 70,000.

The most appealing part of the ground is the *Südtribune*, one of the last covered Kops in Europe. In order to save the character of this stand while still meeting UEFA regulations for European games, the club are investigating the possibility of installing removable seats, so that fans can sit for Champions' League games and stand up for the *Bundesliga*. Such a scheme would doubtless be more expensive than simply plonking in plastic bucket seats as so many clubs have done – but it would typify the approach of a club which marries modern

A derby to end all derbies – Schalke–BVB

including Brazilian Júlio César and Germans Andreas Möller and Jürgen Kohler hammered Dortmund, 6–1 on aggregate, in the final of the UEFA Cup.

Within a year, BVB had signed both César and Möller. Kohler joined in 1995, and another former Juventus man, Portuguese playmaker Paulo Sousa, signed in 1996. Meanwhile, two other former *Serie A* exiles, striker Karl-Heinz Riedle and anchorman Matthias Sammer, were signed from Lazio and Inter respectively.

In the space of four years Dortmund had recruited almost all the German inter-

commercialism with sensitivity to the needs of its fans.

Tickets

BVB have close to 30,000 season-ticket holders and it can be difficult to get a place for the big games. For run-of-the-mill league fixtures, tickets can be bought at the **green huts** which surround the stadium. The club's ticket hotline number is: ☎0231/90 20 15.

If the worst happens and the ground is full, then head for **Friedenplatz** in the centre of town, where a giant TV screen is erected for important sellout games.

Here we go!

The Westfalen is well out of the centre but easily reached by **U-Bahn line U45** from the Hauptbahnhof to its end stop, Westfalenstadion. The journey takes fifteen minutes.

Swift half

The stadium is part of a huge sports complex and park. All around the ground are **stalls** selling beer, sausages and doner kebabs. The best spot for eating and drinking is behind the *Nordtribüne,* just by the side of the old Rote Erde ground. Many fans turn up well over an hour before kick-off to gather here where, as well as a nostalgic view of the past, there is a wide choice of sausages and the excellent local brew, *DAB,* on offer at DM4 for a half-litre. Inside the ground, beer is available at DM7 in the west stand and DM5 in the north, along with sausages and pizza slices.

On the way home, the giant screen inside the Hauptbahnhof shows whichever highlights package is on TV, and several hundred fans may gather there with cans in hand to watch the goals go in again.

After crucial wins, some fans travel to Borsigplatz, the area where the club was formed, to celebrate on the street. If you somehow lose the trail of yellow and black, then take U45 to Kampstrasse, change to tram #404 and head in the direction of Westfalenhütte, getting off at Borsigplatz.

Publications

Borussia Magazin (DM2) is a high-quality colour glossy produced for every home game. The monthly *Borussia Live* (DM4.50) is aimed at a younger, TV audience. *Der Reporter* (DM1.50) is a regional sports magazine with coverage of handball and other sports as well as football. The local daily paper is the *Ruhr Nachrichten,* which carries a well-informed sports page in its Dortmund edition.

In the net

There were more than thirty BVB website at the last count, but the official one is easy to find at: www.borussia-dortmund.de/. It includes the expected high graphics content and online shopping areas but, like so many official sites, it's strangely uninvolving. So try Reinhard Kahle's established fans' site at: www.object-factory.com/dortmund. Unlike the official site, this one includes some English content, along with links to sites from SC Freiburg and Celtic.

Eat, drink, sleep...

Bars and clubs

Dortmund isn't the best night out in Germany but there's still plenty of choice for eating, drinking and dancing. The **local beer** is DAB, best-known for the five-litre barrels of the stuff which Germans take home for their summer garden parties. The girls at the tourist office will also give you the *Lokalführer* – a decent little guide to pubs, restaurants and clubs.

Café Central, Markt 5–7. A popular street café in the summer, but inside there are two TV's; the owner has a subscription to *Premiere*, meaning live *Bundesliga* action and plenty of football talk. Snacks, coffee, beer and a friendly crowd.

Come in, Olpe 33. How can you walk past a place with a name like that? Good little bar, with seating outside in warm weather. Inside there is table bowling and that strange German invention, the electronic dartboard. Cheap menu of sausages and soups.

Gerberschänke, Gerberstrasse 3. If you want to hear CDs of Dortmund footie songs blasted out at full-volume, while downing pints of DAB in the seedy 'kebab and sex shop' part of the city centre, then this is the place. *Heja BVB!*

Liebezeit, Münsterstrasse 71–73. The name means 'love time' but this is no German singles bar. Rather, it's the place to meet up with the Saturday night crowd, have a few to warm up and find out what's on. DJs give the emphasis to dub and jungle.

Soundgarden, Gerichstrasse. Different sounds every night at Dortmund's best disco, which has two separate dancefloors offering contrasting themes. Depending on when you visit, you could face nostalgia from the Eighties, ragga and jungle, jazz and soul or German heavy metal. Also has an adjoining pub and bistro.

Restaurants

Avoid those restaurants obviously geared for the expense-account business trade; Dortmund is a **workers' city** and there's no need to spend a fortune on keeping yourself fed. Look out for excellent *Tagesmenu* lunchtime deals.

Brinkhoffs No.1, Markt. The cooks make use of the market opposite to serve up traditional German food to the masses. Seats for 120 inside, capacity doubles when the terrace opens in spring. The steaks and salads are excellent and there is a lunchtime *Tagesmenu* for around DM15.

Kaktus Jack, Weissenburger Strasse 35/37. Mexican and American restaurant/bar with steaks, burgers, spare ribs, cocktails and a wide range of tequilas. Often has special deals midweek such as happy hours and 'eat-all-you-can'. Open Mon–Fri 5pm–1am, Sat 6pm–3am, Sun 6pm–1am.

La Botte, Beurhausstrasse 21. Word has it this is where several of BVB's former Juventus players come when they pine for some decent *tagliatelli*. High-quality Italian restaurant which, as well as pasta, also specialises in fish. Main courses for DM 18–38. Open daily until midnight.

Marché, Ostenhellweg 3. Popular with a young crowd thanks to its low prices (main meals around DM10) and wide selection. As well as the usual German favourites there are French and Italian dishes, and a self-service bar as well.

Accommodation

You shouldn't have any problems turning up on-spec without a room in Dortmund, but remember that if you want to take advantage of the **football supporters' discount**, you must book in advance. That number again: ☎0231/14 03 41.

Hotel Carlton, Lütge-Brückstrasse 5–7 (☎0231/ 129 955). Slap bang in the centre of town, just five minutes' walk from the Hauptbahnhof. Sports shop downstairs, with an owner who will happily chat about BVB's latest form. Rooms from DM45 including a good cold breakfast.

Parkhotel Westfalenhallen, Strobelallee 41 (☎0231/12 04 555). Ideal if you are just going to the game and aren't planning a night out in the city, as it is located in the same park as the stadium. Wide range of room prices with doubles from around DM100.

Pension 'Cläre Fritz', Reinoldstrasse 6 (☎0231/57 96 23). Cheap and friendly guest house in the centre of the city with rooms from DM45. Only ten rooms, however, so check avalability in advance.

Holiday Inn Dortmund/Rümischer Kaiser, Olpe 2 (☎0231/57 43 54). As you would expect from a big international chain, with sauna, solarium, fitness room and the works. Double rooms from DM148. Central location.

Hamburg

Hamburg SV 232
St Pauli 235

If any city can claim to be the home of football in Germany, that city is Hamburg. While southern and eastern regions of the country reacted with scepticism or outright hostility to the game's popularity at the turn of the century, Hamburg – always, like any major port, more tolerant of outside influences – embraced soccer with open arms.

Germany's first dedicated football club, SC Germania Hamburg, were founded here in 1887. Subsequently the city also pioneered the idea of competition between representative sides from different towns, at a time when the game was still very much confined to regional competitions.

Today Hamburg's two football teams couldn't be more different. Hamburg SV are a famous old club, well-established in the top flight of the *Bundesliga* and playing at a big, purpose-built, out-of-town sports arena. FC St Pauli are the outsiders who have spent most of their life in the regional leagues and play at a tiny ground cramped into the city's famous red light district.

Recent years have seen the relationship between the two clubs change. St Pauli have enjoyed a spell in the top flight and pulled in crowds that almost equal those of HSV, who have been struggling to live up to a long tradition of success at both national and European level. True, St Pauli were relegated (not for the first time) in 1997. But the club's management are boldly going ahead with plans for a new stadium, indicating a confidence of purpose which has been lacking at HSV for years.

Fingered – Kevin Keegan in his Hamburg heyday

It's not just the contrasting stadia and histories that distinguish the two clubs – it's their support. HSV are followed by the traditional working-class fan, while St Pauli attract a mix of anarchists, punks and weirdos that seem totally out of place at a football match. Needless to say, derby games between the two are never anything less than exhilirating.

It all makes for a fascinating clash of football cultures, and regardless of whether you prefer the leather and attitude of St Pauli's 'Happy Fans' or the commitment and loyalty of the HSV boys, there's no doubt that a football weekend in Hamburg can count among the best in Europe.

The thrilling fields

Hamburg SV

Volksparkstadion, Hamburg-Altona
Capacity 61,000
Colours White shirts, red shorts, blue, black and white trim
League champions 1923, 1928, 1960, 1979, 1982–83
Cup Winners 1963, 1976, 1987
European Cup winners 1983
Cup-Winners' Cup winners 1977

The modern German game seems to be full of sleeping giants. Some, like Eintracht Frankfurt and 1.FC Nuremburg, have been asleep so long, they've fallen out of the top flight altogether. Others, such as 1.FC Cologne and Werder Bremen, need to be roused from their slumbers if they are not to suffer a similar fate. Hamburger Sport-Verein fall into the latter camp. The third most successful club in German football history (after Bayern Munich and Nuremburg) are members of an élite group that have never been relegated from the top drawer of the *Bundesliga*, but there is no doubt that something has gone seriously wrong at the Volkspark.

It's almost fifteen years since HSV last won a title, a decade since they won their last honour with a cup win over Stuttgart Kickers in 1987. And, in the past two seasons they have come dangerously close to the drop.

The club were formed in 1919. As with most German cities there were several amateur clubs competing in the regional leagues prior to World War I. Three of them – Germania, Falke and Hamburger SC – merged to form the new club after the end of hostilities. Four years later, HSV won their first national championship, defeating Union Berlin 3–0 in the play-off final.

Hamburg essentials

There are two ways to get from Hamburg's **Fuhlsbüttel airport** into the city centre, 10km away. The *Airport-City-Bus* runs every twenty minutes to the city's Hauptbahnhof (6.30am–10.30pm, journey time thirty minutes, DM8), while the *HVV-Airport Express* (bus line #110, DM3.40) runs every ten minutes to Ohlsdorf S- and U-Bahn stations, about, fifteen minutes from Hauptbahnhof. A taxi into town will cost you DM20.

Most inter-city **trains** also arrive at the Hauptbahnhof, the meeting point for seven S-Bahn and U-Bahn lines. The city's **bus station** is just behind. **North Sea ferries** from Harwich and Hull arrive at St Pauli Landungsbrücken, a short U-Bahn journey into town.

Hamburg's **city transport** comprises S-Bahn, U-Bahn and buses. The network runs 5am–midnight, after which night buses leave every hour from the Rathaus Markt. Ordinary **single tickets** cost DM2.40 for a short journey, DM3.90 for longer trips of about six stops or more. A **day pass** is good value at DM7.50, a three-day version even better at DM20; both are valid Mon–Fri 9am–midnight and all day Sat–Sun. All tickets can be bought from the orange machines at stations or from bus drivers. For a **taxi**, dial ☎040/666 666 or ☎040/221 122. The standing charge is DM3, plus DM1.60 per km.

The main **tourist information office** is at the exit from the Hauptbahnhof into Kirchenallee (open daily 7am–11pm, ☎040/30 05 12 30). You'll find another, smaller one at St Pauli Landungsbrücken, between landing stages #4 and #5 (open daily 9.30am–5.30pm, ☎040/30 05 12 00).

For **listings information**, *Szene Hamburg* (monthly, DM5) is the best. *Hamburger Rundschau* (weekly, DM3) has an entertainment pull-out, while *Hamburger*, a free monthly English-language pamphlet, offers basic, undiscriminating info.

In 1953, HSV left their historical home of Rothenbaum, in the centre of the city, to move out to the newly reopened and redesigned Volksparkstadion ('People's Park stadium') several kilometres outside the city in the district of Altona. While the supporters were less than happy with having to make the long journey out of the city every other Saturday, these were good times on the field. HSV reached two West German championship finals in the late Fifties and lifted the title in 1960, with a side including the legendary West German international striker Uwe Seeler.

Black before the sack – ex-coach Felix Magath (right)

In the following season's European Cup, HSV were involved in a remarkable quarter-final against the English champions, Burnley. At a packed Turf Moor, the Germans were outplayed and lost 3–1. But in the second leg Hamburg pulled out all the stops, and a 4–1 win took them through to play Barcelona in the semis, where they lost out after a replay.

In April 1961, Seeler was approached by Inter Milan who tabled the impressive sum of £600,000 for him. With salaries in Italy soaring way above those in (still semi-professional) West Germany, the club were not going to stand in his way. But Seeler, whose brother Dieter also played for HSV, turned Inter down. He never left the club, playing with them until 1971. Today he is the club president. He went on to lead HSV to the final of the Cup-Winners' Cup in 1968, where they lost 2–0 to AC Milan.

It was to be nine years before HSV got another crack at the same competition. They got to the final after defeating Atlético Madrid in the semis, again despite losing the first leg 3–1. In the final against holders Anderlecht in Amsterdam, goals from Georg Volkert and Felix Magath inside the last twelve minutes clinched the prize.

Within weeks of winning that first European honour, HSV pulled off a major coup in the transfer market when they persuaded Kevin Keegan to leave Liverpool. His first season in Hamburg was mixed –

the team's rigid formation stifled his creativity, and some of his team-mates were envious of the English forward's reportedly massive salary cheques. He also suffered some severe stick from the Kop after Liverpool hammered HSV 6–0 at Anfield in the second leg of the European SuperCup.

Everything changed, however, when HSV appointed the former Bayern Munich coach Branko Zebec as team boss in the summer of 1978. Under Zebec, the team abandoned man-for-man marking and played with a much greater fluidity. It suited Keegan perfectly. In 1979, *Mächtige Maus* ('Mighty Mouse') led HSV to their first-ever *Bundesliga* title. They finished runners-up the following year, while Keegan himself was voted European Footballer of the Year two seasons in a row.

Keegan returned to England, but Hamburg continued to dominate the German game. After Zebec's alcohol addiction had forced him to quit, Ernst Happel took over the coaching reins and HSV won the title again in 1982. In the same season they made the final of the UEFA Cup, but were surprisingly beaten by IFK Gothenburg, their cavalier style swept aside by canny Swedish counter-attacking.

Any disappointment vanished the following season, when HSV defeated Juventus 1–0 in the final of the European Cup. The side, which also retained the *Bundesliga*

Second best – HSV have got beaten to the ball in the Nineties

Here we go!

The quickest and cheapest way to get to the Volkspark-stadion is to take **S-Bahn S3** or **S21** to Stellingen. Your ticket is then valid for the shuttle-bus transfer (*Shuttle-Verkehr*) onto the stadium. Allow yourself a good forty minutes for the trip.

Swift half

As usual with out-of-town stadia, there is an absence of good, local bars around the ground and you will have to make do with the beer and snack stands that appear on matchdays. If you're looking to meet up with HSV fans in town before the game, then visit the **Fanhaus** at Strese-mannstrasse 162, just by Holstenstrasse S-Bahn station (S31). It's a bar/restaurant with football on TV, darts and pool, popular with HSV fans. Sink a pint here and listen to the moans of the loyalists.

title, included Magath (who scored the winner), international sweeper Manni Kaltz, anchorman Wolfgang Rolff (who marked Michel Platini out of the game) and the colossal striker Horst Hrubesch.

Today all that seems a long, long time ago. A West German cup win in 1987 has been the only honour since Europe was conquered, and after several disappointing seasons, in 1997 the club came dangerously close to dropping out of the *Bundesliga*. Crowds have fallen, and with St Pauli continuing to attract more attention despite their own problems, HSV's status in the city has been badly weakened.

President Uwe Seeler knows all too well the high expectations of the club's support. In the summer of 1997 he sacked his old team-mate Magath from his position as coach and brought in the relatively inexperienced Frank Pagelsdorfer.

But with few fresh young players arriving at the Volksparkstadion and the fans desperate for at least a hint of success, the pressure on HSV to wake up grows ever more intense.

Tickets

Ticket prices for standing areas are priced DM10 and DM20, while seats range from DM30 to DM70. The large stadium capacity means there is rarely a problem getting a ticket **at the ground** prior to kick-off. If in doubt, call the *HSV Kartencenter* on ☎040/41 55 141.

Ultra culture

It's hard to generate an atmosphere in a half-empty superbowl, but HSV's organised fan groups (of which there are more than sixty) in the *Westkürve* do their best, and make a fair amount of noise. Away fans are in the *Ostkürve* at the opposite end.

Publications

HSV live aktuell (DM2) is a typical German matchday programme. You may also come across fans selling copies of *Westkürve*, the fanzine of the home end. Other fanzines are *Spree Bier* and *Supporters' News*.

In the net

In the absence of an official website, those in search of the lowdown on matters HSV can head for Jan-Willem Oltmann's offering at: www.hamburg-net.com/hsv. It features a regularly updated news section and a particularly high standard of team and player photos, as well as a fan forum where like-minded souls can exchange condolences. German-language only, though.

 ## St Pauli

Wilhelm Koch Stadion 'am Millerntor', Auf dem Heiligengeistfeld
Capacity 20,000
Colours Brown-and-white striped shirts, brown shorts

Depending on your politics, lifestyle and washing habits, you will be either enchanted or alienated by FC St Pauli and their fans.

Visit the Wilhelm Koch stadium (known to all and sundry as the 'Millerntor'), and you could have the time of your life, waking up next morning with a much sought-after brown-and-white scarf and a hangover that's actually worth having. On the other hand, you might find the whole experience has little to do with football as we know it, and is just an excuse for a bunch of lefty slackers to drink and sing away the dole cheque.

St Pauli were founded in 1910, but the team didn't make the top flight of the *Bundesliga* until 1977. They finished bottom of the table at the end of their first season, and were unable to clamber back up again until 1988. Since then it's been up and down (but mainly down) all the way, the team's latest relegation from the top flight coming in 1997.

In truth, little attention is paid to the team – either in Hamburg or elsewhere in Germany. There are no superstars or boardroom personalities making the headlines here – the focus is on the terraces.

The St Pauli district is home not only to scores of brothels and seedy strip-joints, but also to cheap housing attracting students, anarchists and the 'alternative lifestyle' brigade. In most cities this crowd spend their Saturdays walking dogs on strings, hanging around in alternative record shops, or sleeping. In Hamburg, for some reason, they've acquired an interest in football. St Pauli, ignored and unfashionable, forever scrapping it out in the lower leagues, fit the bill – the small community fighting the eternal struggle against corporate capitalism.

St Pauli fans pride themselves on their anti-racism – the slogan *St Pauli Fans Gegen Nazis* is present on badges, posters and T-shirts – and they also proclaim their internationalism. Some St Pauli fans actually celebrated Denmark's win over Germany in the 1992 European Championship final.

But while the punks and anarchists may make the headlines, there are genuine football fans at the Millerntor who have followed the team from their days in the *Oberliga Nord*. Alongside them are a good number of fair-weather HSV fans who've become tired of the long trip out to the soulless superbowl in Altona. For them, St Pauli is how football used to be – a small, packed ground in the centre of town, with a friendly atmosphere and none of the hype and crass commercialism that has taken over the *Bundesliga*.

Alas, the 'used to be' tag may also soon apply to the Millerntor, for St Pauli are considering moving to a purpose-built stadium of their own within the next few years. The 20,000 capacity of the current ground prevents the club from competing at the highest level – as the 1997/98 season showed. The only questions that remain are whether the 'Happy Fans' (as the media have dubbed them) will still cheer the team on in different surroundings, and whether the football they will be watching is first or second division – or lower.

Tickets

Getting a ticket for any game at the compact Millerntor can be a real problem. Ironically, you may have a better chance at a big game, as clashes with HSV, Bayern, Dortmund and Hansa Rostock are moved to the Volksparkstadion.

At the Millerntor, standing tickets are a snip at DM12, while seats (of which there are only a few thousand) are much more expensive at DM60–120.

A different tariff applies for games played at the Volksparkstadion, where terrace tickets are DM18 and seats are DM40–150.

The St Pauli *Kartencenter* hotline is: ☎040/319 1893.

Here we go!

Take **U-Bahn 3** to St Pauli or Feldstrasse, which are no more than fifteen minutes from the Hauptbahnhof.

Swift half

Where to begin? Where to stop, more like it. Every other building is a bar in St Pauli. The **St Pauli Eck** (corner of Hein-Hoyer Strasse and Simon von Utrecht Strasse) is a typical neighbourhood bar, while **St Pauli Treff**, Detlev-Bremer Strasse 21 has a mirror ball, football scarves and other souvenirs.

The club bar, **St Pauli Clubheim**, is inside the ground but has an entrance on the street. Here a jukebox blares out *White Christmas*, *Be-Bop-A-Lula* and assorted punk classics, while the trophy cabinet is crammed with cups so irrelevant, nobody ever asked for them back.

Publications

The match magazine, *Pauli* (DM1), faces competition from a number of fanzines, the most popular of which are *Übersteiger*, *Splitter* and *Unhaltbar*.

Ultra culture

Go to see a game at St Pauli on a Friday night and you could be forgiven for thinking the New York Dolls had reformed.

Unfeasibly thin people with bug eyes, mauve spiky hair and ripped T-shirts weave their way towards the stadium, pushing shopping-trolleys clanking with booze.

Once match-fit, the crowd join in with the thrash version of *You'll Never Walk Alone* which greets the players as they run out onto the pitch, and after kick-off will rattle their bottle openers to put off opposing corner takers. When St Pauli score, sadly all too rarely in 1996/97, *Ride of the Valkyries* booms over the tannoy, too loud to hear Wagner turning in his grave.

In the net

The official FC St Pauli website resides at: www.fcstpauli.de/home.idc. It's quite a neat little site, with an area devoted to the club's proposed new stadium – though some sections, like the ground, have not yet come to fruition. For the 'Happy Fan' view of life, head for: ourworld.compuserve.com/home pages/MatthiasLw/. Most unofficial soccer sites would welcome some sponsorship, but this one proudly proclaims itself as 'ad free'. Says it all, really.

Eat, drink, sleep…

Bars and clubs

Hamburg has the best nightlife in Germany after Berlin. The heart of it is the Reeperbahn in St Pauli. Although it is better known for its bordellos, the Reeperbahn has a great bar scene, along with a number of techno and trance clubs which open late and close at noon the next day. **U3 St Pauli** or **S1/S3 Reeperbahn** are the jumping-off points.

A more sedate drink can be had in the student bars around Grindelallee (U1 Hallerstrasse). For a quiet lunchtime pint, try the Grossneumarkt (S1 or S3 Stadthausbrücke). The local Hamburg beer is the very quaffable *Astra*.

Café Treibeis, Gaustrasse 25. Up in Altona, a convivial bar for the underground and alternative crowd, particularly after a St Pauli game, with excellent sounds and atmosphere. A short, sharp climb uphill from S1/S3 Altona.

Golden Pudle's Club, St Pauli Fischmarkt 27. Bizarre bar/club in the harbour area, popular with the Hamburg in-crowd, happily entertained by DJs and cabaret artists. S1, S3 or U3 St Pauli Landungsbrücken.

Grosse Freiheit 36, Grosse Freiheit 36. Best live venue in town, with a post-punk leaning, just off the Reeperbahn and adjacent to the site of the old Star Club where the Beatles first made nuisances of themselves. S1 or S3 Reeperbahn.

Painful exit – St Pauli scored three goals in eleven games in 1997

Irish Harp, Reeperbahn 36. Best of the many Irish bars in town, popular with HSV fans and open until late. S1 or S3 Reeperbahn.

Mojo Club, Reeperbahn 1. Excellent, imaginative mainstream club, with acid-jazz, rare grooves and cabaret. Generally a DM10–15 cover charge. Jazz café next door. U3 St Pauli.

Restaurants

Fish plays an important part in the diet of this port city. The classic sailor's dish is *Labskaus*, a cheap mix of mashed potatoes, herring, pickled cucumber and a fried egg. Spicy eel soup (*Aalsuppe*) is also a local favourite.

Hamburg has plenty of **cheap eats**. The streets around the university and the area further south towards Altona, either side of Schanzenstrasse (S21/31 or U3 Sternschanze) offer a particularly wide choice, while the dock area has tasty lunchtime fish bars (S1/3 or U3 St Pauli Landungsbrücken) and, a little further down, a clutch of reasonably priced, unpretentious Spanish and Portuguese diners (U3 Baumwall).

Arkadasch, Grindelhof 17. Friendly, romantic and reasonably priced restaurant in the university area with main courses at DM20 and hearty soups at DM6. Most major credit cards. U1 Hallerstrasse.

At Nali, Rutschbahn 11. Popular Turkish restaurant with an extensive menu, open until 2am. Most major credit cards.

Fischerhaus, St Pauli Fischmarkt 14. Popular and reliable establishment with efficient service, fresh fish a speciality. No credit cards. Open daily 11am–11pm. S1/3 or U3 St Pauli Landungsbrücken.

Klett, Grindelallee 146. Student haunt which tries a bit too hard to be cool, but pleasant nonetheless. No credit cards. U1 Hallerstrasse.

Sagres, Vorsetzen 46. Busy Portuguese diner, full of regulars from the dock area. You may have to wait for a table, but the prices are right and the cuisine is tasty. No credit cards. U3 Baumwall.

Accommodation

Hamburg is one of Germany's **most expensive cities** to stay in. Most hotels cater for the business community, which does at least mean they bring their prices

Pauli girl – a 'Happy Fan' puts a brave face on relegation

Annenhof, Lange Reihe 23 (☎040/24 34 26 18). Basic but clean hotel, not far from the Hauptbahnhof, with shared bathrooms and kitchen facilities. DM50–60 for a single. Breakfasts DM8 extra. No credit cards.

Hotel Kochler Garni, Bremer Reihe 19 (☎040/249 511, fax 040/28 02 435). Large, comfortable single, double, triple and quad rooms, right next to the Hauptbahnhof. Kitchen facilities available. Singles around DM55–70, doubles DM90–100, triples DM120, quads DM140. Breakfast DM10. No credit cards.

Inter-Rast, Reeperbahn 154–166 (☎040/311 591). The perfect place for a weekend's partying, right on the Reeperbahn. Come and go as you please all night – street noise could be a problem if you're retiring early. Singles DM45 without shower, DM60 with. Doubles DM80 including breakfast. S3 Reeperbahn.

down at weekends. The very cheapest hotel room you'll find will be around DM60 for a single room, DM80 for a double.

The area just north of the Hauptbahnhof, around Steindamm, Bremer Weg and Bremer Reihe, has many cheaper pensions, some used for purposes other than rest.

The main **tourist office** in the Kirchenallee exit of the Hauptbahnhof provides a room-booking service for DM6, as does the office in the terminal 4 arrivals lounge at Fuhlsbüttel airport (open daily 8am–11pm, ☎040/30 05 12 40).

The **Tourismus Zentrale** office in town is not open to visitors but can reserve a room for you on ☎040/30 05 13 00 (daily 8am–8pm).

Jugendgästehaus Horner Rennbahn, Rennbahnstrasse 100 (☎040/651 1671, fax 040/65 56 516). A fair way out in the east of town, this is Hamburg's most comfortable and friendliest youth hostel. Open March–December, reception 7.30am–9am, 1pm–6pm & 12.30pm–1am. Dorm beds for under DM30, excellent buffet breakfast included. U3 Horner Rennbahn, then a ten-minute walk.

Pension Helga Schmidt, Holzdam 14 (☎040/28 02 119, fax 040/243 705). Pleasant and comfortable pension near the Hauptbahnhof with spacious rooms, all equipped with a shower and a television. Singles around DM70, doubles DM115. No credit cards. Definitely worth the extra money.

Defending the realm – the career of *der Kaiser*

Defenders are appreciated – they are a necessary part of any successful team. But ask someone to name the greatest players of all time and they will list forwards or, at a pinch, midfield men – Pelé, Cruyff, Puskás, di Stéfano, Maradona. Strikers get the glory, midfielders have the art and craft. But in any list of the greatest there has to be one defender – **Franz Beckenbauer.**

In fact, 'Kaiser Franz' was never just a defender. He began his career in the Bayern Munich youth teams as a schoolboy striker with an impressive goalscoring record. When he made his first-team début for Bayern in 1964, it was as a left-winger. By the time he was called up to the West German side for the 1966 World Cup, he was a central midfielder. And it wasn't until the World Cup in Mexico in 1970 that Beckenbauer was utilised in his **most effective position** – that of **sweeper.**

Object of desire – the *Kaiser* and his cup

Unlike the *libero* that had existed in Italian football in the early Sixties, Beckenabauer was by no means simply a defensive anchorman. Of course, he read the game well and was always there to intercept. But it was in possession that Beckenbauer was so effective – slicing through the opposing midfield, turning defence into attack with a couple of sidesteps and a burst of speed.

On the ball, he was graceful and calm, capable of passing or dribbling with either boot. He had a devastating turn of speed, yet never looked like he was rushing – he just glided past people, his head always raised so that he could pick out the right pass at the right time.

As a player, his **greatest triumph** came in 1974 when he lifted the World Cup in his home town of Munich. His fitness was such that he was expected to be around in 1978 to try to retain the title for West Germany in Argentina. But he chose to retire from international football in 1977. Having quit Bayern for the New York Cosmos in 1978, Beckenbauer briefly went back to playing in midfield. The Americans, in particular the Cosmos board, weren't interested in sophisticated sweeping. "Tell the Kraut to get his ass upfront" was how one Cosmos director reacted to seeing his new signing as the last line of defence. In 1980 Beckenbauer returned to the *Bundesliga* to see out his playing days with Hamburg SV, who needed a big-name replacement for Kevin Keegan. Despite being 35, he gave a good account of himself and some critics demanded he be given another international recall.

Like his contemporary, Johan Cruyff, Beckenbauer made a successful transition to **life as a coach.** In 1990 he became the first man to win the World Cup as both player and coach, and he has had two brief spells in the dugout with Bayern.

Today Beckenbauer lives in Austria but is **president of Bayern** and is regularly used as a **pundit** on German television, as cool and composed under the studio lights as he was on the field of play, 25 years ago...

Greece

The Ancient Greeks had a word for it: pandemonium. Modern Greece has seen its football suffer internecine chaos ever since violent scenes marred a match between representative teams from Athens and Salonika in 1906, and little has changed in the last ninety years.

The only difference has been that, over the past two decades since the introduction of professional club football, various millionaires have flaunted their egos over their favourite football teams, usually one of the big Athenian three of Panathinaikos, AEK or Olympiakos. But, while only four league titles have escaped these clubs since World War II, European success has eluded the Greeks – even under the guidance of a string of expensive foreign coaches.

Internationally, too, Greece can look back on only a handful of modest achievements, the first of which was qualification for the European Championship finals of 1980. The team travelled to Italy as rank outsiders and promptly finished bottom of their group, but under coach Alketas Panagoulias they played some smart football, giving the Dutch a fright in their first match and holding West Germany to a goalless draw in their last.

Fourteen years later, after a sanctions-struck Yugoslavia had conveniently been forced to withdraw from their qualifying section, Greece made it to the World Cup finals for the first time. Panagoulias, now aged sixty, had returned as coach after a spell in America and used images from Greek mythology to bolster his pre-match rhetoric. The stories might have been colourful but they had an unhappy ending. Panagoulias' team of seasoned veterans such as Tassos Mitropoulos, Savvas Kofidis and 37-year-old 'keeper Antonis Minou were no match for the bright young things

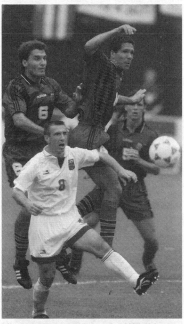

Mitropoulos meets his match – USA '94

of Bulgaria and Nigeria; they lost all three of their matches at USA '94 and failed to score a goal.

Since then, Greek inability to qualify for Euro '96 (and Turkish success in doing so), Athens' failure to win the right to host the centenary Olympics, and rampant price inflation have all served to lower the nation's footballing morale. Meanwhile, fan violence in its modern, callous, organised form, has ruined the domestic game as a family spectacle. Two more Salonika-Athens riots in 1995 left dozens of fans seriously injured. Tough action is needed but the Greek football association, the EPO, are expert wrist-slappers. The imbalance of power between the big Athens sides and the rest means that only big matches attract more than 10,000 fans – and many clubs are in serious debt. The start of the 1996/97 season was delayed by two weeks so that some clubs could arrange their financial affairs, but relatively high ticket prices and live TV games have done little to help falling attendances.

While the Greeks have succeeded in keeping most of their homegrown talent from the clutches of wealthier leagues, quality foreign players are no longer interested in wasting two years of their career in what is becoming a violent football backwater – the result has been a huge influx of cut-price imports from Yugoslavia, Romania, Russia and even Albania.

For the visiting football fan, however, the very chaos and sectarian passion of the Greek game make it as attractive a reason to grab a cheap flight here as any naturist beach or desecrated monument.

Essential vocabulary
Hello *Yassas*
Goodbye *Herete*
Yes *Neh*

No *Ohi*
Two beers, please *Dio bires, parakalo*
Thank you *Efkharisto*
Men's *Andron*
Women's *Gynaikon*
Where is the stadium? *Pou ine yebedon?*
What's the score? *Ta abodesmata?*
Referee *Diedidis*
Offside *Aristeri*

Match practice
Unless the game you're going to is an international or involves one of the big three clubs playing each other, chances are you'll be spending your Sunday afternoon with a few thousand other souls. Whatever the occasion, if you avoid the cheapest seats behind the goal in the *pedalo*, or 'horseshoe', you'll be safe enough. Refereeing decisions may favour the home side to a laughable extent. If you're in Salonika for a game against a side from Athens, take a crash helmet.

As many grounds still have primitive stone seating, most spectators buy a small sheet of polystyrene pillow, a *maxilari*, for a nominal sum. Even the toughest-looking

Blue day – Greece's qualifying campaign for Euro '96 falls at the feet of Scotland

Basics

Citizens of the EU, the USA, Canada, Australia and New Zealand require only a **passport** to enter Greece – but be prepared for a certain amount of hassle at customs if yours contains a stamp from an earlier visit to Turkey.

The Greek unit of currency is the **drachma**, or Dr. There are around Dr470 to £1. You'll find coins for Dr5, Dr10, Dr50 and Dr100, and notes for Dr100, Dr500, Dr1000 and Dr5000. **Credit cards** are generally accepted in major towns, but watch for a high commission charge on cash advances at travel agents and *bureaux de change*.

From outside the country, the international telephone code for Greece is ☎30; Athens is ☎1 and Salonika ☎31. Greek **coin phones** take Dr10 pieces, but most machines are now **cardphones**, for which cards are available at most newsstands for Dr1300. For international calls, dial 00 followed by the country code and number. The cheap rate is between 10pm and 6am. Note that Greece is one hour ahead of Central European Time. You will often find a couple of phones at **newsstands** for public use, though these are slightly more expensive than those in phone boxes. Simply pay the amount clocked up on the vendor's meter.

Buses are the most commonly used form of transport around Greece, since many towns do not have a rail link and trains are pretty slow, anyway. However, the national rail company, OSE, now offers an **inter-city train service** between Athens and Salonika, which takes around six hours and costs about Dr15,000.

Western-style **bars** tend to be more expensive than the traditional coffee houses (*kafenia*) or ouzo dens (*ouzeri*); they also attract a younger crowd, whose favourite tipple is iced coffee – *frappé*. In a *kafenio*, as a foreigner you'll probably be served *Nes Kafe*, naff **powdered coffee** which they have the gall to advertise in neon under the bar sign outside. Throw this back at the barman and demand a *metrios* (medium sweet, strong coffee) or a *sketos* (the same but without sugar).

The *ouzeri* is the place to head for if you're taken by the idea of gambling on **green baize tables** while the waiter serves up snacks (*mezedes*) such as cheese on toast (*sagnaki*) or meat in vine leaves (*dolmadakia*). The *ouzo* itself costs around Dr100–200 and, like its French cousin *pastis*, comes with a small glass of water as a mixer.

Dining takes place in *tavernas*, at their best with simple food, simple furniture and a roof-top setting under the olive trees. The whole caboodle, with half a bottle of resinated wine (*retsina*), shouldn't cost more than Dr2000. *Moussaka* (meat and eggplant) and *souvlaki* (lamb kebab) are the mainstays of any tourist menu.

You should find reasonably-priced **accommodation** even in the height of summer. The Greek National Tourist Organisation categorises hotels according to facilities and quality of service, but you may find a 'B' hotel better than an 'A' one. 'L' is the top of the range. For 'D' class hotels, a single room will cost about Dr5000, a double Dr7000, with a shower in the corridor. If you're paying a bit more – perhaps Dr20,000 for a 'C' or 'B' class double – ask about **air conditioning**.

fan can be seen incongruously wielding his *maxilari*. Few grounds offer much cover from the elements – remember to protect yourself against the Greek sun in late spring and early autumn.

Apart from a short break at Christmas, the season runs between mid-September and late May. With the exception of live TV matches, league games are on Sunday afternoons, with kick-off at 5pm in early autumn and late spring, 3pm in winter. Televised games are on Saturdays at 3pm or Mondays at 6pm.

To compensate Western TV companies for the hour time difference, European games can kick-off as late as 9.30pm, so make sure you can catch the last metro back from the stadium.

The league

The Greek first division, *A' Ethnikis*, has eighteen teams, of which up to half hail from Athens or its port of Piraeus. Three teams go down. The eighteen-team second division, *B' Ethnikis*, operates on a three-up, four-down basis. The third tier, *G' Ethnikis*, is divided into north (*vorras*) and south (*potos*). Two go up from each division and six go down into the regionalised fourth division.

Up for the cup

The cup final, following four two-legged rounds, takes place in the Olympic stadium in May. After the 1995 final between Panathinaikos and AEK, 12,000 seats had to be replaced, the originals having been either burned or broken by irate AEK fans.

Tickets

Hardcore fans tend to enter the stadium early, so unless you're going to a major international, you won't find long queues at the ticket office. The more expensive seats are in the middle numbered section, *arithimena elbigieli*. These are designated according to gate number (*fyra*), sector (*tmima*), row (*seira*) and seat number (*fesi*).

The big three increase prices for derby games, when you might find yourself paying about Dr6000 for a ticket. There are no matchday programmes, but the bigger clubs have their own magazine.

Half-time

Alcohol is generally not available at major league games, so have a beer beforehand in the bars around the ground. On the way to the ground you'll see trays of pistachio nuts, almonds, sunflower seeds and monkey nuts in clearly marked Dr200 or Dr250 bags. Fleshy smoke bellows from grills of kebabs (*gyros*) or sausages (*lukaniko*), both around Dr500 a throw.

Action replay

Each week, two league fixtures are shown live on the cable station Filmnet, on Saturdays at 3pm and Mondays at 6pm. They are then repeated on state TV, ET1 or ET2, later that evening. The best round-up is ET1's *Athletiki Kiriaki* at 10pm on Sundays. State TV shows live European and international games, but note that Panathinaikos have a separate deal with the Mega channel. ET2 shows English Premiership action on Saturday and Monday evenings, while Filmnet has Italian action on Monday evenings. Sky Sports can be seen in many bars in main towns or tourist resorts.

The back page

On any newsstand, particularly on Monday mornings, you'll see a confusing number of colourful sports papers. Of these, the daily *Sportime* (Dr150) is colourful, well laid-out and, for the non-Greek speaker, has results and fixtures which are easy to work out. Its international coverage is the best in Greece and the paper is known for taking a stand when it comes to fan violence. Of the others, *Fos* (Dr150) favours Olympiakos, *Keoko* (Dr150) Panathinaikos, *Ora* (Dr150) AEK; *Filathos* (Dr100) is relatively independent.

The best of the general daily papers for sport is *Ta Nea*, while the English-language *Athens News* is also worth a look.

Ultra culture

Ultras tend to meet at their own fan clubs, then march to the stadium *en masse*, rarely without a police escort for derby matches. Despite thorough searches (you may find your heavy Dr50 and Dr100 coins confiscated), fireworks are somehow sneaked into the ground, helping to create one of the most colourful atmospheres in Europe, and probably the loudest.

In the net

There is no generic Greek soccer website, but you can point your browser in the direction of www.risc.uni-linz.ac.at/non-official/rsssf/results-eur.html, safe in the knowledge that the latest results, complete with scorers and attendances, will all be present and correct, along with a decent-sized slab of stats archive.

Athens

Panathinaikos 246   AEK 249   Olympiakos 250   Ethnikos 251
Ionikos 252   Panionios 252   Apollon 252   Athinaikos 252

Athens, a cosmopolitan capital city of four million people, often feels like a Middle Eastern madhouse of ten times that. Yet, while its transport system might be hopelessly inadequate, its taxi drivers stubborn and its air pollution the stuff of legend, for a major game Athens can still rise to the occasion and has become a justifiably popular venue for European finals.

As for domestic football, despite dwindling attendances, people talk of little else in the *kafenia* and *ouzeri* around town. The great pity, given the natural passion for the game and the millions of drachma poured into it every year, is that that these drinkers have raised a glass to international success so rarely. In place of national flag-waving, victories over traditional club rivals have had to suffice – revenge is a dish best served with *ouzo*.

In town, AEK enjoy the most passionate support, while down in the port of Piraeus, Olympiakos are the team to be seen supporting. Panathinaikos fans, from their traditional base high up in Ambelokipi, north-west of central Athens, tend to look down on the rest. Only hardcore followers make trips from the capital up to Salonika for games against Aris, Iraklis or PAOK.

Despite their dangerous reputation, most fans you meet will be friendly and will gladly talk knowledgeably about football until the stars come out. You'll find stands selling football souvenirs on practically every central street corner, but be careful on matchdays if you're proudly wearing your new AEK scarf, especially around Omonia Square, the city's main crossing point.

The seedy port of Piraeus, at the end of the metro line, is officially considered part of Athens, so its teams have been included in this section. An afternoon around its dockside bars, where Melina Mercouri entertained drunken sailors in the film *Never On Sunday*, makes for compulsive pre-match entertainment. You'll always find Piraeus up for it on Sunday.

Hit and myth – Athens' Olympic stadium is a footballing venue fit for legends

A Pole apart – Pana's Krzysztof Warzycha puts Ajax to the sword, Amsterdam, 1996

The thrilling fields

 ## Panathinaikos

Office Karelas Paiania
Stadio Olimpiako, see p.248
Capacity 76,000
Colours All green with white trim
League champions 1930, 1949, 1953, 1960–1962, 1964–65, 1969–70, 1972, 1977, 1984, 1986, 1990–91, 1995–96
Cup winners 1940, 1948, 1955, 1967, 1969, 1977, 1982, 1984, 1986, 1988–89, 1991, 1993–95

In 1984, Panathinaikos moved home (but not heart) from their old stadium, the intimate Apostolos Nikolaidis, the other side of Athens' Licabettus hill. From the heights of Ambelokipi `– and with the weight of history behind them – Pana fans still view their club as the élite. Originally formed as Panhellenic by English gentlemen at the turn of the century, the club adopted their Greek name in 1908, but stuck to their foreign roots by featuring a shamrock on the team badge – an idea suggested by one of their athletes during World War I.

It wasn't until the Sixties, however, that Pana began to challenge Olympiakos for domestic supremacy, their most successful period coming under the stewardship of former Hungary and Real Madrid star Ferenc Puskás. Double-winners in 1969, league champions again in 1970, Panathinaikos then surprised Everton and Red Star Belgrade to reach the European Cup final at Wembley in 1971. With stars such as centre-forward Anton Antoniadis – scorer of ten European goals that season – and midfielder Mimis Domazos, the Greeks were holding the great Ajax team of the era to a single-goal lead until a late own-goal sealed their fate. Later that year, they replaced Ajax in the World Club Championship, losing 3–2 on aggregate to Nacional of Uruguay.

Like most Greek teams, Pana didn't turn fully professional until the end of the Seventies – five years before their move

to the newly built Olimpiako. Once established there, they resumed their continental adventures, losing to Liverpool in the 1985 European Cup semi-final. (Had the Greeks won that tie, there would almost certainly never have been a Heysel disaster.)

The club had to wait until 1996 to reach the same stage again, when once more Ajax were their opponents. Polish

Athens essentials

Athens' **airport**, Ellenikon, has three termini, East, West (for Olympic flights only) and a charter terminal. There is a shuttle bus service between the two main termini. Blue express bus #091 runs every 35 minutes between Amalias 4, by central Syndagma square, and the termini; the journey takes between thirty and 45 minutes, depending on traffic, and costs Dr160, or Dr200 after 11.30pm. The service runs between 5am and 12.30pm, with buses running infrequently through the night. A **taxi** to or from the airport should cost around Dr2000, but Dr5000 rip-offs are not unheard of. Beware.

The city's two main **train stations**, Larissa (northbound) and Peloponnese (southbound) are adjacent to each other. Trolleybus #1 goes to Larissa, bus #057 to Peloponnese, both from Venizelou, between Syndagma and Omonia squares. The main **bus stations** are at Odos Kifissou 100 (bus #051 into town) and Odos Liossion 260 (bus #024).

With the Acropolis high over the city and the surrounding area of Plaka as its heart, orientation isn't a problem, but transport is. There is only one **metro line**, which runs north-south and completely bypasses the main square, Syndagma. **Tickets** are Dr75 each, available at stations, and should be validated in the orange box as you enter. The service runs from 5.30am to midnight. Luckily, all the main football stadia are near a metro stop.

A system of allowing odd and even number-plated cars into town on alternate working days has alleviated some of Athens' traffic chaos, but even so, the city's blue **buses** and yellow **trolleybuses** can be painfully slow. Tickets (Dr75) are available at news-stands. Stamp them onboard. Route numbers change frequently and no transport map is available. There is a limited service after midnight, but no daily or weekly pass.

Official **taxis** are yellow with red number plates. You should hail a cab as you would hitch a lift, making sure to stand in the right direction for your destination. Do as the locals do and shout your destination from the pavement through the passing car window. It is normal for the driver to pick up other passengers along the way. The meter should start at Dr200, or Dr400 between midnight and 6am, plus an additional Dr40 per item of luggage. Ask a Greek speaker to help you with the Athens **radio taxi service** (☎01/321 4058) or its Piraeus version (☎01/411 5200).

For **tourist information**, dial ☎171 for the 24-hour English-speaking service. There are two EOT tourist offices. One is at Odos Amerikis 2 (open Mon–Fri noon–2.30pm, ☎01/322 3111), the other at Odos Karagheorghitis Servias 2 (open Mon–Fri 8.30am–6.30pm, Sat 8am–2pm, ☎01/322 2545). Both are pretty useless, but the latter, a window hidden in the National Bank of Greece on a corner of Syndagma square, can help with **accommodation**.

There are four main English-language information sources: *Athens News* (daily, Dr250); *Greek News* (Fridays, Dr250); *Athenscope* (Fridays, Dr400) and *Athens Today* (monthly, free). None are particularly helpful when it comes to **nightlife information**.

international striker Krzysztof Warzycha scored a shock late goal to win the first leg in Amsterdam, 1–0. But a Jari Litmanen strike, early in the second leg, then silenced the capacity crowd in the Olimpiako. A more confident and experienced side, under less pressure from their home fans, might have responded differently to such a setback. Pana lost 3–0.

The team's failure to qualify for the Champions' League the following season cost Pana's Argentinian coach, Juan Ramón Rocha, his job, and his fellow countryman, playmaker Juan José Borelli, quit soon after. The 1997 cup final with AEK was lost on penalties and ended with the predictable outburst of violence in the stands, while a fifth-place league finish was insufficient for the club to clamber back into Europe.

But for their fanatical following, who still meet by their beloved old stadium, Pana remain among the élite – in the Greek league, at least.

Here we go!

The Olimpiako is a short walk across the concrete from **Irinis** metro stop, thirty minutes from Omonia. The floodlights loom enticingly as the underground train's journey takes it overland.

Swift half

All you'll find around the ground are dual-carriageway roads and the metro line, but once inside the stadium there's a **bar** virtually at every other gate. Alcohol is barred from sale at crunch matches.

Club shop

A modest store (open Mon & Wed 8.30am–3pm, Tue, Thur & Fri 9am–2.30pm & 5.30pm–8.30pm, Sat 8.30am-3pm, most major credit cards accepted) can be found at gate #11 of the **old Panathinaikos stadium**, the Apostolos Nikolaidis, along Leofros Alexandras.

Ultra culture

Athens Fans Pana, an umbrella organisation embracing thirteen ultra groups, produce a monthly magazine, *Skizofrenia*, available for Dr300 on matchdays. The most likeable group are the 'Mad Boys', who meet in Ambelokipi under a huge banner proclaiming "In Green God We Trust".

In the net

A semi-official website can be found at: www.fnet.gr/panathinaikos. It offers news stories in Greek and contact details for Pana fan clubs around the world.

The Olympic stadium

Stadio OAKA 'Spiros Louis', Irinis
Capacity 76,000 (all-seated)

The **Olimpiako**, Greece's first national stadium since the one built in Athens for the inaugural modern Games of 1896, is a pleasure to visit. Venue for AC Milan's 4-0 supershow against Barcelona in the 1994 European Cup final, the ground should also have hosted the **1996 Olympiad**. The International Olympic Committee's decision to award those games to Atlanta, rather than Athens, still wrankles with the locals, and their loss is made all the more poignant by the venue's official title, OAKA 'Spiros Louis' – Louis was the Greek winner of the first modern Olympic marathon in 1896.

Today, having previously been home to Olympiakos, the stadium hosts Greek international games, fiery cup finals and Panathinaikos home matches. Many Pana fans still mourn the loss of their old stadium and, outside of a big city derby, it's no wonder they feel out of place – the roofless stadium has the feel of a huge bowl.

Yet for big occasions the Olimpiako, built in the early Eighties, comes into its own. Your seat, whether in the upper or lower tier, will afford you an ideal view of the action, played out on the lushest sporting surface in Greece...

AEK

Nikos Goumas stadium, Perissos
Capacity 34,000
Colours All black with yellow trim
League champions 1939–40, 1963, 1968, 1971, 1978–79, 1989, 1992–94
Cup winners 1932, 1939, 1949–50, 1956, 1966, 1978, 1983, 1996–97

Athletiki Enosis Konstantinopoulos were formed in 1924 by Greek refugees who had fled Constantinople, now Istanbul. Having chosen a Byzantine double-headed eagle as their emblem, they built the rough and ready Nea Filadelfia (now Nikos Goumas) stadium in 1936, three years before winning their first Greek title.

Once regarded as the club with money, AEK today have, if anything, the rootsiest support in the city. In the postwar era the team have enjoyed several spells of domestic domination, but have achieved little in Europe save for a run to the semi-finals of the UEFA Cup in 1976/77; their progress was halted by Juventus in 1977.

AEK won three consecutive titles from 1992 and earned themselves a place in the 1994 Champions' League, where they were unlucky to be drawn in the same group as both the eventual finalists, Ajax and AC Milan. The man who took them there, Serb coach Dušan Bajević, controversially moved to Olympiakos for a better salary in the summer of 1996. More than a thousand policemen were on duty for the AEK-Olympiakos clash in January 1997, and while AEK won that game, 2–0, the ease with which Olympiakos went on to take the Greek title enraged the AEK faithful.

A run to the quarter-finals of the 1996/97 Cup-Winners' Cup and a cup final win over Panathinaikos did nothing to stem the tide of discontent, and supporters have begun a campaign to oust AEK president Mihalis Trochanas, boycotting official merchandise and starting a fighting fund to raise money for a buyout of the club.

Despite all this tension, or perhaps because of it, a trip to AEK can be a

Hornets' best – AEK forward Nikolaidis

thrilling affair. Emerging from the metro, you get the distinct impression of having fallen into a hornets' nest. Your ears ring with the buzz of mopeds and your eyes are assaulted by a sea of yellow and black. Once inside the stadium, you'll find home fans at either end, bouncing up and down and throwing things at the pitch for the entire game.

Here we go!

Take the metro to **Perissos**, fifteen minutes north of Omonia. The stadium is five minutes' walk away – but first you have to negotiate the throng under the footway and past the rows of souvenir sellers along Papanastasiou.

Swift half

At the **555 bar** on the corner of Kaplinoleas, with tables outside and food served before and after the match, you'll be sharing a Heineken with the average thirsty fan. The more upmarket **Imperatore** café on Odos Fokon is owned by AEK's international defender Stelios

From AEK to Olympiakos – Dušan Bajević

contains the younger, partying element. Those entering gate #21 are if anything even more wayward, their fanaticism, occasionally helped by chemical influences, celebrated in song throughout the match.

The AEK anthem choruses: "Come on brave men of AEK, shoot and break the goalposts!" Other songs rally against the fish-eating followers of Olympiakos, nicknamed the *Gavroi*, whose stadium is described as "Greece's biggest frying pan", while Panathinaikos supporters are alluded to simply as "vaseline"...

In the net
AEK loyalists run a fine unofficial website at: www.aek.com/. It contains, among other things, a detailed history of the club, a news feed on a virtual 'sports ticker', and info on AEK's basketball and volleyball sides as well as the football team. You can email a form signalling your support for the campaign against club president Trochanas, and since everything is in English, there's no excuse for not signing up.

Manolas. **Ouzeri O Nikos**, Adanon 6, is an excellent pre-match restaurant. All three places are within easy firework-launching distance of the stadium.

Club shop
The **official store** on the corner of Odos Fokon (open Mon, Wed & Sat 9am–3pm, Tue, Thur & Fri 9am–2pm & 5–8.30pm, credit cards accepted) is well stocked, if poorly patronised at present. There's a smaller, family-run shop nearer the metro station on Odos Ignias, open matchdays.

Publications
Dikefalos is a weekly fan paper available on matchdays.

Ultra culture
AEK's following may not have the numbers of Panathinaikos', nor the tradition of Olympiakos', but they make up for this with passion, commitment and a much-tested sense of humour. Choose your gate carefully. The so-called covered end (*skepasti*) is accessed via gates #9, #10 and #11, and

Olympiakos

Karaiskakis stadium, Neo Faliro
Capacity 31,000
Colours Red-and-white striped shirts, white shorts
League champions 1931, 1933–34, 1936–38, 1947–48, 1951, 1954–59, 1966–67, 1973–75, 1980–83, 1987, 1997
Cup winners 1947, 1951–54, 1957–58, 1960–61, 1963, 1965, 1968, 1971, 1973, 1975, 1981, 1990, 1992

With an original support base of blue collar workers, joined in modern times by bikers and heavy metal fans, Olympiakos are Greece's most popular and most decorated club. A game at the Karaiskakis can offer the visitor an unforgettable football experience, against a backdrop of the fairground and harbour lights of Piraeus.

The club are known as *Thrylos* (or 'legend'), after their founders and original five-man forward line, the Andrianopoulos brothers. After helping the team win four of the first six Greek titles, the brothers persuaded the Greek Olympic Committee to convert an old velodrome used for the 1896 Games into an athletics ground of international standard. The ground was the Karaiskakis, and work began on converting it in 1936. After that, the dockers, fishermen and ferrymen were to see their favourites win sixteen further titles, including six on the trot before 1960.

International matches, the 1971 Cup-Winners' Cup final between Chelsea and Real Madrid, and Ethnikos home games were also held at the Karaiskakis, before 21 fans were crushed to death after a game with AEK in 1981. Olympiakos moved their home games to the newly built Stadio Olimpiako the following year, but crowd disturbances there forced the club to move back; a moat had been built at the Karaiskakis in the meantime.

Despite notching up considerably more league titles and cup wins than any other Greek club, Olympiakos' record in Europe is poor, amounting to a string of early exits and a solitary quarter-final appearance in the Cup-Winners' Cup against Atlético Madrid in 1993.

In 1997, however, the club finally ended their decade-long championship drought. Former AEK coach Dusan Bajevic was the hero of the hour, along with the club president who had had the vision (and the guts) to poach him, Sokratis Kokkalis.

Here we go!

The nearest metro stop is **Neo Faliro**, twenty minutes south from Omonia. Turn right out of the station, walk through the underpass, and you'll be greeted by clouds of kebab smoke and flashes of red and white.

Swift half

Look no further than the row of bars along Karaoli Dimitriou. The **nameless café** on the corner of Diamanti is the best of these places, with a gilded framed picture of the

six-time title winning side of the Fifties, and a nervous-looking budgie in a red cage. The **Megali Taverna** next door has an excellent selection of wines, kept in vast barrels along one wall.

Club shop

There's a well-stocked shop at the club's headquarters at Ipsilantou 170, a fifteen-minute walk from Neo Faliro metro into Piraeus (open Mon, Wed & Sat 9am–3pm, Tue, Thur & Fri 9am–2.30pm & 5.30–8.30pm, most credit cards accepted).

Ultra culture

Gate #7 at the Karaiskakis is well policed, and for good reason. This is where the fireworks will be coming from, launched by the likes of *Legenda Gate 7* and the 'Byron City Boys'. Neutrals can take in the whole Olympiakos experience from a seat accessed via gates #2 or #4.

In the net

Manos Tentzeris runs a tidy little unofficial website at: www-personal.engin.umich.edu/~etentz/soccer.html. You'll find a reliably updated fixture schedule and player biographies, and everything is in English.

Groundhopping

From Greece's oldest club to a team that play up the road from the original 1896 Olympic Games stadium, Athens has as many romantic groundhops as it's possible for a single city to have.

Ethnikos

Karaiskakis stadium, see Olympiakos
Colours All blue with white trim
Cup winners 1933

The solitary cup-winning honour in the record books has kept Ethnikos fans going, through thick and much thin, for more than sixty years. Despite being founded in the same year as Olympiakos (1925), Ethnikos are permanently Piraeus' second club – and for that matter, since relegation in 1996, Piraeus' second-division club.

The rundown but calm atmosphere at the **Kaferio O Ethnikos**, on the corner of Tzavella and Skilitsi, five minutes from the Karaiskakis, is in tune with the football you will be watching.

Ionikos

Neopolis Nikea stadium, Voulgari square
Capacity 8000
Colours All blue with white trim

Ionikos, in Athens' south-western suburbs, were only founded in 1965. The cramped Neapolis stadium, with its small but devoted group of fans, saw the team bravely challenge for a UEFA Cup place in 1996 and 1997, with little to back them other than the tutelage of their coach, former Soviet soccer superstar (and European footballer of the year) Oleg Blokhin.

Voulgari square is a 25-minute **#21 bus** ride from Omonia square, and contains **plenty of bars** eminently suited to a pre-match swiftie. The stadium is just behind the square.

Panionios

Nea Smirni stadium, Iannou Xrysostomou 1
Capacity 22,500
Colours All blue with red trim
Cup winners 1979

Stuck out in the southern district of Nea Smirnis, where the mayor is the club president, Panionios at least have history behind them, if not much support. They are the oldest surviving football club in Greece, having been founded in 1890.

They enjoy two other claims to fame: a UEFA cup win over Atlético Madrid in 1971, and a domestic cup victory against AEK in 1979. None of this counted for a thing when they were relegated in 1996.

To share in the latest promotion drive, stand on a crowded **#10 trolleybus** from Syndagma square for thirty minutes or so, heading south. Follow the other fan when he gets off at the square full of sculptures on the right-hand side, along the main Elefteriou Venizlou road.

Nea Smirnis is not the most lively of Athens' suburbs, but any bar along along **Andreou** or **Alexandrou** will prepare you for the half-hour journey back to town.

Apollon

Rizoupoli stadium, Perissos
Capacity 17,500
Colours Blue and white

Characteristically mid-table, Apollon suffer from being in the shadow of AEK, fifteen minutes' walk away. A creditable fourth place in 1995 was marred by a subsequent disaster in their first venture into Europe, when they went out of the UEFA Cup preliminary round to Olimpia Ljubljana of Slovenia.

To see if they can do better next season, take the metro to Perissos. As for AEK, use the passageway underneath the station, but then turn left and head back along the train tracks for ten minutes, after which you'll come to the stadium.

There is **no bar near the ground**, so stop at one of the establishments clustered around Perissos metro station, along Leoforos Ionias.

Athinaikos

Virona stadium, Neas Efessou 6, Kessariani
Capacity 6000
Colours Red-and-yellow shirts, yellow shorts

Founded in 1917, Athinaikos are one of Athens' oldest clubs, founded in 1917. Out in the south-eastern district of Kessariani, their tiny ground has witnessed many a relegation battle since a grass pitch was laid over the sand following promotion in 1990.

The team have troubled the historians only once, when they made the 1991 Greek cup final. They were hammered 5–1 by Panathinaikos, but since Pana did the double that year, the red-and-yellows sneaked into the Cup-Winners' Cup, where they met the holders, Manchester United. Having held Fergie's fighters to a goalless draw at home, Athinaikos came close to taking the lead at Old Trafford before ultimately losing in extra-time.

To follow in United's footsteps, ride **trolleybus #2** for ten minutes south of Syndagma. The ground is a short walk from the bus stop by Agios Nikolaou church, where the main Imitou and Ethnikis Andistasseos roads cross.

Halfway along the #2 trolleybus route, between Syndagma and Kessariani, is where you'll find the **Olympic stadium** from 1896. With its three sides beautifully intact, the 'Panathenic' is a site to stir the blood of any sports fan. Admission is free, and you'll find a **terrace bar** by the entrance.

Eat, drink, sleep…

Bars and clubs

There are two kinds of **nightlife** in Athens: summer and winter. In summer, head for open-air venues in Glyfada and Voula along the Apollo coast, around 10km from town along the main Leoforos Poseidonos road towards the airport. Many players own bars down here, the best being Dimitris Saravakos' late-night **Corte Café** (1 Metaxa 30) in Glyfada.

Bus #129 goes to Glyfada from Leoforos Vassilissis Olgas; a taxi back will cost you around Dr3000. Expect to pay Dr2500–3000 for entry to any club, which includes a drink. Any drink after that may well be Dr2000 a shot.

In town, Exarchia is the best area for bars, though it has lost a little of its underground feel since its early Nineties heyday. Plaka and the Thissio area north-west of the Acropolis also buzz with nightlife.

Berlin Bar, Iraklidon 8. The most popular bar in Thissio attracts a rock crowd, less trendy than

Team spirit – the Athinaikos line-up that almost knocked Manchester United out of Europe, 1991

others in the area. Still, an obligatory port of call for Thissio barhoppers.

Booze, Kolotroni 57. A decent central venue despite the chandeliers, Booze boasts an indie crowd. Dr2000 entrance.

Café Metropolis, Odos Pandrossou. Terrace café with a view of Mitropolan cathedral and Pandrossou's market towards Plaka. Pricy, but traffic-free – just the place to start the day.

Camel Club, Vouliagmenis 268. Successful two-in-one venue, with one large stage for rock music, the other for house and techno. Dr2000 entry, Dr1500 a drink.

Floral, Ogos Arahovis. Probably where you'll end up if you're taken to Exarchion square – a vast wooden pub with two large bar areas, jazz murals and twenty types of beer.

Restaurants

Plaka, the crumbling area of narrow streets and market stalls in the shadow of the Acropolis, is the best area for *tavernas;* food is surprisingly authentic, but most of the live music will be tourist mush.

Apotsos, Odos Panepistimou 10. Just up from Syndagma square, this atmospheric *ouzeri* offers a great selection of *mezedes* against a backdrop of old Greek movie posters.

Cellar of Plaka, Odos Kydathineon 10. Plaka at its best. Stuff yourself silly for less than Dr1500, with wine straight from the barrel. Open evenings only, closed in high season. No credit cards.

Dionysos-Zonar, Lykavittos Hill (☎01/722 6374). Choose a clear evening, reserve a table here and forget it all for the breathtaking view of Athens down below. Dr3000–5000 for a two-course meal, but you won't forget it.

Kouklis, Tripodon 14. Acceptable tourist venue in the heart of Plaka. Main dishes at Dr800. Grab a balcony table, order another bottle of wine and let the afternoon take its course.

Accommodation

If it's summer and you're arriving on spec, you might find a lot of Athens' budget hotels and hostels already full. The **tourist office** in the National Bank of Greece in a corner of Syndagma square (see p.247) will be able to help you, but don't leave it until late in the day.

Remember that although a room in central Plaka or Omonia will solve transport problems, these areas can also be **extremely noisy** until the early hours.

Out of season (ie. when there's football on), some places drop their rates, so if you're staying two nights or more, try and strike a bargain.

Amalia, Leoforos Amalias 10 (☎01/323 7301). For luxury at half the price of the Hilton, and convenience to boot, the Amalia is just off Syndagma square, right by the airport bus stop. The upper back rooms have a view of the Acropolis, most others a view of the National Gardens or Lykavittos Hill in the distance. From Dr30,000 a double, most major credit cards accepted.

Athens Gate Hotel, Leoforos Syngrou 10 (☎01/923 8302). Well-furnished rooms, most with balconies and televisions, for around Dr20,000 a double. Sun deck and roof-garden restaurant. Just across from the temple of Olympian Zeus. Most major credit cards accepted.

George's Guest House, Nikis 46 (☎01/322 6474). Perennial hostel favourite, a short walk from Syndagma square. Doubles at Dr3500, dorm beds at Dr1500.

Omonia, Omonia Square (☎01/523 7211). Clean, budget hotel slap bang in central Athens. Balconies on the higher floors. Dr8500 for a double. Ideal for nightbirds.

Pella Inn, Ermou 104 (☎01/325 0598 or ☎01/321 1229). Cheap, clean and conveniently situated by the Monastikiri metro stop, opposite the flea market and taverns of Plaka, the Pella is ideal for the budget-conscious traveller. Dr8000 for a double room, some with balconies.

Holland

Dutch football is the most remarkable success story of the modern era. For thirty years, Dutch players have entertained us with their precise, visionary passing, their perceptive movement on and off the ball, their explosive free kicks, their attitude of wanting to win in style.

And they have done more than simply entertain. Football in Holland has also contributed significantly to the development of the game. It was Dutch tactical awareness that moved European soccer from its moribund, defensive state in the Sixties, to the fresh new pastures of 'Total Football', with its attacking instincts and all-round adaptability. Today the Dutch are again at the forefront, their emphasis on youth development an example for the continent to follow in the post-Bosman era.

The period has been marked by three generations of awesomely talented players, each of which won a European Cup in its prime: Cruyff's Ajax in 1971–73, van Basten and Gullit's AC Milan in 1989–90 and coach Louis van Gaal's young Ajax prodigies in 1995. Frank Rijkaard, the third of Milan's Dutch trio, bridged the generation gap with his European swansong with Ajax in 1995. This three of them were essential to the Dutch national team's only success to date, the European Championship win of 1988.

Holland has a modest league dominated by three teams and draconian tax laws, so most Dutch stars leave home early. Yet somehow there always seems to be another generation of teenage talent to replace those who have left.

The country's reward will come in the year 2000, when it co-hosts its first major international tournament, the European Championship, with Belgium. If the big three of Ajax, Feyenoord and PSV have their way, this could lead to the setting

Tangerine dream – Gullit and glory, 1988

up of Europe's first multi-national superleague with the Belgians soon afterwards – itself the potential prelude to a border-free, European premier league. And all this from a nation whose football was still amateur when Italy and West Germany had already won three World Cups between them...

Thanks to Holland's proximity to England, Dutch football was the second fastest on the continent to develop, after Denmark. English textile workers first played the game here in the mid-1860s. In 1879, Haarlemse Football Club were the first club to be formed and modest league and cup competitions were inaugurated ten years later. English clubs made regular tours and Holland enjoyed a brief reign among Europe's amateur élite. The Dutch were quick to propose an international football association in 1902 (which became FIFA two years later) and won two bronze medals in early Olympic soccer tournaments. But those semi-final appearances in 1920 and 1924, in what were effectively the World Cup finals of the amateur era, were the last time the national side, *de Oranje*, would feature at international level for fifty years.

Professionalism left Holland behind. Of 26 internationals played between the start of the 1949–50 season and 1955, *de Oranje* won two and lost 22. Defeats by Luxembourg and Northern Ireland kept them out of the latter stages of the 1964 European Championship and 1966 World Cup,

The unsung hero – Rob Rensenbrink, 1978

respectively. It wasn't until the departure of Faas Wilkes (still Holland's leading international goalscorer) for the high salaries of Valencia in 1956 that professionalism was officially sanctioned and a proper national league created.

The new era saw the rise and eventual domination of the *eeuwige rivaals*, 'eternal rivals', Ajax and Feyenoord. Both were blessed with a remarkable crop of young players. Young Ajax forward Johan Cruyff became Dutch football's first modern superstar, his talents honed by the strict coaching of Rinus Michels. Ajax won three straight titles from 1966, and have scarcely looked back since. But it was Feyenoord, with the intelligent Wim van Hanegem in midfield, who won Holland's first European Cup, beating Celtic 2–1 in the 1970 final.

Ajax responded by taking Europe apart for three years. An almost tentative win over Panathinaikos in 1971 was followed by a confident stride through the competition in 1972 and 1973, with the forward-thinking Romanian coach Stefan Kovács at the helm. On paper, Ruud Krol and Wim Suurbier were defenders, Johan Neeskens, Arie Haan and Gerrie Mühren ran the midfield, while Cruyff, Piet Keizer and Johnny Rep led the line upfront. On the pitch, the players constantly interchanged in a flowing 4–3–3 system which left *catenaccio*, quite literally, standing. 'Total Football' had arrived.

With Michels in charge, Holland were the dark horses for the 1974 World Cup. Within a few games they had become the neutral's favourite, too, their popularity soaring still higher after they had beaten a deeply negative Brazil team, 2–0. That result set up a final encounter with the hosts West Germany – pairing Cruyff with Franz Beckenbauer, two interpretations of Total Football. The Dutch were ahead within a minute through a Neeskens penalty, but once the Germans had won a (slightly dubious) spot-kick of their own, Holland's *wanderlust* got the better of them. After Gerd Müller had put the hosts ahead, Holland created few chances.

International swansong – van Basten in the fateful semi-final against Denmark, Euro '92

By 1978, the Ajax stars including Cruyff had gone abroad, allowing Bayern Munich to dominate Europe and PSV Eindhoven the domestic league. It was PSV's van de Kerkhof brothers, Willy and René, who were at the heart of the *Oranje* side which travelled to the World Cup in Argentina that year. Cruyff refused to make the trip, apparently in protest against the Argentine military junta. His replacement was Rob Rensenbrink, who had been forced to leave the 1974 final through injury and who, while less flamboyant, was also less prone to go walkabout.

With a slightly more direct approach and an awesome display of long-range shooting, Holland made their way to the final, where for the second successive World Cup, they found themselves up against the hosts. There, a hostile atmosphere provoked some abonimably weak refereeing, and when Rensenbrink struck a post in the last minute of normal time, the Dutch knew it wasn't going to be their day – Argentina won 3–1.

It was to be ten years before the Rijkaard/Gullit/van Basten triple act, an adventurous formation kept on course by a returning Rinus Michels on the bench, got Holland back to the top. In the 1988 European Championship, just two years after a humilliating play-off defeat by Belgium had denied them a place at the Mexico World Cup, Holland were playing their best football since 1974. A van Basten hat-trick destroyed England, then a single touch from the same player three minutes from time gained the Dutch their revenge over West Germany in the semi-final. In the final, a thunderbolt header from Gullit and an extraordinary far-post volley from van Basten were enough to beat a Soviet Union side who had been weakened since themselves beating Holland earlier in the competition. The *Oranje* had won a major tournament at last.

The Germans would figure prominently in the Dutch bid to win the next two big international events. At Italia '90, Holland's tempestuous defeat by West Germany featured the ugly sending-off of Rijkaard and Rudi Völler. Revenge came at Euro '92, with an easy 3–1 win for the Dutch in a first-round group encounter, but subsequent

Basics

EU citizens and those of the USA, Canada, Australia and New Zealand require only a **passport** to enter the Netherlands.

The Dutch **currency** is the guilder, abbreviated to f, divided into 100 cents. There are coins for 5c, 10c, 25c, f1, f2.50 and f5, and notes for f10, f25, f50, f100, f250 and f1000. There are around f3.5 to £1.

Banks offer the best **exchange rate**, and are open Mon–Fri 9am–4pm, with occasional late Thursday opening in the main cities. *GWK* offices are open much later, and can give cash advances on credit cards. Payment by credit card is widespread.

Phonecards, in f5, f10 and f25 sizes, are sold at post offices and tourist information (*VVV*) offices. From outside the country, the code for Holland is ☎31; for Amsterdam add ☎20, Rotterdam ☎10 and Eindhoven ☎40. Add a 0 before the city code if you're calling inland. From inside Holland, the international access code is ☎00, and the reduced rate for European calls is Mon–Fri 8pm–8am, all day Sat–Sun.

Holland is a small country and few **journeys** take more than three hours. **Trains** are comfortable and efficient, and fares, calculated by the kilometre, are reasonable. A journey of 50km costs around f13, with a 10 percent discount on return fares if come back the same day on a *dagretour*. Buying a ticket onboard incurs a hefty supplement.

Bus stations are nearly always located next to train termini, and local services are equally cheap and efficient. Like all public transport in Holland, buses run on the *Nationale Strippenkaart* system, in which a ticket strip are divided into numbered bars, which the bus driver then stamps according to the length of your journey. Simply tell him your destination when you board.

On **city trams** and **metros**, it's up to you to stamp the ticket in the machine by folding the strip to include sufficient bars. Few urban journeys require more than two. The driver can sell you strips of five, eight and ten bars onboard; more economical 15- (f11) and 45-bar (f32.25) strips are sold at train stations and newsstands.

For all the efficiency of the transport, **cycling** is often the best way to get around. There are bike hire offices at most train stations; they charge about f8 a day, but require a form of ID and f200 deposit. Be sure to use a sturdy lock wherever you park.

Hotels in Holland are not particularly cheap but there is a free **national reservation service**, *Nederlands Reservations Centre* (open Mon–Fri 8am–8pm, Sat 8am–2pm, ☎070/320 5000, fax 070/320 2611. Large towns have a *VVV* tourist office at or near the train station, where you can book a room for f3.50 commission per person. In a two-star hotel, expect to pay around f90 for a double room with a bath/shower. Pensions are about f30 per person, youth hostels f20.

Dutch **cooking** is high on protein, low on variety, relying on fish, meat and dairy produce. *Eetcafés* provide a good-value version of it – look out for the *dagschotel*, the dish of the day, at around f15, or three-course tourist menus at f20–25. The Dutch tend to dine early, so restaurants normally only stay open until 11pm. Most towns have a fair ethnic selection, especially Chinese, Surinamese and Indonesian. Restaurant bills are subject to a 17.5 percent tax surcharge and 15 percent service charge.

The traditional Dutch bar is the *bruine kroeg*, or **brown café**, cosy and tobacco stained. These places serve food until early evening and lager (*pils*) in small glasses with a large head theatrically skimmed off by a plastic knife. *Heineken, Amstel, Oranjeboom* and *Grolsch* are the most common brews, but more adventurous Belgian varieties should also be available. The national spirit is *jenever*, a gin made from molasses and juniper berries. Most bars stay open until 1am, 2am at weekends.

Note that the renowned liberal attitude to **smoking marijuana** in Holland applies only to designated **coffee shops** in Amsterdam.

celebrations and complacency in the semi-final against Denmark proved Holland's undoing.

Euro '92 would mark van Basten's last top-level international appearance before injury. In the run-up to the 1994 World Cup, Gullit withdrew at the last minute, and there was further (now familiar) dissent in the ranks during the tournament itself. Holland went out in the quarter-finals – though not without a fight – to the eventual winners Brazil.

The squad was again divided as it approached Euro '96, with several members of the young Ajax contingent openly at war with coach Guus Hiddink. After a 4–1 crushing by England at Wembley, elimination duly came at the quarter-final stage, in a penalty shoot-out against France.

Since then, the dispersal of the Ajax squad around Europe has made Hiddink's life a little easier, although factionalism remains Holland's greatest enemy – just as it was when the Total Footballers took the world by storm in the Seventies.

The Dutch wouldn't have it any other way, though. Better to be arguing and attractive, they say, than disciplined and dull. On the evidence of history and the immediate prospects for the future, it's hard to disagree.

Essential vocabulary
Hello *Hallo*
Goodbye *Tot ziens*
Yes *Ja*
No *Nee*
Two beers, please *Twee bier, alstublieft*
Thank you *Dank u*
Men's *Mannen*
Women's *Vrouwen*
Where is the stadium? *Hoe kom ik in de stadion?*
What is the score? *Wat is de stand?*
Referee *Scheidsrechter*
Offside *Buitenspel*

Trees, murals and bicycles – the *voetbal* experience

Match practice
The first thing to know about domestic football in Holland is that you can't see any of it without a *Club Card* (see *Tickets*). To counter the rise of hooliganism, this scheme was introduced for all Dutch premier-division grounds in 1996/97. For 1997/98 it is being extended to all first-division grounds.

The system did not prevent some horrendous off-the-ball incidents between Ajax and Feyenoord nutcases in the spring of 1997, but most high-risk matches are so heavily policed, you won't see any trouble at the ground.

In a further move towards turning Dutch *voetbal* into a thoroughly modern spectator sport, all premier-division stadia will be all-seaters by the start of the 1998/99 season. Most of the big grounds – Amsterdam Arena, Feyenoord's de Kuip and PSV's Philips stadium – will be in tip-top shape well before the deadline. Vitesse Arnhem's 30,000 all-seater Gelderland, with its movable roof and floor, should be ready by the end of 1997.

Yet scratch this impressive veneer, discount the big three, and you'll find the average premier-division crowd to be under 8000. Unless you manage to get into *de klassiker*, Ajax-Feyenoord, or a game between either of those and PSV, you'll be

Higher and higher – the Dutch put seven past Wales, 1996

The first-division season is divided into four periods, and the most successful team in each is known as the period champion. These four sides, the clubs finishing second and third from bottom in the premier and the clubs finishing second and third in the first go to make up the two *Nacompetitie* groups. In practice, the play-offs also involve teams finishing fourth or fifth, as invariably period champions finish in the top two or three of the *Eerste Divisie*. The winners of each six-game play-off group go into next season's *Eredivisie*.

At present, no professional club can be relegated to the amateur leagues, but it is hoped that by the end of the century, a system will be in place to encourage movement between the professional and amateur sectors. The latter is strictly divided into Saturday and Sunday leagues, from the days when Christian clubs refused to play on a Sunday. Holland's top amateur club is decided when the Saturday and Sunday champions play each other – on a Saturday!

watching a game in surroundings not far removed from those of an English lower-division match.

The Dutch season runs from mid-August to the end of May, with a one-month break between Christmas and the end of January. Premier-division games take place on Saturdays at 7.30pm or Sundays at 2.30pm. Live televised games are scheduled for 7.30pm on Fridays and 6pm on Sundays. There are a handful of midweek rounds scattered through the season, and Dutch city mayors – who have the right to postpone games unilaterally if they fear crowd trouble – can play havoc with the calendar, causing a pile-up of fixtures at the end of the season.

The league

Holland has two professional divisions, the premier (*Eredivisie*) and the first (*Eerste Divisie*). Both have eighteen teams. At the end of the season, the bottom of the premier swaps places with the top of the first. Other promotion and relegation places are decided in June's *Nacompetitie*, which comprises play-off groups of four teams each.

Up for the cup

The *KNVB Beker* involves sixty amateur and professional clubs. The cup winners and top three league teams from the previous season are exempt from the qualifying group matches in August, when the other 56 are divided into fourteen pools of four teams each. These pools are seeded, with one premier, one first and two lower-first or amateur clubs. After three group matches per team, the top two of each pool join the four exempt teams in the first round proper.

The four rounds (November, January, February, April) to the final are decided on one match, extra-time with sudden death, and penalties.

The final is always played on Ascension Day in May, and always at Feyenoord's de Kuip, irrespective of who the finalists may be. The amateur cup final is played at 2.30pm, then the main event at 6pm.

Tickets

To buy a ticket for an *Eredivisie* game, you must have a *Club Card*, designating you as a member of any of the eighteen clubs. With the help of the cards, a computerised seat allocation system and Dutch national lottery (*Staatsloterij*) outlets, 80 percent of tickets are automatically allocated to the home club, 5–10 percent to away fans and 10–15 percent to neutrals.

If there are tickets available – which, for Ajax, Feyenoord and PSV, there probably won't be – neutrals can buy a token for f10 on the day to allow them to buy a ticket in. Alternatively, you can simply enrol as a member of a lesser-supported club (f10 for two years), which will enable you to see more regular football without any hassle beforehand.

For Holland internationals, members of the official *Dutch Supporters' Association* (f25 for two years) get first priority on tickets, then *Orange Club Card* holders (f10 for two years), then regular *Club Card* holders.

Standing tickets (*staanplaatsen*) will be phased out by August 1998. Seats (*zitplaatsen*) are either covered (*overdekte*) or open (*onoverdekte*). The sector (*vak*) marked *bezoekende* is for visiting supporters. *Verhoogd* matches are the choice games, for which prices are raised slightly.

The cheapest places will be f30–40, a decent seat f50–70. The best view can be had from the *Hoofdtribune*, the main stand. Prices drop dramatically for first-division games, for which f20 will get you the best seat in the house.

Most clubs issue a matchday programme, but don't expect a work of art.

Half-time

The beer on sale at the main Dutch grounds is *malt*, without alcohol, but is still sunk in great quantities. Snacks include *patat met fritesaus* – chips with mayonnaise; if you want them without, just say '*zonder*'. Sandwiches (*broodjes*) come with various fillings, including herring (*haring*). You'll also find waffles (*stroopwafels*) and frankfurter sausages (*fricandel*).

Action replay

The collapse of pay-per-view channel *Sport 7* in December 1996 may have serious repercussions for the future of Dutch league football as a whole. Earlier in the season, smaller clubs were rubbing their hands with glee at the thought of a $1.5 million a season windfall from the proceeds of a new 24-hour-a-day sports channel, conceived by and run in association with the Dutch FA, the *KNVB*. Some clubs planned new stadia, others offered lucrative contracts to keep their key players.

When Ajax and Feyenoord demanded a bigger share of the loot, questioning the *KNVB*'s authority to sell the rights to their games in the first place, a judge backed them up. *Sport 7* collapsed. The clubs saw only six months' money. Bankruptcy or merger now face those who spent what they didn't have.

Weeks afterwards, the *KNVB* made a $43 million-a-year deal with the state *NOS* TV channel for league coverage. *NOS* now has the rights to show the pick of the league calendar, live, at 6pm on Sundays, plus two weekend highlights packages called *NOS-Studio Sport* – on Saturdays at 10.30pm on channel 3, and the most popular show, on Sundays at 8pm on channel 2. The latter also shows Spanish and Italian action from 10pm.

Subscription channel *Supersport* has the rights to show a dozen Dutch premier games live each season, while the commercial *SBS* station shows live cup matches and English and Dutch league highlights on Saturdays at 6.15pm and 10pm, and on Sundays at 6pm and 11pm. *HMG* has the rights to Dutch internationals. BBC and the main German and Belgian channels are easily available all over Holland.

The back page

The main football publication is the authoritative colour weekly *Voetbal International*

(Wednesdays, f4.50), which has fair foreign coverage as well as all the local features, gossip and stats.

A recent and popular innovation, along the lines of *Guadalajara* in France and *Hattrick* in Germany, is *Hard Gras* (bi-monthly, f16.90), a *Granta*-style, pseudo-literary booklet with in-depth interviews and philosophical meanderings on the game.

Of the dailies, the populist *De Telegraaf*, a tabloid dressed as a broadsheet, has all the juicy transfer rumours, and as Holland has no Sunday papers, its *Telesport* supplement on Mondays is pretty much essential.

Ultra Culture

The death of one-time *Ajax F-side* leader Carlo Picornie in March 1997 shocked the nation. A month after Ajax and Feyenoord fans had clashed on the side of a motorway, they arranged a Sunday morning re-match in an empty field in the otherwise sleepy town of Beverwijk. In the short, vicious mêlée that followed, Picornie died after being hit on the head with steel bars. The gangs had arranged their warfare by mobile phone and email to keep ahead of the police.

Much has been done in Holland to counteract the hooligan problem: security fences, strict segregation, the *Club Card* system for buying tickets and, following Picardie's death, an increase in police powers to allow them to infiltrate supporters' groups and tap their telephones.

With PSV's fans scorned for not travelling, the spotlight falls on the bitter Ajax-Feyenoord rivalry. This first saw light of day in the mid-Seventies when groups, modelling themselves on English hooligans and calling themselves *Sides* after the section of terracing they occupied, began to arm themselves every weekend.

With Euro 2000 round the corner, the Dutch authorities have good cause to be worried. Many clubs simply disown the problem, but PSV employ people to work with known hooligans, trying to make them see more to life than the feel of steel against skull.

At national level the picture couldn't be more different – so long as the opposition aren't German. Dutch fans are renowned for their oompah bands ('The Orange Hooters' in particular), good spirit and friendly drinking.

In the net

First port of call must be Joost Schraag's Dutch football homepage at: soccer.boa.nl/. It contains an excellent stats archive and full details of the current season to help you work your way through Holland's usual fixture chaos. It's also a great source of links, a selection of which take you to the online version of *NOS Teletekst*, a great news source which can be hard to access otherwise. Elsewhere, the flashy online edition of *Voetbal International* is at: www.vi.weekbladpers.nl/.

Do we not like orange – Koeman and Platt, Rotterdam, 1993

Amsterdam

Fans visiting Amsterdam find it strangely bereft of football culture. Sure, they love its peaceful vibe, its canals, bars and coffee shops, but...where's the footie?

The answer is at a futuristic superdome on the city's south-eastern edge. Ajax's new stadium, the Amsterdam Arena, was opened in August 1996 with a friendly against AC Milan. Queen Beatrix did the Mexican wave with 51,000 other spectators, all season tickets were quickly snapped up and, despite justified criticism of the turf and lack of atmosphere, plans were laid for an entertainment complex to complement Europe's newest major football venue.

The stadium is packed every game. Ajax, Amsterdam city council and the corporate investors who ploughed f250 million into the project are happy. There is no wire fence, no running track, and the steep-sided stands give a surprisingly intimate feel at a major game.

Yet still visitors beg the question, where's the football? The Jordaan area, where Gullit and Rijkaard played together in the street, has been yuppified. Amsterdam is a one-club town, with none of the tension and colour that a big inner-city rivalry can provide.

It hasn't always been this way. Many local clubs have fallen by the wayside, including RAP Amsterdam, who won the first Dutch title in 1898 and the first double a year later. Ajax's three former cross-town rivals – Blauw Wit, De Volewijckers and DWS – merged to form FC Amsterdam in 1972 (and beat Internazionale in the UEFA Cup two years on), then went their separate ways to operate as amateurs ten years later. The stadium they used, the Olympic, venue for the 1928 Games, was recently rescued from property developers by a campaign group who raised f5 million from donors happy to have their name inscribed on a brick of the

Football ground as flying saucer – the Arena

restored ground. Rebuilding won't be complete until the next century.

Holland's first football ground, the Oude Stadion, was demolished to make way for the Olympic in 1928. Almost sixty years later, Ajax's own De Meer was knocked down to make way for housing. This blunt fact covers a multitude of history. The De Meer not only saw Ajax rise from a modestly successful club side to a major European power – half the players who achieved this grew up within a two-mile radius of the ground. Johan Cruyff's mother, who used to wash the team's shirts, still uses the club shop opposite where de Meer once stood. Fans still drink in the bar next door. Sure, it could barely hold 30,000, and most league matches barely pulled in a third of that. But these

Amsterdam essentials

A fast train service (every fifteen minutes daytime, hourly at night, journey time twenty minutes, single f6) connects **Schiphol airport** with Centraal station, hub of Amsterdam's transport network and a short walk from Dam square. Many trains go on to other cities after calling at Amsterdam Centraal – don't miss your stop.

The seven-and-a-half hour *Eurostar* journey from London Waterloo International (change at Brussels Midi) terminates at Centraal. *Eurolines* buses terminate at Amstel station, a metro journey from Centraal.

Most of central Amsterdam is accessible by foot or bicycle, but **buses, trams** and a three-line **metro** network run on the *Strippenkaart* system. Most journeys you'll make will only take in one zone, so stamp two bars – the stamp is valid for one hour. Transport runs 6am–midnight, after which seven hourly **night bus** routes take over. A day ticket (*dagkaart*, f10) also covers night buses.

Taxis can be ordered from a rank, or by phoning ☎020/677 7777 – you can't hail them down. Cabs are expensive – f5.60 initial charge, then f2.80 per km, rising to f3.25 midnight–6am – and often slow in Amsterdam's crowded streets.

If you want to travel in style, hop aboard the *Canal Bus* (Mon–Fri 10am–8pm in summer, f15 for a day ticket), which serves Centraal station, Leidseplein and Westerkerk every thirty minutes.

If you want to rent a **bicycle**, *Take-A-Bike* at Centraal station charge f8 per day and require a f200 deposit, while *Bike City* at Bloemgracht 70 charge f10 per day, f50 and your passport as deposit.

The *VVV* have four **tourist offices** in town: one inside Centraal station (Mon–Sat 8am–7.30pm, Sun 9am–4.30pm); one just outside it (daily 9am–5pm); another on the Leidsestraat/Leidseplein corner (Mon–Sat 9am–7pm, Sun 9am–5pm) and one at Stadionplein (Mon–Sat 9am–5pm).

The *VVV* produces an English-language **listings guide**, *What's On In Amsterdam* (fortnightly, f3.50). The free Dutch-language monthly *Uitkrant* has more information.

---

people were Ajax through-and-through – not least the *F-side* mob opposite the scoreboard end. The fact that these people are still drawn to de Meer's locale indicates the unease many feel about the move to the Arena.

The club have not been insensitive to fans' feelings. Some have taken their old De Meer seat from the ground and plonked it in their living rooms, so that instead of watching home matches from it, they can now use it to sit back and enjoy away games on the box. Other fans have had their ashes scattered on pieces of De Meer turf donated to a special plot, designed in the shape of a football pitch and planted in the city's Westgaarde cemetery.

Ajax can't help being fashionable. The Arena now attracts media personalities, businessmen, hot shots, people who wouldn't have been seen dead in de Meer – or in Westgaarde cemetery, for that matter. The atmosphere in the Arena, with five times the average gate of the old De Meer, has been subdued not because of the stadium's design, but because a fair few spectators simply don't know what you should do at a football match.

The ground has not brought promised employment to the otherwise economically depressed area of Bijlmer, to which white city workers have been drafted when so much of Ajax's successful modern image has been in bringing young black talent to the fore. But the new development has brought Ajax's famed soccer school superb new facilities in an area known as De Toekomst ('The Future'), a part of the Arena complex. And the future, as Ajax will tell you, is what it's all about.

The thrilling fields

 Ajax

Amsterdam Arena, Arena Boulevard 1
Capacity 51,500 (all-seated)
Colours White shirts, with thick red stripe,
white shorts
League champions 1918–19, 1931–32, 1934,
1937, 1939, 1947, 1957, 1960, 1966–68, 1970,
1972–73, 1977, 1979–80, 1982–83, 1985, 1990,
1994–96
Cup winners 1917, 1943, 1961, 1967, 1970–72,
1979, 1983, 1986–87, 1993
European Cup winners 1971–73, 1995
Cup-Winners' Cup winners 1987
UEFA Cup winners 1992

That thick red stripe on Ajax's white shirts
is a symbol of technical excellence, of faith
in youth and, ultimately, of success. The
club's soccer academy, a production line of
prodigious teenage talent, is the envy of
Europe. Ajax's brand-new stadium, the
Amsterdam Arena, is one of the finest on
the continent.

And yet, with the departure of coach
Louis van Gaal for Barcelona in the summer of 1997, after the club's first trophyless
season since 1991, Ajax have hit a hiatus.

More than half the team who so bril-
liantly took on Europe's best – and won –
in 1995 have gone. Kluivert, Bogarde,
Reiziger, Overmars, Kanu, George, Davids
and Seedorf have taken with them a football education second to none, and a
confidence born of constantly having
proved their worth through those early
years of development. Behind them they
have left a club which, though commercially healthy, has been stung by the
implications of the Bosman ruling and is,
temporarily at least, having to break with
tradition by signing established internationals from foreign clubs.

The last time there was an exodus on
this scale, when Johan Cruyff followed
coach Rinus Michels to Barcelona in 1973,
it took a decade for the team to recover.
For many fans, Cruyff still embodies much
that is forever Ajax: flair, versatility, vision
and a genius bordering on arrogance. At
his peak he led a team which stands alongside Europe's all-time greats.

Ajax celebrate winning the 1995 European Cup in Vienna – but few of this line-up remain

This is how we do it – skipper de Boer shows Dani the ropes

Blankenburg, Gerrie Mühren, Arie Haan and Ruud Krol to raise the club's game to another level. In 1970/71, Ajax beat Celtic and Atlético Madrid in a European Cup run that culminated in a 2–0 victory over Panathinaikos at Wembley in 1971. Michels left for Barcelona. His successor, Romanian coach Stefan Kovács, adapted Michels' attacking *catenaccio* to form a fluid 4–3–3 system which required all outfield players to improvise their positions with constant movement off the ball. Everyone was aware of each other's presence, and could anticipate runs from deep positions, not least by the attacking sweeper. Like an orchestra, it was complicated but, when in full flow, was unbeatable. Like an orchestra, it required a high degree of technical skill and an inspired conductor – Cruyff.

This *Totaal Voetbal* swept aside much of the negativity of the previous decade. In 1972 and 1973 Ajax were simply unstoppable, achieving two European Cup wins over *catenaccio*-driven Inter and Juventus, before Cruyff followed Michels south to Barcelona.

Without their conductor, Ajax floundered – and Franz Beckenbauer's Bayern Munich assumed their mantle. Neeskens also left for Barcelona and soon Haan, Blankenburg and young goalscorer Johnny Rep were gone, too.

It took more than ten years, and the return of Cruyff as coach, for Ajax to regain their strength. As a player, he had come back to lead Ajax to a Dutch league and cup double in 1982/83 – a season during which he had been substituted by a gangly 17-year-old striker, Marco van Basten, who would make a goalscoring début.

By the time van Basten's five-year career at Ajax was over, had scored 128

The Ajax story really begins with Cruyff's début and the appointment of Michels as coach in 1965. Until then the club, formed by businessmen meeting on Sunday lunchtimes in 1900, had been medium-sized fish in a small pond. The Dutch league was of mediocre standard and Holland's international status was on a par with that of Norway. In the Thirties, de Meer stadium was built and the club won five titles under English coach Jack Reynolds. But few outside Holland took much notice.

Even by the mid-Sixties, Ajax were scarcely a name to be conjured with in the wider picture of European football. Michels, a disciplinarian who encouraged freedom of spirit on the pitch, changed those perceptions for good. He introduced a 4–2–4 system, with a young Cruyff moving between midfield and centre-forward. With Piet Keizer on the wing, it began to rain goals at de Meer. Ajax easily won the Dutch title in 1966, then beat Liverpool 5–1 in the European Cup. In 1966/67, Cruyff scored 33 goals in 34 league games.

Ajax were not quite ready to conquer the continent – they were hammered 4–1 defeat by AC Milan in the 1969 European Cup final. It needed Johan Neeskens, Horst

goals in 133 league games. His last strike was the winning goal against Lokomotiv Leipzig in the 1987 Cup-Winners' Cup final – not just van Basten's swansong in an Ajax shirt, but also Cruyff's finale as coach.

Also on the pitch against Leipzig were Frank Rijkaard (who would join van Basten at AC Milan but return to lead van Gaal's prodigies), Dennis Bergkamp and Aron Winter. Before leaving for Italy, the latter two would star in Ajax's UEFA Cup win five years later – the first success of the van Gaal era.

A former youth and reserve team coach, van Gaal relied on Ajax's technical chief, the influential Co Adriaanse, to produce a new generation of players. Adriaanse's graduates were a joy to behold: a group of raw, skilled, committed youngsters who took on the millionaires of Milan in the 1994 Champions' League and beat them – twice. When the two teams met again in the final of the competition in May 1995, it was a nineteen-year-old, Patrick Kluivert, who scored the late winner – his opportunism a fitting tribute to the Ajax philosophy.

Yet by the time the side had lost the following year's European Cup final to Juventus on penalties, storm-clouds of uncertainty were gathering. In 1996/97, Ajax gave up their Dutch title with less than a quarter of the season gone, and after a European Cup quarter-final win over Atlético Madrid, they were destroyed by Juventus in the semi.

While new coach Morten Olsen scours the school playground for new talent, the club counts the cost of the Bosman ruling – Davids, Reiziger and Kluivert all having left for Italy at the end of their contracts, without Ajax receiving a guilder in return.

Tickets

Games at the Arena are a sellout. Of the 50,000 seats available to Ajax fans, 46,000 are taken by season-ticket holders while the remainder are sold to club members and former season-ticket holders. Nonetheless, some black market trading

does go on in the metro concourse. Visitors are generally allocated 1600 tickets, ie. two trainloads, and enter by gate K to sectors #415 and #416 in the corner of the red *Noord* end.

Here we go!

Take **metro line #54** from Centraal, through three zones to Bijlmer. Allow fifteen minutes. The nearby Arena is signposted as you turn left out of the station. Club members can choose from six *Voetbalbus* services (f6 single, f10 return, allow 45 minutes) which leave from various points in the city.

Swift half

By the metro entrance you'll find three soulless, upmarket bars, incongruously spilling out drunken football fans on big matchdays. Of the three, the **Klein Arena**, right out of the metro exit, is the most convivial. In the Arena, no alcohol is on sale. At the stalls for fast food and soft drinks, you'll have to pay for things with an *Arena Card*, available by charging your credit card in the machines, or by exchanging for guilders at a till. The rate is f1.67 to one *Arena*. A small non-alcoholic beer and a burger comes to 4 *Arenas*, or f6.70.

Publications

The Ajax programme (f2.50) is on sale all around the ground. The club also issues *Ajax Magazine*, a thick, glossy men's monthly (f7.50).

Club shop

A large **Ajax superstore** by the main entrance is due to be ready for the 1997/98 season. You'll also find an **Ajax Fanshop** by entrance D (open Mon–Sat 9am–5pm, Sun 11am–5pm, most credit cards).

In town, there are two more official Ajax shops: at the de Kolk shopping centre in Nieuwendijk, not far from Centraal station (open Mon–Sat 10am–6pm, Thurs until 9pm, Sun noon–5pm, most credit cards) and opposite the De Meer site at Middenweg 400 (open Mon–Fri 7.30am–5.30pm,

Sat 8.30am–4.30pm, most credit cards). Both shops are also newsagents.

Club museum

An extensive, two-floor club museum by the main entrance to the Arena is scheduled to open for the 1997/98 season. You'll be able to gain admission to the museum and take a tour of the stadium for a combined ticket (f25).

Ultra culture

The *Ajax F-side*, born of De Meer's southeast end terrace, were the fans who pick up on some (fairly obscure) Jewish influences in the club's history and wave Stars of David as a means of identity. They also spray-painted their end with graffiti and had running battles with police during celebrations on the Leidseplein.

The early Nineties saw fans slowly drifting away from this terrace culture, even before De Meer closed. Many, brought up on clashes with Feyenoord through the Seventies and Eighties, had simply grown out of it – not least when an Austria Vienna goalkeeper was hit by an iron bar thrown from the crowd in 1989, and Ajax were banned from Europe for a year.

In moving to the Arena, the club made no provision to keep the *F-side* together, and this was a major factor in the lack of atmosphere at early games in the stadium. Now other season-ticket holders have been moved from the *Zuid* end and *F-siders* shifted in. The Arena management have even allowed fans to spray-paint images across the advertising hoardings.

The ongoing gang warfare with Feyenoord has been greeted with incredulity by most Ajax fans, the bulk of whom are happy to read their *Ajaxlife* supporters' magazine (monthly, f5.95), drink their beers and dance around to Madness' *One Step Beyond* when Ajax score.

In the net

The official Ajax website is scheduled to open for business at the start of the 1997/98 season. First impressions are of a typically smart but soulless site. You'll find it at: www.ajax.nl/. For a fan's eye view, try the *Ajaxmania* site at: ajaxmania.xs4all.nl/. It includes news and match reports in both Dutch and English. If you still nurse hopes of getting to see Ajax, then check out the latest ticket information at the official Arena website, at: www.amsterdamarena.nl.

Eat, drink, sleep...

Not much, but it was home – De Meer before the diggers moved in

Bars and clubs

Visitors to Amsterdam cluster around three main patches. The red light district (out of Centraal station, go straight up Damrak and turn left at the *Grasshopper* coffee shop) is full of lads on beanos; Rembrandtplein (tram #4 or #9 from Centraal) is neon, tacky and overpriced; and the Leidseplein (tram #1, #2, #5 or #11 from Centraal). **Bars** fall into three main categories: the designer

variety, new and clean; dirty old *bruine
kroeg*, brown cafés; and coffee shops, or
'smokings', which attract tourists.

Nightclubbing is also concentrated
in the centre – check out the flyers at *Mid-
town Records*, Nieuwedijk 104, to see which
DJs are in town.

Bobby Haarms, Utrechtstraat 6. Just off Rembrandtplein, a bar for older-generation fans run by
current assistant trainer and ex-player Haarms.
Packed with souvenirs. Closed Sundays. Tram #4
or #9 from Centraal.

Café Hendrik VIII, Prins Hendrinkstraat 83.
Ajax fans' bar by Centraal station, with framed
posters, scarves, badges and a big screen for TV
games. Diagonally left out of the station.

Café Mono, Oudezijds Voorburgwal 2. Intimate,
friendly spot for local DJs, playing leather-clad
R&R, indie or trip-hop depending on the night.
Short walk from Centraal.

Meerzicht, corner Middenweg/Brinkstraat.
Opposite where de Meer stadium stood, a
friendly, local football bar with a pool table and
signed pic of former neighbour Johan Cruyff.
Tram #9 to Brinkstraat from Centraal.

El Paradiso, Weteringschans 6–8. A former
church that's the best venue in town to see a live
band, especially from a spot on the balcony. Tram
#1, #2, #5 or #11 from Centraal.

Oost-West, corner Zeedijk/Stormsteeg. Brown
café with Heineken at f5 a pint and a perfect view
of the wheeler-dealing in the red light area. Sit
back and pretend you're in *Kojak*. Short walk from
Centraal.

Restaurants
The large concentration of non-Dutch
nationals in Amsterdam means the city has
as wide a **variety of cuisine** as almost any
in Europe. This doesn't make the Dutch
version more exciting, but heavy competition ensures more bargains and better
quality here than elsewhere in Holland.

Balraj, Binnen Oranjestraat 1. Intimate Indian
restaurant off Haarlemerdijk with good vegetarian options. Open until 10pm. Ten-minute walk
from Centraal.

Bojo, Lange Leidsedwarsstraat 51. Fine-value
Indonesian in the tourist-oriented Leidseplein
area. Invariably crowded but open until 2am.
Tram #1, #2, #5 or #11 from Centraal.

El Naranjo, Boomstraat 410. Small, friendly
tapas bar with a menu that changes weekly and
live music on Fridays. Short walk from Centraal.

Keuken van 1870, Spuistraat 4. One-time soup
kitchen, now a cheap, popular, centrally located
eaterie serving Dutch standards. Tram #1, #2,
#4, #5, #9 or #11 from Centraal.

Van Beeren, Koningstraat 54. Excellent
lunchtime choice in the red-light district, with
good value *dagschotel* and large portions of *stamp-
pot*, a traditional Dutch dish of mashed potato
and cabbage which is better than it sounds. Metro
to Nieuwmarkt.

Accommodation
Hotels in Amsterdam are an expensive
proposition. Prices for a double room, with
breakfast, start at around f100. VVV offices
can make on-the-spot bookings for f5.

Amstel Botel, Oosterdokskade 2–4 (☎020/626
4247). Large floating hotel moored close to Centraal station with a late bar. Be sure to get a room
looking out onto the water. Shower and TV in
every room. Singles at around f125, doubles f140,
triples f190, breakfast included. Most credit cards.

Flying Pig Vondelpark, Vossiustraat 46
(☎020/400 4187, fax 020/400 4105). Good-value
hostel near Leidseplein with kitchen facilities and
no curfew. Tram #1, #2, #5 or #11 to Leidseplein.

International Budget Hotel, Leidsegracht 76
(☎020/624 2784). Great canalside location, free
lockers and showers, video lounge. Singles f60,
doubles f110, dorm beds f35. Big breakfast f6.
Tram #1, #2, #5 or #11 to Prinsengracht.

Rotterdam

 Feyenoord 270   Sparta 273
Excelsior 274

The football passions burning in Rotterdam are simply explained. Everyone hates Amsterdam. While Rotterdam works, Amsterdam dreams – that's how the Rotterdammers see it. And that's how they see the football, too – honest, workmanlike Feyenoord against flashy, arrogant Ajax.

Getting one over on Amsterdam has been the priority ever since the city's main stadium was opened in 1937. A favourite with UEFA for staging European finals, 'de Kuip' ('The Tub') has seen a lot of classic football in a fervent atmosphere. But by the end of the Eighties it was falling to pieces, and Rotterdam city council had to step in to give it a complete overhaul, putting up the Maas building for VIPs and sponsors, and making the site more attractive to the business community.

Yet the surrounding Feijenoord area, unlike so much of Amsterdam, still feels like it belongs to the game, its rundown bars embellished with tatty pictures of its beloved soccer-playing stars. This is a football patch *par excellence*, a rare part of Holland where you feel as if football, and doubtless much more, is still being practised in the street.

In fact, Feyenoord attract fans from all over the Brabant and Zeeland regions, which is more than can be said for their city rivals Sparta, who barely attract people from the street next door. On the other side of the Maas river from Feyenoord – and traditionally at the other end of the social scale, too – conservative Sparta have seen demographic change in their Spangen district reduce their average gate to one of the lowest in the *Eredivisie*. The club's laid-back management is generally credited with having allowed Feyenoord to reverse Sparta's once clear dominance in the town without let or hindrance.

Rotterdam's third club, first-division Excelsior, are stuck out east of the centre near Erasmus university.

The thrilling fields

Feyenoord

Stadion Feijenoord, Van Zandvlietplein 1
Capacity 51,000, (40,000 seated)
Colours Red-and-white halved shirts, black shorts
League champions 1924, 1928, 1936, 1938, 1940, 1961–62, 1965, 1969, 1971, 1974, 1984, 1993
Cup winners 1930, 1935, 1965, 1969, 1980, 1984, 1991–92, 1994–95
European Cup winners 1970
UEFA Cup winners 1974

As the advertising hoarding lifts up like some secret launchpad on Tracy Island, Feyenoord's players burst out onto the pitch to a rapturous welcome. Atmosphere is never a problem at de Kuip, but many of the loyal fans who generate it must be wondering why their beloved red-and-whites have been the poor relation of the Big Three for most of the past thirty years. Photos in the club museum show *Feije* fans partying in Lisbon before the 1963 European Cup semi-final with Benfica, and the townsfolk out on the streets after the club's European Cup win of 1970 – the first by any Dutch club in European competition. Yet for all their pioneering spirit, Feyenoord have had a tough time of it in the era of sponsorship, marketing and pay TV.

The club's inferiority complex was first fed in the Sixties. Feyenoord had honest left-winger Coen Moulijn; Ajax had Cruyff, the ultimate maverick trickster. Feyenoord coach Ernst Happel came up with a fluid form of *catenaccio* in 1970; Ajax's Rinus Michels adapted it, called it 'Total Football' and Ajax won the next three European Cups with it.

Only twice since then have Feyenoord fans enjoyed supreme moments of oneupmanship. The first was Wim van Hanegem's superb season in 1973/74, which culminated in a championship and a UEFA Cup triumph (marred by crowd disturbance) over Spurs. The second was Johan Cruyff's shock transfer from Ajax before the 1983/84 season – during which, at the age of 37, Cruyff played some of the best football of his life and won Feyenoord their last double.

The club's rise was a gradual one. Founded by a mining millionaire in 1908, the club played in the lower divisions while Sparta won five early titles, until promotion to the top drawer in 1921. It was at this point that Feyenoord had the advantage of Holland's greatest prewar soccer star, left-half Puck van Heel, who led them to a handful of league titles. This success persuaded president Leen van Zanvliet to build a stadium worthy of champions, with van Heel himself appearing in the ceremony to begin the construction of de Kuip.

After miraculously surviving World War II, de Kuip saw little success until the arrival of Coen Moulijn in 1954. A team was gradually built around him, and Feyenoord won three titles in five years, enjoying Holland's first European run in 1962/63.

It was Ernst Happel's team, later in the decade, that really earned the club its continental reputation. First, with Europe very much in mind, the club's name was changed from Feijenoord to Feyenoord to ease foreigners' pronunciation. Happel then brought in Swedish goalscorer Ove Kindvall, sweeper Rinus Israel and a young van Hanegem. Fans who queued all night for tickets for the team's second-round European Cup clash with holders AC Milan in 1969 were rewarded with a 2–0 win, and an easy passage to the final against Celtic. There, Israel and Kindvall were the goalscorers in an extra-time victory that few outside Rotterdam had expected.

Suddenly, Feyenoord were up there with the Madrids, Milans and Manchesters. Then, just as suddenly, they fell – stumbling out of the following year's competition, on away goals, to UT Arad of Romania.

The enemy within – Cruyff at Feyenoord, 1984

Van Hanegem's triumph, Cruyff's year of magic and the arrival of a young Ruud Gullit from Haarlem have all given the fans something to cheer about. Feyenoord have become known as cup specialists in Holland, and 50,000 fans crammed into de Kuip to watch a live transmission of the game at Groningen that won the title in 1993. Yet the club have manifestly failed to build on their European success.

With Arie Haan in charge and Ronald Koeman in command on the pitch, 1996/97 saw a revival in Feyenoord's fortunes, though the title continued to elude them. A dose or two of European glory before the millennium is out looks well within the club's capabilities – and would be no more than their fans and the improved de Kuip deserve.

Here we go!

On matchdays a **special train service**, the *Voetbaltrein*, runs every twenty minutes from Centraal station to Stadion, opposite the ground – about a ten-minute journey. There are strict controls at the gate, so be sure to stamp your *Strippenkaart* on the

A Nineties hero – Gaston Taument, Benfica-bound

The **Brasserie de Cuyperij**, on the first floor of the Maas building, has a fine collection of mounted pages from sports papers. On matchdays it's open by reservation only, so try during the week.

Tickets
The main **ticket office** is at the corner of the *Stadiontribune* (immediately facing you from the station) and the *Maastribune*. The four stands are colour-coded: yellow for the *Stadiontribune*, home of the Feyenoord boys in sector S and around; orange for the *Maastribune*, with the press and VIP rooms (sectors K, M and V are *genummerde plaatsen*, pricy numbered seats, while sector W is *ongenummerde*, the cheapest in the house); green for the *Marathontribune* behind the goal, with visiting fans in sector GG; and blue for the *Olimpiatribune*, where sector Z is the cheapest.

Publications
Feyenoord Sport Nieuws (f2) is on sale outside the *Stadiontribune*. Also available is *De Krant van Feyenoord* (weekly, f3.25), the club's official newspaper.

third bar. If you miss the train, **bus #49** also runs from outside Centraal to Olympiaweg. Allow 15–20 minutes.

Swift half
Three bars just across the river have the atmosphere of old Feijenoord. One, on the corner of Roetgenstraat and Oranjeboomstraat by the first #49 bus stop over the bridge from town. is actually *called* **Café Oud Feijenoord**. The **Café Schuyer** is on the corner of Slaghekstraat and Beijerlandse. The best of the lot is the **nameless corner bar** nearby, where Laantjesweg and Beijerlandse meet – players' photos line the counter and a parrot in club colours squawks his opinion.

Club shop
Despite 1994's major stadium renovation, the **Feyenoord Fanshop** is little more than a hut by the main entrance, open during training sessions and on matchdays only, no credit cards.

Club museum
De Kuip's **Home of History** (open Wed–Thur 1–5pm, Sat 9am–5pm) is small but entertaining, with a twenty-minute video in the projection room, blown-up front pages from *Het Vrije Volk* newspaper of May 1970, and the ball used for the 'Do I Not Like Orange' Holland-England World Cup qualifying match of 1993. Admission is f5, or f12.50 when combined with a 75-

minute stadium tour (Wed–Thurs 1pm & 3pm; Sat 10am, noon & 2pm).

Ultra culture

The recent, vicious off-the-field wars with Ajax hooligans have soured the memory of the fans who followed Feyenoord peacefully across Holland and Europe in the Seventies and Eighties. The club's support has traditionally been passionate and lighthearted, gathered at either end in sectors S and G. The Feyenoord roar was the first of its kind in Holland, and these days the stadium atmosphere is generated by footstamping and daft songs – largely unthreatening unless Ajax are in town.

Alas, hooliganism is nothing new at de Kuip. The violent scenes which marred Feyenoord's 1974 UEFA Cup final win over Spurs acted as a grim catalyst, the antics of the visitors later being copied by the sector S hardcore, who organised increasingly violent away trips.

In the net

There's no official Feyenoord site, but plenty of unofficial fan-run homepages to choose from. One of the best-established of these is the *Voodoo* site, recently moved to: www.voodoo.demon.nl/index.html. The text is in Dutch only but this is such a well-arranged site that the language barrier is seldom a problem.

Groundhopping

● Sparta Rotterdam

Het Kasteel, Spartastraat 7
Capacity 12,000 (8000 seated)
Colours Red-and-white striped shirts, black shorts
League champions 1909, 1911–13, 1915, 1959
Cup winners 1958, 1962, 1966

Sparta are keepers of a crumbling castle whose base support of old locals who shuffled out of their doors up to the ground has long gone. Now Holland's oldest stadium, het Kasteel ('The Castle'), with its twin towers, would not look out of place as a ghost house in a *Scooby Doo* cartoon.

The Spangen area in which it stands is now home to Surinamese and Antillean families, blissfully unaware of the spooky old football stadium lurking at the end of the road.

Sparta are the fifth most titled club in Dutch history but the last of these honours was won thirty years ago, during a brief period of success – itself forty years after the last one – that saw a handful of European appearances. The most recent of the latter, in 1985, featured a win on penalties over Hamburg SV.

Rotterdam essentials

Bus #33 runs from Rotterdam's small **airport** into town, but since flights are much cheaper to Amsterdam, many visitors arrive via **Schipol**, which is connected to **Rotterdam Centraal station** by an hourly train service (journey time two hours). Centraal is a short walk from Rotterdam's imposing modern centre.

City transport consists of buses, trams and metro, run on the universal *Strippenkaart* system – two bars will take you to anywhere central. There is an extensive night bus network, though some services only run at weekends; tickets are f5 and all routes call at either Centraal station or Zuidplein. To book a **taxi**, simply phone ☎010/462 6060.

The *VVV* **tourist office** (open Mon–Sat 9am–7pm, Fri until 9pm, Sun 10am–5pm) is a ten-minute walk from Centraal station at Coolsingel 67.

For **listings information**, the monthlies *M Magazijn* and *Muziek in Beweging* offer tips on high- and low-brow culture – both are free from the VVV office. For techno and dance events, check out the flyers at the *Virgin Megastore* on Beursplein.

Since then Sparta have had to knock down parts of their grand old pile and man the drawbridge whenever one of the Big Three visit.

Spangen is west of Centraal station. **Buses #38** and **#45**, and **trams #7** and **#17** all run between the two, or catch the metro to **Marconiplein** and take **tram #6** from there.

At Hooftplein 17, where the trams stop, is the **Café Biljart**, with a huge football mural. Nearer the stadium are **het Doelpunt** on Spartastraat and the **Sparta cafeteria** on the corner of Coornherstraat and Spartastraat. Inside the ground, you'll find a bar by the main entrance.

King of the castle – Alfons Groenendijk

⚜ Excelsior

Woudestein stadium, Honingerdijk 110
Capacity 8000 (1000 seated)
Colours Red-and-black striped shirts, red shorts

Excelsior are an impoverished but friendly operation just the other side of the Maas river from Feyenoord, who unsuccessfully took on their neighbours in the 1930 Dutch cup final. Recently they have been trying to avoid sinking as low as professionally possible in the two-tier Dutch league, in which they are the only club to draw average crowds of less than 1000.

Despite this, the team have often featured in the promotion play-offs, even spending the odd season in the premier. Plans are afoot for a ground-sharing scheme with Sparta somewhere in Rotterdam's suburbs. Until they come to fruition, you can take **tram #3** or **#13** from Centraal station eastwards to Woudestein, three stops before the terminus.

The **club bar** is in one corner of the main stand, with a pool table and a window overlooking the pitch.

Eat, drink, sleep…

Bars and clubs

Without the tourists (or the coffee shops), there is a sharper, more determined pace to nightlife in Rotterdam than in Amsterdam. Early evening, the harbour area between Blaak and Willems bridge, Oudehaven, is ideal for a quiet *pils*. By night, the streets Nieuwe Binnenweg and Witte de Withstraat, either side of Eendrachtsplein metro stop, are packed with bars.

Café t'Haantje, Bierens de Haanweg 12. If you want an afternoon in the heart of Feijenoord, this football bar is the one for you. Ernst Happel spent many a card session here with his players in the Seventies. Full menu. Bus #47 or #48 from Zuidplein metro to Spinozaweg.

Dodorama, Rochussenstraat 169. If a Slovenian punk band or avant-garde jazz artist is passing through Rotterdam, this is where they'll be appearing. Admission fl0–15. Metro to Dijkzigt.

Matrix, Mauritsstraat 16. The venue for world music, with African or Brazilian acts. Admission fl0. Ten minutes' walk from Centraal station.

Nighttown, West-Kruiskade 28. Varied disco and concert venue. For DJ nights, expect a fl5–25 door charge. The **Café Popular** next door has jazz and underground music concerts. Five minutes' walk from Centraal station.

Rotown, Nieuwe Binnenweg 19. Multi-purpose restaurant and live music venue in an old Rotterdam townhouse, surrounded by late-night bars. Open until 2am, 3am weekends. Lunchtime specials at fl5. Concerts at 10pm. Tram #4 from Centraal station.

Restaurants

As well as the usual mix of Chinese, Indonesian and Surinamese restaurants, **cosmopolitan Rotterdam** has a decent amount of other options. Cheap lunchtime sitdowns can be found around the Lijnbaan shopping centre, with *dagschotels* around fl3. Unless otherwise stated, the places below take most major credit cards.

de Consul, Westersingel 28. Popular café and restaurant with a film theme and *dagschotels* at fl6.50, to be taken on the large summer terrace overlooking Westersingel. Ten-minute walk from Centraal station.

de Mosselman, Mariniersweg 74a. Reasonably priced, family-run fish restaurant with décor to match – the walls are covered in fishermen's artefacts. Metro to Blaak.

Midnight, 1e Middellandstraat 57b. Late-night, early-morning diner within walking distance of the city's main bar areas, open until 4am Sun–Thurs, 6am Fri–Sat. Tram #1, #7 or #9 from Centraal station. No credit cards.

Restaurant Engels, Stationsplein 45. Bizarre multi-restaurant setup opposite Centraal station, with Tokaj (Hungarian), Beefeater (English), Don Quijote (Spanish) and Engels Brasserie all in one place. Pricey but convenient.

Schieland, Schiekade 770. Mainstream sports café with a giant TV screen and a large, if rather unadventurous, menu. Tram #3 or #5 from Centraal station.

Accommodation

The *VVV* office offers a room-booking service for hotels but not for pensions. If you're stuck, the area a kilometre or so southwest of Centraal station has a number of reasonably priced options close together.

Astoria, Pleinweg 203–205 (☎010/485 6634, fax 010/485 4602). One-star, no-nonsense but friendly joint the other side of the river near the Maastunnel. Late bar, TV room with a massive screen and a former Miss World serving breakfast. What more do you want? Singles f45, doubles f90. Tram #2 from Maashaven metro.

Hotel Bienvenue, Spoorsingel 24 (☎010/466 9394, fax 010/467 7475). Excellent value, small, friendly hotel a short walk north of Centraal station. Ten rooms, all with a telly. Singles at f65 without bath/shower, f70 with.

Hotel Wilgenhof, Heemradsingel 92–94 (☎010/476 2525, fax 010/477 3611). Medium-sized, comfortable three-star hotel with eighty rooms, each with a television. Restaurant downstairs. Singles at f75 without bath/shower, f105 with. Tram #4 from Centraal station.

NJHC City Hostel, Rochunsstraat 107–109 (☎010/436 5763, fax 010/436 5569). Rotterdam's only youth hostel is an inconvient 3km from the centre of town. Eight-bed dorms, kitchen facilities, 2am curfew, lockout 10am–3pm. IYHF members f30, non-members f35, both including breakfast. Metro to Dijkzigt, then bus #39 for a couple of stops. No credit cards.

Eindhoven

PSV 276
EVV 279

Eindhoven is a peculiar town. It is home to Holland's third most successful football team and the huge Philips industrial and research plant that finances it – and little else. Nearly one in five people are employed by the electrical conglomerate and many of these are regulars at the football club.

PSV are the richest team in the land and have a stadium to match. Until the renovation of de Kuip in 1994 and the construction of the Amsterdam Arena, the Philips Stadion was the best in Holland. It still is a very comfortable place in which to see a football match, with superb facilities for the business crowd and rooftop gas heaters warming everyone else down below. Walking around the stadium – the ground level is dominated by a huge *Toys R Us* store – reveals four floors of business lounges and sponsors' restaurants.

For Philips, this expense is an investment – the chance to send the company name around the globe. In any case, PSV is a profit centre in its own right, the club's management having made a serious surplus from the sale of Ruud Gullit, Ronald Koeman, Gica Popescu, Romário and Ronaldo. (Gullit in particular was not happy with having to pose for all kinds of company commercials.)

The club's enormous financial clout also means that the team are the most unpopular in Holland. Ajax and Feyenoord may hate each other, but everyone hates PSV. For this reason, many of the club's younger fans have a chip on their shoulder, and the atmosphere surrounding a big game at PSV can be at best boisterous, at worst downright menacing.

The stadium is a short walk from the train station, so many visits are of the flying variety. Diehard groundhoppers have to cross town to get to the other professional football club, EVV Eindhoven, in the residential southern edge of town.

The thrilling fields

 PSV

Philips stadion, Mathildelaan 81
Capacity 30,000 (28,000 seated)
Colours Red-and-white striped shirts, black shorts
League champions 1929, 1935, 1951, 1963, 1975–76, 1978, 1986–89, 1991–92, 1997
Cup winners 1950, 1974, 1976, 1988–90, 1996
European Cup winners 1988
UEFA Cup winners 1978

Philips Sport Verenigeng were formed in 1913 after a sports event organised by the company to celebrate Holland's independence. They joined the Dutch league a year later and the first division in 1921. Although the club have been relegated just once, in 1925, Philips didn't see any return on their investment until PSV broke the Ajax-Feyenoord monopoly in the mid-Seventies.

Keeping players away from the bright lights of Amsterdam or Rotterdam proved difficult until coach Kees Rijvers came to the club and built a successful team from 1972/73. With Jan van Beveren saving goals and left-winger Willy van der Kuylen scoring them, PSV bided their time until the break-up of Cruyff's Ajax.

A 6–0 cup final romp over NAC Breda in 1974 led to a run in Europe the following year, PSV losing a semi-final to eventual winners Dynamo Kiev. Domestically, with the van de Kerkhof brothers, Willy and René, bought from Twente Enschede, PSV made no such mistake in the league, beating Feyenoord by two points. They won it again, by a one-point margin, in 1976.

The club were twice knocked out of the European Cup by Rijvers' old team Saint-Étienne, but went on to win the UEFA Cup in 1978, overcoming Barcelona

Ronaldo's run – but PSV didn't win the title until after he'd gone

in the semi-final, and Bastia in the final.

A league title that year proved to be the last until the arrival of Ruud Gullit in the mid-Eighties. Gullit ushered in a new and golden era, one of six league titles in seven seasons, a European Cup, and a team of highly paid superstars at odds with each other. Running the show was Hans Kraay, a controversial coach who applied the simple principle that the club should sign players directly from their title rivals, Ajax and Feyenooord, so that the stars would not be playing against them.

After Gullit's and Kraay's departure in 1987, Guus Hiddink took charge of the tam and Wim Kieft was left to score the goals, equalling the club record of 28 in 1987/88. With Hans van Breukelen in goal and Ronald Koeman and Soren Lerby providing passes for Kieft and Gerald Vanenberg, PSV crept through Europe. Almost before anyone knew it, they had reached the 1988 European Cup final against Benfica, which they duly won on

penalties. Outside Eindhoven, theirs was not a popular win – they'd averaged only a goal a game through the tournament and hadn't actually won a match beyond the second round.

At the end of the decade, Romário arrived to bring flair and more than 100 goals in five seasons. Hiddink left the whole circus to Bobby Robson in 1990, but though the former England manager won the title for PSV two years running, the team's failure in the potentially lucrative new European era frustrated club management. With Romário gone to Barcelona and Robson to Portugal, PSV gazumped all-comers to capture the nineteen-year-old Ronaldo for $6 million in 1994. Yet even his goals could not bring the title back to Eindhoven in a 1994/95 season which saw three managerial changes. It took coach Dick Advocaat to steady the ship, steering Ronaldo, Wim Jonk, Phillip Cocu, Jan Wouters and top scorer Luc Nilis to a cup win in 1996, then riding the upset of the

Eindhoven essentials

Eindhoven has a small **airport** 6km west of the centre. Bus #8 runs to and from the train station (journey time thirty minutes), and there is a regular train service to and from Amsterdam, journey time ninety minutes.

Eindhoven is part of the *treintaxi* scheme, whereby rail travellers who have paid an extra f6.50 can take a taxi anywhere in town when they get to their destination. Otherwise the station is five minutes' walk from the centre of town, much of which is pedestrianised. A network of **city buses** runs 7am–11pm, with fares operating on the *Strippenkaart* system. The main routes run after midnight Fri–Sat. To call a **taxi**, phone ☎040/252 525.

Eindhoven's *VVV* **tourist ffice** (open Mon–Sat 9am–5.30pm, Sun 10am–5pm) is right outside the train station. Here you'll find two free Dutch-language **listings** publications, *Eindhoven Info* and the more comprehensive *Uit in Eindhoven*. The local daily, *Eindhovens Dagblat*, also has entertainment information and a good sports supplement on Saturdays.

Brazilian's departure and capturing the title, for the first time since Robson, in 1997.

Today, in addition to Advocaat's quietly persuasive leadership, the positive signs are that young players are breaking through from PSV's training camp, De Herdgang. With f60 million of improvements planned for the Philips Stadion to prepare for Euro 2000, perhaps the time has come for success to be nurtured, rather than purchased.

Here we go!
Either a ten-minute walk as you turn right out of the **station** down Mathildelaan, or take bus **#12, #13** or **#14**.

Swift half
The younger element head for **D'N Berk**, on the corner of Gagelstraat and Mathildalaan, a minute's walk from the stadium. There'll be a couple of bouncers on the door, loud music from the resident DJ and a crowd three deep at the bar.

The **Supporters Home**, up a flight of stairs decorated with PSV murals at gate #11 of the ground, is a better bet. A large bar area has two counters and there's sport on TV, Grolsch beer and pictures of Ronaldo.

Tickets
The PSV **ticket office**, *Hoofdkassa*, by gate #25 is open Mon–Sat 10am–5.30pm and

two hours before a match. You'll need to have a *Club Card*, and expect bigger games to be already sold out. The stadium is sectioned into north, south, east and west stands. The east (*Oost*) end, alongside Stadionplein, gates #12–#21, is with the PSV boys behind one goal. Away fans are herded into *Noord*, along Mathildelaan. The class seats are in the *Hoofdtribune*, through gate #8, in *Zuid* along Frederiklaan.

Publications
Programmes (f2.50) are produced each matchday and there are sellers by the main entrance and gates #11 and #12. The club magazine, *PSV Inside* (monthly, f4.95) is also available at newsstands in town. The fans' magazine is *PSV Supporter* (monthly, f2.50)

Club shop
The **PSV Souvenirshop** by gate #12 is open Mon–Fri 9am–5pm, Sat 10am–noon, two hours before kick-off and an hour afterwards. Perhaps significantly, it sells scarves of other clubs as well as PSV.

Ultra culture
PSV's young *Oost Side* fans are notoriously brash and away support is carefully manoeuvred in from the train station. Security equipment is, naturally, ultra-modern and troublemakers are quickly singled out and dealt with in a special rehabilitation

scheme run by the club. The average PSV fan is otherwise pretty happy with his lot, the company organising a variety of social events through the year. While some 20–25,000 season tickets are sold every year for the Philips Stadion, PSV's travelling support is pretty sparse.

In the net

There's no official PSV website but the *PSV Supporters' Homepage* makes up for it with a good history, a stats archive, nice graphics to download, plenty of English content and online classified advertising. Go to: www.dic.nl/psv/.

Groundhopping

EVV Eindhoven

Jan Louwers Stadion, Charles Roelslaan 1
Capacity 5000 (2000 seated)
Colours Blue-and-white striped shirts, black shorts
League champions 1954
Cup winners 1937

The huge floodlights and superstars at PSV leave little EVV Eindhoven in the shade. Nevertheless, for a mid-table *Eerste Divisie* club pulling crowds of around 2000, EVV's Jan Louwers stadion is well-equipped. All it needs is a team like the one which won their solitary title in 1954, two places ahead of PSV. The team lost the promotion play-offs on goals scored in 1992 but little has been seen of Eindhoven since then.

If you've picked the wrong weekend to be in town, take **bus #171** or **#172** from the train station to Florialaan, or **bus #7** to Alterweg. Either way, allow twenty minutes.

There isn't much around the ground apart from a sports centre and a golf course, so head straight for the **club bar**, *EVV Corner*, under the main stand along Charles Roelslaan, for a pint, team pictures and a friendly atmosphere.

Eat, drink, sleep...

Bars and clubs

Eindhoven's affluence is reflected in the number of **fashionable bars** to have opened in the last couple of years. All are concentrated in the centre, in the streets of Kleine Berg and especially Stratumseind. There are six in a row in one stretch of the latter, of which the *George Taverne* (#43) is the least pretentious. The Big Ben rock club and Trance dance club are opposite. The rest of central Eindhoven features an inordinate number of **biker bars**, probably best avoided.

As for **clubbing**, you have to wonder what poor Romário and Ronaldo did during their spare time here, except lie back and think of Brazil...

Young PSV – Boudewijn Zenden

Baloo's Blues, Kleine Berg 60. One of the few rockers' bars with a bit of spirit to it. Pool table, loud music and Baloo the Bear memorabilia. Short walk from the station.

de Dans Salon, Stationsplein 4. The town's main disco, across from the station, open Thur–Sun. Free entry before 11pm, f5–10 thereafter.

Effenaar, Dommelstraat 2. Left-field culture centre which puts on anything from Desmond Dekker to Test Department. Live music f10–20 admission, DJ nights f5. Just across from the train station.

Muziekcentrum Frits Philips, Heuvel Galerie 140 (corner Hoek Markt and Jan van Lieshoutstraat). The main live venue in town, sponsored by you-know-who, but with a regular selection of jazz and world music acts on the agenda. Most concerts around f30 admission, credit cards accepted. Short walk from the station.

Trafalgar, Dommelstraat 21. Just across from the train station, an English-style pub with a friendly atmosphere, half-decent music and a restaurant section. Guinness on draught.

Restaurants

Eateries are also concentrated down a couple of streets of **central Eindhoven**, especially Kleine Berg. There aren't many takeaway options – try the two late-night Turkish places at #12 (*Sormans*) and #36 (*Aladin*), both open until 3am. All places listed are a short walk from the station.

Ajdanski, Stratumseind 81. Russian and Balkan specialities in this sizeable restaurant at the end of Stratumseind, run by ex-player Petar Ajdanski. Mastercard and Amex accepted.

Charlie's Pub, Dommelstraat 36. Small *eetcafé* where a main course will set you back no more than f20–30. Terrace in summer. Closed Mon–Tues. No credit cards.

Gandhi, Willemstraat 43a. The main Indian restaurant in town, behind the Philips complex, open 5–11pm daily. A decent spread will cost around f50. Most credit cards.

Grand Café Berlage, Kleine Berg 16. Most popular diner in town, with a summer terrace and two side bars. Free live jazz in the evenings. For the price – f20–30 a main course – and the tasteful surroundings, very good value. Open daily noon–11pm.

Pizzeria Romagna, Stratumseind 78. Reasonably priced Italian restaurant at the far end of Stratumseind opposite the hairies at the **Thunder Roadhouse Bikers' Bar**. Most credit cards.

Accommodation

There are precious few cheap centrally located **hotels** in town, but the *VVV* can book you a room on the spot – pay them for your first night, plus f5 commission.

de Bengel, Wilhelmsplein 9 (☎040/244 0752). Modest but pleasant hotel behind the Philips complex and near the PSV stadium. Singles at f75, doubles f125. Most credit cards.

Corso, Vestdijk 17 (☎040/244 9131). One-star hotel along the main drag that runs from the station through town. Singles, doubles or triples at f55, f90 and f125 respectively. Most credit cards.

Oud Eindhoven, Stratumseind 63 (☎040/244 4559). Perfectly located if you're living it up for the weekend, annoyingly noisy if not. One-star hotel slap bang in the area of bars and clubs. Singles at f70, doubles f100. Most credit cards.

Mascotte, Tramstraat 5b (☎040/246 0056). Small pension near the station offering bed and breakfast at f45 per person. No credit cards.

de Zwaan, Wilhelmsplein 4 (☎040/244 8992). Family-run pension which offers B&B at f40 per person. Near the PSV stadium. No credit cards.

Hungary

The decline of Hungarian football is one of the great mysteries of the European game. A nation that produced one of the greatest teams in history, that presented the world with talents such as Ferenc Puskás and Flórián Albert, has for the last decade been unable to qualify for the final stages of any major international tournament. No Hungarian club side has reached the final of any European competition since Videoton lost the UEFA Cup to Real Madrid in 1985.

Hungarian football enjoyed its heyday in the Fifties, but the game had arrived in the country early. The three main Budapest teams, MTK, Ferencváros and Újpest, were formed soon before the national football association and the league in 1901. A year later Hungary took part in the first full international in continental Europe, against Austria – a fixture which was to become an annual tradition. Budapest, Vienna and later Prague became a new, Central European sphere of influence in the development of the international game.

Public interest in early matches was low, however, and the style of play in Hungary lacked tactical subtlety. Lancastrian Jimmy Hogan was the man who changed all that. A former player with Bolton Wanderers, Hogan arrived in Budapest from an internment camp in Vienna at the end of World War I to coach MTK, bringing with him the short passing game from English league football. Thanks to Hogan's revolutionary methods – soon to become known as the Danubian style – MTK won seven consecutive league titles between 1919 and 1925. Interest in the game had risen to such a level that in 1926 Hungary launched

How's the diet? Charlton meets Puskás, Kispest, 1993

a fully professional league. The foundations were laid for an excellent national team which showed their progress by reaching the World Cup Final in 1938, where they were unlucky to lose 4–2 to hosts Italy.

After World War II, Hungarian sport, and football in particular, benefited from unprecedented state backing. Additionally, an extraordinary crop of talented players emerged such as Ferenc Puskás, József Bozsik and Sándor Kocsis, clubmates in the newly formed army side Honvéd. That trio was to become the backbone of a free-scoring national team which would remain unbeaten for four years.

Having arrived at Wembley on a foggy November afternoon in 1953 for a friendly against England, the Magic Magyars gave the old masters a lesson in football. Hogan,

Hope springs eternal – Ferencváros take on Real Madrid in the 1995 Champions' League

having returned to England to take charge of Fulham, was in the stands to witness the fruits of his labour.

The final scoreline of 6–3 barely did Hungary's dominance justice. Faced with opponents to whom perfect close control and precise passing seemed to come naturally, England above all just couldn't fathom how to deal with the visitors' deep-lying centre-forward Nándor Hidegkuti who, unmarked for much of the game, helped himself to a hat-trick.

The bitterness came the following year, only a month after Hungary had repeated the dose in Budapest, destroying England 7–1. Hot favourites to win the 1954 World Cup in Switzerland, but with Puskás playing through an injury in muddy conditions, the Magyars suffered a shock 3–2 defeat to West Germany in the final. Long after the names of the victorious Germans were forgotten, however, the Hungarians would be remembered as a prime example of top-level football at its best. As Tom Finney put it: "The 1954 Hungarian soccer masters did not go into the record books as the champions of the world. But they went into my personal memory file, and that of millions of other football lovers, as the finest team ever to sort out successfully the intricacies of this wonderful game."

Within two years, the magic had gone. The 1956 Hungarian uprising and subsequent invasion of the country by Soviet troops prompted several players, including Puskás and Kocsis, to flee to the West. Worse, most of Hungary's youth team, on tour at the time of the invasion, decided not to return to their homeland. Two generations of soccer talent were lost – and the Hungarians have never fully recovered from this decimation of their ranks.

After the Soviet crackdown, large crowds were still drawn to the big club games. Újpesti Dózsa and Ferencváros had occasional runs in Europe, the latter lifting the Fairs' Cup in 1965. Hungary maintained a respectable presence in international football, winning Olympic titles to add to the gold Puskás and company had won in 1952. At the 1966 World Cup, they reminded the English football public of their quality with a fine 3–1 win over Brazil at Goodison Park, with Flórián Albert an enduring star performer.

Yet by the early Eighties it was becoming clear something was going badly wrong. A series of match-fixing scandals reduced public confidence in the game, and a humiliating 6–0 defeat by the Soviet Union at the 1986 World Cup was the final straw for many fans. Since then, it has been a story of embarrassing failure.

Today the Soviets are long gone but the free-market economics that have replaced them have whisked the best footballing talent abroad at an early age. The legacy of Communism is a bloated league structure, badly managed clubs and a national association incapable of taking the necessary steps to revive the game.

Despite the faded glory and Pelé's assertion that Hungary has "fallen out of love with football", for all the humiliations and the frustrations, the average Magyar fan still loves his game. He may hang his head every November 25 (the anniversary of the 6–3 Wembley win), but he follows international football assiduously. And, at the slightest sniff of victory or hint of a return to the big time, such as Ferencváros' qualification for the Champions' League in 1995/96, the crowds come out in force and hope revives.

Basics

Citizens of the EU, America and Canada require only their **passport** to enter Hungary, and while Australians and New Zealanders need a **visa**, this can be obtained at customs when you arrive.

The Hungarian currency is the **forint** (Ft or HUF), currently Ft280 to £1, divided into 100 fillérs. Forints come in notes of Ft100, Ft500, Ft1000 and Ft5000. There are also Ft1, Ft2, Ft5, Ft10, Ft 20, Ft50, two kinds of Ft100 and Ft200 coins. Fillérs are of so little value that no-one pays any attention to them. Credit-card cash machines are becoming increasingly common – you'll find them outside main banks, supermarkets and shopping centres.

You can also draw money on Visa cards from IBUSZ tourist offices in most major towns, and in Budapest at the American Express office at V Deák Ferenc utca 10 (open Mon–Fri 9am–5pm, Sat 9am–2pm).

Some **telephone boxes** take Ft10 and Ft20 coins but the majority take phone cards, available at newsagents and post offices. They cost Ft500 for 50 units and Ft1100 for 100. The international code for Hungary is 36, the city code for Budapest 1. From Hungary, there is no cheap time for international calls – dial 00, followed by the international code.

For national calls out of Budapest, dial 06, then the area code. To call Budapest from elsewhere in the country, dial 061 followed by the customer number.

Intercity train and bus services are generally cheap, clean and punctual. Main-line **trains** leave from the three central Budapest stations of Nyugati, Keleti and Déli, all of which have metro stations. Fast trains are labelled *gyorsvonat* on timetables; *személyvonat* are stopping services which should be avoided at all costs. Reservations are obligatory on some express and international trains.

International **buses** run by the Volán company leave from Erzsébet tér, while the domestic bus service runs out of Volán's Árpád híd station.

Buses can be quicker than trains between major towns, but could be considerably less comfortable if you don't get your ticket in advance – they can be purchased up to half an hour before departure. Turn up at the last minute and you risk there being standing room only.

Essential vocabulary

Hello/goodbye *Szia*
Yes *Igen*
No *Nem*
Please *Kérem*
Thank you *Köszönöm*
Two beers, please *Két korsó sört kérek*
Men's *Férfi*
Women's *Női*
Where is the stadium? *Hol van a stadion?*
What's the score? *Mennyi az állás?*
Referee *Biró*
Offside *Les*

Match practice

For those used to all-ticket matches, all-seater stadia and expensive, alcohol-free football, Hungary is a refreshing taste of how things used to be. For Sixties prices you can stand on the terraces, drink and swear to your heart's content, with little worry of heavy-handed police stopping the fun. Hooliganism, although occasionally aspired to, rarely rears its head. Neither does quality football.

With a three-month winter break, the Hungarian campaign is split into autumn (early August to late November) and spring (early March to the end of June) seasons. In the shorter summer break you'll find Inter-toto Cup games, pre-season friendlies and preliminary-round cup matches.

TV schedules have started to spread the league programme from traditional Saturday afternoons right across the weekend. There is every chance of a game on both Saturday and Sunday in the capital. In the spring season, games kick-off in the evening – usually 5pm. In winter they start earlier, often at 2pm or 3pm. The practice of staggering matches to allow fans to see two or even three games on a Saturday has declined in the past few years. Kick-off times can change at short notice, so buy Friday's or Saturday's *Nemzeti Sport* newspaper for the latest lowdown.

The league

No other European country has so many teams from its capital city in the footballing top drawer – almost half the clubs in Hungary's *NB1* come from Budapest. In the summer of 1996, the Hungarian football federation increased the size of the *NB1* to eighteen teams in order to include more representation from the provinces.

The second division (*NB2*) is split into Eastern and Western sections which comprise almost exclusively provincial teams, either full-time professional or semi-pro. The third and fourth divisions are regionalised and include both semi-professional and amateur clubs.

The bottom two teams from *NB1* are automatically relegated at the end of each season, to be replaced by the champions of the two second divisions. The runners-up from *NB2* East and West play off over two legs with the 15th- and 16th-placed first-division clubs. Hungary's champions qualify for the preliminary round of the Champions' League; the runners-up and third-placed side take UEFA Cup spots. *NB1* is sponsored by the German machine tools company Kärcher.

Up for the cup

The *Magyar Kupa*, sponsored by Samsung, is a drawn-out non-event. It starts in the summer break with qualification at county level. *NB1* and *NB2* clubs join in mid-July to make up sixteen groups of four teams, seeded to ensure one *NB1*, one *NB2* and two lower-division clubs in each.

Teams play each other once, generally on Sundays and Wednesdays, the top two qualifying for the knockout stage. The rest of the competition consists of straightforward two-legged games, with low crowds and low interest until the semi-finals. The final itself is in June, decided over two legs and played midweek.

Tickets

For all matches, buy your tickets (*belepő*) from the ticket office (*pénztár*) – usually a small hole in the wall by the main entrance. There's little worry of a sellout, even with prices down in the Ft200–350 range. For costlier (but still affordable) internationals and the Ferencváros–Újpest derby, buy your ticket in advance. For a seat (usually a bench) ask for an *üllőhely*; a standing ticket is *állóhely*. The word *tribün* on a sign or ticket generally refers to the main stand. There are few match programmes or fanzines, so for that promised souvenir to the trainspotter back home, look out for a *műsor* – a colour fixture programme with team photo and pen-pictures.

Half-time

With the exception of Ferencváros and MTK, you can buy beer at all grounds in Budapest and at most provincial clubs. In November you can warm up with mulled wine (*forralt bor*). On the way to the ground you will be met by scores of people selling toasted sunflower seeds (*szotyi*), or orange-coloured pumpkin seeds (*tökmag*) – Hungarian football is played to the sound

Kispest-Honvéd meet ÚTE – one of many Budapest derbies

of crackling shells, which carpet the terraces once their contents have been consumed. Food at stadium snackbars is generally restricted to salami sandwiches and savoury scones (*pogácsa*). Ferencváros do sausages (*virsli*), while the spicy cold meatball sandwich behind the main stand at Újpesti TE is the nearest thing you'll find to a hamburger.

Ultra culture

If you wear a British team's shirt or scarf, expect social intercourse. At best you may get a half-decent offer for your gear; at worst, some strange kid will come up to you and tell you in broken English that he is a lifelong Norwich City fan.

Expect to see plenty of banners hung over the fences – these will announce the presence of terrifying-sounding hooligan and ultra groups with names like 'Green Monsters' and 'Viola Kaos'. In many cases the groups consist of nothing more fearsome than a bunch of schoolkids, complete with satchels and sandwiches.

Serious ultra culture has caught on at some clubs, however – Újpest and Debrecen in particular pride themselves on their smokebombs and banners. Sadly, another foreign import, terrace racism, is also on the rise, with African players and gypsies the targets of boo-boys and skinheads. The problem is widespread but particularly prominent at Ferencváros.

Unfortunately, and despite the fact that Hungary is not exactly a huge country, with the honourable exceptions of Debrecen and Békéscsaba few fans from the provinces follow their team to the capital. Unless your match is one of the many Budapest derbies, whatever atmosphere is created will be a little one-sided.

Action replay

In the post-Communist era there has been a fierce battle for the TV rights to both domestic and international games. State TV2 still has one domestic live game per week, usually on a Saturday evening, and the highlights package *Góóól* on Sunday

Fitful inspiration of the national side – Flórián Urbán

evenings. Their unimaginative coverage has none of the fancy camera angles common in the West, and commentator Jenő Knézy is an opinionated reporter whose preference for Ferencváros makes him far from popular with Újpest supporters.

Cable and satellite channel Duna TV has a more imaginative approach, modelling its presentation on that of Sky Sports, although it still has some way to go to

match Western production standards. Duna have a live Sunday afternoon game and are hoping to break state TV's domination of international games. They also have a lively Sunday morning sports magazine show, *Sportpercek*. The Budapest channel MSAT offers an hour-long highlights package of English Premiership action on Monday nights at 9pm, repeated on Tuesdays at 11pm.

The back page

The daily sports paper *Nemzeti Sport* (Ft48.50) is a national institution and deserves its status. It's the best daily sports paper in the former Eastern Bloc, with excellent international coverage. Sunday's edition has Premiership results and scorers, Scottish results, and round-ups from all the major European leagues. Monday's and Tuesday's editions cover the rest of Europe. The Friday and Saturday editions are crammed with line-ups and stats, obviating the need for a matchday programme. In general, domestic coverage has a heavy Ferencváros bias to encourage sales. Aspiring Stattoes will enjoy *Foci Világ* (Ft495), once a cheaply produced fortnightly, now a well-researched monthly book of stats on the Hungarian and international game. The weekly *Sport Plusz Foci* (Ft69.50) is for soccer gossip.

British papers can be bought from the main Budapest train stations and at shops on Váci utca, the city's tourist shopping zone. Bear in mind, though, that with the exception of the international edition of *The Guardian*, these will be the previous day's papers.

In the net

There is no generic Hungarian football website, but stats freaks can get up-to-date results and tables from *NB1* and *NB2* at: pernix.bke.hu/~snobil/nb1-2.htm. The site is carefully maintained by Tamás Karpati but can be difficult to access.

Budapest

Ferencváros 288 Kispest-Honvéd 289 MTK 291
ÚTE 292 BVSC 293 III Ker 294 Vasas 294

With so many top-flight clubs in the city, you almost can't help but see two matches on a weekend trip to Hungary's attractive and atmospheric capital. So long as you are careful to avoid the long winter break and don't harbour any illusions about discovering the new Puskás in the ranks of the local train drivers' club, a relaxed and refreshing football experience awaits you on Budapest's crumbling terraces.

Budapest essentials

Budapest's **Ferihegy airport** has two terminals. Terminal 1 is for British Airways, Terminal 2 for Hungarian Airlines (Malév).

An **LRI minibus** will take you to any address within the city limits for Ft1200. Alternatively, take bus #93 to Kőbányai-Kispest blue metro stop. A ticket dispenser is on the wall by the stop. The taxi company Főtaxi has a freephone (☎0680) and will take you into town for around Ft2000.

Budapest has a fast and efficient transport system. The **metro** is divided into three lines: red (1), blue (2) and yellow (3). There are also buses, trams and trolleybuses. A single ticket, valid for any mode of transport, costs Ft60, or Ft540 for a book of ten, from any station kiosk. Stamp your ticket at the punches entering the metro, or onboard buses and trams.

A **one-day pass** costs Ft400, a three-day one Ft1000. These tickets are valid on the city's extensive **night bus network**.

The cheapest **taxi** firms in town are Főtaxi, recognisable by their cars' rugby-ball shaped lights and checkered sides (☎061/222 2222), and City Taxi (☎061/211 1111).

Ageing but efficient – the city's preferred mode of transport

Budapest addresses are written with a **Roman numeral** indicating the district (*kerület*) number before the street name; thus 'IV Megyeri út 13' means '13 Megyeri út in the fourth district'. All street maps available in the city will have the districts marked on them.

The best place for **tourist information** is Tourinform, next to central Deák tér, at V Sütő utca 2 (open daily 8am–8pm, ☎061/117 9800).

To find out **what's on** in town, the rather dull, local American-language papers, *The Budapest Sun* and *Budapest Week*, have nightlife listings.

The thrilling fields

 Ferencváros

Üllői út stadium, IX Üllői út 129
Capacity 18,000 (all-seated)
Colours Green-and-white striped shirts, white shorts
League champions 1903, 1905, 1907, 1909–13, 1926–28, 1932, 1934, 1938, 1940–41, 1949, 1963–64, 1967–68, 1976, 1981, 1992, 1995–96
Cup winners 1913, 1922, 1927–28, 1933, 1935, 1942–44, 1956, 1972, 1974, 1976, 1991, 1993–95
Fairs' Cup winners 1965

Ferencvárosi Torna Club (FTC) are Hungary's biggest club. They are the most loved, the most hated, the most talked about. There are Ferencváros bars all over

town, and every other taxi driver's mirror has a green-and-white pennant hanging from it. Based in the suburb of Ferencváros in the city's ninth district, the club are known as *Fradi* – a shortened version of its German name, Franzstadt.

The most successful Hungarian team before World War II, under Communism *Fradi* became the unofficial team of the opposition. The anti-Communist pride of the fans was not surprising, since Stalinist dictator Mátyás Rákosi had personally forced the club to play under the name Budapest Kinizsi, after a medieval Magyar hero adopted by the new regime, and wear red – as punishment for the fact that they were the favoured team of the Nazi Arrow Cross, who ruled the country towards the end of the war. The working-class area where the stadium sits was at the centre of the 1956 uprising, and the following year the club won back their name and famous green-and-white shirts.

Due to their marginalised position in the Fifties, the club had few representatives in the Golden Team, although *Fradi* fans never tire of pointing out that a number of the Honvéd side of the period were stolen from them by the military. By the Sixties, though, the club were back at the top. Led by Flórián Albert, they won the Fairs' Cup in 1965, becoming the only Hungarian club to win a European trophy when they defeated Juventus in Turin. Three years later they finished runners-up to Leeds United in the same competition, and that December Albert was named European Footballer of the Year, the only Hungarian ever to win the award. In 1975, inspired by their latest star Tibor Nyilasi, later to become first-team coach, Ferencváros reached the final of the Cup-Winners' Cup, where they lost to Dynamo Kiev.

Since the fall of Communism, *Fradi* have successfully courted pri-

Set in stone – club founder Ferenc Springer keeps watch

vate capital. With easily the broadest fan base in Hungary, they have the financial clout to do what Honvéd did for free in the Fifties and pick up whatever talent they choose from the domestic game. Qualification for the Champions' League in 1995/96 re-inforced the club's position as top dogs in the new Hungary, enabling them to carry out enlargement of their modern, all-seater stadium, Üllői út. Boasting a genuine atmosphere when full, the ground also has a unique feature in the statue of former club president Ferenc Springer, strangely sited behind the goal in front of the players' tunnel.

Here we go!
Blue metro #2 to **Népliget**; take the FTC exit. Allow fifteen minutes from Deák tér.

Swift half
Before the match, many fans gather at the **Bacskai borozó**, IX Üllői út 121, by Nagyvárad tér metro station. It is sometimes closed for major games, however, in which case the **Paracelsus** restaurant at #119 also has a busy borozó and söröző. The **Fradi vendéglő** by the club shop is ideal for pre- and post-match dining. Next-door is a dirt-cheap, traditional Hungarian wine bar and, downstairs, a beer hall.

Publications
The Fradi Újság, published on matchdays, is surprisingly glossy at Ft50, and available from the club shop.

Club shop
The **Fradi Club Shop** (Üllői út stadium, open Mon–Fri 10am–5pm, Sat 9am–7pm, matchdays 9am until after the game, no credit cards) is hardly Bayern Munich's supermarket, but in Hungarian terms it's a treasure trove. There's tack galore, including Fradi cushions, vintage wine, beer, chocolate eggs and umbrellas.

Club museum
Club historian Béla Nagy runs a collection in the main club building which is on view

to the general public by prior appointment. Either turn up in person or phone him on the main club number: ☎061/215 6025.

Ultra culture
Ferencváros have the only serious **hooligan problem** in the country, the more hardline elements of their support having gained a reputation for chauvinism which has badly undermined the image of the club. FTC have received a series of warnings and **fines** from UEFA, but as yet there is little sign that those responsible have learnt their lesson. Avoid sections K and L, the home of the yobs – sections D, E and F of the ground are for away fans.

In the net
Ferencváros are the only Hungarian club to have a substantial presence on the Web, though there is still no officially sanctioned site. Emre Zsoldos hosts a homepage at: ogyalla.konkoly.hu/staff/zsoldos/fradi.html. It offers a rich stats database in English, plus a Hungarian-language archive of match reports. More ambitious, in both content and technology, is a newer Fradi site at: goliat.eik.bme.hu/~garaba/ftcframe.html. Beneath a layer of Javascript trickery and a multitude of useful links you'll find a full news archive, written in English from a fan's perspective, complete with terrace-eye match reports from all competitions.

Kispest-Honvéd

Bozsik stadion, XIX Újtemető utca 1–3
Capacity 15,000 (6000 seated)
Colours Red-and-black striped shirts, black shorts
League champions 1950, 1952, 1954–55, 1980, 1984–86, 1988–89, 1991, 1993
Cup winners 1926, 1964, 1985, 1989, 1996

The former village of Kispest is where Ferenc Puskás learned his football. But the stadium is named after another member of the Fifties 'Golden Team', captain József

Wrong-footed – another year, another European misadventure for Kispest-Honvéd

Bozsik, who won a record 100 caps for his country, and to whom a commemorative plaque now stands before the clubhouse.

Honvéd were the Hungarian army side which, as well as providing the backbone of the Golden Team, also romped to five championships in the first half of the Fifties. After a lean couple of decades in the aftermath of the 1956 Hungarian uprising, they bounced back in the Eighties, winning seven titles between 1983 and 1993, the last as Kispest-Honvéd – the name the club adopted after Communism to reflect their pre-World War II existence as Kispest AC.

Between 1991 and 1994, an ambitious group of Belgians led by players' agent Louis de Vries bought into the club, investing a small fortune on nostalgia value and the hope of a regular place in lucrative European competition. It was not an entirely foolish venture, but since de Vries took his cash home, the business side of the club has collapsed and the team with it. The bulk of the promising 1993 championship squad was sold to Belgian clubs, and today the only surviving legacy of this bold but ultimately doomed first attempt at Western investment in Hungarian football is a VIP bar under the main stand.

Bar aside, the Bozsik is a shabby museum a fair way out of town. "This is Hungarian Dream," says the graffiti by the stadium's main gate and, looking at the overgrown railway lines and tatty buildings beyond, the artist is not far wrong. The cover of Antal Végh's controversial Eighties' book, *Why Is Hungarian Football Sick?*, uses the ghostly atmosphere of the Bozsik well, with a picture of old men standing on a half-empty terrace and the neighbouring cemetery in full view.

Matches here can lack atmosphere, but it's worth paying an extra Ft100 for a seat in the covered stand, where you can clearly see Old Uncle Puskás sleeping his way through the game...

Here we go!
Ride blue metro #2 to **Határ út**, then tram #42 tram for seven stops to the end station. Give yourself half an hour from central Deák tér.

Swift half
The bars down Ady Endre út towards the stadium are cheap and friendly. Try the *borozó* on the corner of Kisviola utca for dirt-cheap spritzers and faded Puskás photos on the walls. After the game, shoot pool at the **Ady Pizzeria** on the corner of Nagysándor utca. Inside the ground, if you can't blag your way into the VIP bar try the fans' equivalent in the 'Hotel Kispest' – the name given to the clubhouse just the other side of the main entrance.

Ultra culture
The **'Kispest Red Boys'**, who gather behind the goal to the left of the main stand, were the subject of a recent art-house documentary film, *Ultra Renaissance*, which showed a series of teenage adventures on an away trip to Debrecen. They were once known as the 'Kispest Sexy Hamburgers.' Draw your own conclusions.

● MTK

Hungária körút, VIII Jávor utca 5
Capacity 24,000 (5500 seated)
Colours Blue-and-white shirts, white shorts
League champions 1904, 1908, 1914, 1917–25, 1929, 1936–37, 1951, 1953, 1958, 1987, 1997
Cup winners 1910–12, 1914, 1923, 1925, 1932, 1952, 1968, 1997

The crowd may be small, but a trip to Magyar Testgyakorlók Köre (MTK) is a must for anyone with a sense of history. As well as featuring the most attractive stand in the land, steeply rising with a view over the BKV ground opposite, Hungária körút has witnessed many of the twists, turns and tragedies of twentieth-century Central European history.

MTK were formed in 1888 by liberal and Jewish defectors from the old national gymnastics club. An intense rivalry with Ferencváros began early on, exacerbated when star player Imre Schlosser moved the short distance from Fradi to MTK during World War I. Once coach Jimmy Hogan had arrived after the end of hostilities, MTK became the dominant force in Hungarian and Central European football.

The team were to pay dearly for their Jewish origins during World War II, when the Nazi Arrow Cross took power and banned the club, sending president Alfred Brüll, one of the founding fathers of Hungarian football, off to his death in a concentration camp along with hundreds of the team's Jewish fans. The period inspired a classic Fifties Hungarian film, *Two Halves in Hell*, while further cinematic exposure arrived thirty years later when Sylvester Stallone and Michael Caine were seen running around the Hungária körút field for the shooting of the kitsch classic *Escape to Victory*.

After the war the club became Vörös Lobogó ('Red Banner'), team of the hated ÁVO Communist secret police. Following the 1956 uprising, the team achieved independence from the henchmen and led a quiet and dignified existence, surfacing briefly in 1964 to reach the final of the Cup-Winners' Cup, which they lost to Sporting Lisbon.

Today MTK are the first Hungarian club to have replaced the old Communist sports club structure with a modern, European-style business setup – the result of a takeover by one of Hungary's first capitalist success stories, the Fotex group. After turning the footballing establishment on its head with a stunning league and cup double in 1997, MTK could be Budapest's team of the future, if only they could find a solid fan base. For now, their crowd consists largely of elderly men and a smattering of enthusiastic young Jewish kids.

Here we go!

Take red metro line #1 to **Népstadion**, then tram #1 or trolleybus #75 to Salgó-tarján utca. Allow about 25 minutes in all.

Swift half

There is no public bar or restaurant at MTK. Fans gather in the **Netovább** ('Go No Further') bar, VIII Hungária körút 5–7, opposite the stadium. After the game, the faithful wander to the welcoming bar of neighbours BKV Elöre, a second-division outfit, on Sport utca.

Újpesti TE

Megyeri úti stadium, IV Megyeri út 13
Capacity 32,000 (12,000 seated)
Colours All white with lilac trim
League champions 1930–31, 1933, 1935, 1939, 1945–47, 1960, 1969–75, 1978–79, 1990
Cup winners 1969–70, 1975, 1982–83, 1987, 1992

Based in the north Budapest port district of Újpest, the once mighty Lilacs have fallen on hard times. The loss of interior ministry funding after the end of Communism has sorely weakened the club's spending power and their influence in the domestic game. Újpesti TE's best resource today is their loyal, passionate, and colourful support, whose fiesta approach offers a refreshing contrast to the grim pessimism of many Hungarian fans.

Újpest did not emerge as a real force until the Thirties, when they replaced MTK as the big rivals to *Fradi*. But the club's golden era came under their Communist-era name of Újpesti Dózsa. Just prior to embarking on a magnificent run of seven straight championship wins, a side packed with internationals such as Ferenc Bene and Antal Dunai met Newcastle United in the 1969 Fairs' Cup final, losing 6–4 in a thrilling, two-legged battle.

During the Seventies Újpest produced one of the last true stars to emerge in the Hungarian game: international winger András Tőrőcsik, whose

Gyula Zsivótzky – goal poacher and 1997 double winner with MTK

light-footed trickery prompted the crowd to shout "Dance Tőrő!" whenever he got the ball. Along with Ferencváros star Tibor Nyilasi, Tőrőcsik was sent off while playing for Hungary against Argentina at the 1978 World Cup. It was a typically controversial moment in a career which would be prematurely ended by drink.

Today, having reverted to their pre-Communist name of Újpesti Torna Egylet, the team are fighting to outdo their sworn enemies, 'The Green Monkeys', as yet with little success. The lowest point came in 1993, when the team were forced to play-off to avoid relegation. The crucial game at the small town of Hatvan was a tense affair, with Újpest's impassioned fans reaching boiling point. The team stayed up – but the club directors held responsible for the decline are still the target of regular "Sack The Board" demonstrations.

However, the team have shown signs of a mini-revival in the past couple of seasons and, if both players and crowd are on song, an afternoon at Megyeri út can be a lot of fun.

Here we go!

Take blue metro #2 to its terminus at **Újpest központ**, then bus #96 or #104 four stops to Megyeri út. Allow half an hour for the whole journey.

Swift half

The **Gold Metro** *söröző* inside the Újpest központ metro station is where many Lilacs meet up for a bevvy before the game. Just out of the station on Árpád út is the **Primo** *söröző*, a decent, straightforward local bar, handily placed next to a brewery depot. The **club restaurant** and supporters' club bar underneath the main stand are convivial options before, during and after the action.

Club shop

Magic Football Shop, VI Teréz körút 40 (open Mon–Fri 10am–1pm, 2–6pm, Sat 10am–1pm, no credit cards) is the only place to buy Újpest souvenirs, though it actually sells merchandise from all Hungarian clubs. The shop is also well-stocked with Italian, German and English gear. Look out for the goalkeeper sign in the courtyard doorway. The store is owned by an Újpest fan who tries hard to smile while selling Ferencváros T-shirts.

Ultra culture

The **'Ultra Viola Bulldogs'**, having adopted fellow purple-wearers Fiorentina as their twin club, behave accordingly, trying ever so hard to create a Latin atmosphere on their crumbling terraces. Twice-yearly pilgrimages to Florence, to stock up on fireworks and memorabilia, reveal the extent of the fans' friendship with the *Collettivo Autonomo Viola*. The UVB can be found in the Bal Terász B.

In the net

An impenetrable, Hungarian-language Újpest site, with minimal graphics and multimedia content, can be found at: goliat.eik.bme.hu/~ute/.

Groundhopping

If you thought some of the bigger names in Budapest football seem to have fallen on hard times, try taking a tour of the smaller grounds. There are plenty to choose from, and you are at least guaranteed top-flight action – of a sort.

● BVSC

BVSC stadium, XIV Szőnyi út 2
Capacity 12,000
Colours All white with yellow and blue trim

For decades the railway workers' team, BVSC (Budapest Vasutas Sport Club) were a minor lower-division club, occasionally producing a tidy player to be sold to the big boys. But in the mid-Nineties, hefty sponsorship from both the state railways and the Dreher brewery enabled the club to become buyers rather than sellers, and climb to unprecedented heights; they even managed a place in the UEFA Cup in 1996. Despite this success, however, the team still rarely attract more than a couple of thousand to home games.

For a place on the terraces alongside the railwaymen, take yellow metro #3 to **Mexikói út**, then go through the subway and you'll find the ground next to the swimming pool. The **Sport Bar** by the main entrance serves a reasonable pint of

Bad hair hero – Újpest's György Véber

the sponsor's brew, plus a full menu. Back at the Mexikói út metro, by the Burger King, you'll find the **Rendevu** bar serving cold Amstel beer on a summer terrace if the weather is warm enough.

III Ker TVE

Hévízi út stadium, III Hévízi út
Capacity 5000
Colours All white with blue trim

III Kerületi Torna és Vívás Egyesület, the Third District Gymnastics & Fencing Club, are another team of minnows now somehow playing in the upper tier. Even more undeserving than BVSC, TVE rely on floating fans coming for a quiet Sunday afternoon beer and a spot of decidedly mediocre football. The ground is tiny and would not be accepted in most of Europe's first divisions. Neither would the chant of "Come On You District!"

If you really must, take blue metro #2 to **Árpád híd**, then tram #1 to the end stop. If not a decent team, Kerület at least have a **decent bar**, on the middle floor of the clubhouse. The window gives out onto the activities on the pitch.

Vasas

Fáy utcai stadium, Fáy utca 58
Capacity 18,000
Colours All red with blue trim
League champions 1957, 1961–62, 1965–66, 1977
Cup winners 1955, 1973, 1981, 1986

Traditionally the team of the iron workers, Vasas are nestled in the district of Angyalföld ('Angel Land'), described by the late Communist leader and Vasas fan János Kádár as "the beating heart of the Hungarian working class movement".

The team have almost always played in the shadow of the bigger clubs but, after winning the title in 1957, they reached the

The Nép stadium

Népstadion, XIV Stefánia út 2 (☎061/251 1222)
Capacity 73,000

Built by the people for the people, Népstadion, 'The People's Stadium', was the flagship of Hungary's Communist, postwar reconstruction. The Olympian statues behind it are a testament to the Socialist-Realist style of the era.

Today, however, the stage for the national team's legendary games of the Fifties is filled only when Michael Jackson or the Rolling Stones bring their rock circus to town.

International football games rarely attract more than 20,000 – mostly Ferencváros fans holding up a wall of flags in the southern end. Visiting support can usually be found to the right of the tunnel.

In the glory days, with no club grounds big enough to hold a 70,000 crowd, the Hungarian football federation would put on double-bills of Ferencváros-Újpest and Vasas-Honvéd

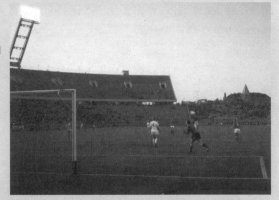

Empty space – full houses are a thing of the past at the Nép

clashes here. Újpest fans would arrive early to cheer on Vasas, forging a friendship which remains strong to this day.

Plans to roof the Népstadion have been put on ice. Until they are defrosted again, possibly with a view to Hungary co-hosting the 2004 European Championship with Austria, the stadium has the same moody, melancholy feel it had on the evening when England's Trevor Brooking famously stuck the ball into the stanchion of the Hungarian net during a World Cup qualifier in 1981.

The Népstadion has **its own metro station** on red line #1 – take the left station exit after leaving the train. Allow ten minutes from Deák tér.

Two decent bars lie at either end of the stadium. The **Stadion**, on the corner of Dózsa György út and Thököly út, has the name but none of the trimmings. The **Félido**, Kerepesi út 24, near the metro exit, has both, with framed black-and-white photos of Flórián Albert and Tibor Nyilasi, who later starred for Austria Vienna in the Eighties, also immortalised here.

semi-final of the European Cup the following season; having thumped Ajax in the quarter-final, they lost out to Real Madrid.

Fáy utcai remains one of the most pleasant grounds to visit in Budapest, thanks largely to the presence of the **Santa Fe** bar/restaurant, an executive box for the masses located behind one goal. Here you can view the action while scoffing hot chicken sandwiches and quaffing cold beer served by Kálmán Mészöly Jnr, son of the former Vasas star and twice national-team boss Mészöly Snr (he'll be the fair-haired one drinking on the balcony above). The crowd are largely pensioners, but the youths and drunks of the 'Vasas Pirates' stand next to the players' tunnel, swigging cheap wine, smuggled into the ground in Pepsi bottles. To join them, take blue metro 2 to **Forgách utca**, then a ten-minute walk down Fáy utca. Warm up for the Santa Fe with a quick one at the **Vasas büfé** on Forgách utca.

Eat, drink, sleep…

Bars and clubs

The Budapest nightlife scene is in a state of flux, with bars opening and closing every week. The 'alternative' scene of the late Eighties is all but dead, the tendency now

Puskás and the 'Golden Team'

The Hungarian Golden Team (*aranycsapat*) are an institution. In a country where the calendar is packed with dates commemorating uprisings, revolutions and wars, the football team of the Fifties have their own day, too. Every year on November 25, the five living members of the '6–3 team' are brought together on *Labdarúgás Nap* – **Football Day**. There are celebrity five-a-side games and speeches, as all the leading figures from the Hungarian football world are rolled out to pay tribute to one of the greatest football teams the world has ever seen.

Worth his weight – Puskás

The star attraction is, of course, **Ferenc Puskás**. Since he returned to the country in the mid-Eighties he has attempted to lead the quiet life. He spent several years living in a simple hotel, rediscovering his love for Hungarian beef stew and wine, and popping to a game or two at the weekend. Apart from a brief spell as **caretaker coach** of the national team for four games in 1993, he has held no official position in the game.

Puskás had three careers. He made his début as a 15-year-old with **Kispest AC** in 1942, and in 349 league games for the club (which later became Honvéd) he bagged 358 goals. When he found himself stranded in Austria at the time of the 1956 uprising, he travelled to Italy in search of a club. But the Hungarian FA refused to pass on his papers to UEFA, and he missed two seasons. In 1958, aged 31, he was offered a contract by **Real Madrid** on the condition that he lose 16 kilos in weight. Like a heavyweight boxer he sweated it out – and went on to enjoy nine years with the greatest club side Europe has known; he also played four games for the Spanish national team. His third career was as a **wandering coach**. From 1967 he worked in nine countries: Spain, the USA, Canada, Greece, Chile, Saudi Arabia, Egypt, Paraguay and Australia. He led Greece's Panathinaikos to the European Cup final in 1971.

Now past seventy, the portly Puskás is still sought after for a quote before any Hungarian international. He always obliges, delivering his opinion amiably enough, then disappearing into a local restaurant for lunch.

The other four surviving members of the *aranycsapat* are rarely heard from these days. Goalkeeper **Gyula Grosics** runs a Budapest sports shop on Szent István körút, and was a member of the Hungarian parliament between 1990 and 1994. **Jenö Buzánszky** is deputy president of the Hungarian FA, **Nándor Hidegkuti** coaches in Egypt, and **Zoltán Czibor** has returned from exile to his hometown of Komárom, next to the Slovak border.

leaning unfortunately towards theme bars and 'pubs'. The zone around Liszt Ferenc tér near **Oktogon** has trendy cafés which buzz in summer. For a bar crawl, the narrow streets between **Kálvin tér** and **Ferenciek tere** are a good bet. The traditional Hungarian drinking hole is the **wine bar** (*borozó*), where people drink white wine spritzers or half-pints of red wine with cola. Because *borozós* are cheap, they tend to attract drunks – beware. A *söröző* is for beer, generally lager or weak brown ale. Of the local brews, Borsodi and Dreher are acceptable. An average half-litre (*korsó*) will set you back Ft120–160.

6–3 Borozó, IX Lónyay utca 62. A typical wine bar whose walls sing the praises of *that* game, featuring three large framed sepia photographs. Ferenc körút metro.

Becketts, V Bajcsy-Zsilinszky út 72. Expat pub, with Irish bar staff, Irish beers and overpriced British food. Central location, Sky Sports. Nyugati pu. metro.

Café Mediterran, VI Liszt Ferenc tér 10. Café bar on fashionable Liszt square serving draught Amstel, fresh sandwiches and great coffee. At its best in summer when the terrace outside is filled with young things. Near Oktogon.

Fél 10 Jazz Club, VIII Baross utca 30. Not a jazz club at all, rather a multi-level disco with mainstream dance sounds. A safe late-night bet. Kelvin tér metro.

Prágai Vencel Vendéglő, VII Rákóczi ut 57a. Large Communist-era restaurant and bar, noted more for its clientèle than its ambience. This is Puskás' favourite watering-hole, and after internationals at the Népstadion, good for star-spotting. Blaha Lujza tér metro.

Restaurants

Hungarian food is not as spicy or exotic as its reputation suggests. Many local joints offer little more than fried **meat with vegetables**. Salads tend to be pickled or

Very Vasas – midfielder Péter Galaschek

vinegared. The world-famous goulash turns out to be a hearty soup rather than the paprika-laden stew you may be expecting; for the latter, ask for *pörkölt*. Budapest has slowly gained a wide range of restaurants serving international cuisine. Expect to pay around Ft500 for a main course.

Bagolyvár, XIV Állatkerti út 2. Next-door to, and partner restaurant of, the famed but overpriced Gundel, the Bagolyvár has a smaller menu and smaller prices to match. Traditional Hungarian food, well-executed. Just by Hősök tere.

Kétballábas étterem, VI Teréz körút 36. Owned by former MTK, Standard Liège and FC Toulon midfielder György Bognár, whose fifty-cap international career is illustrated around the walls. Acceptable mid-range menu. Will happily show football on TV, not least when leading figures in the Hungarian game are invited in to watch major matches. Close to Oktogon.

OK Italia, XIII Szent István körút 20. The most popular Italian restaurant in Budapest, although that may owe more to the micro-skirted waitresses than to the authentic Italian dishes on offer. Five minutes from Nyugati pu. metro.

Remiz, II Budakeszi út 5. Worth the trip out of town in warm weather for its garden grill, steaks, salads and desserts. Bus #22 from Mozkva tér.

Simon Pince, XIII Hegedűs Gyula utca 2. Owned by Tibor Simon, the short-cropped, tough-tackling ex-*Fradi* full-back. His bar is tamer than his tackling ever was, with a restrained display of team photos. Where Ferencváros players come to celebrate a big win. Nyugati tér.

Söröző Szent Jupát, II Retek utca 16 (open 12 noon–6am). Noted for its huge portions of Hungarian food, very late opening hours and cold German beer. Close to Mozkva tér.

Accommodation

Cheap accommodation is plentiful in Budapest thanks to the large number of private *panziós*, or bed-and-breakfasts, which have sprung up since the change to a market economy. A clean double room should be around Ft5000 a night. Bigger hotels charge Western prices, often in Deutschmarks.

Beatrix Pension, II Széher út 3 (☎061/176 3730). Well-established, family-run guest house in the Buda hills. Doubles from DM90.

Citadella, XII Citadella sétány (☎061/166 5794). Youth hostel with a splendid view of Pest from the top of Gellért Hill. From Ft1000.

City Panzió Ring, XIII Szent István körút 22 (☎061/111 4450; fax 061/111 0884). Slick new pension bang in the heart of the city. Around DM50 per room per night.

Hotel Astoria, V Kossuth Lajos utca 19 (☎061/117 3411). Grand old venue, in the centre of town. Headquarters of the Gestapo during World War II, but don't let that deter you. Single rooms from DM140, doubles from DM180.

Mohácsi Panzió, II Bimbó út 25/a (☎061/115 7939). Optional breakfast, easy access to city centre by bus #11. Ask for a balcony which will give you a fair view of Buda. DM50 per night.

The 1997 squad bombed out of sight – but Ferencváros remain Hungary's most popular team

Ireland

The achievements of Jack Charlton's national side at the last two World Cups have changed the status of football in Ireland forever. For two barmy, balmy summers in 1990 and 1994, Irish sports fans the world over were transfixed by their team's extraordinary progress. Ireland's politicians and business community were soon in on the strange new phenomenon, and before long soccer was *the* game to be involved with.

Charlton bowed out in December 1995, his team having been outclassed by Holland in a play-off for a place at Euro '96. His successor, Mick McCarthy, was left with the task of somehow surpassing Big Jack's achievements, with an ageing squad performing in front of fans who, by now, were taking qualification for major tournaments for granted.

Pre-Charlton, the typical fan came from Dublin's working class, gathering with a couple of thousand kindred spirits on rundown terraces before a Sunday afternoon pint. Today international soccer brings Ireland's new business class to Lansdowne Road, the national rugby stadium hired out for the round-ball game. The task facing the League of Ireland is to bridge this two-tier system and attract the new fans, and their families, to regular weekend games.

In 1994, the Football Association of Ireland (FAI) allowed BSkyB to beam English Premiership action throughout Ireland via cable. In return, Sky stumped up IR£1.5 million towards equipping league grounds with floodlights. The consequent scheduling of domestic games on Friday and Saturday evenings has increased attendances, allowing fans to turn up for local action while still following Ireland's three most popular teams – Liverpool, Manchester United and Celtic – on the box. FAI grants from smaller sponsorship deals

Your good health – the American dream, 1994

will go towards a new purpose-built soccer stadium on the outskirts of Dublin, the future home of Ireland's biggest club, Shamrock Rovers. Shelbourne's Tolka Park has seen major renovation, as will Bohemians' Dalymount and Richmond Park, home of St Patrick's Athletic.

The progress is not confined to Dublin. A soccer museum is being built in Galway and the best crowds of all are to be found at the Brandywell, home of Derry City, across the border in Northern Ireland.

Sectarian violence caused Derry to withdraw from the northern Irish League in 1972. The club joined the south's League of

Ireland fifteen years later, and did the Irish double in 1989. But the Derry story was beginning to turn sour until the appointment of Felix Healy as manager in 1995. Under Healy's guidance, Derry won the league again in 1997 and now hope to improve the dreadful record of Irish clubs in Europe.

None of this would have been conceivable before Big Jack. Soccer in the Emerald Isle had traditionally been based in industrialised Belfast. Before the north-south split in 1923, only Dublin's big three of Shelbourne, Bohemians and Shamrock Rovers competed in all-Irish football, mustering just four cup wins in forty years between them.

In the south, the Gaelic Athletic Association promoted the traditional Irish sports of Gaelic football and hurling. Schoolboys were beaten for indulging in the 'foreign' game of soccer and the GAA

enjoyed the lion's share of state funding and favour. Rugby, unaffected by the events of 1923, remained all Ireland's premier international sport.

For much of the postwar era, the League of Ireland was little more than a breeding ground for the English and Scottish leagues. Only record title-winners Shamrock Rovers could pull in reasonable crowds, thanks to stylish football and, in the Sixties and Seventies, some regular European action.

At international level, the game was scarred by administrative incompetence and the reluctance of English and Scottish clubs to release key players. Ireland had the talent – Johnny Giles and Liam Brady to name just two examples – but needed a strong character to bind it together.

That character was Jack Charlton. After pipping Bob Paisley to the post of national-team manager in 1986, Charlton made sure

A man apart – Big Jack keeps the Irish national team on their toes, Florida, 1994

Basics

EU nationals and citizens of the United States, Canada, Australia and New Zealand need only their **passport** to enter the Irish Republic. British nationals born in the UK can enter with a reasonable form of identification such as a driving licence; French, Germans and Belgians need only their ID cards.

The Irish currency is the **Irish pound**, or punt (indicated IR£), divided into 100 pence. Credit card payment is generally accepted and automatic cash machines are widespread. Many shops and businesses also accept payment in pounds sterling, and the two currencies are of broadly equivalent value. Banks are open Mon–Fri 10am–12.30pm & 1.30–3pm, with many open until 5pm on Thursdays.

The international **telephone code** for Ireland is 353. Once inside the country, Dublin is 01, Cork 021 and Galway 091. When calling from Ireland, the cheapest rates are after 6pm. Coin phones take 10p, 20p and 50p pieces, while **phonecards** come in units of IR£2 and IR£5.

Travel around Ireland is slow but reliable, and centralised on Dublin. **Trains** from Dublin to Belfast run from central **Connolly** station, to Cork and Galway from **Heuston** in the west of town. An off-peak return train ticket is almost the same price as a single – around IR£25 between Dublin and Galway.

Buses, operated by the state concern Bus Éireann, are often cheaper than trains, but slow and infrequent; a *Boomerang* ticket, valid from Tuesday to Thursday, allows a return journey for the price of a single. Private operators run **alternative services** on many routes – they're cheaper and usually busier than the state-run buses.

Ireland's players did the simple things right: they closed opponents down, and got the ball forward, fast. Frustrating opponents in Lansdowne's long grass, and displaying a unique team spirit, they were hard to beat. With only a small pool of Irish-born talent to choose from, Charlton encouraged players to exercise their parental – or even grandparental – right to choose the Irish first team over occasional England squad membership. Neither Glasgow-born Ray Houghton nor his then Liverpool team-mate, John Aldridge, had set foot in Dublin before Charlton's first game in charge.

It was Houghton who set Ireland alight with an early winning goal against England in the 1988 European Championship, Big Jack's – and Ireland's – frst major tourna-ment. After drawing 1–1 with the Soviet Union, Ireland went out against the even-tual winners Holland to a late, lucky Wim Kieft goal.

But the team had made its mark, as had its supporters – an exuberant Green Army whose easygoing attitude contrasted so starkly with the ugly demeanour of their English counterparts, and who gleefully car-ried the green, white and orange tricolour on to Italia '90.

In sometimes dour but always indefati-gable style, the Irish progressed to the World Cup quarter-finals in Italy despite failing to win a single match, a David O'Leary penalty beating Romania in the second round and sending Ireland football crazy. Even the staid BBC coverage could not help but be brightened by Liam Brady's emotional commentary.

Although they went on to lose 1–0 to the host nation, Ireland and Charlton were clearly enjoying their spell in the interna-tional football limelight, and the stage was set for another thrilling episode. It could not have been scripted better. For their first game of the 1994 World Cup, the Irish again faced Italy, this time in New York. It was to be the scene of Ireland's finest hour, an early Ray Houghton goal winning the day, just as it had in Stuttgart eight years earlier. Although the team would later wilt in the Florida heat against Holland, history had been made.

Match practice

Irish grounds are primitive. Unless the game involves Derry and/or one of Dublin's big three, the crowd will be small and friendly. The play can be pretty rough, as can the state of the pitch. Any talented youngster will stand out and no doubt be spotted by someone significant in the crowd – scouting is a cottage industry here.

The season begins in late July or early August with lucrative friendlies against English and Scottish clubs. The league generally starts on the last weekend of August, continuing right through until late April, leaving early May free for the cup final and promotion play-offs. In 1996, a spate of late postponements over Christmas and New Year brought the usual calls for a short winter break.

Major games kick-off at 7.45pm on Fridays and 7.30pm on Saturdays, with lesser Dublin Premier Division teams and some First Division sides playing instead on Sunday afternoons.

The league

Ireland's National League has two divisions, both of which contain some semi-professional clubs. The Premier Division's twelve sides have a 33-game season, playing each other home and away and, as far as relegation allows, home and away every other season. A move to expand the Premier to sixteen teams – rejected by club chairmen in 1996 – may yet become reality in 1998/99.

The First Division has ten clubs, playing 27 games in a similar fashion to the Premier. The bottom and top two automatically swap places between Premier and First, while the third-bottom and third-top are involved in a two-legged play-off. The bottom two of the First must apply for readmission to the League at the end of the season.

Up for the cup

The FAI Cup has four rounds, one each month from January. All Premier and First Division clubs are involved, plus ten non-

league teams who enter via an Intermediate Cup played before Christmas. Level scores after extra-time in the first match force a replay, at which there will be both extra-time and penalties if necessary. Home advantage for the semi-final is decided the same way as in the previous three rounds – on the luck of the draw. The final takes place midweek in early May at Lansdowne Road; any replay will normally be a week later at Dalymount Park.

As in England and Scotland, there is also a League Cup to be played for. This takes place in the autumn and involves six groups of four teams – the 22 National League sides plus two non-league sides. The winners of each group plus the best two runners-up go through to a knockout stage, where ties are decided on one game, extra-time and penalties, before a two-legged final in November or December; level aggregate scores lead to extra-time and penalties in the second leg.

Tickets

League football is cheap in Ireland. A typical standing price is IR£4, a seat IR£5. Simply pay your money at the turnstile. For international games at Lansdowne Road, prices range between IR£35 for the best seats and IR£15 for the so-called 'bucket' seats behind the goals. Tickets are only officially available from the FAI, 80 Merrion Square, Dublin 2.

Nearly every club issues a programme, price usually IR£1. Bohemians, Shelbourne and St Patrick's Athletic all have small club shops open on matchdays, but during the week all shirts and souvenirs are available in town at Soccer City, 1 Crampton Quay (☎01/679 1795, Mon–Sat 10am–6pm, most major credit cards).

Half-time

Many Irish clubs survive on bar takings alone. The supporters' club usually has a social function during the week as well as performing its important rôle serving drinks on matchdays. Chocolate is consumed in almost as great a quantity as

Guinness, and vendors will regularly come round with baskets crammed full of gum-threatening goodies.

Action replay

Televised football is woefully lame and the main channel, RTÉ 1, barely touches it. Major internationals are shown on the state's second channel, Network 2, whose coverage of both the 1990 and 1994 World Cups came in for much criticism thanks to the pervasive presence of Eamon Dunphy, an eternal critic of Big Jack at a time when the manager enjoyed a near God-like status in Ireland.

Relax – the Irish prize their pre-match reading time highly

Despite being avoided by most members of the national setup and mistrusted by many fans, Dunphy is still employed by RTÉ and by a new national radio station, *Radio Ireland* – though he no longer contributes his abrasive column to the *Sunday Independent* newspaper.

On Saturdays, Network 2's *Sports Stadium* begins around 12.30pm with a twenty-minute league football preview, followed by news and English results at 6pm. The same channel shows a highlighted Irish game the next day at 10.30pm on its *Sunday Sport* programme.

Most pubs close for two hours on a Sunday afternoon, so you may have to scout around to catch Sky's Premiership game. Network 2 has highlights from the Italian *Serie A* on Tuesdays at 7pm, while the Irish-language TnaG channel offers Spanish highlights at 9pm on Mondays. BBC, Ulster Television and Sky are easily available throughout the country.

The back page

Unless there's an international match looming, at least five times more newsprint is dedicated to the English Premiership than to its Irish counterpart. Most fans read the Irish edition of *The Star* and the Tuesday edition of the *Irish Times*.

The Sunday sports paper *The Title* usually has a page of Irish soccer news tucked away in its back section. The monthly *Irish Soccer Magazine* (IR£1.50) covers the game north and south.

In the net

In the absence of an official FAI site, Thomas Bridge's **Irish Soccer Homepage** is as good a place as any to start surfing. Among other things it offers an MPEG-encoded video of Ray Houghton's USA '94 goal against Italy to download, while the many links embrace club sites from both north and south of the border. Take a deep breath and head for: www.maths.tcd.ie/~thomas/soccer/soccer.html.

For a good old cyber-chinwag, Irish style, try Dale Dermott's generic site at: www.dermott.com. There's plenty of news, debate and general blarney.

Dublin

 Shamrock Rovers *304*   Bohemians *306*   Shelbourne *307*
St Patrick's *309*   Bray *310*   Home Farm *310*   UCD *311*

Provincial sides such as Derry and Cork may attract their loyal followings, but the epicentre of football in the Republic has always been Dublin...

The thrilling fields

Shamrock Rovers

Tolka Park, see Shelbourne, p.307
Colours Green-and-white hooped shirts, green shorts
League champions 1923, 1925, 1927, 1932, 1938–39, 1954, 1957, 1959, 1964, 1984–87, 1994
Cup winners 1925, 1929, 1930–33, 1936, 1940, 1944–45, 1948, 1955–56, 1962, 1964–69, 1978, 1985–87

Ireland's biggest club are both everything that was wrong with domestic football and everything that could be put right. Shamrock Rovers, after a decade in nomadic wilderness, have pinned their future on a new all-seater ground on the outskirts of town. The Tallaght stadium, near Rovers' traditional fan base in south Dublin, should have been ready for the start of the 1997/98 league season, and although problems with planning permission prevented Rovers from starting their campaign there, they are hopeful of being able to move there in the summer of 1998, if not sooner.

The finished Tallaght should finally lay to rest the ghost of Milltown, Rovers' beloved old stadium which witnessed the best football in the league over a sixty-year period before its site was sold to developers in 1987.

Formed in the Ringsend area, Rovers became Dublin's leading club soon after the League of Ireland's inauguration in 1921/22. Their rivalry with nearby Shelbourne attracted record crowds, obliging the club to lease some land in the Milltown area from the Jesuit community, and to build a stand there in 1928.

The Hoops continued to chalk up league and cup wins, but it was the work of player-coach Paddy Coad that won over a generation of fans in the 1950s. 'Coad's Colts', as the young side became known, not only won honours, they played a stylish, passing game that had not been seen in Irish club football before. Pioneers in Europe as well as at home, the team famously restricted the Busby Babes to a 3–2 win at Old Trafford in 1957.

Rovers became cup specialists, winning six straight Irish finals between 1964 and 1969. Yet the Jesuit landlords were unhappy about such craven innovations as floodlights and half-time music, and the team were forced to play their lucrative European games at Dalymount Park.

The Kilcoyne family bought a controlling interest in Rovers in 1972, but invested little money in the club until the arrival of former Leeds United star Johnny Giles as manager in 1977. By then, Rovers were fielding virtually a junior side – they had had to apply for re-election in 1976. Giles' ambition was to build a winning team capable of attracting large crowds to a redeveloped Milltown, raising the profile of the domestic game as a whole. But his slow passing game floundered on bumpy, provincial pitches, while business interests in North America kept him away from Dublin for extended periods.

While Giles' dream faded, the Kilcoynes maintained a steady trade in selling players across the water and buying up all the best Irish ones cheaply. The 'four-in-a-row' title team of the mid-Eighties had the pinpoint accuracy of future coach Pat Byrne in midfield, but the success of that era was brought to a dramatic end when the Kilcoynes sold Milltown. A subsequent groundshare with Shelbourne at Tolka Park proved disastrous, with more Rovers fans on the picket-line outside than on the terraces. A move to the Royal Dublin Society Showgrounds in the early Nineties was a costly half-solution, and a new-look board of directors began work on the Tallaght plan in 1994 – the year the club last won the league, with a team that cost only IR£12,000. The star of that side, Stephen Geoghegan, was soon sold to Shelbourne, but if the move to Tallaght is a success, Rovers may lose their reputation as a 'selling' club, and Irish club football could emerge from the dark ages for good.

Here we go!

To reach Rovers' temporary home at Tolka Park, hop aboard bus #3, #11, #11A, #16 or #16A from O'Connell Street. Allow fifteen minutes and alight in Drumcondra just by the narrow Tolka river.

For the new stadium, buses #49, #54A, #56A and #77A, which depart from Eden Quay, all terminate at The Square in Tallaght, 8km from town. The stadium is across the pedestrian bridge in Sean Walsh Park, on the other side of the main N81 road. From central Dublin allow forty minutes by bus, fifteen by car.

Swift half

In Rovers' early days, fans followed a tradition of walking behind a white horse from south Dublin up to Dalymount Park on cup

Dublin essentials

If you're arriving at the **airport**, the Airlink express bus makes the seven-mile journey south to Dublin's central bus station, Busáras (every 20–30 minutes, 6.40am–11pm, single ticket IR£2.50). Alternatively, a normal city bus #41A or #41C will take you to central Eden Quay in around thirty minutes for IR£1.10. A taxi will cost IR£12–15 to do the same trip.

A more relaxed alternative to flying is provided by two **ferry companies** offering a twice-daily Dublin service from Holyhead in north Wales. The ferries are modern and comfortable, and crossings take around three-and-a-half hours. Irish Ferries/B&I sail to **Dublin port**, where a bus service awaits for the fifteen-minute journey to Busáras; pay the driver IR£1.50. Stena Sealink sail to **Dún Laoghaire**, a twenty-minute journey into town on Dublin's fast overland electric rail line, **DART** (fare IR£1.30). The DART runs every 5–15 minutes, north to south via the city's central train stations, Pearse and Connolly, Mon–Sat 6.30am–midnight, Sun 9.30am–11pm. A one-day unlimited DART travel pass costs IR£3.20.

Dublin's **bus network** comprehensively covers the city, running Mon–Sat 6am–11.30pm and from 10am on Sundays. A bus into the centre will be marked 'An Lár'. Tickets can be bought onboard or at major newsagents. For certain routes, the correct fare is needed. A one-day bus pass is IR£3.30, or IR£4.50 for a combined DART/bus one-day pass. A four-day DART/bus Explorer pass is IR£10, valid Mon–Fri from 9.45am, all day Saturdays and Sundays.

A **night bus service**, *Nitelink*, runs on the hour, Thurs–Sat, midnight–3am, from College Street, D'Ollier Street and Westmoreland Street to a range of suburban destinations for IR£2.50 – pay the driver.

Taxis are hard to find and even harder to flag down. St Stephen's Green is the most likely parking spot. National Radio Cabs (☎677 2222) and All Fives Taxi (☎455 5555); both operate 24 hours.

Dublin's **Tourism Centre**, at the restored former Church of St Andrew in Suffolk Street (Mon–Sat 9am–6pm, Tues from 9.30am, ☎01/605 7777), is friendly and efficient. For entertainment information, *In Dublin* (fortnightly, IR£1.50) is by far the best listings source.

final day. Today the **White Horse**, I George's Quay, is the Rovers pub, right by the River Liffey and swamped in football scarves, memorabilia and framed Italia '90 tickets. Tallaght, when complete, will have its own bar and clubhouse.

Club shop

Rovers' small shop at the Spawell Leisure Complex in Templeogue (Mon–Fri 9am–5.30pm, credit cards accepted) is also the centre of operations for project Tallaght, where a supporters' store will be set up for 1998/99.

In the net

Launched into cyberspace in February 1995, the unofficial Rovers website lays a credible claim to having been the first of its kind in Ireland. News, stats, and jokes at the expense of Bohemians are its strong points, with plenty of debate about the Tallaght move to spice up the mixture. Low on gimmicks, high on content, the site is at: paul.maths.may.ie:8000/rovers.html.

 # Bohemians

Dalymount Park, Phibsborough
Capacity 18,000 (1800 seated)
Colours Red-and-black striped shirts, black shorts
League champions 1924, 1928, 1930, 1934, 1936, 1975, 1978
Cup winners 1928, 1935, 1970, 1976, 1992

The Bohs are the oldest club still in existence in the Republic, and their rivalry with Shamrock Rovers is Dublin's biggest. Fenced in by terraced housing in the wide catchment area of Phibsborough, the Bohs have been playing at Dalymount Park since 1901. They appeared in six pre-1923 all-Irish cup finals, winning one in 1908, and after the separate FA of Ireland was formed, Dalymount Park became the Association's home ground. All internationals and cup finals were played here until the Lansdowne deal was struck in 1971.

Fans still have to trudge along muddy alleyways to get to the ground, with its one main stand and, opposite, cold, open terracing. To the casual visitor, it may seem strange that, in their desire to protect local football from developers, the FAI bought Dalymount Park from Bohemians, rather than the more

Bohemian rhapsody – plenty of rough and tumble at Dalymount

attractive Milltown from Shamrock Rovers. The proposed renovation of Dalymount's old main stand and north terrace has been a long time coming, as has a Bohemians title win – though the team did finish as runners-up in the league in 1996 and 1997.

The team's most consistent performer in recent years has been forward Derek Swan, top scorer for the Bohs on four separate occasions between 1988 and 1996. Even Swan's achievements, however, pale next to those of the club's all-time greatest hero (and future manager) Turlough O'Connor, who hit a club record 120 goals in nine seasons at Dalymount, including 24 in one season the last time Bohemians won the league in 1978.

Here we go!
Take bus #19, #19A or #22 from O'Connell Street, or #10 from Phoenix Park. Allow fifteen minutes for the journey, alighting where the Phibsborough Road, North Circular Road and Dalymount meet. Head through any narrow alleyway toward the floodlights.

Swift half
Two favoured haunts are the **Sir Arthur Conan Doyle**, on Doyle's Corner, with its open fire, cinema memorabilia and substantial lunches, and the neighbouring **Hut**, 159 Phibsborough Road, which has a preservation order on its mahogany bar fittings. The **Bohemian House**, on the corner of Phibsborough and the North Circular, has a large black-and-white photo mural of classic Irish internationals of the Fifties and Sixties. The **supporters' club bar** by the main entrance is open on matchdays and after 8.30pm every evening.

In the net
Bohemians are nicknamed 'The Gypsies' and the club's excellent unofficial website does quite a bit of wandering of its own. It was last spotted at: indigo.ie/~oconnorj/. Webmasters John O'Connor and Brian P Green promise further development, but with a comprehensive history, a picture

gallery, constantly updated news and results and a fetching red-and-black striped background, it's hard to fathom what could usefully be added, save for a more permanent home.

Shelbourne

Tolka Park, Richmond Road
Capacity 9500 (9000 seated)
Colours All red with white trim
League champions 1926, 1929, 1931, 1944, 1947, 1953, 1962, 1992
Cup winners 1939, 1960, 1963, 1993, 1996–97

As the line from *The Commitments* goes: "...And everyone hates Shelbourne!" Be that as it may, the Shels play in Dublin's most pleasant soccer ground, Tolka Park. Shelbourne have always suffered from their reputation as a big-money club, but much of this money has been wisely invested in an all-seater ground that should be the prototype for all Irish clubs.

The biggest Dublin team before the north-south division – Shelbourne won three all-Irish cups – the Shels went through some bleak times in the Seventies and early Eighties before the current influx of new money.

Although Tolka Park is a short bus ride from Dalymount's terraced housing in Phibsborough, Shelbourne's traditional fan base is in the quiet southern district of Harold's Cross, where the club played for most of the Eighties while Tolka was being refurbished. Since then the club have managed only a solitary Irish title, in 1992, but have done better things in the FAI Cup, denying both St Patrick's and Derry City the double by scoring late goals in the finals of 1996 and 1997.

Here we go!
See Shamrock Rovers, p.305.

Swift half
The **Cat & Cage**, 74 Upper Drumcondra Road, a ten-minute walk from Tolka Park,

The national stadium – Lansdowne Road

62 Lansdowne Road
Capacity (for soccer internationals) 34,000 all-seated

Proposals have been flying
thick and fast for a new
National Stadium, but it will be
well into the next century
before Ireland's football team
finds its own place. Until then,
it has to pay its dues on rugby's
home turf, Lansdowne Road.

The FAI's rental arrange-
ment with the Rugby Football
Union has been a successful
one for both parties since the
former moved from Dalymount
Park in 1971. Even at Irish
soccer's lowest ebb, Dalymount
had become too rough and too
cramped for international
matches. Lansdowne Road was
spacious but homely, and an

Old among new – the Lansdowne Road clubhouse

impressive new east stand – built before the Charlton boom years – gave the stadium a
grandeur worthy of the major occasion.

Lansdowne was also handily located near Dublin port and right on the DART line
for supporters arriving from Dún Laoghaire. Alas, the ground's convenience was cruelly
exposed when right-wing English fans eluded security cordons, ripped up seats and
hurled debris on their compatriots below, stopping a friendly international in 1995.

That match had been an evening kick-off under Lansdowne's new floodlights. In
1990, a European Championship qualifier involving the same potentially abrasive sets
of fans had taken place without incident in Lansdowne's convivial afternoon atmosphere. Those were the days when the ground would be full even for a friendly, when it
was party time and everyone wanted to join in. Now the party is simmering down and
all the lights are on – and it might take something more than new seats to generate the
same kind of atmosphere.

Lansdowne Road is three DART stops from central **Connolly station**. The train
service is suspended for twenty minutes before and after kick-off to allow pedestrians
across the tracks. North Terrace ticket-holders should arrive via Havelock Square,
those for the South Terrace via Lansdowne Road.

The immediate area around the stadium is usually fenced off, so the best pubs are a
five- or ten-minute walk from the ground – **Slattery's**, 62 Grand Canal Street, is the
best known. You're almost bound to spot a player after the game here, and there's live
jazz most nights. **Paddy Flaherty's** (formerly *The 51*), 51 Haddington Road, and
Brett's (formerly the *Lansdowne Bar*), 14 Bath Avenue, are old favourites, both with
the benefit of Sky TV.

Inside the ground the **Lansdowne Pavilion**, behind the east stand, is open before
and after the game. You'll find a large, bare bar downstairs, with hot beef rolls sold in
the hallway, and a carpeted bar upstairs whose walls illustrate the history of Irish rugby.

is a fans' pub with its own soccer team and a huge pull-down TV screen for Sky Sports. Dramatist Sean O'Casey was a regular here. **Fagan's**, on the corner of Botanic Avenue and Lower Drumcondra Road, is more rough and ready but nearer the ground. The **supporters' bar** by the main entrance to Tolka Park is open evenings and matchdays.

In the net

Shelbourne have sanctioned the building of their own official website, available at: www.connect.ie/users/shels/shels.htm. The homepage presents you with a pin-sharp team group image, while deeper down there is a selection of MPEG movies of famous Shels goals to download. However, the site is not updated as frequently as many fan-operated pages, so if it's news you're after, you've come to the wrong place.

Groundhopping

With the bigger clubs switching home matches to Friday or Saturday evenings, visitors to Dublin often get the chance to sample a game at one of the city's smaller grounds on a Sunday afternoon. It may not be the perfect antidote to the previous night's excesses, but it will be different…

St Patrick's Athletic

Richmond Park, 125 Emmett Road, Inchicore
Capacity 7000
Colours Red-and-white shirts, white shorts
League champions 1952, 1955–56, 1990, 1996
Cup winners 1959, 1961

When St Pat's won the title in 1990, the small, family club were on the point of

Cup king – Shelbourne's Vinny Arkins shields the ball in the FAI Cup final against Derry City

bankruptcy and playing at a greyhound stadium in Harold's Cross. A committed squad of players and a tiny but dedicated staff dug in, moved back to the club's home ground at Richmond Park, and won the title again in 1996. Since then, St Pat's have spent fresh sponsorship money on a new 2000-seater stand at the Inchicore end of the ground.

Behind much of this progress has been former player Pat Dolan who, as commercial manager, stands as one of the most influential figures in the development of the Irish domestic game. Dolan was appointed team manager in January 1997, and his success could yet have positive repercussions for other Dublin clubs.

To get to Richmond Park, take bus #51, #68A or #78A from Aston Quay; all three stop right outside the stadium after about a fifteen-minute ride. A taxi from Heuston

The English rose – match abandoned, 1995

station will take five minutes and cost IR£2–3.

There are several pubs around the ground, but the **Horse & Jockey**, 107 Emmet Road, has its own pub team and constant football babble. The **supporters' bar** by the main entrance is open evenings and matchdays.

⚽ Bray Wanderers

Carlisle Grounds, Bray, Co Wicklow
Capacity 3000
Colours Green shirts, white shorts
Cup winners 1990

The most appealing Sunday afternoon groundhop is to the end of the DART line down by the sea. Bray have ambitious plans for floodlights and a new terrace, but for as long as the team are bouncing between the premier and first divisions, this is still provincial Irish football at its most charmingly modest – two rusty-roofed terraces, tea and apple-cake served by friendly ladies in the club hut, and the lingering odour of cheap tobacco and Ralgex.

Bray won the cup in 1990, and their subsequent single appearance in Europe, against Trabzonspor of Turkey, is documented in Kodak form inside the hut.

The ground is a minute's walk from the southern terminus of the DART line, about thirty minutes from the centre of Dublin. If you've arrived early, **O'Driscoll's** is the pub with the bright orange front opposite the National Aquarium on the promenade, five minutes' walk from the ground.

⚽ Home Farm Everton

Whitehall, 97A Swords Road
Capacity 3000
Colours Blue shirts, white shorts
Cup winners 1975

As a nursery team for Everton FC (hence the name change in 1995), it is ironic that the most famous player Home Farm have ever produced, Ronnie Whelan, was a star for Liverpool. Home Farm played at Tolka Park until 1990, when they moved up to Whitehall in the far north of Dublin. Despite the bleak surroundings – narrow stone terracing, one crumbling main stand – Home Farm have a tradition of producing fine young players, hence Everton's patronage. Perhaps the English club are beginning to take too many, too young, for the team were relegated at the end of the 1996/97 season...

To see the fledgelings in action before they are swept toward Goodison, take bus #41, #41A, #41B or #41C from Eden Quay in the direction of Dublin airport. Allow a good twenty minutes for the journey to Whitehall.

There are no pubs in the immediate vicinity – only the Home Farm **social club bar** in the main stand.

☕ University College Dublin

Belfield Park, Stillorgan
Capacity 5000
Colours All sky blue
Cup winners 1984

Formerly called Catholic University FC, this team of students plays League of Ireland football of varying quality, depending on the footballing skills of the season's intake. Pressure is not a watchword in the UCD changing room. Still, the club won the FAI Cup, 2–1 in a replayed final against Shamrock Rovers, in 1984. That autumn, the eventual Cup-Winners' Cup victors Everton were held to a goalless draw in Dublin and a 1–0 win at Goodison – UCD's solitary and thoroughly commendable European performance.

Belfield is a fair way from Dublin city centre – take bus #10 from Phoenix Park, #46 or #84 from Eden Quay. Allow a good thirty minutes. The club's main building is full of cheap booze – the *raison d'être* for any good college...

Eat, drink, sleep...

Bars and clubs

The **pub** is at the centre of Irish life and Dublin has over a thousand. Some are large, ornate places, others are binge holes, many serve food, a fair number have live music – but all will slowly serve thick, creamy pints of Guinness, where it tastes best, at around IR£2 a pint. Beamish and Murphys are its competitors, Smithwicks a popular bitter, while lagers are normally limited to Harp, Heineken or Carlsberg. Irish whiskeys such as Jameson's are served in larger measures than in the UK. In the depth of winter a hot whiskey, with cloves and lemon, does the trick.

Pubs are generally open Mon–Sat 10.30am–11.30pm, and from 12.30pm on Sundays, when doors close 2–4pm, although you can probably stay drinking through. Between October and April, pubs close thirty minutes earlier.

In Dublin, the Temple Bar area by the Liffey has a lively pub atmosphere, perhaps a little trendy for some tastes. Right across the river, on Ormond Quay, and further down on the south side, on Sir John Robertson Quay, is where you'll find the clubbing scene.

The Baggot Inn, 143 Lower Baggot St. An old rockers' haunt near St Stephen's Green where U2 learned their chops, this is the pub Jack Charlton took a shine to, bought, and put his son John in charge of. Live music and football chat.

Blue Note Café, Bedford Lane. Laid-back nightclub playing acid jazz, jungle and trip-hop for a young clientèle. Cheaper admission before 11.45pm. Food upstairs. Just off Aston Quay.

Fitzsimmons, 15–18 East Essex St. Spacious two-level sports pub in Temple Bar with a pricey restaurant area near a huge main screen and a smaller bar that gets lively on big-match nights.

The Kitchen, 6–8 Wellington Quay. U2's expensively furnished nightclub, with designer décor and a stream running unfeasibly around it. Decent sounds. Downstairs from the *Clarence Hotel* in Temple Bar.

Mulligan's, 8 Poolbeg St. Said to serve the best Guinness in Dublin, this traditional pub has two floors and no fewer than four bar areas. Near Tara Street station.

O'Donohue's, 15 Merrion Row. Favoured haunt of local band The Dubliners, this pub is a popular centre for traditional Irish music, with concerts every night. Pleasant courtyard open in summer. By St Stephen's Green.

Restaurants

The Nineties have seen a huge variety of restaurants spring up in Dublin, especially in the Temple Bar and St Stephen's Green areas. If you're staying in a B&B, a huge Irish breakfast and a late, cheapish pub lunch will probably keep you going for the rest of the day. If you're spending a bit of money, seafood and vegetables should be deliciously fresh.

Beshoff's, 14 Westmoreland St. A tiled palace of fish and chips, with various similar combinations. Cheap, central, spacious late-night dining. Open until 11pm Sun–Thurs, 3am Fri–Sat.

Bewley's, 78–79 Grafton St. Classic weekend round-the-clock breakfast haunt, with three floors of bustle, the lowest one self-service. Vast choice, and several other branches around town. Mon–Thurs 7.30am–1am, Fri–Sat 7.30am–6am, Sun 8am–1am.

Kilkenny Kitchen, 6 Nassau St. Lunchtime favourite above a crafts store, busy with shoppers tucking into cheap, hearty and well-cooked Irish food, with a view over Trinity College. Open 'til 5pm Mon–Wed, 8pm Thurs–Sat.

Little Lisbon, 3 Upper Fownes St. Cosy diner in Temple Bar serving an interesting choice of Portuguese and Brazilian cuisine. Reasonable prices, bring your own wine – there's an all-night store a minute away in Dame Street. Most credit cards.

The Lord Edward, 23 Christchurch Place. Opposite Christ Church Cathedral, Dublin's oldest and most revered seafood restaurant is above the Lord Edward pub. Cheap set lunches, pricey but tasty dinners. Open Mon–Fri 12.30–2.30pm, Mon–Sat 6–10.45pm. Most major credit cards.

The Old Dublin, 90–91 Francis St. Tucked away among the junk shops in the Liberties area. An atmospheric place replete with open fireplaces, its speciality is a strange but excellent combination of fresh Irish fish done in Russian or Scandinavian styles. Pricey, but try the set menu at IR£10 per head between 6pm and 7pm. Open Mon–Fri 12.30–2.30pm, Mon–Sat 6–11pm. Most major credit cards.

Accommodation

For a reasonably cheap, centrally located room in Dublin your best bet is to try one of the better hostels. Hotels are either expensive or very expensive, while bed & breakfasts tend to be out of town, or centred in the Ballsbridge area.

Whichever option you go for, be sure to book a room well in advance. Most places charge a little more in summer and over rugby weekends. Dublin's Tourism Centre in Suffolk Street (details on p.305) and tourist offices at Dublin Airport and Dún Laoghaire can all book you a room for a IR£1 fee, or arrange credit card payment by phone.

Avalon House, 55 Aungier Street (☎01/475 0001, fax 01/475 0303). Friendly hostel near St Stephen's Green with singles at IR£19, twins IR£25 and dorm beds IR£9. Modest breakfast included. No curfew. Decent café downstairs. Most major credit cards.

Avondale Guest House, 40 Lower Gardiner St (☎01/874 5200). A typical Dublin B&B, with single rooms or the possibility of sharing with a total stranger. Fine breakfast included in the price – around IR£20 per night.

Clarence Hotel, Wellington Quay (☎01/662 3066). Overlooking the river Liffey, this lively hotel was bought by U2 in 1992. Around IR£50 per person per night, but worth it if you want to be in the thick of the action.

Isaac's Hostel, 2–5 Frenchman's Lane (☎01/874 9321, fax 01/874 1574, email isaacs@irelands-web.ie). Well-organised, comfortable and friendly hostel just around the corner from the main bus station. Single rooms at IR£18, twins IR£30, dorm beds IR£8. Breakfast not included. No curfew, but room lock-out 11am–5pm. Self-catering kitchen and restaurant. No credit cards.

Jacob's Inn, 21–28 Talbot Place (☎01/855 5660, fax 01/855 5664). A short walk from the bus station or Connolly train station, this is a new hostel

run by the Isaac's people with prices slightly higher than most hostels. Singles IR£25–29, twins IR£32–36, dorm beds IR£8–10. No curfew. No credit cards.

Lansdowne, 27 Pembroke Road (☎01/668 2522, fax 01/668 5585). Comfortable hotel within shouting distance of Lansdowne Road stadium, popular with visiting sports fans. Satellite TV and bath/shower in every room. Doubles IR£65–80 including breakfast. Most major credit cards.

Leitrim House, 34 Blessington St (☎01/830 8728). Popular B&B, ten minutes' walk from O'Connell Street. Doubles at IR£20–25, large Irish breakfast included. No credit cards.

Flaming youth – David Connolly, the brightest new Irish striker for a generation

Italy

Nowhere in Europe does football matter as much as in Italy. Every Sunday the fate of the nation – not to say billions of lire and civic pride – hangs in the balance. The Italian game, *calcio*, is a weekly celebration of noise and colour, fed by a media hyberbole which would put an American presidential campaign to shame.

Leading politicians, captains of industry, Mafia bosses – all have used the game's exaggerated importance for their own ends. Football's remarkable niche in Italian life sealed Mussolini's popularity in the Thirties. More recently, it allowed media mogul Silvio Berlusconi to climb to the top and become Italian prime minister. The most popular club, Juventus, are as important to the Agnelli family as the wheels on their Fiat cars. The *tottonero*, the illegal gambling racket run by the Mafia, accounts for an annual revenue of at least $3 billion.

The game the world watches – Totò Schillaci, Italia '90

For most of the postwar era, the Italian league has been world soccer's shop window, the stage where the greatest talents parade their skills every Sunday. The transfer market is a twice-yearly week of trading in one of Milan's grand hotels, as frenetic as Wall Street, the commodity being not futures or trusts, but footballers.

In Italy, football really can be a matter of life and death, as sadly proved by the fatal stabbing of a Genoa fan in 1995, which raised serious questions about Italy's ultra gangs – the fans who provide much of the noise and colour essential to every match, and who receive official favour (including match tickets) from many of the biggest clubs.

The ultra phenomenon harks back to the beginnings of the Italian game in sixteenth century Florence. Now played out for tourists every summer, this original *calcio* was a bright, loud and bloody carnival involving fifty Florentine aristocrats violently rucking for a ball, originally a decapitated head.

When the modern version was introduced by English sailors and traders four hundred years later, it was to become the people's art, the aristocracy being left to conduct their business off the pitch. The English influence can be still be seen in the three north Italian cities where the imported game first developed: Genoa and AC Milan carry Anglicised club names, while Juventus of Turin play in a black-and-white striped shirt originally derived from that of Notts County.

Long time coming – Bruno Conti holds the World Cup after Italy had beaten West Germany, 1982

Genoa dominated the first annual Italian championships, played for at the turn of the century. Their mantle was soon taken by AC Milan and that club's rival offshoot, Internazionale. The championship was decided on a north/south/central play-off until the formation of a national league in 1929. Behind the new league lay the workings of a man who did much to hasten football's development in Italy between the wars – Vittorio Pozzo.

Pozzo transformed Italian football. From his early experience in England he brought tactical know-how to Italy, then far behind the Danubian game of their Central European rivals Austria, Czechoslovakia and Hungary. An innovative coach of the national team, the *azzurri*, he couped his players up in regimented training camps, *in ritiro*, away from the trappings of city life. On the field, he introduced the attacking centre-half, a creator and destroyer, a con-

cept embodied in Luisito Monti, an Argentine of Italian extraction whose rugged talents were a prime factor in Italy winning the World Cup they hosted in 1934. If Monti was the anti-hero, then the hero was Giuseppe Meazza, a fast, delicate forward who starred for both Milan clubs. A likable rogue, the popular *Peppino* would receive the posthumous accolade of having the San Siro stadium renamed after him.

At the World Cup, the first to be held in Europe, neither the Austrians nor the Czechs could overcome the awesome Monti, nor cope with his fellow Italo-Argentine wingers, Guaita and Orsi; with a goal from each, Italy beat Austria 1–0 in the semi-final and Czechoslovakia 2–1 after extra time in the final.

The event was a propaganda victory for Fascist leader Benito Mussolini, but it also left a legacy of first-class, modern municipal stadia in many of Italy's major cities.

By the time of the 1938 World Cup in France, Pozzo had discarded most of the 1934 squad, recruiting their replacements from his country's 1936 Olympic gold medal-winning team. His masterstroke was to pair Meazza with Silvio Piola, the Lazio striker who would score five goals in the tournament, including a brace in Italy's 4–2 win over Hungary in the final.

World War II saw the rise of a great Torino side, five times title winners, and captained by their chief goalscorer, Valentino Mazzola. All the team would perish in the Superga air disaster of 1949, when a plane carrying Torino back from a friendly in Lisbon crashed into the side of the Basilica overlooking Turin. The dead were accorded a state funeral.

It would take the Italian national team years to recover from the loss at Superga, but there were other factors at work, not least an influx of star foreigners which accompanied the country's postwar economic boom. When Sweden won Olympic soccer gold at the 1948 Games, AC Milan went out and bought their entire forward trio. To counteract their talents and those of John Charles, Juan Schiaffino, Kurt Hamrin and others, Italian defences of the Fifties adopted the rigid *catenaccio* defensive system of strict man-to-man marking with a *libero* or sweeper behind.

League games became low-scoring affairs, dominated by strong defences and quick counter-attacking. After the demise of the great Real Madrid of the late Fifties, Italian discipline would bring European Cup success for both Milan clubs. It was the Internazionale coach Helenio Herrera who perfected *catenaccio*, his strategies aided and abetted by the brilliant overlapping full-back Giacinto Facchetti and by training methods as strict as any in Pozzo's day. Herrera constructed an infernal defensive trap to frustrate the home side, but the new generation of fans who followed *la Grande Inter* across Europe didn't care.

A fourth successive poor World Cup showing by the *azzurri* in 1962 led to a ban on foreign imports to the Italian league

two years later. For the national side, worse was to follow with defeat by North Korea at Ayresome Park in 1966 – causing a World Cup exit as ignominious as any in the competition's history, and the team to be met by a hailstorm of rotten tomatoes on their return to Italy.

Domestically, however, the ban on foreigners allowed home talents to flourish, like those of Gianni Rivera and Sandro Mazzola in the midfields of Milan and Inter, respectively. Mazzola, son of Valentino who had perished in the Superga crash, would play a key rôle in the event which signalled Italy's return to the top drawer of the international game – victory in the 1968 European Championship. As at the World Cup 34 years earlier, Italy's win (over Yugoslavia in the final) owed a little to luck and much to their hosting of the tournament. But the point had been made – the *azzurri* were a force to be reckoned with once again.

Both Mazzola and Rivera would be used in Italy's run to the final of the 1970 World Cup. In the heat and altitudes of Mexico,

High drama – victory over Yugoslavia, 1968

Basics

EU citizens require only a **passport** to enter Italy, as do Americans, Canadians, Australians and New Zealanders.

The Italian currency is the **lira** (plural lire), abbreviated as 'L' or 'Lit'. There are L50, L100, L200 and L500 coins, and notes for L1000, L2000, L5000, L10,000, L50,000 and L100,000. There are around L2500 to £1.

Italy is still very much a **cash economy**. Major cities have Bancomat machines for cash advances, but credit-card payment for goods and services is relatively rare. Banks are the best places to **change money**, open Mon–Fri 8.30am–1.45pm & 3.30–4.30pm, with restricted working hours before a public holiday.

By law you must **take your receipt** for every purchase. In your change you may find a *gettone* – a token worth L200 for jukeboxes and phone calls from bars. Other coin phones take L100, L200 and L500 pieces. Most public phones will only accept **phonecards**, L5000 or L10,000 from newsstands and *tabacchi* stores designated by a blue 'T' sign. Break off the corner of the card before use.

Calling abroad from Italy is expensive – off-peak times are Mon–Sat 10pm–8am and all day Sunday. To get an international line from inside the country, dial 00. To call Italy from abroad, dial 39, then the city code: Rome is 6, Milan 2, Turin 11, Florence 55, Genoa 10 and Naples 81. As ever, add a 0 to the code if you are calling inland.

The first thing to know about Italian **trains** is that you must validate your ticket in the orange machines by the platform before you board. Services are cheap, frequent and comfortable, if a little confusing. *Pendolino*, *Eurocity* and *Intercity* services connect major towns and require both a reservation and a supplement – indicate the train you are catching when you buy your ticket.

Italian **accommodation** is more expensive than its French or Spanish counterpart. In most towns a double room in a two-star hotel (*albergho*) will cost L70–90,000. A cheaper option is a *pensione* – a family-run guesthouse where a nominal fee is charged for use of the shower in the corridor. Most of these places will ask guests to be in by around 1am, but a double should cost no more than L40–50,000.

Italian **cuisine** is claimed by many to be the best in the world. It is certainly not cheap. A stand-up *pizzeria* will charge around L5000 for a basic slice and up to L10,000 for anything fancier. A *trattoria* – usually slightly cheaper than a *ristorante* – will have first pasta courses at L6–9000, with the main meat course weighing in at L15–20,000. You will also be charged *pane e coperto*, bread and cover charge, and *servizio* of ten percent.

Bars are generally clean, chrome affairs, not designed for passing time in. Standing in a bar for hours is as senseless to an Italian as standing in a hardware store. Alcohol is consumed in good taste, as part of a meal, and wine is (deservedly) the most popular drink. Excessive beer drinking, even if carried out with decorum, is frowned upon. Let none of this deter you. Go to the cash desk (*cassa*), order your drink and pay, then slap your receipt (*scontrino*) on the counter to attract the barman's attention.

Ask for a *birra alla spina* ('beer on draught') and you'll be given a choice of *piccolo*, *media* or *grande* sizes. Of the local brews, **Peroni** and **Nastro Azzurro** are fairly bland but **Moretti**, from the north-eastern region of Friuli, has a distinctive flavour. The national spirit, *grappa*, made from wine-making residues, must be taken in the knowledge that it will leave you a babbling wreck.

Italian **nightlife** is generally dear, derivative and disappointing. Even if you avoid the L15,000 entrance fee by negotiation at the door to a club, you may be charged for membership (*una tessera*), not to say twice usual bar prices inside.

each would play for 45 minutes. With the powerful, prolific Luigi Riva (whose goals had helped Cagliari to a surprising league title that year), the Italian side were Europe's best in the tournament, but still no match for the incomparable Brazil of Pelé, Tostão and Jairzinho.

As the Seventies went on, the absence of foreign stars from the domestic game began to have negative as well as positive side-effects. Italian clubs lost the creative edge they needed to compete in European competition, and at the 1974 World Cup,

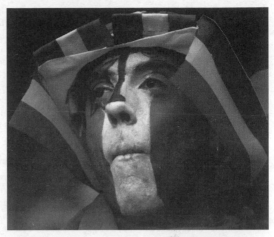

Ultra bright – nowhere is support more colourful than in Italy

the *azzurri*, with their rigidly defensive formation, had no answer to the fluid 'Total Football' of the Dutch and West Germans.

Juventus, nine times title winners between 1972 and 1986, provided Italy's silver lining. The team provided the core of the *azzurri* side who came good under Enzo Bearzot at the 1978 and 1982 World Cups. Paolo Rossi, Roberto Bettega, Franco Causio, Gaetano Scirea and Marco Tardelli were the keys to a fourth-place finish in Argentina in 1978, and to an exhilarating run to the 1982 final – after a stultifyingly slow start – in Spain. After gaining revenge over Brazil in a heart-stopping 3–2 win at the second-round group stage, Italy sealed their third World Cup with a 3–1 victory over West Germany in Madrid. Rossi, who in the mid-Seventies had served a two-year ban for his involvement in a fixed-odds betting scandal, emerged as the tournament's top scorer with six goals.

By then, foreign imports had been allowed back into Italy, and two in particular dominated the Eighties – Frenchman Michel Platini at Juventus, and Diego Maradona at Napoli. Platini's remarkable goalscoring prowess from midfield kept the 'Zebras' at the top in the middle part of

the decade, not just in Italy but in Europe, where they mounted a serious challenge to the then-dominant English game and its prime exponents, Liverpool. The face-off between the two clubs for the 1985 European Cup turned into disaster, however, as English hooligans, Italian ultras and Belgian disorganisation combined in the death of 39 (mainly Italian) fans before the match, then played and almost irrelevantly won by Juventus.

If Platini's skills were mesmerising, Maradona's success with Napoli was no less than the stuff of fantasy. His team's title win in 1987 marked the first time the Italian championship had been won by a team from the deep, impoverished south – a historical footnote given added potency by the regional rivalry that had characterised the game in Italy from its earliest days.

Napoli's success (they won the title again in 1990) was all the more extraordinary considering the contemporary strength of the two Milan clubs. Media mogul Silvio Berlusconi had bought a bankrupt AC Milan in 1986, ostensibly as a tool with which his Canale 5 TV station could challenge the state monopoly of televised football. But the kind of money he made available exceeded expectations, attracting the Dutch trio of Ruud Gullit, Frank Rijkaard and Marco van Basten to the club. Berlusconi didn't just want results – he wanted his viewers entertained. Under coach Arrigo Sacchi, Milan played a fast, attacking style that took the game to the opposing side. Their great *libero*, Franco Baresi, played in front of the defence rather than behind it, while their full-back Paolo Maldini made incisive runs down the flank. In the 1989 European Cup, Milan beat Real Madrid 5–0 in the semi-final and Steaua Bucharest 4–0 in the final. Italy had seen nothing like it in forty years.

Under Milanese influence, zonal marking slowly replaced *catenaccio* and goals flowed in the Italian league. It made great television, and coincided with Italy hosting the 1990 World Cup, the preparations for which saw billions of lire spent on renovating the stadia used in 1934, while all-new grounds were built in Turin and Bari.

Italy began as favourites, and played like it – with rising star Roberto Baggio, a surprise find in goalscorer Totó Schillaci, and

Baresi sublime in defence. It was Maradona who stopped them, in a tense semi-final in Naples, of all places. Just as Baresi and Baggio would do in the 1994 World Cup final, Roberto Donadoni missed in the penalty shoot-out, his unlucky number 17 shirt splashed across the front page of every morning paper, sinking into the turf in grief.

The 1994 side was coached by Sacchi, who had left Milan, leaving former international Fabio Capello to take charge. While Sacchi's *azzurri* prepared for the USA, Capello's Milan won the Italian title three times between 1992 and 1994 – their 4–0 whitewash of Barcelona in the 1994 European Cup final was an awesome demonstration of the chasm in class that existed between the Italian league and the rest of Europe.

Every year between 1989 and 1995, there were at least two Italian clubs in the three European finals. In 1996 there was only one – and although Juventus won the Champions' League, the two stars who had helped them win it, Gianluca Vialli and Fabrizio Ravanelli, were playing in England's

Winning is everything – Roberto Baggio waits for the ground to swallow him up, Los Angeles, 1994

Premiership within months of their victory in the final over Ajax. Despite the vast sums earned from Europe-wide TV rights and sponsorship, Juve could no longer afford the high-figure salaries demanded by Italian stars – England could.

In the summer of 1996, Sacchi made a string of unforced team changes which caused Italy to lose to the Czech Republic and ultimately depart England before the knockout stage of the European Championship. Less than a year later, with the *azzurri* reviving under Cesare Maldini, not one of Europe's club competitions was won by an Italian team.

In 1997, changes in Italian law obliged clubs to turn themselves from informal associations into limited companies. It may be the first of many changes. While their league lacks the TV money of England, the merchandising know-how of the German *Bundesliga* and the massive provincial crowds of the Spanish *Liga*, Italian teams may seek alternative means of finance – including stock-market flotation – to keep up with the European pace.

Yet even if the days of the Italian soccer mogul look numbered, football is still the passion of the people, the one driving force that both unites and divides the nation.

Ultimately, *calcio* is still cool.

Essential vocabulary

Hello/goodbye *Ciao*
Yes *Sí*
No *No*
Two beers, please *Due alla spina, per favore*
Thank you *Grázie*
Men's *Uomini*
Women's *Donne*
Where is the stadium? *Dovè lo stadio?*
What is the score? *Come siamo?*
Referee *Il arbitro*
Offside *Fuori gioco*

Match practice

The first week of September is the big kick-off for a league season that lasts until the first week of June, with a short break for Christmas and New Year. A round of league matches, (*giornata*), takes place on Sunday afternoons. Kick-off time is 4pm in autumn and spring, 2.30pm in winter. One match will be at 8.30pm for live television coverage on Telepiù 2, while teams involved in upcoming midweek European action play on the preceding Saturday evening, usually also at 8.30pm.

The build-up to each Sunday's match starts on the previous Monday. While the media are awash with rumour and counter-rumour concerning the upcoming fixtures, fans dutifully swamp the training grounds before heading off to rehearse their stadium routines back in town.

The grounds begin to fill up from late on Sunday morning. For derby games, the gates may be opened four or five hours before kick-off to allow fans time to put up their banners.

At the turnstiles, security is often tight. Coins and cigarette lighters may be confiscated, and you'll catch your first glimpse of Italy's much-maligned *carabinieri*, the branch of the police responsible for keeping public order. Turnstile searches aren't the only reason to leave yourself plenty of time before kick-off – whatever the quality of the match, you'll be treated to a veritable pageant in the stadium that will live with you long after the details of the game itself have faded from memory.

Remember that Italian football is as exaggerated as everything else in Italy. Outbreaks of violence aren't unknown, but it's easy for the visitor to misinterpret aggressive gestures as provocation – when in fact all you're witnessing is an uncontrollable outburst of local pride.

On full-time (and often sooner), fans of the losing side will take their frustrations out on their mopeds, and are quickly home to watch the highlights on TV. Another Sunday is over – at least until Monday morning.

The league

The top drawer of Italy's *Lega Calcio* – *Serie A* – has been an eighteen-team division since 1988. A team that wins the title earns the right to wear *lo scudetto*, the green, white and red shield, on their shirt for the whole of the following season, and the championship itself is often referred to simply as the *scudetto*. Those who are crowned champions ten times are awarded a gold star above their badge – Juventus are the only team with two stars.

The bottom four clubs change places with the top four from the twenty-team *Serie B*. Teams level on points have their fate decided by the results of matches between them over the course of the season; if these are equal, the relegation spot is determined by a play-off (*spareggio*).

From *Serie B*, four teams go down to the third division, *Serie C1*, which is divided north/south into two groups, *Girone A* and B. The top two from each eighteen-team *Girone* go up automatically, while those finishing second to fifth play off against each other for one place each. Three teams from each *Girone* drop down, to be replaced by six teams rising from the three-section *Serie C2*. The next rung down is for amateur clubs, known as *dilettanti*.

Up for the cup

La Coppa Italia is a half-hearted affair involving all clubs from *Serie A* and B and ten from *Serie C*. Little is left to chance, the draw being structured like a tennis tournament, planned out from the first round in August. *Serie A* clubs do not enter until the second round, and all their games are played midweek.

Ties are decided on one game, extra time and penalties until the quarter-finals in November, semi-finals in January and final in June, all of which decided over two legs.

With no sense of tradition, *la Coppa* generates reasonable crowds only when one of the teams involved in the latter stages have been starved of honours. Fiorentina's successful run of 1996 aroused a rare case of Italian cup fever.

Tickets

Italian football is the most expensive in Europe. The cheapest tickets are with the ultras in the *curva* behind the goals. These cost between L25,000 and L30,000. Larger stadia are divided into rings (*anelli*), with prices ranging from L40,000 to L200,000, depending on the view. To take in both the game and the atmosphere, get a *distinti* – a numbered seat between the *curva* and the expensive *tribuna centrale* over the halfway line – for around L50,000. For derby games and big matches, get an Italian friend to

The Czechs have equalised, Italy are out, Sammer wants to swap shin-pads – Old Trafford, 1996

grab a ticket days in advance from the club shop or from one of the many club bars. Alternatively, do battle with the touts (*bagarini*) outside the ground on matchday. Don't be intimidated – you can always haggle them down – but even when the bargaining is over, you may still be paying more than you ever thought you would to watch a football match...

There are no matchday programmes, but most clubs issue a glossy, monthly magazine; those produced by Juve, Inter and Milan are available at newsstands across Italy.

Half-time

No beer is on sale at Italian grounds. Fans get high instead

Dream ticket? Italy coach Cesare Maldini and his son, Paolo

on *caffè borghetti* – small yellow-topped canisters of heavily sugared, spirit-strengthened coffee.

There'll be no queue for the hot dogs, either. At half-time Italians either smoke nervously or unwrap sandwiches lovingly packed by their mothers, while vendors selling plastic bottles of soft drinks pass through the crowd at regular intervals.

Action replay

Italian state television, RAI, had enjoyed a monopoly of televised soccer until Silvio Berlusconi put his commercial foot in the door in the late Eighties. RAI still have the lion's share of coverage, but they needed to wage a battle royal with Telemontecarlo boss (and Fiorentina president) Vittorio Cecchi Gori in 1996 to hang onto it. In the end, RAI paid L200 billion for the rights to cover *Serie A* football until 1999 – but the deal covers highlights only and even these are 'sub-let' to other broadcasters.

Given the total absence of live action, RAI coax an enormous amount of programming out of each Sunday's *giornata*. From lunchtime, RAI Uno screens six

hours of *Domenica In* – tacky studio entertainment tenuously packaged around the afternoon's half- and full-time scores; the last section, *Novantesimo Minuto* ('Ninetieth Minute'), just after 6pm, offers brief highlights from all *Serie A* games.

This action is analysed on RAI Due's *Domenica Sprint* (8pm). RAI Tre then calls in expert witnesses for *La Domenica Sportiva* later in the evening, and yet more for *Il Proceso del Lunedì* ('The Monday Trial') in the small hours.

Two other non-subscription channels challenge the state monopoly. Berlusconi's Italia Uno has a half-hour Sunday lunchtime preview, *Guida Al Campianato*, a night-time round-up, *Pressing*, and Monday's popular *Mai Dire Gol!* ('Never Say Goal!'). Meanwhile, Telemontecarlo weighs in with a highlights show, *Galagoal*, at 8.20pm.

Pay TV station Telepiù, part-owned by Berlusconi, began live football coverage in 1993 and immediately doubled their subscriber base. As well as showing the evening *Serie A* game on Sunday at 8.30pm, the station usually has a live English Premiership match at 3pm. In 1996/97 the company introduced pay-per-view broadcasts, with the price depending on the importance of the match.

As if all this weren't enough, each major city has a local station with its own football show; those in Rome and Naples attract as many viewers as their nationwide competitors.

European action is divided between all the non-subscription broadcasters – Italia Uno, Canale 5, Telemontecarlo and RAI. Telemontecarlo, which like Britain's Channel 5 can transmit only to a percentage of the country, pulled off a major coup when they won the rights to the England–Italy World Cup qualifier in February 1997 – forcing fans in remote southern towns to hire buses to take them to the nearest screen showing the match.

For real Sunday atmosphere, do as the Romans do and take a radio to the game. *Tutto Il Calcio,* on Radio RAI Uno, has unmissable histrionics.

The back page

Italy boasts three daily sports newspapers, each based in a different city and prone to defend the interests of the region it represents. The pink pages of Milan's *La Gazzetta dello Sport* (L1400) are the most widely read, with average sales of half-a-million, double that on a Monday. The paper has featured some classic sports writing in its time, and its standards remain a cut above – though don't say this in Rome, where *Il Corriere dello Sport* (L1400) is tops. The Turin paper is *Tuttosport* (L1500).

For most of the week – and right through summer – readers of all three papers have to wade through acres of rumour and transfer speculation. Yet, with all those pages to fill every day, none of the three offers anything better than mediocre coverage of the game outside Italy. The all-colour, picture-heavy *Guerin Sportivo* (Fridays, L4000) fills this gap with results and league tables from around the world, as well as international news and *Hello!*-style photo spreads of top Italian

stars, their wives, their villas and their customised Alfa Romeos.

Italian players are theoretically obliged to be as helpful as possible to the media, but the cordial relationship between the two does not always survive the pressure of big tournaments. The *silenzio stampa,* or blanket press ban, issued by coach Enzo Bearzot after vicious reporting of Italy's poor start to the 1982 World Cup, was said to have given his team the boost they needed to win.

Ultra culture

Italy is the home of ultra culture. The movement evolved during the early Seventies and had become an integral part of the game within a decade. The choreography, the colour and the noise of Italian ultras remain unmatched anywhere in the continent, though their fashions have been copied all across Latin America and Southern and Eastern Europe.

Unfortunately, the rise of the ultras has come hand in hand with occasional violence, and the next fan death may push the Italian parliament into taking action to prevent organised gangs travelling to matches.

In the net

Italy plays host to one of international football's foremost generic websites, *Rete!,* at: www.tin.it/rete/. The site boasts some 120,000 pages, each one dedicated to the beautiful game and stored with an efficiency seldom seen on the Web. Still graphics and MPEG videos of goal action are the site's strongest suit, and these extend beyond *Serie A* to other major European leagues. Meanwhile, a vast news and stats archive also covers the globe.

Being so all-encompassing, however, *Rete!* can be slow to access and find your way around. Those interested solely in things Italian might be better off checking out Stefano Rossi's *L'Italia del Calcio* site at: www.mclink.it/com/ies/calcio/indice.htm. You'll find news and stats aplenty for the entire *Lega Clacio,* plus a handy glossary of terms in four European languages.

Milan

AC Milan *328*
Internazionale *333*

Milan is a true football capital. Its stadium, the San Siro, is one of the world's great arenas, shared by opposing city giants AC Milan and Internazionale, who between them have won nearly fifty European and domestic titles.

On March 9, 1998, Milan will be celebrating ninety years of the rivalry, one of Europe's greatest. It was instigated when members of Milan FC formed a breakaway team in protest over the British influence prevalent at the club. Milan FC had been founded as Milan Cricket and Football Club in 1899, by Englishman Alfred Edwards at the *Fiaschetteria Toscana* in Via Berchet. The club became the domain of English sportsmen and well-to-do Milanese, who would meet over cocktails at the *American Bar*.

On March 9, 1908, an Italian and Swiss rebel faction met in a backroom of the *Orologio* restaurant near the Piazza del Duomo, intent on breaking away. They decided to call their club Internazionale Milano, after the multi-national nature of their group.

The rivalry began in earnest with five straight wins for Milan FC, a series interrupted when Internazionale romped to a 5–0 victory in 1910. In time, it would be Inter, as they became known (*never* Inter Milan) who would attract the upper crust, while Milan FC (later AC) appealed to the working class. These criteria have shifted again in the Eighties and Nineties, making the rivalry hard to define. Support for either the *nerazzurri* (the blue-and-black stripes of Inter) or *rossoneri* (the thinner, red-and-black stripes of Milan) has never been a matter of geographical location. Arguments are won and lost over the family breakfast table, making the derby more a domestic tug-of-love than a civil war.

Before the breakaway, Milan FC won three Italian championship play-offs, the

Catenaccio meets 'Total Football' – Ajax v AC Milan, European Cup final, 1969

Punching the air 'til it's black and blue – Inter faithful at the San Siro

last in 1907. Within three years the upstarts of Inter were champions, and two decades later, as Ambrosiana-Inter, they would become the first winners of the all-Italian league. Playing at the Arena behind Sforzesco castle, the *nerazzurri* kept one step ahead of their rivals, who by now were playing in a newly built stadium in the west of the city – the San Siro, whose construction was financed by a former *American Bar* regular from the turn of the century, tyre millionaire Piero Pirelli.

Never mind that Milan had the stadium – Inter had the players, among them top goalscorer Giuseppe Meazza, who played for his country at the 1934 and 1938 World Cups and, at a time of increasingly overbearing Fascist authority, became a symbol of the city's brash individuality. Ironically, the Arena where Meazza gave spectators so much pleasure was used by the Nazis during World War II to round up and shoot local partisans.

After World War II, Inter moved out into the suburbs to share the San Siro with Milan, leaving the Arena, the oldest surviving stadium to have staged first-class

football, to fall into disrepair. It was renovated in 1996, with new press boxes and running track installed, and its main function will be to stage junior athletics.

Inter and Milan both won league titles in the early Fifties, and the San Siro crowd witnessed some tense derbies – the legendary 6–5 game of 1949 was the first that current Inter president Massimo Moratti was taken to as a young boy.

Two key figures helped to turn Milanese football into the modern, multi-million pound business it is today. The first was Inter coach Helenio Herrera, a man who manipulated not just his players but also the press and, by extension, the public. During the Sixties his controversial Italo-Spanish rants made football the main talking point and kept the city buzzing, while on the pitch, Inter's European Cup win over Real Madrid in 1964 proved a turning point in the history of the European game – never again would a Spanish giant overshadow its Milanese counterpart.

Now the city would come alive for big nights of European action, and the San Siro on derby day was a place for high society to be seen. The rivalry between the clubs' two inspirational inside-forwards, Milan's Gianni Rivera and Inter's Sandro Mazzola, gave the fixture added spice.

The second crucial figure was Silvio Berlusconi. After taking over an ailing AC Milan in 1986, Berlusconi put the club on an entirely different commercial footing from the rest of the Italian game. 'Milan' shops, bars, restaurants and clubs were opened across the city, and star players were contractually tied to give them their blessing. The game, and its prime exponents, became a high-profile commercial tool in Italy's business capital. A Martian could visit Turin and not know the city played football. Not so Milan.

In 1989, the trio of Gullit, van Basten and Rijkaard who'd helped Holland win the 1988 European Championship brought AC Milan their first European title for twenty years. That same year, the trio of Klinsmann, Matthäus and Brehme who would lead West Germany to the 1990 World Cup won the title with Inter – the club's first for a decade. Milan was indubitably Europe's football capital.

The San Siro, renamed the Giuseppe Meazza after the popular figure's death in 1979, was given a hundred billion lire refit in order to host the opening ceremony and five other matches of the 1990 World Cup.

Not long after Italia '90, the *rossoneri* pulled away and won three straight Italian titles. Inter couldn't hold a candle to their rivals' earning power from media and merchandising, and while Berlusconi ruled supreme at Milan, boardroom power struggles crucially weakened Inter. In 1994, Milan won the European Cup in supreme style,

Milan essentials

Milan has two **airports** – Linate, 7km east of the centre, and Malpensa, 45km northwest. Both are connected by bus to the main **train station**, Stazione Centrale. From Linate, buses leave every 20–30 minutes, 5.40am–9pm (L4000, journey time 15–20 minutes). City bus #73 also runs between Linate and Piazza San Babila, 5.30am–midnight. From Malpensa, airport buses leave every 30 minutes, 7.30am–12.30pm, and every hour 12.30pm–5.30pm (L12,000, journey time one hour). Three buses a day run between the two airports.

The city has a fast, efficient **metro system** with three colour-coded lines: red (line 1), green (line 2) and yellow (line 3). Lines 2 and 3 cross at the Stazione Centrale, lines 1 and 3 at the city centre, Piazza del Duomo. Lines 1 and 2 cross at Cadorna, near the main **bus station** in Piazza Castello. Buses and trams augment the transport network.

Tickets, available from newsstands and vending machines, cost L1500 each and are valid for 75 minutes on any tram or bus, and for one metro journey. Punch the ticket onboard or when entering the metro. **Carnets** of ten tickets are available, as are **passes** for 24 hours and 48 hours. Transport runs 6am–midnight, with **night buses** following the metro routes until 1am.

Yellow **taxis** can be found outside the main train station or by Piazza del Duomo. To call for one, dial Radiotaxi (☎02/5353) or Autoradiotaxi (☎02/8585).

The two main **tourist offices** are helpful and English-speaking, at the Stazione Centrale (open Mon–Sat 8am–7pm, ☎02/669 0532) and at Via Marconi 1, by Piazza del Duomo (open Mon–Sat 8am–8pm, Sun 9am–12.30pm & 1.30–5pm, ☎02/809 662).

Milan has no **listings magazine**, but the Thursday edition of the daily newspaper *La Repubblica* includes *Tutto Milano*, a booklet containing reasonable concert, restaurant and nightclub information.

The best store in town for **football merchandise** from all over Italy is *Centro Sport Calcio*, Via Procaccini 32 (tram #29 or #30 from M2 Garibaldi, open Mon–Fri 9.30am–12.30pm & 3–7pm, most major credit cards).

with a 4–0 win over Barcelona, while Inter, after a season struggling against the threat of relegation, also won in Europe, beating Salzburg to lift the UEFA Cup. Both sets of supporters celebrated in the traditional way, parading around the Piazza del Duomo – but the chasm in class between the two teams was hard to ignore.

Within two years, however, the rivalry would be alive and thriving once more. Massimo Moratti's determination to re-create *la grande Inter* made the *nerazzurri* the city's sole title contenders in 1996/97, while Milan sank ignominiously into mid-table – their poor form blamed partly on the nightspots the players had been hired to promote...

The thrilling fields

 AC Milan

Office Via Turati 3
Stadium San Siro, see p.330
Colours Red-and-black striped shirts, white shorts
League champions 1901, 1906–07, 1951, 1955, 1957, 1959, 1962, 1968, 1979, 1988, 1992–94, 1996
Cup winners 1967, 1972–73, 1977
European Cup winners 1963, 1969, 1989–90, 1994
Cup-Winners' Cup winners 1968, 1973

For all the criticism that can justifiably be laid at his door, Silvio Berlusconi has revolutionised European football. Over the past decade he has transformed his boyhood favourites, AC Milan, turning them from a shambolic, debt-ridden wreck into the world's greatest club. Along the way his coaches, Arrigo Sacchi and Fabio Capello, have rid Italian football of interminable, defence-first goalless draws. And the president's need to be guaranteed top-class European action for his TV interests has

led directly to the creation of the Champions' League. The arguments surrounding this modern offspring of the European Cup are beside the point. Berlusconi has pushed the game into another financial league and this new money – and the need to make more of it – has given us some breathtaking football, the like of which many in Europe thought they would never see again.

Almost incidentally, Berlusconi, a former cruise-ship singer, used both his football club and his media interests to assist him in becoming prime minister of Italy – albeit briefly – in the early Nineties.

Whether his ambitions have been in broadcasting or politics, Berlusconi's vehicle has been AC Milan. Yet in taking the club relentlessly forward, he has remained true to tradition – even before his arrival in 1986, the *rossoneri* had a reputation for buying the best and attacking with it.

After their formation as Milan Cricket and Football Club in 1899, Milan became the first club to break Genoa's early stranglehold on the Italian game. They won three titles, two as Milan FC, and enjoyed a flow of cash from one of their founding members, car tyre magnate Piero Pirelli. Progress was halted when half the club left to form Internazionale.

Pirelli put his money behind the building of a new stadium, the San Siro, in 1926, but although it saw regular international action, its home club floundered. With their English influence (their origins, Anglicised name and then coach, *il Mister* Burgess), Milan found themselves out of political favour with the Fascist authorities that held sway in Italy in the Thirties.

After World War II, the purchase of Swedish stars Gunnar Gren, Gunnar Nordahl and Nils Liedholm (the so-called *Gre-no-li* trio) helped lift Milan back into the upper echelons of the Italian game. Between 1948 and 1966, Milan finished in the top three of *Serie A* every year but one.

With the inception of the big European club competitions, more foreign stars came to Milan – Uruguayan Juan Schiaffino and Brazilian José Altafini among them. Milan lost to Real Madrid in the 1958 European Cup final, 3–2 after extra time. But there was to be no let-down five years later, against Benfica at Wembley, when two Altafini goals put paid to Eusébio and co.

In the Milan ranks that fine May evening in 1963 was a young inside-forward from Alessandria, Gianni Rivera, who would become the club's figurehead for fifteen years. Alongside him were two men who would make an even greater impact as coaches – Cesare Maldini, later Italian national-team boss, whose son Paolo would star in three European Cup finals, and Giovanni Trappatoni, seven times a *scudetto* winner from the dugout in the Seventies and Eighties.

With Nereo Rocco calling the shots from the sidelines, Rivera running the midfield and two more imported stars, Swedish winger Kurt Hamrin and German full-back Karl-Heinz Schnellinger, spicing up the mixture, Milan won one *scudetto*, two more European trophies and a World Club championship in 1968 and 1969.

Only Rivera remained in the side that beat Leeds in the 1973 Cup-Winners' Cup final – a match tainted by strange refereeing decisions, and one which would give Milan their last European trophy for sixteen years.

Rivera bowed out by helping the club to a star-winning tenth *scudetto* in 1979, but behind the scenes, all was far from well. During the lowest period of the club's history, president Felice Colombo was found guilty of match-rigging during the 1978/79 campaign, and Milan were sent down to *Serie B*. After promotion, they played their way back down again – and Colombo's successor, Giussy Farina, fled to South Africa reportedly owing a fortune in back taxes. British players Mark Hateley, Luther Blissett, Joe Jordan and Ray Wilkins all had the misfortune to be part of Milan during this low ebb.

Berlusconi took over the club in 1986. And while his emphasis on developing the business side of Milan has been well documented, not all of his innovations were

Best in the continent – Marcel Desailly, 1994

driven by the dash for cash. Berlusconi expanded the club's youth structure and invested heavily in the training centre at Milanello, making it the best equipped in Italy. Even more courageously, he entrusted his £20 million investment in the hands of a little-known coach of then unknown Parma, Arrigo Sacchi.

It was Sacchi who bought Dutch stars Marco van Basten and Ruud Gullit, the latter for a world record fee. It was Sacchi who instigated the tactic of 'pressing' the game into the opposition half, attacking the

The San Siro

Stadio Giuseppe Meazza, Via Piccolomini 5
Capacity 85,500 (all-seated)

The Meazza, usually still known by its original name of San Siro, is as rectangular as the day it was first planned. Its pitch is up close to the advertising hoardings, giving the stadium an **intimacy** few others of its stature or grandeur can match. Noise booms around the ground, and smoke hangs in the air with the Milanese mist.

From its **inauguration in 1926**, San Siro has seen three major overhauls, culminating in a £50 million redevelopment for the 1990 World Cup. This gave the stadium a third tier built on a series of cylindrical towers, a plexiglass roof supported by steel girders – and **an overshadowed pitch** which can be about as playable as the trotting track next door. Another £500,000 was spent on drainage and irrigation during the summer of 1995, but the roof, twice-weekly use and **foggy Milanese weather** still play havoc with the playing surface.

San Siro is the name of the district in the west of the city. It was here that Peiro Pirelli built the stadium for his beloved **Milan FC**, its strictly rectangular shape offering no scope for a running track to kill the ambiance. It soon became the leading venue in Italy, the local climate helping the *azzurri* to a muddy semi-final victory over Austria at the 1934 World Cup.

The postwar boom saw another tier added, giving the stadium its **distinctive candy-twist appearance**, in time for the modern age of European competition and televised matches. The San Siro became a household name across Europe before the stands started crumbling in the Eighties. Suitably refurbished for Italia '90, the stadium hosted the tournament's opening ceremony, followed by Cameroon's surprise 1–0 win over holders Argentina. It also hosted a second-round game between West Germany and Holland, in which the teams fielded three players each from Inter and Milan respectively – and all of them playing 'at home'.

The **easiest route** to the stadium is to take the M1 metro line (Molino Dorino branch) to Lotto (fifteen minutes from Duomo), where **stadium buses** will be waiting. In daylight the ten-minute walk alongside the San Siro hippodrome is a pleasant one; after dusk the Viale Federico Caprilli is lined with prostitutes and kerb crawlers.

Getting off the bus, the **Bar Stadio** by the *biglietteria nord* has Forst beer on draught. The **Bar Nuovo Trotto**, by the trotter track on Via dei Rospigliosi 42, is a better bet, with a diplomatic pennant display of both host teams, Heineken on draught and grilled snacks. Pay first at the till, then **shout your order** to the busy barman. In the stadium, the beer is alcohol-free.

As well as the shops and bars listed in the club sections, the Meazza has two main **ticket offices**: *biglietteria nord*, by gates #36/#37, nearest the stadium bus stop from Lotto metro; and *biglietteria sud* by gates #26/#27 opposite, in Piazza Axum.

Apart from big European ties, the Milanese derby, games against Juventus and internationals, **ticket prices** never vary. They are coded in four colours: *rosso* (red, the best tickets, over the halfway line with the press and VIPs); *arancio* (orange, opposite); *blu* (blue, south goal with the Milan fans) and *verde* (green, north goal with the Inter crew). The *3 anello* (third tier) has the **cheapest seats**, with the poorest view from high up. The middle *2 anello* is more expensive, while the *1 anello* nearest the pitch is the dearest of the lot.

Milan diehards enter through gates #17–#22, the **Inter** lads through gates #41–#46, and away fans (regardless of the opposition), tucked in a corner of the south end, through gates #13–#14.

man with the ball instead of falling back. It was Sacchi who laid the groundwork for Milan to pip holders Napoli to the Italian title in 1988.

With another Dutchman, Frank Rijkaard, sweeper Franco Baresi, overlapping full-back Paolo Maldini and midfield creator Roberto Donadoni all maturing into players of world class, the Milan of 1989 were simply irrepressible. Their 5–0 European Cup semi-final thrashing of Real Madrid was the best Europe had seen since their opponents' heyday thirty years before. The 4–0 final win over Steaua Bucharest was a formality – albeit an impressive one.

The work rate involved in Sacchi's pressing game, and the fact that most of his players were involved in the 1990 World Cup, took Milan off the boil before Sacchi's appointment as Italian national-team coach in 1991. After a less convincing European Cup win in 1990, the team made an ignominious exit from the 1991 event – after refusing to take the field after a floodlight failure at Marseille, Milan didn't

just lose the tie – they were banned from Europe for the following season.

Sacchi's replacement was a former Juventus star, Fabio Capello. In his first season, 1991/92, Milan won the league without losing a single game, starting an unbeaten run which would last for 58 games until March 1993 – an Italian record. Before the 1992/93 campaign, Berlusconi bought in bulk. His critics claimed many of the purchases – Gianluigi Lentini, Jean-Pierre Papin, Zvone Boban and Dejan Savićević among them – were made simply to keep the players out of his opponents' clutches. But few neutrals were complaining: that autumn, Milan won 5–4, 7–3, 5–3 and 5–1. Marco van Basten became Italy's all-time highest-scoring foreigner, before sustaining the ankle injury that would eventually – and prematurely – end his career. Clearly unfit, the flying Dutchman was substituted and Milan missed a string of chances in losing the 1993 European Cup final to Marseille.

With the loss of their Dutch trio, it was a solid rather than inspiring Milan that won

Very much so – Ray Wilkins' spell at Milan coincided with the blackest period in the club's history

Second coming – can Capello save Milan?

lo scudetto a third consecutive time in 1994. Their head-to-head clash with Barcelona at the European Cup final in Athens that year was billed as a contrast in styles – hadn't Cruyff's team scored nearly three times more goals that season than Milan? Capello's answer was emphatic. Contrary to all expectations, his team attacked from the start, the final 4–0 scoreline barely reflecting their superiority. Marcel Desailly, recently acquired from Marseille, was outstanding in midfield, Savićević simply sublime.

Crucially, the Montenegrin magician was injured in training before Milan's defence of their European title a year later. Without him, the team retreated into their defensive shell, and were deservedly beaten, 1–0 by Ajax in Vienna.

In the meantime Berlusconi had entered politics, leading his right-wing *Forza Italia* party (named after a football chant) to victory in the 1994 Italian general election. Much of his campaign had been fought using football imagery.

But while Berlusconi's political star rose, that of his football club was starting to fall. In the summer of 1995, Roberto Baggio arrived from champions Juventus, and another new signing, George Weah, got the goals that brought another title to the San Siro. Both men played poorly, however, as Milan were knocked out of the UEFA Cup by Bordeaux, a struggling French side who had entered the competition through back-door of the Intertoto Cup.

At the end of the season, Berlusconi hesitated before offering Capello a new contract, and his coach departed for Real Madrid. Under Capello's replacement, the mild-mannered Uruguayan Oscar Tabarez, Milan's players began to see a little too much of the good life around town. On the pitch, Baresi had lost at least a yard, Maldini was neglecting his defensive duties, and a string of new signings were failing to gel. And, ironically thanks to TV overkill, crowds in the San Siro were down.

After a series of poor league results, Milan needed a draw at home against Rosenborg of Trondheim to set up a meeting with Juventus in the Champions' League quarter-finals. Berlusconi panicked. In the middle of the night he phoned Arrigo Sacchi, who duly appeared back at Milanello, relieved at being given an easy way out of his increasingly untenable job in charge of the *azzurri*. Three days later, Rosenborg won 2–1 and the San Siro fell silent.

Worse was to come. Milan continued to flounder in mid-table as Sacchi's tactical turnarounds confused the players – a 6–1 home defeat by Juventus said it all.

Today Milan have huge debts from awesome wage bills and bonus expenses, and the club is being obliged to convert itself into a limited company. Silvio Berlusconi is out of office, while the team is out of Europe for the first time since the 1993 ban. In 1997/98, returning coach Fabio Capello is back to square one.

Club shop

This is the club with the biggest commercial enterprise in Italy. **Milan Point**, Via

Pietro Verri 8 (M1 San Babila, entrance in Via San Pietro all'Orto, open Mon 3–7pm, Tues–Sat 10am–7pm, most major credit cards), has two floors of class gear, including perfume, Zippo lighters, jewellery, aftershave, long johns and jeans – all gazed down upon approvingly by portraits of Franco Baresi and Silvio Berlusconi. There's a ticket desk upstairs.

Publication

The substantial *Forza Milan!* (monthly, L4000) boasts a circulation of 100,000, an average of seventy for each of the team's 1400 supporters' clubs nationwide.

Ultra culture

The 'Lions' Den', as the lower level of the San Siro's *Curva Sud* has become known, is home to any number of ultra groups, including some of the most feared in Italy – *Fossa del Leoni, Commandos Tigre* and *Brigate Rossonere.*

In 1995, the fatal stabbing of Genoa fan Vincenzo Spagnolo by Simone Barbaglia, of an obscure Milan ultra group called *Barbour,* led to a blanket ban on all sports events across the country the following week. While Barbaglia was sentenced to eleven years in jail – he was caught by security cameras – the very rôle of the ultra movement was brought into question. Milan's ultras, many of whom have left-wing leanings, also saw their status threatened by Silvio Berlusconi's move into (right-wing) politics.

In the net

The club's official website resides at: www.acmilan.it/. It's efficient enough, with news, a picture gallery, ticket information and a sneak preview of the AC Milan CD-ROM among the highlights, but it lacks the vibrancy of some official sites.

Of the many unofficial Milan homepages, one of the best comes from Malta, at: www.geocities.com/Colosseum/4444/. Star of the show here is a splendid rolling news service, in English and with no major piece of gossip omitted. Messy, but rootsy.

Internazionale

Office Via Durini 24
Stadium San Siro, see p.330
Colours Blue-and-black striped shirts, black shorts
League champions 1910, 1920, 1930, 1938, 1940, 1953–54, 1963, 1965–66, 1971, 1980, 1989
Cup winners 1939, 1978, 1982
European Cup winners 1964–65
UEFA Cup winners 1991, 1994

As AC Milan fans are reminded twice a year, Internazionale have never been relegated. That aside, however, there is little ammunition with which to dispute the view that Inter are effectively Italy's third club, and always will be unless either Milan or Juve seriously flounder.

Inter's reputation was built on great sides from two different eras, responsible for six of the club's thirteen titles between them. One man dominated each era: striker Giuseppe Meazza in the Thirties, coach Helenio Herrera three decades later.

Formed by a breakaway group of disgruntled cosmopolitan members of Milan FC in 1908, Inter won their first title two years later almost by default. Their opponents in a title decider, Pro Vercelli asked for the game to be postponed as their best players were involved in a military tournament. When this was refused, they sent a junior team instead. Inter won 10–3.

After a second title ten years later, Inter had to wait until the Fascist era before they again rose to prominence. Ironically their star player, Meazza, was the very opposite of the Fascist ideal – a dedicated man about town who also happened to be a fast, delicate and prolific forward. After his début against the US Milanese club with whom Inter would merge in 1928, his lifestyle would be curtailed by Inter president and Fascist party representative Ferdinando Pozzani. It was to be the first of many interventions. Not only was a strict routine forced on the club, but so was a change of name. The authorities disliked the Leninist implications of 'Internazionale'. So the team became 'Ambrosiana-Inter', after Ambrosio, patron saint of Milan, and under that guise spent the Thirties in a dogfight with Juventus over *lo scudetto*. Matches between the two, which featured several World Cup winners, became known as *il Derby d'Italia*.

Three titles, one cup, 247 Meazza goals and a world war later, Inter got their old name back. They lived up to it with a postwar attack composed of a Dutchman, Faas Wilkes ('The Flying Tulip'), a Frenchman of Hungarian origin, Stefano Nyers, and a Swede, Lennart 'Nacka' Skoglund. In 1950/51 the team hit 107 goals but won nothing. Inter were conceding goals as well as scoring them, until their coach, 1938 World Cup winner Alfredo Foni, devised a solid defensive strategy. In 1952/53 Inter scored 46 goals and won the championship – and a reputation for dour football.

The combination of Foni's discipline and the forward line's spirit kept the title at Inter for another year, often thanks to the considerable talents of the much-loved

Skoglund, whose most tenacious opponent was a bottle of *grappa*.

In 1955, Angelo Moratti became Inter president. A man who had spent his working life in the lubricant oil business and his free time at Inter, his skills were not immediately obvious. Inter fell away in the league and, in an eerie precursor to what would happen in the Nineties, few paid attention to their efforts competing for valueless silverware like the Inter City Fairs' (later UEFA) Cup.

Moratti recognised brass from muck. After a high-scoring defeat by Barcelona, he persuaded Barça's mercurial coach, Helenio Herrera, to leave behind his battle royal with Real Madrid and make Internazionale great again.

With Moratti's millions to oil the wheels, Herrera created an infernal machine. From Barcelona he brought midfield schemer Luis Suárez for a world record fee. In Chile he tracked down the Brazilian Jair, a right-sided winger to play alongside Inter's demon left-winger Mario

Beneath the San Siro lights, Jonk and Bergkamp hail Inter's 1994 Euro win – in 'only' the UEFA Cup

Corso. To meet their crosses was the precocious young talent of striker Sandro Mazzola, whose father Valentino was the biggest footballing loss in the Superga tragedy of 1949. In defence, a junior champion sprinter at overlapping full-back, Giacinto Facchetti, was deployed alongside two henchmen, Armando Picchi and Tarcisio Burgnich. Behind them was Giuliano Sarti, a goalkeeper of rare composure.

Vacuum-tight, man-to-man marking with a solid *libero* and an attack ready to counter – this was *la Grande Inter*. And on the sidelines sat Herrera, *il Mago*, 'the sorcerer', a wizard of hyperbole and sports psychology. He had players chant slogans, he bound the team like a close-knit family, ruled over by a strict Godfather. He introduced the cult of the manager. Above all, he instigated two concepts still relevant today: *ritiro*, a prison-like, three-day training camp far from players' loved ones, and *tifosi* – trainloads of flag-waving fans who would follow Inter's progress around Europe.

The latter were particularly significant. In his early days in Milan, Herrera had missed the atmosphere of the Nou Camp and he persuaded Moratti to encourage organised supporters' clubs. Suddenly, the San Siro was an intimidating place to visit – all the more so when you consider the presence (in the background) of general manager Italo Allodi, Herrera's Mr Fixit, the exact nature of whose dealings with middlemen and referees will probably never be known...

Inter won the league in 1963, then made their way through the European Cup to a final against Herrera's old rivals Real Madrid. Thanks to the *tifosi* the match, held in Vienna, inspired the first mass movement of fans to a major European club game. Past their sell-by date but still potent, Madrid's stars were shackled by Inter's gritty man-markers and Inter won the European Cup at their first attempt, 3–1. They beat Independiente in the World Club Championship later in the year.

In 1965, things got even better. Inter won the league, the European Cup (1–0 at a rainy San Siro against Benfica) and the World Club Championship for a second time. Herrera was the most talked about man in world football.

Although Inter earned their gold star with a tenth title win in 1966, their luck couldn't last. In the European Cup final of 1967, Inter faced Celtic. Without the injured Suárez and Jair, they fell to a superb team performance by the Scottish champions. Liverpool manager Bill Shankly, still smarting from a questionable semi-final defeat by Inter in 1965, took pleasure in taunting Herrera at a post-match dinner.

A few days later, a rare slip by Sarti let in a decisive goal to allow Juventus the title. The magician's spell was broken. Both Herrera and his paymaster Moratti left in 1968.

With a team modified from Herrera's – Facchetti at left-back, Mazzola as midfield playmaster – Inter regained their domestic title in 1971. But Europe was beyond them this time. Their road to the 1972 European Cup final was rocky enough (a 7–1 defeat by Borussia Mönchengladbach was nullified by a beer can thrown from the crowd at an Inter player), but in the final they were swept aside by the exciting Total Football of Ajax.

The 1971 side featured Roberto Boninsegna, a centre-forward in the classic mould. Nine years later Inter would have another, Alessandro Altobelli, to help them to the 1980 title. Again, though – and despite the presence of West German international Karl-Heinz Rummenigge – Inter's European progress was limited.

With further influence from Germany in the shape of Lothar Matthäus, Andreas Brehme and Jürgen Klinsmann, Inter won the title again in 1989, and the UEFA Cup two years later. But the pressure was on to keep pace with Berlusconi's Milan, and Inter just couldn't keep up. Debts rose, further expensive imports flopped, and the club's catering millionaire president Ernesto Pellegrini lost interest.

A UEFA Cup win in 1994 looked good on paper, but served only to disguise a season of boardroom struggle and near

Off the ball – Schalke beat Inter to the 1997 UEFA Cup

beaten on penalties by Germany's Schalke – a team that cost a fraction of Moratti's star-heavy squad.

Hodgson jumped before he was pushed, to be replaced by the former Napoli coach Luigi Simoni. Moratti, meanwhile, was planning some even bigger signings. *Lo scudetto*, alas, is not for sale.

Club shop

The **Inter shop** by gate #21 of the San Siro is open only on matchdays. At other times head for **Football Team**, Via Rubens 26 (M1 Gambara, open Mon–Sat 9.30am–12.30pm & 3.30–7.30pm, most credit cards).

Publication

The glossy *Inter Football Club* (monthly, L4500) can be found at most newsstands.

Ultra culture

Of the big clubs, Inter's ultras have featured least in unsavoury incidents over the last twenty years. The *Interisti* are traditionally on the right-hand side of the political sphere, with no few skinheads in their midst. Split into groups like the *Forever Ultras Inter* and the *Irrudicibili*, they occupy the *Curva Nord* of the San Siro.

Inter fans need their sense of humour. At a Milanese derby in 1995, large black sheets with holes cut in them were hung over the *nerazzurri* faithful, who then did a collective moon towards the opposite end.

In the net

Perhaps surprisingly, Inter's official website has a good bit more zap to it than the Milan equivalent, with a daily news update, online version of the club magazine and an extensive virtual shopping mall, all at: www.inter.it.

Like Milan, Inter benefit from a fine unofficial Malta-based site, this one being at: www.geocities.com/Colosseum/3832. Graphically it's a tad ambitious, but the essentials are all there.

relegation in the league. The following year was no better, and Pellegrini sold the club for a mere $25 million to Angelo Moratti's son, Massimo.

A ninetieth-minute goal in the last game of the 1994/95 season kept Inter in Europe. Moratti put Facchetti, Mazzola and Suárez on the payroll. But after Inter lost to Lugano of Switzerland in the 1995/96 UEFA Cup, he hired Englishman Roy Hodgson as 'technical director'. With Hodgson in charge, midfield destroyer Paul Ince's game improved no end, and Inter again qualified for the UEFA Cup.

To bolster Inter's challenge, Moratti spent prodigiously, recruiting another galaxy of foreign stars including the spectacular French striker Youri Djorkaeff and his spectacular goals. Hodgson tried manfully to work the ingredients into a convincing mixture, but without success – Inter never seriously challenged for the title in 1996/97, and in what should have been the season's saving grace, their third UEFA Cup final appearance of the decade, they were

Eat, drink, sleep…

Bars and clubs

Drinking in Milan need not be as exclusive as its big-business image would have you believe. The city *does* have its fair share of upmarket joints for the mobile phone brigade, but can also offer unpretentious **pubs** and reasonable **live music**.

In a hangover from the nineteenth century, *aperitivi* are taken in the early evening, when many places keep the tradition of providing selections of free snacks on their bar counters. Remember – Campari is a Milanese invention.

In line with sponsors' demands on players to make personal appearances in town, a good few bars and clubs have a **football connection** of some kind.

The best, and most atmospheric, area for **nightlife** is south-west of the centre, alongside the city's canals (*navigli*), near Porta Genova train and metro station.

English Football Pub, Via Valpetrosa 5 (signposted on Via Torino). A great success since it opened in 1996, a large pub with a remarkable collection of old English football souvenirs, Inter and Milan memorabilia, and Premiership and *Bundesliga* TV action. Full menu, most major credit cards. M1/3 to Duomo.

Hollywood, Corso Como 15. The place to go if you fancy a dance with a Milan player. House DJ is Ringo, Paolo Maldini's best mate, who was spinning the tunes when the player met his future bride here. Stars passing through town often stop by. Prices to match. In the same building around the corner is the **Loolapaloosa Pub**, an Irish-style pub with a decent selection of whiskies, popular among the sporting fraternity. M2 to Garibaldi.

La Belle Aurore, Via Castelmorrone. Named after Rick and Ilsa's last drink in Paris, an atmospheric corner bar which buzzes during the *aperitivi* hour. Closed Sundays. Ten-minute walk or bus #60 from M1 Lima.

Osteria del Pallone, Viale Gorizia 30. Atmospheric football bar overlooking the canal. San Miguel and Guinness on draught, framed front pages of *La Gazzetta* from after each World Cup victory, and a huge line drawing of Tardelli's manic celebration after scoring in 1982. Downstairs, framed poems dedicated to the 4–3 semi-final win over West Germany in 1970. Closed Mondays. M2 to Porta Genova.

Racaná Pub, Via Sannio 18. The best of the city's pubs, its genuine atmosphere engendered by simple furniture and regular clientèle. Cider and darts available. M3 to Porta Romana.

Restaurants

Lunchtime sees Milanese office workers swarm around the multitude of **fast-food joints** in the city centre. Join them if you must. Many restaurants close in the afternoon, before the relaxed tradition of cocktails and an evening meal. Milanese **specialities** include *risotto giallo* (rice with saffron), *cotoletta alla Milanese* (veal cutlet in breadcrumbs) and *cazzouela* (pork and cabbage).

Collina Pistoiese, Via Amadei 1. Once owned by the father of Inter star Sergio Gori, and a haunt for the football community of the Sixties. You still might find a few old sports writers in here. Fish specialities at L25,000–30,000, *piatti espressi* at L25,000. Closed Fridays. Most major credit cards. M3 Missori.

Ibiza, Corso Garibaldi 108. Part-owned by Milan players Sebastiano Rossi and Alessandro Costacurta, this is where the team celebrated Franco Baresi's twenty years in a red-and-black shirt. Large, simple interior, starters at L10,000, main courses at L25,000. Guinness on draught and thirty types of cocktails. Evenings only. Most major credit cards. M2 Moscova.

Lucca, Via P Castaldi 33. Romantic French *bistrot*, film director Wim Wenders' port-of-call when he's in town, with first-rate cuisine at fair prices. Lunchtime specials. Crayons provided for you to draw caricatures of the clientèle – the best ones decorate the walls. Closed Wednesday. Most major credit cards. M1 Porta Venezia.

Pizzeria Nueva Arena, Piazza Lega Lombarda 5. Milan players' favourite haunt, but no-one talks shop once they're inside. No posters, no pennants, just damn fine pizzas. Kitchen closes 11.30pm. Closed Tue–Wed.

Stalingrado, Via Biondi 4. Former haunt of disaffected left-wing youth, now a bustling two-floor Irish tavern serving Guinness, Tennants and main courses at L15,000. Open until 2am. Closed Sundays. Ten-minute walk or bus #78 from M1 Lotto.

Accommodation

Milan gets booked up quickly so reserving a room in advance is always advisable. The tourist offices will check for vacancies, but **Hotel Reservation Milano** (Via S Palestro 24, ☎02/76 00 60 95) can actually reserve a room for you.

Antica Locanda Solferino, Via Castelfidardo 2 (☎02/65 70 129, fax 02/65 64 60). Luxury at half the price, a two-star, centrally located hotel with pleasant rooms, some with baths. Singles

L80–90,000, doubles L125–140,000. No credit cards. M2 Muscova.

Hotel Nettuno, Via Tadino 27 (☎02/29 40 44 81). Pleasant, friendly, quiet pension near the main train station, with showers in the corridor and the usual 1am curfew. Singles at L55,000, doubles L85,000. No credit cards. M1 Lima.

Hotel San Tomaso, Viale Tunisia 6 (☎02/29 51 47 47). On the third floor of a building halfway between the main train station and the centre. On the sixth floor is the **Hotel Kennedy**, which is more comfortable but has a midnight curfew. Both places L45–50,000 a single, L75–90,000 a double. No credit cards.

Ostello Pietro Rotta, Viale Salmoiraghi 2 (☎02/39 26 70 95). Best hostel in town, out near the San Siro. IYHF members L20,000 for a dorm bed, non-members L25,000. No credit cards. Ten-minute walk from M1 QT8.

San Francisco, Viale Lombardia 55 (☎02/23 61 009, fax 02/26 68 03 77). Basic rooms, but all have a TV and most have a bath. Singles L80–90,000, doubles L125–140,000. Most credit cards. M2 Piola.

Matchday routine – enjoy your view from outside, as well as inside, the San Siro

Florence

Unlike most Italian cities, Florence manages to exude both calm and affluence. The narrow streets of the old city are filled with treasure houses of art, and in summer are flooded with tourists heading for the galleries and popping into town from cottages in the Tuscany countryside. Without serious local rivals (the nearest major city is Pisa, whose team have spent most of their life in the lower divisions), the local football club, Fiorentina, and the ground at which they play, the Stadio Comunale, might be expected to have an easygoing atmosphere, reflecting that of their surrounding environment.

Nothing could be further from the truth. Belonging to neither the north nor the south of Italy, rather than be ignored Fiorentina find themselves in the position of being disliked by almost every other supporter in the land. The relative geographical isolation of the club has created a strong local patriotism, which finds an outlet in the stadium. A series of controversies involving Juventus and Fiorentina over the past fifteen years has created a new derby in Italy, at which tensions often boil over into violence. Crowd trouble has continued to be a major problem in Florence, with the club suffering a series of fines and punishments – the latest a consequence of the team's exit from the 1997 Cup-Winners' Cup.

Yet the fanaticism of support here has a positive side. Local stars are idolised to extremes, and the ultras produce some outstanding firework and choreographed displays. On its day, the Stadio Comunale can provide one of the most intense experiences in football – its atmosphere, like the match itself, poised on a knife-edge.

Lilac wine – portrait of a young Baggio in Fiorentina purple

The thrilling fields

Fiorentina

Stadio Comunale Artemio Franchi, Campo di Marte
Capacity 47,000
Colours All lilac with red and white trim
League champions 1956, 1969
Cup winners 1940, 1961, 1966, 1975, 1996
Cup-Winners' Cup winners 1961

Florentines will tell you that theirs is a club on its own – always producing sides with flair, often ignoring trends pursued by the rest of Italy, and following a tradition of attacking football. Take a trip to a game in Florence and you will understand why the defensive, slow-motion football that dominated Italy for so long never had the chance to establish itself here. This is a city where the fans don't just shout and sing – they roar their team on with the passion, and the impatience, of a Spanish or English crowd.

Although Florence was the birthplace of the original game of *calcio*, the region was slow to pick up on the English rules which first became popular in Europe in the late nineteenth century. Lacking the industrial and cosmopolitan influences of northern Italy, Tuscany had only three teams competing in the early series of regional play-offs for the national championship – Livorno, Pisa and Lucca. Florence itself had two minor clubs who had failed to make much impact – Palestra Ginnastica Libertas, founded in 1887, and Club Sportivo Firenze. A British expatriate team known as Firenze Football Club had also been founded, but achieved little.

Enter Luigi Ridolfi, a local aristocrat from a grand old Tuscan family, who had fallen in love with the game he had seen on his travels to England. A young man of 31 committed to developing sport in the region, he persuaded the two major clubs, Libertas and Club Sportivo, to merge and form a team capable of competing in the newly formed Italian championship. On September 19, 1926 the new club was founded, and the team quickly worked their way up the football pyramid, finding themselves in *Serie A* after just five years.

The timing couldn't have been better – Florence's new stadium, designed by the respected architect Pier Luigi Nervi, had just been completed. The Stadio Comunale Giovanni Berta (named in honour of a local Fascist leader), a breakthrough in stadium design with its functional, modernistic approach, was inaugurated on September 13, 1931 with the visit of Austrian side Admira Wacker. The game also marked the début of the first of Fiorentina's many South American stars, Uruguayan striker Pedro Petrone, known as *l'Artillero* – 'The Gunner'. Petrone's scoring record was outstanding, but he had a poor relationship with the club's management and was released in 1933.

Problems both inside the club and on the field came to a head in 1938/39 when the *Viola* were relegated to *Serie B*. They bounced back at the first attempt and then, in 1940 and with most of Europe at war, they won their first silverware, lifting the *Coppa Italia* after hammering Milan, Lazio and Juventus before beating Genoa 1–0 in the final. At last, President Ridolfi had

Florence essentials

Florence has no major international **airport** so those arriving by air are likely to land at **Pisa**. There is a regular train connection from Pisa airport to Florence's **Santa Maria Novella** train station in the heart of the city. If you do fly into Florence it will be to the small **Perétola** airport, 5km outside the city and connected by bus to the main bus station, which is adjacent to the train station.

Public transport consists only of buses, run by ATAF. **Tickets** must be bought in advance from ticket booths at main stations, at *tabacchi* kiosks across the city and from automatic ticket machines.

The main **tourist information centre** is at Via Cavour 1 (Mon–Sat 8am–7pm), close to the cathedral (*duomo*). There is another close to the train station at Piazza della Stazione (daily 8am–2pm) and a third at Piazza della Signoria (Mon–Sat 8am– 2pm).

Pick up a copy of *Concierge*, a useful **listings pamphlet** updated each year, and the monthly cultural guide *Firenze Spettacolo*. The tourist offices will also provide free maps and book **accommodation** for a small charge.

The main **post office** is at Via Pelliceria (Mon–Fri 8.15am–7pm, Sat 7.15am–noon). There's a smaller branch office at Via Petrapiana 53–55, keeping the same hours.

'I never touched him' – Fiorentina's Robbiati feels the force of Barcelona's Sergi, Florence, 1997

something to show for twenty years of effort in building up the club.

The cup win didn't just put Fiorentina on the map – it established the club's reputation as innovators. The success of the 1940 side, coached by Beppe Galluzzi, was based on a radical change in tactics, Fiorentina (along with their fellow cup finalists Genoa) being the first to abandon Italy's favoured *Metoda* formation of 2–3–5 in favour of the 'WM' system developed by Herbert Chapman at Arsenal.

With the help of what become known in Italy as the Sistema formation, Fiorentina hoped to increase their power base within the game. But World War II intervened, and after it, the club had to start again.

The stadium had been damaged by bombing, but care was taken to repair the ground in keeping with Nervi's original design and the Fascist name was dropped from the ground's title. Enrico Befani took over as president in 1951 and Fiorentina became regulars in Italy's top five. In 1955/56, they won their first *scudetto,* going 33 matches without defeat and losing only in the last game of the season, when the title was in the bag – the *Viola* finishing twelve points clear of their nearest rivals, Milan. Coach Fulvio Bernardini's side was

outstanding in defence, conceding just six goals at home all season. But Fiorentina's fans still cared for goals above all else. Among the heroes who were greeted in the Piazza della Repubblica (to this day a meeting point for *Viola* fans) was the title-winning strike partnership of 21-year-old Beppe Virgili and Miguel Montuori. The latter, nicknamed 'Pecos Bill' because of his obsession with cowboy comics, was born in Argentina to an Italian mother. Despite his mixed parentage, he spoke no Italian and during Bernardini's lengthy tactical discussions, he would simply stare, uncomprehending, into space. He went on to score 72 goals in 162 appearances for the club, before injury cut short his career at the age of 29.

Providing the ammunition for the front two was Brazilian winger Julinho Botelho. As a player with São Paolo he had earned a place in the Brazilian national team and was a star of the 1954 World Cup side. Bernadini spotted him there and for the next twelve months, Fiorentina tried to persuade him to leave Brazil. He finally arrived in the summer of 1955 and was an instant hit in the no. 7 shirt. Homesickness led him to return to Brazil in 1958, but his three seasons of magical wing-play had earnt him an eternal place in the hearts of all *Viola*. The picture of Julinho leaving the field after his last game, against Padova in 1958, tears streaming down his face, is tucked away in scrapbooks across Tuscany.

In truth, Fiorentina's title-winning side was packed with stars. Six of the *azzurri* side which played against West Germany in Rome in 1955 came from the Florence club, and against Yugoslavia in 1957, there were no fewer than 9 *Viola* in Italy's starting line-up.

Yet European success just eluded them. In the 1957 Champions' Cup, Fiorentina beat Grasshoppers and Red Star Belgrade but lost 2–0 to holders Real Madrid in the final. The penalty award with which Alfredo di Stéfano gave Madrid the lead twenty minutes from time – given by a visibly nervous Dutch referee – in front of 125,000 in the Bernabéu – still raises voices in Florentine cafés.

Fiorentina's championship side quickly fell apart. Bernadini left in 1958, after which there would be four coaches in as many years, former Hungarian international Nandor Hidegkuti among them. Julinho was replaced by Swedish international winger Kurt Hamrin, who would go on to Milan and Napoli after nine years at the Stadio Comunale. It was Hamrin, a remarkable goalscoring winger, who was the most influential figure in the *Viola* side which, in 1961, won the club's only European honour to date. In the Cup-Winners' Cup they defeated Lucerne and Dinamo Zagreb, before beating Rangers home and away in the final, Hamrin scoring the last of four Fiorentina goals in the tie.

A year later the *Viola* defeated Újpesti Dózsa in the semi-finals of the same competition, then became the first in a long line of clubs to just fail to retain that particular European crown, losing out in a replay to Atlético Madrid.

Contenders rather than champions during the mid-Sixties, Fiorentina held their own under the stewardship of Giuseppe Chiapello while never remotely threatening another *scudetto*. All that was to change in 1968/69, when Bruno Pesaolo was brought in as coach and immediately abandoned Chiapello's caution and fielded four strikers. Widely criticised as naïve, Pesaolo's tactics worked – not just because of the team's instinct for goal, but because their attacking movements were co-ordinated from the back, by the brilliant sweeper Giuseppe Brizi. It was a unique combination, good enough to win Fiorentina their second Italian title. Yet within two years, Brizi would be a hero in entirely different circumstances – his goal against Inter saving Fiorentina from relegation to *Serie B*.

Once again, the club had allowed a successful squad to break up before it had had a chance to leave a lasting impression on the game – and the consequences were serious. For Fiorentina, the Seventies were a decade of frustrating mediocrity, relieved only by the artful playmaking of international midfielder Giancarlo Antognoni, drafted into the ranks of the *azzurri* by old boy Bernardini, by now coach of the national team.

For the 1981/82 season, Giancarlo de Sisti, Fiorentina's former Italian international, was brought in as coach by new president Ranieri Pontello. To play alongside the ageing but still capable Antognoni, de Sisti blooded fresh talent in the formidable shape of stopper Pietro Vierchowod and target man Daniele Massaro – future Milan players both. The new-look team led the Italian table for most of the season but on the last day of the campaign, Fiorentina were level on points with Juventus. 'The Old Lady' had to visit Catanzaro while the Lilacs were at Cagliari. At half-time both games were scoreless and the Italian championship was heading for a rare play-off. But in the second half two events occurred which determined the outcome of the title. Bertoni scored for Fiorentina but his goal was disallowed. In the other game, Juventus were awarded a disputed penalty in the 75th minute. The title went to Turin, and Florence all but exploded with rage.

Ask anyone in the town today about that season and you will hear any variety of conspiracy theories – the most popular being that both referees had been bribed by Juve officials. The protests, official and unofficial, went on for weeks, but the Italian FA stood by the results and the *Viola* had been denied a third title.

The city's loathing of Juventus began with that season and only intensified in the coming years. In 1985/86, Fiorentina signed a promising youngster by the name of Roberto Baggio from Vicenza. Baggio, along with resourceful Brazilian Dunga, was the inspiration in a side that reached the final of the 1990 UEFA Cup, where they were to meet Juventus in an all-Italian clash. Juve won the first leg in Turin, 3–1, but there was an outbreak of violence from the travelling support, and the Italian FA were ordered by UEFA to play the second leg at a neutral ground. The site chosen was Avellino – a town without a major team but, according to Fiorentina, with a large traditional support for Juve. Again the club protested, but to no avail. The second leg finished scoreless and Juve lifted the trophy.

Within a matter of weeks, even that ignominy would seem irrelevant. On the eve of Italia '90 Juve announced they had signed the darling of the *Viola* – Baggio – for a world record transfer fee of £8 million. The city went wild with anger. Baggio, along with fellow international Nicola Berti (who had left Fiorentina for Inter the previous season) were targeted by local fans when the Italian team came to their training camp at Coverciano, close to Florence. Not only had Juve 'stolen' a *scudetto* and a major European trophy – now they had nicked Fiorentina's star, too.

The fans launched a successful campaign to oust President Lorenzo Righetti, who was

replaced by film producer and businessman Mario Cecchi Gori.

During the following season, 1990/91, Baggio's return to Florence in a black-and-white striped shirt required a massive police mobilisation. With Fiorentina ahead, Juve were awarded a penalty. Baggio, who had been taking penalties all season, turned his back. In the incredibly hostile atmosphere, he dared not score against his old club. As a Juve team-mate of the time, Thomas Hässler, put it: "For the first time

Pleading with the gods – the 'Angel Gabriel', Batistuta

Little fluffy clouds – the Fiorentina flag touches the sky from its position atop Nervi's tower

in my life I felt we were playing not against another team, but against an entire city."

Intimidating the fans may have been – the team were anything but. Despite high-profile signings like Marius Lacatuş, Stefan Effenberg and Brian Laudrup, Fiorentina could not mount another challenge for the title, and in 1993 they were relegated to *Serie B* for the first time since World War II. The following year, President Mario Cecchi Gori died, leaving the post to his son, Vittorio.

With their backs against the wall, the men in purple hit out, returning effortlessly to *Serie A* at the first attempt, with Argentinian striker Gabriel Batistuta their leading scorer. The long-haired goal-poacher, nicknamed *Batigol*, was the man who finally buried the memory of Baggio. His dedication was admired – he had resisted lucrative offers from elsewhere and stuck by the club in *Serie B*, determined to help get them back where they belonged. And his instinct for goal was lauded not just in Florence but the length and breadth of Italy.

On Fiorentina's return to the top flight in 1994/95, Batistuta scored 26 goals,

including one in each of the first eleven games – a *Serie A* record. It was Batistuta's goals, coupled with the understated but intelligent coaching of Claudio Ranieri, which brought Fiorentina victory in the *Coppa Italia* in 1996, and an excellent run in the Cup-Winners' Cup a year later.

In the semi-finals of that tournament, however, Florence's inability to lose gracefully was again thrown into sharp relief. This time there were no excuses – if anything, the refereeing in Fiorentina's second-leg home defeat by Barcelona had favoured the *Viola*. Yet the ultras could not contain themselves. Barça coach Bobby Robson was hit by a bottle, and the referee threatened to abandon the match.

The result? A hefty UEFA fine, a ban on staging European ties, suspensions for key players who insulted the match officials.

With Ranieri gone, Batistuta restless and Cecchi Gori increasingly preoccupied by his media interests, the Fiorentina ship is once again sailing close to the rocks. But then, in a city where football, like art and life itself, is followed with so much passion, breaking up never has been hard to do.

Tickets

With a stadium capacity of only 45,000 and a large number of season ticket holders, arriving in town without a ticket can mean problems. Tickets can be bought from the stand at Piazza della Repubblica in the centre of town from the Tuesday morning of the week prior to the game. They officially go on sale at 9am but are usually all snaffled up by touts within an hour.

Alternatively, you can travel out to the stadium where the ticket office is open 10am–4pm weekdays. The safest bet is to call the club's ticket information line on ☎055/587 858, well in advance.

If the worst comes to the worst there are plenty of touts operating outside the stadium on the morning before kick-off. Ticket prices at the Comunale range from L27,000 behind the goals to L163,000 for a top seat in Nervi's famous main stand.

Here we go!

The stadium is on the east side of the city in the parkland and sports complex known as Campo di Mare. From the train station, bus #10 makes the journey in around 25 minutes. Other buses heading for the ground from different parts of the city are #3, #17 and #20.

Swift half

Just opposite the main stand, on the other side of Via della Manfredo Fanti, are the two traditional meeting places for *Viola* fans. The **Bar Maresi** is a must, any day of the week. Morning, noon and evening it attracts an elderly clientèle of supporters with nothing else on their minds than the next game and the last six hundred. There's bottled beer as well as the usual coffee concoctions, and in fine weather the football forum moves out on to the street. If this self-appointed purple parliament drags you outside to join them, make sure you don't miss the interior – the photos on the wall, including team line-ups of both title squads, old shots of the Comunale and stars of past and present, amount to a free Fiorentina museum.

At the crossroads, the **Bar Stadio** has less character but better coffee, live football on TV and doughnuts to die for. It also attracts a younger crowd, including women. Creamy cappuccino, fresh doughnuts and plenty of *la bella figura* in lilac – *sempre!*

Publications

The Florentines pay little attention to the sports papers which are so revered elsewhere in Italy. On matchdays, you can pick up a copy of *Gazzetta Viola,* an official weekly tabloid containing lengthy interviews with club officials. *Viola!* is a glossy monthly magazine perfect for the pull-out Rui Costa poster, and *Sindrome Viola* is a freesheet given out inside the ground.

Ultra culture

Collettivo Autonomo Viola, founded in 1978, are the boys gathered in the *Curva Fiesole* behind the goal. They were responsible for the stunning 1991 choreography which displayed a silhouette of the city's outline in lilac, and more recently built a statue of Batistuta which is, alas, beginning to fall to pieces. Unfortunately, Fiorentina fans also have a reputation for less peaceful displays of loyalty, of which see opposite.

Unlike many ultra groups who have far-right connections, CAV are supposedly sympathetic to the left and the Italian Communist Party. Their symbol is an American Indian.

More mainstream fans are organised into *Viola Clubs,* of which there are more than a hundred nationwide. The *Centro Coordinamento Viola Club* brings them all together.

In the net

With a couple of unofficial sites having recently gone AWOL, web surfers have no choice but to take the party line from: www.cecchigori.com/fiorentina/index.htm. Actually it's a smart site, with a good club history in Italian (including profiles of classic players such as Antognoni and Baggio) and links to other companies within the Cecchi Gori empire.

Eat, drink, sleep...

Bars

The advice is simple – avoid the tourist traps and you'll be fine, though Florence doesn't have the range of **nightlife options** available in, say, Milan or Turin.

Dublin Pub, Via Faenza 15. A decent effort at the Irish pub theme, packed with a young crowd doing what you are supposed to do in a pub – drinking beer and talking to each other. If you've had enough of Italian bars where people do neither of these things, a pint of Guinness here will do the trick. Open 5pm–1am.

Meccanò, Piazza Vittoria Veneto. Popular city-centre disco with guest DJs and one-off nights throughout the year.

Snackbar '50 Rosso', Via dei Panzani 40. No posers, no tourists, no mopeds parked outside – the perfect antidote to Italian café life. Scruffy and frequented by beer-drinking losers, it offers Heineken, Tetleys and toasties, all served up by one of the grumpiest hosts this side of Blackburn. Near Santa Maria Novella train station.

Totocalcio 'Viola Club', Salvemini 3. A perfect place to start the day. Purchase your *Gazzetta* from the newsagents down the road and enjoy a morning coffee, surrounded by men agonising over their *Toto* coupon. Plenty of *Viola* memorabilia scattered around. Just off Piazza Gaetano.

Restaurants

Traditional **Tuscan cuisine** is a straightforward mix of meat and vegetables, often served as stews and with the emphasis on fine ingredients. However, Florence's restaurants mostly cater to tourists, so dull **pizza** and **pasta** predominate. If you really want to pig out, jump on a bus and head for the suburbs.

Dante, Piazzi Nazoria Sauro 10. Said to serve the best pizza in Florence, though the pasta is

pretty good, too. Busy at weekends and attracts a good crowd of locals.

La Lampa, 8 Via Nazionale 8. Excellent pizzas, but the house speciality is grilled meat served with fresh salads. Main courses from L9000.

Trattoria Casalinga, Via Michelozzi 9. A genuine *trattoria* serving genuine Tuscan food at low prices – soups, stews and salads all outstanding.

Trattoria Sergio, Piazza di San Lorenzo. A lunchtime spot (open 10am–4pm) right in the heart of tourist land which does a good trade with local residents as well. Main courses from L9000, excellent three-course lunch for L18,500.

Accommodation

Florence has a longer **tourist season** than any other major Italian football city. Anytime between April and October, there could be a serious shortage of places to stay. If you turn up on spec, the best bet is to try to book through one of the **tourist offices** listed on p.340.

Alessandra, Borgo Santi Apostoli 17 (☎055/283 438). Classy, upmarket two-star hotel in a sixteenth-century palace. A fine escape from the tourist crush and the buzzing mopeds. From around L100,000 for a double.

Azzi, Via Faenza 56 (☎055/213 806). In a street full of small hostels and pensions, this is in a block jam-packed with accommodation. Clean and very well priced – L60–75,000 per person per night.

Donatello, Via V Alfieri 9 (☎055/245 870). Smart and set in a quiet but central area, between Piazzale Dontalle and Piazza d'Azeglio. No curfew, plenty of eating and drinking places within ten minutes' walk. Around L90,000 per person.

Ostello Archi Rossi, Via Faenza 94r (☎055/230 2601). Youth hostel in the centre of town, five minutes' stroll from the train station. Modern, clean – but best of all, there's a TV room with a giant screen where you can sit down with a few bottles and watch the big game...

Turin

"It was not until we moved to Turin on the day before the match that we felt the full intensity of the rising tension. Turin at the time seemed to be a city of carnival. About the only ones who went to sleep that last night were the players of both sides and their officials. For the rest it was gala time. There was music all through the night, the city lights never went out and the parks were full of those who had poured in from all parts of Italy."

So wrote Geoffrey Green in *Soccer, The World Game*; his subject – a friendly international between England and Italy in 1948. Today, as then, the heart of Turin's football culture lies in the city centre, and not, as one might expect, at the Stadio delle Alpi shared by the town's two big clubs, Juventus and Torino.

Built at awesome expense for the 1990 World Cup, the delle Alpi is a white elephant, bereft of any of the atmosphere Green found five decades ago. By the year 2000 it may have ceased to host football and become a concert venue, leaving Juventus and Torino to go back to their roots at their Comunale and Filadelfia stadia.

These two grounds face each other across the Corso Unione Sovietica which leads south from town, dividing the vast Fiat car plant from the Mirafiori housing estates opposite. The Fiat factory employs some 50,000 workers in Turin, many of whose families live on the Mirafiori estates. Behind Fiat lie the Agnelli family who have been financing Juventus since 1923. Their club are the most successful in Italy, with seven million supporters, two million of them in the south. Many of their hometown fans are also originally southerners, economic migrants who, like the team's current coach, Marcello Lippi, came to Turin for work.

The rest of Agnelli's employees, however, are loyal Torino folk, supporting the working-class club across the road whose

Migrant worker – Juve coach Marcello Lippi

five years of football fame were cruelly ended by the Superga air crash of 1949. The scene of that disaster, the Basilica, looks down over the city from its 700m-high vantage point on the other side of the river Po.

Torino FC had been formed in 1906 by disgruntled members of Juventus, and by the fusion of two teams who had featured in the finals of the first three Italian championships: Internazionale Torino and FC Torinese. The former had been Italy's first football club, founded by noblemen two years after local Edoardo Bosio had come back from London with a football in 1887. It was Genoa who won those first three titles, but when the Italian Football Federation was set up in 1898, their headquarters were in Turin.

Behind Torino FC (later simply Torino) was Vittorio Pozzo, who was born nearby. Coach of Italy's World Cup winning sides of the Thirties, Pozzo also worked for many years behind the scenes at Torino. He would see the club win just one prewar title, in 1928, Juventus having conspired to nullify one the year before; Agnelli's club claimed Torino officials had tried to bribe Juve defender Luigi Allemandi, and the Federation, by then moved to Rome, came down in Juventus' favour. A great soccer rivalry was born.

With Agnelli's financial backing, Juve left their neighbours firmly behind in the years to World War II, winning five titles in a row with the best players money could buy. Oddly, though, during the war Torino's emerging side was nurtured not only by wise old Pozzo but by the Agnelli family, who gave the players nominal jobs at Fiat to keep them out of the Italian army.

It was a generosity of spirit the Agnellis would regret, for Torino would win five titles between 1943 and 1949, and would surely have gone on to dominate the city's footballing life had the Superga crash not intervened. After the disaster, Juve reasserted their old dominance, but clashes

between the two sides in what had become known as *Il Derby della Mole* were always closely fought, not least after Toro came good again in the Sixties.

The mercurial talents of Torino's exceptional young forward, Gigi Meroni, had the crowd on their feet many times on derby day, before he was killed by a car while crossing the city's busy Corso Re Umberto in 1967. For the derby game a few days later, Toro refused a Juve offer of another player in his place. Before the match, as the colours of each team were entwined all around the Comunale, flowers were laid where Meroni would have stood.

In 1976, when Torino won their first and so far only post-Superga title, it was Juve who were pushed into second place – not least thanks to two derby-day defeats. The following year the positions were reversed, in what would be the last post-war Turin one-two.

Torino managed to do the double over Juve again as recently as 1994/95, but by that time the club were in deep trouble; a year later the team would be relegated, in

Long and winding road – matchday flag-sellers line the route out to Turin's Stadio delle Alpi

Turin essentials

Caselle **airport** is 12km north of Turin. A bus service (L7500) runs into town, calling at the two **train stations**, Porta Susa and Porta Nuova, every forty minutes, 6.30am–11.30pm. Buses from town are more frequent and leave earlier. A **taxi** will cost about L50,000 lire to do the same journey.

Porta Nuova is the main train station and lies at the crossroads of two of Turin's main avenues, Corso Vittorio Emanuele II and Via Roma, the latter leading on to central Piazza San Carlo and Piazza San Castello; Vittorio Emanuele leads to the main **bus station** at Corso Inghilterra 3, 1.5km away, and down to the river Po, 1km in the opposite direction.

The city is laid out on a grid system, criss-crossed by a network of buses, trams and fast trams, running 6am–11pm, with no night transport. Free **route maps** are available from the information offices at Porta Nuova and Porta Susa. You can buy **tickets** there, and at *tabacchi* designated by an 'ATM' sign, and also from automatic machines at main tram stops.

A single ticket (*ordinario urbano*) is L1400, valid for seventy minutes – stamp one end in the yellow box onboard, then the other end if you're continuing your journey on another route within the seventy minutes. A book of ten costs L13,500; a one-day ticket (*giornaliero*) is L4200; and a 'shopping' ticket, allowing four hours' travel between 9am and 8pm, is good value at L2400.

You should find taxis parked either side of Porta Nuova on Via Nizza or Via XX Settembre, or in the main square by the river, Piazza Vittorio Veneto. To phone for one, dial ☎011/5737 or ☎011/5730. The standing charge is L5000, after which it's L1300 per km, with a L3500 night tariff and L1500 surcharge on Sundays and public holidays.

Turin has two **tourist offices**. The central one is at Via Roma 226 (open Mon–Sat 9am–7.30pm, ☎011/53 59 01), with a smaller branch at Porta Nuova station (open Mon–Sat 9am–7pm, ☎011/53 13 27).

The Turin daily *La Stampa* has a high-brow **entertainment section** on Thursdays. In town, look out for the free weekly pamphlet *Spettacolo News*, which has comprehensive bar and club **listings**.

---

the same season as Juventus, under Lippi, were winning both the *scudetto* and the *Coppa Italia*.

If the two clubs are currently poles apart in terms of league status, they are at least united in their desire to leave the Stadio delle Alpi and return 'home'. Torino's beloved Filadelfia stadium, which last saw *Serie A* action in 1963, is overgrown with weeds, ivy and faded Toro banners – walking around it is like exploring a shipwreck. Yet fans still share memories in the bars opposite the ground, and 25,000 of them will be able to fit into the Filadelfia when it is rebuilt, 75 years after its initial construction was funded by Count Cinzano.

Juve's Stadio Comunale is in better shape – after all, the two clubs shared it for 25 years until the eve of the 1990 World Cup. Currently used for Juve training sessions, it can still hold 65,000 at a pinch. But, like the Filadelfia, the ground still needs serious work before it is fit to host top-class *calcio* in the new millennium.

In the meantime, and with their nationwide appeal, Juventus could, and do, play major games anywhere. Home legs of their 1995 UEFA Cup semi-final and final ties were played in Milan's San Siro. And the venue for the second leg of the 1997 European Super Cup against Paris Saint-Germain was as far from Turin as is possible without leaving Italy altogether: Palermo in Sicily. The tie, a foregone conclusion after the Zebras' 6–1 away win, attracted 90,000 requests for 40,000 tickets.

The thrilling fields

 Juventus

Office Piazza Crimea 7
Stadium Delle Alpi, see p.354
Colours Black-and-white striped shirts, white shorts
League champions 1905, 1926, 1931–35, 1950, 1952, 1958, 1960–61, 1967, 1972–73, 1975, 1977–78, 1981–82, 1984, 1986, 1995, 1997
Cup winners 1938, 1942, 1959, 1960, 1965, 1979, 1983, 1990, 1995
European Cup winners 1985, 1996
Cup-Winners' Cup winners 1984
UEFA Cup winners 1977, 1990, 1993

Italy's biggest club are celebrating their centenary year in 1997. On November 1, 1897, pupils from the well-to-do Massimo d'Azeglio Grammar School formed a sports club, settling on the name Football Club Juventus two years later. Twenty-four titles, two European Cups and dozens of other trophies later, the bench the boys were said to have met on stands, battle weary, in front of the club's heavily guarded offices on Turin's Piazza Crimea.

Juventus – literally 'Youth' – mean many things to many people. For their thousand supporters' clubs worldwide, they are a point of contact with the *calcio* they see on satellite TV. For the Agnelli family, whose Fiat car company bankrolls the club, they have been a fantastic showroom but a 75-year loss maker. For seven million Italian fans, many from the south, they are *La Vecchia Signora* – 'The Old Lady', a symbol of devotion. For everyone else, *La Juve* are a callous hussy, buying their way up the ladder to worldwide fame.

Juventus won their first Italian title in 1905, but lost players to the newly formed Torino the following year and had to wait for the Agnellis' funds to kick in before they won another one. Then, just as now, talented players were attracted by a huge signing-on fee, a decent wage and a new Fiat car. Argentines Raimundo Orsi and Luisito Monti, Italians Luigi Bertolini and Giovanni Ferrari – all to win the 1934 World Cup with Italy – were teamed with goalkeeping captain Giampiero Combi and a goal-a-game youngster by the name of Felice Borel. It was a setup not unlike today's, and millions of fans followed their progress to five straight titles from 1931.

The Juve years set the newly shaped Italian league alight. The Zebras, nicknamed after their black-and-white striped shirts, were loved or hated by all. As this great side aged, however, their neighbours Torino rose, and it was not until the season after the Superga disaster that Juventus won their next title, with further expensive imports in the shape of Danish forwards John Hansen and Karl Præst.

The club stayed in the hunt all through the Fifties, with striker Giampiero Boniperti as the figurehead. Boniperti would subsequently lead the club into the modern era, as its managing director from 1972 to 1994. As a player he scored a goal every other game for more than a decade. But his playing career was coming to an end when a complementary striking pair were imported to bring Juventus three more titles between 1958 and 1961: John Charles, the Welsh gentle giant who cost a record British transfer fee to buy from Leeds; and Omar Sivori, a brilliant but temperamental Argentine. Over five years, Charles became a folk hero in Turin, famed for his power, bravery and subtle ball skills. Sivori was a magician, European Footballer of the Year in 1961. Each topped the league's scoring charts for one season.

But when Charles left and Sivori faded, for once the Bank of Agnelli could not find a winning return on their investment. Juventus were overshadowed by the Milan giants in the league, and were no more than also-rans in the emerging European competitions – they reached two UEFA Cup finals in 1965 and 1971, but lost them both, to Ferencváros and Leeds respectively. Unusually, Juve were out of the limelight, and Italy's ban on foreign transfers prevented the club from buying their way back into it.

At the start of the Seventies Juve learnt to buy wisely in safe Italian (or Italo-naturalised) stock: José Altafini, a European Cup-winning goalscorer with Milan in 1963; a 1968 European Championship winner, Pietro Anastasi, as his partner upfront; and another 1968 gold medallist, Dino Zoff, in goal.

With their help, the team carved out a narrow title win over Milan and Torino in 1972. The victory encouraged Juventus to nurture a core of players who would go on not just to dominate the domestic game, but to represent a regenerated Italian national team. Wily forward Roberto Bettega and midfield creator Franco Causio may have been on the losing side when Ajax beat Juve in the 1973 European Cup final, but they would still be around four years later, as part of the team that lifted the 1977 UEFA Cup – Juve's first European silverware.

Black-and-white classic – Michel Platini in full flight

That same year saw the arrival of coach Giovanni Trapattoni – *Il Trap* – a former canny wing-half with AC Milan who set about constructing an iron defence and tightly sprung attack which would bring Juve six titles in ten years. Italy's national-team coach, Enzo Bearzot, used practically the entire Juve team for the 1978 World Cup, and seven of them were still there to win it for him in 1982 – including the old-warhorse Causio, brought on as a late sub in the final against West Germany.

At various points in the Seventies and Eighties Juventus could call on Antonio Cabrini, Gaetano Scirea and Claudio Gentile in defence, Romeo Benetti and Marco Tardelli in midfield, and a rejuvenated Roberto Boninsegna in attack, later replaced by Italy's hero of 1982, Paolo Rossi. When foreigners were allowed back into the Italian game, Juve imported flair – men like Liam Brady, scorer of a late penalty in his last game in 1982 which won

Juve two stars for their twenty *scudetti*; the rapid-fire Pole, Zbigniew Boniek; and the matchless Frenchman, Michel Platini.

Platini's contribution was awesome. In three successive years between 1984 and 1986 he was Italy's top scorer – from midfield. More than anyone else, he spearheaded Juve's quest for the European Cup. In 1983 they had been outwitted by Ernst Happel's Hamburg. In 1985, having won the Cup-Winners' Cup in between, they set up a long-awaited head-to-head with Liverpool – but the match was to be rendered irrelevant by the deaths of 95 fans at the Heysel stadium disaster. Platini accepted the cup after his penalty had given Juve a hollow win. "He never talks about it," his wife said later. "In his head was the fact that a Frenchman, who died at Heysel, had come to see him play. That broke Michel in two. He wanted to give everything up."

As Platini faded, Juve disintegrated. The club moved to the Stadio delle Alpi, having crowned the Comunale era with a UEFA Cup win over Fiorentina in 1990.

But they did not get a sniff of the title for ten years.

As the Nineties unfolded, it was clear Juve would have to buy bigger than ever to match the Milanese. Italian internationals Roberto Baggio, Gianluca Vialli and Dino Baggio, plus Germans Jürgen Kohler and Andreas Möller, were in the side that won the UEFA Cup in 1993.

Like Boniperti before him, Roberto Bettega then moved upstairs to direct affairs, and within months coach Marcello Lippi was in the Juve dugout after performing miracles at Napoli. Journeyman striker Fabrizio Ravanelli came through to earn his place alongside Vialli, and while Kohler and Möller had gone back to Germany, Juve were blessed by the arrival of a prodigious young playmaking talent, Alessandro del Piero, from Padova.

This was the backbone of the team that did the Italian double in 1995, and though Parma beat them in the UEFA Cup final that year, Bettega and Lippi had the sights set on higher things – the laying to rest of the ghost of Heysel. A year later their goal was achieved, thanks to a penalty shoot-out win over Ajax in Rome – an untainted European Cup was Juve's for the first time.

That summer, with old Gianni Agnelli demanding belt-tightening, Bettega and Lippi bought and sold wisely, surprisingly selling Ravanelli and Vialli to England. In came Nicola Amoruso, Christian Vieri Croatian Alen Bokšić and Frenchman Zinedine Zidane, a new breed of players with an average age of 24.

The move worked perfectly – up to a point. Juve comfortably won back a *scudetto* that had been lost to Milan in 1996, but after playing some magnificent football in the 1996/97 Champions' League, their ambitious bid to retain Europe's premier footballing honour failed at the hands of their reckless goalkeeper Angelo Peruzzi and at the feet of Borussia Dortmund's super-sub, Lars Ricken, in Munich's Olympic stadium.

Within weeks of that European Cup final defeat, Bokšić and Vieri had been off-loaded, and 'The Old Lady' was about to embark on another new round of squad-building to cement her reputation as Italy's *numero uno*.

An untainted triumph – skipper Gianluca Vialli lifts the European Cup for Juventus, Rome, 1996

Publications

Two monthly magazines can be found on most Turin newsstands: *Hurrá Juventus!* and *Forza Juve!* (both L5000).

Club shop

Near the ground is the **Juve Shop**, Strada Altessano 57 (open Tues–Sat and match-days 9am–9pm, Mon 2–9pm, no credit cards) and in town you'll find others at Via Soggia 42 (open Tues–Sat 10.30am–7pm, Mon 1–7pm, most credit cards) and at Via Massari 189 (same opening hours, no credit cards).

Club museum

The club's long-awaited centenary museum has yet to materialise, but an exhibition will be staged to commemorate the anniversary during winter 1997/98 – details from the club office at Piazza Crimea 7 (☎011/65 631).

Ultra culture

Lo Juventus Club were one of the earliest ultra groups to be founded in Italy, during the early Seventies. Splinter groups like the 'Black & White Supporters' brought drums and rattles to the old Stadio Comunale, but it wasn't until the post-Heysel forma-tion of the *Drughi* that ultra culture became a lively issue. Competition became fierce with the foundation of *i Viking*, especially when the rival groups had to scrap for ter-ritory at the new Stadio delle Alpi. Now you'll see the 'Black & White Supporters' and *Drughi* in the *Curva Scirea*, and *i Viking* at the other end.

In the net

The official Juve website resides at: www.juventus.it/. Work your way through the sponsors' notices, corporate propa-ganda and language choices (including, significantly, Japanese) and you may feel the content itself is a little thin. Marco Vet-terello's unofficial site is more like it – simple, info-packed pages including a superb Euro Cup stats archive, at: www.eikon.e-technik.de/~sutnev.ju/juve.html.

 # Torino

Office Corso Vittorio Emanuele II 77
Stadium Delle Alpi, see p.354
Colours Claret shirts, white shorts
League champions 1928, 1943, 1946–49, 1976
Cup winners 1936, 1943, 1968, 1971, 1993

The fact that Torino are part of the four-team, twin-city triumvirate that has won all but ten Italian titles since World War II does not hide the fact that the club are in sorry shape now. Shifting between first and second divisions, their faithful fan base barely covering the *Curva Maratona* of the Stadio delle Alpi, forever selling their best players, Torino have all the trappings of a small club from Italy's southern provinces.

Fewer and fewer fans have been coming to see the team since *Il Grande Torino*, prod-uct of the coaching genius of Vittorio Pozzo and the business acumen of agriculture mil-lionaire Ferruccio Novo (and perhaps the greatest club side in Italian football history), were cut down in their prime by the 1949 Superga air disaster.

The shadow of Superga lay heavy over the postwar period until the form of *La Granata* ('the clarets') slowly picked up in the Sixties. An unlikely striking partnership between Joe Baker and Denis Law was responsible for a few goals – and no few beers – in 1961/62, until it ran aground after a post-party car prang.

Not long after, the club moved from Campo Filadelfia to share with Juventus at the Stadio Comunale. There was no lack of atmosphere – the arrival of coach Nereo Rocco from Milan, and his signing of the genial prodigy Gigi Meroni, saw to that. In 1965, a play-off defeat by Munich 1860 was all that separated the club from a place in the European Cup-Winners' Cup final against the eventual winers, West Ham.

Meroni's death in a road accident two years later saw the city in mourning once more. It was to be a decade before his ghost and those of the Superga victims were finally laid to rest, after coach Gigi Radice had taken hold of a side featuring

The Stadio delle Alpi

Strada Altessano 131
Capacity 71,000

Expensive, unwanted and unloved,
the delle Alpi stands in Turin's
northern outskirts, home to two football clubs who desperately desire
not to play in it. Its construction, for
the 1990 World Cup, cost three
times the originally estimated L60
billion. But to Juve and Toro, the
real cost has had to be borne since –
the company that built the ground,

Doomed – the ground is spectacular but unpopular

Acqua Marcia, have a contract with the Turin city council, which administers it, to take
three-quarters of stadium advertising revenue.

Money is not the only problem. The atmosphere at the stadium is as cold as the
wind that howls through it. With the running track, there is a twenty-metre gap between
the spectators and the players, who complain that they cannot hear the crowd at all.

The stadium *is* accessible, but only if you're coming by car from out of town. The
journey from the city centre is fertile ground for pickpockets who eagerly fill the tram
as it slowly winds its way through Turin's dark streets for what seems like an eternity.

Ironically, given that the decision to build the delle Alpi was taken in an atmosphere of post-Heysel paranoia, security is another complaint laid at the stadium's door.
The exits are too narrow, and segregation is not as tight as it could be.

Who will remember the place with affection when football moves out in the year
2000? Not **Paul Gascoigne**, so famously reduced to tears here after his booking in the
Italia '90 semi-final between England and West Germany. Certainly not Stuart Pearce
or Chris Waddle, England's failures in the shoot-out that followed.

To reach the scene of that calamity, take tram #9 or #12 across the road from Porta
Nuova **train station** to the terminus at Piazza Stampalia, then a ten-minute walk down
Strada Druento. Allow yourself a good forty minutes from town. Leaving the ground,
you'll find tram #9 waiting on Corso Grande Torino, along the west side of the stadium.

Before and after the action, many fans head for the **Self-Service delle Alpi**, Strada
Altessano 146 (facing the east side of the ground), a large, soulless cellar serving three-
course lunches at L16,000, with a bar on one side and a TV in the corner. Further
along, at Strada Altessano 55, **L'Elite** is indeed a far classier option. It has a lively bar
area, which sells match tickets and cans of Boddingtons, and a self-service restaurant
behind. For a genuine football bar, **Italia '90**, Strada Altessano 42, has colour pictures
of the stadium under construction and noisy card games going on in the background.

The **Stadio Service** behind the south end, at Via Sansovino 229 (open Mon–Fri
9am–noon & 2.30–5.30pm, ☎011/455 9691), sells **advance tickets**, as do the club
shops. On matchdays the stadium has eight ticket gates and can suffer from dreadful
queueing. Many deal with touts merely because they can't be bothered to wait.

There are **three tiers**, the highest (*3 anello*) far too high, the lowest (*1 anello*) too
low. The *tribune est* and *ovest* are over the halfway line, the most desired place to be for
the neutral, especially the middle tier. If you're willing to spend a reasonable amount of
money for a reasonable view, *distinti centrale* seats are the best. You'll find Toro fans in
the *Curva Maratona*, behind the north goal; Juve's are in the *Curva Scirea*, opposite.

the goalscoring partnership of Paolo Pulici and Francesco Graziani. Winning all but one of their home games, Torino took their first and only post-Superga *scudetto* in 1976, and the city went ape.

The best Torino team since the title-winning line-up of 1976 emerged in the early Nineties. With the right blend of foreign (Belgian Enzo Scifo, Brazilian Walter Casagrande, Spaniard Martín Vázquez) and Italian (Gianluigi Lentini) influences, the side looked anything but an outfit that had just scrambled out of *Serie B*. Lentini was the key – a tricky young winger who had come through Torino's junior squads to take on the best. In 1991/92 Lentini was at his sublime best, taking Torino to the only European final in their history (a UEFA Cup showdown with Ajax, lost on away goals) and third place in the league.

Then the fans took to the streets. President Gianmauro Borsano was selling Lentini! This 23-year-old winger, the very symbol of the new Torino, had become no more than a multi-billion lire bargaining chip, eventually going to Milan for a world record £12.8 million. The sale provoked near-riots, a fans' boycott of home fixtures, and a miserable exit from Europe at the hands of Dynamo Moscow.

Without Lentini, Torino still managed to win the 1993 *Coppa Italia*, on away goals after a remarkable 5–5 aggregate draw with Roma – their first trophy since 1976. The following season they narrowly lost to Arsenal in the quarter-finals of the Cup-Winners' Cup.

But by then, despite the proceeds from the Lentini sale, the club were heavily in debt. The team, further weakened by out-going transfers, were finally relegated in 1996 and never looked likely to bounce straight back.

In the summer of 1997, the appointment of Graeme Souness as coach and the return of Lentini – after a lean spell at Milan, a near-fatal car crash and a revival at Atalanta – provoked a new optimism among fans. Whether or not it is misplaced remains to be seen.

Rover's return – Gianluigi Lentini, Torino idol

Swift half

Campo Filadelfia (bus #14 from Piazza Solferino) is the Toro fans' old stomping ground. Close to the decaying stadium, **Sweet Bar**, Via Filadelfia 31, has a huge colour picture of Toro fans and old men playing cards in the back room. The old curiosity shop next door hasn't sold a rusty nail in years, but has framed photos from the Forties, plus a certificate for the L100,000 public subscription recently asked of fans to help rebuild the Filadelfia.

Publication

Alé Toro (L5000) is the club's full-colour monthly publication, available around town.

Club shop

The **Toro Shop** is in the centre of town, at Via Nino Costa 3 (a tiny street next to Piazza P Le V Fusi, open Tues–Sat

9am–12.30pm & 3–7pm, no credit cards). It has a display of the usual paraphernalia, plus some more off-the-wall items including leggings and frisbees.

Ultra culture

A rainy, windswept game against lowly opposition in *Serie B* is a thoroughly depressing experience – a fact not lost on the *Ultras Granata*, whose choreography, particularly in derby games against Juventus, was once among the best in Italy. The vast 12-million lire *bandierina* exclaiming 'From Here To Eternity', with two bulls' heads and a heart, was a classic of its time. The day these boys can make the rebuilt Filadelfia come alive, the better for Italian football culture.

In the net

There is no official Torino Web presence, but never mind – Valerio and Cristiano Muzi operate a superb unofficial site at: www.aginet.msoft.it/ospiti/torino/toro.htm. The pages feature imaginative but not memory-hungry graphics, meticulously updated stats, transfer news and gossip, newspaper cuttings, copious links and much more – and, perhaps most impressive of all, everything is in a choice of Italian, French and English languages.

Eat, drink, sleep…

Bars and clubs

Turin is laid-back rather than lively. The main area for nightlife is the Murazzi, a quay of lock-up warehouses alongside the Po, under the far edge of Piazza Vittorio Veneto (tram #13 from Porta Susa, tram #15 from Porta Nuova), but it only gets going after midnight. If you can avoid the occasional presence of the *carabinieri* and blag your way in to places without paying a hefty membership fee, you can have a fair time club-hopping.

On the other side of the Po are a row of cheap(ish) bars, less pretentious than those in town. If you're on a real budget, nip into a *vineria* – a cheap wine bar. As in Milan, early evening is *aperitivi* hour, when better establishments stack their counters with free snacks to go with your vermouth.

Alcatraz, Lungo Po Murazzi 37–41. Popular and spacious two-floor nightclub in the Murazzi with alcove tables overlooking the Po, a vague prison theme and bearable music. Tram #13 or #15.

Bar Baspas, Corso Casale 16. Down-at-heel *Totocalcio* bar opposite the Murazzi and overlooking the Po, with faded team line-ups on the wall and lively conversation on a Sunday night. Closed Wednesdays. A walk across Emanuele I bridge from town, or buses #61 or #66.

Bar Ciao 90, Corso Regina Margherita 181. Large football and betting bar between the Stadio delle Alpi and central Turin, embellished with posters, pennants and a large photograph of the Queen Mother pulling a pint. Tram #3.

Caos, Corso Francia 229. Stuck out in Turin's western outskirts, the only half-decent techno club in town, with regular guest spots by foreign DJs and no membership charge. Open Thurs–Sat. Bus #36 from Piazza Statuto.

Doctor Sax, Lungo Po Murazzi 4. The Murazzi's world music bar, occasionally dabbling in jazz and rather unfortunately in rock, with standard beer prices and a decent atmosphere. Nightly from 10pm. Tram #13 or #15.

Newcastle Pub, Largo Cibrario 9. By Piazza Statuto near Porta Susa station, the best of Turin's many expatriate bars, with a Scottish theme, despite the name. Decent if pricey selection of whiskies, and the only bar in town selling Newcastle Brown. Open nightly until 2am. Tram #1, #10 or #13.

Restaurants

Turin cuisine is heavy on polenta – a cornmeal porridge, covered with butter and cheese or meat sauce – risotto and *farinata* (fried corn batter). Everything here is fried in butter, not olive oil, and many restaurants have a distinct French influence. The local pasta dish is *agnolotti* – ravioli with lamb and cabbage. To help digest the starch, the local red wines, Barbera and Barberesco, are excellent.

Many places close mid-afternoon and before 10pm. For something cheaper, you'll find plenty of takeaway snack bars around Via Nizza, near Porta Nuova station.

Brek, Piazza Carlo Felice 22. Quality self-service diner opposite Porta Nuova train station, closed Sundays. No credit cards. Tram #1, #4, #12, #15 or 18.

Pizzeria Bochicchio Rodolfo, Via Monferrato 7c. A rarity in Turin – an excellent, reasonably priced pizzeria near the Piazza Gran Madre on the far bank of the Po, also serving a decent range of pasta dishes. L12–15,000 should cover you for a pizza and a beer. No credit cards. Closed Thursdays. Bus #61 or #66.

Taverna Fiorentina, Via Palazzo di Città 6. Centrally located, reasonably priced home cuisine at around L7–10,000 for a main course. Closed mid-afternoon and on Saturdays. No credit cards. Tram #4 or #12.

Trattoria Amelia, Via dei Mercanti 6. Cosy home cooking and friendly service, a short walk down Via Garibaldi from Piazza Castello. Main dishes at L8–10,000. Closed mid-afternoon, then open until 9.30pm, closed Saturdays. No credit cards. Tram #12 or #13.

Accommodation

Both tourist offices can provide hotel and pension information. If you're turning up on spec, the streets to the right as you come out of Porta Nuova station are full of one-star hotels, but after dark this area can be a little seedy. Opposite, around Piazza Carlo Felice, is safer if a little more expensive. The area west of Piazza Castello also has a few reasonably priced rooms. Frustratingly, the quietest time to come to Turin is in summer, when

there's no *calcio*. Note that the skiing crowd passes through Turin in mid-winter.

Albergo Versilia, Via San Anselmo 4 (☎011/65 76 78). Pleasant, clean pension around the corner from Porta Nuova station, with a bar downstairs and a decent café a couple of doors down. L45,000 a single, L65,000 a double, L70,000 a double with a shower. No credit cards. Tram #9.

Hotel Bellavista, Via B Galliari 15 (☎011/66 99 121, fax 011/66 87 89). Round the corner from the station, spacious rooms, each with a TV and radio. Singles at L65,000, doubles L110,000, or L140,000 with shower. Triples available on request. No credit cards. All transport to Porta Nuova, then turn right down Via Nizza – you want the second street on the left.

Magenta, Corso Vittorio Emanuele 67 (☎011/54 26 49, fax 011/54 47 55). A little pricier than most around Porta Nuova, all rooms in this two-star hotel have a TV and telephone. Bar downstairs. Singles with shower L75,000, doubles without L65,000, with L95,000. Most major credit cards. Left out of the station or tram #1, #9 or #15.

Ostello Torino, Via Alby 1 (☎011/660 29 39, fax 011/66 04 45). Up in a quiet, hilly part of Turin, a tidy and comfortable youth hostel with dorm beds at L18,000 for members, L23,000 for

Every step you take – Baggio's last Turin derby, 1995

non-members, breakfast and linen included. Cur-
few 11.30pm in summer, 10.30pm in winter.
Lockers and laundry facilities available. No credit
cards. Bus #52 from Porta Nuova – get off after
Piazza Crimea over the bridge, turn right up
Corso Giovanni Lanza, then up Viale Enrico
Thouvez. Via Alby is the narrow road to the right.

San Carlo, Piazza San Carlo 197 (☎011/56 27
846). Fourth-floor pension on a main square, a
short walk straight up from the main Porta
Nuova train station. Can get a little noisy. Singles at L60,000, with bath L80,000, doubles
L80,000 without, L100,000 with. No credit cards.
Tram #4, #12 or #15.

Italy's postwar legend – *Il Grande Torino*

At 5pm on May 4, 1999, the city of Turin will come to a standstill. It will be fifty years
to the minute since a plane carrying the entire Torino squad, plus journalists and club
officials, crashed into the side of the Basilica on top of Superga hill outside Turin.

All 31 onboard were killed, including the pilot, whose decision not to land at Milan
Malpensa and to fly on to Turin has never been explained in half a century. Teeming
rain, high winds and mist swept over the city that afternoon and visibility was poor.
When the plane hit the church, built to honour Turin's resistance to the French in
1706, it was flying in the wrong direction. The team bus, which had taken the Torino
players around Italy for four title-winning seasons, stood empty and waiting at
Malpensa. Vittorio Pozzo, the coach whose tactics paved the way for Torino's postwar
scudetto monopoly, had the task of identifying the bodies.

Turin went into mourning, the players were given a **state funeral** and the whole
country shut down for a week. Torino's junior team played out the last league fixtures of
the season against their counterparts from the other clubs, and a record fifth title went
to a grieving Campo Filadelfia.

Fifty years on, *Il Grande Torino*'s place in history is inevitably shrouded in myth,
but the historical importance of the team cannot be over-stressed. After twenty years of
Mussolini's Fascism, Italians needed something great and good to look up to. They
found it in Torino, and especially in the side's greatest star, **Valentino Mazzola**.

A bullish but light-footed inside-left, Mazzola had struck up a productive forward
partnership with **Ezio Loik** while helping little Venezia to win the *Coppa Italia* in
1941. The duo's mutual understanding had curious origins – both men were born on the
same day, January 26, 1919. Pozzo persuaded Torino president Ferrucio Novo to snap
the pair up, and they duly helped Toro **win the double** in 1943.

With Pozzo's organisation, and with much of Italian football still in disarray, Torino
won another title in 1945. By 1947 they were simply unstoppable, etching a ten-point
winning margin over Juventus in the league; that May, they provided all ten outfield
players for Italy's 3–2 defeat of Ferenc Puskás' Hungary in Turin.

In 1948 Torino's winning margin was sixteen points over Milan, and over the course
of the season the team scored nearly **fifty goals more** than anyone else; the Filadelfia
crowd, including the team mascot, Valentino's son Sandro, saw nineteen wins in twenty
home games. After Superga, seven-year-old Sandro was taken under the wing of the
Internazionale youth programme, from which he would rise through the ranks to global
fame at the 1970 World Cup.

To **visit Superga**, take tram #15 from outside Porta Nuova station to the terminus
across the Po at Sassi. From here a small train chugs up the steep hill to the cathedral,
every hour on the half-hour (April–Oct daily 9am–8pm, Nov–March weekdays 10am–4pm,
L5000 return). Inside the cathedral (open April–Sept 9.30am–noon & 3pm–6pm,
Oct–March 10am–noon & 3pm–5pm) is a memorial to the victims of the 1949 crash.

For a reflective beer nearby, the **Ristorante Superga** (Strada Basilica di Superga
45, closed Wed) offers a panoramic view of the city.

Genoa

Genoa 360
Sampdoria 362

Sea ports, with their big immigrant communities and working-class populations, always seem to create vibrant football towns, and Genoa is no exception. A cramped, messy city with buildings crawling over hills and crowding into valleys, it barely seems to have any space in which to kick a ball about. No surprise, then, that there is room for only one stadium.

Yet history has blessed the city with two big football clubs, of dramatically differing contemporary status, but each with its place in Italian soccer history.

The Genoa Cricket and Athletic Club were formed in 1893, exclusively for British expatriates. Four years later, locals were allowed into the club and the football team met a select eleven from Turin in the first inter-city game ever played in Italy.

The boy David – Platt lifts the *Coppa Italia* for Sampdoria, 1994

Genoa dominated the early Italian league competitions but soon faced a local challenge from Andrea Doria and Sampierdarenese – the two teams who would later merge to become Sampdoria.

In the modern era Samp have become one of the élite in *Serie A*, boasting a long line of foreign stars and with a record of making astute buys in the domestic transfer market. Meanwhile, Genoa have bobbed up and down between the top two divisions, occasionally promising a revival but usually failing to deliver.

Yet despite the presence of more glamorous neighbours – perhaps because of it –

Genoa have managed to hang on to their support throughout the barren years. Naturally there is a competitive rivalry between the two clubs, but it has rarely spilled over into violence, and in recent years there has been a suspicion that a large number of fans are actually watching both teams. Nonetheless, the local *Derby della Lanterna* ('Lighthouse Derby') remains a passionate affair – when it is played.

The ultra movement, once powerful in the city, has quietened a great deal of late, particularly since the death of Genoa fan Vincenzo Spagnolo, after fighting with Milan supporters in 1995.

The thrilling fields

 Genoa

Office Via Roma 7/3
Stadium Luigi Ferraris, see p.363
Colours Red-and-blue halved shirts, blue shorts
League champions 1898–99, 1900–04, 1915, 1923–24
Cup winners 1937

There are two plaques outside the Stadio Luigi Ferraris. One is in tribute to Dr James Spensley, one of the founders of the Genoa club. The other is to Genoa fan Vincenzo Spagnolo, who was stabbed to death by Milan hooligans in 1995. Between them, they sum up the two Genoas. The first is a

The last Genoa hero – Czech striker Tomáš Skuhravý

reminder of the long-gone era when Genoa dominated the Italian championship, the latter of more recent times when there have been little but bad memories.

It would be easy to dismiss Genoa as dinosaurs. Easy, but unfair. It may be more than sixty years since they last won a trophy, but Genoa are survivors. Plenty of European clubs enjoyed success in the early days of organised league football but vanished in the era of professionalism or in the face of fresh local competition. Thanks largely to the loyalty of their supporters, Genoa are not a footnote in the history books, but a major organisation – albeit one that has a lot to do to recapture its long-lost status.

With the good Dr Spensley in goal, Genoa won six of the first seven Italian championships, although at that stage the competition consisted of a series of regional play-offs, rather than a national league. After World War I the club won two more titles – in what was now a much more competitive championship. The first of those post-WWI campaigns was particularly impressive, seeing Genoa unbeaten throughout the season. The side included several of the early Italian national team – notably goalkeeper Giovanni de Prà and striker Aristodemo Santamaria.

In 1929 the club were forced to change their name. Italy's Fascist authorities didn't like the English sound of 'Genoa', and until the end of World War II the team played under the name Genova 1893.

Psychologically, the name change could scarcely have come at a worse time, for the club were already beginning to fade from the limelight. In 1934, the unthinkable happened and the mighty *Grifone* ('griffins') were relegated. The fans couldn't believe it, but over time their children and grandchildren would become accustomed to such yo-yoing between divisions.

A cup win in 1937 seemed to show that the club were still capable of

Genoa essentials

Genoa's **airport** is 6km out of the city at Sestri Ponente. Buses link up with all flights and take you to Stazione Principe on Piazza Acquaverde, one of two big **train stations** in town; the other is Stazione Brignole, on Piazza Verdi. Both stations are very central and are served almost hourly by buses returning to the airport.

Public transport is limited to **buses** run by the local transport authority, ATM Genova. Services run from 5.30am to midnight on most major routes. A standard one-way ticket costs L1400, available from any ATM kiosk. The city's 24-hour tourist ticket is good value at L5000 – it's valid for all bus services and local trains around the city, and in the nearby region.

The main **tourist office** is at Via Roma 11 (open Mon–Thurs 8am–2pm & 4–6pm, Fri–Sat 8am–1pm). There are smaller offices at the two train stations (both open Mon–Fri 9am–noon & 3–6pm, Sat 9am–noon) and at the airport (open Mon–Sat 8am–noon & 2–8pm).

The local daily newspaper *Il Secolo XIX* is a decent source of **nightlife listings**, and the tourist office also puts out occasional free 'what's on' pamphlets.

matching the best, but today it remains Genoa's last piece of silverware.

After World War II the club got their old name back, but struggled to establish themselves in *Serie A*. The Fifties saw a string of relegations and promotions, and Genoa spent the whole of the period between 1965 and 1973 outside of the top flight, enduring a year in the amateur ranks of *Serie C* in 1970. Throughout the Seventies and Eighties the club's existence revolved around the fight against relegation from *Serie A* – a battle joined with varying degrees of success.

In 1989, a promising young side won the *Serie B* title and there was optimism that a genuine revival might be around the corner. It proved justified.

In 1990/91, with Osvaldo Bagnoli as coach, midfielder Stefano Eranio pulling the on-field strings and a colourful Italia '90-inspired strikeforce of Czech Tomáš Skuhravý and Uruguayan Carlos Aguilera, Genoa had their best season for half a century, finishing fourth in the league.

Typically, their local rivals Sampdoria stole the show, winning the title. But fourth place was enough to earn Genoa European qualification for the first time in the club's history. The following year's UEFA Cup campaign provided enough memories to sustain another generation of supporters.

Wins over Real Ovideo and Dinamo Bucharest were followed by an impressive victory over a strong Steaua Bucharest side, to set up a quarter-final with Liverpool. Anfield fans may have long since forgotten the tie, but the Genoa *tifosi* consider their team's 4–1 aggregate win the club's greatest postwar success. Skuhravý in particular terrorised the Merseysiders' defence, earning his team copious praise in the Italian sports press, while their opponents were dubbed 'Little Liverpool'.

The victory earned Genoa a semi-final date with Ajax. With Sampdoria heading for the final of the European Cup, the city's football heart was beating as never before. Genoa were looking forward to the prospect of an all-Italian UEFA Cup final, against their old northern league rivals Torino. But Ajax, themelves showing the first signs of their great Nineties revival, hadn't read the script – Genoa were out, and the party was over.

Within a few years it was back to the old struggle. Bagnoli was sacked, and by 1995 Genoa were facing a relegation play-off against Padova, in which an overweight Skuhravý, shambling around the park in the desperate hunt for the goal that would avoid a penalty shoot-out, seemed to symbolise the decay that had set in. The shoot-out duly came, Genoa lost it, and while Padova were themselves relegated the following year, that was scant consolation for the proud Genoa club and their unswervingly loyal supporters.

Publications

Minigol (weekly, L2500) is a magazine dedicated to local football which gives both Genoese teams plenty of coverage, as well as regional and amateur sides. *Genoa News* is a glossy monthly produced for the club. Programmes are sold outside the stadium on matchdays.

Club shop

Souvenirs can also be bought in town at **Genoa Point Nervi** in Via Nervi. On matchdays there are plenty of *Grifone* products on sale at stands around the stadium car park, which houses an official club shop.

Ultra culture

Serie B football and the death of Vincenzo Spagnolo have both had an impact on the ultra scene. The club's main ultra group are *Fossi dei Grifone*, who gather in the *Curva Nord* of the Luigi Ferraris.

In the net

Click on a screen-wide image of the *Curva Nord* to enter the unofficial Genoa site at: www.promix.shiny.it/genoa. The text is in Italian only, but this is a fair stab at a fan-run site, with smart graphics, a decent club history and a well-maintained stats archive.

 **Sampdoria**

Office Via XX Settembre 33/1
Stadium Luigi Ferraris, see p.363
Colours Blue shirts with white, red and black hoops, white shorts
League champions 1991
Cup winners 1985, 1988–89, 1994
Cup-Winners' Cup winners 1990

Although most Italian clubs managed to survive Fascism and WW2, and the post-

war Italian league contained many of the same names as the prewar championships, the city of Genoa had a new club around for peacetime.

In 1946, two of the clubs who had been struggling to compete with Genoa merged to form Sampdoria. Andrea Doria and Sampierdarenese had had their moments – both had played in *Serie A*, Sampierdarenese had come close to winning the title in 1922, and Francesco Cali of Andrea Doria was the first captain of Italy.

In 1927 the two clubs decided to unite, under the grandiose name of Dominante, in an attempt to dislodge the Anglophiles of Genoa from their seat of power in the city. But in their first season Dominante were relegated. The club changed their name to Liguria (the region of which Genoa is the capital) and finished fifth in *Serie A* in 1939. But in the last championship before World War II, the team finished in bottom place.

Immediately after the war the two clubs re-emerged under their original names and with separate structures, but on August 1 1946, they united once more, choosing the name which has survived to this day, Sampdoria Unione Calcio, and moving in to share the Stadio Luigi Ferraris with Genoa.

The new club could boast nothing like Genoa's level of support, but in their first season 'Samp' won both city derbies, setting a pattern for the coming seasons in which the upstarts would regularly finish above their more illustrious neighbours in the *Serie A* table.

One of the stars of the early postwar sides was striker Adriano Bassetto – 'The Dwarf' – who despite his lack of height notched 93 goals in seven seasons with the team that had become known as the *Blucerchiati* – literally 'blue-and-hoops', after their distinctive blue shirts with white, red and black hoops. (The strip was a compromise between Sampierdarenese's blue-and-white and the red-and-black of Andrea Doria.) The other favourite of the Fifties was Argentinian international Tito Cucchiaroni, whose name lives on in the title of Sampdoria's main ultra group.

The Luigi Ferraris

Stadio Luigi Ferraris, Via del Paino 9
Capacity 42,000 (all-seated)

There has been a football stadium on this site in the **Marassi** district of the city since Genoa began playing here in **1910**. It has been rebuilt three times since then, and was renamed 'Luigi Ferraris' after a former Genoa centre-half killed during World War I.

The last remodelling was by **Vittorio Gregotti** for the 1990 World Cup. It included the construction of four brick-red towers which stand at each corner of the ground, and from which fans get a dramatic if rather eccentric view of proceedings on the pitch.

The ground is by no means the biggest in Italy, but it is certainly one of the easiest to **fill with atmosphere** – as Ireland supporters discovered when their team played Romania here at Italia '90.

Buses #37 and #47 go from **Stazione Principe** to the ground. On matchdays these are augmented by a special bus service, beginning around two hours before kick-off; this latter ride takes around twenty minutes and deposits you at the ground. If you take either of the regular city buses, get off at Marassi and head down Via Giuseppe Bertucioni – it's a five-minute walk to the stadium.

With Genoa and Sampdoria currently in different divisions, ticket prices vary depending on which team is at home. For **Genoa** games, the cheapest seats in one of the *Curvas* behind the goals are around L20,000, with prices rising to L100,000 for the best seats in the house. For **Sampdoria** matches, these prices go up to L25,000 and L150,000, respectively.

To check on seat availability in advance, call one of the two **ticket hotlines**: Genoa's is ☎010/540547, Sampdoria's ☎010/564880 or 585343.

There are plenty of opportunities for passing an hour with a **pint** or a **cappuccino** close to the stadium. The **Key Pub** (Via Giuseppe Bertucioni 2) has an 'English' theme that isn't rammed down your throat – Caffrey's, Bass and Cera Danish lager are on tap, and there are toasties and other bar snacks.

Nearer the stadium, at Corso Alessandro de Stefani 63, is **Bar Europa**, the only establishment in the area specifically targeting Genoa fans, serving Cera lager and a range of cocktails, including one called *Frappè Everton*.

The **Bar Stadio** (Via Tortosa 3) gets packed before games and is also a popular midweek meeting point, for supporters of both clubs. This being Genoa, the debates are usually friendly, but maybe the regulars have some influence – one former Genoa coach reportedly blamed the patrons for his sacking.

Although they enjoyed a successful year in 1961, when they finished fourth thanks largely to 27 goals from striker Sergio Brighenti, Samp suffered from instability for much of the early Sixties, and in 1966 they were relegated to *Serie B*. They bounced back within a season but were down in *Serie B* for half of the Seventies, and the dream of a fresh football force in the city seemed to be fading.

All that changed in the Eighties with the appointment of oil magnate Paolo Mantovani as club president. Mantovani didn't just bring cash to Samp – he also brought a rare (for a sporting entrepreneur) insight into the game he was financing. In 1982 he made his first inspirational signing – Roberto Mancini. The arrival of *Mancio* coincided with the club's return to the top flight. He was the archetypal Italian attacking midfielder, with style, imagination and the ability to score goals – especially from set pieces. All he needed was a striker to feed – and in 1984 he got that when Mantaovani signed 20-year-old Gianluca Vialli from Cremonese. Vialli, whose wealthy

So near yet so far – Roberto Mancini, Wembley, 1992

Berne. The Italians were stunned by a fourth-minute strike from Salinas, however, and when Recarte struck eleven minutes from time, the trophy was Barça's.

Boskov was undaunted, and the pain of defeat was eased immediately in the same competition the following year, when Samp beat Grasshoppers and Monaco on the way to a final with Anderlecht in Gothenburg. Playing a less open game than in Berne, Sampdoria took the match into extra time, in which two goals from Vialli were enough to give the club their first European title.

Ever ambitious, Mantovani continued to augment the squad, adding balding wide man Attilio Lombardo and the tough-tackling Slovenian midfielder Srećko Katanec to the mix before an all-out assault on the Italian title in 1990/91.

Lombardian family background gave him a relaxed air perfect for situations demanding a cool head in front of goal, soon struck up a lethal forward partnership with England international Trevor Francis. With Scottish midfielder Graeme Souness signed from Liverpool and the massive Pietro Vierchowod marshalling the defence, Mancini now had all the supporting cast he needed.

In 1985 Samp earned their first piece of silverware, defeating Milan in the final of the *Coppa Italia*. Veteran Brazilian Toninho Cerezo was signed from Roma in 1986 and another cup win followed two years later.

By this time the team were playing to a tune orchestrated by Vujadin Boskov, an unassuming Yugoslav coach who turned out to be another of Mantovani's shrewd investments. Boskov's ability to change his team's formation to suit the occasion was particularly useful in Europe, and in 1988/89 reached their first continental final, in the Cup-Winners' Cup against Barcelona in

With Katanec acting as Boskov's eyes and ears on the pitch, Vierchowod an unbreachable barrier at the back, and Mancini and Vialli netting more than thirty league goals between them, Samp's first *scudetto* was duly won with something to spare. Almost 200,000 fans gathered in the Genoa streets to celebrate the title win.

Sampdoria found themselves in the European Cup just as it was beginning its transformation into the Champions' League. After edging past Kispest-Honvéd by the odd goal in seven, they entered group one of the new mini-league system. They lost just one game (against Anderlecht away) and finished top of their group above holders Red Star Belgrade, who were defeated home and away.

The final at Wembley pitted them against Barcelona again. There were plenty of chances for Samp, but the game went to extra time and in the dying seconds, Ronald Koeman's epic free-kick allowed Barça to foil the *Blucerchiati* once again. Vialli departed for Juventus, and in 1992/93 Samp failed to hold on to their title.

Recent years have seen stars come and go. Boskov was replaced by another canny foreign coach, Sven Göran Eriksson. For 1993/94 Ruud Gullit was brought to the Luigi Ferraris, along with two former Red Star Belgrade stars, Siniša Mihajlović and Vladimir Jugović, while the club broke their record transfer fee to lure David Platt from Juventus. The result was another *Coppa Italia*, followed by a run to the semi-finals of the Cup-Winners' Cup where Samp lost out on penalties to Arsenal. To add to the disappointment, Vierchowod, Jugović and 'Popeye' Lombardo all joined Vialli at Juventus at the end of the season, while Platt returned to England.

Following the death of Paolo Mantovani in October 1994, the club passed into the hands of his son, Enrico. One of his first acts was to bring young striker Enrico Chiesa back from loan, to see him score 22 goals in 27 games in 1995/96. They weren't enough to lift Sampdoria back into the European frame, though, and Chiesa was sold to Parma in the summer of 1996.

Twelve months later, the club reached the end of an era with the departure of both Eriksson and the immortal Mancini. But the arrival of another glamorous import, Jürgen Klinsmann, and a return to the European stage confirmed Sampdoria's unlikely but stubbornly held position among Italian football's front rank.

Publications

Samp (L3000) is a glossy magazine produced for home games. The weekly paper *Ettimara Sport* has extensive coverage of Samp news and results.

Club shop

There is a well-stocked **shop** at the north end of the stadium where, among other things, you can buy a famous 'Samp For Peace' replica shirt, worn by players in solidarity with the victims of the Bosnian war.

Ultra culture

As at Genoa, the fan scene has died down lately, but the *Ultras Tito Cucchiaroni* in the south end can still put on a fine show for a big game. There are many active *Samp Clubs* around the region, and a number of them have taken the name of Roberto Mancini into their title.

In the net

The official site is at: www.sampdoria.it/. Like the club which sponsor them, the pages are smart but unpretentious, with the highlight an excellent English-language history, conveniently divided into players, presidents and so on. There's also online shopping in the *Solosamp* area. Less commercial, and only really worth a peek if you're a confirmed Samp anorak, is Tamás Karpati's 'ultimate Sampdoria history', at: www.risc.uni-linz.ac.at/non-official/rsssf/tables/sampdoria-html. No graphics, no photos but, by the same token, no Samp fact omitted.

Eat, drink, sleep...

Bars

A potent mix of students and immigrant dock-workers gives Genoa a varied and unpredictable nightlife. The port area is full of scruffy little bars in which the non-Italian population does some serious drinking – usually wine, sunk while standing. Beer is preferred in the student areas but, as in most Italian cities, alcohol is a side issue to the serious business of eating.

In clubs, dance has yet to really catch on and live music is generally preferred – though look out for leaflets and posters announcing one-off events.

Albatros, Via Roggerore 8. Popular live music venue for local acts, with a range of bottled beers and a cosy, jazz-club feel.

Bar Universita/La Caffeteria, Via Balbi. Two ideal spots for an early morning wakener or a mid-afternoon freshener. Draught lager, cheap snacks and plenty of fliers with details of events, clubs and gigs. Largely student crowd.

Brittania Pub, Vico Casana. Expat pub just off Via San Lorenzo which seems more popular with the locals than the expats. Promises English football on TV in the near future. Choice of Guinness stout and Tetley bitter.

La Divina Commedia, Via Galata 116. Genoa's often seedy port area specialises in strange shops – one sells only scissors, another only door handles. There is also a dirty little stand-up bar (at Via di Pre 55) which sells nothing other than wine and soda water. *La Divina Commedia* has more than that, offering fine sandwiches and snacks, a giant-screen TV (with football action) and colourful sea-dogs aplenty.

Restaurants

The Liguria region is famed for *pesto*, a basil sauce made with pine nuts and parmesan. It is most often used as a pasta sauce but finds its way into many other dishes. Fish is also popular – look out for it in *carpione*, marinated in vinegar and herbs. There are plenty of snacky places around the port

Towering inferno – Samp flags at the Ferraris

and also lots of small joints selling soups and stews. Chill out – dining is much less formal in Genoa than in many Italian cities.

Ciao/Spizzico, Via XII Ottobre 24. Self-service cafeteria with meat and pasta dishes – basic, cheap and tasty. Fast food Italian-style.

Corona di Ferro, Vico Inferiore del Ferro 11. The best place in town for tasting *pesto* and other local specialities. Busy crowd all day.

Florida, Via Doria. If you get off the train famished, then this is the perfect place to feed your face. Just down the road from the Stazione Principe, it serves all the favourites including a wide range of excellent and affordable pizzas.

Trattoria African Bar, Via San Bernardo 7/9. Interesting mix of local and African cuisine, with special offers on three-course set lunches and dinners. Bohemian atmosphere.

Accommodation

There's no shortage of affordable hotel rooms in Genoa, but many are pretty seedy. If you turn up on spec, then Via XX Settembre, near Brignole train station, is as good a place as any to start.

Bel Soggiorno, Via XX Settembre 19 (☎010/581418). Cheap, comfortable hotel, close to the old town. The **Bruxelles Margeherita** and the **Switzerland** are two other budget options in the same street.

Bristol Palace, Via XX Settembre 35 (☎010/592541). At the better end of the street, a classy four-star hotel worthy of its high charges – L140–280,000 per person per night.

Ostello Genova, Via Constanzi 120 (☎010/24 33457). New hostel which provides a stunning view of the city. From Stazione Principe, take bus #64 up the hill. Don't even think about walking.

Veronese, Vico Cicala 3 (☎010/202551). Small, acceptable two-star place with rooms in the L40–70,000 range.

Rome

Rome is Italy's eternal city, stages the country's most important international fixtures and generates its fiercest derby – but it is not its football capital. In terms of tradition, success and finance, Milan and Turin are in a different league. Only three titles have ever come Rome's way, and the road to and from them has been littered with corruption, mis-management and political wrangling.

Like Milan and Turin, Rome is a two-club, one-stadium city. Lazio and Roma share the Stadio Olimpico, built for the 1960 Games. Across the river Tiber is the Flaminio, venue of *Serie C* minnows Lodigiani, and home to the big boys during the political upheavals either side of World War II.

Italian Fascism was centred on Rome. Mussolini wanted to re-create the city in its ancient imperial image and football was too important in the public consciousness to escape involvement. *Il Duce* was a Lazio man, taking his kids to games when the club were based at their Rondinella stadium, at the base of the heights of Pairoli, a leafy, residential area of northern Rome which is still firm Lazio territory today.

An abandoned Stadio Nazionale stood near the Rondinella, and this was to be the site for Mussolini's Stadio del Partito Nazionale Fascista, or PNF. After staging a friendly with Hungary in 1928 – Italy's first home game south of Bologna – the PNF would be the venue for Italy's (and Mussolini's) triumphant 1934 World Cup final.

Lazio were also based at the PNF by then, having left the Rondinella three years previously. Shortly before then, local patriot and Fascist politician Italo Foschi had been behind the merger of four clubs to form Roma, a club intended to represent the city in name and colour.

Foschi died after being taken ill while watching a Lazio game. His beloved Roma made their home at a wooden stadium, Campo Testaccio, in Via Zabaglia. The district of Testaccio is everything Pairoli is not – shabby, urban, and still Roma through and through.

Reasonable success on the pitch led to a huge rise in Roma's popularity at their overcrowded stadium, and they joined Lazio at the PNF as war broke out in 1940. Mussolini needed to promote Rome as the capital of a new, rationalised Italy, football included. When Roma were topping the league in 1941/42, authority favoured the leaders. In the vital Lazio–Roma game that January, some strange refereeing decisions and a weird last-minute own goal went Roma's way – as did the title in May.

Without political interference – save for the bungling and backhanders that got the Stadio Olimpico finished and improved upon thirty years afterwards -- Rome saw its footballing rôle reduced to a big events venue and little else.

The Eighties saw a rise in the local ultra movement, some of it developing into violence as bored Roma youth from the Fascist-built housing project at EUR clashed with their disaffected counterparts from Lazio. The divisions were political as well as geographical – Lazio fans being predominantly suburban right-wing, Roma's inner-city left.

The violence has lessened, but first-time visitors shouldn't be surprised to see losing fans attempt to burn down their section of the ground before the final whistle of *Il Derby Capitale*. Preparation for the ever more ostentatious ultra choreography starts months in advance, donation boxes appearing at either end for materials to be gathered for the big day.

The next day's papers will have reports on either end's show, and these are given almost as much prominence as the football itself. Which, given the recent lack of success enjoyed by the participating teams, is somehow appropriate.

The thrilling fields

Roma

Office Via di Trigoria, km 3600
Stadium Olimpico, see p.370
Colours All burgundy with yellow trim
League champions 1942, 1983
Cup winners 1964, 1969, 1980–81, 1984, 1986, 1991
Fairs' (UEFA) Cup winners 1961

Associazione Sportiva Roma are celebrating their seventieth anniversary in 1997. Formed from the Alba, Fortitudo, Roman and Pro Roma teams in 1927, the club soon earned a loyal fan base in the poor, tatty Testaccio area of the city. Roma boasted two members of Italy's 1934 World Cup-winning team – right-winger Enrico Guiata and half-back Attilio Ferraris

IV – and were virtually unbeatable at their cramped home, Campo Testaccio. Goalscorer Rodolfo Volk, whose century-plus of strikes for Roma was bettered only in the Eighties by Roberto Pruzzo, was the club's first folk hero, nicknamed *Siggefrido* ('Siegfried') because of his Wagnerian appearance. In their first seven seasons at the Testaccio, Roma never failed to finish in the top six of *Serie A*.

The move north to the PNF was a practical but unpopular one, sweetened by the arrival of centre-forward Amadeo Amadei, who hit exactly a hundred goals for the club and, with a little push from the Fascist authorities, helped win Roma their first title in 1942.

I Lupi ('the wolves') fell away after that, even going down to *Serie B* at one point, despite signing Alcide Ghiggia, scorer of Uruguay's winning goal in the 1950 World Cup final. Cup football was the fans' biggest cheer – two Argentine forwards, Antonio Angelillo and Pedro Manfredini, gained the club the Fairs' Cup of 1961 and the *Coppa Italia* in 1964.

Two men changed Roma's fortunes around after Italy's ban on foreign imports was lifted in the Seventies. Brazilian Falcão, he of the immaculate shoulder dummy in the 1982 World Cup game against Italy, ran a busy midfield, engineered by Swedish coach Nils Liedholm.

Aided by winger Bruno Conti and Roberto Pruzzo, three times *Serie A* top scorer, Roma had their best side since the Thirties. Back-to-back cup wins at the start of the Eighties were followed by Roma's first postwar title in 1983.

Alas, the team froze on their big night – the 1984 European Cup final on home turf against Liverpool. It was a poor game, lost on penalties to Bruce Grobbelaar's wobbling knees. Almost as quickly as it had arrived, Roma's moment had gone.

During the last decade Roma's fans have enjoyed watching some star

A prince among wolves – Giuseppe Giannini

names upfront – Rudi Völler, Daniel Fonseca, Abel Balbo – and sustained a long love affair with midfielder Giuseppe Giannini, *Il Principe* ('the Prince'). His presence wasn't quite enough to turn things round in the club's last European final, a 2–1 aggregate defeat by Inter in the 1991 UEFA Cup.

That year Roma lifted the *Coppa Italia* again, but there has been no sniff of silverware since then. In 1996 the club said farewell to Giannini, and within a year, incredibly, Liedholm was back in charge, now in his seventies, as a stopgap before the arrival – from Lazio, of all places – of new coach Zdeněk Zeman. As well as all sorts of prejudices to overcome, the new man has a long drought to end.

Publication

LaRoma (L5000) is the glossy club monthly, sold at newsstands across town.

Club shop

The **official shop** at Via Paolina 8 (open Mon 3.30–7.30pm, Tues–Sat 9am–1pm & 3.30–7.30pm, Visa cards only) sells tickets and souvenirs. To reach it, take metro line B to Cavour, then a short walk up Via Cavour to Piazza Esquilino. Other club outlets can be found at via 7 Chiese 133 and at Via Sampiero di Bastelica 12.

Ultra culture

Only five years ago, Roma's ultras were among the fiercest in all Italy. The main

Rome essentials

Rome has two **airports**, one for scheduled flights, the other for chartered. The former, **Fiumicino**, also known as Leonardo da Vinci, is 30km south of the city, and connected to Rome's main train station of Termini by an hourly direct express rail service (L13,000, daily 7am–9.15pm, journey time thirty minutes). A more frequent stopping service runs until 1am (L7000, journey time forty minutes) and calls at Ostiense, by Piramide metro. An overnight bus (L7000 from automatic machine) runs to Tiburtina metro station, almost hourly from opposite the arrivals hall entrance. A taxi will set you back some L70,000.

The other airport, **Ciampino**, is 15km south-east of the city, connected by a half-hourly COTRAL bus to Anagnina metro station (L1500, daily 6am–10pm).

Rome has **buses, trams** and a two-line **metro**, all running 5.30am–11.30pm. Metro lines A (red) and B (blue) cross at Termini. Tickets must be bought in advance from the machines at major stations or from *tabacchi*. A single ticket ('BIT', L1500) is valid for 75 minutes from validation on all orange buses, and for one metro journey. A day ticket ('BIG', L6000) is valid for all city transport until midnight of the day it is stamped. For the city's 28 night bus routes (marked N), you can buy a BIT ticket onboard.

Licensed **taxis** are either yellow or white. Make sure the meter is switched to zero when you pick one up from a rank, which will be marked with a blue taxi sign. As you set off, the meter should indicate the minimum fare (currently L6400) for the first 3km or nine minutes of the journey, followed by L1200 per km. There are various surcharges at night, on Sundays and holidays, and for pieces of luggage. To call a cab, dial ☎06/4994 or ☎06/3570, giving your whereabouts. You will be given a taxi code-name, a number and a time. The meter will start running from the time of your call.

The city's EPT **tourist office** has three branches. The central office is at Via Parigi 5, by the *Grand Hotel*, diagonally left out of Termini (open Mon–Sat 8.15am–7.15pm, ☎06/48 89 91, fax 06/481 93 16). The second, between platforms #2 and #3 at Stazione Termini (open daily 8.15am–7.15pm, ☎06/487 12 70), often has huge queues. The third branch is at Fiumicino, by customs (open daily 8.15am–7.15pm).

Thursday's edition of *La Repubblica* newspaper has a free **entertainment** supplement, *Trova Roma*. Less high-brow **listings information** can be found in *Roma C'è* (Thursdays, L1500), which has an end section in English.

The Stadio Olimpico

Via dei Gladiatori
Capacity 82,000 (all-seated)

Italy's **national stadium** will be a multi-purpose, seven-day-a-week, American-style leisure centre before the end of the century. Chains of shops, pizzerias, bars, restaurants... What would poor Benito have made of it? Put them in uniform and stop them eating pasta had been Mussolini's motto.

Historic – the ground is a favourite for Euro finals

A sports complex, the so-called Foro Mussolini, had been constructed in the leader's honour during the Thirties – an obelisk announcing a grand, marble, tree-lined walkway leading to a fountain and, it was planned, a 100,000-seater modern-day Colosseum. The latter was never built, but the grand **Fascist entrance** still stands, Mussolini dedications and all. Behind it lies the modern Stadio Olimpico, begun in 1952. It was then that the area, and the smaller sports stadia around it, became known as the **Foro Italico**. The complex played host to a successful Olympic Games in 1960, the 80,000-capacity Olimpico staging athletics events, the nearby Flaminio some of the football.

Home to Roma, Lazio, every third Italy home game and various European finals (including two Liverpool victories in 1977 and 1984), the Olimpico has a **tremendous setting**. With the sun sinking over Monte Mario, the Tiber and the Eternal City as the backdrop, the stadium's vast open bowl presents a picture not easily forgotten.

To host Italy's intended march to the **1990 World Cup final**, the Olimpico needed a roof and individual seats. After the usual politics and doubling of estimates, a translucent roof was added and space made by extending each end nearer the pitch. Now the *azzurri* had their stage. Nobody who went to one of Italy's games in 1990 will forget the wall of **noise and colour** at the Olimpico – it was as if the opposition were being fed to the lions, the kind of spectacle that had them going time and time again in Nero's day.

Italy never made the final, alas, but Juve's win over Ajax in the 1996 European Cup Final gave the Olimpico an Italian victory to celebrate. There will surely be many more.

To reach the stadium, take **metro line A** to its terminus at Ottaviano, and on leaving the station, turn away from the Vatican into Via Barletta, with the #32 bus stop in the middle of the street. Head towards **Maresciallo/Cadorna**, and the Olimpico will be on your left after about ten minutes.

For **tickets**, your best bet is to get an advance (*prevendita*) ticket from an individual club outlet – although around L3000 dearer, it will save you a lot of headaches on matchday. At the stadium, Lazio's office is in the *Curva Nord*, Roma's in the *Curva Sud*. You'll pay around L25,000 to sit at either end. Away fans are placed in the *distinti* section opposite the home boys. For neutrals, the *Tribuna Tevere laterale* are fair value at around L50,000, while the better-placed *centrale* cost around L80,000.

The **best seats in the house** are in the *Tribuna Monte Mario*, under the press and VIP section, at L80–120,000.

The Foro Italico, planned for *Il Duce*'s sporting minions, was not designed for pre-footie **bar crawls**. The best you can do are the *caffès* on Piazza Mancini, the other side of the Duca d'Aosta bridge. The **Cerbara** at no. 5 is friendly enough.

bunch, the **CUCS** (*Commando Ultras Curva Sud*), were an imposing and colourful presence at any Italian stadium. Derby day became something akin to standing on the launchpad of Cape Canaveral at take-off.

Since the CUCS' heyday, *Boys Roma* and sympathisers of the neo-Fascist *Movimento Sociale Italiano* have infiltrated the ranks, creating minor pockets of havoc. At one point the right-wingers even held the club to ransom, threatening to cause terrifying disturbances in Prague for a UEFA Cup game against Slavia in 1996, unless they received tickets and were allowed to travel with the team...

In the net

Andrea Michelini runs a comprehensive and totally unofficial Roma site at: www.pelagus.it/calcio/roma/asromaen.htm. It's a good, clean informative chunk of Web space, with a good club history and well-maintained stats, plus graphics and movies borrowed (with permission) from the *Rete!* server.

 Lazio

Office Via U Novaro 32
Stadium Olimpico, see p.370
Colours Sky-blue shirts, white shorts
League champions 1974
Cup winners 1958

The *biancocelesti* (literally 'white-and-skies') were founded as a multi-sports club in 1900 on stout Victorian principles by Luigi Bigiarelli, a military man who chose the club name from that of the region surrounding Rome, and whose choice of club colours was inspired by the Greek flag.

Among Lazio's handful of early venues was a military parade ground, and their core fan base is still in the quiet, green-belt northern outskirts of Rome, now pestered by the revving-up of sports car engines and the bleeping of mobile phones.

For all their early ancestry, Lazio were also-rans until the modern era. Before

World War II, rare highlights included moving from their Rondinella ground to the then sumptuous PNF stadium in 1931, and the arrival of 1938 World Cup hero Silvio Piola – the most prolific striker in *Serie A* history with 290 goals to his name. Generally, though, Lazio were overshadowed in the league by new boys Roma.

A cup win in 1958 and an occasional promotion from *Serie B* kept fans hungry until the arrival of Giorgio Chinaglia from Swansea Town in 1969. A big, affable lunkhead of a forward, Chinaglia had been born in Italy but raised in South Wales. He was delighted to be given the chance to move back to his homeland, and certainly made the most of it. Diving in bravely where Italian defenders trod – and most local forwards dared not – he was idolised by the fans.

By now Lazio were being coached by Argentine Juan Carlos Lorenzo, who learned his football with the notorious Estudiantes side of the Sixties. His win-at-all-costs attitude saw Lazio improve their derby record and qualify for Europe for the first time, but at a cost to club discipline. A fiery home Fairs' Cup clash with Arsenal ended in a fight between players at Rome's *L'Augustea* restaurant – some say engineered by Lorenzo. The coach left but the malady lingered on. Fans now began to occupy the *Curva Nord* in serious numbers, and Rome derbies became ferocious.

When Ipswich Town came for a UEFA Cup game in 1973, leading 4–0 from the first leg, Lazio went 2–0 ahead on the night before they had a penalty refused. One was then given to the English, duly converted, and the match finished 4–2 in Lazio's favour. No favours were done afterwards, as fans rained anything they could get their hands on down on the departing players, who began to set upon each other in the tunnel. Lazio were banned from Europe for a year – which just happened to follow their solitary Italian title.

Chinaglia was top *Serie A* scorer in that championship season of 1973/74, partnered by Renzo Garlaschelli upfront, provided for by midfielder Mario Frustalupi, and guided by the team's Darlington-born captain, Pino Wilson. Chinaglia was practically chained to the Fiumicino runway when he left for New York Cosmos two years later. Without Chinaglia, Lazio declined further into tragi-comedy. Young midfield prodigy Luciano Re Cecconi was shot dead in a jeweller's store in 1977, when he walked in disguised as a robber and pretended to heist it for a joke. Two years later a Lazio ultra was slain by a firework at a derby game.

The club began the Eighties by being relegated for their part in the Milan match-fixing scandal, came back up, then went down again. In 1986/87 Lazio had one foot in *Serie C1*, maintaining their second-division status only with a 1–0 play-off win over a village side, Campobasso.

By the time Paul Gascoigne arrived in 1992 – after a year on the operating table – Lazio's fans were desperate for success. Gazza's three seasons in Rome were the usual mixture of controversy and injury off the pitch, wayward genius on it. But he was surrounded by great players, thanks to financier Sergio Cragnotti's millions, which brought Alen Bokšić, Karl-Heinz Riedle, Thomas Doll and Aron Winter to the club.

The fans' favourite was 'Beppe' Signori, his little legs running like dynamos, his mind constantly devising new attacking ideas. He and Czech coach Zdeněk Zeman had both come from Foggia. With Signori's goals – 49 in his first two seasons from 1992/93 – and Zeman's adventurous, three-upfront formation, Lazio became regular top-five finishers for the first time in their history.

Such was Signori's popularity that fans swarmed Rome's Piazza del Popolo to prevent Cragnotti selling him to Parma in the summer of 1995. Two years later Signori was still a Lazio man, but Riedle, Doll, Winter, Gazza and Zeman had all gone, and Italy's 1982 World Cup goalkeeping hero, Dino Zoff, was caretaker coach, pending the arrival of Sven Göran Eriksson – the latest to take on the task of turning Lazio from nearly men into a team of winners.

Publication

Like Roma, Lazio publish their own glossy club magazine – *Lazialità* (monthly, L5000) is available throughout the city.

Club shop

The main **Lazio Point** is at Via Farini 34 (open Mon 3.30–7.30pm, Tues–Sat 9am–1pm & 3.30–7.30pm, Amex accepted) and sells both tickets and souvenirs. Take metro A to Vittorio Emanuele, then walk up Via Napoleone III. There is a Monteverde branch is Via Portuense 544, and a Prati one at Via Cipro 4/1.

Ultra culture

Lazio fans started hanging around the *Curva Nord* in groups in the early Seventies, fired by the political tensions of the day and by the bullish success of Chinaglia's champions of 1974. The movement became focused on one main group, 'Eagle's Supporters', who copied a lot of English fashions, not all of them good. The arrival of the *Irriducibili*, predominantly Fascist, swung the club's support firmly to the right. Fights between rival Lazio groups took place in the early Nineties – the *Irriducibili* won out and now dominate the *Curva Nord*.

In the net

The official website is at: www.sslazio.it/. The English-language area is still 'under construction', but the Italian area offers up its considerable content via a graphic in the form of a Rome restaurant 'menu', which is more appealing than it sounds. For a fan's-eye view, head for: www.icom.it/lazio/. A good-looking site, it offers plenty of chat and gossip, and has a separate area for female Lazio fans.

Eat, drink, sleep…

Bars and clubs

La Dolce Vita has long gone. The buzzing café culture around Via Veneto, captured on celluloid by Federico Fellini, belongs to

Licked into shape – Lazio's Luca Marchegiani is attacked by an unknown assailant, Rome, 1995

the Fifties. In its place is the exclusive film star hang-out around Santa Maria della Pace (any bus to Corso Vittorio Emanuele or Corso Rinascimento), where you'll find Robert de Niro if he's in town.

For something more downmarket, the Trastevere area (bus #710, #718 or #719 from Piazza Venezia) has a decent range of unpretentious **bars**, while Testaccio (metro B to Piramide) is full of popular and reasonably priced clubs, open until dawn.

Bar San Calisto, Piazza San Calisto 3. The jewel in Trastevere's crown, serving cheap beer which you can buy at the bar and take to the terrace. Inside are old shots of both teams and signed boxing photos. Around it all, moped gangs, local wrinklies and less trustworthy characters. Classy it ain't, but a visit here and you've definitely been to Rome. Closed Sundays. Any bus to Trastevere.

Soul II Soul, Via Aurelia 601. Black music club that provides a decent selection of rap, reggae and soul. Open Thurs–Sun, admission L15,000. Bus #46, #49 or #45N.

Villaggio Globale, Lungotevere Testaccio. Set in the old slaughterhouse of Mattatoio, this *Centro Sociale* features live bands on Fridays, DJs on Saturdays. The Mattatoio bar opposite opens at dawn. Metro B to Piramide, then tram #13 down Via Marmorata.

Yes Brazil, Via San Francisco a Ripa 103. Latin bar in Trastevere with live bands from 10.30pm and dancing until 2–3am. No entrance fee but drinks (one obligatory) are L12,000 a throw. Closed Sundays. Any bus to Trastevere.

Restaurants

Roman food is traditionally reliant on offal, brains, tripe and such – a hangover from ancient times when commoners lived on leftovers. Traditional Italian mainstays are also available, but prices are high, as restaurateurs make their killing from tourists.

You'll find most restaurants open 12.30–2.30pm and 7.30–10.30pm, closing one day a week. Credit-card payment is not as common as in the north.

Al Cardello, Via del Cardello 1, off Via Cavour. Rare reasonably priced diner near the Colosseum, with a three-course tourist menu at L25,000 and tables outdoors. Closed Sundays, most credit cards. Metro B to Cavour.

Da Giovanni, Via della Lungara 41a. Busy, cheap two-room diner near the Tiber in Trastevere. Roman dishes at L10–15,000. Closed Sundays, no credit cards. Bus #23, #41, #65 or #280.

Mario's, Via del Moro 53. Excellent pasta dishes for under L10,000, tourist menus at L20,000.

Closed Sundays, most credit cards. If full, try the Taverna at no. 43. Bus #23, #65 or #280 along Lungotevere.

Perilli a Testaccio, Via Marmorata 39. Straight out of a Fellini film, a family-run *trattoria* serving huge portions of local delicacies. About L25,000 for two courses. Closed Wednesdays. No credit cards. Metro B to Piramide.

Accommodation

Rome has a shortage of mid-price hotels. Always try to reserve a place well in advance, and allow for the possibility of it not being available for the length of time originally agreed. **Enjoy Rome** (Via Varese 39, ☎06/44 51 843, fax 06/44 50 734, open Mon–Fri 8.30am–1pm & 3.30–6pm, Sat 8.30am–1pm) offers a free hotel booking service – turn right out of Termini. The station itself is full of absurd **hustlers** offering rooms – official tourist board agents will have ID and a map.

Foro Italico, Viale delle Olimpiadi 61 (☎06/32 36 267, fax 06/32 42 613). Rome's main youth hostel is right up by the Stadio Olimpico. Dorm beds for IYHF members at L25,000 (L5000 extra for non-members), breakfast and showers included. Midnight curfew. No credit cards. Metro A to Ottaviano, then bus #32 to Cadorna.

Fawlty Towers, Via Magenta 39 (☎06/44 50 374). Pensione-cum-hostel with no curfew, terrace and sitting room with a satellite TV. Dorm beds at L25,000, doubles at L65,000, with bath L80,000. No credit cards. Turn right out of Termini.

Pensione Germano, Via Calatafimi 14a (☎06/48 69 19). Singles around L40,000, doubles with bath L65,000, triples and quads also available. Visa/Mastercard accepted. Off Via Volturno, facing Termini.

Pensione Piave, Via Piave 14 (☎06/47 43 447, fax 06/48 73 360). More comfortable than most *pensioni* in the area; all rooms have bath and telephone. Singles around L50,000, doubles L75,000. No credit cards. Ten minutes out of Termini.

The sticker picker – Giuseppe Panini

Every September, the school playgrounds of Europe become a hive of activity. Trading is as frantic as any stock exchange. The commodity? Self-adhesive **football cards** (*figurine* in Italian), bought, collected, swapped and stuck into albums, manufactured by **Panini** and individually modelled for different domestic markets across Europe.

It all began in **1960**, when a newsagent from Modena was faced with a pile of unsold football players' cards. Putting each card into a red-bordered white envelope, Giuseppe Panini sold **packs of two** for **ten lire** apiece. They went like hotcakes. An industry was born.

Giuseppe enlisted the help of his three brothers to produce and distribute the cards. Benito was in charge of shipping, Umberto took care of typography, inventing a machine which could both print and package cards at the same time, and Franco dealt with administration.

The business grew until Panini had a $60 million annual turnover and was selling in **forty countries**. Each September brought a new album cover, each trip to the newsagents a thrill of anticipation, each packet opening – with its accompanying heady smell of gloss print and adhesive – a buzz unbettered until girls came along. World Cup editions were a special treat. Suddenly, every kid in class knew where El Salvador was.

Giuseppe Panini was the definitive self-made man. Before his death in October 1995, not long after the latest deal with the Italian players' union had been struck, he bequeathed **three-quarters of a million cards** to Modena city council.

The 1998 World Cup should see Panini's design department pulling out all the stops, frantically trawling in images and information from Tunisia to Brazil. See you down the newsagents…

Naples

Football in Naples must be seen in a different context from the rest of Italy, probably from the rest of Europe. Naples is one team, 70,000 season-ticket holders against the world. Naples, of course, *was* one man, whose seven seasons here are almost the stuff of fiction. From the hysteria of his arrival to the ignominy of his departure, Diego Maradona took this benign madhouse to the top and back down again. Whether the club, Napoli, can ever take the city back to the top of the Italian football tree is a subject as hotly debated here as the date of the next eruption of Mount Vesuvius, the volcano which dominates the city.

Saint turned sinner – Maradona KOs Italy, Naples, 1990

The thrilling fields

 Napoli

Stadium San Paolo, Piazzale V Tecchio
Capacity 72,000 (all-seated)
Colours Azure-blue shirts, white shorts
League champions 1987, 1990
Cup winners 1962, 1976, 1987
UEFA Cup winners 1989

The history of Napoli can be divided into 'am' and 'pm' – before and after Maradona. Before his arrival in 1984, the club had relied on the occasional European run to appease Italy's most manic support.

It was a Cunard sailor, William Poths, who organised the first football team here at the turn of the century. Poths' Naples FC had a rival, Internazionale, but over pizza and wine at the city's *d'Angelo* restaurant, the two agreed to merge in 1926.

The newly formed Internapoli, later Napoli, had a poor start in life. Their first season in the southern regional division was so disastrous, fans turned the city's symbol of a proud horse into the club's unofficial one of a little donkey. The club moved grounds up to the tranquility of Vómero, but crowd disturbances soon had the place closed and the authorities sought to build a secure venue where Neapolitans could vent their passions. They chose a spot in the west of the city, outside an area of toxic gases and extinct volcanoes known as Campi Flegrei.

With the backing of shipping magnate Achille Lauro, a huge bowl, the Stadio San Paolo, was built in 1959. Lauro, *Il Comandante*, bought the South American strike partnership of José Altafini and Omar Sivori from Gianni Agnelli's Juventus, in a deal which gave Fiat the contract to motorise Lauro's ocean liners.

At last, Naples had a team to challenge the north. Napoli won the *Coppa Italia*,

Diego's Napoli foil – Brazilian striker Careca

their first major honour, in 1962, made second place to Milan in the league in 1968, and the following year went out to Leeds in the Fairs' Cup on the drawing of lots. In 1975 they lost a title decider to Juventus on a last-minute goal – scored by the team's former hero, Altafini.

By this time Corrado Ferlaino was Napoli president, and it was he who brought Diego Maradona to the club. The transfer of the little Argentinian from Barcelona was fraught with difficulties, not least a $1 million shortfall in the fee, overcome in one day after the club appealed to fans to make personal donations, and people queued round the block, savings books in hand. Maradona was flown into a packed San Paolo by helicopter; everyone in the crowd paid L1000 to attend.

Diego's arrival made little immediate impact on the team. But in 1986/87, after his triumphant World Cup in Mexico, Maradona was on top of his game and Napoli's first-ever *scudetto* seemed within reach. With ex-player Ottavio Bianchi, a strict disciplinarian, as coach, Ciro Ferrara at the back, the gritty Fernando de Napoli

in midfield and Brazilian Careca partnering Maradona upfront, Napoli kept ahead of the pack and the city prepared to party. Naples had waited sixty years for this moment. When it came, with a 1–1 draw against Fiorentina on May 10, 1987, hundreds of donkeys were let loose around the town, no-one slept for a week, let alone went into work, and Maradona himself partied as hard as anyone – a prelude to the drugs-and-prostitutes hell into which he would sink within four years.

In 1989 Maradona's Napoli beat Jürgen Klinsmann's Stuttgart to win the UEFA Cup, and a year later they were champions again, thanks to a two-point award after another of their South Americans, Alemão, was struck by a coin at Atalanta – TV cameras caught Napoli's masseur shouting to the Brazilian: "Keep down on the ground!"

In many Italian eyes, this incident tarnished Napoli's reputation. Their 1987 *scudetto* had not been unpopular elsewhere in the country, but now the honeymoon was over, and divorce seemed the only possible outcome after Maradona's Argentina knocked Italy out of the 1990 World Cup. Before the semi-final between the two teams at the San Paolo, Diego had exhorted Neapolitans to cheer for his side as the underdogs against an Italian line-up comprised almost entirely of northerners. The plea did not go down well, either in Naples or elsewhere.

Less than a year later, after testing positive for cocaine, Maradona took a privately chartered plane to Buenos Aires and never set foot in Naples again. Without him, the club stumbled from one financial crisis to another and were unable to hang on to the prodigious talent the Argentinian had left behind – players like Ferrara, Careca, Uruguayan striker Daniel Fonseca, and Diego's understudy, Gianfranco Zola. As Napoli's coach of the mid-Nineties, Marcello Lippi, explained: "We played without salaries for six months and with lawyers in the dressing room."

In 1997, the San Paolo drew its first capacity crowd in years for the first leg of the *Coppa Italia* final against Vicenza. Napoli won 1–0, but lost the tie overall...

Getting a ticket

Since the post-Maradona decline, gaining entry is no longer an issue at Napoli. Apart from the club's outlets in town, there are **ticket offices** immediately facing you as you approach the San Paolo. Napoli ultras are in *Curva B*, and visiting fans are placed in the *distinti* furthest from them. The *tribuna laterale* is a reasonably priced spot for neutrals; the *tribuna Posillipo* is for the press and Neapolitan dignitaries.

Here we go!

Take the Gianturco-Bagnoli branch of the 'FS Metropolitana' train line from Garibaldi (inside the central train station), seven stops to **Campi Flegrei**. The stadium is a short walk between the palm trees of Piazzale Tecchio.

Swift half

The best bar is the tiny **Caffè Cumana** on the traffic island between the station and the stadium, with a table outside if you're there early enough. At Via Giambattista Marino 13a, to the right of the stadium as you approach from the station, is the **Caffetteria degli Azzurri**.

Ultra culture

For the decisive game with Fiorentina in May 1987 that won Napoli their first *scudetto*, the **CUCB** (*Commando Ultra Curva B*) organised a banner of such size it made the *Guinness Book of Records*. At the time they also had their own local TV show and the blessing of Diego Armando himself. Still fiercely loyal, the CUCB put out a monthly ultrazine, *UltrA'zzurro* (L5000).

In the net

The unofficial Club Napoli Internet can be found at: www.x4all.nl/~elio/napoli.htm. The site is a bit of a mess, to be frank, but have patience – keep digging and you'll find news, links, chat, and an email form should you want to join the Club. Choose from English, Spanish, Italian and Neapolitan dialect as your preferred language.

Naples essentials

Naples' Capodochino **airport** is 4km north-west of town. Bus #14 (L3000) calls at both international and domestic terminals and then runs on to Piazza Garibaldi, the square outside the main **train station**, Stazione Centrale. Buses run every fifteen minutes, 6am–midnight, journey time thirty minutes. A taxi will cost at least L20,000.

The best way around Naples' narrow streets and back alleys is to **walk**. Towards the bay, the Stazione Centrale is a twenty-minute hike across Piazza Garibaldi and down Corso Umberto. Otherwise there are five modes of **transport**: buses, trams, metro, a high-speed suburban train and funiculars up to Vómero. A single ticket for an inner-city journey on any of these is L1,200, from transport offices and *tabacchi* – stamp it onboard or before entering the train or metro; it is valid for ninety minutes. A **half-day ticket** (6am–2pm or 2–11pm) is L2000, an **all-day ticket** L4000. Transport runs 6am–11pm, and a few night buses leave from Piazza Garibaldi or Parco del Castello.

Taxis (☎081/570 70 70) are yellow, and some of them are metered. Either barter first or watch the meter like a hawk. Journeys should cost L3000 plus L500 per minute, with supplements for night-time, Sundays, holidays, and items of luggage.

There are EPT **tourist offices** at the station (open Mon–Sat 9am–8pm, Sun 9am–1pm, ☎081/26 87 79), in town at Piazza dei Martiri 58, Scala B, 2nd floor (open Mon–Fri 8.30am–2.30pm, ☎081/40 53 11), and at the airport (daily 8.30am–2pm & 5–7.30pm). All should be able to provide free copies of the weekly poster *Posto Unico*, and monthly *Qui Napoli*, both of which offer reasonable **entertainment** details. The daily *Il Matino* has a **listings guide** every Thursday.

Eat, drink, sleep...

Bars and clubs

Start the day with the finest **coffee** in Italy – Neapolitan bar owners warm their cups in special machines under the counter. In the city's **maze of streets**, anything could be around the next corner, a devil's head or an oasis of football talk in a bar.

Bar Messico, Piazza Amedeo. Large bar/disco with Latin music and drinks, popular with young Neapolitans. Metro to Amedeo.

Caffè Dumas, Via A Dumas 1. High up on the incline overlooking Castel dell'Ovo, a light, airy, modern café. Tram #1 or #1B to Galleria della Vittoria.

Maschio Angioino, Via Martucci. One of Naples' many pub/discos with reasonable prices, heavy clouds of dope smoke and old-fashioned music. Popular with *tifosi*. Metro to Amedeo.

Oasis Pub, Via Giovanni Bausan 30. Incredibly friendly bar with big wooden tables and a decent selection of music. Metro to Amedeo.

Restaurants

Naples is the home of the **pizza** – wafer-thin crust, fresh local tomatoes and lashings of mozzarella cheese. You'll find street stalls serving up **slices** at L1500 a throw, and you won't want to walk inside your local chain of pizza restaurant ever again.

Although the best spots to dine are at the pricey end of Mergellina **on the bay**, take the metro to Mergellina and it will drop you just inland in a neighbourhood full of reasonably priced *trattorie*.

Avellinese da Peppino, Via Silvio Spaventa 31/35. Piazza Garibaldi is full of pricey, mediocre diners for tourists; its side-streets are full of marvellous, moderately priced places for locals – such as *Peppino's*, with outdoor tables and outstanding *spaghetti alle vongole*. Open daily until midnight. No credit cards.

Osteria Castello, Via S Teresa a Chaia 38. Cosy restaurant with a literary feel and two courses for under L15,000. Open mid-afternoon. Most major credit cards. Tram #1 or #1B to Via Acton, then cross Piazza del Plebiscito by Palazzo Reale.

Pizzeria da Michele, Casale Sersale 1/3. A local institution which sticks by a menu of two varieties of pizza, *margherita* and *marinara*, at L4000 each, L5000 with extra mozzarella. Closed Sundays. Short walk from Piazza Garibaldi.

Pizzeria Port'Alba, Via Port'Alba 18. The oldest *pizzeria* in Italy, tucked in the Port'Alba arch. Superb range of pizzas, most under L10,000, with a fair array of other offerings. Open Thurs–Tues 9am–2pm. No credit cards. Metro to Cavour, then a short walk down Via Costantinapoli.

Accommodation

Although Naples has the cheapest accommodation of all major Italian cities, it pays to **splash out** a little more on comfort and safety. There are many cheap *pensione* around Piazza Garibaldi, but quite a few are hired out by the hour and it can get noisy. The area near the university, between Piazza Dante and the cathedral (down from metro Cavour) is a better bet, but even so, watch yourself at night. Wherever you stay, check the locks before you check in.

Hotel Casanova, Corso Garibaldi 333 (☎081/268 287). Comfortable single, double, triple and quad rooms, roof-top terrace with bar service. Doubles L45,000, with bath 55,000. Most credit cards. Short walk up from Piazza Garibaldi.

Ostello Mergellina, Salita della Grotta 23 (☎081/761 23 46). Comfortable youth hostel with two-, four- and six-bed rooms, all with bath. L20,000 for IYHF members, L5000 extra non-members. Curfew 11.30pm. Metro to Mergellina.

Pensione Margherita, Via Cimarosa 29 (☎081/556 70 44). Away from the chaos downtown, a smart place up in Vómero by the *funiculare centrale* stop. Singles at L45,000, doubles L75,000. No credit cards. Midnight curfew.

Norway

As the twentieth century draws to a close, Norwegian football is still enjoying what many consider to be its golden age. The club sides are no longer the cannon fodder they were during the formative years of European competition, and the national side maintains its reputation of being a gritty, super-fit team of combatants. Norway are a new footballing force, if not to be feared, then certainly to be respected.

The key to Norway's arrival at the top table of international football can be traced back to 1984, and a long-term state plan to produce sporting excellence. When the so-called *Elite Sport* venture began, it focused mainly on track and field athletics. The results were impressive: Olympic and European championship medal hauls doubled, and a huge increase in grassroots participation.

Part of the *Elite Sport* philosophy could be summed up as 'win at all costs' – then something of a novelty in a country where so much sporting activity was still strictly amateur. The philopsophy was transferred to team games, including football. If the previous generation of Norwegian players were content to travel to Benfica or the Bernabéu as lambs to the slaughter, *Elite Sport* ensured that the next one would not.

In 1990, Egil Olsen was installed as coach of the Norwegian national squad. Nicknamed 'Drillo' after his ability to drill low passes around the midfield, as a player, Olsen took the *Elite Sport* teachings a stage further and incorporated them into what he called 'effective football'. Olsen, a controversial figure who claimed to make more money from playing poker than coaching soccer, told his players to chase every lost cause and get the ball forward early. It was, in effect, a refinement of the long ball game, and was immediately criticised by fans.

The baby-faced bomber – Ole Gunnar Solskjær

But effective it was, and in 1994 Norway appeared in their first World Cup finals since 1938, after finishing top of a qualifying group that included Holland and England – neither of whom could beat Olsen's side. Graham Taylor's England, in particular, were completely nonplussed by Norway's limitless running during a vital defeat in Oslo in the summer of 1993.

At USA '94, Norway beat Mexico, lost to Italy and drew with Ireland. It was a respectable performance, but not one that won many plaudits. In truth, the heat in America had made it impossible for the Norwegians to play the game as they wanted, and without any back-up plan in the locker, they simply wilted in the sun.

Norway needed another tactical string to their bow, and the mass export of players to the English Premiership looked as though it would provide it. Now a little more flexible in their approach, Olsen's team got off to a flier in their qualifiers for the 1996 European Championship. But a late equaliser by Jan Suchopárek for the Czech Republic in Oslo, with the Norwegians just three minutes from the finals, proved a telling blow; after away defeats by both the Czechs and the Dutch, Norway missed the boat to Euro '96.

While the exodus of key players had produced some positive results, Norway needed a more sophisticated domestic game to give Olsen the strength in-depth he needed. The club that provided that sophistication were Rosenborg of Trondheim – tough, efficient, professional, forward-looking, all the things, in fact, which up until now had been anathema to Norwegian club sides.

With Rosenborg and SK Brann of Bergen both reaching the quarter-finals of European club competitions in 1997, and the national team very much back on track (their latest victims being Brazil, beaten 4–2 in Oslo), all that remains is for the last vestiges of the amateur code to be swept away from the domestic game.

In truth, there is still some way to go, for cultural, historical and geographical reasons. Skiing and other winter pastimes have always dominated the sports calendar in Norway, and football, with its necessarily short summer season, didn't get a national championship until 1937 – a year after the national side had beaten Germany in front of Hitler at the Olympic Games in Berlin. Even then, the title was decided by a series of play-offs; a fully fledged league didn't start up until 1963.

Matches in that first league season were watched by an average of 8000 fans, which delighted the Norwegian FA. But the game's popularity wasn't sustained. The modern TV era, combined with the departure of star names such as Rune Bratseth and Erik Thorstvedt, made European foot-

Stalemate in the sun – Erik Thorstvedt saves for Norway against Ireland, USA '94

Basics

EU, US, Canadian, Australian and New Zealand citizens require only a valid **passport** to enter Norway for up to three months.

Like other Scandinavian countries, Norway has a reputation for being one of the most expensive European destinations. The Norwegian currency is the kroner, one krone (crown, indiactated here as Nkr) being divided into 100 øre. There are notes for 50Nkr, 100Nkr, 500Nkr and 1000Nkr, while the coins in circulation are 50 øre, 1Nkr, 5Nkr and 10Nkr. There are around 12Nkr to £1.

The best places to **change money** are banks, savings banks and major post offices, which all offer competitive rates. On arrival, you will also be able to change foreign currency and travellers' cheques at airports, harbours, train stations and hotels, but expect a less generous rate and higher commission charges. **Credit cards** are widely accepted in major towns.

Norwegian cities are connected by the train services of *Norges Statsbaner* (*NSB*), the efficiently run state rail company. In places, the rail network is extended by a train-bus service, with connecting coaches continuing on from train stations. A one-way train ticket from **Oslo** to **Trondheim** costs around 550kr for the nine-hour journey. Special **discount fares** are available for long-distance journeys if booked at least one day in advance; enquire about any other special deals before booking. If you have more time to spare and the geography allows, travelling by **ferry** or coastal steamer can be a relaxing alternative.

Norway's **telephone service** is likewise efficiently run by *Telenor* and you'll have no problem making international calls from public phones. These take 1Nkr, 5Nkr and 10Nkr coins, or phonecards (*TeleKort*) which can be bought from shops and kiosks and come in three sizes: 35Nkr, 98Nkr and 210Nkr

From outside the country, the **dialling code** for Norway is ☎47; city codes are part of the customer number. From Norway, the dialling prefix for international calls is ☎00 followed by the country code; reduced call rates, offering a 15 percent discount, apply from 10pm to 8am daily.

ball, and the English game in particular, more attractive than the domestic variety. Meanwhile, Norway's terrain and long distances between cities deterred travelling support. And the inability of Oslo to generate an influential club (locals blame a lack of training facilities in the capital and the cosmopolitan distractions of the big city) has deprived football of its biggest natural catchment area of support.

Assuming that a challenger from Oslo – probably Lyn or Skeid – can be found to compete with Rosenborg, Brann and ambitious Molde for honours, then the future looks bright for Norwegian football. The exodus of star names shows no sign of letting up, but at the same time, neither does the flow of fresh talent from the clubs' excellent youth policies – a lasting legacy of

the *Elite Sport* programme. And if Norway's men need any further inspiration to make future progress, they need look no further than their womenfolk. Football is far from being a single-sex sport here – there are more than 50,000 girls' clubs up and down the country, and in 1995, Norway won the Women's World Cup for the first time.

Match practice

Like their Scandinavian neighbours, Norwegian fans have been brought up on a diet of overseas football. Their long winters are illuminated by live television coverage from England and other countries, and most Norwegian fans have a favourite English club. No surprise, then, that with the exception of Rosenborg, Norwegian fans ape the songs of British supporters.

The Norwegian season begins in mid-April and finishes towards the end of October. By the time most of Europe is approaching its halfway stage, Norwegians are raising a glass of beer to their newly crowned champions.

The league

Norway's twelve-team premier division is known as the *Tippeliga*. Below this comes the first division, a fourteen-team competition from which the top two teams gain promotion each year, swapping places with the bottom two of the premier. Further down the ladder, the second division is highly regionalised, with eight groups of twelve almost entirely amateur teams.

Up for the cup

Like all Europe's long-established knock-out tournaments, Norway's is a mammoth competition and is entered by all clubs from second-division level upwards. *Tippeliga* clubs enter at the third round. The action starts in May and all ties are single-match affairs, with extra-time and penalties if necessary, until the semi-finals which are two-legged. The tournament ends in October with a single-game final at the Ullevål stadium in Oslo.

Tickets

Outside of big domestic games involving Rosenborg and/or Brann, you should have no difficulty just turning up on-spec and buying your ticket immediately before the match. Admission prices vary, but the average standing place is around 80Nkr, while a decent seat will 110Nkr.

The back page

Football competes with skiing for media attention. Norway's leading newspapers, *Aftenposten* and *Dagbladet* both offer decent coverage of the local game, but curiously, it is Norway's ephemeral-looking tabloids that carry the in-depth soccer features.

For a round-up of what's going on both locally and abroad, try the weekly magazine *Bladet Fotball*.

Action replay

Until recently, Norwegian state *NRK* had the rights to live *Tippeliga* coverage, but with the Norwegian FA now realsing the commercial potetial of the game, a more lucrative deal, in keeping with subscription packages elsewhere in Europe, looks likely. Subscription channel *TV 3* has Champions' League rights, with other European competitions being shared around according to individual club deals.

Ultra culture

Crowd behaviour tends to be very disciplined, with good-natured singing but otherwise a rather refined appreciation of the game.

There are few organised fan groups in Norway outside of officially sanctioned supporters' clubs. With so few fans able to travel to watch their team and only a handful of local derbies in the calendar, there's little potential for trouble.

With typical fair-mindedness, clubs and supporters' groups have always acted together to supress any hooliganism that may surface from time to time. When a few coins were thrown at a Lillestrøm match recently, there was a major outcry – an indication of how unused Norwegians are to living with the spectre of soccer violence.

In the net

Lars Aarhus runs a reliable and very extensive Norwegian football server at: www.unik.no/~larsa/football.html. The site contains an extraordinary stats archive embracing international, amateur and women's football, and the news section is regularly updated in English.

Norway is also host to one of the most useful football servers anywhere on the web, *Soccercity*. The site has changed owners recently but has now been substantially rebuilt and contains thousands of links to footie sites all over the world. Each country gets its own 'homepage' of links, which are further divided into clubs if need be. Head for: athene.net/soccercity/.

Trondheim

With the capital Oslo continuing to lag behind the pace of Norwegian football, it falls to the northern city of Trondheim to act as the nation's soccer hotbed. This is the place where Norwegian Kings are brought for their blessing, and it is also the home of the country's kings of football – Rosenborg BK. Their dominance in recent years has completely overshadowed the city's other clubs, of whom only Nardo, Strindheim and Byasen play above the regional leagues.

Trondheim celebtrated its millennium in 1997, but the city has become used to letting its hair down and having a party – the success of Rosenborg has seen to that.

The thrilling fields

 Rosenborg BK

Lerkendal Stadion
Capacity 28,000
Colours White shirts, black shorts
League champions 1967, 1969, 1971, 1985–86, 1988, 1990, 1992–96
Cup winners 1960, 1964, 1971, 1988, 1990, 1992, 1995

When Rosenborg Boldklub were founded in 1917, much of Europe was in the grip of new political teachings. In keeping with the spirit of the times, they extolled the virtues of a people's club. Yet in the Nineties, while they continue to enjoy close links with the local community in Trondheim, the club are also in the forefront of the push towards full professionalism in the Norwegian game.

The team first earned their share of the limelight around the time that Norway began a league championship for the first time, winning two titles and two cups in

All wrapped up – scarves are not for show here

the Sixties. They remained leading contenders domestically through much of the following two decades, but in European terms, RBK were an obscure footballing backwater, even less well-known than the amateur sides of Oslo and Bergen.

The arrival of coach Nils Arne Eggen in 1990 acted as the catalyst for change. Eggen had led unfashionable Moss to the title in 1987, and his methods soon paid dividends at Rosenborg. Like his national-team counterpart Egil Olsen, Eggen emphasised teamwork, discipline in defence and the long, aerial pass as a means of bypassing the opposition. He also instigated a clearout of the squad, favouring young players for their superior fitness.

At home RBK quickly became near-invincible. They have won all but one of

appeared in the Champions' League for the first time in 1995. They beat England's millioniare champions, Blackburn Rovers, at the Lerkendal stadium, and while they failed to progress to the knockout stage, they had served notice of their intentions.

Just twelve months later they were back, beating IFK Gothenburg to affirm their position as Scandinavia's strongest club, then taking their greatest scalp so far with a 2–1 win over the Italian champions, AC Milan, in the San Siro. They then pushed European champions Juventus to the limit in the quarter-finals, despite having lost several key players to foreign clubs during the long winter break.

Norwegian players have almost become a fashion accessory in Britain, and a sizeable percentage of the incoming players are from Rosenborg. Steffen Iversen, Stig-Inge Bjørnebye, Bjorn Kvarme and Øyvind Leonharden all hail from the Lerkendal academy. But, happily for Rosenborg, there seem to be plenty more where they came from.

Climbing frame – Rosenborg outjump Milan, 1996

the championships to be decided during the Nineties, and today no team in Norway can match them for organisation or commercial know-how.

Rosenborg's reputation began to spread to European competition when they

In addition to money from transfers and Champions' League sponsorship, Rosenborg's crowd figures alone (11,000 people watch home games at the Lerkendal, compared with a *Tippeliga* average

Trondheim essentials

Trondheim **airport** is 35km northeast of the city at Vaernes, and airport buses (45kr) run to the main train station, Sentralstasjon, in the city centre, a 45-minute ride.

Transport in town is by **buses** and **trams** (flat-fare tickets 15Nkr), but you can just as easily walk around the city. However, if you're planning to venture outside the centre, the unlimited 24-hour public transport ticket is worth having (35Nkr from the tourist office – see below); it is valid on all local buses and trams.

The city **tourist office** (open daily 10am–6pm, until 8pm in summer; closed winter weekends) is at Munkegaten 18, on the corner of the city's main square, Torvet. They can assist you with accommodation in private houses and sell maps and other guides. The office also issues the free *Trondheim Guide*, the only local source of entertainment and nightlife **listings**.

of less than half that) give them a competitive advantage over those who would usurp their crown in Norway.

The next step, as Eggen acknowledges, is to make a serious bid for European silverware, in the hope that Trondheim can host the kings of the continent as well as the local variety.

Here we go!

Board any bus trailing black-and-white scarves in the centre of town. Lerkendal is a five-minute ride away.

Swift half

Your best bet is to sink one in Trondheim city centre before boarding the bus. Try the lively (but pricy) **Amsterdam Bar** of the Hotel Residence on the main square, Torvet.

Ultra culture

The Norwegians like their songs, and while the rest of the country is happy to crash its way through British terrace standards, Rosenborg's *Kuernen* have a vast repertoire to call upon, including two written specifically for them by local composer Dag Ingebrigtsen – *Rosenborgboogie* and *Vi skå slukke Brann*.

In the net

The official Rosenborg website is at: home.sn.no/~terjerix/rbk/. The pages are efficient and matter-of-fact in a typically Scandinavian way, but there's plenty of information here and everything is available in English as well as Norwegian. To swap song lyrics with the *Kuernen,* head for their unofficial fans' site at: colargol.idb.hirt.no/~tommyi/rhk/.

Eat, drink, sleep...

Bars and clubs

As in other Scandinavian countries, alcohol is **heavily taxed**, rationed almost, in Norway – a half-litre of beer costs around 35Nkr, and the distribution of wines and

spirits is strictly controlled by a state-run monopoly. Beer (øl) is sold in supermarkets at about half the price you'd pay in a bar. The strongest (class III) beer can only be purchased from state-controlled shops, known as *Vinmonopolet* (open Mon–Fri 10am–4pm, Sat 10am–1pm). The best brands are *Hansa* and *Ringsnes*. The favourite spirit is Aquavit, 40 percent proof and served in ice-cold glasses.

In Trondheim, you'll be able to keep drinking in bars until at least 1am, or as late as 4am in some places – but you'll probably **run out of money** first.

The city's large student population ensures a lively (for Norway) nightlife scene with the pick of the bars and clubs along Dronningens gate, around the Britannia hotel.

Breiflabben, Kjøpmmanns gate 7. Below the Havfruen restaurant, a club catering for a slightly older crowd, playing live jazz on the weekends.

Carl Johan Møteplass, Olav Tryggvasons gate 24. Stylish bar, packed at weekends and a good place to meet with celebrating RBK fans after the big match.

Dubliner, Nordre gate 23. The city's only 'Irish pub'. Don't come here for the Guinness.

Exit, Dronningens gate. Very popular bar and nightclub with varied sounds and a similarly varied clientèle.

Restaurants

Those on a tight budget have problems eating out in Norway and Trondheim is no exception. However, the mobile fast-food stalls, concentrated around the Sentralstasjon and on either side of Torvet, are a good bet if you're peckish and penniless.

At lunchtime, take advantage of cheaper set menus or the *koldtbord* (Norway's answer to the *smörgåsbord*) where for around 120–170Nkr you can eat as much as you like during the three or four hours that the food is on the table.

Havfreun, Kjøpmanns gate 7. A great fish restaurant near the cathedral. Good-value main courses from 170Nkr. Can get busy.

Hos Magnus, Kjøpmanns gate 63. Just along the road from Havfreun and worth a look if the latter is full. Fish are again the speciality, with the herring especially recommended.

Ni Muser, Bispegata 9. Modern European cuisine in a relaxed, fashionable café atmosphere. Reasonable prices. Open until midnight. Closed Mon.

Trubadur, Kongens gate 34. Traditional food, with bargain daily specials such as fishballs and reindeer at lunchtime, right by St Olavs gate.

Accommodation

Norwegian hotels are of the highest standard – neat, clean and efficient and offering huge breakfasts – but they don't come cheap. There are, however, budget alternatives such as youth hostels, guest houses (*gjestgiveri*) and private rooms which could keep you from bankruptcy. Discounts are also offered in summer, which is handy for the visiting football fan.

Pensions (*pensjonater*) charge around 350–450Nkr for a single room and 450–550Nkr for a double, while youth hostels start from 100kr for a bed and 50kr for breakfast. In Trondheim, **private rooms** are good value, although many of them are a fair way out from the centre; book them at the **tourist office**, where the rate is fixed at 330Nkr per double per night, plus a 20Nkr booking fee.

Britannia, Dronningens gate 5 (☎73 53 53 53, fax 73 51 29 00). Bang in the middle of town and with magnificent *Art Nouveau* architecture. Comfortable rooms, but pricey – around 900Nkr for a double. Summer discounts.

Jarlen, Kongens gate 40 (☎73 51 32 18, fax 73 52 80 80). Basic pension, bargain prices. Central location. Less than 500Nkr for a double.

InterRail Centre, Elgester gate 1 (☎73 89 95 38). Basic B&B accommodation in a large house with a couple of hundred rooms. Operated by the university's student society. Take bus #41, #42, #48, #49, #52 or #63 along Prinsens gate and ask for the *Studentersamfundet*. 90Nkr per person per night.

Rainbow Trondheim, Kongens gate 15 (☎73 50 50 50, fax 73 51 60 58). Popular chain hotel in an attractive old city-centre building. Reasonable value, lively bar. Around 700Nkr for a double room. Sizeable summer discounts.

Poland

Suffering from familiar post-Communist blights – rising corruption and hooliganism, dwindling crowds and insufficient finance – Polish football needs another decade to find the right ingredients for a healthy domestic game and international success.

Today's Polish game seems a long way from the thriving industry that fostered three notable World Cup campaigns between 1974 and 1982, a golden era which had its roots in the gifted side that were crowned Olympic champions in 1972. That was the team which, in the qualifiers for the 1974 World Cup, shocked group favourites England with a home win, then came to Wembley on October 17, 1973, needing only a draw to deny Alf Ramsey's men a place at the finals. Goalkeeper Jan Tomaszewski confounded the critics – including TV pundit Brian Clough, who had described him as a clown – by somehow keeping the ball from crossing the goal line until it was too late. At the other end, the most capped goalkeeper in English history, Peter Shilton, flopped weakly to a Domarski shot – 1–1 and Poland were through.

Kazimierz Deyna, Robert Gadocha, Grzegorz Lato and Andrzej Szarmach would then emerge as world stars of the side that made the semi-finals a year later, losing out to eventual winners West Germany in atrocious playing conditions. Deyna and co were joined four years later by the most successful Polish player of modern times, Zbigniew Boniek, and had it not been for Argentine striker Mario Kempes' punch off the line in their opening second-phase match, the Poles might well have gone on to play in the final instead of the host nation.

Boniek was back at the next World Cup in Spain 1982, but was suspended for

Gone but not forgotten – Kazimierz Deyna

the crucial semi-final against Italy; the Poles, as in 1974, would have to be content with victory in a meaningless third-place play-off, where the veteran Szarmach was among the goals against France.

In those halcyon days of the Seventies and Eighties, Silesia, Poland's footballing heartland, could boast packed stadia and the most popular team in the land, Górnik Zabrze. Since then the region's heavy industry has severely declined and, with it, the subsidised entertainment (like football) which once kept the workers happy. Górnik have faded, and even the national stadium in Chorzów was closed following a crowd riot and subsequent UEFA investigation in 1993.

Two sides have dominated Polish league football in the Nineties: Legia Warsaw and Widzew Łódź. Legia were involved in a comical match-fixing scandal at the climax to the 1992/93 season, when both they and their co-table toppers LKS Łódz won their final matches by daft scorelines, against teams who were clearly content to provide no more than token opposition. The belated PZPN (Polish FA) decision to award the title to Lech Poznań has resulted in a grudge between hardcore Legia fans and the rest of Poland, and the more volatile element of Widzew's support has been quick to take up the fight. The two sets of fans created havoc at Poznań and Wrocław respectively one black Saturday in October 1996, raising public order questions in parliament, bringing security cameras into first-division grounds, and causing both home stadia to be declared out of bounds for the remainder of the 1996/97 season.

Although never one for the terraces, one particular Polish football fan should not be left out: former goalkeeper Pope John Paul II, whose team, Cracovia, are Poland's oldest surviving football club and were the country's first champions in 1921.

Essential vocabulary

Hello *Dzień dobry*
Goodbye *Do widzenia*
Yes *Tak*
No *Nie*
Two beers, please *Proszń dwa piwa*
Thank you *Dziekuj'e*
Men's *Dla Pano'w*
Women's *Dla Pań*
Where is the stadium? *Gdzie stadion?*
What's the score? *Jaki jest wynik?*
Referee *Sędzia*
Offside *Spalony*

Match practice

Poland is a fundamentally Catholic country – players touch the turf like Italians and

Playmaker Piotr Nowak – a rare jewel in the crown of contemporary Polish football

Basics

Americans and most EU nationals now need only a **passport** to enter Poland. Australian, New Zealand and Canadian nationals still require a visa, valid for ninety days. Check with your Polish embassy for details.

The Polish currency is the **złoty**, divided into 100 groszy. The current exchange rate is around 4.50zł to £1. Coins come in denominations of 1, 2, 5, 10, 20 and 50 groszy, and 1, 2 and 5 złoty; notes in denominations of 10, 20, 50, 100 and 200 złoty. Exchange booths (*kantors*) are everywhere and give better rates than the banks. In Warsaw, you'll find a 24-hour *kantor* at the airport and main train station.

In general dollars and Deutschmarks are preferred, but most places will accept **sterling**. Credit-card payment is slowly catching on, but most places prefer cash. Most cash machines in Warsaw only accept cards from their particular bank, but large hotels such as the *Mariott* in the centre of Warsaw have Amex, Visa and Mastercard cash advance facilities.

The international **telephone code** for Poland is 48. The city code for Warsaw is 2, Kraków 12, Łódź 42 and Poznań 61. To make an international call from Poland, dial 00 then the country code. There are two types of public telephone in Poland: old-style ones for local and inland calls, and the increasingly common cardphones. You'll need a handful of tokens (*żetony* – size A at 17 groszy for calls in town, size C at 1.70zł for cross-country calls) for the old-style version; wait for an answer before you slide the token in. Phonecards come in units of 25 (4.28zł), 50 (8.56zł) and 100 (17.12zł). There is no cheap time for international calls.

Transport in Poland is cheap. Inter-city **trains**, marked in red on timetables, are reasonably comfortable and have a buffet car. Seat reservations are compulsory. Leave yourself plenty of time for queueing at the ticket office, and specify the train you're catching once you reach the window. The two **bus** companies are the older, cheaper PKS and the newer Polski Express. Orbis tourist offices dotted around major towns can help with all transport enquiries.

cross themselves while stepping out into bleak, empty, Communist-built stadia. But, unlike most Catholic nations, the Poles prefer Saturday to Sunday as the day for league action. The season runs from the end of July to the end of November, then from the beginning of March until the end of June. Only a handful of grounds have floodlights, so kick-off times can be as early as 11am or noon at some grounds either side of winter, 3pm or 4pm at other times of the year.

Security has been tightened at many grounds, especially Legia, Poznań and Widzew Łódź. Football is an easy excuse for Poland's jobless youth to vent their frustration against a rival town and/or its police force. Whether beer is available or not – depending on the club's security rating – you'll see plastic bottles of clear liquid

passed around the terraces. More romantically, flowers are often exchanged between teams before matches. As in Russia, every ball-boy has his own ball to keep the game in constant play whenever there's a throw, corner or goal-kick. Stadium commentators follow the match vigorously, trying to raise enthusiasm among home supporters.

The league
The first two divisions of the Polish league are fully professional. Four teams go down automatically from the eighteen-team *I liga*, to be replaced by two each from the eighteen-team east and west divisions of the *II liga*.

The *III liga* comprises eight *makroregions*, whose top teams replace four each from the two second divisions.

Up for the cup

The *Puchar Polski* begins in July, with ties decided over one game, extra-time and penalties. First-division clubs enter at the fourth-round stage, with ties taking place at the lower-ranking club's ground to allow for cup surprises. The final takes place at a neutral venue in late June – one of the last major events in the European calendar.

Tickets

At better stadia, there'll be a covered stand (*trybuna kryta*) and an open one (*trybuna otwarta*). At Legia, the most expensive example, you'll pay 30zł for a plastic seat under cover, 20zł for a spot on a wooden bench in the open. At grounds with no cover, tickets will generally be divided into *bilety normalny* (a spot on a wooden bench) for 10–15zł, and *bilety na miejsca stojace* (a standing space on concrete terracing) for 5–10zł. Most clubs issue a free programme which will be given to you with your ticket.

Half-time

The traditional match snack is the *kiełbasa* – a long sausage cooked on the grill, served with bread, mustard or ketchup for 5zł. Alcohol is available only at certain grounds. Tea (*herbata*) at 1zł is a popular, cheap and bearable substitute. Coffee (*kawa*) is generally undrinkable.

Action replay

Canal Plus' move into the Polish market has given television coverage of football a long-awaited touch of professionalism. The channel shows a league game live on most Saturday afternoons, plus a live English Premiership game at 5pm on Sunday. State television, TVP, has the rights to show highlights of another Polish game on *Studio Sport* (Saturday, 8pm). On those Saturdays when Canal Plus is not showing a live match, TVP presents short highlights of the first half of a game followed by the whole of the second half live.

The best round-up programme is *Gol* (Monday, 4.30pm) on TVP2. TVP also has Champions' League rights. Western Poland can easily pick up German television, while you can get Russian and Ukrainian TV in the east of the country.

The back page

The staple diet is the broadsheet sports daily *Przeglád Sportowy* (90 groszy), heavy on text, short on pictures. Its foreign results coverage is excellent, however, and the Monday edition has reports, scorers and line-ups from all English Premiership and *Bundesliga* games, with results from their respective next lower divisions. The weekend edition (Fridays, 1.50zł) is tabloid format. Its provincial rival, *Sport* (90 groszy), concentrates on news from around its Silesian base of Katowice.

Piłka Noźna (1.50zł) is an all-colour weekly magazine, with a thicker monthly edition, *Piłka Noźna plus* (2zł).

British, French, German and Italian football papers are available in Warsaw at EMPIK, ul Marszałkowska 116/122 (Mon–Thurs 9am–10pm, Fri & Sat 9am–11pm, Sun 10am–4pm).

Ultra culture

Polish fan culture is more about sporadic violence than organised support. Widzew Łódź–Legia games are the most notorious, and any match between Legia and a Silesian team is liable to provoke tension of some kind.

At international matches, as the 1993 riots at Chorzów proved, the main problem is fighting between rival gangs of Polish fans. Meanwhile, the poorly paid, demotivated police force have their own axes to grind.

In the net

Pawel Mogielnicki runs a generic site at vlo.waw.ids.edu.pl/~mogiel/index.html. Stats are the strong point, but there's English and Spanish signposting, plus news stories and match reports in Polish. Other highlights include transfer-market updates and a huge number of links to one-club sites in Poland, only some of which will actually be functioning at any one time.

Warsaw

Unlike many East European countries, Poland boasts a good spread of top-flight clubs throughout its territory. But, thanks to Polonia's revival and the continuing strength of Legia, the capital, Warsaw, remains the best bet for an introduction to Polish football.

The thrilling fields

 Legia

Woiska Polskiego stadium, Ul Łazienkowska 3
Capacity 25,000
Colours All green with red and white trim
League champions 1955–56, 1969, 1970, 1994–95
Cup winners 1955, 1956, 1964, 1966, 1973, 1980, 1981, 1989, 1990, 1994, 1995

Legia Warsaw are the archetypal Communist army side, still led by steadfast generals whose stern portraits gaze down from the club's 80th-anniversary display on the main stand wall. Inside the ground you'll find a heavy following from modern Warsaw's economically depressed suburbs.

It's a meeting of the old and the new – a contrast thrown into sharp relief whenever those generals are obliged to face the music after another rumpus by Legia's lads.

The match-fixing scandal of 1993, and subsequent title-stripping decision by the PZPN, has set Legia's following on a collision course with the Polish football authorities and their power base down in Silesia. Regular outbreaks of hooliganism have forced Legia to up ticket prices and have driven away the floating fan.

Meanwhile the sponsors, whose heavy investment refloated Legia's sinking ship when the team faced relegation in 1990, have fallen out with the generals and left in acrimony. The subsequent financial woes saw half of Legia's team leave immediately after the club had done the double in 1995, yet the goals of Jerzy Podbrozny and

Endangered species – Marek Jozwiak is one of the few internationals to stay faithful to Legia

A tough nut to crack – Alan Shearer struggles to get past Legia's Jacek Bednarz, 1995

Cezary Kucharski were still enough to propel the team past Rosenborg and Blackburn Rovers to a Champions' League quarterfinal berth in 1996.

Partly as a result of their European exertions, however, Legia lost their title – and subsequent potential earnings in Europe – to Widzew Łódź later in the year. Twelve months later they were again involved in a head-to-head with Widzew. Two up against 'the enemy' in a six-pointer one round from the end of the 1996/97 season, Legia somehow contrived to concede three goals in the last four minutes, and another title chance had slipped through their fingers.

That defeat sparked yet another wave of trouble on the terraces. Yet the sad thing is that Legia, founder members of the Polish league in 1916 and still the nation's most popular club, also have among their following a generation raised during the Deyna era. Under Kazmierz Gorski, later coach to Poland's 1972 Olympic team and 1974 World Cup semi-finalists, Legia were Poland's first modern-day footballing heroes. With Kazimierz Deyna in midfield and Robert Gadocha on the wing, they

won the league in 1969 and 1970, the year they also made the European Cup semifinals. Deyna and Gadocha both ended up in America, via Manchester City and Nantes respectively, but the older fans in the main stand still remember them...

Here we go!

Legia's base, Łazienkowska, is just south of the city centre, below the Armii Ludowej highway. Several buses go there including #159 (four stops from Pl Konstitycji) and #155 or #166 from Nowy Swiat.

Swift half

No alcohol is allowed in the ground and security is strict. One of the many popular pre-match places for the older or neutral fan is the **Blues Bar**, in Łazienkowski park. A converted public toilet, the Blues offers EB beer and a relaxed atmosphere. After the game, you'll find journalists and players consuming beer and fine cheesecake in the nearby **Garaz**, Mysliwiecka 1.

Publications

The bog-standard *Legiagol* is issued free with your match ticket.

Club shop

In an innocuous-looking building, tucked in from Czerniakowska, behind the *Komis* used-car lot, is a modest shop decked out in green. Called simply **'Legia'** (Mon–Fri 9.30am–4.30pm, Sat 10am–2pm, no credit cards), it offers the usual souvenirs plus badges from all over Eastern Europe; solid silver Legia ones are 500,000zł, gold ones a cool couple of million.

Ultra culture

Scowling on the wooden benches behind one goal are **'Forever Legia'**, who spend each match waiting to take on the few of their opposite number huddled in the scoreboard end. You have been warned.

In the net

The official Legia homepage is only sporadically available. Gabriel Kutz maintains an unofficial site (from Florida) at www.naples.net/~nfn01005/files/legia.html. This is essentially a stats service but there are some neat links to other Polish footie web sites.

Groundhopping

If the tension of Legia gets too much, both the city's other professional clubs offer a more relaxed environment in which to watch a game...

◐ Polonia

Polonia stadium, Ul Konwiktorska 6
Capacity 15,000
Colours Red shirts, black shorts
League champions 1946

Polonia are the traditional Warsaw club, set in quiet surroundings above Nowe Miasto, the 'new town' which actually dates back to the fifteenth century. Originally the

The national stadium

Ten Years Stadium (Stadion Dziesęciolecia), Al KS Józefa Poniatowskiego
Capacity 100,000

There is talk of revamping this, the former national stadium, to boost Warsaw's interesting bid to host the Olympic Games in 2012.

Let's hope the members of the IOC observation committee bring their shopping bags, because around its top level and for a kilometre north, all they'll see is Europe's biggest flea market.

The pitch, which always suffered severe drainage problems anyway, is today hired out by local

Crowds fill the balconies – but to see the pope, not football

companies for friendly matches, while helicopter-sized crows hover above. To join them, take tram #7, #22, #24 or #25 along Al Jerozolimskie just the other side of the Wisla across Most K S J Poniatowskiego.

railway workers' team, they won the league in 1946 but then received none of the financial support afforded to Legia during Poland's decades of totalitarian rule.

They faded into the obscurity of the lower leagues, before picking up sponsorship and local support in the Zoliborz and Praga areas of town after the collapse of Communism. Polonia were finally promoted back to the top flight in 1996, and even got a taste of European action in the 1997 Intertoto Cup.

Crowds are still low, but pleasant to share an afternoon with. A *Hey Polonia* **programme** will be handed out with your 10zł match ticket. Beer is on sale at the **Restauracja Remis**, straight on from the main entrance, which also offers a full menu and Polonia scarves and pennants. Take tram #2, #4, #15, #18, #31 or #36 along

Gen Wł Andersa, up to the crossroads with Z Słominskiego.

Gwardia

Racławicka stadium, Ul Racławicka 132
Capacity 12,000
Colours Blue shirts, white shorts
Cup winners 1954

The Warsaw police department have more to worry about than propping up their team, Gwardia. Cup winners in 1954 and in occasional European competition for two decades afterwards, Gwardia are now festering in Poland's regional third division. Their matches kick off at noon on Saturdays. Admission is 3zł, and the **Bufet Gwardia** is in the main building behind

Warsaw essentials

A 1zł ticket will get you from Okęcie international **airport** to Warszawa Centralna train station in thirty minutes – the service is run by bus #175 in daytime and #611 at night. Alternatively, Airport City buses run every twenty minutes from the airport to major city centre hotels; tickets are available at 4zł from the Orbis desk at the airport or at the LOT desk inside the *Hotel Mariott*.

Municipal transport tickets (*bilety*) are available from the *Ruch* kiosks scattered about everywhere. A *normalny* ticket is 1zł and should be validated in the ticket puncher onboard – large baggage will cost you an extra 1zł. A **24-hour pass** is fine value at 3zł. Night buses (#601–611), which run from beside the Palace of Culture every half-hour, require three *normalny* tickets.

Warsaw's one **metro line**, #11, runs from Politechnika south to Kebaty and takes the same *normalny* tickets, to be punched at the entrance. The metro runs 4.30am–11.30am. By the end of 1997 the line will be extended through the city centre north to Młociny.

In town, **taxi** drivers can only charge 3zł for the first kilometre, then 1zł per kilometre thereafter, though rates rise by 50 percent after 10pm. *Radio Taxis* (☎919) accept credit cards for longer journeys; *Express Taxis* (☎9626), *Super Taxis* (☎9622) and *Sawa Taxi* (☎644 4444) are also generally reliable.

The main **tourist office** is at ul Marszałkowska 142 (Mon–Fri 9am–6pm, Sat 9am–1pm, ☎02/827 8031). Other tourist information in Warsaw is available at a small office in the old town, pl Zamkowy 1/3 (Mon–Fri 9am–6pm, Sat 10am–6pm, Sun 11am–6pm, ☎02/635 1881).

Warsaw is blessed with an excellent English-language **city guide**, the monthly *Warsaw Insider* (4zł), by far the best source for tips on entertainment and nightlife. Of the other publications, the *Warsaw Voice* (3.50zł) is aimed at the foreign business community, while the monthly *What Where When Warsaw*, issued free by the tourist board, has reliable practical information.

Never mind the footie, where's the fight? Rival factions are separated by police, Chorzow, 1993

the goal. The club's crumbling Racławicka ground is near the Zolnierzy Radzieckich cemetery, down Żwirki i Wigury by bus #114, #136, #175 or #188.

Eat, drink, sleep…

Bars and clubs

Not that long ago, Poles had a serious drink problem: they wanted vodka by the bucketful but there weren't any places to drink it in. Everyone drank at home.

Now everyone's still thirsty, but at least there are bars. Many are cheap dives with greasy food, but a reasonably lively, modern bar culture has developed in the major cities. It's still fairly cheap, too. Expect to pay about 4zł for a **beer**, of which Okocim, EB and Żywiecki are acceptable local brands. **Vodka** still rules, however – neat, chilled and downed in one. Zwykla, Wyborowa or Polonez are all too drinkable, as is the flavoured Żubrówka.

Akwarium, Ul Emilii Plater 49. The best jazz club in town, decked out with classic record sleeves. Local talent plus Western guest appearances. 10–15zł admission. By the Palace of Culture.

Big Fish, Ul Marszałkowska 55/73. A great cheap find in the centre of town, this basement is both a bar and a fishing tackle shop. Friendly and laid back, the perfect daytime stop for a quiet pint.

Blue Velvet, Ul Krakowskie Przedmieście 5. A techno club by night and a beer garden by day, this is the place for party animals. Basement dance action until dawn (Wed–Sat, 10zł). Between Nowy Swiat and the old town.

Café Blikle, Ul Nowy Świat 33. Along a boule-vard full of elegant shops and cafés, the Blikle is the oldest and the best. Breakfast here is an affordable luxury, served from 8.30am, 10am on Sundays. Décor and toilets that would put many top-class hotels to shame.

Ground Zero, Ul Wspólna 62. Main disco in town, open Wednesday to Saturday, 10–20zł entrance fee. Just south of the Centralna train station.

Irish Rover, Ul Waliców 13. A housing estate on the corner of Waliców and Grzybowska is where you'll find Ollie's bar, run by Warsaw's most pop-ular Irishman. An expat favourite, 'Ollie's' has a genuine pub feel, unlike other more expensive places in the same genre. Ollie plans a similar venture in town by the end of 1997. Tram #157 from Centralna.

Restaurants

Eating out in Warsaw is inexpensive, if rarely adventurous. International cuisine has arrived, much of it catering for local *nouveaux riches*. The mainstay for every-one else is the **milk bar**, cheap and rarely cheerful, though you're guaranteed a soup, a slab of pork and potatoes for under 3zł. **Restaurants** tend to close early, but cen-tral Warsaw fairly bristles with late-night takeaways.

Flik, ul Pulawska 43. A lunchtime favourite, serv-ing reasonably priced Polish cuisine and with a buffet worth investigating. Reservations recom-mended (☎02/494 434). Credit cards accepted.

Pod Barbakanem, Mostowa 27/29. Milk bar by the Barbican in the Old Town, clean and with outdoor seating. Give your order to the cashier and take your receipt to the hatch, where your food will be served a couple of minutes later. Dirt cheap but far from nasty.

Taj Mahal, Ul Brzozowa 27/29. Best Indian restaurant in town, in a quaint side street in the Old Town, near the river. Tandoori specialities. Main courses around 20zł, credit cards accepted.

U Barssa, Rynek Starego Miasta 14. An Old Town square favourite – three floors with a wine cellar and a piano bar. French feel, Polish and European cuisine. 50–75zł for a three-course meal, credit cards accepted.

U Szwejka, Pl Konstytucji 1. At the *Hotel MDM*, a Sixties-designed beer hall with a standard menu, perhaps a little heavy on the pork. Open until 1am on Fridays, 2am on Saturdays. American Express accepted.

Accommodation

This can be a problem in Warsaw, espe-cially in summer. For low-budget travellers, the city's few youth hostels have early curfews, and cheap hotels are generally a fair way from the centre. One option is to arrange a **private room** with a family. The **Syrena** office by the *Grand Hotel* at Ul Krucza 17 (Mon–Sat 9am–7pm, Sun 9am–5pm, ☎02/628 7540 or 628 5698) offers a single room for 35zł, a double for 53zł. Be sure to check your room's location on the map before you sign up.

For those with more to spend, even mid-range accommodation is overpriced and often fully booked. **Orbis hotels**, gen-erally soulless but functional, may be the best bet. Check with their main office at Ul Marszałkowska 142 (Mon–Fri 9am–6pm, Sat 9am–1pm, ☎02/827-8031) for availability.

Gromada Dom Chłopa, Pl Powstańców Warszawy 2 (☎02/625 1545, fax 625 2140). Best option for mid-range accommodation, centrally located in a quiet square, with a restaurant, health club and all-night pool hall. 160–200zł a night for a double, credit cards accepted.

Harenda, Ul Krakowskie Przedmieście 4/6 (☎02/262 625). Best budget deal in town, just south of the university. Rooms with or without a bath, student bar at the back. No credit cards.

HI, Ul Smolna 30 (☎02/278 952). The only youth hostel close to the centre, near the National Museum. Curfew at 11pm, lockout hours

10am–4pm. 115 beds, 15 zł for one person, 20 zł a head in a two- or three-person room.

Praski, Al Solidarności 61 (☎02/184 989). Just over the bridge from the Old Town, clean, basic accommodation with a restaurant downstairs.

Around 100zł a night for a double. Credit cards accepted.

Victoria, Ul Królewska 11 (☎02/657 8011, fax 657 8057). Best-loved of Warsaw's top-range hotels, renovated in 1996. Credit cards accepted.

'Beauty of the Night' – Poland's soccer saviour

In an era when Polish football does battle with a general malaise of corruption, hooliganism and a mass export of players, one man stands out above it all. **Zbigniew Boniek**, Poland's first international superstar, has enjoyed a hero's welcome since returning home from Italy in the mid-Nineties. His image has been used on every other billboard across the country as part of a publicity campaign by a Poznań brewery to save the game; he is actively involved in an annual children's football tournament; his voice gives learned TV analysis for major games; and his marketing agency, *Go And Goal,* negotiates TV rights for major sports events.

Voice of reason – Boniek as pundit

The flame-haired forward shot to fame in 1978, his star rising while Kazimierz Deyna's declined at the **Argentina World Cup** that year. By the 1982 finals he was at the peak of his form, having just led Widzew Łódź to two consecutive Polish titles. After a slow start, he scored a hat-trick against Belgium. Then, against a backdrop of **Solidarity flags** in the crowd, Boniek received a yellow card against the Soviet Union to disqualify him for Poland's ill-fated semi-final with Italy – he spent the game sitting in the crowd next to Claudio Gentile, also suspended, who would have been marking him on the pitch.

That summer Boniek became Poland's biggest export – and Eastern Europe's **first million-dollar footballer** – when he left Łódź for **Juventus**. In his first season, Boniek's new team faced his old Widzew one in a European Cup semi final, which Juve won, then flopped in the final against Hamburg. The following year, 1984, Boniek scored the winning goal against Porto in the European Cup Winners' Cup final, and both goals in a 2–0 SuperCup win over Liverpool.

Juventus president Gianni Agnelli nicknamed him **'The Beauty of the Night'** because of his superb form in floodlit European games – although in the tight marking régime of *Serie A* he needed all his legendary pace to gain the merest inch of space.

In 1985 Boniek was sold to Roma, where he was gradually withdrawn deeper into the formation before spending an acclaimed final spell as a **sweeper** in 1988. An unimpressive Italian coaching career ended down in *Serie C1* with Avellino in 1995.

Today Boniek's position in the new Poland bodes well for the otherwise shaky future of the game there, and his influence off the pitch could be as crucial to Poland's effort for World Cup 2002 as it was on it twenty years earlier.

Portugal

Portugal is a refreshingly idiosyncratic country whose footballing reputation was built on the riches of its former colonies. Africans, particularly the incomparable Eusébio, were the stars of Portugal's golden era. Eusébio's club side, Benfica, won the European Cup in 1961 and 1962 and the national team made a stunning début in international competition at the 1966 World Cup finals.

Top scorer of that 1966 tournament, Eusébio still dominates the Portuguese game, in spirit if not in fact. His statue stands outside Benfica's Stadium of Light, his reputation as football's endearing ambassador still shining. Fans not only remember his speed and ferocious shot, they revere him for having led cavalier teams whose free-scoring approach surprised the established opposition of the day. Benfica's European Cups were won 3–2 and 5–3 against Barcelona and Real Madrid respectively, and Portugal's adventurous style saw them knock reigning champions Brazil out of the 1966 World Cup, 3–1.

Having broken Spain's stranglehold on the European Cup, then Brazil's on the World Cup, the way was open for Eusébio and his colleagues, among them fellow Mozambican and national-team captain Mário Coluna, Angolan forward José Augusto and centre-forward José Torres, to be crowned kings of the footballing world. In the World Cup quarter-finals, North Korea scored three shock early goals before Eusébio scored four, Portugal's 5–3 win setting them up for a semi-final clash with the hosts, England. At Wembley, Portugal's hopes were dashed against the rocks of Nobby Stiles' brutal marking job on Eusébio, sterling performances by England's defence and two remarkable goals by Bobby Charlton – 2–1

Ambassador – Eusébio in full marketing flow

to England, Eusébio's famous parting tears and an eventual third place for Portugal.

Thirty years on, and the likelihood of Portugal ever attaining the same status as a football power seems remote. There have been a string of corruption scandals, the first of which broke in the autumn of 1996, involving referees, club chairmen and a former head coach of the national team. Attendances have plunged to a postwar low. After flattering to deceive at Euro '96, the national side is toiling shapelessly in its bid to qualify for the 1998 World Cup. Most of the squad now play abroad, particularly in Spain, from where weekly televised league action exposes the fact

Brothers in arms – but will Portugal's national team ever live up to their potential?

that, for Portuguese fans, the grass is indeed greener on the other side – a group of leading media personalities have even signed a petition, expressing their disgust at the current domestic scene and pledging their support for Barcelona.

So what happened in thirty years? In truth, the generation of '66 quickly waned. Portugal failed to qualify for the World Cup in either 1970 or 1974. Eusébio's emigration to America in 1975 coincided with revolution at home, and the subsequent independence of former Portuguese colonies in Africa slowed the influx of talent from that region into the domestic game. Portugal had to turn towards Europe in an attempt to rediscover its old glories. Clubs queued up to import players and coaches to take on the continent's big boys who, by then, had bigger bank accounts than most Portuguese teams could ever aspire to.

An entertaining revival in the 1980s centred on a squad which seemed to contain the perfect mix of experience (in the shape of Rui Jordão and the veteran striker Nené, a former team-mate of Eusébio's)

and youthful exuberance (from the likes of Diamantino and Paulo Futre). Portugal danced their way to a classic semi-final with France at the 1984 European Championship, and though that game was ultimately lost to the genius of Platini, hopes soared of a new Portuguese dawn.

They were swiftly dispelled. Two years later, in what would become known as the Saltillo Affair, Portugal's squad for the 1986 World Cup gathered in a Mexican mountain retreat to demand extra appearance money from their federation officials. Some of the demands were met, but after a 3–1 defeat by Morocco brought the team's campaign to a premature end, eleven of the squad were suspended by federation president Silva Resende, who claimed their lack of discipline had contributed to the team's poor performance. The remainder of the players withdrew their services from the national side in protest and Portugal competed (unsuccessfully) for a place at the Euro '88 finals with what amounted to a third-choice team.

On the club front, a European Cup win by Porto in 1987, followed by appearances in the continent's premier final by Benfica in 1988 and 1990, kept Portugal in touch with the élite without ever threatening full membership of it. From time to time during the Nineties, Porto have successfully humiliated some of the greatest names in the European game, only to fall flat again within a few months.

The country continues to produce great natural talent, its Under-20 side having won the World Youth Cup in 1989 and 1991 – the latter in front of 120,000 at the Stadium of Light. But turning that talent into a senior team capable of taking on the world's best remains a circle Portugal have still to square.

Domestically, the staid three-club domination of Porto, Benfica and Sporting has given way to a Porto monopoly. Many clubs are in dire financial difficulty, having to make ends meet at the cheaper end of the Brazilian and East European transfer markets.

Today Portugal's football, played out every Sunday in huge, echoing theatres,

Basics

A passport is sufficient for citizens of the EU, the USA, Canada, Australia and New Zealand to gain entry to Portugal.

The Portuguese currency is the **escudo**, divided into 100 centavos. A $ price sign is normally used to delineate escudos from centavos. There are around 250$ to £1. You'll find coins in denominations of $50 (50 centavos), 1$ (one escudo), 2$50, 5$, 10$, 20$, 50$, 100$ and 200$. Notes come in denominations of 500$, 1000$, 2000$, 5000$ and 10,000$. Credit-card cash machines are widespread and generally charge less exchange commission than the banks.

Telephones take 10$, 20$ and 50$ coins. Most bars will have a phone – simply pay the barman for the number of impulses used. Phone cards come in 50-unit (750$) and 100-unit (1725$) denominations. For international phone calls, cheaper between 10pm and midnight and cheaper still between midnight and 8am, dial 00 followed by the country code. From outside the country, the code for Portugal is 351, followed by a 1 for Lisbon or a 2 for Porto.

Most **trains in Portugal** are classed as *regional* – they're cheap but stop everywhere. Faster and more expensive are the *intercidades*, while the fastest of all are the *rápidos*, such as the **Alfa service** which runs between Lisbon and Porto. A ticket for the Alfa, including a compulsory reservation, costs around 3000$. There are four Alfas a day and the journey takes just over three hours.

Buses can be a good alternative to trains – the network is more extensive and fares are competitive. In contrast to rail services, most major inter-city bus routes are run by private companies.

Accommodation is cheap and plentiful. **Pensions** (*pensões*) are fine value and are graded according to a star system; a double room in a two-star pension will cost between 3500$ and 5000$.

Drinking, dining and clubbing are similarly cheap. **Fish**, **seafood** and **pork** are the mainstays of Portuguese cooking, which can be a little on the bland side – though the portions are never less than generous. **Wine** is invariably tasty, either red (*tinto*) or white (*branco*). The slightly sparkling *vinho verde* from the Minho region is justifiably popular everywhere.

Beer, probably either **Super Bock** or the sweeter **Sagres**, is served in a small glass (*fino*), a medium glass (*imperial*) or a half-litre (*caneca*). In most bars a *fino* will set you back no more than 150$.

Coffee is the classic pick-me-up, served either black, espresso-style (*bica*), or with a dash of milk (*garoto*). Tea (*chá*) is also popular and is better in Portugal than anywhere else in southern Europe.

might be a turn-off for the local fan but, for the visitor, this instinctive, one-touch game is as attractive now as it was in 1966.

Essential vocabulary

Hello *Olá*
Goodbye *Adeus*
Yes *Sim*
No *Não*
Two beers, please *Dois cervejas, por favor*
Thank you *Obrigado/Obrigada*
Men's *Homens*
Women's *Senhoras*
Where is the stadium? *Onde esta o estádio?*
What's the score? *Como esta o jogo?*
Referee *Árbitro*
Offside *Fora de jogo*

Match practice

Although the current downturn and corruption scandals have forced many fans away from grounds, interest in the game itself has not wavered. Every Sunday, you'll see Portuguese menfolk in the bars, radios pressed to their ears.

The big clashes involve Porto, Benfica and Sporting. Most other games, if poorly attended, should still offer a high level of skill and tactical awareness, not least from the large stock of Brazilian, Balkan and African players on show. As in Spain, an outstanding piece of play – or a poor performance – brings out the waving of the white handkerchief, a custom borrowed from bullfighting.

The season runs from September to May. Most games take place at 3pm on a Sunday afternoon. There'll be one league game played later, normally at 8.45pm, to be screened live on television.

The league

Portugal's top flight is the *I Divisão* which has eighteen teams, as has the next rung down, the *II Divisão de Honra*; teams are promoted and relegated on a three-up, three-down basis. Three teams are relegated from the *II Divisão de Honra* into the *II Divisão B*, itself divided into three regional

eighteen-team zones – the winners of the *Zona Norte*, *Zona Central* and *Zona Sul* are promoted. The final rung, *III Divisão*, has six zoned leagues, from each of which two clubs are promoted to accommodate the four bottom teams dropping down from each zone of the *II Divisão B*.

Up for the cup

La Taça de Portugal has six rounds, then quarter-finals, semi-finals and a final, all decided on one match each time. Extra time is played after the first replay. First-division clubs enter at the third-round stage in December. The final is in May at the otherwise underused Estádio Nacional on the outskirts of Lisbon.

Tickets

Portugal's larger clubs are multi-disciplined sports organisations. Benfica alone can boast more than 150,000 members (*camarotes*) who get the first pick of tickets for major games. There will usually be a special window for members at the ticket office (*biheteiria*). In practice, given the huge size of the major Portuguese stadia, sellouts are rare.

Best seats will be in the *tribuna central*, which offers the clearest view overlooking the halfway line. The benches alongside, the *bancada lateral*, are the next dearest. The cheapest places, confusingly called *superiores*, are behind the goal; if there are any hardcore fans, this is where you'll find them. *Coberta* indicates covered seating, *descoberta* open.

For an average league match, a ticket in the *tribuna central* will cost you around 3000$; in the *bancada lateral*, 2000–2500$; and in the *superiores*, 1500$. Expect to pay 1500–2000$ more for big matches.

Half-time

Beer and wine are sold at most grounds, both generally on draught (*de pressão*). Snacks come in the form of roasted chestnuts (*amendoins*), peanuts (*amendoins torrados*) or butter-beans (*tremoços*). At hamburger vans you'll get a choice of pork steak sandwiches (*bifanas*), fatty pork (*entremeadas*) and fried pigskin (*coiratos*), each for around 200–300$.

Action replay

The nature of the Portuguese domestic setup was never better illustrated than by the announcement in early 1997 of a pay-per-view TV deal involving Olivedesportos, a powerful media company, and the Portuguese FA. At the time of the announcement, the head of Olivedesportos was Joaquim Oliveira, while his brother António, who led the national team to Euro '96, was coach of Porto. The new deal is due to begin in 1998.

What time can you make it…? Sellouts are rare in Portugal

In the meantime, state TV2 has *Jornada Na 2*, with matchday previews on Sundays at 2.30pm, results and news at 5.30pm and a full round-up and highlights at 11pm. State TV1 has the live match, generally at 8.45pm. On Mondays at 3pm, also on state TV1, there is *Golo Europa* with action from the main European leagues. Sky Sports, DSF, Eurosport and Spain's Canal Plus are all popular and readily available.

The back page

The leading sports paper is Lisbon's well-established *A Bola* (daily, 120$). Although its domestic content leans heavily on the comings and goings at Benfica, its international coverage is excellent. *A Bola* also publishes an eponymous colour monthly magazine (300$).

There are two other sports dailies. *O Jogo* (120$) publishes separate Lisbon and Porto editions, and fans in the north tend to prefer the latter above all other papers. *Record* (120$) is the paper that broke the 1996 controversy over the falsification of international licences.

Ultra culture

Fan culture is as dependent on the three main clubs – Porto, Benfica and Sporting – as the league title has always been.

Games involving these three, especially between Porto and one of the two Lisbon giants, can often spark something off.

Sporting, whose last league title dates back further than the birthdate of many in the *Juventude Leonina* group, have the most passionate ultras, with scars to prove it. Two Sporting fans were killed in 1995 when a ledge gave way before a crucial league game against Porto, and another died at the 1996 cup final with Benfica.

Most matches, however, take place in complete safety. As in Spain or Italy, ultras spend their week working out their routines and making flags (*faixas*) and banners (*bandeiras*). Many fans enjoy a wine or a beer, but outright drunkenness is a rarity.

In the net

The best source for Portuguese soccer info on the Web is InforDesporto Online at: www.infordesporto.pt/ids/inicio.asp. It's a little heavy-handed with the graphics but if you and your browser have sufficient patience, you'll find up-to-date news, stats and match reports (in Portuguese only), still images of the major games, an online chat area and plenty more besides.

Many Portuguese newspapers have online versions and the best for soccer is *Diário de Notícias*, which offers match reports and stats updated daily. Bypass the politics and go straight to the sports pages at: www.dn.pt/des/sintdes.htm.

Lisbon

Benfica 404   Sporting 407
"Os Belenenses" 409

It may lack the smooth machinations of Milan, the partisan frenzy of Barcelona and London's strength in depth, but Lisbon is one of Europe's legendary football capitals, its fame spread by Benfica's glory years in what was once the continent's largest venue, the Stadium of Light. Though the football legends may have faded, Lisbon itself is still a great city for a weekend's entertainment, like a jumble-sale version of Barcelona – full of the cheap, the weird and the exotic.

Lisbon has no real football centre as such. Both Benfica and Sporting moved home several times around the Campo Grande, Benfica and Alvalade areas in the far north before both settling on their current neighbouring homes on the highway near the airport. Four bus stops, along the #33 and #50 routes, are all that stand between the city's two giants.

The thrilling fields

Benfica

Estádio da Luz, Avenida General Norton de Matos
Colours Red shirts, white shorts
Capacity 92,000 (all-seated)
League champions 1936–38, 1942–43, 1945, 1950, 1955, 1957, 1960–61, 1963–65, 1967–69, 1971–73, 1975–77, 1981, 1983–84, 1987, 1989, 1991, 1994
Cup winners 1930–31, 1935, 1940, 1943–44, 1949, 1951–53, 1955, 1957, 1959, 1962, 1964, 1969–70, 1972, 1980–81, 1983, 1985–87, 1993, 1996
European Cup winners 1961–62

Crossing the Norton de Matos airport highway to Benfica's Stadium of Light is like coming across a lost empire. The vast eagle over the entrance, Eusébio's statue in kicking action on a grass plinth, the club motto *E Pluribus Unum* and the museum inside – it's a treasure trove from another age.

In the summer of 1961 Portugal's most popular team, nicknamed the Eagles, were set to grab the mantle of the legendary Real Madrid as Europe's team of the new decade. After surprisingly beating Barcelona 3–2 in the European Cup final that May, Benfica then signed Eusébio from under the noses of their city rivals, Sporting. The Mozambican immediately scored a hat-trick in a pre-season tournament game against Pelé's Santos.

The scene was set – an arena worthy of worldbeaters in the expanded Estádio da Luz (the name, incidentally, derives from its location in the Lisbon suburb of Luz, not from any 'light' that may emanate from it), a master coach in Hungarian-born Béla Guttmann, and a 20-year-old African prodigy who could outshoot Pelé. Eusébio it was who scored the last two goals to beat Real Madrid 5–3 in a classic European Cup final of 1962.

But then it all started to go wrong. A dispute between the Benfica management and Guttmann over bonus payments, and the coach who had built the team was gone. His departure, coupled with scene-stealing displays by Milan's two *catenaccio*-based European Cup-winning sides (AC Milan in 1963, Inter in 1965), took the red carpet out from under the Eagles' claws. Benfica's dream of European domination was over.

From now on, there would be only heroic defeats in Europe – Alex Stepney's late save for Manchester United in the 1968 final, Celtic's coin toss the following year – though Benfica continued to dominate at home, winning the title twelve times in fifteen seasons. Even so, when he left for America in 1975, Eusébio must have been reflecting on what might have been.

Lisbon essentials

The **Aerobus** makes the twenty-minute journey between Lisbon's **Portela airport** and central Praça do Comércio, also calling at Rossio train station. The service runs every twenty minutes, 7am–9pm, and costs 420$ – which also covers a day's transport use in the city, except for the metro. A taxi will cost you 1000–1500$. Buses #9 and #46 connect Rossio with the main **Santa Apolónia** train station, fifteen minutes' walk from Comércio and point of departure for trains to Porto, Madrid and Paris.

Most of the modern city centre, the **Baixa**, which runs down to the river Tagus, is pleasantly walkable. The steep twists and turns up to the old town, the **Alfama**, are negotiable by century-old trams #12 and #28 – a thrilling way to see the city. Lisbon's transport system, **Carris**, specialises in glorious anachronisms. In addition to the trams, there is a giant lift (*elevador Santa Justa*) and a funicular (*elevador da Glória*),

Avoid the jams – take a tram

either of which will take you up to the main area for nightlife, the **Bairro Alto**, from the centre of town below.

There are also 'ordinary' buses and a single two-forked metro line which stops at both main football stadia – the line runs 6.30am–1am. A ticket for one metro journey, to be stamped before you enter the platform, is 70$, a book of ten 500$. Bus and tram tickets are 140$ for two journeys – stamp one end as you board – and are available at metro stations and at larger newsstands. For the lift and funicular, buy a ticket for 150$ onboard.

At the **main transport office**, Rua Jardim do Regedor 50 (open daily 9am–5pm), you can buy passes for all buses, trams, lifts, funiculars and the Aerobus, valid for 24 hours (420$) or 72 hours (880$). A **Lisboa Card** adds the metro and gives you free entry to most museums – it costs 1200$ for 24 hours, 2000$ for 48, 2600$ for 72. Validate your pass as you make your first journey.

The minimum **taxi** fare is 250$, with a night tariff between 10pm and 6am and at weekends. All cabs have meters and no journey in the centre of town should run to more than 600–800$. Call ☎01/793 2756 or ☎01/815 2016 if you can't see a cab near a main square.

The main **tourist office** is at Palácio Foz, Praça dos Restauradores, near Rossio station (open Mon–Fri 9am–8pm, Sun 10am–6pm, ☎01/346 3314). Neither of the free monthly listings publications available there, *Agenda Cultural* and *Lisboaem*, is particularly good for nightlife information.

After a string of European flops, Benfica's management decided to act. The club had been formed in 1904 by a group of rich kids from Belém, headed by the Anglophile Cosme Damião, from two separate organisations; one had a club with an eagle emblem but no ground, another had the Benfica village football pitch but not enough players to use it. Damião laid down the rule that Portuguese nationals only should play for his *Sport Lisboa e Benfica* – a rule subsequently bent to include stars from the colonies such as Eusébio. Some time after Portugal lost its colonies following the 1974 revolution, Benfica turned to Swedish coach Sven-Göran Eriksson to bring European stars to the club. It was Eriksson's side that did the double in 1983 and narrowly lost the UEFA Cup final to Anderlecht the same year. This was followed by European Cup final appearances in 1988 and 1990, although both games were lost.

Benfica's management have been progressively less astute as the Nineties have worn on. In 1993 the club sold its TV rights to buy Paulo Futre, but were then unable to pay his or other stars' wages. A year later there was a repeat performance, when only a last-minute intervention by Benfica's then-sponsors Parmalat enabled Claudio Caniggia to be bought and paid for one, desperately disappointing, season.

In the meantime, Porto keep clocking up the titles and the lucrative Champions' League appearances. The Benfica party is over, and someone has to pay for it. Tax bills mount, new stars are produced and, almost immediately, sold. And still the football goes on, in Europe's most romantic sporting venue, with its three tiers and near-perfect view open to the sunshine.

By the end of the century the stadium, part of a huge sports complex, will be renovated with the introduction of 85,000 individual seats. Whether their occupants will again be watching Europe's best is another matter.

Here we go!

Metro to the terminus **Colegio Militar**, fifteen minutes from central Restauradores. As you exit, the stadium will be visible on the other side of the highway.

Swift half

There are no bars around the stadium complex but quite a few inside it. **Ponto Vermelho**, opposite gate #9, is a bar/restaurant, the bar section having a colourful collection of pennants and draught Amstel beer. Pay at the cash till first. Credit cards are accepted at the restaurant which, like the bar, is open every day. The bar/cafeteria **O Benfica**, between gates #10 and #11, is more down-to-earth – grilled hamburgers, white wine on draught in various measures and Super

A classic arena – but the shadows of past riches loom over Benfica's Stadium of Light

Bock beer. The beer hall next door has a meat-heavy tourist menu plus an assortment of framed, classic team line-up shots.

Publications

The official weekly newspaper is *Benfica* (Wednesdays, 120$). Produced by the club, it has a stablemate in the all-colour monthly *Benfica Ilustrado* (350$). Both are widely available at newsstands.

Club shop

The **Loja do Benfica** (open Mon–Fri 10am–8pm, Sat 10am–7pm, most major credit cards) is by gate #11. Souvenirs include tins of Benfica biscuits called 'Benficookies', red toy buses and cars, the eagle in various poses, several players' biographies and cassettes of the club anthem, *Orfeão do Sport Lisboa e Benfica*.

Club museum

A vast portrait of club founder Cosme Damião dominates the entrance to the **Museu** (open Mon–Fri 9.30am–1pm, 2–6pm, Sat 9.30am–1pm, admission 250$), up the stairs from the main doors. You'll find a vast display of gold and silverware from all sporting disciplines, but not, strangely, Benfica's two European Cups. Construction began on a redesigned museum in November 1996; when open, it will feature interactive games including one in which visitors will be able to face Eusébio's fearsome shot.

Ultra culture

The **No Name Boys** and the **Diabos Vermelhos** both occupy the area behind the west goal.

In the net

The absence of a really comprehensive Benfica website is one of the great mysteries of Internet life. Until the suits at the Stadium of Light deign to countenance the building of an official site, we'll have to be content with Pedro Pimentel's at: www.uninova.pt/UNIAGUA/ppf/slb/slbindex.html. There are some neat graphics, an excellent history and a decent stats archive but, as with many Portuguese soccer sites, you might wait all season for the latest news and results.

Sporting

Estádio José Alvalade, Rua Francisco Stromp
Capacity 75,000 (all-seated)
Colours Green-and-white hooped shirts, black shorts
League champions 1941, 1944, 1947–49, 1951–54, 1958, 1962, 1966, 1970, 1974, 1980, 1982
Cup winners 1923, 1934, 1936, 1938, 1941, 1945–46, 1948, 1954, 1963, 1971, 1973, 1974, 1978, 1982, 1995
European Cup-Winners' Cup winners 1964

The lions of Portugal have been waiting to roar for too many years. Sporting Clube de Portugal, the most loyally and vociferously supported team in the land, have lifted just one trophy this decade – thanks to a cup final win over Marítimo in 1995.

The club is not without resources. With the help of disenchanted former Benfica members, the Viscount of Alvalade founded Sporting in 1906, on land owned by his family. Sporting then spent fifty years moving around the Campo Grande area, until the Alvalade fortune built the stadium which still bears the family name in 1956.

Yet the Lions were at their most successful just before, winning seven titles in eight years from the end of World War II – their last a year before the inauguration of the European Cup.

The era of pan-European football has coincided broadly with the club's gradual decline. Sporting's only European success has been a Cup-Winners' Cup trophy in 1964 – won on a lucky corner in a replayed final against MTK Budapest.

The last domestic title arrived under Malcolm Allison's fiery rule in 1982. Since then there have been promises aplenty from a string of ambitious club presidents, and the club have continued their tradition

Hoops and glory – Cadete leads Sporting out to face Benfica

election as the club's president at the start of the decade, carving his name over garish monuments like the huge lion and cascade of water that now guard the main entrance. Cintra was also the first club president to sack Bobby Robson, when Sporting were leading the league in December 1993. Robson headed north to guide Porto to a cup final win over Sporting five months later and to the Portuguese title in 1995 – leaving Cintra's lion to keep a sad and solitary watch over the bulldozers, shacks and shanty huts which still litter a neighbouring plot of land, cleared for a hotel complex which has yet to be built.

In 1996 Sporting passed back into the family, albeit only briefly. New president José Roquette, grandson of old Alvalade, quickly announced that Sporting would be the first Portuguese club to be floated on the Lisbon stock exchange – a rare innovation for a team that seems to have one boot firmly stuck in the past. The flotation cash has yet to deliver silverware, however.

of nurturing young talent in the shape of Jorge Cadete and Luis Figo, among others.

They have also, arguably, been more astute in signing players from outside Portugal's former colonies than have Benfica. Yet still the championship eludes the men in hoops.

Today Sporting attract both Lisbon's youth and the city's upwardly mobile élite; board members tend to see the club as a springboard into local politics.

The mineral water millionaire José de Sousa Cintra made a great show of his

Here we go!
Metro to **Campo Grande**, fifteen minutes from central Restauradores. The stadium will appear as you approach the modern metro complex.

Swift half
The best bars around the stadium are by the corner of Rua Francisco Stromp and Avenida Linho de Torres. Opposite the

rundown church is **O Dificil** and, by former player Stromp's name in mosaic tiles on the pavement, the **O Magnico**. The **Tipe-Tope**, on the next corner, is a smaller, less pretentious bar with green-and-white trimmings.

In the stadium, above gate #8, is the **Toca do Lagarto** bar/restaurant, serving Sagres beer and meals every day. The **Sala do Socios** nearby is theoretically for members only, but on a quiet afternoon you'll probably be allowed in for a game of pool or a glass of port, the latter best enjoyed while relaxing into one of the many green leather armchairs.

Club shop
The **Loja Verde** (open Mon–Fri 10.30am–1pm and 2–7pm, and two hours before a match, most major credit cards) is by gate #2. It offers only a fairly modest range of merchandise but is a treat for furry lion collectors.

Club museum
The **Sala de Trofeus** (open Mon–Fri 10am–1pm and 2.30–6.30pm, Sat 10am–1pm) is usually reserved for members but a smile should get you in free. There's a huge collection of pennants, four rows of trophies, a framed picture of the 'Five Violins' strikeforce of the Forties and a replica of the Cup-Winners' Cup.

Publications
The weekly newspaper, *Sporting* (Tuesdays, 100$), is published by the club and is available at most newsstands in the city.

Ultra culture
The **Juventude Leonina** who faithfully troop through gate #10 to the *superior sul* are proud of their reputation as Portugal's most passionate following. A plaque dedicated to the two fans who died in the 1995 tragedy stands outside the ground.

In the net
Proudly proclaiming its presence on the Web since November 1993 is Rui Bastos'

Sporting site at: sporting.di.uminho.pt/. This is a solid, no-nonsense site with plenty of English signposting and an electronic mailing list for interested parties to join, though the 'latest results' may be nothing of the kind. If up-to-date stats are required, it's worth waiting for your screen to alternate between green and white backgrounds for a minute or so before you gain access to supporter Fernando Amaral's site at: camoes.rnl.ist.utl.pt/~fmfa/index4.html. GIF images, audio interviews and a fine history in English are all present and correct.

"Os Belenenses"

Estádio Restelo, Avenida do Restelo, Belém
Capacity 42,000 (all-seated)
Colours Azure blue shirts, white shorts
League champions 1946
Cup winners 1927, 1929, 1933, 1942, 1960, 1989

Belenenses are the only club outside the country's 'Big Three' ever to have won the Portuguese championship. Their one-point victory of 1946 is remembered by only a tiny minority of today's fans, yet it still reverberates through the residential district of Restelo, overlooking the magnificence of Belém in the far west of the city.

The walk from Belém station up the hill to the club's stonewashed denim-coloured stadium leads you past the finest building in all Lisbon, the Jerónimos monastery. Looking down from the stadium restaurant, the monastery is merely a blip in the panorama of the River Tagus and opposite shoreline – the backdrop for Vasco da Gama's men as they set sail for India five hundred years ago. The suspension bridge is a recent but still poetic addition.

As for the compact stadium, two grandstands cover the side terraces. The lower seats are stone slabs, the superior *bancada* blue plastic ones. By the main office is a large carving in a stone wall of José Manoel Soares, the idol of Belenenses. His glory days were shortly before the introduction of the national league in 1934, but his goals took Belenenses to three Lisbon titles before he died in mysterious circumstances in 1931. Blue and white flowers embellish the large dedication, while a much smaller plaque marks the pope's visit in 1991.

There have been no honours for "Os Belenenses" to celebrate since the Pontiff came and went, but an occasional UEFA Cup appearance – along with the odd derby victory over Benfica or Sporting – keeps spirits high.

Here we go!

Take the suburban train from Cais do Sodré to **Belém**, a seven-minute journey. Trains run every thirty minutes and a return ticket is 210$. Cross the pedestrian bridge over the rails, cut by the park along Rua de Belém towards the monastery, then hike up Rua dos Jerónimos. Allow a good ten minutes – it's a steep old hike.

Swift half

The bars along the Rua de Belém are geared up for the groups of package tourists visiting the monastery. **Os Jerónimos**, at #78, is the best bet, with fair-priced food. The nameless bar at #54 Rua dos Jerónimos, opposite the stadium, has a large fixture list on the wall. Inside the ground, the **Restaurante Varandazul** under the main grandstand has *that* view from its far window. It serves draught Sagres and Carlsberg and offers a full menu.

Club shop

The modest **Loja Azul** (open Mon–Fri 10am–1pm, 2–5pm and on matchdays, no credit cards) does a nice line in Belenenses ties, mirrors and watches.

Ultra culture

The club's grandiosely named **Furia Azul** gather behind the riverside goal, which is just as well – the other goal has a large stone wall behind it.

Unequal struggle – João Pinto and Benfica storm the Restelo

Eat, drink, sleep...

Bars and clubs

Lisbon nightlife is lively, varied and goes on 'til dawn. The best place for bars is the **Bairro Alto**, high up over the town centre. Getting out of your lift or cablecar from Praça dos Restauradores, Rua do Ouro or Cais do Sodré station, you'll find an area criss-crossed with streets dotted with cheap restaurants, corner grocers, sex shops and the occasional salsa procession. Most of all you'll find **bars** – of all shapes, sizes and sexual persuasions.

Here and on the opposite hill of Alfama you'll also find **fado houses**. Originally a vibrant, cathartic folk music characterised by shawls, wailing and twelve-string guitars, fado is now mainly tourist mush at inflated prices. But if you catch authentic fado, you won't stop boring your friends about it.

Another great Lisbon institution is the **ginjinha**, the ginja house. These are ornate palaces specialising in cheap, sticky cherry brandy; it tastes sweet, but it knocks your socks off. For nightclubbing, the **Alcântara** area and **Avenida 24 de Julho** by the river are the best bet.

A Brasileira, Rua Garrett 120. Famed coffee house decorated with paintings, statues and wood carvings. Newspapers and coffee ready for the breakfast crowd from 8am. Centrally located.

Benfica Bar, Rua Jardim do Regedor 9. Above the club office in the city centre, with a giant eagle dominating the entire block, this first-floor bar/restaurant open to the public is laughably cheap. Scarves, pennants and a model of Gorbachev in a Benfica shirt. Next door is a members' bar with pool tables and classic team line-up shots.

Capela, Rua da Atalaia 45. The jazziest bar in the Bairro Alto, this is a converted chapel now decorated with framed bats and old gramophones, with live jazz music and waitresses in bacofoil skirts.

Cervejaria, Rua do Salitre 38A. Nameless bar opposite the popular central **Choupal**, with football blaring out of a large television balanced on a teetering pile of Super Bock crates, watched by old men with football-shaped radios pressed to their ears and beer to their lips.

Kremlin, Escadinhas da Praia 5 (alleyway off Avenida 24 de Julho). The most reputable techno house in town, home of DJ Vibe and clubbers on cheap weekend flights from England. Santos suburban train station, one stop from Cais do Sodré.

Portas Largas, Rua da Atalaia 105. Possibly the best bar in all the Bairro Alto, announced by a huge neon *Record* sign outside. Autographed tiled walls, a collection of old transistor radios, great Brazilian music, and hectic bar staff mixing vicious *mojito* cocktails.

Restaurants

Lisbon is a remarkably cheap place to eat out and, as elsewhere in Portugal, meals are served in huge quantities; you may find a half-portion (*meia dose*) enough for one. Look for a three-course tourist menu (*ementa turistica*) or dish of the day (*prato do dia*), always served promptly for around 2500$ and 1500$ respectively.

Apart from the **Bairro Alto**, there are dozens of inexpensive places within five minutes of **Rossio station**, especially along the Rua San José/Portas de Santo Antão stretch. **Cacilhas**, by the ferry stop on the opposite shore of the Tagus, has a string of cheap fish restaurants.

Adega do Ribatejo, Rua Diário de Notícias 23. *Adegas* are places with local specialities and fado music. Most are to be avoided, but the Ribatejo is probably the best fado house in the Bairro Alto, and certainly the most reasonably priced. Open until midnight, most major credit cards.

Cervejaria Trinidade, Rua Nova do Trinidade 20c. Gorgeous old fish restaurant/beer hall decked out in local *azulejo* tiles. Kitchen open until 1.30am. Centrally located.

Sol Nascente, Rua de São Tomé 86. In the old Alfama quarter, under ancient São Jorge castle, a reasonably priced restaurant with a perfect view of a sandy five-a-side pitch and, beyond that, the huge sweep of the Tagus estuary.

Tronco, Rua das Portas de Santo Antão 147. If there's a match on, it'll be showing in this cheap diner. The waiters will happily talk football until closing time at midnight, and probably afterwards. Substantial portions. No credit cards.

Accommodation

Conveniently, the central **Rossio** area is the best area for cheap pensions. You may have to shop around in peak season, but the **tourist office** by Rossio station can help you out – their reservation service will book you a room at no extra charge if it's priced at more than 5000$ per night.

Hotel Borges, Rua Garrett 108 (☎01/361 953). Charming, quiet, centrally located hotel, each room with its own bath. 7500$ for a double, most major credit cards.

Residencia Campos, Rua Jardim do Regedor 24 (☎01/346 2864). Perfectly located, clean, cheap pension, immediately opposite the Benfica club office and within a minute's jog of Rossio station. Part of a family-run chain which has three other centrally located places if this one is full. 4500$ for a double.

Hotel Eduardo VII, Avenida Fontes Pereira de Melo 5 (☎01/353 0141, fax 01/353 3879). If you're going to splash out, this three-star hotel might just be the place to do it. Cable TV and bath in every room, panoramic view from the rooftop restaurant. Near the Rotunda stop where the metro line divides. 15,000$ for a double, most major credit cards.

Pensão Globo, Rua do Teixeira 37 (☎01/346 2279). Clean and efficiently run, in a quiet part of the Bairro Alto near the *elevador da Glória* terminal. Shared bathrooms. 4500$ a double.

Pousada de Juventude de Lisboa, Rua Andrade Corvo 46 (☎01/353 2696) The city's only youth hostel is near Picoas metro stop. Curfew at midnight and 2–6pm.

Time out – sports papers proliferate at Lisbon's bars and cafés

The Estádio Nacional

Avenida Pierre de Coubertin, Caxias
Capacity 60,000 (all-seated)

It was here, at this bizarre amphitheatre cut deep into the pinewoods 10km out of
Lisbon, that Bill Shankly turned to Jock Stein and said: "John, you're immortal!"
The occasion was Celtic's European Cup win over Internazionale, the two Scots
managers hailing the first British team to win Europe's premier trophy.

Even for those
not there that
sultry May
evening in 1967,
a visit to the
Portuguese
**national stadi-
um** can be a
moving occasion
– it was also the
venue for the
great Torino's last
game before the
Superga air crash
of 1949.

For most of
the year, all is
quiet on the west-
ern front, beyond

Green victory – Boavista celebrate a cup final win over Porto, 1992

the city limits of Lisbon along Pierre de Courbertin avenue. The only sporting
events that take place here now are the **Portuguese cup final** and minor
athletics meetings.

All around are sports facilities, and the only disturbance during the short walk from
the tram stop to the ground will be the rush of air caused by the
occasional passing jogger.

Once you're through the old-style turnstiles, the stadium spreads out in a
horseshoe shape. There is no stand on the east side of the ground at all, but rows
of simple, stone benches gradually rise up to a marble rostrum dominating the
far, western, side. The changing rooms, toilets and Bar Saida nearby are overgrown with weeds.

Down below, however, the **stadium office**, with its huge picture of Eusébio in
classic '66 form, is in full working order, as is the small **refreshments stand** by
the reception area. Shankly, Stein and Valentino Mazzola have a rightful place
among football's immortals, and a celebratory beer with their ghosts in the
peaceful forest of Caxias is a rare pleasure.

To get to Caxias, ride the rickety wooden #15 tram to its terminus from
Sodré (30min) or Belém (15min). Stamp both sides of your ticket; this journey
crosses two of the city's public transport zones. From the terminus, cross the stone
bridge away from the shanty huts and keep walking along the main road into the
woods, away from Lisbon.

The sports complex is occasionally signposted. The stadium, away to your left,
is fifteen minutes' walk.

Porto

FC Porto *414*   Boavista *418*
Salgueiros *419*

The city of Porto is a strange setting for the new power base in Portuguese football. The first-time visiting fan gets none of the immediate sense of grandeur and football history served up by Lisbon – the main footballing areas are tucked far from the old centre's narrow streets.

To the north, along Rua da Constituição, is where you'll find FC Porto's roots. The Campo da Constituição is where the Dragons played for thirty years. The other side of a huge white wall dotted with plaques, signs and badges is the dusty training pitch once used in earnest by Portugal's first trophy winners. (Porto won both the inaugural cup competition in 1922 and the first national league title in 1935.) The club's youngsters now play there, and a small shop, *A Loja do Dragãozinho*, sells souvenirs to the Young Dragons. The club was formed a few hundred metres away back in 1906.

A kilometre or so to the east is Porto's modern home, the Estádio das Antas. The affluent setting for a three-year title monopoly and a series of impressive runs in the Champions' League, it is a hive of activity in an otherwise sleepy district, and rapidly becoming a regular fixture in the calendar of Portugal's national team.

To the west is Bessa, enticingly run-down, whose club, Boavista, are Porto's poorer relations. Support in the city itself is polarised and is barely affected by tiny Salgueiros, the town's third club.

Local rivalries are nothing, however, compared to the strength of feeling against Lisbon. Many fans in the city, for example, regard the media revelations of possible corruption involving their club's coach,

Porto essentials

Regular bus service #56 runs between central Praça de Lisboa and the city's **Exponor airport**. The journey should last no more than forty minutes but it's a stopping service and, depending on the traffic, it can take more than an hour.

Porto has two main train stations. **Campanhã** is for mainline trains, while the central **São Bento**, gorgeously decked out in *azulejo* tiles, is for local ones. All trains from São Bento stop at Campanhã, but not vice versa. Bus #35 runs between the two.

Buses are the mainstay of the city's transport system, though there are a few trams still running. Tickets, available at major newsstands, cost 80$ for a single, or 1200$ for a strip (*módulo*) of twenty. Stamp the ticket onboard, where otherwise the charge is 160$. If you're staying a while, a four- or seven-day *Passe Turistico* might make sense. A few major routes have a night service until 2am.

Taxis have a standing charge of 125$, but a journey in town should not cost more than 500–750$. Phone ☎02/488 061 for a *Radiotaxi* if you can't see a cab nearby – although if you have time on your side the city, with its winding, cobbled streets and imposing bridges, is best explored on foot.

There are two main **tourist offices**, neither of which is particularly useful. One is in the city hall at Rua Clube dos Fenionos 25 (open Mon–Fri 9am–5.15pm, Sat 9am–4pm, ☎02/312 740) while the other is the more upmarket ICEP, Praça D João I 43 (open Mon–Fri 9am–7pm, Sat 9.30am–3.30pm, ☎02/317 514). Unhelpful English is spoken at both.

Minimal **entertainment information** can be found in the free monthly pamphlet **No Porto 12**, available in bars, cafés and cinemas.

António Oliveira, as a sideshow deliberately set up by a vengeful capital to distract
attention from Porto's successes.

Meanwhile this eccentric city, with the
crumbling streets of its old town facing the
port wine lodges of Vila Nova de Gaia
across the deep gorge of the river Douro,
just gets on with the job in hand.

The thrilling fields

FC Porto

Estádio das Antas, Avenida Fernão de Magal-
hães
Capacity 76,000
League champions 1935, 1939–40, 1956, 1959,
1978–79, 1985–86, 1988, 1990, 1992–93,
1995–97
Cup winners 1922, 1925, 1932, 1937, 1956,
1958, 1968, 1977, 1984, 1988, 1991, 1994
European Cup winners 1987
World Club champions 1987

Portugal's team of the Nineties, FC Porto
are set upon building a football empire
reminiscent of Benfica thirty years ago –
after decades of living in the shadow of
their great Lisbon rivals.

Like Benfica and Sporting, Porto moved
from their traditional home during the
Fifties – to a new stadium, das Antas – as
the era of European competition was about
to dawn.

Yet the Sixties were to be lean times
for the Dragons, without a domestic trophy
or a European run of any note. It wasn't
until former player José Maria Pedroto took
control of the side in the late Seventies
that things picked up. Under Pedroto, two
title wins and a UEFA Cup final appearance
were notched up, while the das Antas got
a new stand and extra sports facilities. A
key factor on the pitch was the goalscoring
prowess of Fernando Gomes, twice Golden
Boot winner as the top scorer in Europe,

Made in Brazil – Edmilson takes on Milan

a Porto player since signing as a 15-year-
old apprentice in 1971, and a member of
the side which lost the Cup-Winners' Cup
final to Juventus in 1984.

The team's star performance came
three years later, under the inventive
coaching of Artur Jorge. Surprise European
Cup finalists against Bayern Munich in
Vienna, Porto conceded an early goal, then
packed their midfield to soak up over an
hour of pressure before hitting back with
two late strikes to win the game 2–1.
Algerian-born Rabah Madjer and Paulo
Futre were the stars, and Madjer stayed
on, combining with Mendes in the Tokyo
snow to help beat Peñarol of Uruguay 2–1
in the World Club championship. Add a

Porto in a storm – the corruption charges

In late 1996, the incestuous and secretive world of Portuguese football was rocked to its foundations when charges of corruption, bribery and match-rigging were levelled at some of its most senior figures.

First in the firing line was **António Oliveira**, the man who took the Portuguese national team to Euro '96 and who succeeded Bobby Robson as coach of FC Porto. In a private conversation with journalists from the daily sports paper *Record*, Oliveira claimed he still had the rubber stamp which was used to forge documents in the 1987 transfer of Zairean striker **N'Dinga Mbote** from Académica Coimbra to Vitória Guimarães. The

Pointing the finger – Oliveira

stamp had been needed to falsify internationally recognised licences in the deal, and the implication was that similar acts of deception were commonplace throughout Portugal.

Such stories paled into insignificance, however, compared with the allegations levelled at Porto club president **Jorge Nuno Pinto da Costa**. First, it was alleged he had bought a £3000 holiday for a local referee and his family. Then it was claimed he had tried to bribe the Romanian referee of a 1984 **Cup-Winners' Cup** semi-final against Aberdeen – to the tune of some £30,000.

Pinto da Costa strenuously denied the stories but, in an attempt to quell the storm of criticism which was enveloping him and his club by the spring of 1997, he relinquished his post as **president of the Portuguese league** and the subsidiary organisation which appoints referees for domestic competitions.

Meanwhile, Portuguese police and UEFA mounted separate investigations into the allegations, amid rumours that further revelations were no more than a few surreptitious phone calls away.

European Supercup win over Ajax, and the team had notched up a hat-trick of international honours unique in the history of the Portuguese game.

Still dominating at home, Porto were now carving serious (and increasingly lucrative) inroads into Europe, first under Tomislav Ivic, then under Bobby Robson who arrived as coach in February 1994, embittered at his shock dismissal from Sporting. Not only did his new charges beat his former employers in that year's cup final, they hammered Werder Bremen 5–0 in Germany to qualify for a Champions' League semi-final. They lost that match to Barcelona, but ran away with the league for the next two seasons.

Robson left for Barcelona in the summer of 1996 but the money his side earned

in Europe has financed a major overhaul of the stadium, which now boasts a new club headquarters and an office complex – the sort of development the Lisbon giants can only dream of.

A crushing 4–0 defeat by Manchester United in the '97 Champions' League quarter-finals added a dose of realism to Porto's advance – as did the £40,000 fine imposed on the club by UEFA for the roughing-up of United fans by police and stewards in the goalless return leg. Porto, however, are convinced these will come to be regarded only as minor setbacks.

Here we go!
Das Antas is in the far east of town. Bus #21 from Rotunda da Boavista, or #78 between Hospital de S João to the north

and Avenida dos Aliados, the commercial centre of town, stop right by the stadium.

Swift half

There are a number of bars along the main road from town, Avenida Fernão de Magalhães. **O Braseiro das Antas** at #1532 is a cheap, friendly place for a beer and a bite, specialising in tripe *à la Porto*. **Cafeteria Satelite**, at #1556, has footie on cable television.

The fans' favourite is the **Restaurante Azul e Branco**, nearer town at #227. Here, blue and white cover everything, including the toilets, and on the wall sits a caricature of the 1987 European Cup-winning team. Right by the stadium is the **Cafeteria Peão**, Rua do Estádio 568 – compact and simple, with Porto souvenirs on sale behind the bar. Inside the stadium, the bar above the *bilheteiria norte* does not sell alcohol.

Club shop

The **Loja Azul** by gate #6 (open Mon–Fri 10am–1pm and 3–7pm, Sat 10am–1pm and on matchdays, no credit cards) sells small bottles of port in presentation boxes bearing the club badge, and a range of crockery in the local *azulejo* style.

Club museum

Disappointingly, the museum two levels above the *bilheteiria norte* is open by appointment only.

Publications

Dragões is a full-colour monthly at 400$, available at newsstands throughout town.

Ultra culture

For most games, the **Super Dragões** occupy the *superior sul* (gates #4, #6 and #10) behind one goal; the away support the *superior norte* (gates #5, #7 and #9) behind the other. On that far side, the anti-Benfica graffiti is outstanding, the heavy-handed policing – as scores of Manchester United fans discovered in March 1997 – rather less so.

In the net

The official Porto website has recently moved to: www.fcporto.pt/menu.html. It's one of the best official sites around, with megabytes of stats, a comprehensive (if

Welcome to Portugal – Porto were fined for the brutal policing which greeted United fans

slightly biased) history, an online version of *Dragões* magazine and a virtual *Loja Azul* shopping mall, just in case you can't survive another week without those replica socks. If you're fed up with the party line, try Alexandre Miguel's unofficial site at: www.geocities.com/Colosseum/8085/. Straightforward and easy to get around, it suffers from the common Portuguese Web ailment of not being regularly updated.

Boavista

Estádio do Bessa, Rua O Primeiro de Janeiro
Capacity 26,000
Colours Black-and-white chessboard shirts, black shorts
Cup winners 1975–76, 1979, 1992, 1997

Regular if unsuccessful performers in Europe, and without a league title in their

Hip to be square – Boavista's timeless attire

entire history, the city's second team, Boavista Futebol Clube, command a passionate local following.

Giving the impression that a boom and crash are happening at the same time, the Boavista area, with its rundown bars and bric-à-brac shops, is one of the more charming parts of Porto. The club were founded here in 1903, drawing their support from the surrounding factories and agricultural businesses.

The team achieved nothing for decades, but not long after the homely Estádio do Bessa was built in 1972, Boavista began to take on the big boys. Three cup wins in quick succession – the black-and-whites missed out on the double by two league points in 1976 – pointed to a bright future in the Eighties but, despite the arrival of João Alves, the black-gloved Portuguese international, the club were always playing in the shadow of the Big Three.

João Pinto, the striker who captained Portugal to victory in the World Youth Cup of 1991, had joined Boavista eight years earlier at the age of 12. He led them to a 2–1 cup final win over Porto in 1992, before departing for Benfica.

In the post-Pinto era, respectable UEFA Cup runs in 1993/94 and 1996 have given Boavista fans a look at Internazionale, Lazio, Karlsruhe and Dynamo Tblisi.

Here we go!
All routes, it seems, lead to Boavista. Take bus #3 from central Praça da Liberdade, tram #18 from Rua do Ouro by the river, bus #78 from Avenida dos Aliados or bus #21 from Porto's das Antas stadium.

Swift half
The unnamed **club bar** by the *bilheteiria*, decked out in black-and-white tiles, has the feel of a fish-and-chip shop. Pay for your order at the till first. There's Golden Beer on draught, though not on major matchdays. Bars between the Rotunda and the stadium tend to be tacky, but those down the other side of Rua da Boavista, towards town, can be enchantingly tatty.

Salgueiros

Estádio Vidal Pinheiro, Rua Álvares Cabral
Capacity 11,000
Colours Red shirts, white shorts

The most working-class club in town, SC Salgueiros are an odd fish. Their fan base is south of the Douro, but they're planning to move to a new stadium between the Cintura Interna highway and Rua de Monsanto, not far from their current ground on the north side of the river.

Past the washer women, barking dogs and car repair sheds along a muddy dirt track, you'll come across the proud graffiti: "Ten Years Of Love". This is the kind of place the Taylor Report warned you about. Ominously, the only shop nearby is one selling flats in the tower blocks which will surely swallow the humble stadium.

On paper there is little to distinguish this team of exiled Serbs, naturalised Brazilians and earnest local lads from any other mid-ranking Portuguese side. Yet after memorable wins over Porto and Benfica, Salgueiros found themselves in contention for a UEFA Cup place in 1997.

Here we go!
While the stadium still stands, take bus #79 from central Avenida dos Aliados, getting off at **Paragem**.

Swift half
The **Café Rogerito**, Rua da Alegria 715, is happy to stick flyposters around the stadium announcing its loyalty to the club, but it's a modern mess of a bar, a good fifteen minutes' walk away. You can buy match tickets there for 800$ each. For better bars, head for where Rua de Costa Cabral meets Rua do Dr Joaquim Pires de Lima.

Ultra culture
The Gerafon ('Carafe') Boys have a reputation for being the biggest drinkers among the city's ultras, their name referring to the large bottles of wine they bring to matches.

Eat, drink, sleep…

Bars and clubs
The two main areas for nightlife are to be found either side of the Douro, in the **Ribeira** (north bank) and **Vila Nova de Gaia** areas. From under the seedy scaffolding that props up Ribeira, the bright, expensive lights of Vila Nova de Gaia entice you across the Dom Luis I bridge. The port wine company names dominate the hillside in Hollywood-sized letters, but while many wine lodges offer free samples during the day, their cafés charge a fortune at night. In contrast Ribeira, especially Rua Fonte Taurina, is a dank hive of cheap bars and artful dodgers.

Many Porto **nightclubs** run a slate system of payment. You'll receive a ticket at the door which is your tab for the night. Pay the whole amount at the cash till on your way out. KAOS are the mob who hire out clubs and bring over Europe's best DJs – look out for their flyers around town.

100% Bar, Rua Canastreiros 16. Slap in the middle of dark Ribeira, an intimate venue with an unusual mix of alcoholics playing draughts and old-time waltzing. Ring the bell for entry at the bright red door.

Café Aviz, Rua de Aviz 59. Large tea room in the town centre with pool tables downstairs and breakfast served from 7am.

Cosa Nostra, Rua S João 74. Between São Bento station and Ribeira, the best of three popular neighbouring clubs. Two floors without any real dance area, but plenty of smoky alcoves. Free entry, 300$ a beer, open 'til early.

Da Lapa, Rua da Boavista 22. Down from Lapa church towards Boavista, a local football bar *par excellence*, with dozens of framed line-ups and pub league trophies.

Encontro dos Amigos, Rua Fonte Taurina 78/80. Genuine football hangout in the heart of

Ribeira, embellished with scarves, cheap food and local colour.

Indústria, Centro Comercial do Foz, Avenida do Brasil 843. Entertaining mainstream disco down in Foz, the university area. Bus #78 from Avenida dos Aliados drops you nearby.

Restaurants

Fourteenth-century legend has it that Porto's residents gave away all their meat to feed the lost expedition to Ceuta, now Spanish Morocco. The **tripe** could not be transported, and the local cuisine has been based around it ever since. Fish – particularly cod (*bacalhão*) – is also a staple diet.

Café Luso, Praça Carlos Alberto 91. Atmospheric, theatrical-style café serving cheap snacks and lunches, in an area packed with daytime workers' caffs.

Casa da Filha da Mãe Preta, Cais da Ribeira 40. Busy place overlooking the Douro, perfect for an early evening bite before plunging into Ribeira. Good-value tourist menu at 1600$. No credit cards.

Galiza, Rua do Campo Alegre 55. Just west of the centre, Campo Alegre has several late-night eateries. This is probably the cheapest, with a tourist menu at 1600$. Cod a speciality. Open until 2am, no credit cards.

Terreirinho, Largo do Terreirinho 7. Fish restaurant tucked away in Ribeira and owned by Porto club president Pinto da Costa. Cod and salmon are the specialities. Most major credit cards.

Accommodation

Invariably the cheapest rooms are near **São Bento** train station, but be sure to have a look at yours first. You'd be better off, and probably safer, spending a little more money either side of **Avenida dos Aliados**. The tourist offices mentioned above can provide a list of phone numbers.

Hotel Antas, Rua Padre Manuel Nóbrega da Costa 111 (☎02/525 000). A stone's throw from Porto's das Antas stadium, this three-star hotel charges 10,500$ for a double – ideal if you're a journalist on expenses. Most major credit cards.

Pensão Astória, Rua Arnaldo Gama 56 (☎02/200 8175). Excellent value at 4000$ for a double, this stylish pension is in a quiet area between São Bento station and the river. Reservations necessary.

Pensão Estoril, Rua de Cedofeita 193 (☎02/200 2751). The best value in town. Double rooms at 4500$, all with private bathroom and television. Cafeteria and billiard room downstairs. A ten-minute walk from the Torre dos Clérigos. No credit cards.

Pousada da Juventude, Rua de Rodrigues Lobo 98 (☎02/606 5535). The city's only youth hostel, off the main Rua de Júlio Dinis towards Boavista. In peak season it is often full by noon. Clean rooms, curfew at midnight. Twenty-minute walk from the centre or bus #3, #20 or #52 from Praça da Liberdade, getting off at Praça da Galiza.

Vera Cruz, Rua de Ramalho Ortigão 14 (☎02/323 396). Slightly upmarket at 7500$ for a double, but comfortable and centrally located.

Romania

'There could have been a revolution that night," was how one Steaua Bucharest supporter reflected on the celebrations which followed his team's triumph in the 1986 European Cup. For the first time in decades, thousands of people filled the streets of the capital, singing, drinking and revelling in success, without the presence of Nicolae Ceauşescu and his cronies pushing them into line and telling them how lucky they were to be Romanian. It was spontaneous. It was liberating. For a few hours, the people of Bucharest controlled the streets – and there must have been more than a few nervous generals wondering whether the success of their own army team would end in tears.

In the end, there was no need for tanks or show trials – the celebration of Steaua's victory remained just that, and it was to be another three years before the army had to decide which side it was on.

The Romanian revolution of 1989 allowed the nation's footballers to pack their bags and cross the once strictly-guarded borders into the world of sports cars, luxury villas and agents' commissions. The generation of Gheorghe Hagi, 'Gica' Popescu, Dan Petrescu and Marius Lăcătuş moved abroad *en masse*. Even with the dictator dead and buried, life was hard in Romania and there was no way the likes of Steaua could stop their stars from going West. After parading their talents at Italia '90, these players had a chance not only to boost their bank balances but to develop their skills, tactical awareness and profes-

Only one way to stop him – McCarthy and Hagi, Italia '90

sional mentality. The results were plain for the world to see four years later, as the Romanians, along with their Bulgarian neighbours, turned the World Cup form-book on its head with display after display of fluent, attacking football. With Yugoslavia in crisis, USA '94 signalled a shift in power in the Balkan footballing world, and the former grand old hotels of Bucharest, which once attracted traders from across the continent, were suddenly filled with the cigar smoke of players' agents.

Like other Balkan leagues, the domestic Romanian competition has suffered as a result of these defections to the West, but despite all the problems, the talent just seems to keep on coming through. To a

Basics

Romania is a country still trying to pull itself out of the mess left by one of Communist Europe's most maniacal dictators. In post-Ceauşescu Romania, you no longer have to worry about *Securitate* agents tracking your movements, and the private sector is offering more choice. But when it comes to making use of **state services** such as transport, banks and the post, the problems of the old regime are still very much apparent.

American citizens can enter Romania with only their **passport**, but those of many EU countries (including Britain and Ireland), Canada, Australia and New Zealand require a **visa**. Check with your local **Romanian embassy** for the latest cost and time of purchase details.

The Romanian **currency** is the leu, plural **lei**. Massive inflation has played its usual havoc, but at the time of writing there were coins for 20, 50, 100 and 200 lei, along with notes of 500, 1000, 5000 and 10,000. There are around 12,000 lei to £1. Generally the best rates for changing money are found at banks rather than exchange offices, but queues and slow service can make the private dealers seem a better option. Cash machines are impossible to find outside of Bucharest and few establishments accept credit cards. **Never** change money on the black market.

Travel between cities is best accomplished by **train**. Services may be slow and the cleanliness of trains may leave a lot to be desired, but the appalling state of Romanian roads (and vehicles) makes for bumpy and uncomfortable long-distance **bus journeys**, and train fares are nothing if not cheap.

Taxis are likewise reasonably priced, but as a foreigner you run a better-than-evens risk of being ripped off. **Agree a price** beforehand and don't pay a leu until you're sure you've arrived at your intended destination.

To call Romania from outside the country, the international code is ☎40, followed by a ☎1 for Bucharest. Direct-dialling abroad is **almost impossible** from Romanian payphones, so head for the nearest major post office or public telephone exchange, or dial ☎071 for the **international operator**.

Accommodation in Romania is expensive, its quality low. Expect to pay four-star rates for hotels which wouldn't deserve a star in the seediest districts of most Western cities. You'll find two hotel rates advertised – one for locals and another, much higher figure for the rest of us. You may be able to negotiate a **discount** if you are paying in hard currency.

working-class Romanian lad, a career in football offers much more than a decent salary – it holds out the possibility of the kind of lifestyle even the highest state official in the land could not imagine. Perhaps that explains why, like their counterparts in Belgrade or Istanbul, Bucharest kids kick a ball around on any spare patch of land they can find – real coats-for-goalposts stuff.

Attendances for Romanian league games may be low and match-fixing may still be endemic, but public interest is high and the careers of foreign-based players are closely chronicled by a number of new sports papers and TV shows that have sprung up in recent years.

This corner of the Balkans, then, differs from much of post-Communist Eastern Europe. In Russia, Poland, Hungary and Slovakia, the local footballing greats are captured in fading photos and appear only for cheesy team reunions. In Romania the legends are living, and international matches draw huge crowds keen to get re-acquainted with their heroes.

It's not just the power of the present that reduces the need for nostalgia – there isn't much of a past to speak of. Until the emergence of the Hagi generation, Romania had rarely produced players of note. While East European football was booming in the days of Stalinism, Romania sat on the sidelines, and it wasn't until the era of *glasnost* (which passed Romania by) that the country began to make an impression on the international scene.

Which is not to say that Romania has no footballing tradition. The game arrived at the turn of the century via British workers who, while developing industry in Western Romania and commerce in Bucharest, demonstrated football to the locals. In 1908 the Romanian FA was formed, and two years later a national competition was begun.

Bucharest teams dominated from the start, but in the early years the oil town of Ploieşti and the industrial cities in and around Transylvania could boast teams capable of challenging the capital's supremacy. Between the wars, Bucharest had four major teams (Olimpia, Colentina, Venus and Juventus), Ploieşti produced United (later Prahova), and Timişoara had two successful clubs, Ripensia and Chinezul, the latter winning seven titles in a row in the Twenties. The spontaneous growth of clubs across the country created some fascinating local derbies, while the diverse ethnic nature of prewar Romania saw the creation of Jewish, Hungarian, Serbian and German sides.

Sadly, few of these teams survived World War II and the subsequent Communist restructuring of football. The Soviet-backed authorities wanted each provincial city to be represented by only a single team, and created giant, centralised ministry sports clubs in the capital. The consequences were predictable. Barring occasional successes for UT Arad, Petrolul Ploieşti and Universitatea Craiova, the Romanian championship became the preserve of Steaua Bucharest (backed by the military) and their city rivals Dinamo (supported by the interior ministry). And, by and large, it has remained so ever since.

In the international arena, the Romanians have tended to plot their own idiosyncratic path. The national team did not take the field until fourteen years after the founding of the FA, and even then they rarely ventured further than the Balkans. By the early Thirties, however, Romania was keen to embrace international competition, and the team gladly accepted an

Bad old days – Germany's Rummenigge feels the force of Romania's Bölöni and Ştefănescu, 1984

The world at his feet – Florin Răducioiu grabs Romania's late equaliser against Sweden, USA '94

invitation to the inaugural World Cup in Uruguay in 1930. They failed to get past the first round in Montevideo, and suffered the same fate in Italy in 1934 and in France four years later.

Romania's Communist authorities were less enthusiastic about testing their footballers' mettle. Between 1947 and 1955 the national side played only against other Communist states, and though they reached the quarter-finals of the inaugural European Championship in 1960, they did not enter the 1962 World Cup at all.

After finishing top of their qualifying group for the 1970 World Cup in Mexico, Romania were drawn in an impossibly tough section alongside reigning champions England, the eventual winners Brazil and a strong Czechoslovakia. There was never any hope of progressing but the Romanians beat Czechoslovakia and lost their other two games by only a single goal.

It was to be twenty years before they made the final stages of the World Cup again. In between, Romania made a brief and rather ugly appearance at the 1984 European Championship finals in France.

But at Italia '90, despite again being drawn in a tough group, they began to show another side to their game. Inspired by the diminutive Hagi, the Romanians beat the Soviet Union with two goals from Lăcătuş in their opening game, then bounced back from defeat by Roger Milla's Cameroon to draw 1–1 with Maradona's Argentina. That took them through to the second round, where Hagi's creativity was stifled by the strong-arm tactics of the Irish midfield; the game finished goalless and Romania went out on penalties.

If their football in Italy had been tasty, it turned out to be only an appetiser for what was to come. Four years later, in the USA, Romania were simply the most attractive side in the competition. They attacked from the start in their opening game against one of the favourites, Colombia, winning 3–1 thanks to two goals from Florin Răducioiu and an extraordinary long-distance curler from Hagi. A 4–1 defeat by Switzerland in the next game might have knocked earlier Romanian sides out of their stride; but under the astute coaching of Anghel Iordănescu the squad regrouped, and a 1–0 win over the host nation took them through to the second round – and a rematch with Argentina which would prove the game of the tournament. The score was 2–1 to Iordănescu's men after just eighteen minutes, with left-winger Ilie Dumitrescu having scored both Romanian goals – the first a Hagi-style lob, the second the outcome of a stunning, length-of-the-field counter-attack. In the second half, Hagi made it three and though the Argentinians fought back with a goal from Balbo, Romania held on for a famous win.

The team's quarter-final with Sweden was similarly packed with incident. With his side trailing by the only goal, Răducioiu scored with just two minutes left to take the game into extra-time, and five minutes into the extended game he scored again. Alas, Romanian 'keeper Florin Prunea suffered a rush of blood to the head, seven minutes from time, to allow Kennet Andersson to equalise and force another shoot-out. All the world bar Sweden was hoping for a Brazil–Romania semi, but they reckoned without the acrobatics of Swedish 'keeper Thomas Ravelli, whose grinning face still haunts fans the length and breadth of Bucharest.

Despite the disappointment, the Romanian team returned home to a heroes' welcome. Politicians and press alike lapped up the international tributes – within the space of a month, Romania had attained the status of a major footballing power.

While still showing sparks of magic, Romania were disappointing at Euro '96. The side has aged, and not all the players' individual careers have gone as planned. Răducioiu and Dumitrescu in particular have gone off the rails after unsuccessful spells in England. Hagi and the team's elegant sweeper-cum-anchorman, Popescu, are playing out their careers in Turkey. Coach Iordănescu, a national hero who has earned himself the rank of honorary colonel in the Romanian army, worries that the next generation of stars have left the country too soon in their careers.

Yet when the side began their qualifying programme for the 1998 World Cup, they were soon back to their spirited, indulgent, almost arrogant best. The confidence is well-founded – anyone peeking their heads into the scruffy grounds up and down Romania will see that there's plenty more where Gheorghe Hagi came from.

Essential vocabulary

Hello *Salut*
Goodbye *Ciao*
Yes *Da*
No *Nu*
Two beers, please *Dovă beri vă rog*
Thank you *Mulţumesc*
Mens' *Toaletă bărbati*
Women's *Toaletă femei*
Where is the stadium? *Unde este stadionul?*
What's the score? *Cî este scorul?*
Referee *Arbitru*
Offside *Ofsaid*

Match practice

The rather predictable nature of the Romanian championship is slowly breaking up, with the emergence of stronger clubs in Bucharest, particularly Rapid and Naţional, to take on the Communist-era giants, Steaua and Dinamo.

Universitatea Craiova are the strongest team in the provinces, but there is hope that new private capital might boost the footballing fortunes of cities such as Timişoara, Ploieşti, Constanţa, Arad, Bistriţa and Cluj, recreating the much more interesting competition of the prewar era.

Stadium facilities in Romania are predictably poor. Many of the grounds are in an advanced state of disrepair. Crowds are low, but the big derbies in Bucharest can pull in over 20,000, while any major international will probably sell out.

Romanian economic development in general has been much slower than in many former Communist countries, and there has been little growth in football-related business such as merchandising. The flip side of this is that ticket prices remain incredibly cheap.

Spartan army – soldiers fill seats left unoccupied by fans

first round proper in August. There are no replays – if the game is level after ninety minutes it goes straight to extra-time and is then decided on penalties if necessary. The final is played in late May in Bucharest, usually (but not always) at the national stadium.

Tickets

Expect to pay between 2000 lei for a normal league game and 20–30,000 lei for a top international. Tickets are bought at kiosks outside the ground. For the rare occasions when games look likely to sell out, go to the ground in advance and buy a ticket there.

The Romanian season follows the classic East European model, beginning in mid-August, taking a break in November, then restarting in late February to finish late in May.

Kick-off times vary, but are usually 3pm or 4pm on a Saturday afternoon. One match will be rescheduled for Sunday to be shown live on television. In late autumn and early spring, games often start at 1pm – or even in the morning – to avoid the costly use of floodlights.

The league

The first division (*Divizia Naţională*) consists of eighteen teams, the bottom two of whom are relegated at the end of the season. They are replaced by the champions of the two regionally divided, eighteen-team second divisions that make up *Divizia A*. The bottom two of each of the second divisions are replaced by the champions of the four regional leagues in *Divizia B*. The fourth tier consists of a series of county and city leagues.

Up for the cup

The *Cupa României* is played on a straight one-leg knockout basis. There are a series of preliminary rounds in July before the

Half-time

Sunflower seeds (*seminţe*) are hawked around grounds by gyspies, who seem to have a monopoly on the pet-food-for-fans service sector in the former Eastern Bloc. Better stadia will have a kiosk selling simple sandwiches and soft drinks. and if you're lucky you might find a street trader grilling up Turkish-style meatballs.

Alcohol is now banned from all football grounds, although the police usually turn a blind eye to a hip flask; watch closely and you will often see the police passing one among themselves.

There is no tradition of fans drinking together in bars before matches, but local restaurants attract a brisk trade after the final whistle.

The back page

Once upon a time there was only *Gazeta Sporturilor*, the sports daily throughout the Communist era, but there are now a plethora of football and sports publications on the market. *Sportul Românesc* (1000 lei) is the most popular daily. It's an unattractive read, with dense text, low print quality and grainy pictures, but it is a reliable source of information, particularly on match details and fixtures. The paper recently suffered from the defection of a large number of its staff to set up a new paper, *Pro Sport*, which was due to start publication for the 1997/98 season.

Sport Magazin (3500 lei) is an excellent glossy monthly with in-depth features and fine photography. When buying a ticket for a game you will be offered a copy of *Stadion Magazin* (1000 lei), a monthly tabloid full of bizarre statistics such as players' birthdays and elementary football crosswords. *Stadion Intergame* (1000 lei) is just crosswords and other puzzles, but could probably be flogged to a daft programme collector back home.

Action replay

As with printed media, the choice of football on TV has widened dramatically in recent years, with a number of private cable channels now offering soccer action. State channel *TVR* is still hanging on in there, though; the station has the rights to the Champions' League until the year 2000, and shows either delayed coverage of a Romanian league game or a highlights package on Saturday evenings. The excitement of USA '94 was too much for veteran *TVR* commentator Cristian Şopescu, who retired after the World Cup. His replacement is Emil Grădinsecu, whose fast-talking style goes down well.

Live domestic league action is shown on *PRO TV*, which also has Italian *Serie A* live games on Sunday afternoons. *7ABC* has live English games on Sunday afternoons or Monday evenings, and also has the rights to the German *Bundesliga*, while *Antena 1* has Spanish action on Saturday nights. Almost every tower block in Bucharest has cable, so you'll find listings for all these channels in the daily press.

Ultra culture

The idea of independent fans' organisations, like the idea of independent organisations in general, was anathema to the old Commu-

nist regime. Since the revolution loose fan groups have sprung up at many clubs, and away travel has become much more popular. Ultra groups do exist at Steaua and Rapid, but they are very loosely organised and some amount to little more than a big banner. There have been waves of hooliganism, however, and the Steaua-Rapid derby can be hairy on occasions.

The most well-organised and colourful ultras hail from Politehnica Timişoara. Their friendship with fans of Rapid Bucharest has led to a party atmosphere at matches between the two, but Politehnica's relegation in 1997 has called a halt to the festivities, at least temporarily. Romanian fans are extremely knowledgeable about the European game and large numbers of young people speak foreign languages – a quick word with the lad in the scarf on the tram should provide you with an expert commentator for the game and, more than likely, a companion for post-match drinking and analysis.

To get up to date on the latest gossip, take a trip to Cişmigiu Park in the centre of Bucharest, close to Eroilor metro stop. Here you will find old men playing chess, drinking coffee and arguing furiously about players and tactics. As many as a hundred old-timers gather at a time in what for decades has been the unofficial open-air forum of Romanian football.

In the net

Alex Tóth's long-running *Romanian Soccer Page* is the best generic website, at: www.webcom.rom/~timis/soccer.html. There's a feast of stats and historical info, and each top-flight club gets a miniature homepage of its own. You'll also find the latest transfer news courtesy of the Timişoara paper *Fotbal Vest*, soccer stories (in Romanian) from the daily *Ziua*, and an audio link to Radio Bucharest. Alex himself is a long-suffering Politehnica fan who inscribes his homepage with the words: "You do not support your team because they are the best, or because they are successful, but because you have grown up with them and they are part of you." Amen to that. For a less comprehensive (but, for precisely that reason, quicker to access) site, have a peek at Romulus Filip's efficiently updated *Soccer Romania*, at: www.niuguni.com/filip/foot.html.

A family affair – football and the Ceauşescus

Romania's entrepreneurs are busy trying to market one of their country's most notorious historical figures – a certain Count Dracula. But while the fanged one from Transylvania might be the man featured on bottles of spirits and tacky T-shirts, it is a **modern-day monster**, former president Nicolae Ceauşescu, whose influence remains more visible in the country. And, like so many dictators, Ceauşescu just couldn't keep his blood-stained hands out of football.

Nicolae Ceauşescu was executed on Christmas Day, 1989, along with his wife Elena. He left behind two sons. One, Nicu, died in Vienna in 1996, after years of alcohol and drug addiction and allegedly sexually abusing young female Olympic gymnasts. The other, Valentin, now leads a quiet life in business in Bucharest.

But back in the Eighties, Valentin was what locals call the 'unofficial sponsor' of **Steaua Bucharest**. He was a lifelong fan of the army team and, through his membership of the first family, he wangled his way into a position of power within the club.

In the 1986 **Romanian cup final**, Steaua were leading their city rivals Dinamo 1–0, in front of a packed crowd in the national stadium, when in the dying seconds Dinamo equalised. Steaua players protested that the goal was offside but the referee blew the whistle to take the game into extra-time. As the teams gathered for a swig of water and a quick pep-talk from their coaches, Valentin sent a message down from the stands. The Steaua team then **refused to take the field**, in protest at the referee's decision. With players standing around and the referee trying to persuade Steaua to return, the TV commentary went dead. Everyone knew that Valentin was behind the protest, but in Romania it wasn't done to launch into criticism of a Ceauşescu live on television. Dinamo defender Ioan Andone was unimpressed, however, and made his silent protest by **dropping his trousers** and mooning at Ceauşescu Jr.

It couldn't have much fun being on the Romanian FA committee that had to make a judgement on that final. A verdict in favour of Dinamo would enrage the Ceauşescus but, on the other hand, Dinamo were the team of the feared *Securitate* **secret police**. A replay would have raised eyebrows at UEFA, however, so the bureaucrats followed the rule book – Dinamo were awarded the game as Steaua were judged to have forfeited the match. But, just to appease Valentin and family, poor old mooner Andone was banned for a full season.

It was not the first time the Ceauşescus had tried to influence the outcome of a match. Nicolae Ceauşescu's birthplace was a small village by the name of Scorniceşti. For years the local team, **Viitorul**, had played in the county league like other village sides. But in the mid-Seventies Nicolae decided it was time socialism delivered top-flight football to Scorniceşti.

Four years in a row they won promotion, and by the 1978/79 season they were in the second division. But something had gone wrong. In the last round of the season, Viitorul needed to win by **twelve clear goals** to win promotion on goal difference. Perhaps spurred on by the presence of their village's most famous son, the lads from Scorniceşti duly romped to an impressive victory of **exactly 12–0** to secure a place in the top flight. In an attempt to conceal their humble origins, they changed their name to FC Olt, and remained in the top tier until 1990 – when a patch of inexplicably bad form, following the death of the great dictator, resulted in relegation.

Today the team are known as **FC Olt '91** and play in the regional third division.

Bucharest

 Steaua 429   Dinamo 431
Rapid 434   FC National 435

It may no longer live up to its Twenties nickname of 'the Paris of the Balkans', but neither is modern Bucharest the living nightmare it was under the Ceauşescu regime. And, despite the obvious poverty of most of its clubs, it remains a city where football is taken seriously, and where the long tradition of a resourceful and flamboyant style of play is studiously upheld.

The thrilling fields

Steaua

Stadionul Ghencea, Bdul Ghencea 35
Capacity 30,000
Colours Red shirts, blue shorts
League champions 1951–53, 1956, 1960–61, 1968, 1976, 1978, 1985–89, 1993–97
Cup winners 1949–52, 1955, 1962, 1966–67, 1976, 1979, 1985, 1987–89, 1992, 1996–97
European Cup winners 1986

The gloves are on – Steaua entertain Juve, 1995

Few army teams from the former Eastern Bloc have survived to thrive in the free-market Nineties. But, unlike Dukla Prague or Budapest's Honvéd, Steaua (the name means 'Star') have maintained a position as their nation's most popular, most successful and most powerful club.

Part of the reason for this continued success is an excellent youth system, which year after year manages to replace the stars who have headed west. Steaua can draw on some of the best coaches in the land, and have a network of scouts across the country. In recent years they have ploughed income from successive Champions' League appearances into modernising their stadium and training facilities – something most Romanian clubs can only dream of.

But Steaua's survival as number one was also helped by the fact that, under the post-Communist regime of Ion Iliescu, the army – as his main ally – were allowed to maintain their influential position in politics, the economy and sport. Under Iliescu's reign there was never any question of halting state funding of Steaua in the same way that, say, Dukla or Honvéd saw their traditional patronage terminated.

Today, however, military reform is part of a package of changes promised by President Emil Constantinescu, and Steaua may have to adapt to stay at the top.

The club were formed as Armata in 1947 but two years later changed their name to CSCA, subsequently shortened to CCA. They became Steaua in 1962. Although successful in the late Fifties and, early Sixties, they played second fiddle to Dinamo from the mid-Sixties on – a change, which according to some local observers, reflected a shift in the balance of power between Romania's army and the interior ministry, which ran Dinamo.

It was a totally different story in the Eighties. But, while many fans might have predicted that Steaua's league and cup double win of 1985 would be the launchpad for an era of prolonged domestic domination for the club, few foresaw the scale of the glory that would come the team's way only a year later. Almost unnoticed, Steaua beat Rangers and Anderlecht on their way to a European Cup final rendezvous with Terry Venables' Barcelona in Seville. With 70,000 Spaniards baying for their blood, Steaua set their stall out early, and concentrated on defence. An ethnic Serb, Miodrag Belodedici, swept up calmly at the back, while a Hungarian who just happened to be Romania's most-capped international, Ladislau Bölöni, sacrificed his usual rôle as a forward to snap at the heels of the opposing midfield.

Even so, a Barça side containing Bernd Schuster and Steve Archibald was beginning to make inroads until, in the second half, Steaua coach Emerich Jenei brought on Anghel Iordănescu as a substitute. Iordănescu was a 36-year-old veteran who had played for Romania at the 1970 World Cup. Barcelona thought he had retired – after all, he hadn't featured in any of the previous rounds in the European Cup, and he was listed on Steaua's team-sheet as an assistant coach. But he was still registered as a player, and now on he came to ensure there would be no slip-ups at the back until the game was safely taken to extra-time and penalties.

With the home crowd now tensed into a nervous silence, there was a certain inevitability about the shoot-out. Barça missed every one of their spot-kicks, while Marius Lăcătuş and Gavril Balint made no mistake. Steaua were champions of Europe. It was the first time that a team from a Communist country had lifted the top prize in European club football, and to this day it remains the greatest achievement of any Romanian team.

That summer, Steaua strengthened their squad with the signing of Gheorghe Hagi – an ethnic Macedonian whose size-five left boot was the sweetest in the Romanian league – from Sportul Studenţesc. He promptly led them to the first of three consecutive league and cup doubles, and in 1989 Steaua were back in the final of the European Cup. There they had the misfortune to meet the AC Milan of Gullit and van Basten in their prime, and were destroyed 4–0. Yet this Steaua was almost certainly a better side than that of 1986. Jenei had moved on to coach the national team, and been replaced by Iordănescu, who introduced a more attacking approach, based around the creative genius of Hagi. On their way to the final Steaua had been electrifying, defeating Sparta Prague 5–1, Spartak Moscow 3–0, IFK Gothenburg 5–1 and Galatasaray 4–0.

Following the departure of several of their star players immediately after Italia '90, Steaua staggered, failing to win the title for three seasons. But it wasn't long before the club were back to winning ways. During the Nineties Steaua have participated in four Champions' League group stages, without really threatening to come close to winning a second European title.

Like most successful clubs, Steaua are the most loathed as well as the most loved in their country. Supporters of other Romanian clubs are full of tales about how their star player was 'conscripted' for Steaua during the Eighties. And even now, nine years after the death of the dictator, Rapid fans still refer to Steaua as the Ceauşeii – 'Ceauşescu's Kids'.

Ironically, it is the man who masterminded Steaua's greatest moment, Emerich Jenei, who is now doing most to threaten their position in Romanian football. In his new rôle as the country's sports minister, Jenei has proposed ending all state support for clubs. That would mean the end of the link between the army and Steaua, and would force the club to compete for sponsors and players in the same way as other teams. The prospect of seeing his beloved Steaua opened up to such competition was too much for coach Dumitru Dumitriu, who quit in a fit of pique at the end of the 1996/97 season – casting a shadow over the team's latest double win.

Here we go!
Yellow metro M3 to Gorjului, then tram #41 to the stadium. As you emerge from the metro you need a tram heading right.

Swift half
Just by the tram and bus terminal there are a number of **small kiosks** serving hot and cold drinks and snacks. On the opposite side of the road is the **Drumetul restaurant** where fans head for a pint after the game. It's a fairly typical Bucharest street corner restaurant, with a limited menu and few people eating.

Club shop
Steaua are the only Romanian club to boast a real **souvenir shop**, in the centre of the city at Str Brezoianu 15 (open Mon–Fri 10am–6pm). It's a dark, dusty place that attracts scant custom and seems to offer little more than a few scarves and hats. Look a little further into the gloom, however, and you'll find an anniversary poster issued to commemorate the European Cup win and bearing the words *Ten Years of the Romanian Miracle.* If that doesn't tempt you to part with your lei, nothing will.

In the net
Radu Mirel Victor runs a decent unofficial Steaua website at: members.tripod.com/~rmv/ steaua.html. There are match reports in English, news stories in Romanian, and a quirky collection of links.

Dinamo

Stadionul Dinamo, Bdul Ştefan cel Mare 7–9
Capacity 18,000
Colours All red with white trim
League champions 1955, 1962–65, 1971, 1973, 1975, 1977, 1982–84, 1990, 1992
Cup winners 1959, 1964, 1968, 1982, 1984, 1986, 1990

Dinamo, like most clubs in Eastern Europe carrying that name, were the team of the interior ministry and the police. The connection remains, even though the ministry's brutal *Securitate*, one of Eastern Europe's most notorious secret-police units, have been disbanded. For the average Romanian fan, Dinamo, more than Steaua, were the team of the repressive Communist-era state. Somehow, despite their Ceauşescu connections, Steaua were viewed as a people's team, while Dinamo and their *Securitate* friends were the enemy.

Midfield Dinamo – Costel Pană against Galatasaray, 1991

The club were formed in 1948 from the merger of prewar clubs Unirea Tricolor and Ciocanul. Unirea Tricolor had won the last title before the war in 1941 and appeared in two Romanian cup finals. The new club were given a prime venue for their stadium – an area of parkland off the busy Ştefan cel Mare boulevard.

Although Dinamo lifted their first title in 1955, it was not until the Sixties that they established themselves as the second force in Romania. From 1962 they won the title four years in a row, doing the double in 1964. In the late Sixties the club produced three of Romania's top internationals – Cornel Dinu, who made 75 appearances

for the national team and is now club president; prolific striker Florea Dumitrache; and Mircea Lucescu, who went on to forge a successful career as a coach with the national team and the Italian club Brescia, for whom he signed Gheorghe Hagi.

Dinamo won three titles in the Seventies, during which their undisputed star was frontman Dudu Georgescu. In 1975 he became the first Romanian to be placed top ten in the voting for European Footballer of the Year, and on three occasions he won the *Golden Boot* award as top scorer in Europe – including the 1977/78 season when he scored 47 goals in the Romanian league. The precise rôle played

Bucharest essentials

Bucharest's Otopeni **airport** is 16km north of the city centre. Bus #783, which leaves from right outside the arrivals terminal, makes the 25-minute journey to the centre of town every half an hour. A ticket costs 3000 lei – pay the driver. The end stop of the bus line is Piaţa Unirii, which is a **metro interchange**.

Alternatively, a **taxi** shouldn't cost an exhorbitant amount, but beware – a cartel operates at the arrivals gate, restricting the number of cabs that can pick up there. Your best bet for taxis is to head up to the departure lounge and haggle a price with a driver dropping someone off – they'll be glad of the business.

Before leaving the airport, you may wish to use one of Bucharest's two *Bancomat* **cash machines** (the other is at Piaţa Universitaţii), in the baggage claim area.

If you're arriving by train you'll come into the infamous Gara de Nord, Bucharest's main **train station** and a popular meeting place for pimps, black marketeers and dodgy characters of all persuasions. There is an ONT **tourist office** at the station (open Mon–Fri 7.30am–8pm, Sat 7.30am–3pm, Sun 7.30am–2pm), and another at Bdul Magheru 7 with the same hours. Both will book **accommodation** for you in exchange for a small commission.

There are three lines to the **metro system** which is the quickest and safest way to get around town. Ticket prices are very cheap – a ten-journey card, which must be stamped before each journey, costs 7000 lei. You can get **transport maps** from the ticket offices inside metro stations. (If you want a detailed **street map**, buy one before you come as they are extremely hard to find in Bucharest.)

There are also **trolleybuses, trams** and **buses**, the last only worth using if you are in the suburbs. There is a flat rate of 700 lei per journey. Tickets can be bought at small *Billet* offices next to main stops (open 5am–8pm) and must be punched on entrance. It's worth stocking up on a few of these tickets as there are no day cards for overground transport, and metro tickets are not valid.

Street crime is rife in Bucharest. As well as pickpockets and muggers, there are more sophisticated criminals. Some operate as 'policemen', accusing foreigners of changing money on the black market, demanding to see the cash and then quickly disappearing with it. **Watch your pockets**, especially on public transport, and keep your wallet in a secure place. If someone approaches you on the streets of Bucharest, just ignore them.

Rail trouble – the sponsor has changed, but Rapid are still lining up in the shadow of the big boys

by the *Securitate* in elevating Georgescu's goals tally – and that of another Dinamo *Golden Boot* winner, Rodion Cămătaru, in the Eighties – may never be known.

Dinamo's titles in 1982 and 1983 paved the way for a decent European Cup run (Romania's first) in 1983/84. In the second round they defeated the holders, Hamburg, and then squeezed past Dynamo Minsk in the quarter-finals. They ran up against the brick wall of Liverpool in the semis, and lost both legs.

The title was retained that summer, but after that Dinamo had to take a back seat to Steaua. Many Dinamo fans argue that the late-Eighties side, with Florin Răducioiu upfront, was one of their best ever, but that the strength of Steaua ruled out any hope of silverware. That view is strengthened by Dinamo's run in the 1989/90 Cup-Winners' Cup, in which Panathinaikos were hammered 6–1 in Bucharest and Partizan Belgrade were dismissed with almost equal ease. Alas, Dinamo lost both legs of their semi to Anderlecht, and Steaua's record as the only Romanian team to reach the final of a European competition stayed intact.

In the aftermath of the Romanian revolution, Dinamo briefly changed their name back to Unirea Tricolor, and saw their much-maligned nursery club, Victoria, disbanded by the new authorities.

Since their last title win in 1992, Dinamo have slumped. Virtually all the team's stars have been sold to foreign clubs, generating revenue which fans believe has been squandered by the bureaucrats who run the club. Discontent among supporters has spilled over into increasing fan violence – Dinamo fans set fire to a stand at Steaua during a derby match in 1997. And the club's proud European record counted for nothing when, in July that year, the team were knocked out of the UEFA Cup preliminary round by KR Reykjavík of Iceland.

Here we go!
Red M1 metro to Ştefan cel Mare – a fifteen-minute ride from any central station.

Swift half
The **Ştefan cel Mare restaurant** on block #14 at the crossroads to the right of the stadium's main entrance, is the traditional meeting place for older Dinamo

fans. The food is nothing much, but the beer is cheap. There are some **snack bars** in the shopping area on the other side of the crossroads, including a bakery and a burger joint which serves decent coffee.

Club shop

There is a small **sports shop** at the stadium entrance which sells the odd scrap of pennant and hat. It's open 10am–6pm weekdays, but closed matchdays.

In the net

You'll find a simple Dinamo homepage, with text in Romanian only, at: www.geocities.com/colosseum/5471/dinamorom.html.

Groundhopping

● Rapid

Stadionul Giuleşti, Calea Giuleşti 18
Capacity 23,500
Colours All white with claret trim
League champions 1967
Cup winners 1937–42, 1972, 1975

East European dictatorships were not renowned for providing choice. But while you can have a one-party state, you can't have one-team football. Soccer was one of the few areas of life where people could exercise freedom of choice. And for football fans in Bucharest opposed to the Ceauşescu regime, there was one simple outlet for frustrations – Rapid Bucharest.

A hangover from the prewar era, Rapid somehow avoided being merged into a police or army side and were there-

fore seen as disassociated from the party state. *"Hai Rapid!"* was one of the few slogans that could be shouted without a dictate from above. Rapid were, are and always will be a genuine workers' team, with their traditional support base coming from railwaymen (*feroviarii*) who live in the Giuleşti district and work at the Gara de Nord just down the road.

Although Rapid never won a championship before World War II, they were cup specialists, winning the competition six times in a row between 1937 and 1942. The Communists got their hands on Rapid in 1950, when the ministry of transport took over the running of the club. Choosing a new name wasn't difficult – until 1958 they played under the predictable title of Locomotiva. Having won their name back, Rapid enjoyed their most successful postwar spell – they finished runners-up in the league three times in a row from 1964, and in 1967 won their first and so far only title.

Although there were cup wins in the Seventies, Rapid quickly faded and even spent a couple of spells in the second division. As anyone who has ever driven in Romania will testify, the ministry of transport was not one of the biggest spenders in the country and they certainly lacked the resources to outbid the army and the *Securitate* for players.

Yet despite the lack of success, Rapid maintained their popular support. After

Home banker – Naţional's first European campaign ends in Bruges

The Stadionul Naţionul

National stadium, Parcul de Cultură şi Sport
Capacity 65,000

Formerly the 'August 23', named to commemorate the victory of Communist forces in Romania, the national stadium remains a potent symbol of the country...it is falling to pieces. Anyone who has ever visited an abandoned ground will find the scene familar – an uninspiring bowl filled with **rotting wooden benches**, clumps of grass and weeds, crumbling concrete and faded notices.

The stadium's main feature is the pavilion in the west stand, where Ceauşescu used to speak to **the assembled masses** on May Day and, of course, August 23. Although it is no longer the setting for political rallies, the stadium is still used for international football – though the smaller but vastly superior Steaua stadium is preferred for games against minor nations.

The stadium has **great natural acoustics** and a capacity crowd can create a great atmosphere with the sound 'trapped' inside the ground. But the ground badly needs repair and redevelopment if it is to survive as a major venue, and in these days of IMF austerity packages, Romania has more pressing priorities.

To visit the stadium, take the **red M1 metro** to Piaţa Muncii, turn right outside the station and head towards park – the ground is a fifteen-minute walk into the park. Behind the east stand is the **Teraca Stadionul,** a small bar with a terrace serving snacks and bottled beers.

the 1989 revolution, politicians of all colours including President Iliescu, rushed to associate themselves with the club.

Local businessman George Copos, head of the Samsung company's Romanian operation took control of the club in the early Nineties but although the clarets have established themselves in the top half of the league, the much-anticipated Rapid revival has yet to materialise.

Copos' cash has provided a new stand at the south end of the Giuleşti, ending the three-sided 'horseshoe' appearance of the ground. But the rest of the stadium is in a shocking state. The rickety wooden benches are broken, the claret paintwork is fading and the toilets are without doubt the most pungent in European football.

For all these drawbacks, Rapid remain the most romantic club in Romania, their rebellious spirit well illustrated by the plaque at the main entrance which pays tribute to three young Rapid sportsmen who were killed in the revolution. "We'll never forget you" says the message under their portraits. The *feroviarii* live in hope

there will soon be some heroism to watch on the field.

Follow the workers from Gara de Nord train station on **tram #11, #22** or **#44** to the ground – the journey takes around ten minutes. The **Tonady,** at Calea Giuleşti 49, is a decent spot for a swift one, while the **Nemecu Billiard Restaurant** on 9 Mai, just off the main road, offers pool, pints and pizza.

FC Naţional

Stadionul Cotroceni, Str Dr Lister 37
Capacity 16,000 (all-seated)
Colours White shirts, blue shorts
Cup winners 1961

In stark contrast to the dereliction to be found at Rapid and at the national stadium, the home of FC Naţional is an example of what can be achieved if the cash is there. A modern, all-seater (with seats, not benches) arena, the Cotroceni is flanked by an equally impressive tennis centre. The ground development was financed by a consortium of banks, primarily the Romanian national bank, who are the major backers of the club.

FC Naţional were formed as Lafayette in 1934, became Grafica in 1948, and two years later were renamed Spartac. They adopted the name Progresul in 1954, and stuck with it until after the 1989 revolution. Like many Romanian clubs in the postwar period the team were linked to the trade unions, but Progresul had the unusual distinction of being the team of the Romanian hairdressers' association! Well trimmed they might have been, but they seldom cut a dash on the field. They finished third in the league in 1955 and 1962, and won the Romanian cup in 1961. Throughout the first two decades of Communism, the club enjoyed a decent level of popular support as, like Rapid, they were clearly not a favoured team of the regime.

But in the mid-Eighties the heart was ripped out of the club by a familiar figure. Between 1984 and 1989, a large area of central Bucharest was demolished to make way for Nicolae Ceauşescu's grotesquely impressive Victory of Socialism Boulevard, a giant road lined with huge tower blocks and terminating at the massive House of the Republic – the third largest building in the world. This ludicrous project saw the demolition of 9500 houses, fifteen churches and the Stadionul Republica – the charming, downtown home of Progresul.

The Republica was a prewar stadium, with an English feel and a grand main stand, and for the older generation of Progresul fans, going to a game was like being transported back in time to a Bucharest where there was no Ceauşescu, no Communist Party and no ration coupons. Perhaps that was why the tyrant razed it to the ground.

Anyway, for much of the rest of the Eighties, Progresul played in the lower divisions, sharing grounds wherever they could and playing bigger games at the national stadium.

Now, with a superb ground, a healthy bank balance and a team capable of rivalling Steaua and Dinamo, FC Naţional are emerging as the club of the future. They entered Europe via the UEFA Cup for the first time in 1995/96, and finished runners-up to Steaua in both the league and the cup in 1996/97.

If Romania does develop into a healthy capitalist nation, then no football club will better symbolise the transtition than FC Naţional. And yet, with their traditional support dying out and crowds remaining low in the absence of that elusive first title, one wonders whether – as with MTK in Budapest – the nascent capitalists have chosen the right target for their investment.

To get to the Cotroceni, take **yellow metro M3** to Eroilor (from the centre, take trains heading for Industrillor). From the metro stop, cross the road and head down Str Doctor Lister – the stadium is on your left. The bankers may have put individual seats in the ground, but they neglected to arrange for a handy bar to be constructed anywhere near the stadium. Have one in town before you go.

Eat, drink, sleep…

Bars and clubs
Bucharest hardly has the reputation of being a slamming night out, but you can have a good time here if you're prepared to search for it. The best thing to do is think of the kind of place you'd like to be in, then look for the opposite. If you're after a cheap place just to sink a few pints and have a natter, then choose a **restaurant**. If you want to eat, try a **bar** or, alternatively, one of the new venues that are springing up with names like *Uncle Sam's Pizza Café-Bar Deutsche Billiard Music Pub.*

Wherever you end up, there's no excuse for doing what Rangers fans did in 1995 – camp in McDonald's all night with thirty bottles of vodka.

Hanul Manuc, Str Iuliu Maniu 62. An ancient inn with a huge courtyard perfect for outdoor

Tough on the streets – football is the hot topic among most of Bucharest's populace, young or old

drinking and ideal for groups. Only open in good weather, but if you can get a table you might be here all night. Near Piaţa Unirii.

The Dubliner, Bdul Nicolae Titulescu 8. Sky Sports, Guinness, Western consultants and Irish stew – the best of several expat pubs. Just off Piaţa Victoriei.

Lapteria Enache, Piaţa Universitaţii. Find the double glass doors to the right of the *Dominus Art* building, which is attached to the national theatre, and take the lift to the fourth floor... After all that you'll need a beer, and this is a small, dark, café bar popular with students from the nearby university. Live music on weekends (with cover charge) and it's open late.

Restaurant Tic Tac, Bdul M Kogalniceanu 15. You lost 3–0, it's raining, the phones aren't working and the banks are closed. You have 10,000 lei in your pocket and a packet of Marlboro Lights, and you need a few beers. This will do

the job. The 'Restaurant' is nothing of the sort – it's a scruffy little drinking den for depressed former factory workers and alcoholic housewives with shocking make-up. The 'Café-Bar Tic Tac' in the same building is similar, but for younger, less depressed people.

Salt & Pepper Bar/Bistro, Bdul Nicolae Balcescu 15–17. Naturally this is not a bistro, but a restaurant serving American-style dishes. Most people come here simply to be seen and to drink from the wide range of imported beers, including Budweiser and Corona. Fashionable young crowd.

Restaurants

Although pizzas, burgers and the like are now widely available in Bucharest, it's well worth searching out a decent traditional Romanian restaurant. Gone are the days (in Bucharest at least) when all you could expect was a greasy slice of pork and a pile of fatty chips. **Romanian cuisine**, which struggled to survive in the era of rations, is enjoying a comeback here. Dishes to look for include *samrle* (cabbage stuffed with rice and spiced, minced meat) and *muşchi poiana* – beef filled with mushroom, bacon and peppers and served with a tangy vegetable and tomato sauce. **Soups** and **stews** are especially good, but if you want something a little less rich, most places will serve simple grilled meats with salad. The local wine and beer are quite acceptable.

Bradet, Bvd Carol Davila 60 (☎01/638 6014). Excellent Lebanese restaurant with vine leaves, kebabs, humus and various spiced meat dishes. Very busy, so worth calling to reserve in advance.

Carul Cu Bere, Str Stavropoloeos 5. Its name means 'the beer cart' which, as you might have guessed by now, means this is a place to dine in style. The spacious interior resembles a medieval castle and there is usually a folk dance and music performance thrown in. Traditional Romanian dishes, cheap beer – and nobody objects to you staying on well into the night.

Casa Romăna, Calea Victoriei 12. Quality Romanian restaurant with the emphasis on traditional dishes rather than the usual 'international' menu. Outstanding soups, courteous service.

Sherriffs, Bdul I C Brătianu 44. The most central of this popular chain of fast-food joints. The burgers aren't up to much but the pizza is fresh and tasty, the various kebabs are excellent, and the cappuccino and pastries are just perfect for breakfast.

Tandoori, Str Budai Deleanu 4. The better of the two Indian restaurants in Bucharest, serving authentic curries, tandoori-cooked meats, fresh salads and wonderful bread.

Accommodation

The city's hotels tend to be extremely expensive and you don't always get what you pay for – always inspect the room before agreeing a price. The **tourist information** people might be able to sort you out with a private room if you're staying for two or three nights. As prices are almost always subject to negotiation, call the hotel in advance and start haggling.

Hotel Casa, Victor Campia Turzii 44 (☎01/222 9436, fax 01/312 9424). Owner Mihai Oancea is a friendly chap who runs an excellent, mid-range hotel with high standards of cleanliness and service. Close to Piaţa Victoriei.

Hotel Continental, Calea Victoriei (☎01/614 5348). Classy, central and pricy. If your budget is flexible enough and you want a top-quality room, then this is the place.

Hotel Triumpf, Şos Kiseleff 12 (☎01/222 3172, fax 01/223 2411). Situated in the old town, this is a beautiful old hotel offering modest rooms at very reasonable rates. Book well in advance.

Universal, Str Gabroveni 12 (☎01/615 82 33). Dirt cheap boarding house used as student accommodation most of the year, but with some rooms to rent. Clean and central.

Russia

Soccer in Russia is up for sale. Shabby market stalls occupy many of Moscow's main grounds, forcing teams to share stadia, while players raise their game only in the shop window of European football. Corruption is rife. In the new 'market' economy, the balance of football power has shifted away from Moscow to the provinces, where Rotor Volgograd and Alaniya Vladikavkaz play to packed houses in modern arenas that put the capital's marketplaces to shame – and nobody questions where the money for the new grounds has come from. Alaniya, the pride of North Ossetia, near war-ravaged Chechnya, won the title in 1995, and should have retained it a year later – they were beaten by Spartak Moscow in a play-off.

Spartak, the people's team, are the only club to attract reasonable custom in the capital. Young Muscovites remember little and care less about the days of exciting domestic football in the old Soviet league, the break-up of the USSR having deprived them, and the older generation of fans, of classic battles between Moscow sides and top Ukrainian and Georgian teams such as Dynamo Kiev and Dynamo Tblisi. A modern indoor tournament, held in Moscow every January and involving the flagship teams of all the former Soviet republics, barely does history justice.

After its introduction by English mill-owners in 1887, football slowly developed in Moscow and St Petersburg, with neither help nor hindrance from the ruling tsars. City teams played each other in representative fixtures, but Russia's vast distances and long, harsh winters stood in the way of rapid, nationwide growth – the Olympic team lost 16–0 to Germany in 1912.

After the 1917 revolution, the Communist authorities saw organised sport as

The latest 'new Yashin' – Sergei Ovchinnikov

a cheap way of keeping workers fit, disciplined and entertained. Although yet to be established on the factory floor, football had been part of the sports curriculum in Moscow's better schools and colleges. The Moscow clubs Dynamo, Spartak, CSKA, Torpedo and Lokomotiv were quickly formed in the Twenties, and the first all-Soviet league was organised in 1936.

Even then, football in this part of Europe was rarely 'clean'. So-called agreed (*dogovorni*) matches, in which the outcome was little more than a formality, were a familiar trait under Communism, and two key figures, Spartak founder Nikolai Starostin and Torpedo star Eduard Streltsov, spent time in gulag camps for refusing to buckle under the authoritarian might of the KGB (represented by Dynamo Moscow) and the Red Army (CSKA).

International appearances were not encouraged until after World War II, when Stalin hoped to capitalise on the propaganda victories of Dynamo Moscow's tour of England in 1945, and the Olympic team's début in 1952. After Stalin's death, the USSR won soccer gold at the 1956 Olympics, encouraging the new Soviet leader, Nikita Khrushchev, to allow the full national team, the *sbornaya*, to play in the World Cup finals of 1958. Under captain Igor Netto, the Soviets bowed out at the quarter-final stage, but progress was clearly being made.

Two years later, the team won the first-ever European Championship by beating Yugoslavia in Paris – although the scale of their achievement was undermined by the non-participation of the likes of England, Italy and West Germany in a tournament then seen as having little potential by the European football élite. The Soviets' hero in Paris was their goalkeeper, Lev Yashin,

a six-foot-plus giant dressed in black who would become his country's most enduring footballing legend. A veteran of the 1958 World Cup, Yashin was still in goal when the Soviets finished as European runners-up in 1964 and as semi-finalists at the 1966 World Cup.

After the Sixties, however, the USSR would earn a reputation for being under-achievers at international level, perennial 'dark horses' who faded before the final hurdle. Bad luck certainly played its part – shocking refereeing denied them in 1986, and the team travelled to Italia '90 with an unfeasibly long injury list. But lack of support also took its toll. In those days, whatever voices could be heard in the world's stadia urging the *sbornaya* forward were those of diplomats and spies.

At club level, meanwhile, Moscow's domination was being successfully challenged by clubs from outside the Russian republic. Khrushchev's favoured team

Early glory – the Soviets, with goalkeeper Yashin top left, win the 1960 European Championship

Basics

To enter Russia you need a **visa**, pre-arranged with considerable hassle at your Russian embassy back home. For those on **package tours**, this will be sorted out by the travel company. For individual travellers, there are three choices: a **tourist visa**, valid for a specific number of days providing you have pre-booked accommodation for that period; a **business visa**, valid for up to sixty days without the need to pre-book accommodation; and a private, **individual visa**, which may take up to four months of bureaucratic wrangling to obtain. Check with your local embassy for current details on visa application and cost.

On arrival in Russia, you will have to fill out a **currency declaration form** stating how much money you have with you. On departure you will have to fill out a similar form, declaring how much money you are taking out.

The Russian currency is the **rouble**. At the time of writing there were around 8000 roubles to £1. The rate is little different at the airport or at any of the **currency exchange places** on every other Moscow street corner; all deal in dollars and marks, but sterling is often accepted. By law you can only pay for goods and services in roubles, although most shops and bars will accept dollars in small denominations. Only smarter businesses take **credit cards**. You'll find your pockets full of roubles, in differing notes to the value of 100, 200, 500, 1000, 5000, 10,000, 50,000 and 100,000, and coins of 1, 5, 10, 50 and 100 roubles.

For local **phone calls** in Moscow, buy a handful of brown plastic tokens (*zhetoni*) at 1500 roubles each from metro station ticket offices. Nearby you'll see a row of old-style telephones (*taksofoni*) – dial your number first, then drop in the token as soon as you hear someone's voice. For **international calls**, main metro stations have card phones; the lowest denomination of phonecard on sale is 75,000 roubles. To dial out of Russia, dial 8 (pause)10, then the country code. Calls are cheaper after 10pm and on Sundays. Remember that Moscow is two hours ahead of Central European Time.

Gone are the days when foreigners were obliged to travel around Russia according to specific 'tourist' routes. Today your freedom to **explore the country** is more likely to be limited by the threat of armed conflict – before you board that plane for Vladikavkaz, check with the Foreign Office or local equivalent that you stand a decent chance of making the return journey.

Russia's provinces are best reached by **train**, from one of Moscow's eight mainline stations. St Petersburg is eight hours away, a journey most conveniently done overnight – though beware that petty crime is rife on Russian sleepers. Train tickets are almost laughably cheap, but as a westerner you may be asked to **pay a supplement** on long-distance and international routes.

Dynamo Kiev, became the first non-Moscow side to win the Soviet title in 1961. And while Russian clubs could only muster one appearance in a European final, the Ukrainians of Kiev and their Georgian counterparts, Dynamo Tblisi, would both win the Cup-Winners' Cup during the Seventies and Eighties, as well as making an impact in other European competitions.

Ukrainian players such as Oleg Blokhin, Igor Belanov and Oleg Protasov formed the backbone of the *sbornaya* until the squad was effectively disbanded by the break-up of the Soviet Union in the early Nineties. After competing under the CIS ('Commonwealth of Independent States') banner at Euro '92, many top non-Russian players chose not to play for the newly independent nations of their birth, reasoning they would have a greater chance of honours if they represented Russia. While the players' decision reduced the

Georgian and Ukrainian national sides to the status of European minnows, Russia duly qualified for the 1994 World Cup – but seven players, Ukrainian-born Andrei Kanchelskis included, then refused to play after a row with team management.

There was similar acrimony at Euro '96, when an intriguingly creative squad failed to deliver under the authoritarian rule of the former Spartak Moscow coach Oleg Romantsev, and were eliminated after the group stage.

Kanchelskis' generation have long since fled Russia for west European clubs, and the next one will not hang around for long. In Moscow, fans face a stark choice between paying to see action of variable quality at the big clubs, or spending the same money on winter coats for their children in the market outside the ground.

Essential vocabulary

Hello *Zdravstvuyte*
Goodbye *Do svidaniya*
Yes *Da*
No *Nyet*
Two beers, please *Dva piva, pazhalysta*
Thank you *Spasiba*
Men's *Muzhskoy* (МУЖИ)
Women's *Zhenskiy* (ЖЕНЫ)
Where is the stadium? *Gde stadion?*
What's the score? *Kak schyot?*
Referee *Sood*
Offside *Nye igri*

Match practice

The Russian season runs from early March to early November, with a break in June if the national side are involved in the finals of a major tournament. Games generally take place on Saturdays at 5pm, but with CSKA/Dynamo and Spartak/Lokomotiv sharing the same stadia, there is invariably a Sunday game in Moscow.

Security is tight for the Spartak-CSKA clash and whenever a Moscow side are hosting Alaniya Vladikavkaz, who attract large numbers of expatriate Chechens and Ossetians. Otherwise, the loudest noise you'll hear all afternoon is laughter.

Outside the stadium you'll see a swift trade in badges, scarves and old programmes. If available, a programme for the current match will be on sale at the *kassa* (RFCCF), where you buy your ticket.

Some teams still proudly stride out to the 'Footbolniy March', a rousing Soviet pre-match theme dating back to the Thirties. During the game, a ball is thrown back by the ball-boy nearest to where it went out of play, ensuring quick goal-kicks and throw-ins – and no rest for thirsty players.

From your seat in the stands you'll hear shouts of *"Maladtsi!"* ("Excellent!") after a goal, *"Davay!"* ("Go for it!") as an attack breaks, and *"Durak!"* ("Idiot!") at any given player for the other 88 minutes. You should also have little trouble hearing the players' instructions to each other – league crowds are low (entire sectors may be filled with bored soldiers), and the atmosphere can be eerily quiet.

The league

The Russian league is made up of four main divisions. The premier (*Vischaya*) has eighteen teams, the last three being replaced by the top three of the twenty-team first (*Pervaya*) division. Five teams drop from the first into the three-zone second (*Vtoraya*); two teams go up from each of the Western and Central zones, plus the top club from the weaker Eastern zone. The third (*tretyaya*) division has six zones.

As illustrated in 1996, teams finishing equal on points at the top of the *Vischaya* have to play off for the title, irrespective of goal difference.

Up for the cup

To allow for the huge number of participating teams, preliminary rounds for the Russian cup take place just before the previous year's cup final in May. These early ties are decided over one game, extra-time and penalties if necessary, and often attract vast crowds to provincial grounds.

Premier-division teams join two rounds before the quarter-finals, which take place over two legs the following April. The semi-finals are decided over one game on neutral ground, while the final in Moscow, which had been played at the Dynamo stadium but will soon return to the rebuilt Luzhniki, is decided over a single game.

Tickets

A ticket (*bilyet,* displayed as БИЛЕТ) should cost between 15,000 and 25,000 roubles and grant you access to any spot on a tatty wooden bench in the sector of your choice. In most grounds, sectors are indicated by north, south, east or west. Unless the fixture is a Moscow derby, visiting fans are rare, so the only seating problem is cured by taking along that day's newspaper as a precaution against any embarrassing splinters.

Half-time

Follow the plumes of smoke to the nearby kebab (*shashlik*) grill, where some 15,000 roubles should see you OK. Risk the *khot dogs* (3000 roubles) if you must. A newspaper cone full of sunflower seeds is the essential accoutrement to a summer evening's entertainment. Most stadia will have a small buffet van for sandwiches (*butterbroti*), filled with either ham or caviar, and beer – about 4000 roubles for a bottle of domestic brew, 6000 for a can of imported lager.

Vendors will pass around the ground during the game with trays of beer and soft drinks, but most drinking is done before the match at a stand near the ground – a hangover from the Soviet era when bars were practically non-existent. You'll see supporters sharing a bottle of vodka (about 15,000 roubles all in) or knocking back beer at 5000 roubles a time.

Action replay

One league match a week is televised live throughout Russia, on national Channel

Travelling fans – expect plenty of colour if Vladikavkaz are in town

1, ORT, or the Rossiya channel, RTR. This will be at the same time as most other matches, Saturday at 5pm – a piece of programming hardly conducive to filling empty stadia.

Late on Sunday evenings, ORT show a round-up of the previous day's league highlights, *Footbolnaya Obrazrynyie*; RTR's *Footbol Byez Granitsi* ('Football Without Frontiers'), on Sunday afternoons, is more analytical. *Footbol Klub*, on Moscow's commercial channel NTV early on Monday evenings, has a smattering of other European action, and most cable TV stations deliver Eurosport and the BBC World Service TV channel for Premiership news.

The back page

The launch in 1992 of the daily *Sport Express* swept the red carpet from under the feet of the staid *Sovyetski Sport*, the classic old-style Communist daily put out by the Olympic Committee. The best journalists went straight across to the *Express*, which now boasts a circulation of almost a million. Its bumper Tuesday edition (neither daily comes out on Sundays or Mondays) has excellent foreign coverage if someone can help you out with the Cyrillic. Variable prices will be displayed from vendor to vendor – around 3500 roubles should cover you.

As for the weeklies, Sunday's *Footbol* is good on analysis – especially if the doyen of Russian football writers, Lev Filatov, feels like putting pen to paper – but short on humour. Its rival, Wednesday's *Footbol Review*, is lighter but respected.

The fan-level monthly *Tvoi Footbol* is sadly no longer with us, but its star journalist Sergei Mikulik, the brightest of Russia's new generation of football writers, launched his own glossy monthly *Gala Sport* in Moscow in September 1996. Its rival is the monthly *Match*.

Ultra culture

Gone are the days of pitched battles between Spartak Moscow and Dynamo Kiev fans on the streets of either city. These days the average Spartak fan is barely out of primary school socks, no longer plays football in the yard, and probably won't stay for the whole game, preferring to mooch around different parts of the stadium with his mates. Spartak fans, with a minor right-wing element, do make a noise but don't have the wherewithal to splash out on colourful banners and fireworks.

In the net

The Russian national anthem will boom sombrely out of your computer's speaker system as you access Oxana Smirnova's excellent generic football site at: www.quark.lu.se/~oxana.football.html. When the music has stopped, you'll find the latest news in both English and Russian, a history of the national game, a plethora of club links and a meticulously maintained stats archive.

The official RFU (Russian Football Union) site is at: www.feesmg-football. ru/index.htm. Still very much 'under construction', this is a smart-looking site which promises sections devoted to other member states of the CIS, as well as to Russia itself – worth keeping an eye on.

Falling before the last – internal feuding hit Russia's dark horses at both USA '94 and Euro '96

MOSCOW

Thin crowds, dilapidated grounds, second-rate players...why would anyone come to Moscow to watch football? There are all sorts of reasons. The game here is steeped in history, while the football itself will never have anything less than a cultured aim, even if it is sometimes clumsily executed.

Above all, though, Moscow is the biggest, most exciting football city in Europe to play its football in the summer – which, as any local will tell you, can be a surprisingly warm and inviting time to be in Russia's capital.

The thrilling fields

Dynamo

Dynamo stadium, Leningradski prospekt 36
Capacity 51,000
Colours All blue with white trim
League champions (USSR) 1936 (autumn), 1937, 1940, 1945, 1949, 1954–55, 1957, 1959, 1963, 1976 (spring)
Cup winners (USSR) 1937, 1953, 1967, 1970, 1977, 1984
Cup winners (Russia) 1997

Few club histories are as colourful as that of Dynamo Moscow. Their tale involves Victorian millowners from Blackburn, the founder of the KGB, Stalin's henchman, the Cold War and the greatest goalkeeper in the history of world football.

The game first came to tsarist Russia in 1887 thanks to Clement and Harry Charnock, whose family ran the Morozov cotton mills in Orekhovo Zuyevo outside Moscow. Lifelong fans of Blackburn Rovers, the Charnocks formed a factory team and kitted them out in their beloved blue-and-white. As the Russian game expanded at the turn of the century, the *Morozovtsi* won

the Moscow league five years running before being renamed Orekhovo Klub Sport and relocated to Moscow itself. Once there the club quickly became a front for anti-tsarist activities, and it was these that attracted the attention of Felix Dzerzhinsky, the man who, after the 1917 revolution, would become leader of Lenin's secret police – the forerunners of the KGB.

In 1923 Dzerzhinsky changed the team's name to Dynamo Moscow, affiliating the club to the electrical trades' union. But the VIP box at the open, functional and all-bench Dynamo stadium, built in 1928, played host not to an élite band of electricians but to the hierarchy of Stalin's secret police – among them his soon-to-be chief henchman, Lavrenti Beria. A keen Dynamo fan, Beria watched his team share prewar Soviet league titles with the Spartak side of his sworn enemy, Nikolai Starostin. Beria would subsequently be fundamental in arranging Starostin's exile to the gulags.

After World War II the club would become the rôle model for secret police ('Dynamo') teams across the former Eastern bloc, from Berlin to Bucharest. Just as importantly, it was Dynamo whom Stalin sent to Britain in November 1945, for a four-match tour cloaked in fog, mystery and fast-flowing football. The team returned to Moscow in triumph, having won the first leg of Russia's propaganda war with the West.

Star of the tour was goalkeeper Alexei 'Tiger' Komich. Four years later, Tomich was idly watching Dynamo's ice-hockey team when his eye was caught by a promising goal-minder called Lev Yashin. Yashin was promptly converted to football, and would become the hero of the postwar Soviet soccer era, the very embodiment of success and sportsmanship. Over two decades he played in three World Cups and two European Championship finals for his country, and led Dynamo to five titles and three cup wins. He was named European footballer of the year in 1963 – the first and so far only goalkeeper to attain the honour. A one-club man, Yashin played his farewell match (between Dynamo and a FIFA World XI in front of 100,000 at the Luzhniki) in 1971.

After that he worked 'upstairs' at the club, even after he'd had a leg amputated as a consequence of a long-held knee injury in 1986. He died four years later, still a Dynamo employee.

Ironically, it was a year after Yashin's retirement that Dynamo became the only Russian side to take part in a European club final, losing a Cup-Winners' Cup clash to Rangers in 1972. After that there were

two fallow decades before the dissolution of the Soviet Union in 1992.

These days Dynamo share their peeling ground with CSKA, the army side down the road. The ubiquitous market surrounds the stadium, which was finally given undersoil heating in early 1997. The installation proved a mixed blessing: while it enabled Dynamo to continue their ground-sharing arrangement with CSKA, the heat scorched the grass. After a string of injuries, most notably to Russian international Omari Tetradze during a World Cup qualifier, Dynamo were forced to re-lay the turf to provide a softer, safer playing surface.

Grass aside, the ground is in desperate need of modernisation, but it did at least

Moscow essentials

Arriving at Moscow's international **airport**, Sheremyetevo 2, is a sharp introduction to the realities of life in Russia. Don't pack any valuables in your hold luggage, and watch your bags at all times.

Once through customs and with roubles in your pocket, from the airport you have three choices: go with one of the **taxi sharks** hassling you as soon as you pass through customs (cost $70–100 for the 28km journey south-east into town); step outside the airport concourse and **strike a bargain** with someone going into town anyway (around $30 is reasonable); or take bus #551 to its **Rechnoi vokzal** terminal, where green metro line 2 starts (4000 rouble ticket available onboard, stamp both sides in the puncher machine afterwards). The bus runs 8am–1am; at night, the shark option is safest.

If you're coming in by train from Berlin or Warsaw, you'll arrive at the city's Belarus **train station**, served by Belorusskaya metro where the circle line connects you with ten of Moscow's eleven-line metro system, possibly the world's finest – buy a handful of green plastic tokens (*zhetoni*) from any station at 1500 roubles each. At the metal gates above the escalators, throw a *zheton* into the slot – it is valid for any journey until you come back above ground.

The **metro** is clean and fast, and runs 6am–1am. Stations are marked with a large letter 'M'. Get a little Russian-language metro map from a newsstand to follow the station names, which are indicated only in Cyrillic letters.

The city's **buses, trams** and **trolleybuses** take tickets (*taloni*) at 1500 roubles each, available from newsstands. A single ticket is transferable from one route to the next during a single journey – stamp your ticket in the puncher every time you board.

In a **taxi**, agree a price – in dollars – before the driver sets off. Westerners are open game for Moscow's taxi mafia, so a cheaper way is a paid hitch across town, flagging down any driver and agreeing a price.

For **tourist and listings information**, you'll have to rely on the English-language press: the *Moscow Times* and *Moscow Tribune* appear daily except Mondays, and their Saturday editions feature information about the week's entertainment in town. Both papers are available free of charge at expatriate bars and hard-currency shops, where you'll also find copies of the weekly *Living Here*, with club information.

see the club return to winning ways with a Russian
cup victory in June 1997 –
a much-needed tonic for
the few diehards who
gather at the top of the
west stand.

Here we go!
Take green metro line 2 to
Dynamo – the station interior is richly adorned with
sporting figurines.

Swift half
People gather by the row of
stand-up bars between
the main ticket office and
the stadium behind. One
bar has a side terrace with
tables and chairs, where
threesomes lay into a bottle of vodka, a plate of dried
fish and a few beers to wash
it all down.

Inside the stadium, the
Restoran Dynamo is
open to VIPs only, but has
wonderful shots of Yashin
in its entrance.

Policeman's ball – Yuri Kuznetsov puts in a cross for Dynamo

The **bar** above gate #2 is similarly
exclusive, but do your utmost to get past
the man on the door to the buffet just
below – during the match, a tray comes
round offering large cans of Zipfer at 7500
roubles each.

Club shop
On matchdays you'll find dozens of football **souvenir sellers** on the concourse
in front of the ticket office and the north
stand. Just inside the main gate is a **kiosk**
(open Tues–Thurs, 10.30am–4pm and
before matches) selling videos, magazines
and badges.

Publication
The club publishes *Park* magazine, produced
for important matches only, price 5000
roubles a copy.

Club museum
Just in front of the north stand, the
Dynamo museum (open Mon–Fri
9am–5pm, admission 1500 roubles) has
two floors with displays covering almost
every sporting discipline.

On the first floor you'll find the football
and Felix Dzerzhinsky exhibits, the former
with a fabulous set of Soviet badges. The
Lev Yashin display, on the second floor, is
unmissable.

In the net
A tasteful Blackburn-style blue-and-white
background adorns Sergei Ukladov's unofficial but useful Dynamo site at:
www.soccer.ru/dinamo/. There's an efficient news and stats service in English, plus
newspaper reports and player interviews
in Russian.

Down and out – Spartak's Tsymbalar (left) and Kechinov impede Makelélé of Nantes, 1996

 Spartak

Club offices 1st Koptelsky pereulok 18/2
Stadium Lokomotiv, see p.451
Colours All red with white trim
League champions (USSR) 1936 (autumn),
1938–39, 1952–53, 1956, 1958, 1962, 1969, 1979,
1987, 1989
Cup winners (USSR) 1938–39, 1946–47, 1950,
1958, 1963, 1965, 1971, 1992
League champions (Russia) 1992–94, 1996
Cup winners (Russia) 1993

The people's team do not belong to one class of Moscow society, nor to any particular area, nor even to one home ground, but to the memory of the most dedicated figure in the history of Russian football.

It was the vision of Nikolai Starostin that the city should have a team which could operate independently of political interference. Having helped to create Spartak from the Moscow Sports Club that had been based in the Luzhniki park since the early Twenties, Starostin then coached the team, and even managed to play one match in the club's first Soviet championship win in the autumn of 1936. His three footballing

brothers, Alexander, Andrei and Pyotr, also played for the team and for the USSR.

Officially the club was affiliated to the Moscow food producers' co-operative, but Starostin ensured that Spartak's relationship with the authorities was, at best, ambivalent. He would spend much of the next six decades combing the country for young talent and coaxing it away from other, more politically favoured, clubs.

Starostin's resolute stance against the KGB (represented by Dynamo Moscow) and the Red Army (CSKA Moscow) cost him dear – he spent ten years in Stalin's gulags after being charged with "the promotion of bourgeois sport", and was released only after the personal intervention of the dictator's son, Vasily.

Nikolai Starostin died in February 1996, shortly before his 94th birthday. But his legacy lives on. Spartak's nationwide popularity, reputation for attractive football and freedom from any rusting state authority have helped them face the modern age.

Backed by Gazprom, the huge state gas and oil company, Spartak won the first three Russian titles after the break-up of the Soviet Union, and took part in three consecutive Champions' League campaigns. In 1995/96, under coach Oleg Romantsev (now the club's president), Spartak shocked everyone by taking maximum points to top their group, only to sell four key players – goalkeeper Stanislav Cherchesov, defenders Viktor Onopko and Vasily Kulkov, and forward Sergei Yuran – in the winter break and fall at the quarter-final stage.

A cut in sponsorship funds from Gazprom had forced Spartak to hit the selling trail. But for once, the club found political influence operating in their favour when, just before their Champions' League exit, the mayor of Moscow, Yuri Luzhkov, issued a decree enabling the team to sign players from outside the city without paying local tax. Their squad suitably reinforced on the cheap, Spartak mounted a fine blindside run to win back their Russian title from Alaniya Vladikavkaz, beating the provincials 2–1 at a play-off in St Petersburg in November 1996.

With their spiritual home, the Luzhniki stadium, considered unfit for their return after reconstruction, Spartak's fans still have to follow their club to Lokomotiv Moscow – as the "Spartak We Love You" graffiti on the ticket-office wall testifies. They mull around in the east (*vostok*) stand overlooking the opposition goalmouth, with the harder element in sector A, and continue to provide the team with the best support in the city.

None of that popular favour counted for a thing in June 1997, when Spartak's director-general Larissa Nechayeva was murdered at her *dacha* outside Moscow. Both Nechayeva and her personal manager were shot in the head, victims of a gangland assassination which, it was reported, may have been connected to Spartak's reluctance to sign away TV rights.

For Spartak, it seems, refusing to play the game according to the rules will always carry a bitter penalty – no matter which ideology is running Russia.

Here we go!

To avoid the ramshackle market by the stadium, turn left out of **Cherkizovskaya** metro (red line 1), where you'll be two minutes from the ticket office and Lokomotiv's main gate.

Swift half

There is a **buffet** between sectors 1 and 2 of the stadium, selling sandwiches and cans of Holsten at 7000 roubles, and a **shashlik grill** opposite. Ticket prices are the same price for Spartak as they are for Lokomotiv – 25,000 roubles each.

Club shop

As you enter the main gate of Lokomotiv's ground on Spartak matchdays, you'll see a **van** surrounded by covetous lads and selling Spartak scarves, shirts and pennants. A wider selection of memorabilia can be found at the **club headquarters**, 1st Koptelsky pereulok 18 (open Mon–Fri 11am–5pm, Sat 11am–2pm, no credit cards). The store was opened by Spartak management last summer as a way of making money in the long winter months. To reach it, take the orange line metro to **Sukharevskaya**.

Publications

While Spartak are playing at Lokomotiv's ground, **programmes** are only produced – and snapped up – for European ties and major league fixtures. Availability and price will be indicated at the window of the ticket office.

In the net

As befits Russia's most popular club, Spartak have more websites devoted to them than any other team in the country. The official homepage is at: spartak.home.ml.org, but can occasionally play hard to get.

A better bet might be Mike Dryomin's American-based unofficial site at: www.colombia.edu:80/~aib7/spartak.html. Mike's aren't the prettiest pages your browser will ever display, but they're functional enough, with everything in English and Russian, including a regularly updated news section. Also based Stateside is Dmitri Blagin's multi-frame offering at:

euclid.math.fsu.edu/~dblagin/spartak.html. Though a little too clever for its own good, this is an attractive site guaranteed to contain the latest results, and with a nifty historical archive.

 Torpedo

Luzhniki stadium, Luzhniki park
Capacity 80,000
Colours Green shirts, white shorts
League champions (USSR) 1960, 1965, 1976 (autumn)
Cup winners (USSR) 1949, 1952, 1960, 1968, 1972, 1986
Cup winners (Russia) 1993

A club whose roots are in a working-class district of south-east Moscow, Torpedo are named after the first Soviet-built production car, and until recently were sponsored by ZiL – erstwhile purveyors of Fifties-style limousines to the politburo. In 1996, as Russia's new political class exercised its right to choose a Mercedes over the home-grown product, ZiL found they could no longer support the club and for a few months Torpedo faced extinction.

Salvation arrived in the form of the owners of Moscow's Luzhniki stadium, itself privatised in 1992. After gaining permission from the city council, which retained a 49 percent stake in the Luzhniki, the entrepreneurs took control of Torpedo and set about transforming the club from a post-Communist relic into a modern sporting organisation.

One of their first actions was to move the team from their modest ground on Avtozavodksaya to the Luzhniki itself – even though Moscow's biggest ground, still officially called the 'central Lenin stadium', was in the middle of a massive refurbishment programme. By hook or by crook, the Luzhniki's owners managed to clear the stadium of both the diggers and the scores of market stalls which had covered it while the development work was being carried out, in time for the start of the 1997 season. They also invited Spartak to move back to the stadium – an invitation that was politely declined, Spartak officials claiming that the new-look Luzhniki was unsafe.

In fact, only the first stage of the Luzhniki's redevelopment is complete. There is new individual seating and a roof has been built over the stands, to comply with UEFA regulations should the Russian FA bid to host a European final or, as is rumoured, the 2004 European Championship. The second stage, ambitiously targeted for the year 2000, calls for the building of a retractable dome – though whether the Luzhniki

Sea battle – Torpedo blow United out of the water, 1992

consortium can raise sufficient funds for this remains to be seen.

What is also not yet known is whether a plaque will be mounted to commemorate Europe's worst-ever stadium disaster here in 1982, when 340 Spartak fans were crushed to death in an icy corridor as a UEFA Cup match against Haarlem of Holland was drawing to an exciting finish. Details of the tragedy only came to light seven years later.

As for Torpedo themselves, the squad has been rebuilt following the collapse of ZiL and, like Lokomotiv, the club have placed the emphasis on nurturing new talent – a policy that bore fruit earlier in the decade, when the club knocked Manchester United out of the UEFA Cup in 1992.

Today's young lads have the reputation of an awesome historical figure to live up to – the 'Russian Pelé', Eduard Streltsov. Like Spartak's Nikolai Starostin in an earlier era, Streltsov fell foul of Soviet authority. On the eve of the 1958 World Cup he was 'invited' to join either CSKA or Dynamo. His refusal to leave Torpedo led to his expulsion from the national team, and he was subsequently charged with "criminal behaviour" and sentenced to seven years in the gulags.

After his release, Streltsov led Torpedo to the Soviet title in 1965 and a cup triumph three years later. Even had he not returned from the camps, his name would have lived on among the fans – his trademark back-heel pass is still known as a 'Streltsov' in Russia.

Here we go!

Take red metro line 1 to **Sportivnaya**, then follow the exit signs to Stadion I Lenina. The stadium is a five-minute walk immediately ahead of you.

Swift half

Sadly gone is the football fan's meeting-place bar on the stadium grounds. These days, turning sharp left out of the metro station, you'll find a quiet **terrace bar** serving Holsten beer and sausages.

Diesel power – Lokomotiv meet Bayern, 1995

Groundhopping

The grounds will be huge, the crowds tiny at Moscow's lesser clubs. But there are compensations – not least in the stalls selling vintage footie ephemera, the professional cynicism of the fans, and the *frisson* of seeing Russia's Red Army team in action...

Lokomotiv

Lokomotiv stadium, B Cherkizovskaya 125a
Capacity 30,000
Colours Red shirts, white shorts
Cup winners (USSR) 1936, 1957
Cup winners (Russia) 1996

Moscow's railway workers' team boast a wonderfully kitsch stadium decorated with train motifs in the north-east of the city. Currently also used for Spartak home games (see p.448), this well-maintained ground, extensively used in the Coca-Cola 'Eat Football' TV commercials, has under-soil heating and two stands, east and west – Lokomotiv and Spartak fans both watch their side from the east stand.

Lokomotiv seldom troubled the statisticians during the Soviet era, but in the Nineties the club have proved themselves smart spotters of young talent. Four of the new breed of Russian internationals have cut their footballing teeth beneath the sign of the diesel engine – defender Igor Chugainov, midfielders Alexei Kosolapov and Andrei Solomatin, and goalkeeper Sergei Ovchinnikov, the latest man to earn the 'new Yashin' tag and beneficiary of a lucrative move to Benfica in the summer of 1997.

A season earlier, these four were at the heart of an enterprising side which beat Bayern Munich in Germany in the first leg of a UEFA Cup tie, then won their first post-Communist domestic honour by lifting the 1996 Russian cup. They reached the final again the following year, only to lose to Dynamo.

CSKA

Club offices Leningradski prospekt 39
Stadium Dynamo, see p.445
Colours Red shirts, blue shorts
League champions (USSR) 1946–48, 1950–51, 1970, 1991
Cup winners (USSR) 1945, 1948, 1951, 1955, 1991

Not so long ago CSKA could claim to be Moscow's third club, with a reputation based on a postwar side said to have been the greatest team of the Soviet era. Today, though, the club are in a mess. Although they have their own stadium a couple of tram stops down from Dynamo's, it now hosts a huge market – essential modernisation works have a completion date pencilled in as "the end of the century". In the meantime, all home games take place at Dynamo.

As well as having two grounds, on the eve of the 1997 season CSKA also appeared to have two teams. The club's board, still run by the Red Army which has overseen the team since formation in 1923, dismissed coach Alexander Tarkhanov and replaced him with the former Russian

Which CSKA? Many of this 1996 UEFA Cup line-up have since followed their coach to a new club

national-team boss Pavel Sadyrin. But Tarkhanov refused to go quietly, submitting his own 'CSKA' team-sheet to the Russian FA, complete with many of the club's best players. The row was settled when Tarkhanov's side renamed themselves FC CSKA 97 and took a place in a lower division. The official CSKA, meanwhile, began the season with a desperately weakened side and a clearly demoralised Sadyrin in charge.

It's all a far cry from the Forties and Fifties, when the club won five Soviet titles in six years and provided all but one of the players for the USSR's first international competitive appearance at the Olympic football tournament of 1952.

Since then, honours have been few. The defensive strength of international captain Albert Shesternev helped CSKA win the league in 1970, and the team also won the last Soviet title in 1991. A year later, they knocked holders Barcelona out of the European Cup with an away-leg comeback which silenced the Nou Camp.

Today CSKA's fan crew, the Red-Blue Warriors (essentially composed of kids who haven't done their military service yet) get most of their kicks from watching early- and late-season football in the club's indoor sports complex, with its full-size pitches and warm, dry air. If you want to join them, take tram #6, #23 or #28 three stops out of town from the **Dynamo** metro stop, looking out for the huge poster of Lenin by the Mercedes-Benz flag. The strange **Samovolka bar** in the back of the ice-hockey stadium, with its bizarre military exhibits, is a comfortable but expensive winter warmer.

Eat, drink, sleep…

Bars and clubs

Moscow survives on a dollar economy and can be as expensive as Tokyo. When it comes to nightlife it is certainly ten times as tacky. The average **nightclub** can cost anything from $30 to $100 admission and will probably feature gorillas on the door, mafia flunkies at the bar and ladies of ill repute on the dancefloor. Keep your wits about you at all times, not least when staggering out of any club and into a taxi.

There *are* decent **bars** in town, charging around 25,000 roubles for a foreign beer, slightly less for a Russian one – **Zhigulovskoe** is the most acceptable home brand, **Tverskoe** if you prefer dark beer. When leaving town, the Irish bar in the departure lounge of Sheremyetevo 2 is well worth a visit.

Byedniye Lyudi, Bolshaya Ordnika 11/6. It's officially members only, but a quiet word at the door will get you into this intimate two-room pub, with occasional live music and a full menu. For Moscow, the atmosphere is unusually laid-back. Tretyakovskaya metro.

Hungry Duck, Pushechnaya ulitsa 9. Where the expat crowd loosens its tie and sinks a few pricey beers. Can get wild, will certainly get sweaty. Next to Kuznetsky Most metro.

Krizis Zhanra, Prechistensky pereulok 22/4. Hip cellar bar tucked away in a courtyard, five minutes' walk from Kropotinskaya metro station. Live music until 9pm.

Rosie O'Grady's, Znamenka ulitsa 9/12. The best of Moscow's handful of Irish bars, with a regular crowd and jazz on occasional weekdays. Arbatskaya metro.

Sports Bar, Novy Arbat 10. The only sports bar in town, American-style with pool tables and dartboards. May have televised soccer in the near future, as may the nightclub/casino **Metelitsa** across the street at #21. Arbatskaya metro.

Restaurants

Moscow's eateries reflect the city's economic extremes. Few locals can afford to eat out, but those who do spend a small fortune doing it. If you're on a budget, or into social observation, the *stolovaya* – a **cheap slop** for the masses – is the place for you. Otherwise, expect to pay $15 upwards before drinks, for a two-course meal which will probably include an excellent soup and a meat-heavy main dish.

Café Margarita, Malaya Bronnaya ulitsa 28. Intimate eaterie with imaginative décor. Russian specialities. Mayakovskaya metro.

Guriya, Komsomolsky prospekt 7/3. If you're going to try ethnic cuisine, then moderately priced, spicy Georgian fare is your best option, and this is one of the best places to try it. Park Kultury metro.

Moosh, Oktyabrskaya ulitsa 2/4. Authentic Armenian cuisine at affordable prices, with a lively atmosphere and friendly service. Novoslobodskaya metro.

Moscow Bombay, Glinishchevsky prospekt 3. Best Indian deal in town – tandoori dishes a speciality, vegetarian options, lunchtime bargains. Most major credit cards. Pushkinskaya metro.

Ogni Arbata, Arbat ulitsa 12. Dark café in the heart of the Arbat – once Moscow's underground heartland, now home to talentless painters and tacky souvenir stalls. Cheap soups, reasonably priced drinks. Arbatskaya metro.

Skandia, Radisson-Slavyanskaya Hotel, Berezhkovskaya Naberezhnaya 2. Possibly the best buffet breakfast deal in town – omelettes, waffles and hangover-slaying fruit juices, 7–11am. Kievskaya metro.

Accommodation

The type of **room** you find depends on the kind of **visa** you have arranged; those coming on a business visa will do best to opt for private or hostel lodgings. Unless your trip has been organised through a package deal, you'll find most hotels laughably overpriced.

Arena, 10-Letiya Oktyabrya 11 (☎095/245 2802). Perfectly located for the Luzhniki, this is a no-frills hotel, clean, safe and prostitute-free. Around $50 a night for a double. Sportivnaya metro.

Belgrad Hotel, Smolenskaya Ploshchad 5 (☎095/248 1643, fax 095/230 2129). Pleasant, clean, safe hotel block in the Arbat area. Around $80 for a double, breakfast included. Smolenskaya metro.

Moskva Hotel, Okhotniy Ryad 7 (☎095/292 1000, fax 095/925 0155). Classic Communist hotel block within sight of the Kremlin, reasonably priced if you don't pay their expensive reservation fee – try turning up on-spec out of season. Okhotniy Ryad/Teatralnaya metro.

Prakash Guest House, Profsoyuznaya ulitsa 83, korpus 1, entrance 2 (☎095/334 2598 or ☎095/333 8263). Comfortable hostel on the third floor of a block, twenty minutes from the city centre. Clean rooms, plus the bonus of a small restaurant serving Indian food. Prices vary according to facilities, but $40 should see you tucked up safe and sound. Belyayevo metro.

Travellers' Guest House, Bolshaya Pereslavskaya ulitsa 50 (☎095/971 4059, fax 095/280 7686, e-mail tgh@glas.apc.org). A godsend in a wilderness of dodgy, service-free central accommodation, the Travellers' can not only sort you out a single room for $30 or a double for $35, but will also help with your visa, your laundry, train tickets and lodgings in St Petersburg for a small service charge. Four-bed dormitories also available. Turn left from Prospekt Mira metro, take a right for 400 metres towards the chimneys ahead of you, then turn left into Bolshaya Pereslavskaya. The hostel is on the tenth floor.

Scotland

Football – along with the legal system and education – is one of the few areas of Scottish life independent from English rule. The sense of independence goes back a long way. While the English may have invented the modern game, it was the Scots who provided much of the man-power for their early professional clubs. Take a look at any English line-up from the early part of the century, and you'll find plenty of Scottish names. And the Scots did more than simply supply personnel – they developed the tactics, the skills and techniques that trans-formed the sport from 'hacking and punting' into a sophisticated game of short passing and dribbling.

The Scots were also keen mis-sionaries, their players and coaches travelling across Europe to spread the word at the turn of the century. The enormous influence of Scottish coaching on the English game has

Victory in defeat – the national side, Euro '92

continued to this day, yet despite the stream of talent constantly heading south, and the near total dominance of the Glasgow clubs, the Scottish league remains well supported.

Perhaps all this goes some way to explaining the intense pride taken in the achievements of the national team and of Scotland's club sides in European compe-tition – though there has been precious little of the latter in recent seasons.

The Scottish Football Association was founded in 1873, and a year later a national cup competition was launched. Few of the clubs which dominated those early ama-teur years thrived once professionalism was given the nod in 1893. Queen's Park of Glasgow are a surviving remnant of those

early years, but have spent decades in the lower reaches of the league. Others, such as Third Lanark and Vale of Levan, have long since departed from the scene.

The first year of the professional league saw Glasgow's Celtic lift the title, finishing just one point ahead of neighbours Rangers. The battle between the 'Old Firm', with Celtic representing Irish Catholics and Rangers the Protestant community, has dominated the domestic game ever since – between 1905 and 1947, the title went to another team only once. The sectarian and often violent character of the Glasgow rivalry is one of the most unattractive aspects of Scottish football, but arguably, the dominant position of the two teams on the field has been more damaging.

The Scottish national team took part in the first-ever official international game when they drew 0–0 with England in 1872. They won the first Home Championship, the annual competition between the four nations of the United Kingdom.

But it wasn't until 1929 that Scotland played a continental side. Like England, the Scots also ignored the prewar World Cups, making their first appearance in the finals in 1954 – they lost 1–0 to Austria and were hammered 7–0 by Uruguay.

It was at club level that the Scots made their mark on the international scene. In 1967, Celtic defeated Inter Milan in Lisbon to become the first British side to win the European Cup. A week later Rangers lost out in extra-time to Bayern Munich in the final of the Cup-Winners' Cup. And Scotland so nearly a trio of finalists in Europe that year, as little Kilmarnock made it to the semi-finals of the Fairs' (now UEFA) Cup – their performance an indication of the strength of Scottish club football at the time.

But with the exception of the 'Lisbon Lions', Scotland has been known for its outstanding individuals rather than its great teams – players such as Denis Law of Manchester United, Kenny Dalglish of Celtic and Liverpool, John Robertson of Nottingham Forest. A remarkable percentage of English championship sides have included a Scottish midfield general – George Graham at Arsenal and Billy Bremner at Leeds in the early Seventies; Graeme Souness in the great Liverpool side of the early Eighties; and Gary McAllister, also at Leeds, in the early Nineties.

The list of great managers is equally impressive – Bill Shankly of Liverpool, Matt Busby of Manchester United, Jock Stein of Celtic, and in the modern era the three most successful managers in the English game – Graham, Dalglish and, of course, Alex Ferguson.

In recent years the tide of talent flowing southwards has slowed. English clubs can now find cheaper players of equal or higher standing from the continent, and

Big man, big occasion – Duncan Ferguson takes on the Austrian defence, 1996

there has been less talent emerging from Scotland's Boys Clubs and junior teams.

Yet still the Scottish national side defies the prophets of doom by keeping its head above the international waterline. The Scots qualified for five World Cups in a row between 1974 and 1990, and though they failed to advance beyond the group stage in any of them, they provided English fans with a surrogate team to 'support' – and a lot of vivid memories. Like Archie Gemmill's solo goal against Holland in 1978, David Narey's toe-poke against Brazil four years later, and Jim Leighton's vain attempt to keep out Careca's late strike for the Brazilians at Italia '90.

The Scots turned in what some regard as their best-ever performance at an international tournament at Euro '92, yet still failed to make it past the first round. They did not qualify for USA '94 at all. But two years later all those battling qualities of discipline and team spirit were on show again, at Euro '96 – and once more Scotland somehow contrived not to qualify for the knockout stage, Patrick Kluivert's late consolation goal for Holland against England saving Dutch bacon while the Scots could only beat Switzerland 1–0 and went out on goal difference.

Scotland's continued ability to deliver the goods internationally is all the more remarkable when one considers the stagnation of the domestic game. The Eighties saw the Glasgow stranglehold broken, with Jim McLean's Dundee United and Alex Ferguson's Aberdeen enjoying domestic and continental success. But the Nineties have witnessed a return to the old pattern, with Rangers winning every title since 1989 and Celtic apparently the only side capable of challenging them.

Some voices have begun to suggest that Rangers and Celtic might be better off joining the English Premiership. However, most Scots know that if this were to happen, it would signal the end of the Scottish league as a credible European championship. And the history is surely too rich for that to be contemplated.

Match practice

The days of whisky bottles being passed around the terraces are gone. Alcohol is banned from all grounds, police and stewards will eject drunken supporters, and most Scottish stadia have been upgraded to all-seaters with modern facilities – clubs here having been quicker to modernise their grounds than their counterparts in south of the border.

The season begins in early August and ends in mid-May. Weekend games are played on Saturdays at 3pm, with live TV matches on Friday evenings, Sunday afternoons or Monday evenings, depending on the schedules. Midweek fixtures (usually Tuesday or Wednesday) kick-off at 7.30 or 7.45pm.

The league

The Scottish League has gone through various mutations over the years. In 1975, in a bid to increase the number of competitive games played by the top clubs, the Scottish Football Association introduced an élite ten-team Premier Division. In 1994 the League was restructured from top to bottom. A new Third Division was created, and all divisions were reduced in size to ten teams.

The bottom side from the Premier Division are automatically relegated, to be replaced by the champions of the First Division. The runners-up of the First Division play-off with the ninth-placed Premier Division side over two-legs.

In all other Divisions, the top two teams change places with the bottom two.

Up for the cup

The Scottish Cup began in 1874, two years after the English FA Cup, but the Scots preceded the English in developing a second knockout competition when their League Cup began in 1946. Unlike their English counterparts, the two Cups do not run simultaneously.

The first round of the League Cup is in the first week of August and involves sixteen clubs, excluding the Premier Division

Basics

If travelling from England by train, the *Intercity* announcer will tell you when you are **crossing the border** but, in fact, little changes in terms of practicalities once you arrive in Scotland.

Customs **entry requirements** are the same, as is the **currency** – although you will be given Scottish £5 and £1 notes; both are legal tender throughout the UK, but few shops in England will accept the latter, so spend them before you head south.

The **telephone code** for Glasgow is ☎0141, for Edinburgh ☎0131.

The best way to get from one Scottish city to another is by **train**, although, as in England, the equivalent buses and **coaches** can be substantially cheaper.

The most attractive legal difference between the two 'countries' is the pub opening hours: Scottish pubs are not tied by restrictive **English licensing laws** and most stay open until midnight, some well beyond that.

sides and fourteen other sides who receive a bye. The second round in mid-August includes Premier Division teams. All games are single-leg and there are no replays, results being decided on the day by extra-time and a shoot-out if necessary. The final is played at a neutral ground in November.

Family viewing – the terrace whisky has gone

The Scottish Cup kicks off with a first round proper in mid-December, although non-league sides begin qualification in August. Premier Division sides join the competition in the third round, traditionally in the last week of January, and the final takes place in the last week of May at Hampden Park – reconstruction permitting. All ties are single-leg with one replay, after which it's extra-time and penalties.

Tickets

Football is a tad cheaper here than in England. Ticket prices range from £10 to £20 and for big games should be bought well in advance. The major clubs operate telephone credit-card booking services.

The back page

Scotland has a long tradition of serious football writing. At the turn of the century magazines such as *The Scottish Referee* and *Scottish Sport* featured intelligent discussion on the development of the game. Today, alas, there is no exclusively Scottish football publication, though there is an excellent fanzine, *The Absolute Game*.

The *Daily Record* is Scotland's daily tabloid, *The Scotsman* and *The Herald* the national broadsheets. Each, in its own way, offers comprehensive coverage of the game in Scotland. In recent years, the London-based tabloids such as the *Daily Mirror* and *The Sun* have produced more local soccer material for their Scottish editions.

As with players, Scotland has exported many of its best sportswriters to England. Perhaps the most respected football writer in Britain today is Hugh McIllvanney, of the *Sunday Times*. A recently published book, *McIllvanney on Football*, is a collection of his best writing over the last thirty years and includes portraits of some of the great names in the Scottish game. McIllvanney's fellow Scot, Patrick Barclay, is also well worth reading in the *Sunday Telegraph*.

Hope over expectation – the Tartan Army

Action replay

While obviously tempted by the prospect of a major cash injection from the sale of TV rights, the *SFA* have made a conscious effort to limit the number of games shown on live television. The consequence is that the satellite channel *Sky Sports* and terrestrial *Scottish Television* (*STV*) share live coverage, with *Sky* getting two Old Firm games a year and *STV* one.

BBC Scotland have a Saturday night highlights show, *Sportscene*, usually shown around 10pm, which in addition to extended highlights and goals from the day's Premier Division and First Division games, includes a selection of English matches.

Sunday afternoon's *Scotsport* show on *STV* has highlights of all Scottish Premier and First Division games and the occasional live game. *Sky* shows one game from each round of the Scottish Cup, but the final is also screened by the *BBC*.

Ultra culture

The absence of drink and bottles has meant that the hooligansim which once blighted the Scottish game has all but disappeared.

The Edinburgh and Glasgow derbies remain tense, hostile affairs, but with few visiting supporters now allowed in to such games, you are more likely to see violence on the pitch than in the stands, even if the Catholic and Protestant communities remain bitterly divided.

Strangely, football unites those groups as well as dividing them, since Celt and Ger alike stand proud in their support of the Scottish national team. In contrast to the right-wing thug element which has infiltrated followers of England, the Tartan Army, are renowned for their gregariousness, good-natured drinking and ability to laugh in the face of footballing tragedy.

After a World Cup qualifying defeat by Yugoslavia in Zagreb in 1989, a lone Scottish piper stood on his hotel balcony to play a lament, and soon found he had a crowd of hundreds listening to him in the square below. A year later, Scots cheerily joined in an all-night samba party alongside fans of the Brazil team which had just knocked their heroes out of Italia '90.

In the net

For a quick update on all that's going on north of the border, the best place to look is the Scottish area of the *Daily Mail*'s *Soccernet* site, at: www.soccernet.com/scottish/index.html. Each Premier Division club has its own homepage, including news and match report archives. An area devoted to the national team is promised.

Glasgow

Rangers 461   Celtic 466
Partick Thistle 469

With the possible exception of the Madrid/Barcelona rivalry, there is no game in Europe that arouses as much passion and hatred as the Glasgow derby.

Its roots lie in the violent Irish political struggle whose divisions and loyalties were transferred to Glasgow with the large emmigration of Irish workers to Scotland in the late nineteenth century. Rangers are the team of the city's Protestant community, Celtic represent the Roman Catholics. Rangers were the first to be formed in 1873, with Celtic setting up some fifteen years later.

Celtic, formed from an amalgamation of Catholic Boys' Club sides at the prompting of Brother Walfrid of the Marist Order, made no attempt to hide their affiliations – their name, their colours (emerald green and white) and the Irish tricolour that flew above their main stand, along with close links to the Roman Catholic clergy, were all designed to appeal to one particular section of Glasgwegian society.

By contrast, in their early years Rangers had not shown a great deal of interest in religion. But the foundation of Celtic made them the focus of Protestant support. It was Rangers' unwritten rule of not signing Catholic players, or indeed employing Catholics in any position, that made them the focus of so much criticism, as Scottish authorities struggled to tackle the increasingly violent clashes at derby games between the two teams.

The term 'Old Firm' refers to the profitable nature of the rivalry. The sectarian divide intensified a local rivalry and ensured huge crowds – and revenues – whenever the two sides met. With today's Premier League structure, the two are guaranteed to meet four times in the league season and, given their domination, they usually meet in one or both of the cup competitions (although, as Edinburgh fans are keen to point out, rarely in the semi-finals).

Violence at Old Firm games long preceded the worst of the British hooligan era but, following a series of incidents in the Seventies and a particularly gruesome riot after the 1980 Cup Final, pressure mounted on the clubs to at least reduce the tension, if not renounce their identities. Still Rangers continued to refuse to sign any Catholics, and Celtic, though they had always signed Protestant players, refused the counterdemand that they remove the Irish tricolour from their ground.

Glasgow essentials

Glasgow **airport** is 14km west of the city; bus #500 makes the forty-minute journey every ten minutes to the central **bus station** at Buchanan Street.

There are two main train stations, Queen Street and Central. Trains to and from Edinburgh come in to Queen Street while those from England terminate at Central.

There are plenty of **city buses**, but beware that you have to put the exact change into the slot on entrance – no change will be given. Buses run until around 11.30pm, after which there is a skeleton network of night buses after that. Glasgow also has an **underground** with a flat fare of 65p per journey.

The main **tourist information centre** is at the corner of George Square near the top of Buchanan Street (open Mon–Sat 9am–6pm).

Information on **nightlife** can be found in *The List* – an excellent fortnightly listings magazine covering Glasgow and Edinburgh, it costs £1.80 and the same staff also produce an annual eating and drinking guide to both cities (£1.50).

In 1989, Rangers manager Graeme Souness, having announced on his appointment that religion would play no part in his recruitment of players, shocked Rangers' hardcore Protestant support when he signed Catholic Maurice Johnston. Johnston, a former hero at Celtic, was probably not the ideal choice to break the tradition. A day before he put pen to paper at Ibrox, he had posed for press photos in a Celtic shirt and announced that he would be returning to Celtic Park. In addition, at a derby in the Eighties he had been criticised for crossing himself after scoring.

Although the Old Firm games (two of which are always held at New Year and Easter) are still a focal point for sectarians, with extremist political pamphlets on sale and religious and political songs much in evidence, they are no longer the dangerously violent encounters they once were. Glasgow is no longer divided into Catholic and Protestant districts, and many Rangers and Celtic fans are now neighbours. Nor are the officials of either club any longer afraid to denounce bigotry.

Two's company – the Old Firm boils over

recent years, they have become a wealthy business, too – the first club in Scotland capable of bringing in players from England and the continent. Yet one thing still rankles at Ibrox: unlike Celtic, Rangers have never managed to lift the continent's premier club trophy, the European Cup.

While always among the front-runners from the early days, Rangers firmly established themselves as the top club in the inter-war years when they won fifteen league titles, with sides featuring goalscorers such as Bob McPhail, who scored 233 goals between 1927 and 1939, and Sam English, who hit 44 in the 1931/32 season alone. This was also a period of massive crowds, and the club's record attendance of 118,567 was set at an Old Firm derby in 1939.

Following World War II, Rangers faced a stronger challenge from Edinburgh than from Celtic, but with a side marshalled by the big centre-half George Young, they won three of Scotland's first four postwar championships.

The Sixties saw the 'Gers begin to make an impression in Europe. In 1961 they reached the final of the Cup-Winners' Cup, losing out to Fiorentina. Defeat in the final of the same competition in 1967 was more

The thrilling fields

Rangers

Ibrox Stadium, Edmiston Drive
Capacity 50,500 (all-seated)
Colours Blue shirts, white shorts
League champions 1891, 1899, 1900–2, 1911–13, 1918, 1920–21, 1923–25, 1927–31, 1933–35, 1937, 1939, 1947, 1949–50, 1953, 1956–57, 1959, 1961, 1963–64, 1975–76, 1978, 1987, 1989–97
Cup winners 1894, 1897–98, 1903, 1928, 1930, 1932, 1934–36, 1948–49, 1950, 1953, 1960, 1962–64, 1966, 1973, 1976, 1978–79, 1981, 1992–93, 1996
Cup-Winners' Cup winners 1972

Forty-six titles and counting. Rangers are Scotland's most successful club, period. In

All that glitters – trophies aplenty, but Ibrox wants more

by cup wins, the exciting wing-play of Davie Cooper and the emergence of talented striker Ally McCoist.

But the Rangers of the Seventies and Eighties was an institution in decline. Ironically, for a club which had been a strident campaigner against old-fashioned amateurism at the turn of the century, Rangers had become conservative and unprofessional.

Their policy of not employing Catholics was increasingly under fire from the media and politicians. But aside from the moral and political aspects of the unwritten rule, it just did not make footballing sense. Rangers missed out on two of Scotland's key players of the late Seventies and early Eighties – Celtic and Scotland full-back Danny McGrain, a Rangers-mad youngster who many believe was ignored simply because of his name, and Kenny Dalglish, another Rangers fan as a schoolboy who was snapped up by Celtic. Something had to change.

The elderly board received a shake-up when millionaire entrepeneur David Murray arrived on the scene in the mid-Eighties, determined to introduce modern business methods. Murray wanted change on the field too, and his appointment of Graeme Souness as manager delivered plenty of that. When Souness arrived in 1986, he talked big. His mission was to reverse the pattern of transfer trade with England, end the club's title drought and make Rangers a competitive force in Europe.

But Souness was not a Rangers man. Unlike Greig, he had never played for the club; indeed he had never played in the Scottish league. He started out as player-manager and his own tough tackling, along with those of imported hatchet men such as Englishmen Graham Roberts and Terry Hurlock, gave the impression that Souness was out to create a team of cloggers. Yet the cash provided by Murray also allowed

painful, however. A week before, Celtic had lifted the European Cup and Rangers had the perfect opportuniy to keep the gloating to a minimum – but an extra-time goal by Bayern Munich ended hopes of an Old Firm double in Europe.

In 1971, Ibrox Park had its second tragedy. Fifty years earlier it had been the scene of the world's first football disaster, when a wooden terrace collapsed, killing 26 people. On 2 January 1971, 66 fans leaving Ibrox by stairway #13 at the end of an Old Firm derby were crushed to death, and 145 were injured. It was the worst tragedy in Scottish football history and one which united Rangers and Celtic fans in mourning.

A year after the disaster, Rangers had their greatest moment, finally getting their hands on the Cup-Winners' Cup. Revenge was gained over Bayern in the semi-final and two goals from Willie Johnstone helped win the final against Dynamo Moscow, 3–2, in Barcelona's Nou Camp. Though the club's masterful midfield playmaker Jim Baxter had retired, this Rangers included Alfie Conn, Willy Henderson and full-back John Greig in its ranks.

Greig went on to manage the side in the early Eighties, during a lean spell in which the club failed to win a title between 1978 and 1987. The era was brightened

Souness to bring in more creative English players such as Trevor Francis, Mark Walters and Trevor Steven.

The strategy paid off. Rangers won the title in 1989 and have not let go of it since. The signing of Maurice Johnston was the final confirmation that Souness had no time for the old way of doing things. But the European success demanded by Murray didn't follow. The team hardly had the luck of the draw – they were knocked out of the European Cup in the first round by Bayern Munich in 1989/90, and the following season they succumbed to eventual winners Red Star Belgrade in the second round.

Following Souness' departure for an ill-fated spell in charge of Liverpool in 1991, Rangers continued to look outside Scotland for playing talent under the management of Walter Smith. In 1992/93, they qualified for the quarter-final group stage of the Champions' League, thanks to a memorable two-leg 'Battle of Britain' victory over Leeds United.

Rangers remained unbeaten in the Champions' League. Their 2–2 home draw with Marseille was a classic, played in a frenzied atmosphere, and throughout the campaign the Scottish champions, often with key players missing through injury, and with the three-foreigner rule also depleting their squad, perfomed with great enterprise and guts. Ultimately, Marseille beat them to a place in the final by a single point, gained in their last match against Club Bruges – a game which has since been the subject of a UEFA match-rigging inquiry.

Needless to say, expectations were high for greater things in the coming seasons. But despite continued domination on the home front, Rangers flopped in Europe. In 1993/94 they were knocked out before the Champions' League stage by Levski Sofia, and the following year they were beaten 3–0 on aggregate by AEK Athens in the qualifying round.

Since then, the expansion of the Champions' League has made it easier for Rangers to qualify, but once there, performances have been embarrassingly inept. Some critics of the Scottish League have suggested the gap between domestic competition and Europe is simply too large for

One thing at a time – McCoist celebrates a Champions' League qualifying win in Vladikavkaz

any team to bridge effectively, while some fans have questioned Rangers' style of play and tactical approach.

Chairman David Murray has dismissed suggestions that Rangers may seek to join the English Premiership, preferring to see Rangers as Scotland's representative in a future European League – of which the club have been passionate advocates.

Ibrox, transformed in the late Eighties into an attractive, modern all-seater stadium which has since served as a model for many post-Taylor Report redesigns in England, can boast a fantastic atmosphere when the result is in doubt. But the ease with which Rangers are winning Scottish titles has made the crowd strangely quiet, greeting goals with the nonchalance that assumed victory brings.

Only 'Old Firm' games and European nights see the volume turned up, although the 1997/98 campaign, which sees Rangers trying to break Celtic's record of nine successive national championships, is expected to be more raucous, regardless of the club's European exploits.

Here we go!

Take the **underground** from St Enoch's Square to **Ibrox**. Allow fifteen minutes.

Swift half

Right opposite the Ibrox underground station is **Stadium** which, despite its cheap Seventies exterior, is an attractive pre-match venue with plenty of 'Gers stuff to gaze at while downing a pint. The **Stadium Chip Shop** opposite is a popular meeting place, as the piles of greasy newspaper wrapping floating their way up to the stadium prove.

If you have time to kill, a trip down **Paisley Road** will reveal several pubs packed with fans on matchdays.

Publications

As well as the *Gers* matchday programme at £1.50, the club produces *Rangers News* (also £1.50) a popular monthly magazine which, for an official publication, is also a surprisingly good read. The fanzine *Follow, Follow* (£1) is the established voice of the Ibrox faithful.

Born to be British – Ibrox is one of the few venues in Scotland where you will see the Union Jack

Hampden

Hampden Park, Mount Florida

Scotland's national stadium is effectively **out of action**, as wholescale redevelopment takes place. The decision of the Scottish FA to spend £60 million on rebuilding the ground seems a little strange. With Ibrox and the new Celtic Park, Glasgow already has two stadia suitable for interna-

Return of the roar – Hampden's lights will soon be back on

tional competition. And across in Edinburgh, Murrayfield is a magnificent and badly underused venue.

But Hampden has a history that the FA was not prepared to abandon in the name of economic logic. Until the Fifties, it was the **largest football ground in the world**. Almost 150,000 people paid to see Scotland play England here in 1937 – still a record for any European game, and one unlikely to be surpassed. Arguably the greatest game to take place at Hampden had no Scottish involvement at all. In May 1960, a crowd of 130,000 saw **Real Madrid**, with Puskás and di Stéfano, destroy Eintracht Frankfurt 7–3 to win their fifth consecutive European Cup.

Safety restrictions imposed following the Ibrox disaster saw Hampden's capcity reduced to little more than 70,000, and with modern stadia appearing across Britain during the Eighties and Nineties, scruffy old Hampden had lost its appeal.

Until the stadium is reopened sometime in 1998, Scottish internationals are being played at a range of venues including Ibrox, Celtic Park, Aberdeen's Pittodrie and Kilmarnock's Rugby Park. The only football being played at Hampden at the moment is by the stadium's owners, Queen's Park, who still faithfully stage Third Division games here in front of a few hundred loyal souls.

To join them for a taste of history, take **bus #45** or **#57** from the centre of town – the journey takes around twenty minutes.

There is a **lack of pubs** in the area around Hampden and most fans tend to drink in their 'club' bars before internationals. On the bus route you'll pass the **Brazen Head** at 1–3 Cathcart Road, which proclaims itself to be Europe's only Irish-Italian bar. The theme is illustrated on the walls with a collection of Italian soccer shirts and Gaelic football memorabilia.

Club shop

The **Rangers Shop** at 21 Trongate in the centre of town is open Mon–Sat 9.30am–5.30pm, Sun midday–5pm. At the ground, the **1873 Superstore** has a bigger range. It's open Mon–Sat 9.30am–5.30pm.

In the net

Pending the arrival of an official website, one of the best sources of online info is the so-called *Rangers Webzine* at www.x-static.demon.co.uk/rangers. It's superbly presented and offers results, fixtures, player biogs and news stories from Glasgow newspapers. Also worth a peek is Sandy MacKinnon's eccentric homepage at: wkweb4.cableinet.co.uk/smackinnon. Sandy is a Rangers fan who promises "tedious things like football, drinking and music," on his site, and delivers in spades.

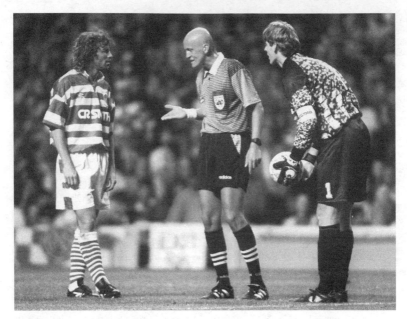

Lord shave us – another Celtic European run comes to an end before it has started

 ## Celtic

Celtic Park, 95 Kerrydale Street
Capacity 47,500
Colours Green-and-white hooped shirts, white shorts
League champions 189–94, 1896, 1898, 1905–10, 1914–17, 1919, 1922, 1926, 1936, 1938, 1954, 1966–74, 1977, 1979, 1981–82, 1986, 1988
Cup winners 1892, 1899, 1900, 1904, 1907–8, 1911–12, 1914, 1923, 1925, 1927, 1931, 1933, 1937, 1951, 1954, 1965, 1967, 1969, 1971–72, 1974–75, 1977, 1980, 1985, 1988–89, 1995
European Cup winners 1967

Nowhere is the transformation of a football club from central component of a working-class community to a multi-million pound business more evident than in the East End of Glasgow, home of Celtic Football Club.

Not so long ago, the area around the ground was home to shipbuilders and factory workers, who on a Saturday afternoon would pour out of the terraced houses and corner pubs to make their way to Celtic Park. Today, the shining plastic and steel of the redesigned stadium stands in the middle of an area of extreme social problems. Boarded-up houses blight the nearby streets, while inside the ground, the terraces have been replaced by new stands and executive boxes.

Disturbing though Celtic Park's environment might be, the new stadium also symbolises the revitilisation of one of Britain's most famous clubs. After a decade of decline, discontent and defeats by Rangers, Celtic are at last in shape to launch a serious challenge on the hegemony of their rivals.

As Celtic fans are keen to remind themselves, Rangers' run in the Nineties is the second time that one of the Glasgow clubs has enjoyed a decade of domination. From 1966 on, Celtic lifted nine consecutive titles – a record equalled by Rangers in 1997. But it was the European title they won during this era which is most fondly remembered. In 1967, Celtic reached the final of the European Cup for the first time, where they met Inter Milan. Inter were clear favourites – with the defensive *catenaccio* system mastered by their coach Helenio Herrera, they had won the competition in 1964 and 1965 and had narrowly lost in the semi-finals in 1966. Celtic manager Jock Stein was determined that the game would be a battle of styles. Before the game, he told the *Observer* reporter Hugh McIlvanney: "We want to win it playing good football, to make neutrals glad we've done it, glad to remember how we did it."

How they did it was to go at Inter and give a display of passionate, attacking football allied with the traditional ruggedness of Scottish sides. Little red-haired winger Jimmy Johnstone, with his jinking runs and pace, provided the creativity, Bertie Auld in midfield and Tommy Gemmell at left-back typified the graft and effort that Stein inspired. Celtic's 2–1 victory made them the first British side to lift the continent's premier club trophy, but the 'Lisbon Lions' were acclaimed across a continent delighted to see the death of Inter's dull tactics.

Three years later, in the semi-final of the same competition, Celtic defeated Don Revie's Leeds United – a side as unpopular as Herrera's Inter – in front of 136,000 at Hampden. But the elation of victory in the 'Battle of Britain' was soured when the Bhoys lost in extra-time to Feyenoord in the final.

Within a year, Stein had dismantled the squad and begun creating a new side for the Seventies, including forwards Kenny Dalglish and Lou Macari, who

were to go on to lengthy careers at Liverpool and Manchester United respectively.

The departure of Dalglish in 1977, coupled with Stein's resignation a year later, marked the end of the Celtic glory years. One of Stein's old charges, Billy McNeill, created a championship-winning side in the early Eighties, but financial problems at the club were beginning to have an impact on the team. Top players such as Charlie Nicholas, Brian McClair and Maurice Johnstone were lured away by English clubs.

In the late Eighties and early Nineties, the club had a string of unsuccessful managers and an ongoing boardroom battle. A takeover bid by former director Brian Dempsey, who had wanted to take the club to a new stadium in the Robroyston district, divided the board. The club's need to redevelop or move their stadium in the wake of the Taylor Report was one of the points of conflict, but while the arguments were raging, Celtic were slipping further and further into debt.

In March 1994, the Bank of Scotland announced they were ready to call in the receivers – but at the eleventh hour, the club was sold to a Canadian businessman, Fergus McCann.

The new chairman kept his pledge to redvelop the existing stadium and to provide cash to spend on imported players, recognising that to try to conquer Europe

Down we go – former player and coach Lou Macari shows the way

Hoop springs eternal – Alan Stubbs

as Jock Stein did three decades ago – with what was essentially a team of Glasgow Boys' Club players – is impossible in the modern era. But McCann's sacking of coach Tommy Burns before the end of Celtic's trophyless 1996/97 campaign divided fans, and led to the acrimonious departure of the very stars the chairman's money had brought to the club – among them the popular Italian, Paolo di Canio.

Already a fragile entity, the new sense of optimism at Celtic Park may not endure beyond another season of disharmony in the dressing room and failure on the pitch.

Here we go!
From **Argyle Street** in the centre of town, take one of **buses #61s, #62b** or **#62c** down London Road, getting off at Springfield Road. The journey takes around fifteen minutes.

Swift half
There are a couple of rough pubs on Springfield Road but most fans looking for a pint head for the **Barrowlands area,** which is along the bus route to the ground or a ten-minute walk from Argyle Street. **Baird's Bar**, next door to the market at 244 Gallowgate, has non-stop football from *Sky Sports* or Celtic videos on the TV screens, features live music at weekends and has an enormous collection of Celtic scarves. You could well catch Jimmy Johnstone in post-match discussion.

Johnstone and his team-mates are the theme at **Bar 67** across the road at 257 Gallowgate – a tribute bar to the Lisbon Lions. The **Hoops Bar** at 227 Gallowgate promises "you"ll never drink alone" at its entrance. It offers live Irish folk music during the week and is cluttered with Hoops memorabilia.

If you are sick of the sight of Shamrocks then the **Hielan Jessie** at 370 Gallowgate is a small, spartan pub, with the rarity of a Celtic-supporting landlord who has a true blue son.

Publications
As well as the matchday programme, the club produce *Celtic View* (£1.40) a long-established monthly newspaper. The latter's rather conservative approach explains the title of the most popular Celtic fanzine, *Not The View* (£1). *Our Day Will Come* (also £1) is a joint Celtic-Manchester United fanzine.

Club shop
There are three official outlets for green-and-white merchandise. The **Celtic Shop** at 21 High Street is the most central (open Mon–Sat 9.30am– 5.30pm), but there is also a fair-sized shop by the stadium at 95 Kerrydale Street (open Mon–Sat 9am–5pm, later on matchdays) and a rather smaller store at 40 Dundas Street (open Mon–Sat 9am–5pm).

In the net
You need to register to get the best from the official Celtic website, but 'guest' users can have a peek at: www.celticfc.co.uk. What's on offer is a slow but extremely comprehensive site, complete with multimedia areas and a 'Boot-room' chat forum.

Groundhopping

⚫ Partick Thistle

Firhill Park, 80 Firhill Road
Capacity 22,000
Colours Red-and-yellow striped shirts, black shorts
Cup winners 1921

Forever in the shadow of Glasgow's big two, Partick Thistle have nonetheless produced a number of top players, the club acting as a safety net for those ignored by Rangers and Celtic. Long-time Scottish national-team 'keeper Alan Rough spent the greater part of his career at Firhill; elegant Liverpool defender and later TV pundit Alan Hansen began his career with here; and Maurice Johnston also started out in the a red-and-yellow striped shirt.

The Jags won the Scottish Cup in 1921 and the League Cup in 1971, but have spent much of their life bobbing up and down between the top flight and the next rung down. The team are currently in the First Division, their games attracting a number of Rangers and Celtic fans enjoying the relaxed good humour of the Firhill support, which prides itself on being anti-sectarian.

Take the **underground** as far as **St George's Cross** and you will see the ground, five minutes' walk away. There are a couple of **pubs** where Thistle support can sink a swiftie free from the jibes of greens and blues – the **Star & Garter** on Garstube Road and the **Munns Vaults** on Maryhill Road.

Eat, drink, sleep…

Bars and clubs
In recent years, Glasgow nightlife has improved significantly with the city gaining a strong reputation for its **dance clubs**. Irish theme bars have popped up all over the city, along with European-style **café bars**. But the traditional **Glasgow pub** survives in the suburbs, serving malt whisky, Scottish bitter 'heavy' and the traditional bar snack of stovies and meat pies. All the places listed below are centrally located.

Café Cini, 81 Renfield Street. Close to St Enoch's Square and owned by former Chelsea and Arsenal striker Charlie Nicholas, this café bar serves light meals and sandwiches until 7pm when the DJs take over with pre-club sounds. Occasional happy hours for cocktails.

McNeill's, 106 Torrisdale Street. Twice manager of Celtic (and one of the many who tried and failed at Maine Road), former Bhoys midfielder Billy McNeill has followed the familar career path into pub management. Masses of memorabilia, along with a full menu and wide choice of whisky. Open until 11pm midweek, midnight weekends.

Beaten up Jag – Thistle suffer more than most from relegation blues

Sub Club, 22 Jamaica Street. Packed out on sweaty Saturdays but busy throughout the rest of the weekend as well, a friendly club with a full range of dancefloor sounds, respected resident and guest DJs.

The Arches, Midland Street (off Jamaica Street). Popular dance club with guest DJs from all over the UK and Europe popping in for weekend sessions of house and techno.

The Mitre Bar,12–16 Brunswick Street. Intimate ittle bar just off Argyle Street with football shown in downstairs. Upstairs is a comfortable lounge. Offers an incredible three-course lunch of decent pub food for £3. Open until midnight.

Restaurants

Long gone are the days when eating out in Glasgow meant a hot haggis or else. These days the city prides itself on being Scotland's **culinary centre** although, that said, you could still do a lot worse than the local fish and chips.

The Buttery, 652 Argyle Street. Renowned Scottish restaurant specialising in game, venison and salmon, with a wide range of vegetarian options and excellent country soups. Three-course lunch deal for around £15. Closed Sunday.

Crème de la Crème, 1071 Argyle Street. Glasgow has plenty of quality Indian restuarants to choose from, but this one differs in that it is located in a converted cinema, meaning plenty of room. Full range of Asian dishes. Open daily until midnight.

Panini's,186 West Regent Street. Ideal breakfast or lunch place in the centre of town. Rolls, bagels, croissants and a range of breads with all kinds of fillings, simple and exotic. The home-made pasta and Italian soups are a good, cheap lunch option. Closed weekends.

The Ubiquitous Chip,12 Ashton Lane. If you're going to splash out on a taste of Scotland, then do it here at Glasgow's most famous restaurant. Haggis, steak, salmon, stews and game. Expect

to pay around £25 for a three-course lunch during the week, but there are Sunday lunch deals for around £15. **Upstairs At The Chip** is a smaller, more affordable bistro version, offering variations on the same theme. Closes 11pm.

Walfrid Restaurant, Celtic Park, 95 Kerrydale Street. A stadium restaurant that has been given the seal of approval by Glasgow's culinary reviewers. Traditional Scottish menu with three-course lunches for £10 and three-course dinners for £15, served in a room with tasteful and restrained memorabilia. Open until 9pm. Closed Sundays. Book in advance if you want a post-match meal or the £18.95 Saturday cabaret and meal in the adjacent Jock Stein Lounge: ☎0141/551 9955.

Accommodation

Glasgow has plenty of low-cost B&B options plus some more upmarket places aimed at the business community which do good **weekend deals**.

Albion Hotel, 405–407 North Woodside Road (☎0141/339 8620). Small hotel offering B&B for £36 a single, and £23 per person in a double/twin. Just a mile from the city centre, easily accessible by underground to Kelvinbridge.

Argyll Hotel, 973 Sauchiehall Street (☎0141/337 3313). Just by Kelvingrove Park, a recently refurbished period hotel, with bar and restaurant. B&B from £50 single, £30 per person in a twin.

Hampton Court Hotel, 230 Renfrew Street (☎0141/332 6623). Small B&B in the centre with a fixed price of £17 per head. Just three single and four double rooms, so book ahead.

Holiday Inn Garden Court, 161 West Nile Street (☎0141/332 0110). Opened in 1995 and in the theatre district, next to the Royal Concert Hall and the Theatre Royal. Pricey but comfy. Around £60 per room.

IYHAF Youth Hostel, 7–8 Park Terrace (☎0141/332 3004). Handily placed in the West End of the city, and open all year round. Cardholders only.

Edinburgh

🌑 Hibernian 472
🌑 Heart of Midlothian 474

The Scottish capital boasts the nation's largest and most impressive stadium, but the 65,000-capacity Murrayfield is the home of Scottish rugby union. The stadium is filled every year for Five Nations rugby championship games, while Edinburgh's two round-ball teams – Hibernian and Heart of Midlothian – both struggle to fill their two grounds. Not since the Fifties, when both clubs won titles, has Edinburgh been a real force in Scottish football.

The two clubs both aim to become Scotland's third force, behind the Old Firm. It was a

Lonely vigil – a few Hibs loyalists keep watch at Easter Road

status they took turns to hold until the early Eighties, when Aberdeen and Dundee United emerged as new challengers from the north. Although those two clubs have faded in the Nineties there has been no resurgence in Edinburgh, with occasional cup runs the only hints of possible success.

The rivalry between Hibs and Hearts is nowhere near as intense as that of the Old Firm, but has a similar background. Hibs preceded Celtic as being the club of Scotland's Irish Catholic immigrants, but in the modern era, the club's owners have sought to distance themselves from their origins. Likewise, though Hearts are labelled a Protestant club, today you are unlikely to hear much in the way of Loyalist chants or see union jacks at Tynecastle.

Today's Edinburgh rivalry has more to do with location. Hearts draw their traditional support from Gorgie in the west, Hibs from the port of Leith to the east of the city. Nor, contrary to many English misconceptions, do fans of the Edinburgh clubs automatically have sympathies for their Glasgow equivalents. Hearts have lost many good players to Rangers down the years,

and Hibs to Celtic. If anything, a strong anti-Glasgow feeling binds Edinburgh's football fans together.

Until recently there was a third club in the capital. Meadowbank Thistle emerged out of the works team Ferranti Thistle but never managed to get anywhere near worrying the traditional two. In 1995 they gave up, moving out of the city to become Livingston FC.

Edinburgh's football scene was almost radically altered in 1990 when the then Hearts chairman, Wallace Mercer, announced his intention to take over and then close down Hibernian. The attempt provoked fierce opposition from Hibs supporters who rallied to save their club from extinction. It wasn't only at Easter Road where the plan was opposed – the idea of losing the derby didn't appeal much to Hearts fans, either.

Although neither club can hope to compete with the Old Firm in the transfer market, Edinburgh fans hope they may yet see a return to the *status quo* of the Sixties, when Europe's finest travelled regularly to the city with justified trepidation.

The mean green – Chris Jackson lets fly

The thrilling fields

 Hibernian

Easter Road Stadium, Albion Road
Capacity 16,000
Colours Green shirts with white sleeves, white shorts
League champions 1903, 1948, 1951
Cup winners 1887, 1902

Hibs are the original club of Scotland's Irish Catholic community. Formed in 1875, they took their name from the Roman word for Ireland and it was stated in their constitution that all players must be practising Catholics. So close were their Irish connections that the club were actually barred from the early Scottish competitions.

In recognition of their status, Hibs were invited to be the opposition for the opening of Celtic's ground. But the fraternal relations between the two clubs did not last long. When Celtic poached half the Hibs players, the team never recovered

and after a few struggling seasons, the club folded in 1891. Two years later Hibs were reformed (without the sectarian clause in their constitution), and the new team continued to play at the old club's Easter Road ground.

Hibs' golden era came after World War II. They lifted the title with a young side in 1948, then again in 1951 and 1952. The team included a frontline tagged 'The Famous Five' – Gordon Smith, Bobby Johnstone, Lawrie Reilly, Eddie Turnbull and Willie Ormond. It was a team that played the Scottish game at its best – positive, attacking football full of flowing passing and neat, swift movement off the ball.

In 1955 Hibs became the first British side to enter the European Cup, reaching the semi-finals where they lost to the French side Stade de Reims. It would not be the club's last continental adventure – indeed, Hibs' performances in Europe have been impressive for a club that have won so little on the domestic front.

In 1961 they reached the semi-finals of the Fairs' Cup, after a thrilling 7–6 aggregate win over Barcelona. In the same competition seven years later they defeated Porto home and away, then played one of the most memorable games in the club's history – trailing 4–1 down to Napoli from the away leg, Hibs destroyed the Italians in Edinburgh, putting five goals past a visiting 'keeper by the name of Dino Zoff.

There has been little joy for the Hibees since the early Seventies. Badly managed at both boardroom and dugout level, the club entered a deep decline which resulted in relegation for the first time in 1980. They bounced back after a season quickly, but it took the hostile takeover bid from Hearts in 1990 to truly awaken the club. Faced with the prospect of their team's extinction, dormant fans came crawling out of the woodwork in order to ensure the club survived. The protests and fundraising gave Hibs an unlikely boost, and in 1992 they won their first trophy for almost twenty years, clinching the League Cup. But that team, created by manager Alex Miller, failed to develop and by the mid-Nineties the club was in trouble again, flirting with relegation.

Ground developments have spoilt the traditional feel of Easter Road and obscured the famous view of Arthur's Seat, an extinct volcano in nearby Holyrood Park. The Hibees may be a frustrated bunch but they are grateful that at least their fire didn't go out for good.

Here we go!
Bus #1 from the Royal Mile will take you to Easter Road; **bus #6** makes the journey back. Alternatively, from Princes Street take **bus #75, #106** or **#108** along London Road, getting off at Easter Road. After walking down Easter Road take a right down Albion Road to the ground.

Swift half
Easter Road is almost as famous for bars as for its football ground. **Middletons** at #71 has a big-screen TV and fading black-and-white Hibs photos. The **Royal Nip** (#171), on the corner of Albert Street, has the Hibs logo built into its bar. The area also boasts **The Chocolate Shop**, 28 West Norton Place, on the corner of Easter Road and London Road, serving all kinds

of traditional boiled sweets, magnificent fudge and handmade chocolates.

The club's **Forthview Restaurant** in the new north stand is not open for pre-match meals. It is open, however, for lunch during the week and Sundays (noon–2pm) and Friday and Saturday evenings for dinner (7.30–10.30pm). If you fancy a post-match nosh-up, then reservations are recommended: ☎0131/661 3618.

Publications
The matchday programme costs £1.50. There are two fanzines, *Hibees Here, Hibees There* and *Mass Hibsteria*. The latter is particularly strong on info about the latest boardroom problems.

Club shop
The store at the stadium (Mon–Fri 9am–5pm, Sat 9.30am–5.30pm) has all the essential Hibee fashion, plus one of the most preposterous footie videos of all time, *Hibernian – The Club That Refused To Die*; this romanticises the fight against the Mercer takeover and glorifies the 1992 League Cup win, as well as featuring those famous Hibs fans, folk-pop duo The Proclaimers.

In the net
The club have kept everything nice and simple on the Hibs official homepage, at: www.hibs.co.uk/home.htm. The site has up-to-date ticket information as well as the usual attributes. For a more off-the-wall look at Hibee life, try: www.mmse.napier.ac.uk/~jfairley/hibby.html.

Edinburgh essentials

Edinburgh **airport** is 14km west of the centre, the airport buses provides a frequent service into town, around the clock– the journey takes around half an hour. Travelling from England, you'll come into he main train station, Waverley, which is slap bang in the centre with Princes Street and the castle on either side.

At St Andrews Square you'll find the **bus terminal** for both local and inter-city services. The city is well-covered by **local buses**. As in Glasgow, make sure you have exact change for the slot on entrance as no change is given. Services run until around 11.30, and there are a few night buses after that.

The main **tourist information centre** is just up the steps from the train station at 3 Princes Street (open daily 9am–5.30pm).

🌐 Heart of Midlothian

Tynecastle Park, Gorgie Road
Capacity c18,000 (after reconstruction)
Colours Maroon shirts, white shorts
League champions 1895, 1897, 1958, 1960
Cup winners 1891, 1896, 1901, 1906, 1956.

Heart of Midlothian were named after the dance hall in which the club was formed. The name springs from the nickname for an old prison by St Giles' Cathedral, which was taken as the title for a novel by Walter Scott and was adopted by several civic organisations. Today, three of these remain – a swimming club, a budgerigar lovers' club, and the football team.

Hearts made an immediate impact, winning two league titles and two cups around the turn of the century, when Bobby Walker emerged as one of the early stars of the Scottish league. Yet it was just as Walker was hanging up his boots that Hearts wrote their name into history. At the outbreak of war in 1914, the entire team, then top of the league, volunteered for the armed forces – a move which encouraged many of their supporters to follow suit. Seven of the squad were killed in action and their names are honoured at a memorial at the Haymarket, where supporters gather to pay their respects every Armistice Day.

In the seasons immediately after World War II, Hearts attracted record crowds across the country to watch their attractive and attacking football. Titles followed in 1954, 1957 and 1959 – the club's best postwar period. Tommy Walker's side included Dave Mackay, who went on to a successful career with Tottenham and Derby County. Mackay was the classic hardman, powerfully built with a fearsome tackle, yet also with the ability to distribute the ball.

The Jam Tarts, as Hearts are known, lost their way in the Seventies. bobbing up and down between the top two flights. After returning to the Premier in 1983, the club built a new-look team around the defensive stability of Dave McPherson and the goals of striker John Robertson. This was to be the side which, in 1986, had a league and cup double in sight but ended with nothing after losing their last two games of the season. McPherson and Robertson left for Rangers and Newcastle, respectively, but both have since returned to see out their careers at Hearts, with Robertson becoming the club's record goalscorer.

Stadium redevelopment at Tynecastle was long overdue but one consequence of the latest work at the Gorgie Road End has been to end the free matchday views for residents of the apartments behind that goal. The change is a particular blow for the resident of a third-floor flat who for years has taunted visiting fans by dangling a maroon scarf from the safety of his bedroom.

Here we go!

From the Waverley Centre on Princes Street, take **bus #3, #3a, #21** or **#33** to Tynecastle. The journey takes about twenty minutes.

Swift half

The **Tynecastle Arms** at 1 McLeod Street is the nearest pub to the ground and as a result gets packed on matchdays. A better bet is the **Athletic Arms** at 1–3 Angle Park Terrace; until a few years ago, the thirteen beer pumps here were reserved exclusively for Eighty Shilling, and while concessions have been made to lager and Guinness drinkers, you can still just ask for "two" and the bar staff will know what you mean. Worth visiting even if there is no game at Tynecastle, the pub, known locally as 'Diggers', has a collection of framed Hearts and Scotland team photos, a knowledgeable clientèle and hot bar snacks – it closes at 6pm on Sundays.

Publications

As well as the well-produced matchday programme (£1.50), there are a couple of fanzines – *Always The Bridesmaid* and *No Idle Talk*.

Club shop

The **Hearts Shop**, on the corner of McLeod Street behind the north stand (open Mon–Fri 9am–5pm, Sat 9am–3pm) has a limited range of Jambo gear. Look out for the trader who operates on match-days at the corner of Murieston Lane – he has an excellent range of European enamel club badges as well as Hearts T-shirts.

In the net

The club's official website is located at: www.heartsfc.co.uk. Though not particularly original, it has all the basics and is smart-looking, with the new club badge – subject of some dissent among fans – very much to the fore. Meanwhile, proudly displaying the old logo is the *Electronic Jam Tart* at: www.ednet.co.uk/~rkw/index.htm, a friendly, unofficial news-and-links site.

Eat, drink, sleep...

Bars and clubs

While it may not enjoy quite as high a reputation as Glasgow for its nightlife, Edinburgh is a **good night out**, with an increasingly cosmopolitan scene. As with Glasgow, check out *The List* magazine for the latest on clubbing.

The Caley Sample Room, 58 Angle Park Terrace. Just down the road from Tynecastle, this is an ideal venue for watching games on TV. *Sky Sports* plus Caledonian ales, cask whiskies and pub grub. Live music once the game has finished.

Carwash, 11 North Bank Street. The lilac exterior makes this a must for Fiorentina and Újpest fans. Inside you'll find kitsch Seventies décor, cocktails and American snacks. DJs most nights make this a good warm-up spot before clubbing. Open until 1am.

La Belle Angele, 11 Hasties Close. Top spot for house, techno and mainstream dance. The Yip Yap nights with imported DJs are the main attraction, along with *Club Latino* on Fridays. £5–6 cover charge.

Mathers, 25 Broughton Street. Offering good guest ales along with the usual Scottish bitter, this is one of the more down-to-earth of Edinburgh's central pubs – the sport on TV is a rarity in this part of town. Open until midnight.

King of the Jam Tarts – John Robertson just misses out on silverware once again

French lesson – Hearts 'keeper Rousset

St James Oyster Bar, 2 Calton Road. There are a number of oyster bars in Edinburgh and this is the biggest. As well as the fresh oysters, traditional bar food and tex-mex snacks supplement a good range of real ales and bottle beers. Close to the Playhouse Theatre. Open until 1am.

Restaurants

Eating-out **standards are high** in Edinburgh, but many restaurants are geared heavily toward the tourist trade, and during the International Arts Festival in late August and early September, anywhere around the Royal Mile will be intolerable. If you can't avoid hitting town at this time, try to eat somewhere suburban...

Alfredo's, 109 Hanover Street. Unpretentious Italian place with plenty of fish dishes on the menu. Good-value lunchtime deal gets you a three-course meal for around £5.

Bay of Bengal, 164 High Street. Right in the centre of the city, this is a popular lunchtime spot

thanks to its £5 three-course business lunches. Indian and Bangladeshi flavours, as you'd expect.

Bronx American Café, 9 Baxters Place. Daft name, excellent fast food. All-day breakfast, baked potatoes, burgers and chips are the staples. Eat in or take out.

City Café, 19 Blair Street. Now famous as the venue for the pub fight scene in *Trainspotting*, the café offers excellent coffee and hot or cold club sandwiches.

Jackson's, 209 High Street. Most of Edinburgh's Scottish restaurants target the business and tourist markets and their prices reflect this. Jackson's offers the oysters, salmon, haggis and lamb at more reasonable prices. The daily lunch menu is excellent value at around £6, but set dinners are around three times that price.

Accommodation

The advice is simple – avoid Festival time. Though it may be tempting to try to catch some **footie before autumn** takes a hold, you've got no chance of finding anywhere to stay. Rest of the year, you should have little difficulty.

Edinburgh Backpackers Hostel, 65 Cockburn Street (☎0131/337 1120) £10.45 a head in four- to eight- bedded rooms, in the city centre. Price includes breakfast. Closed December.

King James Thistle Hotel, 107 Leith Street (☎0131/556 0111). Large, fairly upmarket hotel just off Princes Street with en-suite B&B from £60. Close to all the main tourist attractions. Restaurant and *Boston Bean Company* bar.

Jarvis Mount Royal Hotel, 53 Princes Street (☎0131/225 7161) En-suite B&B from £45, in a large hotel on the city's busiest shopping and tourist street.

Royal Circus Hotel, 19–21 Royal Circus (☎0131/220 5000) Quiet but central location, offering B&B from £26 and good deals on single rooms. Easy walk to all the major sights.

Slovakia

The 'velvet divorce' that separated Slovakia from its Czech neighbours on January 1, 1993 created another new member of UEFA from the former Communist bloc. But Slovakia should not be dismissed as just another minor East European nation with poor prospects in international football. Slovak players had been a regular part of the Czechoslovak national team, while Slovak clubs had represented the country in Europe, at times with great success. This may have been a 'new' country in the political sense, but in footballing terms Slovakia was already well established.

Independence created a number of headaches for the local game, however. A national league had to be set up in a country where little more than half a dozen clubs had spent any length of time in the top flight of the old Czechoslovak league. And a national team had to be thrown together in time for the Euro '96 qualifiers.

The upheavals caused by these changes should not be under-estimated but, after fears that the game might lose support and that there wasn't the strength in-depth for a competitive domestic league and a strong national team, Slovak football is on the up. Attendances are rising, the quality of football has improved and the national team have gelled into a respectable side.

Prior to World War II, in the first Czechoslovak republic, Slovak teams failed to make any impact on the nationwide league between its establishment in 1925 and the outbreak of hostilities. Bratislava, then a cosmopolitan city made up of Germans, Jews and Hungarians as well as Slovaks, had a number of teams based on ethnic lines, such as the Hungarian club Pozsonyi TE. With the exception of PTE, which went on to become Petržalka, none of these minority clubs survived the war

Slovakia's first coach – Jozef Vengloš

and the 'Slovakisation' of Bratislava. This took place during the period of Slovak 'independence' between 1939 and 1945, when the country was ruled by the Fascist dictator Jozef Tiso and was little more than a puppet state of Nazi Germany. A national league was briefly played for and was dominated by Slovan, then playing under the name of SK Bratislava. The Slovak national team played sixteen games in this period, the bulk of them against allies Croatia, Romania and Germany; they won only three times.

After the war, the Communists reunited Slovakia with the Czech provinces of Bohemia and Moravia. In the second Czechoslovak league which then emerged, Slovan became a respected force, winning three titles in the immediate postwar period. By the Sixties, 1.FC Košice and Spartak Trnava had also become Slovak clubs to be reckoned with. Between 1968 and 1975, the championship trophy never left Slovak soil. Indeed, in 1973 the top three clubs were all Slovak.

This dominance was reflected in the make-up of the Czechoslovak national team, and the Czechoslovakia squad which won the 1976 European Championship was dominated by Slovak players. Little wonder, then, that when the Czech Republic reached the final of Euro '96, supporters in both Bratislava and Prague were wryly describing it as Czech football's best-ever achievement.

Today, having initially struggled under the idealistic leadership of the former Czechoslovak national-team coach (and Aston Villa manager) Jozef Vengloš, the modern Slovak national side are beginning to at least punch their own weight –

although qualification for a major finals still seems a long-term project.

At club level, while Slovan remain the best-resourced team in the land, the past couple of seasons have seen a revival in the fortunes of Spartak Trnava and 1.FC Košice. The city of Trnava may have a population of only 72,000, but that doesn't prevent Spartak from pulling in average gates of around 15,000, and most of them seem to travel away for the big games in Bratislava and Košice.

In Košice itself, the VSS ironworks back the local favourites and their money has enabled the club to attract some talented players. In February of 1997 the team caused a stir when they signed Hungarian international András Telek from Ferencváros, and Košice's ambitious owners, who also have a controlling interest in Sparta Prague, appear intent on acquiring more clubs in former Communist Europe.

Basics

Americans and EU nationals need only a **passport** to enter the Slovak Republic. Australian, New Zealand and Canadian citizens require a **visa**, available at your local Slovak embassy or at border crossings.

The **Slovak crown** – or koruna, abbreviated as Sk – is divided into 100 almost worthless heller. Coins come in denominations of 1, 2, 5, 10, 20 and 50, with 20, 50, 100, 200, 500 and 1000 crown notes. There are about 50Sk to £1.

The Slovak crown is not convertible in the West, so **keep your receipts** to change currency back when you leave.

Banks give the best rates for **currency exchange**, at the desk marked *zmenáreň*. They are generally open Mon–Fri 8am–5pm. You'll find at least one **cash machine** in most main Slovak towns – don't count on finding it in a hurry. In Bratislava there's one in the main train station, inside the entrance to the right, and a handful along the main streets of Špitálska and Laurinská.

The **telephone code** for Slovakia from abroad is 421; add a 7 for Bratislava. From inside Slovakia, dial 00 to call abroad, followed by the country code. There is no cheap time to make an international call, but the Slovak telecom company recently dropped their United Kingdom call rate to 29Sk per minute.

Most public call boxes now take **phone cards**, available at newsstands and post offices at 100Sk for 50 units or 200Sk for 100. Coin phones are only really useful for local calls and take 2Sk or 5Sk coins.

When it comes to travelling around the country, Slovak **trains** are cheap, reliable and generally preferable to **buses**, though still a tad sluggish. A *rýchlik* is the faster and more expensive between towns; an *osobný* will stop everywhere.

International through trains may be delayed at borders and will require a seat reservation (*miestenka*).

All change – after six years with Ferencváros András Telek was tempted to move to Slovakia

Essential vocabulary

Hello *Ahoj*
Goodbye *Do videnia*
Yes *Áno*
No *Nie*
Two beers, please *Prosím si dve pivá*
Thank You *Dakujem*
Men's *Páni*
Women's *Dámy*
Where is the stadium? *Kde je štadión?*
What's the score? *Aký se stav?*
Referee *Rozhodca*
Offside *Mimo hry*

Match practice

Crowds for the first two seasons of the Slovak league were dreadful, with few games attracting more than 3000 and a depressing number failing to pull in four figures. It was a stark contrast to the days when matches against the big Prague teams (Sparta, Slavia or Dukla) would attract 30,000 or more Czech-baiting Slovaks.

More recently, however, matches between Slovakia's own big three – Slovan, 1.FC Košice and Spartak Trnava – have brought in crowds of over 20,000, fuelling hopes that those who turned their backs on football after independence can be persuaded to return to the game they love.

Slovak football takes a long winter break. The first half of the season starts in the first week of August and runs until the last week of November. The second half kicks off in the first week of March, and the final round of games is not played until the end of June.

Matches are usually played on Saturday afternoons; kick-off times vary throughout the season but are usually around 4–5pm, except in November when many games start at 1.30pm to avoid expensive floodlight use. One game from each round is usually played on a Sunday afternoon for TV purposes, while some smaller clubs play on Sunday mornings in an attempt to maximise crowds.

The bigger Slovak stadia are better than most in Eastern Europe, but facilities in general are limited. Don't come expecting executive boxes, wheelchair access or sophisticated half-time 'entertainment'.

Quick feet – Slovakia's playmaker Peter Dubovsky

Yet the gamble has paid off. There is now less pressure on the smaller clubs, whose development has enabled the Slovak league to become a truly national competition for the first time since independence, while rising attendances have lessened the impact on the big boys of what is a potentially less attractive fixture list.

The bottom two of the top flight go down at the end of the season, to be replaced by the top two from Slovakia's eighteen-club second division. The third division is split into four regional groups – West, Central, East, and Bratislava, each with eighteen clubs – and every year the champions of each division are promoted to replace the bottom four in the second division. The fourth tier consists of district leagues.

Up for the cup

Slovakia had its own cup competition as long ago as 1970. Between then and the break-up of Czechoslovakia, the winner of the Slovak Cup played off against the winner of the Czech Cup to decide the overall Czechoslovak Cup, which was known as the *Interpohár*. These days the first round of the *Slovenského pohár* takes place in the first week of August and involves 32 teams. Most matches are single-leg, and if the scores are level after ninety minutes there are penalties with no recourse to extra time. The semi-finals are two-legged, with extra time if necessary. The final takes place at a neutral ground in the first week of June, with extra time and penalties if needed.

The league

After independence in 1993, the Slovak championship was modelled along Swiss lines. Twelve teams played each other home and away, after which the top six went off to form a championship group and the bottom six were sent into a relegation section.

For the 1996/97 season, the Slovak FA decided to drop its 'two-halves' season and adopted a conventional sixteen-club first division. The move was strongly opposed by the major clubs and by most leading personalities in the game. The arrival of four weak teams from the second division was deemed unnecessary, and the fact that the top clubs would meet each other only twice a year clearly had financial as well as footballing drawbacks.

Tickets

As there is rarely danger of not getting in, tickets are bought at the stadium. A standing ticket costs upward of 15Sk, a seat no more than 35Sk. The crucial wording on your ticket will be *tribúna* (stand), *stane* (terrace), *rady* (row) and *sedadlá* (seat).

Half-time

No surprises here – it's that staple of Central European football cooking, beer and sausages. Both tend to be good, though. If you're lucky the beer will be Czech, though Slovak brands aren't a bad second best. Sausages come in two main varieties. The *klobása* is a chunky affair that can be boiled or grilled – the latter is better. The *párky* is a thinner, boiled, frankfurter-style number. Popcorn is catching on, as are potato crisps; nationalists among the crowd enjoy *Slovakia Chips*, surely the only bag of crisps to be named after a nation state. If you need perking up before the game and a cup of espresso coffee won't do the trick, then try *Semtex* – the Czech hi-energy drink.

Action replay

After prolonged negotiations between the Slovak FA, the clubs and a number of private stations, state-run STV has lost its monopoly on football coverage. Cable company VTV, which has the same owners as Spartak Trnava, now has the rights to some live games which are broadcast on Sundays at 5pm or 6pm. VTV promised to present football in a modern way but chose tradition in signing up commentator Karol Polak, for more than twenty years the voice of Slovak football before he quit STV in 1992. STV still has the rights to a highlights package, *Tango*, shown on Sunday nights at 8pm on STV2. This is a no-frills collection of goals featuring the occasional studio pundit in a bad suit. STV also has the rights to the Champions' League.

Eurosport is widely available in bars, as are Czech, German and Austrian channels. You'll find the Hungarian-language station Duna TV in towns with large Magyar communities, and Hungarian state television is also available in bars – walk into one on a matchday and you'll most likely be rubbing shoulders with a group of Ferencváros fans looking up at the screen.

The back page

Slovaks may not have had their own state but throughout the Communist years they had their own sports paper, *Dennik Sport* (Mon–Sat, 7Sk). The paper's support for the Slovak cause once carried a hint of subversion, but today it is a typically dry East European read, and the lack of a Sunday edition means you have to wait until Monday morning for a full round-up of the league programme.

In the absence of the excellent weekly *Futbal-Sport* which closed recently, those in search of something a little less worthy have a choice between a new glossy monthly, *Futbal Magazin* (20Sk), and the weekly *Profik* (10Sk). The former carries a full results round-up of both domestic and foreign leagues, while the latter is aimed squarely at *toto* (pools) tippers but none the worse for that.

In Bratislava, the Interpress newsstand at Laurinská 9 carries a decent range of foreign sports papers.

Ultra culture

Organised fan groups were once almost non-existent in Slovakia, but the recent vogue for travelling to away games – instigated by Slovan fans but now taken up enthusiastically by followers of Spartak and Košice – has brought supporters closer together. Even so, there is little in the way of well-developed ultra gangs.

Sadly, Slovak football has also attracted a racist skinhead element, particularly evident at Slovan. Trouble at the team's home games is rare, but Slovan fans have been involved in several violent incidents away from home.

In the net

The presence of Slovak football on the Web is discreet, to put it diplomatically. There is no generic site dedicated to the local game and no Slovak clubs have their own homepages, official or otherwise.

Stats fans will, however, find an up-to-date first-division table, complete with results, scorers and goal timings of all rounds played so far, buried deep inside the RSSSF archive at: www.risc.uni-linz.ac.at/non-official/rsssf/results-eur.html.

Bratislava

 Slovan 482   Inter 485
Petržalka 486

Literally just across the river from Austria and a mere 15km north of Hungary, the capital of Slovakia is somehow not quite the heaving melting-pot of a metropolis that its location suggests. It has few splendours to match those of its great rival Prague, yet from a football point of view, Bratislava can claim to have at least as rich a heritage as the Czech capital. The old Czechoslovak national side was always cheered more enthusiastically here, and

when full, the city's Tehelné pole stadium can still be one of the most raucous in Central Europe.

The thrilling fields

Slovan Bratislava

Štadión Tehelné pole, Junacka 2
Capacity 32,000
Colours Blue-and-white shirts, blue shorts
League champions (Czechoslovakia) 1949–51, 1955, 1970, 1974–75, 1992
Cup winners (Czechoslovakia) 1962–63, 1968, 1974, 1982
League champions (Slovakia) 1994–96
Cup winners (Slovakia) 1994, 1997
European Cup-Winners' Cup winners 1969

With the possible exception of Croatia Zagreb, no team in Europe is so closely identified with the nation it belongs to as ŠK Slovan. They wear the Slovak national colours of blue and white, their club badge is almost indistinguishable from the national emblem, their ground is the *de facto* national stadium and the headquarters of the Slovak FA are based just next door in Slovan's sports complex. Add to all this the fact that the first Slovak national team was made up almost entirely of Slovan players, and it is little surprise that the club helped themselves to the first three Slovak championships after independence.

Bratislava is the only major city in Slovakia and Slovan are the only major team in town. For much of the Communist era, they were the Slovaks' only hope of stopping the big Czech clubs, and benefited accordingly. Assured of serious financial support from local industry and government authorities, they were able to take their pick from the best players in the land.

Slovan veteran – stopper Dušan Tittel

Bratislava essentials

Bratislava's Štefánika **airport** is for domestic and Prague flights only, although services are planned from Vienna and Munich. Bus #24 runs between Štefánika and the Sportová hala in Nové Mesto.

International trains arrive at Bratislava's main station (*hlavná stanica*), from which tram #1 will take you into the centre of town in ten minutes. Some local trains arrive at Nové Mesto in the north-east of town, near the Slovan stadium. The main **bus station** is just east of central Bratislava on Mlynské nivy.

Boats and **ferries** to and from Vienna or Budapest land at the Danubius station, Fajnorovo nábreži 2, between SNP and Starý bridges.

Bratislava has three forms of **transport**: buses, trolleybuses and trams. Tickets, valid for each at 7Sk per journey, are available from the yellow machines at major stops and at most newsstands. Stamp your ticket as you board.

A **24-hour pass** (*24-hodinový*, 35Sk) can be bought from the transport offices just outside the main train station and at Štúrova 5. The clerk will time-stamp your ticket for you. Transport runs 5am–11.30pm, with a night bus from the main station into town at midnight, 1am and 3.20am.

Taxis can be found at the station and in námestie SNP. Dial ☎07/253 333 for Non-Stop Taxi or ☎07/566 5050 for Yellow Expres. The old town (Staré Mesto) is pedestrianised and outside of this, the centre is too small for you to spend more than 150Sk on a cab ride.

The English-speaking **Bratislava Information Service** (open Mon–Fri 8am–4.30pm, Sat 8am–1pm, ☎07/533 3715) is at Klobúčnícka 2, with a smaller branch in the main train station that can help with accommodation.

A weekly English-language newspaper *The Slovak Spectator* (Wednesdays, 16Sk) prints restaurant and bar listings. The monthly *KAM V Bratislave* (9.60Sk) has Slovak-language information on movies and live music events.

The club were founded in 1919 as First Czechoslovak Sports Club Bratislava (I.CŠK Bratislava). The name reflected the fact that until then, most of the sports clubs in Bratislava had been based around the large Hungarian, German and Jewish populations. When the first Czechoslovak state was dismembered by the outbreak of World War II in 1939, the club shortened their name to ŠK Bratislava. The official name was altered several times under Communism but the team have been popularly known as Slovan since 1953.

From 1945, Communism brought with it organisation, resources and a determination to create a truly 'national' competition in Czechoslovakia. In contrast to the prewar years, in which the team never progressed beyond amateur leagues, Slovan made a real impact – winning the Czechoslovak title three years in a row

from 1949 under the guidance of coach Leopold Štastný.

After the Soviet invasion of Czechoslovakia in 1968, Štastný defected and went on to coach the Austrian national team for seven years. But a year after his departure his old club had their greatest moment, winning the Cup-Winners' Cup and becoming the only Czechoslovak team to win a major European club competition.

In the wake of the Soviet invasion, UEFA had attempted to separate the early rounds of the Cup along East/West lines. The Soviets called for an Eastern Bloc boycott of the competition in protest, and only Slovan and Dinamo Bucharest disobeyed. In the second round, Slovan defeated Porto 4–1 on aggregate, and in the quarter-finals they caused another upset, defeating Torino home and away before sneaking past Dunfermline Athletic to set up a final with

Barcelona in Basle, where a 3–2 win gave a demoralised nation a much-needed boost.

Slovan ended Trnava's run of titles with championship wins in 1974 and 1975. It was this side, now coached by Josef Venglóš, which formed the basis for the Czechoslovak squad who were crowned European Champions in 1976; indeed six of the team who beat West Germany in the final in Belgrade came from Slovan, with two more on the bench.

From the mid-Seventies onwards, however, the club entered a decline as the Czechs regained their dominant position in the league. Slovan won the penultimate Czechoslovak title in 1992, but all they'd had to show for the previous seventeen years was a solitary cup win in 1982.

When Slovakia woke up to find itself a new football nation in 1994, it did so with only Slovan capable of making any sort of impression in Europe. To add to the frustration of fans bored by the domestic league, however, UEFA did not rate the new republic of Slovakia worthy of a place in the qualifying round for the Champions' League, ruling out a possible source of excitement and revenue for the club.

The loss of some key players to foreign clubs during the 1996/97 season caused Slovan to slip behind Trnava and Košice in the championship race for the first time since independence. But with backing from the country's biggest bank, the largest fan base in the country and an excellent stadium, the team should be enjoying top-class European football again soon.

Here we go!

Tram #2 takes you from the main train station to the stadium, while trams #4, #6 and #10 all make the ten-minute journey from the city centre along Vajnorská.

Swift half

Pivnica Otvorená, Ulica Moskovská 1, is full of pennants, flags and scarves and even has an excellent Slovan drum; unfortunately it is also full of skinheads. It should definitely be avoided for international games. If you can stomach the heavy nationalist overtones you might find a few friendlier English-speaking types before a league match. Trolleybus #210 takes you to the ground from the bar.

A lighter atmosphere prevails at the **Hysteria Pub** on Odbojárov, just by the tram stop and only five minutes' walk from the ground. It's a fairly scruffy place that seems to do little business other than on matchdays. On the same street, nearer the stadium entrance, is the **Buffet Slovan**, which does snacks as well as beer.

For more substantial eating, the **Reštarácia Štadión**, by the bus station courtyard on the Bajkalská side, opposite the stadium, is a large restaurant with a small summer terrace offering reasonably priced Slovak food and beer before kick-off on matchdays.

Once inside the ground you'll find there are **buffet hatches** dotted around the place, all selling *pivo* (beer) at 15Sk, *párky* at 20Sk and *klobása* at 25Sk.

Publications

Slovanista is a free matchday programme, cheaply printed and text-heavy, but with all the essentials.

Club shops

There are two **Suveníry ŠK** hatches, at opposite ends of the ground, open on matchdays only – no credit cards.

Ultra culture

Few clubs have a 'home' end so dominated by skinheads as Slovan. At the south end you'll see row upon row of youths in black bomber jackets, short-cropped hair and black leather boots.

Their chants reveal a predictable dislike for gypsies, Jews and Hungarians, while 'Pressburg' emblems on their sleeves reveal their political preferences – Pressburg was the German name for Bratislava during World War II. *Belasi Fanatici* ('Light Blue Fanatics') is the name of the most prominent ultra group, but all are probably worth going out of your way to avoid.

Groundhopping

As the balance of power in Slovak football swings away from the capital, the minor Bratislava clubs have been labouring in mid-table with little hope of imminent improvement. Despite this, or perhaps because of it, both have their own colourful appeal.

⚫ Inter Bratislava

Pasienky stadium, Vajnorská 100
Capacity 15,000 (3000 seated)
Colours Yellow-and-black striped shirts, black shorts
League champions (Czechoslovakia) 1959
Cup winners (Slovakia) 1995

Literally overshadowed by their next-door neighbours Slovan, AŠK Inter Slovnaft are a club that have never truly found an identity or a support base. Five name changes, including a spell in the Fifties as Red Star

Bratislava, haven't helped; nor has the lack of success or link to any particular district of the city.

They won their only Czechoslovak title as Red Star in 1959, with a side that included international striker Adolf Scherer, who later moved to Slovan. In the following season's European Cup they beat Porto home and away before losing out to Rangers in the second round.

Inter's best run in Europe came in the 1975/76 UEFA Cup, when they defeated Real Zaragoza and AEK Athens before unexpectedly falling to Stal Mielec of Poland in the third round.

After merging with ZTS Petržalka to become Internacionál ZTS, they enjoyed a mini-revival in the late Eighties, winning the Slovak Cup in 1988 and in 1990, the year they also finished third in the Czechoslovak league.

Having demerged from Petržalka and returned to their own stadium, in the new Slovak championship they finished runners-up in 1994 and third in 1995, but on both occasions they were a long way off Slovan's

Rare highlight – Martin Kuna of Inter scraps with Zaragoza's Gustavo Poyet, September 1995

pace and never seriously threatened to win the title.

The revival of Slovakia's provincial clubs has pushed Inter even further out of the frame during the past two seasons, and with tiny crowds and little cash, the club are struggling to regain past glories.

To get to Inter, take any of the trams listed under Slovan above – the Inter stadium is the smaller of the two grounds you can see as you jump off.

As well as a few **beer stands** around the ground, there is a **club bar** underneath the main stand. Strictly speaking it is for officials and sponsors, but a smile and a foreign language should get you in to view the old team photos and a smattering of pennants from UEFA Cup and Intertoto campaigns.

There's a **club shop** adjacent to the ground with a modest selection of yellow-and-black gear. When Real Zaragoza came here for a Cup-Winners' Cup tie in 1995, they liked Inter's shirt so much, they adopted it as their away kit the following year. Buy one for yourself and keep the club treasurer happy.

✪ Petržalka

Ihrisko Petržalka, Krasovského 1
Capacity 12,000 (1800 seated)
Colours Green-and-black shirts, black shorts

Slovakia's first professional football club were founded in 1892 as Pozsonyi Torna Egyesület ('Bratislava Gymnastics Club' in Hungarian). Bratislava was then part of Hungary and the team played in a Hungarian regional league before the creation of Czechoslovakia between the wars, when the club became Polgári ('Citizen'). During this period the team became the subject of a long-running dispute between Hungarians and Slovaks, but in 1938 Hitler's Nazi authority ended the argument.

In 1945, with Czechoslovakia once again on the map as an independent, unified

state, the club became ZTS Petržalka, after the area to the south of the city centre – the team has been playing next to the Starý Most ('old bridge') on the south side of the Danube since 1900. Sunderland visited in 1913, and along with the many Hungarians who played here were a couple of more exotic foreign imports – Scottish brothers Colin and John McInnes.

The club survived a 1986 merger with Inter Bratislava, and ten years later, as 1.FC Petržalka, they gained promotion to Slovakia's expanded top tier.

Today Petržalka are enjoying a revival. They play on Sunday mornings in front of a congenial crowd, many of whom are here as much to cure their hangover as for any partisan reason. There are no floodlights but you've a choice between two covered stands behind the goals, one of which has a booze warehouse underneath.

Bus #52 from the other side of Starý Most, by the Kácacia fountain, stops right outside the stadium. Alternatively, bus #23 from the train station stops a two-minute walk away.

The **Restarácija Anita**, just behind the ground, has a terrace and a PA system for outdoor discos in summer. Inside you'll find a large old wooden bar offering friendly service, Czech Budweiser beer and darts. Nearer the bridge, inset from the Jantárová cesta, is the **Bufet Pri Starom Moste**, a modest bar open until 11pm with Corgoň beer, food and an earthy clientèle.

Eat, drink, sleep…

Bars and clubs

Slovakia is unpretentious. Bars are cheap – you should pay no more than 15Sk for a **beer**, which will usually be a drinkable local brew, invariably light (*svetlé*), on draught, with a pricier popular bottled Czech beer also available. In Bratislava, most bars will have a Czech beer on draught at 20–25Sk. The average pub (*pivnica*) will close around

10pm, a wine bar (vináreň), a couple of hours later. A thousand years of Hungarian rule have given the Slovaks a taste for **wine** – Furmint is just one of many decent local whites. Slovaks are also big on **shorts**, the favourites being slivovica and borovička, strong plum and pine-nut brandies. **Tacky discos** are the meat and potatoes of Slovak nightlife, but Bratislava can offer a few more interesting alternatives.

Charlie's Pub, Špitálska 4. Mainstay of Bratislava nightlife, a late pub and disco in a leisure complex next to the Hotel Kyjev. Small entrance fee, open until 4am every day except Sundays.

Danglar, Hviezdoslavovo námestie 19. Cellar bar near the SNP bridge for Bratislava's alternative types. Smoky, crowded, with big wooden tables and inside knowledge on what's happening in town that night. Open until 2am.

The Dubliner, Sedlarská ulica. Bratislava's first Irish pub opened in 1997, in a renovated building opposite the French Embassy in the Old Town. Open daily until 1am, 65Sk a Guinness.

Nightmare Pub, Františkánské námestie 10. Silly dungeon-style decor, but a popular bar in the Old Town in the same building as a famous vináreň. The courtyard turns into a live jazz venue in summer. Open until midnight.

U-Club, NAG Ludvíka Svobodu. An old air-raid shelter underneath Bratislava castle turned hardcore techno haunt of Bratislava's body piercers and weirdos. Near SNP bridge, open until 2am, later on Fridays and Saturdays.

Restaurants

Slovak specialities suffered under forty years of collective cooking and nowadays a reštaurácia menu will differ little from its Czech counterpart – in other words, dumplings (knedl'e) with everything. Hungarian spices still feature, though, especially in soups (polievky) and meats (masá). In most places you'll pay around 150Sk for a two-course meal, 200Sk with drinks.

Dušan Galis – ex-boss of Slovan and Slovakia

Arkádia, Zámocké schody. Elegant restaurant halfway up to the castle, where you can dine for around 400–600Sk, with a view overlooking the Danube, St Martin's Cathedral and the SNP bridge. Open daily 10am–10pm, most major credit cards.

Bistro Magda, Panenská 24. Excellent, friendly, cheap lunchtime venue near the Hotel Forum. Only room for a handful of people, so get there early. Open Mon–Fri 10am–5pm.

Mamut/Stará Sladovňa, Cintorínska 32. A vast beer hall five minutes' walk from the Hotel Kyjev, in a converted malthouse which was once the pride and joy of the Bratislava beer industry. Now sadly party to an upstairs bingo hall and oompah bands on the ground floor. Decent range of food, but the kitchen closes around 9pm.

Vináreň Velkí Františkani, Františkánské námestie 10. Bratislava's most famous wine cellar in the Old Town, with beef and pork specialities.

There's a cover charge for the gypsy violinists, but this place is not as expensive as it looks – around 300Sk all in. No credit cards.

Accommodation

Bratislava is not endowed with a vast number of **cheap digs**. Private rooms are less widespread than in Prague, and most centrally located hotels charge inflated rates. The **BIS offices** at the main train station (☎07/533 4370, open Mon–Fri 8am–4.30pm, Sat 8am–1pm) will give you a price list. In July and August, the **CKM office**, Hviezdoslavovo námestie 16 (☎07/331 607, open Mon–Fri 9am–noon, 1–4pm) can arrange a cheap bed in a student hostel.

CKM, Ružinkovská 1 (☎07/220 441). Youth hostel open all year round. IYHF members 200Sk per person; non-members 500Sk a single, 850Sk a double. Tram #8 from the main train station.

Hotel Dukla, Dulovo námestie 1 (☎07/526 9815). Semi-renovated Communist-era hotel overlooking a quiet square. 1000Sk for an old double, 2000Sk for a new one, breakfast included. All rooms have baths, new ones have a TV. Most credit cards. Bus #23 from the train station.

Hotel Kyjev, Rajská 2 (☎07/322 041; fax 07/326 820). Tower block hotel which dominates the centre of Bratislava. Rooms with satellite TV and bathroom. *Luna* night bar open until 3am. Off-peak singles at 1850Sk, doubles 2000Sk. Most major credit cards.

Junior Sputnik, Drieňova 14 (☎07/234 340). Also run by CKM (see opposite), this is a better bet but also more expensive than the hostel on Ružinkovská. Bus #22 from the train station.

Spain

Spain is a nation divided by language, culture – and football. Each of the country's main clubs are the flagship of their region, particularly Real Madrid (Castille) and Barcelona (Catalonia). These two giants of world football have been battling out their differences on and off the pitch since before the Spanish Civil War. In doing so, both have built vast football empires around palatial superstadia, and paid extraordinary transfer fees and salaries in building teams to play there. The likes of di Stéfano, Puskás, Cruyff, Kubala, Kocsis, Maradona, Romário, Stoichkov and Ronaldo have all performed for one or other club, in fantastic amphitheatres of colour and competitive fervour.

Real and Barça have won 37 of the last 50 championships between them. But the problem remains that few Spanish players (and even fewer homegrown coaches) have ever scaled the same heights as the imports.

Club culture – regional rivalries dominate the game

A match between the two great rivals is the highlight of the Spanish footballing calendar, more thrilling and eagerly anticipated than any fixture involving *la selección*, the long-suffering national side. In fact, the overwhelming power of the club game in Spain has contributed to its national team's continued lack of success over the years. Club rivalries may be between two sides from the same city (Real Madrid-Atlético or Sevilla-Betis) or, more potently, between regions (Real-Barça). Many of the ethnic tensions that surround the latter are tied up with the Civil War and its aftermath, the country's postwar Francoist regime having suppressed regional identities and

forbidden the open use of Catalan and Basque. This in turn helped to create Spain's first football boom in the Forties and Fifties, as huge crowds rallied round their team as an identifiable local cause.

Before Franco, the picture couldn't have been more different. A professional national league wasn't set up until 1928, but at international level, Spain regularly beat France and Portugal in friendlies, and in 1929 became the first continental team to beat England in a full international.

Football had come to Spain via British mining workers in the Basque country, from where the game spread to Madrid, Barcelona and Valencia. In a regionalised cup competition whose play-off winners were regarded as national champions,

Champions of Europe – Madrid, 1964

Basque flagship side Athletic Bilbao won one in every three prewar tournaments, earning their reputation as cup fighters.

The hero of the day was goalkeeper Ricardo Zamora, whose acrobatics won Spain a silver medal at their first international appearance in the 1920 Olympics, and who scarcely missed a match for his country until 1936. He might have been able to prevent Italy from winning the 1934 World Cup, but injury ruled him out of the replay his acrobatics had earned when Spain drew 1–1 with the hosts. After a successful playing career with Barcelona and Real, and postwar, title-winning management at Atlético Madrid, Zamora died in 1978, a hero in both cities.

Rare is the player who has earned such an honour. In the hothouse atmosphere which prevailed in the Spanish game of the Forties, Fifties and Sixties, players were Barça or Real, never both. Argentine footballing maestro Alfrédo di Stéfano had to choose, opting for Madrid over Barcelona in 1953. Real president Santiágo Bernabéu's friends in high places may have helped the decision process, because Barça, with the classy Ladislav Kubala, had by far the more successful team prior to then.

The national side produced their best-ever World Cup form in Brazil in 1950, finishing fourth. With Barça's Ramallets in goal and Bilbao's Zarra upfront, Spain brushed aside the England of Finney, Milburn and Matthews, and drew a thriller, 2–2 with the eventual winners Uruguay. Drained of both strength and ideas, they were then hammered 6–1 by the hosts.

Back home, football was becoming more popular than bullfighting – and would remain so. Real Madrid and Barça both had outstanding teams, but Bernabéu's poaching of di Stéfano would prove the masterstroke. Bernabéu built his team around di Stéfano, built a great stadium around the team – then added the Hungarian Ferenc Puskás to the mixture. Real won the European Cup five times with a side that would go down as one of the finest in football history. At home, they dominated the league but were by no means the only class act – Spanish clubs won 13 of the 25 titles contested in the first ten years of European competition.

Though neither was actually Spanish, both di Stéfano and Puskás travelled to the 1962 World Cup in Chile for their adopted country. In the event, only Puskás would actually play – and there was nothing he could do prevent the Spaniards exiting at the first round, having lost to Czechoslovakia and Brazil.

Two years later, it was a very different *selección* which won the European Nations' Cup, forerunner of the modern European Championship, in Madrid. The final pitted Spain against a Soviet side Franco had refused his team permission to meet in the same competition four years earlier. Now he was in the stands along with 120,000 others at the Chamartín (now Bernabéu) stadium to see Spain win comfortably, 2–1. Stars of the victory were forwards Luis Suárez and Amaro Amancio; missing was the speedy, evergreen Real left-winger Francisco Gento, equally among the candidates for the accolade of finest postwar Spanish player.

The next major tournament Spain staged was altogether less successful, in terms of both organisation and the home side's performance. Visiting teams cursed the 1982 World Cup for its blistering heat and tortured logistics (the Spaniards used sixteen stadia in thirteen different cities), while local fans, desperate for a victory that would confirm the country's post-Franco renaissance, imposed a burden of pressure that Spain's modest side simply could not cope with.

They drew with the rank outsiders, Honduras, in their opening game, took advantage of some imaginative refereeing to beat Yugoslavia in their second, then lost to Gerry Armstrong's breakaway goal for Northern Ireland in their third. Defeat by West Germany and a goalless draw with England drew the whole unhappy chapter to a close.

Within two years there was to be a surprisingly upbeat sequel. At the 1984 European Championship in France, an almost identical side to that which had hosted the World Cup seemed to be heading for its customary early exit when, in injury time in the last group game against West Germany, Maceda launched himself at a cross from Señor and gave Spain an unlikely 1–0 win. The Spaniards then beat Denmark on penalties in the semi-finals, and were making a decent fist of the final against the host nation until their goalkeeper and captain, Luis Arconada, allowed Michel Platini's curling free-kick to slip out from under his body and crawl over the goal line. The match finished 2–0 to France.

The addition of Real Madrid striker Emilio Butragueño, *El Buitre* ('The Vulture'), allowed Spain to build on their progress of

1984. At the Mexico World Cup of 1986, four goals from *El Buitre* beat a much-favoured Denmark team, but, having done all the hard work, Spain then surprisingly went out to Belgium after a shoot-out in the quarter-finals.

At club level, meanwhile, Spanish teams had long since ceded their domination of Europe, initially to Italy. Like the Italians, the Spaniards banned foreign imports from their domestic game for a while. But in 1973 the ban was lifted as local teams struggled to keep pace with the advances being made by clubs in Holland, West Germany and, towards the end of the decade, England.

After a brief reign by hard-tackling Basque teams in the early Eighties, which put paid to the challenge of Maradona's Barcelona, Butragueño's Real Madrid won five Spanish titles on the trot. Terry Venables and Bernd Schuster won Barça the championship in 1985, the club then lost the subsequent European Cup final on

Italia '90 – Rafael Martín Vázquez pulls clear

Basics

Citizens of the EU, USA, Canada, Australia and New Zealand require only a **passport** to enter Spain. Arriving in the country by train you may be delayed by **anti-terrorist measures**, but these are unlikely to amount to much.

The Spanish unit of currency is the peseta (pta), of which there are around 230 to £1. Coins are named in units of five, a *duro*. A silver 25-peseta coin is five *duros*, useful for phone calls. There are coins for 1, 5, 10, 25, 50, 100, 200 and 500 pesetas, and notes for 1000, 2000, 5000 and 10,000.

Spain has the most advanced **credit-card system** in Europe, but plastic payment is not as widespread as in the UK. Cash can be advanced from machines just about anywhere, and most machines take all kinds of cards. Banks and savings banks (*cajas de ahorros*) are the best places to **change money**. Hours are Mon–Fri 9am–2pm.

After the Expo and the Olympics of 1992, transport in the country has been greatly improved. **Buses** are comfortable, air-conditioned and charge around 1000ptas per 100km, while the pride of the **train fleet** is the *AVE* high-speed link between Madrid and Seville, a luxury journey of two-and-a-half hours costing around 7000ptas. The Barcelona-Madrid trek is three times as long for about the same price, but if you're in a hurry you'd be better off taking the air shuttle service – Spain has some of the **lowest domestic air fares** in Europe. On trains, there are a range of discount fares on so-called **blue days** of the calendar.

Coin phones take 5, 25 and 100 peseta coins, and most bar-owners won't mind you using their phone without buying a drink – look for the **yellow telephone sign** outside. Otherwise, telephone cards come in 1000- and 2000-peseta units.

From outside the country, the code for calling Spain is ☎34. The major **city codes** are Madrid ☎1, Barcelona ☎3, Bilbao ☎4, Seville ☎5 and Valencia ☎6. For inland calls town-to-town, dial a ☎9 before the city code. To call internationally from Spain, dial ☎07 before the country code. While local calls are staggeringly cheap, phoning abroad is not, so stick to the off-peak times – 10pm–8am, seven days a week.

Accommodation is very reasonably priced in Spain. In almost any town you can get a double room for under 4000ptas and a single for about half that. The most basic lodgings are *hospedajes*, then *pensiones*, then *hostales* – which must offer at least a sink in each bedroom. An English-language accommodation information service (daily 10am–8pm) is available by calling ☎901 300 600 from anywhere in Spain.

Spanish **food** is rich in regional variety. The mainstays include *paella*, a rice and seafood dish originally from Valencia, and *tortilla*, potato omelette. A set menu (*menú del día*) should be around 800–1000ptas. Lunch is the main meal of the day.

Social life revolves around the **local bar**, which serves reasonably priced alcohol for unfeasably long hours. Customs vary from area to area, but draught beer will generally be served in a 250ml glass (*una caña*) for around 100–150ptas. A longer glass is *un tubo*, 200–250 ptas. The most popular brews are *Mahou* (Madrid), *Estrella Damm* (Barcelona) and *Cruzcampo* (Seville). **Wine**, either red (*tinto*), white (*blanco*) or rosé (*rosado*), will cost around 150ptas for a glass.

On the bar will be a selection of *tapas*, hot or cold snacks for around 300–500ptas a plate, although these are given free in some regions – wait a while before ordering your food, just in case. A larger portion (*una ración*, 500–1000 ptas) will be easily enough for lunch. The **drinking and snacking time** (*el tapeo*) finishes around midnight, after which you'll be drinking *copas* – spirits liberally poured from a great height over huge ice chunks in tall glasses. The biggest problem with bars in Spain is **leaving them**. Stick around for breakfast, hot chocolate and fritters (*chocolate y churros*), and the smell of the new day's football press.

penalties to Steaua Bucharest, and the chance to build a new European power had gone.

Barcelona would have to wait until 1992, forty years after losing di Stéfano, to finally lift the European Cup. Dutchman Johan Cruyff, whose exploits as a player under Rinus Michels had given Barça an emphatic and stylish title win in 1974, came back as coach in 1988. His influence would transform Spanish club football and spark a second postwar boom in the domestic game's popularity.

Cruyff assigned equal importance to home-produced players and top foreign stars.

The big tissue – hankies are waved in ecstasy or exasperation

The success he attained with an arrogantly adventurous side – four titles in a row, two European trophies including the European Cup – encouraged other club presidents to hire attack-minded trainers, who in turn were urged to raise cheap local talent.

The outcome of all this has been that football has become a fashionable pastime, attracting the major players of modern, democratic and economically buoyant Spanish society. In the early Nineties, three nail-biting title finishes, one featuring the perennial underdogs of Deportivo La Coruña, made great TV and helped to arrest the growth of basketball. Today TV companies are effectively underwriting the game, allowing debt-ridden clubs like Real Madrid to spend millions on the finest playing and coaching staff money can buy.

Perhaps inevitably, there has been a reaction against all this conspicuous consumption. When Ronaldo fled Barcelona for Inter Milan at the end of the 1996/97 season, fans at the Nou Camp paraded banners reading: "No more foreigners who don't love our colours!"

There has been no such disharmony among the members of *la selección*, currently prospering under the leadership of Javier Clemente. While the coach has drawn light-hearted criticism from the media for picking too many fellow-Basques, his team have been displaying a rare unity of purpose.

They might already have had some silverware on the shelf, had it not been for some questionable refereeing decisions in key matches. At the 1994 World Cup, Luis Enrique had his nose broken by Mauro Tassotti in the Italian penalty area – an off-the-ball incident that went unpunished. At Euro '96, Spain outplayed England at Wembley only for Kiko's 'goal' – replays proved it was on-side – to be cancelled out by the linesman.

Essential vocabulary

Hello *¡Hola!*
Goodbye *Adiós*
Yes *Sí*
No *No*
Two beers, please *Dos cañas, por favor*
Thank you *Gracias*
Men's *Caballeros*
Women's *Señoras*
Where is the stadium? *¿Dónde está el estádio?*
What's the score? *¿Cómo va el partido?*
Offside *Fuera de juego*
Referee *Árbitro*

Match practice

Spanish football is a celebration of noise, colour and alcohol. Sunday is when football provides the excuse to eat, drink and be merry. Corner bars fill with wide-eyed kids in nylon shirts; fans (*hinchas*) devour copious afternoon beers and *tapas*; and old men press their ears to *Carrusel Deportivo* on the radio, swearing quietly to themselves.

Traditionally, women prepared dinner at home while all this was going on. But Spain's *fútbolmanía* is attracting a wider audience. In the stadia, crowds are more mixed than ever before, and the first duty of the head of any family is to buy club membership cards for the wife and kids. Today's Spanish game is a family affair.

Inside the grounds, cushions (*almohadillas*) and white handkerchiefs (*pañuelos*)

are the pre-requisites. The former are thrown onto the pitch to express displeasure at a refereeing decision or a particularly inept display by the home side. The latter, in a tradition borrowed from bullfighting, can be waved to express either exasperation or satisfaction after a stunning goal or move.

Regional tensions can make for a cracking atmosphere, which rarely spills over into violence – though expect Spanish nationalist chants wherever Barcelona are the visiting side. The natural Spanish sense of fun rarely lets pride stand in the way of a good party. High tackles, hilarious refereeing and flashy latin antics all add to the ambience. Ace foreign stars (Spain imports more than any country in Europe) invariably win the top goalscorer title, *el Pichichi*, providing the icing on the cake.

The league season runs from early September until mid-June, with a short break for Christmas and New Year break. Most top-flight games take place at 5pm on Sundays (7pm in late spring and early autumn). Some matches – those at Rayo Vallecano in Madrid, for example – kick-off at noon so as not to clash with bigger rivals across town.

One top game will kick-off a couple of hours later for live coverage on satellite television, while another is brought forward to Saturday night at 8.30pm for free-access regional TV channels. Monday nights host the last match of the weekend, screened by *Antena 3*. Note that match posters often list the away side first. Line-up information is distributed in handouts at some clubs.

The league

The first division, *la Primera Liga*, is gradually being scaled down to eighteen clubs. A bureaucratic bungle before the start of the 1995/96 season had extended it to 22 teams

USA '94 – Miguel Ángel Nadal engineers a Swiss miss

and the consequent 42-game season crippled major clubs also trying to balance a cup run and European football. There were a relatively manageable twenty teams for the 1997/98 campaign.

Below, *la Segunda División A* also contains twenty sides, including some of the top clubs' reserve outfits, who cannot be promoted to the first. Otherwise the two top teams swop with the bottom two in the *Primera,* while the third- and fourth-place finishers enter two-leg play-offs with the third and fourth from bottom in the top drawer.

Outside broadcast – TV crews gather at the Bernabéu

Not for nothing do Spaniards call their lower divisions *El Pozo,* ('The Well'). Below the *Segunda A* lurk the depths of the semi-professional *Segunda B* – four leagues of twenty teams each, roughly divided geographically, from which it is almost impossible for former big-name clubs to emerge. Only one team from each section gains promotion, via play-offs between each group's top four teams.

Four drop from each *Segunda B* down to the fourth tier, *Tercera División,* which is divided into seventeen impenetrable regional zones.

Up for the cup

La Copa del Rey was initiated by King Alfonso XIII in 1902. For nearly thirty years it was Spain's only tournament, and it continued to be held in high esteem until the fixtures started piling up in the Eighties.

Currently *La Copa* is decided on eight two-legged rounds. Fifty teams from the *Segunda B* and the *Tercera* kick things off, followed by those from the *Segunda A* and the *Primera,* except for clubs involved in European competition who are allowed a bye until the last sixteen.

The single-game final is at a neutral venue, decided when the finalists are known. It is always played as the last game of the season, in late June or a little earlier if there is a major international tournament in the summer.

Extra-time and penalties decide drawn games throughout. The winners go through to the *Recopa,* as the Spanish rather elegantly call the Cup-Winners' Cup.

Tickets

At big clubs, members (*socios*) often number nearly as much as the stadium capacity. However, all clubs put aside at least ten percent of tickets to go on sale a few days before the match, so for a major tie, go to the club office as early as possible. Bear in mind that prices may vary according to the class of opposition.

On the day, tickets are bought at ticket offices (*taquillas*). The cheapest, around 3000ptas, are standing on the seats behind the goal in the *fondo,* normally either north (*norte*) or south (*sur*). Some grounds still have ordinary standing tickets – *de pie.*

Alongside the pitch, there are various kinds of *tribuna lateral* tickets: lower (*baja*), higher (*alta*) and, in larger stadia, the topmost *anfiteatro,* these last going for around 4–6000ptas. Numbered (*numerada*) seats with the best view are known as *preferencia* and weigh in at 6–8000ptas. Contrary to

Euro '96 – Kiko tucks the ball under Seaman, but the man with the orange flag, he say no goal

popular myth, it does rain in Spain, and in wet weather a place which is covered (*cubierto*) is obviously preferable. On your ticket, *puerta* is the gate, *sección* the sector, *fila* the row and *asiento* the seat.

Half-time

Bars around the ground will be packed before and after matches, but at half-time, the beer on sale inside will be alcohol-free. Some bars have hatches that sell *minis* – plastic mugs of booze, either beer or mixed spirits, for glugging down outside the ground before kick-off. Inside, you may see a *bota* being illicitly passed around the crowd – a large pouch made out of hide that squirts wine down the throat of the uninitiated drinker.

By the stadium, you'll find sunflower seeds (*pipas*) or dried fruit (*fruta seca*), being sold in different-sized bags decorated in club colours. Snacks include sausages (*salchichas*), hot dogs (*perritos*) and the self-explanatory *hamburguesas*, all on offer for around 300–500ptas.

Action replay

Spain's right-wing government recently ditched its free-market principles to stop pay-per-view television getting a stranglehold on football. New legislation ensures that there will be at least one free-access live match per week for the foreseeable future – though precisely which channel it will be on is anyone's guess.

The new law's enactment was a triumph for *Antena 3*, the consortium which represents regional, terrestrial channels, and a defeat for *Canal Plus*, the satellite station which wanted to pursue an exclusive pay-per-view deal similar to the one it has already instigated in France.

Now it looks as though any future (non-exclusive) pay-per-view developments will be handled by an unholy alliance of the two companies, after successful trials were carried out during 1997.

All existing TV contracts are due to expire in June 1998, but until then, the division of games is fairly straightforward. State *TVE 1* has the live Saturday evening game at

8.30pm, plus highlights from the Sunday afternoon action in *Solo Goles* (9.30pm). *Canal Plus* shows a live Spanish game at 7.30pm on a Sunday, then *Antena 3* takes over for the Monday night game at 8.30pm.

Many complain that there is too much football on Spanish television, not least the National Association of Restaurant Owners, who claim they are losing trade to bars with *Canal Plus*. Such bars are well worth seeking out – in addition to the live Spanish action, the channel shows a live English Premiership game on Saturday afternoon at 4pm, while their excellent *El Tercer Tiempo* ('The Third Half', Sundays around midnight) has action from top Italian, English and Argentinian matches.

Meanwhile, *TVE* screens international games live, along with Champions' League matches. *Antena 3* is the place to go for live *Copa del Rey* action.

The most popular show is *El Día Después* (*Canal Plus*, Mondays, 8pm), featuring former Liverpool striker Michael Robinson in a double act with Lobo Carrasco, cracking weak jokes about the past weekend's main incidents.

The back page

There are four main sports dailies. *Marca* (110ptas) is by far the most popular – outside Catalonia. Unless there is any shattering news elsewhere, the first six pages usually concern Real Madrid. The paper's circulation of two million is the highest of any sports paper in Europe, but don't be caught reading a copy in a Barcelona bar. Surprisingly, *Marca's* foreign coverage is only average.

The equivalent in Catalonia is *El Mundo Deportivo* (110ptas) which, naturally, has its first few pages dedicated to news from Barcelona. Its international coverage is more balanced, and while it is Catalan-run, the paper is printed in Spanish and is on

sale throughout the country. The other two papers are the Madrid-based *As* (100ptas), with smart graphics, and the Catalan-language *Sport* (110ptas).

The national daily *Diario 16* has a colour sports supplement, *Campeónes 16*, while the Seville edition of *ABC*, with its Monday sports supplement *Campeón*, is the most widely read down south.

Don Balon (Mondays, 325ptas) is the leading football weekly, with posters and 'at home' features appealing to a younger readership, but some serious columnists.

Ultra culture

Supporters in Spain are organised in clubs called *peñas*, which organise tickets, away trips and social gatherings. In any town, the *peña* bar will be a place to hang out and catch up with all the soccer gossip.

Alongside and occasionally overlapping with the *peñas* are the *ultras*, similar to their Italian counterparts – although the fashion took off in Spain much later. In Madrid, Atlético and Real ultra groups were set up around 1982. The first fanzine, *Ultras*, was produced in 1985 as the movement swept through all the main clubs. Outbreaks of violence, mainly away from

Supermarket sweep – try a taste of Beaujolais Nou Camp

grounds, were becoming more frequent when the Spanish FA decided to ban alcohol at grounds in 1990, and fireworks in 1992.

If there is one factor mitigating against further development of the ultra concept, it is the vast distances between clubs which make away travel so difficult in Spain. The fans' choreography also tends to be less ambitious than in Italy, although the big boys can still put on a big show.

Super Hincha (monthly, 300ptas) has all the inside ultras info.

In the net

Spain's printed sports media were quick to jump aboard the internet bandwagon. The daily *Marca* runs a *Digital* version at: www.recoletos.es/marca/. It's an ambitious, graphics-heavy site that takes a while to load, but your patience will be rewarded with a selection of the day's news stories (choose from a range of headlines) and a modest stats archive covering both national and European competitions. Unlike its printed equivalent, *Marca Digital* gives equal weight to basketball, tennis, cycling and other sports as well as football.

Much the same can be said of the online version of *El Mundo Deportivo,* at: www.elmundodeportivo.es/. It's a simpler site than its *Marca* rival, but still looks smart thanks to Neville Brody's groundbreaking graphics. Choose your news stories from the *Tema del Dia* section, or head straight for areas dedicated to Barça and Espanyol.

Away from all this hurly-burly, the *Servifútbol* site offers a wealth of useful soccer links, including scores of club sites and areas dedicated to the transfer market and the pools. Go to: www.servifutbol.es.

History tour – the mosaic outside Sevilla's stadium incorporates the badges of Spain's finest clubs

Madrid

Madrid is a member of football's aristocracy. Like the Real club which dominates it, its importance as a football city owes much to the work of Don Santiágo Bernabéu. *Los Meringues'* most famous president took the club from relative mediocrity to European superstardom, building an arena which would go on to host a World Cup final, a European Championship final and three European Cup finals. Today, the Bernabéu stadium's position on one of the city's main avenues befits the club's regal name and status in the game.

If you're an ambitious club president, it helps to have friends in high places. The rôle of Spain's dictator General Franco in Real's rise could be overstated, but it is said he could reel off old line-ups like any good statto. Don Bernabéu was one of his associates, and used the situation to his advantage – Barcelona were always wealthier, but Real were Franco's pet.

The area around the Bernabéu is one of elegant plazas and palaces. A little to the south is la Plaza de Cibeles, where Real fans go and celebrate – a major city landmark that Atlético followers threatened to paint black the night their team won the title in 1996.

The Mattress Makers (*los colchoneros*), as Atlético are known, have almost always lived in the shadow of their wealthier neighbours. Their urban, working-class support have followed them from Vallecas in the south-west of the city, to Reina Victoria in the north-west, then down to their present home at the Manzanares in the industrial south-east.

The club, an offshoot of the Madrid FC team that would become Real, first played their former team-mates in 1905; the game finished 1–1. Atlético had the audacity to win a couple of titles at the start in the Forties and early Fifties. But from the day

Raúl Madrid – the club's teenage superstar

Bernabéu signed Alfredo di Stéfano in 1953, Real were on a different plane. By the end of the decade, they didn't even deign to give Atlético the status of rivals – that position had been taken by Barcelona.

Atlético's best crack at taking Real down a peg or two was the European Cup semi-final of 1959. Both won their home leg by the odd goal, and it took a play-off at Zaragoza for Real to edge it over their neighbours, 2–1.

For *Atléti*, further ignominy was to follow. Jealously coveting Real's palace up the road, Atlético planned to build one of their own, raising money – as Bernabéu did – by membership subscription. While negotiating the sale of their old Metropolitano stadium, Atlético's scheme hit the rocks when funding dwindled, and the club were

Higher and higher – the Bernabéu bears the name of Real's visionary former president

forced to go cap in hand to Real and play their home games there for a season. Yet it was around this time that Atlético hit a rare patch of consistency, beating Real in consecutive cup finals in 1960 and 1961. They won the Cup-Winners' Cup of 1962, made the final of the same tournament a year later, and fell to Juventus in the 1965 Fairs' Cup semi.

Atlético eventually moved into their new stadium at Manzanares in 1966, the year of Real's last European Cup victory. Since then, only the public outbursts of controversial club president Jesús Gil y Gil have kept Real from dominating the headlines – though the historic title win of 1996, black fountains or no, was still a moment for the Mattress Makers to savour.

Madrid's third team are Rayo Vallecano, from the tight-knit, working-class neighbourhood of Vallecas. The club regularly exercise their right to be relegated and promoted, the last time in 1997 when they dropped out of the top flight after a play-off defeat by Mallorca. The club are propped up by the eccentric Ruiz Mateos family, far out on the south-western edge of the city.

The thrilling fields

 Real Madrid

Estadio Santiágo Bernabéu, Avenida Concha Espina 1
Capacity 106,000
Colours All white with purple trim
League champions 1932–33, 1954–55, 1957–58, 1961–65, 1967–69, 1972, 1975–76, 1978–80, 1986–90, 1995, 1997
Cup winners 1905–8, 1917, 1934, 1936, 1946–47, 1962, 1970, 1974–75, 1980, 1982, 1989, 1993
European Cup winners 1956–60, 1966
UEFA Cup winners 1985–86

Spain took the field at the 1978 World Cup wearing black armbands. Don Santiágo Bernabéu, club president at Real Madrid, had passed away, and the national team's gesture was much more than a token one.

It was Bernabéu who pulled Real Madrid from post-Civil War austerity up to the rank of aristocracy. For five years in the second half of the Fifties, Real dominated Europe as no other ever team will, their white strip becoming as feared as any in the game's history.

Those white shirts also came to represent the repressive right-wing régime of the day. For Catalan and Basque alike, General Franco's favoured team of international all-stars were the Castillian overlords, while Bernabéu himself was reviled as an out-and-out Francoist. Catalans would claim that the one player instrumental to Real's rise, Alfredo di Stéfano, was kept away from Barcelona by political manoeuvering.

For the neutral, though, Real Madrid will always mean class, a bastion of attacking football whose finest hour, their 7–3 destruction of Eintracht Frankfurt in the 1960 European Cup final, is etched into the consciousness even of fans who were born after it was played...

Don Santiágo and his brother Marcelo played for Madrid Football Club as teenagers, when games were played by a rubbish tip at a ground known as Campo O'Donnell – now the site of a Walt Disney theme park. Madrid FC had been formed by students at the turn of the century. They moved from ground to ground, at one point playing next to a bullring and changing in the toilets of the bar next door.

The club regularly topped the regional *Campeonato del Centro*, which qualified them for the *Copa del Rey*. Madrid celebrated four straight victories in the cup from 1905 – before the Bernabéus had begun their playing career. King Alfonso XIII gave Madrid his royal (*Real*) blessing in 1920, and the club turned professional with the inauguration of the Spanish league in 1929.

By now the team had found a permanent home, the purpose-built Chamartín stadium, south of the main train station of the same name. Don Santiágo was on the board, and it was he who decided to splash out a world record transfer fee on goalkeeper Ricardo Zamora in 1930. Zamora's Real proved a hardy defensive unit, and the club won their first two league titles in 1932 and 1933.

The Spanish Civil War interrupted the run, and when Bernabéu took over as club president in 1943, his first task was to rebuild Chamartín, which had been all but destroyed by fighting. At this time, *la liga* was dominated by Real's two biggest rivals, Barcelona and Aviación Madrid, later to become Atlético. After a brush with relegation, Bernabéu vowed to make Real the best in Spain, playing in a new Chamartín. Raising money from a bond issue among supporters – and with possible state assistance – Bernabéu built a stadium worthy of champions, between the old ground and Avenida del Generalísimo Franco, today's Castellana.

To help hire these champions, there was club treasurer Raimundo Saporta and Bernabéu's political connections. Saporta's first task was to draw up a contract with Millonarios of Colombia for forward Alfredo di Stéfano, formerly of River Plate in the Forties – a team considered by his fellow Argentines to be the greatest in their football history.

Di Stéfano had learned his trade by dribbling with the ball at speed down Buenos Aires' grid-pattern streets. Direct, gifted and ambitious, he was football's complete player. Money had lured him to Colombia's breakaway league, and $50,000 brought him to Spain in 1953. Barcelona had also drawn up a contract – but with River Plate, not the Colombians. Amid the confusion, the Spanish FA decided that di Stéfano should play for Madrid and Barcelona in turn, each for a season at a time. The ruling pleased nobody. Saporta manoeuvred with the powers-that-were, and after the player had spent six weeks with Real, Barcelona dropped their option. A day later, Di Stéfano scored four against them in Real's 5–0 win.

Alongside di Stéfano were Héctor Rial from Uruguay and former Santander winger Francisco Gento. Behind them as the team's engine was Miguel Muñoz, who would become coach before the decade was out. Real won four titles in five years. But it was the European Cup that made them.

Bernabéu had been behind the competition from the start, meeting in Paris with Gabriel Hanot when the blueprint was drawn up. The first of his club's five consecutive victories in it began in 1956, with a difficult win over Stade de Reims in Paris. The French had scored two in the first ten minutes, and it took a surprise run and strike from centre-back Manuel Marquitos to level the scores, before Madrid went on to win 4–3.

Bernabéu duly bought Reims' Raymond Kopa, di Stéfano dropped a little deeper, and three more Cups were won. Uruguay's José Santamaría anchored the back, former Betis striker Luis del Sol buzzed upfront, Brazil's Didi came and went. But it was the arrival of Hungarian exile Ferenc

Vulture on the swoop – Eighties hero Emilio Butragueño

Puskás that completed the best-loved Real line-up. Although he only played in one winning final, that of 1960, it was in a display so exquisite that the scoreline alone has come to suggest Madrid's showcase football – 7–3 to Real, four to Puskás, three to di Stéfano. "We were scoring goals and they stood and watched us," said Puskás of the opposition, Eintracht Frankfurt. Also standing and watching were 135,000 fans at Glasgow's Hampden Park, every one of them entranced by what they saw.

The 'Galloping Major', who had starred in another scoreline milestone, Hungary's 6–3 mauling of England in 1953, had been exiled from his homeland since the 1956 uprising, drifting round Europe before happily assuming a rôle complementary to di Stéfano's at Real.

It took a very special Barcelona team to beat Madrid in the following year's tournament, and an even better Benfica to edge the 1962 final 5–3 – a game in which Puskás scored a hat-trick in 20 minutes yet still finished on the losing side.

The turning point came in 1964. Puskás and di Stéfano, both 38, weren't quick enough to slip Internazionale's tight marking. Their era had given way to *catenaccio* and the cult of the manager.

Gento stayed on to captain the team to a record sixth European Cup win in 1966. He was still there five years later, when Real lost the Cup-Winners' Cup final to Chelsea after a replay.

Throughout the Seventies and early Eighties, Real's Spanish players were good but not great – Pirri, Camacho and Amaro Amancio in midfield, Juanito and Carlos Santillana upfront. Their expensive imports were patchy – Bernd Schuster was under the thumb of his domineering wife, while Lawrie Cunningham's dragged him around Madrid's nightclubs when he should have been at home nursing an

Madrid essentials

Madrid's Barajas **airport** is 16km east of the city. Airport buses leave from all terminals (every fifteen minutes, 4.45am–1.30am, 325ptas, journey time one hour) and make six stops on the way to their terminus at Plaza Colón. A taxi costs around 2000ptas – only use those from official ranks outside each terminal.

The city has two main **train stations**. Chamartín serves France, northern Portugal, Catalonia and northern Spain; Atocha serves the rest of Spain, Lisbon and the high-speed *AVE* trains to Seville. Confusingly, some trains call at both. International and long-distance **coaches** terminate at c/Canarias 17, next to Palos de la Frontera.

Madrid's **transport system** is excellent. The colour-coded, **ten-line metro** is quick, clean and safe. Its only drawback is the long pedestrian tunnels at major station interchanges, which can add ten minutes to your journey time. A single **ticket** is 130ptas, a ten-journey one (*un bono*), 645ptas, and the network runs 6am–1.30am daily. There is also a city **bus network**, which issues separate tickets but has the same price structure. Drivers can sell you singles, but *bonobus* tickets are sold at EMT kiosks and newsstands. The network runs daily, 6am–midnight. Twenty *búhobus* **night routes** run from Plaza de Cibeles (every half-hour midnight–3am, then every hour until 6am), with tickets and fares the same as during the day.

Taxis are white, with a diagonal red stripe on the door. The minimum fare is 180ptas, then it's 80ptas per km, with supplements 11pm–6am, at holidays, for luggage and for journeys to the main stations or the airport. Cabs can be flagged down, found at ranks marked with a blue T-sign, or booked on: ☎91/445 9008 (*Tele-Taxi*, Visa card accepted) or ☎91/547 8500 (*Radioteléfono Taxi*, Amex and Visa accepted). Give the name of the bar, restaurant, hotel or street corner, and your name – the **meter starts running** when the call is answered.

The main city **tourist information office** is at Plaza Mayor 3 (open Mon–Fri 10am–8pm, Sat 10am–2pm, ☎91/588 1636, M1/2/3 to Sol). The **regional authority** also has four offices, including one at Duque de Medinaceli 2 (open Mon–Fri 9am–7pm, Sat 9am–1pm, ☎91/429 4951, M2 Banco de España), and others at the international arrivals hall of Barajas airport and near platform 14 of Chamartín station. None can book hotels but all will provide useful information of some sort.

The best **listings magazine** is the weekly *Guía del Ocio* (Mondays, 125ptas). *Enjoy Madrid* (bimonthly, 200ptas) is in Spanish and English but is nowhere near as comprehensive. For a city-run telephone information line, dial ☎010 (☎91/366 6605 from outside town, open Mon–Fri 8.30am–9.30pm); you may have to wait a short while for an English-speaking operator.

Madrid has two specialist **football stores**. *Fútbol Total*, c/Cardenal Cisneros 80 (open daily 10.30am–2pm & 5–9pm, most credit cards), near Quevedo metro, has kits from all over Europe. *Deportes Aguila*, Palencia 3 (open Mon–Sat 10am–2pm, & 5–8.30pm, most credit cards), near Cuatro Caminos metro, specialises in local gear.

injury. But Mexican Hugo Sánchez regularly topped the league goalscoring list, while Argentine forward Jorge Valdano and German anchorman Uli Stielike both played with conviction.

In the mid-Eighties, *la quinta del Buitre* – 'the Vulture Squad' – rose through Real's competitive ranks to win the club five straight titles. Butragueño, Michel, Sanchis,

Martín Vázquez and Gordillo became first-team regulars for the best part of a decade which, in addition to a bulging trophy room, also saw major renovation to Bernabéu's stadium.

Behind the glossy exterior, however, Real were being subjected to scandalous financial mismanagement. In the early Nineties, president Ramón Mendoza all but

Renaissance man – Jorge Valdano contemplates his handiwork as Real climb back to the top, 1995

bankrupted the club, spending money that wasn't in the bank, then forging a series of disadvantageous marketing deals which robbed the club of huge potential earnings when they entered the Champions' League in 1995. That was the year when, having gifted two consecutive titles to Barça by losing the last match of their season at Tenerife, Real won a long-awaited title with the thoughtful Valdano as coach.

The Argentine's premature dismissal midway through the 1995/96 season saw the club miss out on Europe altogether the following year. So new president Lorenzo Sanz went for broke – investing in Davor Šuker, Clarence Seedorf, Roberto Carlos, Christian Panucci, Predrag Mijatović and coach Fabio Capello.

It worked – for a season. But Capello's subsequent swift departure back to Milan, after the 1996/97 title had been won, served only to highlight the uphill task facing a club which last won the European Cup three decades ago.

Here we go!
M6 metro to **Lima**. As you emerge, the Bernabéu is on the right-hand side, where Avenida Castellana meets Avenida Concha Espina.

Swift half
The Bernabéu is **ringed with bars**. Many fans hang out down c/Marceliano Santa Maria, the second street on the right down Avenida Concha Espina, in any of half-a-dozen bars or just swigging wine on the street. Nearer to the metro, **OK Madrid**, at c/San Juan de la Salle 5, has a great wall of classic black-and-white Madrid pictures. **Birrä**, Concha Espina 8, is definitely a cut above, an upmarket bar full of Forties Americana, with table football (Real-Atlético!) and a huge selection of beers.

On the other side of the stadium, the **Orsay**, c/Doctor Fleming 6, is packed with fans knocking back cheap *cañas* and *vino tinto*. No alcohol is on sale within the ground itself.

Tickets

The main **ticket office** is at gate #61
(open Mon–Fri 10am–1pm & 5.30–7.30pm
and two days before each match, no credit
cards). Unless it's raining, the best view is
from the *anfiteatro lateral*, the uncovered
main stand, divided into two tiers with
prices scaled accordingly – you'll pay
around 4–6000ptas.

The Real ultras can be found in the
fondo sur (season-ticket holders only)
behind the goal nearest Avenida Concha
Espina. The *fondo norte*, opposite, also has
Real fans, with visiting supporters heavily
policed into the tier above them. For games
against Barcelona, there is a 1km security
cordon around the ground.

Before big games, ticket **hustling** takes
place between B and C towers (*torres*), by
the car park on Avenida Castellana.

Publications

A *Programa Oficial* is issued free of charge,
available all around the ground. The club
also produce a glossy magazine, *Real Madrid
Monthly*, 500ptas from newsstands.

Club shop

The official shops on three corners of the
stadium are rather modest kiosks (open
Mon–Fri 10am–1.30pm & 4.30–8pm, Sat
10am–1.30pm and on matchdays). The
Tienda Estádio by gate #61 (open
Mon–Fri 10am–1.30pm & 5–8pm and on
matchdays, most credit cards) is equally
unimpressive for a club of Real's stature.
The **Todo Fútbol** van, parked at the corner of Concha Espina and Castellana on
matchdays, has a better selection.

Club museum

La Sala de Trofeos (open to the public
Mon–Fri 6.30–7.30pm, but not if there's a
game on) is a poorly annotated Aladdin's
cave of 550 pieces of silverware. You can
get to it through gate #61.

Ultra culture

The **Ultras Sur**, a permanent fixture in
the *fondo sur* since 1982, are the most

notorious in Spain and probably the loudest, too. Unlike many Spanish fan groups,
this lot have always travelled widely.
Throughout the Eighties, tensions rose
whenever the *Ultras Sur* came to town. At
home, Real were heavily fined after missiles rained down on Bayern Munich players
during a European Cup match in 1987. A
group with right-wing sympathies, the *Ultras
Sur's* natural allies are Espanyol's *Brigadas
Blanquiazules*.

In the net

The official website has been a long time
coming and was still not ready for the start
of the 1997/98 season. It's probably worth
going periodically to: www.realmadrid.es/.
Of the many unofficial sites floating around
in cyberspace, Luis Allende Fernandez's
symphony in lilac is one of the best, with a
good club history, squad information, latest
news and the expected stats archive. It's
at: www.geocities.com/Colosseum/4568.

Important import – Montenegro's Mijatović

Atlético Madrid

Estadio Vicente Calderón, Paseo Virgen del Puerto 67
Capacity 62,000
Colours Red-and-white striped shirts, blue shorts
League champions 1940–41, 1950–51, 1966, 1970, 1973, 1977, 1996
Cup winners 1960–61, 1965, 1972, 1976, 1985, 1991–92, 1996
Cup-Winners' Cup winnners 1962

One baking hot afternoon in June 1996, nearly a quarter of a million people took to the streets of Madrid to join with Jesús Gil y Gil in celebrating a victory few had thought possible. Atlético had won the title for the first time in nearly twenty years, a decade after the controversial mayor of Marbella had taken over as club president.

Gil had given the Spanish press ten years' worth of lively copy. As *el Atléti* consistently failed to match Real and Barça, Gil sacked 29 coaches. He had publicly

Bernd oak – Schuster at the Calderón

punched, sworn and insulted his way to notoriety. Now he had the last laugh.

For his coach, a Serb-born former Luton Town supersub called Radomir Antić, revenge also came sweet. A superb motivator, he had taken Real to the top of the *liga* table in 1991, and got the sack for his trouble. He then turned mediocre Oviedo into one of the most attractive club sides in Spain, before ignoring everyone's advice and taking the job at Atlético in 1995.

While planning a new-look team for Gil, Antić had seen his compatriot, midfield playmaker Milinko Pantić, on TV. The same under-achiever he had brought from third-division Jedinstvo to Partizan Belgrade in 1985 scored a hat-trick that day for Greek club Panionios. Just half-a-million dollars secured his transfer. Valencia's third-choice goalkeeper, Francisco Molina, was another cheap acquisition that somehow got past Gil. Bulgarian striker Ljuboslav Penev came with him on a free, and Antić urged existing players like striker Kiko and midfielders José Luis Caminero and Argentine Diego Simeone to give their all.

In the 1995/96 season, Atlético stayed top of the league from the first game to the last. Before the final whistle was blown on their decisive 2–0 win over Albacete, Gil was bathing in champagne. Outside, the Manzanares stadium, so rarely full these last ten years, made up for lost time.

The double was then won with an extra-time Pantić goal beating Barcelona. Fans of *los colchoneros* – the 'Mattress Makers' – had never slept so soundly.

Atlético earned their nickname because of their red-and-white striped shirts, originally borrowed from Athletic Bilbao when the club was formed by disgruntled members of Madrid FC in 1903. Initially a subsidiary of the Bilbao club, 'Athletic de Madrid' were drifting into obscurity when the Civil War came along. Relegated then promoted by default, the club were merged with the Spanish air force team, Aviación, with backing from the authorities. Former star goalkeeper and national hero Ricardo Zamora was put in charge, and as Atlético

Aviación the team won back-to-back titles in 1940 and 1941.

Another star coach, Helenio Herrera, was responsible for two further titles ten years later, but the newly named Atlético de Madrid received no further favours from General Franco. Real Madrid did them few favours, either. The first time the poor relations got a sniff of continental glory, in the semi-finals of the 1959 European Cup, Real brushed them aside in a replay.

'I have today given my vote of confidence to the manager' – Jesús Gil

Few clubs could have lived in such a shadow as Real's over Atlético. Even the team's single European success, in the 1962 Cup-Winners' Cup, slipped by almost unnoticed, their victorious replay against Fiorentina coming four months after the first game.

At around this time, Atlético's prospective move from the cramped Metropolitano to Manzanares at the other end of the city became bogged down in debt. The club's hard-working president, Vicente Calderón, bailed them out after they had spent a season grumpily ground-sharing with Real. The team returned briefly to the Metropolitano and the club's last season there fittingly saw the title won in 1966.

The new stadium, built over a ring road on the banks of the Manzanares river, by an old gasworks and surrounded by the smells of the Mahou brewery, saw some brutal football. First, Austrian disciplinarian Max Merkel instilled a tight, defensive game. Then, to add insult to inflicting injuries, Juan Carlos Lorenzo took control. The Argentine was known the world over for producing teams in the style of the Estudiantes side he played for in the late Sixties: vicious and unrepentant. Three of his players were sent off against Celtic in the 1974 European Cup semi-final, yet

Atlético won the tie, and came within a minute of lifting the trophy itself. At the final in Brussels, a speculative long-range shot by Bayern Munich defender Georg Schwarzenbeck in the last minute of extra-time tied the final at 1–1, after Luis had given the Spaniards the lead four minutes earlier. Bayern easily won the replay, 4–0.

Calderón, rewarded for his efforts by having the stadium named after him, would only live to see one more Spanish title, attained by a single-point margin over Barcelona in 1977.

The next major assault on the European Cup came as the 1996 celebrations were dying down. A confident breeze to the top of their Champions' League group, which included a win over the eventual winners Borussia Dortmund, earned Atlético a classic quarter-final pairing with Ajax. With the aggregate score tied at 2–2, a Pantić penalty looked to have given his side a semi-final meeting with Juventus. But on 100 minutes, Ajax equalised and, with chances going begging at either end, sealed the the the tie with a goal a minute from the end of extra-time.

Gil had gambled that the 1996 double-winning side was good enough to take on Europe. He quickly owned up to the error, signing Juninho, Christian Vieri and Jordi Lardín for the 1996/97 UEFA Cup.

Here we go!

Take **M5 metro** to Pirámides, cross the large roundabout of Glorieta Pirámides, then walk downhill towards the river for five minutes.

Swift half

Several bars dot the industrial area around the Manzanares. From Pirámides metro, the **Bar Santos** is the best of three in a row on Glorieta Pirámides. But it's worth holding out until the **Bar Resines**, Paseo de los Melancolicos 7, nearer the stadium, which sports pennants, scarves and a superb, framed colour aerial shot of the ground.

If you want the whole Atlético experience, cross the river and head for Paseo Quince de Mayo, left after the bridge. **Bar de la Peña** at #18 and **Bar Figón de Gredos** nearby are classic football bars, with colours and pub trophies to prove it.

Inside the stadium, the **Restaurante Rojiblanco** is next to the trophy room, up three flights of stairs from the main office at Puerta O.

Tickets

The main **ticket offices** are at gates #8 and #68, and unless Real Madrid or Barcelona are the visitors, turning up to buy yours on matchday shouldn't be a problem.

The most prestigious area is the *preferencia* stand, above the highway that runs under the stadium and colour-coded blue. The most expensive seats are in the *palco preferente B*, followed in descending order of price by the *tribuna de preferencia*, and *tribunas superiores baja* and *alta*.

On the other side is the *lateral*, colour-coded orange, in which the *anfiteatro* upstairs is divided into *primer* and *segundo*, the comfortable *tribuna* is just below, and the *grada* is at pitch level.

Visiting fans are allocated sections 405/6 and 505/6 in the *tribuna superior* of the *preferencia* (gates #3 and #4), and sections 417/8 and 517/8, opposite in the *lateral* (gates #31 and #33).

Publications

Atlético Madrid's eponymous magazine (monthly, 300ptas) is available at their club shops. You'll also see a fanzine, *Super Atléti* (300ptas), being sold at the ground most matchdays.

Club shop

The main club shop, **Tienda Estadio Oficial** (open Mon–Fri 10.15am–2pm, 4.30–8pm, Sat 10.15am–2pm and matchdays, Visa cards accepted) is by gate #14 of the Calderón. It's nothing special but the place to go for that much longed-after postcard portrait of Jesús Gil. There are **smaller stores** on the corner of Paseo Virgen del Puerto and c/del Duque de Tovar, and by the ticket office at gate #68.

Ultra culture

El Frente Atlético, based in the *fondo sur* behind one goal of the Calderón, are one of Spain's best-organised ultra groups. Their colourful choreography is certainly among the top three in the land and their away support is, for Spain, impressive.

In the net

The club run an excellent official website at: www.at-madrid.es/. Smart-looking and well maintained, it gives you the chance to book tickets and order replica shirts online, and also contains less commercial material like information for disabled fans.

Groundhopping

☙ Rayo Vallecano

Nuevo Vallecas, Payaso Fofó
Capacity 19,500
Colours White shirts with red sash, white shorts

This sympathetic working-class team from the downbeat district of Vallecas, former home of Atlético, are permanently stuck in the lift between Spain's first and second divisions. Their latest trip down occurred in the summer of 1997, when they lost a relegation play-off to Real Mallorca on away goals. The team have had six different coaches in the past two years alone, the sackings being conducted, Gil-style, with the minimum of ceremony by Spain's only female club president, Maria Teresa Rivero.

Unlike their counterparts at Atlético, Rayo loyalists make no grand claims about the level of support their team enjoys in the city. Not that they don't enjoy putting one over the big boys – Rayo's 2–1 league win at the Bernabéu in January 1996 was a key factor in the sacking of Real coach Jorge Valdano.

The last big star to play here was the Mexican international and former Real Madrid striker Hugo Sánchez, who averaged a goal every other game in 1993/94. Nigerian goalkeeper Wilfred Agbonavbare was a popular mainstay until his departure in 1996.

The immediate environs, with their Maoist graffiti and bingo halls, are about as unlikely a prelude to a big football team as you can get. Then again, so is the idea of Rayo becoming a credible third footballing force in the Spanish capital.

To watch the latest promotion struggle unfold, take **M1 metro** to Portazgo, two stops from the terminus. The metro stop is right next to the stadium.

The road c/Teniente Muñoz Diaz, which runs from the Portazgo metro exit round to La Colonia Virgen del Castañar, is full of bars. The **Blanco y Rojo** at #5 is a little upmarket for its own good; its **nameless rival** next door, and another at the next corner of the street, are brimming with old *Vallecasos* debating relegation, surrounded by the waft of cheap tobacco, draught Mahou and faded old football pictures.

Eat, drink, sleep...

Bars and clubs
La movida, the underground, post-Franco cultural explosion that earned Madrid nightlife its fame, is no more, but new habits die hard in this city. The **sheer volume** and variety of bars and clubs here matches anything in Europe.

Although city council rulings have since seen bars close earlier, you're still spoilt for choice at 2am. The Huertas area, embracing Sol, Sevilla and Atocha metro stops, and the slightly seedier Malasaña and Chueca between Bilbao and Chueca stations, have more bars than anyone could ever wish for.

'Discobars' don't charge admission but their beer will be twice the price of

Dance with me – Rayo's Cota clings on to someone famous

regular bars. Full-blown **clubs** demand
1500–2000ptas cover. In fine weather, the
terraza bars down Castellana are the place
to be.

Café Jazz Populart, c/Huertas 22. Possibly the
best jazz bar in town, with live reggae, salsa,
African and Brazilian music, too. Either 250ptas
cover, or extra for those Sol or Paulaner beers.
M1 Antón Martín.

La Habana, c/Atocha 107. Salsa, reggae or
world music accompanied by wicked Mojito or
Daiquiri cocktails. M1 Antón Martín.

Pachá, c/Barceló 11. A refurb and a swerve away
from that inane Spanish techno, *Bacalao*, has kept
this classy disco on top of its game. Open until
5am Wed–Sun. M1/10 Tribunal.

Stella, c/Arlabán 7. Run by local punk hotshot
Alaska from the *movida* days, the Stella is a reliable
dance club with house music on Saturdays and
a bowling alley downstairs. M1/2/3 to Sol. Also
check out the tackier, leopard-skin clad **Morocco**

under the same ownership, the other side of the
Gran Vía at c/Marqués de Leganés 7.

Viva Madrid, c/Manuel Fernández y González
7. Ideal starting point for a night around Santa
Ana, a large, popular tiled bar which buzzes with
anticipation. Open 8pm–3am. M1/2/3 to Sol.

Warhol's Club, c/Luchana 20. Keeping the sensible hours of 5–10am (or until noon on Sundays),
this spacious bar is packed with wobbly people
who kept 1250ptas back for admission and
another drink. M1/4 Bilbao.

Restaurants

Madrileño cuisine is traditionally heavy,
reliant on **stews** and **offal**. *Cocido Madrileño*
is a classic dish – a chickpea stew with
chorizo sausage – as is *caldereta de cordero*,
lamb stewed with tomatoes and peppers.

Eating out here isn't cheap, but look
out for a lunchtime *menú del día* at around
1000–1500ptas, or check out some of the
budget restaurants around M3/4 Argüelles

Mattress power – Atlético ultras threatened to paint the town black when their team won the title

and M3 Moncloa, near the university. *Tapas* bars are popular, but a few *raciones* (small platefuls) during an evening can be surprisingly dear. Local favourites include potatoes in spicy pepper sauce (*patatas bravas*), pig's ear (*orejas*) and tripe (*callos*).

De La Riva, c/Cochabamba 13. Open weekday lunchtimes only, a popular restaurant in the shadow of the Bernabéu where the talk is all Real. Varied, imaginative menu which changes regularly. Main courses around 2500ptas, Visa cards accepted. M9 Colombia.

Las Batuecas, Avenida Reina Victoria 17. Family-run place serving reasonably priced home cooking, including tripe and other local delicacies. Set lunch at 1000ptas. No credit cards. M1/2/6 Cuatro Caminos.

Las Bravas, Pasaje Matheu 5. One of the many places that claim to have invented *patatas bravas*, this friendly restaurant and *tapas* bar also serves up a mean octopus (*pulpo*). Outdoor tables. No credit cards. M1/2/3 Sol.

Museo del Jamón, c/de Alcalá 155. A Madrid institution (with six similar branches around town), a *tapas* bar and restaurant decked head to trotter in ham hocks, which dangle enticingly from the ceiling. Fabulous smoked meats, set lunches at 1000ptas. No credit cards. M1/2/3 Sol.

Nueva Galicia, c/de la Cruz 6. One of Madrid's many Galician restaurants, this one serves an excellent (and cheap) *caldo gallego* – vegetable and ham soup, *Canal Plus* TV and endless football chat. The bar area is open long after everything else around Sol has closed. No credit cards. M1/2/3 Sol.

Accommodation

Madrid is still a fairly **cheap city** to stay in, with most of the budget accommodation conveniently centred around the main nightlife areas.

Puerta del Sol and Plaza Santa Ana (M1/2/3 Sol) and c/Fuencarral (M1/5 Gran Vía) are all good stomping grounds, where

you can expect to pay 4–5000ptas for a double room in a *hostal* or *pensión*.

The *Brújula* accommodation agency, c/Princesa 1, 6th floor (open Mon–Fri 9am–7pm, Sat 9am–1pm, ☎91/559 9705, M2/3/10 to Plaza de España), can book you a room for a 250ptas fee. They also have a branch at the airport bus terminal in Plaza de Colón (open daily 8am–10pm, ☎91/575 96 80, M4 Colón).

If you arrive in hot weather and have a little more money to spare, make sure your room has **air conditioning**.

Albergue Juvenil Santa Cruz de Marcenado, c/Santa Cruz de Marcenado 28 (☎91/547 4532). Modern, quiet youth hostel in the university area, dorm beds at 1000ptas including breakfast, 800ptas for under-26s. Three-day maximum stay. Curfew 1.30am. *Pensión* facilities also available. No credit cards. M3/4/6 Argüelles.

Hostal Jeyma, c/Arenal 24, 3rd floor (☎91/541 6329). Surprisingly quiet *pensión* in the Sol area, singles at 1500ptas, doubles 2800ptas. No credit cards. M2/5 Opera.

Hostal Sud Americana, Paseo del Prado 12, 6th floor (☎91/429 2564). With a great location by the Prado museum, this small *hostal* has elegant fittings and high ceilings. Singles around 2500ptas, doubles 4000ptas. No credit cards. M2 Banco de España.

Hotel Monaco, c/Barbieri 5 (☎91/522 4630, fax 91/521 1601). If you've a little extra to spare and have a sense of humour and history, this is the place for you – a former celebrated bordello that is now a quaint, quirky hotel frequented by pop video directors and lifestyle photographers. In spite of this, it's very reasonably priced, especially if you haggle. Doubles around 8000ptas. Air conditioned. Most major credit cards. M5 Chueca.

Pensión Poza, c/Nuñez de Arce 9 (☎91/522 4871). Laughably cheap if basic *pensión* two steps from all the nightlife action, with another floor of rooms a few doors down. No credit cards. M2 Sevilla.

Seville

Sevilla FC 513
Real Betis 516

Deep in the south of Spain, in the region's fiery capital of Seville, burns the country's fiercest cross-town footballing rivalry. Away from the title battles between Madrid and Barcelona, the city's two clubs, Sevilla and Real Betis, have been enjoying their own private feud since one club broke from the other at the turn of the century.

The vast, hot southern province of Andalucía first saw football being played around the same time as the Basque country in the far north. Recreativo de Huelva were the first club, playing a game against a Seville select XI consisting mainly of British employees of the Riotinto mines. It was these employees who formed Sevilla Football Club in 1905, their directorship taken from the native land-owning classes that ruled Andalucía. When one director refused to hire a local factory worker at the club, there was a revolt and Betis were founded by the dissident members.

Betis merged with Sevilla Balompié in 1914, and made King Alfonso XIII their honorary president. They became Real Betis Balompié, taking their new title from their royal patronage and the old Spanish name for football, and met Sevilla for the first time on New Year's Day, 1916. Against a political backdrop of disputes over land reform and Andalucían autonomy, the first derby game, which finished 2–2, saw flare-ups of violence all over Seville. The next eighty years saw Sevilla generally holding the upper hand, until the Betis revival of the mid-Nineties.

Although both have moved around town since their early days at the Prado de San Sebastián, their deep divisions are typified by their current respective geographical locations. Sevilla's impressive Sánchez Pizjuán is in the commercial district of Nervión, surrounded by fast highways; Betis' Benito Villamarín is in working-class Heliópolis, south of town on the 'wrong' side of the river Guadalquivir.

Both grounds were originally named after their area, then renamed after influential club presidents. Both underwent renovations for the 1982 World Cup. And both will long be remembered for the games they hosted: Betis' for David Narey's toe-poke for Scotland against Brazil; Sevilla's for the epic semi-final between France and West Germany.

Until recently, both grounds were also used regularly for Spain's international matches. The tradition began with a bizarre 12–1 win over Malta in late 1983, which enabled Spain to qualify for Euro '84 above Holland on goals scored. Playing in Seville became known as *un talisman*, a lucky charm, the team apparently galvanised by the raucous atmosphere generated and fervent flamenco handclapping. Free from any of the ethnic tensions felt elsewhere in Spain, the Andalucían crowd was solidly behind *la selección*.

After Malta, Spain won 20 out of 23 qualifying matches in Seville. But it was a thin, frustrated crowd which witnessed a narrow 1–0 win over Armenia in June 1995, causing the Spanish FA to rethink and stage important games elsewhere.

Of the two, the Benito Villamarín has the edge on ambiance, and of late its hosts have had the better time of it, making regular excursions into Europe. Former prime minister Felipe González is Betis' biggest fan, and it has become fashionable to follow the *verdiblancos*.

Sevilla fans have accused Betis of plotting to get their club relegated by 'going easy' against another struggling side, Sporting Gijón, in 1997. But when Sevilla finally did go down that summer, nobody worried more than Betis president Manuel Ruiz de Lopera, who knows the derby is good for business – he had, after all, been the first to stand behind his counterpart when Sevilla were threatened with relegation by the FA over bureaucratic irregularities in 1995.

The thrilling fields

 Sevilla FC

Estadio Sánchez Pizjuán, Avenida Eduardo
Dato
Capacity 68,000
Colours All white with red trim
League champions 1946
Cup winners 1935, 1939, 1948

The grand mosaic which dominates the
entrance to the superb Sánchez Pizjuán
stadium incorporates badges from teams
who have visited the ground. But while it's
true that many visitors have left with their
tails between their legs, Sevilla's shocking
away form has contributed to their meagre record in modern times.

With no domestic trophy since 1948,
no decent European run to speak of the
prospect of second-division football in
1997/98, Sevilla hardly do justice to their
position as the leading team in Spain's
fourth city. Which is a shame, considering
the venue, the depth of support in it, and
the kind of footballers who have played
there in the last few years.

The club's early progress, after their
foundation in 1905, was halted by half the
team leaving to form Betis two years later.
Seville was the first city to fall to Franco
in the Civil War, and Sevilla took advantage of their stadium staying open by
winning the cup in 1939, their only league
title in 1946, and the cup again two years
later. While Betis declined, Sevilla kept their
passionate home crowd happy by taking
the occasional big scalp at the Sánchez
Pizjuán. Their only major European victory,
however, was a 3–1 win over Benfica in
the pre-Eusébio days of 1957.

There has been much endeavour but
little to show for it since. Like so many
Andalucían workers, Sevilla's homegrown
players have tended to leave for the bright
lights as soon as they've been given the
chance. Yet until recently the club was not

An expensive flop – Diego Maradona, 1993

without resources, and in the Eighties and
Nineties recruited a series of expensive
foreigners to the Sánchez Pizjuán.

Their fortunes were decidedly mixed.
Russian international 'keeper Renat
Dasayev settled in well, staying on to run a
sports shop in town. Toni Polster, Daniel
Bertoni, Bebeto and Ilie Dumitrescu all flitted in and out. Perhaps the saddest of all
was Diego Maradona, brought here by his
fellow Argentine, coach Carlos Bilardo,
partly to cure his cocaine addiction, and
partly to keep world attention focused on
Seville after the Expo had finished at the
end of 1992. Unfit and unsettled, Maradona
proved an expensive flop. His 26-game stay
resulted in five goals, two red cards – and
an awful lot of shoe leather on the part of
the private detectives hired by the club to
follow him around the city's nightclubs and
bordellos.

Much more successful was Davor Šuker,
the Croatian striker who scored more than
sixty goals in four seasons at the Sánchez

Davor Šuker, Sevilla hero

Pizjuán. Towards the end of the 1995/96 camnpaign, Šuker signed a pre-contract with Real Madrid. But the Sevilla faithful refused to turn against him. In his last game for the club, he scored a hat-trick against Salamanca to keep the team in the top flight and was carried head-high from the field, a modern-day flamenco hero.

Sevilla received around £7 million for Šuker, but all it did was pay off old debts. When the club tried to buy another Croatian, Robert Prosinečki, from Barcelona later in the summer of 1996, their cheque bounced.

It was Sevilla's inability to secure bank guarantees that almost led to their automatic relegation in 1995; thousands took to the streets in protest, and the club's reinstatement gave rise to Spain's unwieldy 22-club first division.

By June 1997, however, Sevilla had done the FA's job for them, after a season which saw three coaches come and go, a series of bad-tempered boardroom squabbles, and relegation.

Here we go!

Several buses pass down the highways surrounding the Sánchez Pizjuán. The **#21, #22** or **#23** from the main municipal bus crossroads at Plaza Nueva stop at the corner of Avenida de Eduardo Dato and c/de Luis Morales. Allow fifteen minutes from town. The new **Santa Justa** train station is not so far as the crow flies, but a pig to negotiate if you're new in town.

Swift half

On matchdays the otherwise business-like atmosphere around the stadium is transformed into a party zone. The narrow streets leading off Avenida de Eduardo Dato, on the south side of the stadium, throng with activity. Three bars are particularly worthy of note. **Casa Antonio**, c/Jose Luis de Casso 4, on the east side of the stadium, has one wall of budgerigars, another of football scarves and great local characters within it. **Bar Jota**, c/Puerta Carmona 52, is a Sevilla supporters' bar. And **Bar Buenos Aires**, Divino Retentor 10, run by ex-player Acosta, is a little staid but does great pre-match mussels and seafood.

Tickets

The Sánchez Pizjuán is huge, but even in their relegation season Sevilla pulled in average crowds of more than 45,000, so don't assume you'll just be able to turn up on the day. The **ticket office** is by the main entrance. Cheapest places are in the *Baja Gol Sur* and *Norte*, while the *Fondo* is a little pricier and the best seats in the house are in the *Preferencia Tribuna*. Visiting fans are placed in the *Grada Alta* of the *Gol Sur*.

Publication

El Sevillista (bi-monthly, 300ptas) is the club's glossy, available at most local newsstands.

Club shop

The **Tienda de Regalos** (open Mon–Fri 11am–2pm & 6–8pm, Sat 9.30am–1.30pm and matchdays, Visa cards only) is by the main office entrance. In among the usual paraphernalia you'll find Sevilla-badged lingerie for those hot Andalucían nights.

Ultra culture

The **peña Biri-Biri** are named after an African player who was with the club in the Seventies. The group is divided into *Norte* and *Sud*, and the two sections indulge in choreographed chants which echo around the Sánchez Pizjuán The *Norte* section count among the most fervent fans in Spain – videos of their activities are on sale in the club shop, and they produce their own fanzine, *Mágico Nervión*, available at the ground on matchdays.

In the net

There's no official Sevilla website, but Javier Gayán Guardiola runs a fine alternative at: ibgwww.colorado.edu/~gayan/futbol/tsevilla. html. It's a deceptively simple-looking site, with news, stats archive and animated goal action, all delivered with pride and passion.

Seville essentials

Expo '92 in Seville brought fast, new transport links with the rest of Spain. The city's San Pablo **airport** is 12km northeast of town, connected by the EA Airport Bus (twelve buses daily, thirty minutes journey time, 750ptas) to central Puerta de Jerez. A taxi will come to about 2000ptas.

A spanking new **train station**, Santa Justa, has been built east of the centre, and is where the new luxury high-speed *AVE* train arrives from Madrid Atocha. The service is expensive – about 15,000ptas return – but takes just two-and-a-half hours. Other trains cost two-thirds as much to do the same journey, taking around six hours. To get into town from Santa Justa station, take bus #20 to Plaza Nueva.

Five trains and nine buses a day run from **Málaga** to Seville, taking between three-and-a-half and four-and-a-half-hours each. From Málaga airport, take the electric train to the main RENFE train station, one before the terminus at Guadelmedina (journey time 25 minutes). Málaga's bus station is nearby.

Seville's main **bus station** is at Prado de San Sebastián, a ten-minute walk or short bus journey (#25 or #26) to Plaza Nueva in town. Seville's buses run 6am–11pm in winter, until midnight in summer. Two circular lines – #C1/2 and #C3/4 – run outside the centre of the city. A limited night bus service runs from Plaza Nueva at midnight (winter only), 1am and 2am.

Ordinary **tickets** are issued onboard and cost 115ptas. A *Bonobus* book of ten is 575ptas, available from newsstands and *Tussam* kiosks. *Bonobus* tickets are valid for one hour – you can change as often as you like so long as you don't go back to your original line.

Official **taxis** are white with a blue stripe. The driver will prattle away in fluent *Andaluz*, a lifestyle away from your GCSE Spanish, and will charge around 800ptas for a journey from Santa Justa to somewhere central. Officially the flat fare is 120ptas, plus 60ptas per km, with supplements according to time, luggage and mood. To call a cab, dial ☎95/462 2222.

The **tourist office** is near the cathedral at Avenida de la Constitución 21 (open Mon–Sat 9am–7pm, Sun & holidays 10am–2pm, ☎95/422 1404, fax 95/422 9753). The staff are friendly but practical information is thin on the ground.

You'll find Seville's only **listings publication**, the free monthly *El Geraldillo*, woefully short on concert and nightclub information. The English-language press also available here caters for retired expatriates on the Costa del Sol.

 **Real Betis**

Estadio Benito Villamarín, Avenida de Heliópolis
Capacity 47,500
Colours Green-and-white striped shirts, white shorts
League champions 1935
Cup winners 1977

Real Betis Balompié, or *Er Beti* as they are known in the local rapid-fire, swallow-all dialect, are the most popular Spanish provincial team of the Nineties. This mini-boom has been instigated by owner and president Manuel Ruiz de Lopera, who has turned a debt-ridden second-division club into a profitable, fashionable but still down-to-earth outfit who could yet take a few big European scalps, such is the tempestuous atmosphere at the Benito Villamarín.

In this contemporary golden age, a nice bonus for the *verdiblancos* has been to look far down the *liga* table and find their city rivals Sevilla at the opposite end of it. Apart from a narrow title win in 1935 and a cup final triumph on penalties over Athletic Bilbao in 1977, Betis have spent much of their ninety-year history in the shadow of their neighbours. Some thirty years have been spent in the lower divisions, and the club nearly went under altogether in the Fifties.

Historically, Betis were not designed to shine in the Franco era. Born of the social prejudice of turn-of-the-century Andalucía by breakaway group from Sevilla FC, the club have always attracted left-wing sympathy. That solitary title win came on the eve of the Civil War and the killing of Andalucían republican poet Federico García Lorca; Betis fans should have known that the glory wasn't to last.

Whereas now it is hip to declare your love for *Er Beti*, it's not that long ago that such support would have been frowned upon. The main star the club produced in the Franco era was Luis del Sol, and it is significant that his finest hour came not in green and white but while playing for Real Madrid in their 7–3 win over Eintracht Frankfurt in 1960. By comparison, Betis themselves have been non-entities in Europe, their only win of note coming over AC Milan in the first round of the Cup-Winners' Cup in 1977.

Such a lack of big-time experience did nothing to deter coach Lorenzo Sarra Ferrer, nicknamed *El Brujo* ('The Wizard'), who came from Real Mallorca in 1994, gained the club promotion, then kept them in and around the UEFA Cup placings for three seasons. In addition to expert coaching, the club's easygoing nature and passionate support have kept star names eager to stay and compete. In 1996/97, Nigerian World Cup star Finidi George and Croatian wing-back Robert Jarni provided the service that allowed striker Alfonso to stay just behind Ronaldo in the *Liga* scoring charts.

All three were in tears after Betis lost the final of the *Copa del Rey* to Barcelona after extra-time at the end of the season. But so long as Lopera remains ambitious, and so long as the team keep playing their electric, every-inch-of-the-pitch brand of attacking football, it is surely only a matter of time before Betis make a European semi-final.

Here we go!
Take **bus #6** or **#35** from Plaza de España, or **#34** from Plaza Nueva, towards the university. Allow a good fifteen minutes from the city centre.

Swift half
There are cheap bars all the way down c/de Reina Mercedes on the way to the stadium, some offering set lunches for as little as 600ptas. The **Colmu** at #17 is probably the liveliest.

The **Bar Parada** on the corner of Avenida del Padre García Terejo is another stop, its name referring to the bus rather than the goalkeeping variety.

The **Bodeguita Castulo** at Terejo 17 is a classic Betis bar, cramped and hotter than an Andalucían launderette, but full of team photos and bullfighting graphics.

Tickets

Sellouts are a serious problem at the Benito Villamarín. The main **ticket office** is between gates #5 and #25. The Betis ultras go behind *Gol Sur*, away support with the cheaper tickets in *Gol Norte*. The most expensive seats are in the *Anfiteatro Numerado*; the *Tribuna Numerada* is slightly cheaper but still offers a decent view.

Publication

El Mundo Bético (monthly, 300ptas), is the club's glossy mag available at newsstands.

Club shop

La Tienda Oficial del Betis Balompié (open matchdays and theoretically Mon–Fri 9am–2pm & 5–8.30pm), is basically just a kiosk by gate #18 of the stadium.

Ultra culture

There's a family atmosphere at the Benito Villamarín, and the *Supporters Gol Sur* do little more than let the odd green-and-white painted rabbit onto the pitch.

In the net

You'd expect an unofficial Betis website to be fun, and Francisco Rojas Pulido's offering is just that, at: www.geocities.com/Colosseum/8611. The usual news and stats are overshadowed by exhortations to join the *Cyberbéticos* internet fan club and by the wacky *Planeta Betis* chat forum.

Eat, drink, sleep...

Bars and clubs

The Andalucían summer takes no prisoners. The only way to survive from April to September is by knocking back life-giving glasses of draught *Cruzcampo*, the excellent **local beer**. The average bar is run by some shuffling old *Andaluz*, who'll chalk a running tab on the counter. Service will be desperately slow, but friendly.

That said, Sevilla is a tourist city and the places in central Barrio Santa Cruz can

From Triana to Europe – Betis' Alfonso gets away from Uche Okechukwu of Fenerbahçe

¡Musho Beti eh! **The faithful at the Benito Villamarín are among Spain's friendliest footie fans**

be pricey. Just across the river from here is Triana, a more down-to-earth district full of *tapas* bars, and a Betis stronghold. The places along c/Betis by the river's edge are lively, as are those around the Plaza de Toros opposite.

Discos, many located on the former Expo site at La Cartuja, are too dear for most, so people organise *botellonas* – improvised open-air parties with cheap rum sold out of car boots.

The only people you'll see in the city's **Flamenco clubs** are tourists willing to part with up to 3000ptas for a show.

Blanco Cerrillo, c/Dr Jiménez Díaz 16. A bit out of the centre, but a great football bar with caricatures of the pub team on the wall, signed pix of old Betis stars and a crowd for games on *Canal Plus*. The regulars know their football. Bus #11 or #12 from central Encarnación.

Kiosko de las Flores, Puente Isabel II. Classic Triana bar overlooking the river with outdoor tables. A little pricey, but worth it for the atmosphere. Closed Mondays. Tucked into the bridge – circle line buses #C1 and #C2 run nearby.

La Carbonería, c/Levies 18. Atmospheric traditional flamenco bar which operated illegally in Franco's time, with a terrace and patio. Tucked away near Santa Cruz church.

P Flaherty, c/Alemanes. In a tiny street by the cathedral, the best Irish bar in town, with a TV room showing English Premiership action on Saturdays at 4pm, and Spanish games on *Canal Plus*. Full Irish breakfast at 850ptas, Guinness at 500ptas, open until 3am if there's a crowd.

Sopa de Ganso, c/Pérez Galdós 8. Popular music bar with live bands on Thursdays and an original range of *tapas*. Gets pretty crowded, so grab a table early. Open until 3am. Just off lively Plaza Alfalfa in the centre.

Restaurants

Andalucía is the home of *tapas* – small snacks to go with your drink – and a full restaurant meal is generally reserved for special occasions here. There are *tapas* bars on virtually every street, offering small platefuls of meat or fish for 300–500ptas, or larger *raciónes* for 500–700ptas; a couple of the latter is a meal in itself, washed down with beer, wine or fino (dry) sherry.

Andalucían cooking is fresh and light. Seafood is prominent, being used in *zarzuela* (fish stew) and *arroz marinero*, the local fish paella. But a set *menú del día* three-course lunch (around 750–1000ptas) will probably feature meat for main course.

The other local delicacy is the famous *gazpacho* – cold tomato, pepper and garlic soup, served in glasses clinking with ice and a lifesaver on a July afternoon.

Cervecería Giralda, c/Mateos Gago 1. Not cheap, but a classic *tapas* bar behind the cathedral with a wide selection of main courses and smaller portions. Open until midnight. No credit cards.

El Aragonés, c/Juan Manuel Rodríguez Correa 15. Just up from the Red Cross building on the circular #C1 and #C4 bus routes, notable for serving the best *patatas bravas* in town and some of the cheapest *tapas*. No credit cards.

La Albahaca, Plaza Santa Cruz 9. All the romantic trimmings in this converted mansion slap bang in the middle of Seville, with tables outside, three dining rooms inside and great variety on the menu. Expect to pay 4500ptas for the full splurge, but the *menú* at 3500ptas is money well spent. Closed Sundays. Most major credit cards.

Los Gallegos, c/Capataz Franco. In an alleyway just off c/Martín Villa, near c/San Eloy, a cheap but high-quality restaurant where locals eat away from the tourist traps in town. No credit cards.

Mesón La Barca, c/Santander 6. Small, reasonably priced restaurant serving decent portions of fish and venison dishes, near the Torre del Oro. Open until midnight, closed Saturdays. No credit cards. If you feel like splashing out, the **Bodegón Torre del Oro** at #15 has superb set meals with wine at 3000ptas.

Accommodation

Seville is not cheap to stay in at any time of year. If you're thinking of coming during *Semana Santa,* the festival between Palm Sunday and Good Friday, or the April Fair, book yourself a room months in advance – and be prepared to pay double.

For the rest of the year, the area around the old train station, particularly c/de San Eloy, is the best hunting ground for reasonably priced accommodation. The Barrio Santa Cruz is a little more expensive, but equally reliable. **Air conditioning** is a luxury worth paying extra for.

Albergue Juvenil Fernando el Santo, c/Isaac Peral 2 (☎95/461 3154). Comfortable youth hostel out towards the Betis stadium, with no lockout or curfew. Beds at 1000ptas for IYHF members under-26, 1200ptas those over-26 and 3000ptas for non-members. Three-day maximum stay. Bus #34 from Plaza Nueva.

Goya, c/Mateos Gago 31 (☎95/421 1170). Good-value hotel with a decent variety of rooms, all of a fair size, and only two of which face onto the noisy street. Doubles at 6000ptas with shower, 5000ptas without. No credit cards. Near the cathedral.

Hotel Murillo, c/Lope de Rueda 7 (☎95/421 6095, fax 95/421 9616). Simple but comfortable hotel in a restored mansion. Doubles at 12,000ptas with a shower, 7000ptas without. Most major credit cards. In the heart of Barrio Santa Cruz.

Hostal Plaza Sevilla, c/Canalejas 2 (☎95/421 7149, fax 95/421 0773). Designed by Aníbal González, the architect of the Ibero-Americana Exhibition held in the city in 1929, this comfortable hotel has a splendid façade, air-conditioning and an on-site hairdresser. Doubles at 10–16,000ptas. No credit cards. Within a stagger of the bars of c/San Eloy.

Hotel Simón, c/García de Vinuesa 19 (☎95/422 6660, fax 95/456 2241). A bargain out of season, the Simón is in a restored 18th century mansion with a fabulous courtyard and dining room. Double rooms at 6000ptas, 9000ptas with bath. Breakfast extra. Laundry service available. No credit cards. Off Avenida de la Cónstitución, near the Cathedral.

Valencia

Valencia CF 521

The vibrant fiesta city of Valencia was one of the first to pick up on football after the game filtered south from the Basque country. Its main club, Valencia CF, are the fifth most-titled in Spanish history, with three European honours to their name.

The club were formed by foreign residents and students in 1902, then reformed with local players in 1919, but didn't make the first division until 1931, and only won their first honour, the *Copa del Rey*, ten years later.

Valencia's stadium, La Mestalla, was used for the host nation's three group games at the 1982 World Cup. It had been intended that Spain would remain in Valencia for the second-round group, too, and *la selección* played no fewer than six warm-up friendlies here to acclimatise themselves to the atmosphere. But in their last group match, Gerry Armstrong gave Northern Ireland a 1–0 win which pushed the Spaniards into second place in the table – and packed them off to Madrid for the second stage.

Since then, Valencia has hosted matches in the 1992 Olympic soccer tournament, but has only occasionally been used by the national side and as a neutral venue for the Spanish cup final.

Current club president Paco Roig is big-talking and publicity-hungry in the Jesús Gil y Gil mould. His latest plans include restyling and expanding the Mestalla to a 75,000 capacity, with a commercial area, offices and executive boxes. How this will suit Valencia's most famous fan is another matter. 'Manolo', the fat drummer on whom the cameras focus at every World Cup, is a resident of Valencia, and has dedicated himself to forever drumming up support for his local team. His bar near

Valencia essentials

The official **language** of Valencia is a local brand of Catalan, which is being fiercely promoted by the regional government, but Spanish is used and understood everywhere.

Valencia's **Manises airport** is 15km south-west of the city. *Cercanías* trains run from here to Estación del Nord (Mon–Fri every half hour, Sat–Sun hourly, thirty minutes' journey time, 165ptas). It's a short walk from the train station down Avenida Marqués de Sotelo to central Plaza de Ayuntamiento. A *CVT* bus runs to the main **bus station** at Avenida Menéndez Pidal 13 (hourly 6am–8pm, journey time thirty minutes, 250ptas), which is across the river by bus #28 from town.

From **Mallorca** and the other Balearic Islands, **ferries** connect with Valencia's Estación Marítima, from which bus #4 goes to the Plaza de Ayuntamiento.

Valencia has a new four-line **metro system** and a network of *EMT* buses, half of which leave from Plaza de Ayuntamiento 22. Both the metro and buses run 6am–10.30pm, after which there is a limited night bus service through Plaza de Ayuntamiento every forty minutes, 11pm–1.20am only.

An ordinary single **ticket** for the metro costs 120ptas, while a *bonodiez* of ten is 1000ptas. Buses are cheaper – 90ptas for one journey (pay onboard or buy in advnace from newsstands), 625ptas for ten. **Taxis** are generally found in Plaza de Ayuntamiento, or call ☎96/370 3333 or ☎96/357 1313.

The main **tourist office** is at Plaza de Ayuntamiento 1 (open Mon–Fri 8.30am–2pm & 4–6pm, Sat 9am–12.45pm, ☎96/351 0417). The daily *Levante* (125ptas) puts out a weekly arts events supplement, *La Cartelera Turia*, but the best publication for nightclub and concert details is *¿Qué y Dónde?* (weekly, 125ptas).

the ground is well worth a visit. It's not known whether he also has a soft spot for Valencia's minor neighbours, Levante UD, who have occasionally sneaked into the first division but were last spotted somewhere deep in the regional leagues.

The thrilling fields

 ## Valencia CF

La Mestalla, Avenida Aragón 33
Capacity 49,000
Colours White shirts, black shorts
League champions 1942, 1944, 1947, 1971
Cup winners 1941, 1949, 1954, 1967, 1979
Cup-Winners' Cup winners 1980
Fairs' (UEFA) Cup winners 1962–63

Valencia president Francisco Roig has the notion to ride the current boom in Spanish football and create his own soccer empire just north of the Costa Blanca.

It was Roig's money which prompted the arrival of Brazilian striker Romário at the club in 1996, against the wishes of then coach Arsenio Iglesias. Romário himself unsuccessfully tried to get Iglesias sacked. Both parties left the club, Romário going on loan back to Brazil (perhaps never to return), Iglesias to be replaced by the more attack-minded Argentine, Jorge Valdano. In the chaos, Valencia missed out on a European place.

The disappointment in the city is tangible. The reconstruction Roig has planned for the tight, friendly Mestalla stadium will cost some 4 billion pesetas, 3 billion of which is being borrowed from the local council – and European football is vital to whole project.

Valencia were late developers – the club's first title came 25 years after their recognised foundation in 1919 – but regular European football has come to be expected here, following a tradition which began when the club reached three con-

Romário indicates the size of his pay-cheque

secutive European finals between 1962 and 1964. *Los Ches* won a European trophy at their first attempt, with Brazilians Chicão and Waldo and inside-left Vicente Guillot in their side. Guillot got a hat-trick in the 6–2 home win over Barcelona in the first leg of the Fairs' Cup final, and the trophy was successfully defended the following season against Dinamo Zagreb. The 1964 final was decided on one match in Barcelona against Real Zaragoza, when the 2–1 scoreline going against the holders.

In those days Valencia's football was crisp and cavalier in the style of the great

Take that – Valencia oust Bayern from the UEFA Cup, 1996

International defender Miguel Tendillo wasn't asked to take one that night in Brussels, but it was his penalty which saved Valencia from relegation three years later – and prevented Real Madrid from winning the title.

Though there have been no similar scares, mediocrity has been the keynote since. The closest Valencia have come to silverware in the Nineties was in the *Copa del Rey* final of 1995, when 10,000 *Valencianos* travelled to Madrid to see just fourteen minutes of football, after the initial game had been abandoned in torrential rain – it was just long enough for their opponents, Deportivo La Coruña, to net the winning goal.

Knocking holders Bayern Munich out of the 1996/97 UEFA Cup was a major achievement, but it did not disguise the fact that the club has some serious rebuilding to do on the pitch as well as off it. Spain's most-capped international, goalkeeper Andoni Zubizarreta, is approaching retirement, and it remains to be seen whether Roig's cash will be enough to keep some of the more talented outfield players in Valencia.

Real Madrid team of the era. When one of the key members of that Madrid side, Alfredo di Stéfano, coached Valencia to their only title in modern times in 1971, they were playing a dour, defensive game; after finishing level on points with Barcelona, their low 'goals against' total earned them the championship.

Valencia have scarcely had a sniff of the title since, and Europe has also been an unhappy hunting ground, save for a Cup-Winners' Cup triumph in 1980. In what was the first European club final to be decided on penalties, a side containing 1978 Argentine World Cup hero Mario Kempes and the 1974 tournament's influential German, Rainer Bonhof, beat Arsenal after 120 tense, goalless minutes. Goalkeeper Carlos Pereira saved Graham Rix's final penalty (he was in good company – both Kempes and Liam Brady failed to convert), and the cup was Valencia's.

Here we go!

La Mestalla is the other side of town from the dried up Turia river, along Avenida de Aragón. The **buses** which go from town are the **#12, #21, #71, #89** and **#90**, but leave yourself at least twenty minutes – the traffic can be murder. From the train or bus station, take the *Via Circular* bus to the bottom of Avenida de Aragón, then a ten-minute walk from there. If you're running late, a **taxi** might be able to weave down the backstreets – it'll cost around about 750ptas from the city centre.

Swift half

Drummer Manolo has his own bar/museum, **Museo Deportivo de**

Manolo el del Bombo, on the Plaza Valencia CF by the stadium. Otherwise there are bars all down Avenida de Aragón, Avenida Suecia, c/Artes Gráficas and c/Micer Masco. For a football theme, try the **Bar Penalty** at Suecia 27, opposite the ticket office, or the **Mestalla** at Micer Masco 13.

Tickets

The main **ticket office** is on the corner of c/Artes Gráficas and Avenida Suecia. The *Palco Preferiente* has the most expensive seats, the *Tribuna Numerada* is best for the neutral, and the *Fondo Sur* behind the goal is dirt cheap – as in many Spanish grounds, the terracing in the *Fondo* is high above the seating area rather than the other way around. **Visiting fans** are allocated seats in sector 27, the highest part of the *Tribuna* overlooking the sideline.

Ultra culture

Los Yumos in the *Fondo Norte* like a beer. Formed in 1983, they were the first in Spain to choreograph with coloured cards, and their originality is widely recognised. Their sworn enemies are Barcelona, the empathetic groups the *Gavnas Sur* from Logroñés and the *Ultra Boys* from Gijón.

In the net!

The official Valencia website is at: www.valenciacf.es/. Click on the appropriately coloured swooping bat (the club's symbol) for your choice of English, Spanish or Valencian Catalan. You'll find little that deviates from the party line, but the official news and fan club areas are worth a peek.

Eat, drink, sleep...

Bars and clubs

Valencia has some of the **best nightlife** to be found in mainland Spain – no idle boast. Another plus is that there are few tourists here outside *Fallas*, the week-long festival (March 12–19) of fireworks and processional floats.

The central area around the cathedral is quite dead after dark and can give the false impression that nothing goes on in town. In fact, the action is taking place around Plaza Cánovas Castillo, an area full of music bars, each with its own particular style – including *bacalao*, the rather sad Spanish form of techno that was invented in Valencia.

In summer, the bars lining Malvarrosa beach are the places to be – take bus #19 from Plaza del Ayuntamiento.

Drinks-wise, **cocktails** (*combinadas*) are particularly popular, with *Agua de Valencia* (orange juice, champagne and vodka) the locals' favourite.

Café Malvarrosa, c/Ruíz de Lihoro. Just off c/de la Paz, a pleasant café which serves its own *Agua de Malvarrosa* cocktail, made with lemon instead of orange.

Cervecería de Madrid, c/de la Abadía de San Martín 10. Just below Plaza de la Reina, an old-fashioned bar with walls full of paintings, where they serve the orthodox *Agua de Valencia*.

Circuito Oliag, c/Circuito Oliag 6. Definitive Valencia supporters' bar, full of scarves, photos and footie talk. Don't be put off by the constant headache of the fruit machines.

Vivir sin Dormir, Paseo Neptuno. Best bar in the quieter area between Paseo Neptuno and the new Paseo Maritimo, next to the port. Pool and candlelit tables.

Woody, c/Menendez y Pelayo 37. A typical *Valenciano* disco – 1500ptas entry, with the music either mainstream *bacalao* or old-school dance tunes from the Seventies. Bright lights and loons. Open Fridays and Saturdays only, until dawn.

Restaurants

Valencia is the home of *paella*, a dish traditionally eaten at midday, which means that it is sometimes difficult to find after dark. Paseo Neptuno is lined with small hotels, all of which have their own *paella* and *marisco* **restaurants**. The city beach, Playa Levante, also has plenty of possibilities. For *tapas* and **budget eating**, head for the Barrio del Carmen.

Barbacoa, Plaza del Carmen 6. Serves a wonderful *menú del día* including barbecued meat for 1500ptas. Be prepared to wait as it's small and very popular. Bus #5.

Bar Cánovas, Plaza Cánovas Castillo. One of the city's best *tapas* bars, perfect for a pre-club bite, around Valencia's liveliest *plaza*. Bus #1, #2, #3 or #4.

Bar Pilar, c/Moro Zeit. Just off Plaza del Esparto, a traditional place for *mejillones* (mussels). They serve them up in a piquant sauce and you throw the shells into buckets under the bar. Bus #60, #62, #70 or #72.

Casa Mundo, c/Don Juan de Austria 7. Run by a former member of Valencia's legendary *Delantera Eléctrica* ('Electric Forward-line') and in a central, pedestrianised shopping street, this is a perfectly themed football *tapas* bar with decent variety on the menu.

Accommodation

Valencia is not a tourist city, so there are plenty of **cheap rooms** all year round except during the *Fallas* festival in March.

Budget accommodation is centred around the train station, in c/Bailén and c/Pelayo, parallel to the tracks off c/Játiva. C/Pelayo is the quieter of the two streets, but the area is not exactly charming.

For nicer and not much more expensive places, head for the centre of town, around the market and out near the beach. You'll find an **information**

point with a hotel reservation service at the train station.

Hospedería del Pilar, Plaza Mercado 19 (☎96/331 6600). Crumbling, central pension. Doubles around 2250ptas. Most credit cards.

Hostal Moratín, c/Moratín 15 (☎96/352 1220). Just off c/Barcas from the Plaza de Ayuntamiento, a good-value, *hostal* with clean and comfortable rooms, and excellent *paella* served in the dining room. Singles at 1750ptas, doubles 3000ptas, triples 4500ptas. Most credit cards.

Hotel Alkázar, c/Mosén Femades 11 (☎96/352 9575). Dependable town-centre hotel, near the post office. All rooms with shower. Doubles around 2500ptas. Most credit cards.

Hotel La Marcelina, Paseo de Neptuno 72 (☎96/371 3151). Comfy hotel in a lovely spot near the sea, all rooms with bath. Around 5000ptas a double. Most credit cards.

Valencia views – high tech and high terracing at La Mestalla

Barcelona

If you're young, free and football mad with it, there is no better destination in the whole of Europe than Barcelona. After forty years of subjugation from Madrid, Catalonia, with Barcelona as its capital, now has a degree of autonomy unthinkable in Franco's day. Barcelona feels independent, and wants the whole world to know. And one of the ways in which it expresses that feeling is through its football club, FC Barcelona.

This last decade has seen the city strike a few blows against the old empire. On the football field, Johan Cruyff's Barcelona team won four titles in a row and captured a previously elusive European Cup in 1992. The celebrations in the city's Plaça Sant Jaume were as much for a triumphant Catalonia as for a victorious Barça. Away from football, the staging of the 1992 Olympics sealed Barcelona's century-long love affair with sport, and legitimised the city's status as one of Europe's great capitals – albeit one that is still without a country.

Times change; nationalist sentiment doesn't. Between World War II and the dictator's death in 1975, Franco's régime suppressed the use of the Catalan language and the show of identifiable Catalan symbols. Barcelona was Catalonia's flagship team, and games against the Franco-favoured Real Madrid became statements of national intent, an excuse wantonly to fly the Catalan flag. FC Barcelona was, in effect, an empire in opposition, a huge structure built up around a palace of a stadium, the Nou Camp.

Catalonia is also Spain's most industrial province, with a businesslike attitude that contrasts with the *mañana* culture of the rest of the country. In the post war era, the region attracted thousands of migrant workers from Andalucía and elsewhere. To earn brownie points with their colleagues and neighbours, many joined Barça as club members, during Spanish football's boom

Hmm...Hristo – the bull of Barcelona

years of the late Forties and Fifties. Those workers whose sympathies were more inclined to Madrid (either through their status as employees of public companies or because they were on the winning side in the Civil War) supported Barcelona's rivals, Español – literally, 'Spanish'.

Both clubs were formed at the turn of the century. Barcelona owe their formation to a Swiss national, Joan Gamper. In October 1899, he placed a classified ad in the paper *Los Deportes* – desperately seeking 'Foot-Vall'. A team called FC Barcelona were duly gathered and dressed in blue and grenadine (*azúlgrana* or *blaugrana* in Catalan), the colours of Gamper's native Swiss canton of Ticino. They lost 1–0 to an English select XI at the Bonanova velodrome. Still with Gamper playing upfront, they

Centre of an empire – the Nou Camp, Europe's largest footballing arena

enjoyed their first victory when they beat Català 3–1 on Christmas Eve, 1899.

Local students then formed another club, naming it Español in mockery of Barcelona's Swiss connections, and *soel derbi barcelonés* was born.

Playing in grounds at the Hotel Casanovas, both teams competed in the Catalan championship until it was interrupted by the Civil War. By then, Barça and Español had already happily scrapped it out on the pitch itself. In 1912, the two clubs severed relations for the first time after a brawl between players in a cup match. Within ten years both had settled in stadia a kilometre apart – Barça at Les Corts, Español at Sarrià. Barça's modern home, the Nou Camp, is in this same square mile of the city, just north of Sants train station.

Although Español rarely challenge for honours, derby matches between the two are traditionally tense and unpredictable.

Scores of fans were injured in 1952 when the crowd surged forward after an Español goal. In March 1973, with Barça and Español first and second in the league, a dubious penalty was enough for the underdogs to beat the leaders at home, and let Atlético Madrid in to win the title. It was a similar story in 1982, when Barcelona lost 3–1 at home to Español, and effectively lost the championship.

The changing political climate has drawn some of the sting from the occasion. With a rampant Catalan renaissance going on all around them, Español have had to move with the times, in more ways than one. They are now known by the Catalan version of their name, 'Espanyol', and have moved from Sarrià to the Olympic stadium at Montjuïc. The last derby at Sarrià, in 1997, ended in a win for the home side – a bittersweet finale for the ground's loyal supporters, and another telling blow to Barça's title ambitions.

The thrilling fields

FC Barcelona

Camp Nou, Avenida Arístides Maillol
Capacity 118,000
Colours Blue-and-grenadine striped shirts, blue shorts
League champions 1929, 1945, 1948–49, 1952–53, 1959–60, 1974, 1985, 1991–94
Cup winners 1910, 1912–13, 1920, 1922, 1925–26, 1928, 1942, 1951–53, 1957, 1959, 1963, 1968, 1971, 1978, 1981, 1983, 1988, 1990, 1997
European Cup winners 1992
Cup-Winners' Cup winners 1979, 1982, 1989, 1997
Fairs' (UEFA) Cup winners 1958, 1960, 1966

Barcelona are the biggest and richest football club in the world. Few teams mean as much to their city as Barcelona's. Though the club's membership of more than 100,000 is spread all over the world, it was the vast local contingent who put up the wherewithal to build Europe's biggest football stadium, the Nou Camp.

It is a venue whose grandeur befits the cosmopolitan adventure of Barcelona's football. It is also a monument to Catalan pride and business sense. The Nou Camp is effectively the national stadium of Catalonia, and its trophy cabinets have been filled by the world's best: Diego Maradona, Johan Cruyff, Ladislav Kubala, Sándor Kocsis, Romário, Hristo Stoichkov, Johan Neeskens, Luis Suárez, Ronald Koeman and Ronaldo. Foreign influence has been the key to Barcelona's success. The club were formed by a Swiss national, Hans Gamper (he later changed his first name to the Catalan 'Joan'), in 1899, and their first president was an Englishman, Walter Wild. Of the club's fifty-odd managers, more than half have come from abroad. All the coaches who have won Barcelona a title in modern times have been foreigners: Helenio Herrera, Rinus Michels, Terry Venables and Johan Cruyff.

Barcelona were without question the best team in pre-championship Spain. In the Twenties they were regular cup winners, with Ricardo Zamora in goal, Josep Samitier and Philippino-born Paulino Alcántara up front. As supporters' membership

Derby daze – Barça's Jordi Cruyff feels the bite of the city's eternal underdogs, Espanyol

crept into five figures, Barcelona moved to the Estadi Foixarda at Montjuïc from their cramped quarters at Carrer de la Industria. When Foixarda became too small, Gamper bought land around Les Corts and built a stadium that was to be the club's home either side of the Civil War. Hungarian Franz Platko replaced Zamora in goal, and would become a folk hero during a decade of playing service and two spells as coach. He later died in desperate poverty in Chile, his last years sustained by handouts from his former employers.

Barcelona became the first Spanish club to turn professional and were winners of the inaugural Spanish championship in 1929. But Spain's economic recession in the Thirties forced Barça to sell key players, Samitier going to Real Madrid, and the subsequent Civil War nearly destroyed the club completely. Many players stayed abroad after a tour of North America in 1937, and the Spanish FA named a Francoist, Enric Piñeyro, as club president in 1940. He immediately changed the name to the Castillian 'Club de Fútbol Barcelona'

Barcelona essentials

Although the official language of Barcelona is firmly **Catalan**, everyone understands and most people speak ordinary Castillian **Spanish**.

From El Prat de Llobregat **airport**, 12 km south-west of the city, there's a half-hourly rail service to the main train station, Estació de Sants, (6am–10pm, journey time twenty minutes, 300ptas). There's a welcoming little *tapas* bar on the platform if you've just missed one. Some trains run on to the metro stop of the main square, Plaça de Catalunya. An *Aerobus* (6am–10pm, every 15–30 minutes, journey time thirty minutes, 450ptas) calls at Plaça de Catalunya, Sants and Plaça Espanya. A **taxi** will cost around 2500 ptas. The other mainline **train station** is Estació França, close to Barceloneta metro stop.

The **city transport** system, made up of a metro, a suburban railway, various funiculars, cablecars and buses, is excellent. Free maps are given out at most stations. **Tickets** are valid across all lines – a single is 130ptas, a *targeta multiviatge* of ten 680ptas. A day pass, covering all transport, costs 450ptas, a three-day version 1150ptas and a five-day one 1700ptas.

The metro runs 5am–11pm, and until 1am on Friday and Saturday nights and before holidays. From 11pm there is an extensive *nitbus* system, with most routes running through Plaça de Catalunya – tickets are available onboard at 145ptas.

The city's yellow-and-black **taxis** are quick and cheap. If his cab is free (*Lliure*), the driver uses a set of lights on the roof to indicate how far he will travel – a green light means anywhere in the city limits. Each zone carries a 300ptas minimum charge, plus 150ptas per km, and there are night and holiday tariffs on top of this. To call a cab, dial *Barna-Taxi* on ☎93/357 7755 or *Fono-Taxi* on ☎93/300 1100.

The main **tourist offices** are at the airport, near the customs exit of the international terminal, (open Mon–Sat 9.30am–8pm, Sun 9.30am–3pm, ☎93/478 4708); at Sants train station (open daily 8am–8pm, ☎93/491 4431); and at Gran Vía 658 near Plaça de Catalunya (open Mon–Fri 9am–7pm, Sat 9am–2pm, ☎93/301 7443). All are efficiently and helpfully manned. City information is also available 24 hours by dialling ☎010 – ask for an English-speaking telephonist.

The main weekly **listings magazine**, *Guía del Ocío* (Fridays, 125ptas), is the best for cinema and restaurant information. For concert and club action, pick up a free copy of the monthly newspaper, *a Barna*, distributed around the city's bars. You may also find the monthly *Interrock* pamphlet, a surprisingly snappy concert guide put out by the local council; their English-language *Cultural Information* monthly booklet is pretty staid, however.

(as opposed to the Catalan 'Futbol Club Barcelona') – and so began forty long years of football in opposition to the totalitarian régime in Madrid.

For these four decades, Catalonia existed for ninety minutes every other Sunday. This was fine when Barça had a team as stunning as that which won five titles in eight years from 1945. With Antoni Ramallets in goal, Estanislao Basura and Ladislav Kubala upfront, Catalans could satisfy their desire for nationhood through support of the *blaugrana*. For much of the thirty years that followed, however, that desire remained unfulfilled – Madrid not only ruled by law, but also by football, constantly humiliating Barcelona on the field of play.

The arch-rivalry between Barça and Real Madrid was at its peak in the Fifties, when both clubs had their most talented sides. Fate (and Franco) favoured Madrid, not least after Alfredo di Stéfano had opted out of a 50-50 agreement with both clubs and stayed with Real from 1953 onwards. Barça had Kubala, signed after touring Spain with a team of Hungarian exiles in 1950, but he contracted tuberculosis in the year of di Stéfano's transfer.

From then on, Barça were always one step behind. Their attack included Hungarian stars Kocsis and Czibor; Real had Puskás. From South America, Barça had Brazilian Evaristo; Real had di Stéfano. Barça won the first two Fairs' Cups; Real won the first *five* European Cups.

When Barcelona finally got a crack at the continent's premier club trophy in 1960, they lost to Real in the semi-finals. Coach Helenio Herrera was chased out of the club by furious fans. When he went to Inter, he took with him Luis Suárez, Barcelona's greatest young prospect – and together, they would take the European Cup to Italy.

A diving header from Evaristo put Real out in 1960/61 – their first elimination from the European Cup. Here was Barça's chance to get even, drawn against an inexperienced, almost unknown Benfica side in the final. It was superb end-to-end stuff,

Cruyff senior – big shouts from a big mac

punctuated by slips from Ramallets – 3–2 to Benfica.

Backed by prosperous local industry and the deep pockets of all those loyal members, Barcelona continued to throw serious money at their inferiority complex. They added a new tier to the Nou Camp (and built another stadium, for reserve-team games, alongside it). Yet still the Bernabéu was grander. In the Seventies they paid a world record transfer fee for Johan Cruyff, having already established his old Ajax boss Rinus Michels as coach. In the early Eighties they paid another record fee for Diego Maradona, getting in his old boss, César Menotti, as coach. Then they got an English coach, Terry Venables, and British forwards, Steve Archibald, Gary Lineker and Mark Hughes. *Still* no European Cup – not even when they were

Shine on – trophies of all ages and sizes in the Nou Camp museum

playing the final in Spain, against little-fancied Steaua Bucharest, in 1986.

Behind the scenes, Basque-born Barcelona chief José Luis Núñez wielded an authority that antagonised star players and coaches alike. Such was the political scenario after Franco's death that the club president of Barcelona became the biggest civilian post in all Catalonia.

All along, there were small crumbs of comfort for the fans. Like a Cruyff-engineered 5–0 win at the Bernabéu in 1974; a cup final victory over Real, conjured by Maradona and Bernd Schuster in 1983; and a handful of Cup-Winners' Cup triumphs, the last of them under Cruyff, who had come back as coach in 1988.

Cruyff recognised that giving home-grown players the same attention as the foreign stars raised the game of both. As Barcelona progressed inexorably to the 1992 European Cup final, young midfield orchestrator Josep Guardiola was as creative as Michael Laudrup or Hristo Stoichkov, José-Maria Bakero as solid as Ronald Koeman.

For the final against Italy's Sampdoria, London was transformed into a city of carnival, Wembley a sea of continental colour. In truth, the game was not a classic. But a

rocket of a Koeman free-kick in the last minute of extra-time was all it took for a forty-year itch to be scratched. Joy at Wembley, ecstasy at Plaça Sant Jaume. At home, with Koeman's boot safely encased in the club museum, the team won four Spanish titles on the trot – three by the skin of their teeth. Twice Tenerife beat Real on the last day to hand the title to Barça. Then, in 1994, a last-minute missed penalty by Miroslav Djukić cost Deportivo La Coruña a once-in-lifetime shot at the championship The Nou Camp was no longer the place for nationalists with an axe to grind. Cruyff's Barcelona had won everything. The fans grew tired of the daily grind of competing for domestic honours, but any notion that an era of European domination might be beckoning was swiftly disabused by AC Milan's 4–0 thrashing of Romário, Stoichkov and company at the 1994 European Cup final in Athens.

Cruyff fell out with Núñez; everyone fell out with Romário. Barcelona was a dull place to be until Ronaldo came along in the summer of 1996. The young Brazilian not only scored fantastic goals, he made football fun again and gave the city a fresh appetite for the game. He also won them silverware – the Cup-Winners' Cup and the *Copa del Rey* of 1996/97.

Barcelona approach their centenary year with Núñez's presidency open to election, the club preparing to plough money into their own TV channel – and still, following a long-held tradition, with no sponsorship or advertising on the shirts.

But with former Ajax coach Louis van Gaal moving in and Bobby Robson moving upstairs, backroom politics may yet hinder Barcelona's attempts to prove their true worth where it matters most – out on the Nou Camp pitch.

Here we go!
Metro to **Collblanc, Maria Cristina** or **Les Corts** (each about ten minutes' ride from Espanya), then a five-minute walk, excluding bar time.

Swift half
Of the many bars near the Nou Camp, off Travessera de Les Corts you'll find the two best Barça ones are the **Gent del Barri** (carrer Arizala 53) and the **Bar J Tous** (carrer del Comte de Güell 31).

The former fills early with friendly, drunken fans. Jordi, the club mascot, is presented at intervals, as is the landlord's proud picture of a visit by the Macclesfield branch of the Barça supporters' club.

In the street parallel, the cramped J Tous has a few tables in the back for pre-match dinners. On the walls are dozens of team shots which, like the clientèle, are taken from various eras.

At **the ground**, the beer on sale is non-alcoholic Damm. The most popular snack is *butifarra*, Catalan blood sausage on bread spread with *sofregit* – tomato and garlic – at 500ptas.

Tickets
With nearly as many *socis* as seats in the stadium, the small percentage of tickets available for each match are sold pretty quickly. The black market trading along Travessera de les Corts can get pretty fevered before a big occasion.

The main **ticket office** is where Les Corts meets Avenida Aristides Maillol (open Mon–Fri 10am–1pm & 4–8pm, and two hours before kick-off). *Entrades generals* are for non-members.

The cheapest seats are behind *Gol Sud* (gates 16–19) and *Nord* (gates 1–8), where around 4500ptas should get you a reasonable view. Another couple of thousand and you've a place in the *Lateral* (gates 20–21), while the best seats are in the *Tribuna* (gates 9–15). The details

on your ticket will be printed in Catalan – *seient* is seat, *fila* is row, *boca* is section, *acces* is gate.

Club shop
Barcelona sell more merchandise than any other club in Spain, some $30 million worth a year. Plans are afoot for the club to have a hundred outlets all over the country, but until that day, you can find stores all down the Ramblas and at the shopping centre down by Port Olimpic.

At the stadium, the main store is **La Botiga** (open Mon–Sat 10am–6.30pm, Sun & holidays 10am–2pm, most major credit cards), a modern, efficient operation across the car park from gate #9. Items include the local *cava* sparkling wine (vintage 1992, naturally), a range of toiletries and cassettes of *Cant del Barça*, the club song.

Club museum
The **Museu Estadi** (open Tues–Fri 10am–1pm & 3–6pm, Sat–Sun 10am–2pm, closed Suns in summer, 400ptas) is one of the most visited museums in the city. Its displays trace the history of the club with explanations in Catalan, Spanish and English. The items are laid out chronologically,

Danish tasty – Michael Laudrup in full Barça flow

starting with a large painting of founder Hans Gamper, and everything is well presented. Huge photos, models of Barça's main two stadia, Koeman's boot, Cruyff's shirt, medals, season tickets, programmes and a hundred other mementoes are in the main room, while a running video history is in a small cinema to the side. Entrance through gate #9.

Ultra culture

Although there are hundreds of Barça *penyas* all over the world, some visitors have returned home disappointed about the lack of atmosphere at the Nou Camp. "The loudest noise you'll hear is the sandwiches being unwrapped at half-time," complained one Scottish regular in the early Nineties.

Recently the stadium has been brought back to something like its fiery self, but for all that, after some ritual pre-match singing a cinema hush falls over the crowd, broken by the odd ripple of occasional, knowledgeable applause.

However, if you're standing with the **Boixos Nois** or younger, more fiery **Penya Almogavers** behind either goal, you'll be made more than aware of the kind of passion that kept alive football's greatest arch-rivalry. The **ICC** (*Inter City Culés*) are Barça's travelling support.

In the net

The official Barcelona website is everything you'd expect it to be – smart, fast and full of panache. You've a choice of Spanish, Catalan, French and English language. There's plenty of info on official supporters' clubs and full biographies of all the board members, but otherwise the site is a bit dull. You can find it at: www.fcbarcelona.es.

Unofficial Barça sites come and go with depressing regularity, but one that has been around for a while is Xavier Garanyó's at: www.bcn.servicom.es/~garanyo/barsa/. This is a no-nonsense stats site with a wide variety of links, which also gives you the chance to join an electronic mailing list of like-minded souls.

 # RCD Espanyol

Estadi Olimpic, Montjuïc
Capacity (for football) 30,000
Colours Blue-and-white striped shirts, blue shorts
Cup winners 1929, 1940

Espanyol are firmly Barcelona's second club. While they have often snapped at the heels of their wealthier neighbours, their history is one of almost total failure. They enter the new millennium having had to change name from their proud Castillian 'Español' to its Catalan equivalent, despite their students founders' intention of winding up the 'foreigners' at FC Barcelona.

Worse, the club have had to sell their beloved, intimate Sarrià stadium to make way for developers. Apart from the epic Italy-Brazil tie in the 1982 World Cup, sorry old Sarrià had seen precious little top-level excitement since its opening in 1923. But that wasn't the point. To the club's traditional inner-city support, Sarrià was home – a shabby but unpretentious antidote to the hyperbole of the Nou Camp down the road.

Among the Sarrià memories set to be blurred by the bulldozers, perhaps the most precious is that of goalkeeper (and national hero) Ricardo Zamora. He reluctantly left Español for Real Madrid in 1930, but not before leading the Barcelona club to a 2–1 cup final win over his future employers.

Apart from another narrow win over Real at the 1940 cup final, *Los Periquitos* ('The Parakeets') have had little to squawk about since Zamora's day – although each decade has produced at least one half-decent team.

In the mid-Seventies, under former Real star José Santamaria, Español twice made the UEFA Cup and played good football in the process.

A decade later, with a young Javier Clemente as coach, the club came desperately close to a European honour. With

Cameroon's Thomas N'Kono in goal and Dane John Lauridsen upfront, they beat Borussia Mönchengladbach and both the great Milan clubs on the way to the 1988 UEFA Cup final, where they met Bayer Leverkusen. In the first leg at Sarrià, the Parakeets were on song, and won 3–0. Yet their domination of the game was so total that they could have scored more, and their profligacy would prove costly when the West Germans won the second leg by the same score. Español lost the resulting shoot-out, and the players left the Ulrich-Haberland pitch in tears, knowing a lifetime's opportunity had been blown.

The 1988 side was so pre-occupied with Europe that they almost got relegated, and there were several more battles against the drop – not all of them successful – in the early Nineties. But with José-Antonio Camacho in charge, the team bounced back in 1994/95, their first season as 'Espanyol'. With Spain's Olympic gold medallist Toni in goal, Romanian Florin Răducioiu upfront and young talent Jordi Lardín pulling the midfield strings, they even approached derby games in a higher league position than their city rivals, and a return to European action duly came the following season.

Espanyol began the 1997/98 campaign without Lardín (sold to Atlético) but with Camacho back in the coaching saddle. The team are now playing at the otherwise underused Olympic stadium at Montjuïc. Built for the 1929 International Exposition and a venue for the Alternative Olympics of 1936, it was completely overhauled for the 1992 Games. It's a huge arena, but Espanyol's decision to dedicate the areas behind the goals to advertising hoardings has halved its normal capacity to 30,000.

The move to Montjuïc had been mooted – and bitterly opposed by hardcore fans – for some time. The stadium's position, high above the woods overlooking the Mediterranean, couldn't be more spectacular. Whether it's the right kind of cage for the Parakeets remains to be seen – and heard.

The parakeet-in-chief – Jordi Lardín

Here we go!

There can be few finer journeys in European football than the **funicular** from Paral·lel (winter 11am–8.15pm, summer noon–2.45pm & 4.30–9.25pm, 175ptas single, 300ptas return,) up to Montjuïc. Another option, between June 10 and October 1, is the **cablecar** (noon–9pm, 350ptas single, 550ptas return) that runs between Montjuïc and Mirador. The club will also be running a special bus service from Sarrià.

Swift half

Fans look set to keep with tradition and meet around the old stadium, particularly at the **Bar Sarrià 82**, Avinguida de Sarrià 129, facing the old site. At Montjuïc, there is a bar overlooking the action upstairs in the main building.

The bald truth – Barça's Iván de la Peña takes PSG apart in the 1997 Cup-Winners' Cup final

Tickets

As well as the club shop listed below, tickets are on sale at the office in the main stand at Montjuïc. The plan to fit the usual Sarrià crowd into the two main stands of the Estadi Olimpic looks good on paper – *gol sur*, ultras and standing spectators on the lower level of the far *anfiteatro*, *gol norte* regulars in the upper – but how it works in practice will be decided as the 1997/98 season rolls on. Habitués of the old Sarrià *preferencia* seats, press and VIPs will be placed in the main stand at Montjuïc.

Club shop

The modest Espanyol shop by the main entrance of **Sarrià** may still be in operation in 1997/98. The (strictly theoretical) opening hours are Mon–Fri, 9.30am–1.30pm & 5–8pm.

Ultra culture

The relegation battles of the early Nineties caused the rowdier elements of Espanyol's support to give vent to their feelings, and a nasty right-wing element still lurks in their midst. The **Brigada Blanquiazules**, with their hardcore sub-section, **Los Irre-**

ductibiles, could give a mean show of strength.

Things turned particularly nasty towards the end of the 1996/97 season, as the anti-Montjuïc protests reached their crescendo. Visiting goalkeepers standing in front of the *gol sur* were invariably pelted with missiles and Espanyol's final game at Sarrià, in which they successfully staved off relegation by beating Valencia, had to be interrupted and saw scores of arrests by police in riot gear.

Traditionally at the Sarrià, the *gol norte* was more Catalan, home of the slightly more peaceable **Pericos Catalans**.

Eat, drink, sleep…

Bars and clubs

Measure for measure, Barcelona is as lively as any city in Europe. Champagne bars, cocktail lounges, designer clubs, down-and-out harbour dives – this town has it all.

The economic boom of the late Eighties was one big party in Barcelona, and no-one has turned the lights off yet. The pulse of the city can be taken along the **Ramblas**, the main drag which by day sings with the sounds of street performance and caged birds, but which by night becomes the domain of the strange, the deranged – and the innocent backpacker. The nearer you get to the lap of the Mediterranean, the seedier it gets. Keep your wits about you. The **Barrí Gótic**, just off the Ramblas, is crammed full of bars and small restaurants, as is the Ribera area nearby.

Along Carrer de Balmes the scene is more upmarket, and further west in the Eixample you'll find designer bars and clubs where serious money gets spent on fun. The Port Olimpic also buzzes all summer long. Flashier venues have a strict dress code and an entrance charge of up to 5000ptas. However, bar prices, while the most expensive in Spain, are bearable. Estrella Damm is the local beer.

Apolo, Nou de la Rambla 113. Bright, noisy dance club in an old theatre with a balcony for sorting out a spot for your next bop. Reasonable admission prices. Music is either pounding and electronic, or latin and funky. Open Thurs–Sat from 1am. Metro to Paral-lel.

Bar Cayuco, Vidrieria 3. Down by Barceloneta, a tiny, rundown bar whose walls are full of pictures of Barça stars posing next to the landlord's grandson. Counter two deep in local characters talking football. Metro to Jaume I.

Glaciar, Plaça Reial 13. A former haunt of punks, junkies and bikers in an off-Ramblas square which is a springboard into the Barrí Gótic. These days the *Glaciar* is much calmer – pleasant, even. The music of choice is jazz, blues and reggae, and you'll find all the concert information you need posted above the pinball machines. Metro to Liceu.

Miramelindo, Passeig del Born 15. Flash cocktail bar in a square full of them. Huge lounge, glamorous clientèle, magnificent cocktails. Enjoy a few latin tunes, let them mix up another *mojito*, and damn the expense. Metro to Jaume I.

The Quiet Man, Marquès de Barberà 11. The best of Barcelona's three Irish bars. Large bar area, with a reception room at the back. Guinness 475ptas, Cruzcampo 300ptas for a large glass. Metro to Liceu.

Restaurants

Dining out is as expensive here as anywhere in Spain. If you baulk at the cost of a full blowout, don't panic – the Barrí Gótic and Port Olimpic are dotted with little *tapas* bars, where you'll find bread coated with tomatoes, oil and garlic – *sofregit* – also used as a sauce in many Catalan dishes.

In restaurants, most **specialities** are pretty meaty, bloody affairs, like *butifarra amb mongetes*, sausage with haricot beans, and *casuola*, a meat-heavy casserole. These are best washed down with the local 'black' wine, *venedez*.

Barcelona also has plenty of seafood – *bacallà a la llauna*, salt cod with tomato and garlic, is the most popular dish.

Las Caracoles, Calle Escudellers 14. Possibly the best-known restaurant in town, its two floors plastered in photographs of famous guests like Ingrid Bergman and Edward G Robinson. For all that, it is reasonably priced for the superb quality of the food on offer. Snails (*caracoles*), *paella* and mussels are the specialities. Open daily 1pm–midnight. Most major credit cards. Near Plaça Reial, metro to Drassanes.

Los Pescadores, Carrer de l'Arc de Santa Eulàlia 3. Cheap fish restaurant with two floors – upstairs is candlelit and romantic, but downstairs has footie on the box. Metro to Liceu.

Màgic Barça, Passeig Maritim de la Barceloneta 36. The first themed sports bar/restaurant in town, opened in 1996 in the Port Olimpic. Two floors, bar area, TV room, terrace and shop. Food reasonable but a little overpriced. Open until midnight, 1am Fri–Sat. Between the beach and Hotel Aris. Metro to Ciutadella.

Restaurant Pitarra, Carrer d'Avinyo 56. Famous meeting place for writers, artists and politicians, and former home of the Catalan poet of the same name. Food exquisite (especially the smoked salmon) and reasonably priced. Closed Sundays. Most credit cards. Metro to Drassanes.

Xampanyet, Carrer Montcada 120. Classic *tapas* bar, often deservedly crowded. Blue tiles on the walls, sawdust on the floor, fridges packed with *cava*, the local champagne, sold at 150ptas a glass. Huge range of tasty eats. Metro to Jaume 1.

Accommodation

Barcelona is the most expensive city in Spain for accommodation, the clean-up for the 1992 Olympics having cleared a lot of the town's rundown old pensions. If noise isn't a problem, then anywhere just off the Ramblas will be adequate and affordable. **Ultramar Express**, in the hallway of Sants train station (open daily 8am–10pm, ☎93/491 4463), can book a room for 200ptas and take a deposit which will then be chalked off your final hotel bill.

Alberg Juvenil Palau, Carrer Palau 6 (☎93/412 5080). Small, friendly hostel in the Barri Gòtic.

Two-to-eight bed rooms, 1500ptas a bed, breakfast included. Metro to Jaume 1.

Hostal Dalí, Carrer Boqueria 12 (☎93/318 5580). Perfectly located a few paces off the Ramblas, a perennial favourite cheapie with singles around 2300ptas doubles at 3300ptas, both with shower. Most credit cards. Metro to Liceu.

Hotel Jardí, Plaça del Pí 5 (☎93/301 5900). Pleasant, slightly upmarket pension in a quiet market square. Bit of a climb up to the higher rooms, but nice and airy inside. Most credit cards, Metro to Liceu.

Hostal Capitol, Les Rambles 138 (☎93/301 0872, fax 93/412 3142). Near Plaça de Catalunya, a slightly pricier two-star pension with cable TV and telephones in each room. Doubles 5000ptas with shower, singles and quads also available. Most major credit cards. Metro to Plaça de Catalunya.

Pere Tarres, Numancia 149–151 (☎93/410 2309). Within walking distance of the Nou Camp, a simple hostel with beds at 1200–1500ptas. Metro to Les Corts or Maria Cristina.

Inner city blues – Espanyol's Sarrià ground, now sold to developers

Clause and effect – Ronaldo's season in Spain

The longest-running transfer saga involving the world's greatest young footballer ended in July 1997, when FIFA ruled that Internazionale of Milan should pay more than the **$25 million** they had already handed over to Barcelona in order to buy **Ronaldo** out of his contract with the Catalan club – and Inter reluctantly caved in. The fact that the finer points of his release clause claimed more column

Best of friends – Robson and Ronaldo, Rotterdam, 1997

inches than the finer points of his game was a hint of the kind of multinational, conglomerate hole football might dig for itself before the century is out.

Never mind PSV, Barcelona, Inter or Brazil. Ronaldo is, more than anything, **a Nike player**. The sports goods company have him tied to the same kind of personal contract as basketball's Michael Jordan and golf's Tiger Woods. They signed the Brazilian during his first European season with PSV Eindhoven, when he was just seventeen years of age, and he is theirs for $10 million over the next decade.

Nike have also paid the Brazilian FA $400 million over the next ten years, for the world's most glamourous national side to represent them – which meant that a friendly game with Mexico in April 1997 was no more than a **promotional exercise** for Nike to launch their new *Ronaldinho* range of sports gear. By the time Ronaldo's contract with Inter runs out, the World Cup could well be played out between representative teams of the planet's two leading sports good companies.

Ronaldo may only have spent **one season at Barcelona**, but it was enough to shake the club out of its post-Cruyff slumber and double his value at the same time. Easy winner of *El Pichichi*, Spain's top goalscorer award, with 34 goals in almost as many games, Ronaldo burst onto the scene in a way that neither Maradona nor Romário ever did. He was young, immensely popular with his team-mates, the crowd and the media, and his **behaviour was exemplary**. He eschewed smoking, drinking and drugs, and rarely indulged in gamesmanship. *Ronaldomania* was all the rage in Spain in 1996/97, his goal of the season against Compostela endlessly re-run on TV, his contract battles with club president Núñez regularly splashed across the front pages of the main four sports dailies. His winning penalty goal in the Cup-Winners' Cup final against Paris Saint-Germain was apt, as it was scored in the same Feyenoord stadium where he bade farewell to **PSV Eindhoven** in the Dutch cup final a year before.

PSV had paid $10 million for him in 1994 and, despite injury, he scored 55 goals in 56 games for them – an improvement on his already phenomenal 58 in 60 during one season at **Cruzeiro**. Ronaldinho, as he is known in Brazil, began his career at Social Ramos Clube in Rio, his early ambition to play for his beloved Flamengo having been thwarted when the club refused to pay the untried youngster's **bus fare** to their training ground. Inter, by comparison, could have bought several fleets of buses for what the player cost them in 1997. Then again, buses don't sell sportswear, do they…?

Bilbao

Bilbao is the home of Spanish football. Its team, Athletic, are both a throwback to the British influence on the game's introduction a hundred years ago, and the figurehead of Basque national pride.

Unlike their near neighbours Real Sociedad, from San Sebastián, Athletic have never signed a non-Basque. The arrival of French international defender Bixente Lizarazu from Bordeaux in the summer of 1996 raised eyebrows – his was the first transfer of a foreign-national Basque, and the move suggests that the club may yet adopt a more open policy as they approach their centenary year in 1998.

The Basque boy wonder – Julen Guerrero

The British influence in Bilbao is still apparent, in both the club's anglicised name (although Franco had it changed to the Spanish 'Atlético' during his dictatorship) and their red-and-white striped shirts. English foundrymen and mining engineers working in the Basque country during the industrial boom at the turn of the century introduced the name and the shirt, the latter taken from the greatest English side of the era, Sunderland. They began playing alongside local merchants' sons who had been sent to school in England and learned the game there.

In 1902, a Bilbao select XI were invited to participate in a tournament organised in Madrid by King Alfonso XIII, which they duly won. Today, no team in Spain have won more *Copas del Rey* than Athletic de Bilbao – 23 to date.

The 1902 win sealed not just Bilbao's position as leading exponents of the game, but that of the Basque country as a whole. Ciclista San Sebastián, Racing and Real Union Irún, and Bilbao's city rivals Arenas Getxo all won the cup in the early days, and a local Basque Cup is still competed for in earnest every summer.

Athletic were ahead of the game in many ways. Their San Mamés stadium was such a revelation when it was built in 1913 that it immediately earned the title *La Catedral*, a name which has stuck. It was laid with English turf and staged Spain's first home international in 1921.

One of Athletic's leading strikers, Rafael Moreno, nicknamed *Pitxitxi*, died young and as well as a street running alongside the San Mamés, Spain's top goalscorer award, *El Pichichi*, is still named after him.

Perhaps because of the influence of their other national game, pelota, Basques have provided generations of great goalkeepers, including José Iríbar and Andoni Zubizarreta, who amassed over 150 Spanish caps between them. Iríbar is now goalkeeping coach at the club, but whether the straitjacket of the Basque-only policy will produce another like him in modern-day competition is another matter.

The thrilling fields

 Athletic Bilbao

San Mamés, Avenida Alameda Mazarredo 23
Colours Red-and-white striped shirts, black shorts
League champions 1930, 1931, 1934, 1936, 1943, 1956, 1983–84
Cup winners 1903–4, 1910–11, 1914–16, 1921, 1923, 1930–33, 1943–45, 1950, 1955–56, 1958, 1969, 1973, 1984

"I'd like to celebrate the centenary with *la Copa del Rey* or a place in Europe," said Athletic coach Luis Fernandez of his aims for 1998. The title, last won under the firm managership of Javier Clemente in 1984, is not even in Fernandez's sights. And how could it be, with Athletic trying to match the resources of Real Madrid and Barcelona with a team of Basque nationals, season after season?

For all the enormous pride associated with the club and its still relevant heritage, the fact remains that Athletic Bilbao haven't won a thing in more than ten years and haven't put together a decent European run in twenty.

The fact that Athletic are finding it hard to compete with the money men of *La Liga* is not surprising. What is extraordinary is the way they kept on winning titles, well after the end of their domination of the early amateur era. The team's cup form was never in doubt, but to win the pro-

fessional league eight times, finishing in the top three every third year, in a league in which seven clubs have played in European finals, is a remarkable achievement.

What is also remarkable is the way the club have been able to hang on to their Spanish international midfielder Julen Guerrero – though perhaps the tax advantages of living in the Basque country have made their job easier.

Guerrero's historical counterpart, and the first modern-day Athletic star to take the national side by storm, was Telmo Zarraonandia, or 'Zarra' – still the fifth highest scorer in a Spanish shirt, and hero of the 1950 World Cup campaign.

Like so many Bilbao stars before and especially since, Zarra was part of a team that played a rugged, English style, on a pitch well-watered by the local heavy rain or, in times of drought, by canny groundstaff. Both style and surface have occasionally troubled European opponents. After knocking Honvéd out of the European Cup in 1956, Bilbao beat Manchester United's Busby Babes 5–3 at home, before falling 3–0 at Old Trafford. Liverpool were beaten 2–1 at San Mamés in the Fairs' Cup in 1968, Rangers 2–0 a year later.

The only time Bilbao ever made a European final was in the UEFA Cup against Juventus in 1977. En route, with little Dañi upfront and the veteran Iríbar in goal – and the weight of the Basque country behind them at San Mamés – Athletic beat AC Milan (4–1!) and Barcelona in home legs. But another home win, 2–1, in the second leg of the final wasn't enough to counter Juve's 1–0 victory in Turin, and the Italians won the trophy on away goals.

The political terrorism in the Basque country after Franco's death in 1975 led to a tense atmosphere at some domestic matches. That tension, coupled with the iron discipline and attention to detail of a young Javier Clemente as coach, brought Bilbao the title in 1983 and 1984. Clemente's side was fearsomely aggressive, with a hatchet man, Andoni Goikoetxea, was nicknamed *The Butcher of Bilbao*.

Bilbao essentials

The language you'll hear on the streets of Bilbao is **Basque**, but most people here are bi-lingual and will easily (if sometimes grudgingly) switch to Spanish if that's all you can muster.

From Bilbao's **airport** at Sondika, 9km from town, the A-3247 *Bizkaibus* runs to the **bus station** on c/Sendeja, alongside the river next to the Puente del Ayuntamiento (every forty minutes, 6am–10.30pm, forty-minute journey time, 150ptas). You can get off the bus on its way through town, at the Plaza de España by the main **train station** of Abando. A taxi will take fifteen minutes to do the journey and cost around 1750ptas.

Coming **overland** into Bilbao can be confusing, since there's a welter of different bus and train stations. Most of them are near the bridge which links the Plaza de España, in the new part of town, with the Plaza Arriaga and the old quarter, the Casco Viejo. Local train services to San Sebastián use the Estación Atxuri (Achuri), on the other side of the river, south of the Casco Viejo, while *FEVE* services along the coast to Santander stop at Estación Concordia, on the riverbank below Abando. It is planned that all major train lines will stop at Estación de Abando by 1998.

Most long-distance and international **bus routes** are covered by *ANSA*, c/Autonomía 17, with a bus-station entrance around the corner at Alameda de Recalde 73, south of the centre in the new town. There are at least half-a-dozen other bus stations in town run by various private companies.

The **P&O ferry** from Portsmouth docks at **Santurtzi**, across the river from Getxo. Local trains run from nearby Portugalete, or you can cross over the hanging bridge which transports cars and passengers every 10–30 minutes to Las Arenas, site of a zone B metro station.

Bilbao's newly built **metro** (Mon–Sat 6am–2am, Sun 7am–11pm) has just one line, running from the Casco Viejo through the new town and up to the coast. Zone A covers any travel in town – 125ptas for a single ticket, 750ptas for a strip of ten.

The metro is augmented by the *Bilbóbus* network (daily 6am–11.30pm); tickets are 85ptas, payable onboard, or 520ptas for a ten-ride strip, available at newsstands. There is no night service, but you'll probably find a **taxi** by Plaza Arriaga; if not, call for a *Radio Taxi Bizkaia* on ☎94/416 2300 or *Radio Taxi Bilbao* on ☎94/444 8888.

The main **tourist office** is at Plaza Arriaga (open Mon–Fri 9am–2pm & 4–7.30pm, Sat 9am–2pm, Sun 10am–2pm, ☎94/416 0022, fax 94/416 8168).

The 1984 cup final between Athletic and Barça ending in a free-for-all fight in front of King Juan Carlos and millions of TV viewers. Bilbao won the match – and their last piece of silverware to date.

Since then, while the Basque-only policy has been rigidly enforced among the playing staff, a selection of foreign coaches have passed through San Mamés with varying degrees of success. Dragoslav Stepanović and Guus Hiddink flopped; Jupp Heynckes and Jean Fernandez performed well under the circumstances; Howard Kendall was unsuccessful but well-liked, famously rejecting the penthouse apart-ment he was offered by the club in preference for a more spartan one that overlooked Athletic's training ground.

As for San Mamés, president José Maria Arrate is trying to convince club members that it is too small and unsuitable for the modern era. Making it all-seater for 1997/98 is one thing, but move from San Mamés? They'll be fielding Spaniards next.

Here we go!

San Mamés has its own **metro stop**, three stops from Abando train station. Coming out of the metro, the ground is a two-minute walk down Luis Briñas.

Swift half

C/Licenciado Poza, which leads to the stadium, and its surrounding streets boast more than fifty bars. Try the **Ziripot** (Poza #40) or **Bar Gales** (#49) as a starting point. At Avenida de Sabino Arana 3 is the English-style **City**, where you can order a *Kendall*, a mix of gin and orange named after the English manager.

At c/Luis Briñas 3 you'll find the **Bar Flower**, where the speciality is *kalimotxo*, a mix of Coke and wine, and there's a great old photo of the original San Mamés. Not far away along the same street you'll find **Bar Estadium, Bar Campeón** and **Bar Club**.

Tickets

Outside of visits by Real Madrid or Barcelona and the Basque derby against Real Sociedad, getting into San Mamés isn't too taxing. The **ticket booths** are on the corner of the *Tribunas Norte* and *Este*, the other side of the stadium from the metro.

The most expensive seats are in the *Tribuna Principal*, the main stand with the arch over it, and in the *Tribuna Este* opposite. Seats with a slightly poorer view alongside the pitch are the *Preferencias Laterales*. The cheapest places behind the goals, the *Gradas Norte y Sur*, were due to be converted to seated areas for the 1997/98 season. Away fans are allocated places in the *Tribuna Norte* and in the *Preferencia Este Cubierta*.

Club shop

There's a small-ish, official store next to the ticket booths (open Mon–Sat 10.30am–1.30pm & 5–7.30pm, and on matchdays, most major credit cards).

Ultra culture

Bilbao is full of supporters' bars. Athletic have the reputation of being everyone's second favourite team in Spain, and a weekend in Bilbao is a treat for the neutral visitor. In the stadium, the two main ultra groups are the **Herri Norte** (*Grada Norte* section), the **Abertzale Sur** and the **Tri-**

Luis Fernandez – Athletic's French-born coach

pustelak (*Grada Sur* section). In 1996/97, a firecracker thrown from one *Grada* group hit Real Zaragoza goalkeeper Otto Konrad, briefly closing San Mamés and forcing the introduction of $750,000 worth of closed circuit TV equipment.

In the net

The official Athletic website is under construction. When it's finished, you should be able to find it at: www.athletic-club.es.

Eat, drink, sleep...

Bars and clubs

The best place to start in Bilbao is near the San Mamés stadium, especially around the junction of c/de Licenciado Poza and Gregorio de Revilla, an area known as **Pozas**, and popular during the day.

For a relaxed drink in the early evening, head for the outdoor tables in Plaza Nueva or in the lively areas of the new town. The places around the Plaza de España have a slightly smarter atmosphere, particularly along c/Ledesma, a street inviting you in with dozens of bars.

The Casco Viejo is perfect for exploration deep into the night, by which time quick shots of the local spirit, *pacharrán*, will be doing the rounds.

Café Boulevard, Paseo del Arenal 6. Classic Bilbao coffee house near the Teatro Arriaga, preserved from the last century. Popular meeting place. Metro to Casco Viejo.

Café Irúña, Colón de Larreategui. Atmospheric café founded at the turn of the century, with authentic décor. Metro to Abando.

Lamiak, c/Pelota. Popular student café-bar playing decent sounds, and worth a visit just to check out the notices for new clubs and upcoming events. Metro to Casco Viejo.

Taberna Txiriboga, c/Santa María 13. Lively bar in the old town with a decent range of small *tapas*. Metro to Casco Viejo.

Restaurants

Basque **cooking** is the most sophisticated in Spain, varied and tasty, and Bilbao is the best and cheapest place in the whole region to dine. The most enjoyable way to eat is to move from **bar to bar**, snacking on *tapas*. Casco Viejo is the best area to head for, with almost wall-to-wall places on c/Santa María and c/Barrencalle Barrena.

For a full meal, *bacalao a la vizcaína*, salt cod in tomato sauce, and *chipirones en su tinta*, cuttlefish in its own ink, are the local **delicacies** to seek out.

Aji Colorado, c/Barrencalle 5. Bilbao's only Peruvian restaurant, and a good one, if a little pricey. Specialities include raw fish and peppered chicken. Closed Sundays. Most credit cards. Metro to Casco Viejo, then a ten-minute walk.

Café-Restaurante Kalean, c/Santa María. Ideal place to try *nueva cocina vasca*, the new Basque

cuisine now popular all over Spain but still at its best in its region of origin. Reasonable prices. Most major credit cards. Metro to Casco Viejo.

Herriko Taberna, c/de la Ronda 20. For no-nonsense home cooking at reasonable prices. Excellent *menú* deals, fervent Basque atmosphere. Most credit cards. Metro to Casco Viejo.

Taberna Aitor, c/Barrencalle Barrena. Lovely old *tapas* bar with football trimmings, in the Siete Calles area down by the river. Metro to Casco Viejo, then a pleasant ten-minute stroll across the cathedral square.

Accommodation

Bilbao's **festival season** in August happily coincides with Spanish football's summer break. At all other times of the year you should have no problem finding a reasonably priced place to stay. The best places are almost all in the **Casco Viejo,** especially along c/Bidebarrieta, which leads from Plaza Arriaga to the cathedral, and in the streets around it.

Hostal Laredo, c/Lotería 1, 4th floor (☎94/415 0932). Reasonably priced, friendly pension with modern furnishings. Metro to Casco Viejo.

Hostal Roquefer, c/Lotería 2, 2nd and 4th floors (☎94/415 0755). Don't be put off by the dingy building – the rooms inside are fine, and some have a view of the cathedral square. Doubles around 2500ptas, 3000 with bathroom. Most major credit cards. Metro to Casco Viejo.

Hotel Ripa, c/Ripa 3 (☎94/423 9677). Great-value one-star hotel, over Puente del Arenal from the Casco Viejo, down by the waterfront. All rooms with bath and TV, doubles around 3000ptas. Most major credit cards. Metro to Abando.

Pension Mendez, c/Santa María 13, 4th floor (☎94/416 0364). Centrally located pension in the Casco Viejo by the *Bolsa* building, clean and reasonably priced. Most major credit cards. Metro to Casco Viejo.

Sweden

The Nineties saw the standard-bearers of Scandinavian football arrive in the modern world. After decades of patient and carefully planned effort, Sweden finished third at USA '94 and a nation that had long considered football to be just one of many athletic pursuits began to take the game seriously. Now Swedish business has finally realised the benefits of backing football, TV companies are starting to compete for rights and the bigger clubs can offer salaries which at least tempt key players to stay at home.

Yet despite the interest generated by the national team's successes and the improved performance of Swedish clubs in European competition, the domestic league, the *Allsvenskan*, remains a low-key affair. There are no full-time professional clubs (although IFK Gothenburg are edging towards that status), league crowds rarely top 5000 and football culture is under-developed. For adults, it is simply entertainment; for a growing number of kids it is a chance to act hard.

Football arrived relatively early in Sweden, with the game taking root in Gothenburg in the 1870s thanks to the usual missionaries – English engineers and railway workers. But the game didn't begin to take off until pioneer Victor Balck, founder of the Swedish National Sports Federation, travelled to England in the 1880s. On his return he penned a book, *Sports Illustrated* – his description of English football as "not a game for the weak and timid" proving to be a prophecy for the future style of Swedish football.

Initially the game met with opposition from the austere gentlemen of Sweden's Gymnastics Federation, a body dedicated to developing fit, healthy young men. They saw football as a dangerous phenomenon

Don't blame me – the incomparable Ravelli

and were willing to accept it only on the understanding that when players kicked the ball they alternated between their left and right feet, in order to ensure balanced physical development.

Under the auspices of an unofficial FA, a national championship, in knockout format, began in 1896 and the game found a place in the 1912 Stockholm Olympics – at which Sweden were knocked out in the early stages. A league began in 1925, dominated by Örgryte, from near Gothenburg, and by the Stockholm clubs AIK and Djurgårdens.

It wasn't until the end of World War II that Sweden began to make an impact on the international scene, a 3–1 victory over Yugoslavia winning them gold at the 1948 London Olympics. Sweden's success, with a side managed by Englishman George Raynor, resulted in a number of players being lured away from the strictly amateur Swedish league for the seriously professional *Serie A*. Indeed, the entire front three of the Olympic side – Gunnar Gren, Gunnar Nordahl and Nils Liedholm – was snapped up by AC Milan in 1949. The Milanese nicknamed them the *Gre-no-li*, making an Italian-sounding word from the beginnings of their surnames, and they went on to bag a collective 329 goals for their club – even though only Liedholm chose to remain with Milan for the whole of the Fifties.

With the departure of others such as Kurt Hamrin, who played for five Italian clubs, and Lennart Skoglund, who went to Inter, the Swedes banned professionals from the national team and went into the 1950 and 1954 World Cups without their top players. Despite this self-imposed handicap, they managed third place in Brazil. But when Sweden hosted the 1958 World Cup, the FA was pressured into recalling the pros. Ten years after they last appeared in national colours, the veterans of the

Olympic side gave local fans a taste of what they had been missing. After dismissing the USSR in the quarter-finals, the Swedes drew a capacity crowd to Gothenburg's then-new Ullevi stadium to witness a highly physical 3–1 crushing of West Germany. The 1958 Swedes were a great side, but their opponents in the Stockholm final – the Brazil of Didi, Garrincha and a 17-year-old Pelé – were on another plane and hammered the hosts 5–2.

Attendance records were smashed at the World Cup, which saw the Swedes use a number of small provincial grounds in order to create a close-knit, 'family' atmosphere. In 1959, the local FA switched the club programme to a summer season in an attempt to keep the fans who had turned out in such force the previous year, but the move failed. With the retirement of the *Gre-no-li*, the national team faded and the Sixties were a barren time for Swedish football.

In the Seventies the national team maintained their consistency in qualifying for

The host with the most – Tomas Brolin scores for Sweden against Denmark at Euro '92

Basics

A full, valid **passport** is sufficient for EU citizens and those of the US, Canada, Australia and New Zealand to gain entry to Sweden.

The Swedish currency is the **krona** (plural kronor) or crown; the exchange rate is roughly 10kr to £1. All banks change money and standard opening hours are Mon–Fri, 9.30am–3pm. Outside those hours cash machines (*Bankomat*) are good for both Visa and Mastercard. *Forex* exchange offices are open late in the cities and charge a commission of 20kr on cash, 15kr on travellers' cheques.

Sweden has a fast and reliable **public transport** system. Swedish state **railways**, SJ, cover the country; second-class trains cost 25 percent more on Fridays and Sundays. There is a maximum fare of 610kr for all journeys over 815km. If you are travelling from the UK and intend to use the Swedish rail system extensively, the **ScanRail pass**, which must be bought in advance and is available from NSR Travel in London, offers five days' travel for £125 and good deals on longer periods.

The domestic **bus** system, run by Swedbus, is cheaper than its rail equivalent. For weekend city-to-city travel the company's *Expressbuss* services are your best bet.

You can make **international phone calls** from public kiosks. Most payphones will take both cards and coins. Dial 009 to get an international line. The minimum domestic charge is 2kr, and phones take 1kr and 5kr coins. Cards (*Telefonkort*) are available from newsagents (*Pressbyran*), priced 40kr, 60kr and 100kr. All operators speak English and both domestic (☎07975) and international (☎0019) directory inquiry services are fast. In summer, take advantage of the *Turist Telefon* scheme which offers half-price domestic calls between June and August at specially marked booths. From within Sweden, the code for Stockholm is ☎08, while Gothenburg is ☎031.

As elsewhere in Scandinavia, **eating out** can be an expensive business. Stoke up at breakfast time, then take advantage of a *Dagens Rätt* (set lunch) on offer in many restaurants. Open sandwiches (*Smörgåsar*) are a good-value snack but the celebrated self-service *Smörgåsbord* cold buffet can be costly.

If food is expensive, **drink** is positively prohibitive. **Beer** is divided into three classes according to its strength. All are available in bars but beware that Class I is virtually non-alcoholic. Class I and Class II beer is sold in supermarkets, Class III only in state-run off-licences (*Systembolaget*), where you will need to be over 20 and show ID to get served. Expect to pay 40kr for a glass of beer or wine in a bar.

the final stages of major competitions but, save for an epic 4–2 defeat by the hosts at the 1974 World Cup in West Germany, they failed to make much impact.

Club sides were making more progress, however. In 1979, Malmö FF finished as runners-up to Nottingham Forest in the European Cup. In 1982 came the big breakthrough – IFK Gothenburg slaughtered Hamburg to lift the UEFA Cup and become the first Swedish club side to win a European competition. They won the same trophy five years later with a 2–1 aggregate win over Dundee United.

Swedish fans got another chance to see top-class football when the country hosted Euro '92. Stadiums across the land were upgraded and the finals coincided with the emergence of an attractive new national team coached by Tommy Svensson. The side performed well, reaching the semi-final stage before the Germans gained their revenge for '58. The damage to national pride was increased when Sweden's neighbours Denmark, whom the Swedes had earlier beaten in a group game, won the final.

Two years later, at the World Cup, Svensson's side at last fulfilled its potential. Traditional physicality was complemented by the verve of target-man Kennet Andersson, the guile of midfielder Tomas Brolin and the eccentricity of 'keeper Thomas

Ravelli. Again, it was only the Brazilians who could stop them – this time in the semi-finals. Few people remember third-place play-offs, but in Los Angeles, the Swedes trounced Bulgaria 4–0 in a performance which ensured they returned home to thousands of cheering fans in Stockholm's Ralambshovsparken.

As in 1948, the bulk of the squad swiftly departed for more lucrative leagues, leaving the domestic competition starved of stars. The national team failed to qualify for Euro '96, but in the meantime, IFK Gothenburg's performances in the Champions' League have amply demonstrated the rewards of greater professionalism.

Essential vocabulary
Yes *Hej*
No *Adjö*
Two beers, please *Två öl, tack*
Thank you *Tack*
Men's *Herr*
Women's *Fru*
Where is the stadium? *Var ligger stadion?*
What's the score? *Vad står det?*
Referee *Domare*
Offside *Offside*

Match practice
If you brought a book and opened it after five minutes of a Swedish game, no one would look at you twice. Sit down. Pull a tartan rug over your legs. Open a flask of coffee. Apart from the rowdies – usually behind the goals and burdened with a ridiculous gang name – the Swedish football experience is sedate and relaxed.

People don't argue about football in the pub, wives don't curse their husbands' domination of the remote control and you won't catch Ace of Bass in the stands. With an upbringing like this, it's no wonder Lennart Johansson, Swedish president of UEFA, has a vision of football as nicely packaged, family entertainment.

But things *are* changing. Just as Swedes brought the idea of pubs and bars back from holidays outside Scandinavia, fans have got a taste of what supporting a team

means from abroad. IFK Gothenburg's fans have been travelling all over Europe in Champions' League campaigns, and Europe came to Sweden in 1992. All this has resulted in a growth in supporters' clubs and, alas, in a sad fad for hooliganism.

Although much of the action takes place on Saturday and Sunday, there is no set day or kick-off time for league games. Monday and Friday nights are also popular. Kick-off time for evening games tends to be 7pm, with afternoon games at 3pm.

The Swedish football season begins in April and runs until the start of July, when it breaks for a month. It restarts in August and, including the play-offs, continues into mid-October.

The league
The *Allsvenskan* is Sweden's fourteen-team premier league. Teams play each other home and away. Between 1982 and 1990, the championship was decided in a two-leg play-off between the top two sides in the table. Below the *Allsvenskan* is the first division, consisting of two leagues of fourteen, split into North and South. At the end of the campaign, the champions of North and South are promoted, replacing the bottom two clubs from the Premier League. Runners-up from North and South play-off over two legs with 12th and 11th from the *Allsvenskan*, so as many as four teams can lose their top-flight status in a single year. Below the first divisions are a series of regional leagues.

Because Sweden's league campaign doesn't end until after the main European competitions have begun, Swedish teams entering the Champions' League and UEFA Cup book their places by their position in the previous year's season.

Up for the cup
The *Svenska Kupa* is extremely low-key. Preliminary rounds begin around the same time as the league campaign with around 250 clubs involved. The first round proper, with 128 teams including all top-flight clubs, is in August, and the competition runs right

through to the end of the league season, beginning again the following spring with a last-sixteen round in March.

The final is at the end of May and, like all the games, is a single tie with sudden-death extra time and penalties if necessary. It is held at a neutral stadium, the venue changing from year to year depending on who's playing. Unlike the other two European competitions, the Cup-Winners' Cup sees Sweden's cup holders enter the continental equivalent the same year as they won their domestic honour.

Tickets

Domestic games almost never sell out. Tickets are bought at the stadium. On average they cost 120–140kr in the main stand and 70–100kr behind the goals. A stand will be indicated as *tribun*, while the area behind each goal is a *kurva*. A seat is *sittplats* while a spot on the terraces is a *ståplats*.

Half-time

You'll find standard hot dogs and sausages, with hot tea and filter coffee in the autumn. Before the game, a good warmer is the traditional Swedish short – vodka and loganberry *lonnbar*. The original home-brewed stuff is hard to find in Gothenburg or Stockholm but you might get lucky at a provincial game.

Action replay

State SVT1 has its major football show on Mondays at 7.15pm. This is usually a live game with highlights of the week's other action. During the close season in Sweden, TV4 has a live English Premiership game on Saturdays at 4pm. The subscription-only Sports Kanel has Sky Sports games plus German, Spanish, Scottish and Italian action. As well as live and delayed full-length games it also has regular highlights packages from those leagues. SVT1 has the rights to the Champions' League.

The back page

There is no daily sports paper in Sweden, but two tabloids offer decent coverage.

Chill out – Swedish football is relaxed

Sunday's *Expressen* has the full wrap on Saturday's games while *Aftonbladet* on Monday evenings has a round-up of the whole weekend. As Swedes are big gamblers on football and there are no local matches to bet on in winter, you'll find piles of stuff on foreign leagues. *Fotbolls Extra* (25kr) is a glossy fortnightly. The newsagents at the main train stations in Gothenburg and Stockholm are well stocked with international papers, sports press included.

Ultra culture

All teams have their 'Fan Club' or 'Support' and at the bigger clubs these have an official or semi-official relationship with the club, with reduced-price tickets in an allocated section of the stadium for members. These groups are generally well organised and often run souvenir shops as well as arranging away travel. Hooliganism has become hip in the past few years and some clubs are reviewing their relations with fan groups. Following trouble at Djurgårdens and at IFK Gothenburg, the tabloid press has jumped on the issue and has created a moral panic out of a handful of incidents.

In the net

Sweden has a high rate of modem ownership, and Swedish football clubs are well represented on the Web. Erik Goethe's *Svensk Fotboll* site has piles of stats and links to many Swedish club sites. Go to: www.student.nada.kth.se/~nv92-ego/.

Stockholm

AIK 548   Djurgårdens 550
Hammarby 551

Although Gothenburg is the heartland of Swedish football, it is the capital which is its official centre. The national stadium, the Råsunda, is in the Solna district of Stockholm and is home to the Swedish FA as well as most national-team games. The choice of the Råsunda rather than Gothenburg's Ullevi for the final of Euro '92 provoked anger among Gothenburg's fans, who are increasingly annoyed at what they see as unjustified privileges going to a footballing backwater that seems more interested in ice-hockey and its outdoor equivalent, bandy.

Perhaps it is not only convenience that lies behind the FA's desire to play so many internationals in Stockholm. For without the internationals at the Råsunda, football interest in the capital could have withered away from success starvation. AIK's title win in 1992 was the first championship for a capital side in 26 years, and the city's most popular team, Hammarby IF, have never won anything at all.

But while Stockholm has never produced teams to compete with IFK Gothenburg or other successful provincial sides like Malmö FF or IFK Nörrkoping, it boasts an interesting if somewhat genteel football scene.

The residents of the Råsunda, AIK, were one of the first teams to be formed in Sweden and have remained an influential if not consistently successful force since. Patronised by the Swedish royal family, attracting major sponsors and producing several leading administrators, AIK are the Stockholm club most disliked in the provinces.

More successful since World War II, with four titles and a crop of famous internationals to their name, have been Djurgårdens IF. But the last time they finished top was in 1966, and residents of their wealthy, leafy district pay little attention to the goings-on at the Olympic stadium. Mention Djurgårdens to a Swedish sports fan and he or she will presume you are talking about ice-hockey.

It is on the south side of the city where Stockholm's prewar working-class football scene survives. Attracting punks, drunks, skinheads and bohemians, as well as their traditional constituency of factory workers, Hammarby IF are a charming reminder that not everything in Stockholm is Volvos and *Smörgåsbord*.

The thrilling fields

 AIK

Råsunda Stadion, Solnavägen 51
Capacity 36,000 (all-seated)
Colours Yellow-and-black shirts, white shorts
League champions 1900–01, 1911, 1914, 1916, 1923, 1932, 1937, 1992
Cup winners 1949–50, 1976, 1985, 1995–97

As you will be pedantically told as soon as you mention 'AIK Stockholm', despite being the capital's most famous club and lying just a ten-minute tube ride from the city centre, AIK actually come from the nearby town of Solna. The club's full name is Allmänna Idrottsklubben ('General Sports Club'), but don't bother trying to master the pronunciation – only their patron, His Royal Majesty King Karl Gustaf, ever uses the full title.

AIK is the largest sports club in the country, with 11,000 members and several sections including a popular ice-hockey team. As the team of the royals and of the capital's élite, they enjoyed their best days before World War II, when Swedish sport was no more than amateur recreation. With professionalism sneaking its way in from the Fifties on, the strictly amateur

AIK struggled to attract talent. By the late Seventies members began to realise that professionalism needed to be increased if the club was to stay competitive. One of the administrators who took up the call was Lennart Johansson, chairman of the club for sixteen years prior to becoming UEFA president. Johansson is currently AIK's honorary chairman.

In 1992, AIK won their first title for 55 years, sparking hope that the club might at last give the capital a period of success. They quickly returned to mid-table, however. The Råsunda received a facelift the same year but remains soulless. From the outside it looks like an office block (it is home to several sports federations) and inside the seats are painted in seven colours – the club's black has been overlooked. As crowds rarely top 5000, the atmosphere is as poor as the decorating.

Here we go!
Take the blue tube from T-Centralen in the direction of Akalla, get off at Solna and follow signs for Råsunda. The tube journey takes around ten minutes.

Swift half
The Råsunda has lacked a local bar ever since the Irish pub opposite the main entrance on Solnavägen closed. It may reopen in another guise in the near future.

Publications
Programmes (15kr) are produced for all home games. There are two fanzines – *Svartgult* ('Black-and-yellow') and *Gnagaren* ('Rat'), both available from the club shop.

Club shop
To the right of the main entrance on Solnavägen is the **AIK-Shopen**, staffed by Black Angels and selling a combination of football and ice-hockey merchandise, as well as back issues of programmes. It's open 10am–4pm weekdays and up until kick-off on matchdays.

Ultra culture
The local lads are the **'Black Angels'**. They are closely connected to the club and produce their own souvenirs, available from stalls underneath the south end.

Who said the Swedes don't party? AIK celebrate their 1997 cup final win over Elfsborg

In the net

AIK's official homepage is at: www.aik.se. The football is hard to find among all those head-and-shoulders portraits of ice-hockey stars, but it's worth the search.

 Djurgårdens IF

Olympiastadion, Lidingövägen 1
Capacity 12,500 (all-seated)
Colours Light and dark blue striped shirts, dark blue shorts
League champions 1912, 1915, 1917, 1920, 1955, 1959, 1964, 1966
Cup winners 1990

Even if Djurgårdens aren't at home, it's worth visiting their ground. The Olympiastadion, known locally as the Stockholms or *Klocktornet* ('clock tower'), is one of the quaintest venues in Europe. A listed historical site, it maintains the romantic aura it had when built for the 1912 Stockholm Olympics, untouched by the whims of twentieth-century architecture. The perimeter walls are covered with ivy and the two towers at the east end evoke a medieval castle. The east end was knocked down in the Fifties and a terrace block built in its place, but in 1991 this was bulldozed to make way for an exact replica of the original 1912 tribune. The result is a beautifully proportioned, refined little ground.

Djurgårdens moved here in 1936, having previously played at the Traneberg stadium. The team were at their best in the late Fifties and early Sixties, when they lifted four championships with sides skippered by Gösta Sandberg, the club's record scorer.

But after spending three seasons from 1988 playing at the Råsunda, while restoration work was carried out on the Olympiastadion, the club have bounced between the premier and first divisions. The football section of the sports club became independent in 1991, but in the face of declining attendances and financial problems, the team were relegated (again) in 1996.

Stockholm essentials

Arlanda **airport** is 45km north of Stockholm. A direct rail link to the city centre is currently under construction. Until it opens, a 60kr, 45-minute bus ride takes you to the Cityterminalen, adjacent to the City's Central train station. The bus leaves every fifteen minutes, 4.30am–10pm. Alternatively, take a local train to Märsta and then a ten-minute bus ride to the city centre.

Trains arrive at Central station, which is the hub of all public transport. All three lines for the tube system (*Tunnelbana*) meet at the Central station's T-Centralen. Tickets are available at newsagents and from machines. A journey in one zone costs 13kr, with 6.50kr for every additional zone. You can buy strips of twenty for 85kr – stamp the appropriate number of tickets for your trip prior to entering the tube. Once stamped, tickets are valid for an hour.

An easier option is the **tourist ticket** at 56kr for 24 hours, or 107kr for 72 hours. The **'Stockholm Card'**, at 175kr, is valid for 24 hours and offers free museum entry, discounts on boats, ferries and tours, as well as free use of public transport. All tourist cards are available from the **tourist information office** inside Central station. The main office is in the *Sverigehuset* building at Kungsträdgården (June–Aug Mon–Fri 8am–6pm, Sat & Sun 10am–5pm; Sept–May Mon–Fri 10am–6pm, Sat & Sun 9am–3pm; ☎08/789 2490).

There is a central **taxi** booking number, ☎08/150 000, but you can avoid the 30kr booking charge by hailing down a cab. A fifteen-minute trip across the city centre will cost around 90kr.

Here we go!

It's a ten-minute tube ride on the red line in direction of Mörby Centrum, getting off at **Stadion**. Follow signs for Stadion.

Swift half

Stay on the tube for one more stop beyond Stadion, getting off at Östra. Go up to ground level to the train station. On the first floor, the **Jarnags restaurangen** is a simple café, serving meat and two veg and pints of draught Pripps beer. Although there are no scarves, posters or any other signs to suggest it, this is actually where Djurgårdens fans meet before and after the match.

Ultra culture

Having prided themselves on a good relationship with their younger, more volatile supporters, 'The Blue Saints', Djurgårdens have now broken off contact with the group. The decision followed a game with Halmstads in 1995, when a Saint ran onto the pitch and karate-kicked the referee. The tabloid press leapt on the story, nicknaming the fan 'Terrorist Tommy'; while he became a celebrity, the FA launched an inquiry into safety at the stadium and fined the club.

The Saints no longer get cheap tickets and coffees with the club president, but they still gather at the north end.

Publications

Jarn Kaminen ('Iron Stove') is the Blue Saints fanzine, produced on an irregular basis.

In the net

Peter Landhage maintains an extensive, unofficial Djurgårdens football site at www.mds.mdh.se/~adb93ple/djurgarn.htm. The homepage takes a while to download but, once done, your browser will show a charming sepia-tinted image of one of the stadium's clock towers.

The news is in Swedish only but there is an English section and, for some bizarre reason, links to sites for Lazio and Wolverhampton Wanderers.

The clock tower's playmaker – Zoran Stojčevski

Hammarby IF

Söderstadion, Arenavägen, Stockholm-Globen
Capacity 10,200
Colours Green-and-white shirts, green shorts

If AIK are the establishment of Swedish football, Hammarby are the underclass. Despite a history of total and utter failure, they remain the most popular team in Stockholm and the one club everyone would love to see back in the *Allsvenskan* – not least AIK, for whom Hammarby would be the source of lucrative local derbies. The club averaged crowds of nearly 9000 during the season they were relegated in 1995 – almost twice the national average.

Hammarby have a strange history and can boast a passionate support unlike any other in Sweden. The club's nickname is *Bajen* ('village') and the village of Hammarby was where they were formed. But the team have never played in Hammarby, having spent all of their life in Södermalm, the traditionally working-class south side of Stockholm.

In 1918, 21 years after their foundation, the club were involved in a curious merger with Stockholm side Johanneshofs IF. Hammarby kept their name, but in return the president of Johanneshofs made Hammarby sign an agreement that they would wear his club's yellow-and-black striped shirts for sixty years.

Despite the fact that their rivals AIK wore identical colours, Hammarby kept their side of the deal. In 1978 they reverted to their own green-and-white, but still wear the yellow as a change strip. Their stadium is dwarfed by a huge spherical ice-hockey

and concert venue, the Globen, which was built on Hammarby's old training ground.

A record crowd of 14,221 turned out for Hammarby's biggest moment – a 1982 league play-off final defeat by IFK Gothenburg. Since then *Bajen* have bounced between the premier and the first-division north, their latest disaster being a play-off defeat by Trelleborgs in 1996. The fans' once-famous good humour and patience have run out, and there have been angry campaigns against the board. In one incident, a pig's head was placed outside the club's offices.

That's a strange thing for Swedes to do, but then again, Hammarby are a very strange club.

Here we go!
It's a twenty-minute ride on the green line tube from T-Centralen to **Globen**. Cross

Going down, staying down – a play-off defeat in 1996 was Hammarby's most recent disaster

From San Siro to a Södermalm park bench

Before every important game, Hammarby fans indulge in a strange ritual which involves congregating on Katarina Bargata, in Södermalm, and praying at the feet of an iron statue of the **club's most famous player**. On his back is the number 11 and the word 'Legend'. He stands in front of a full-size iron goal, and there are iron footballs dotted on the ground around him.

This is **Lennart *Nacka* Skoglund**, and he stands outside his old home at #42, just around the corner from where he and Södermalm's most famous female, Greta Garbo, went to school.

Skoglund began his career kicking a ball about in the rough streets of Stockholm's south side during World War II. After impressing at **Hammarby** he was snapped up by **Inter Milan** in 1949, and later played for **Sampdoria**.

The poster of *Nacka* behind the bar at the **Kvarnen** portrays him as the ultimate Swedish footballer – strong physique, short hair, serious expression. But it wasn't just his talent that endeared him to the Hammarby faithful – he was one of them, a working-class underdog. He returned to Hammarby at the end of his career but after his retirement from the game in the Sixties he spent much of his time in bars, telling tales of *Serie A* and singing **folk songs**, a collection of which were recorded and are available today on cassette in the club shop.

Skoglund's temper was ferocious and, after several rows with Hammarby officials, his complimentary season ticket was withdrawn and he spent the last years of his life standing on the terraces, shouting abuse with the rest of them. He became a penniless alcoholic, and today every drunk in Södermalm claims it was they who found *Nacka* lying dead on a park bench...

the bridge, turn left at the dome, and you're there.

Swift half

Although the **Globen Star**, an ice-hockey theme bar next to the arena, is well placed for a pre-match pint, the **Kvarnen** at Tjaäshovsgatan 4, close to the Medborgarplatsen tube station, has for decades been *the* Hammarby bar. It is one of the few working-class vodka and soup bars left in Stockholm. Two of the district's famous sons are framed on the walls: Joe Hill, who left Södermalm for America but took its radical politics with him and became a folk singer, and *Nacka* Skoglund, the Hammarby hero (see above).

Publications

Hammarby iten is an occasional official colour newspaper. There are programmes for big games and fanzines – *Bajen Fanzine* and *Bajen Vralet* – available at the ground and the club shop.

Club shop

Hammarby-Shopen, Gotgatan 91, is a high-street souvenir shop.

Museum

Just behind Hammarby's Globen is the **Swedish Sport Museum** (open daily 10am–4pm, admission free). It is a modern, interactive series of presentations, including a small football section, with a re-created wooden stand and a collection of old shirts and boots. The bookshop has some reissues of classic Fifties Swedish sport magazines such as *Idrottsbladet*.

In the net

All Hammarby's sports clubs, including the football one, can be found on the official website: www.hammarby-if.se. It's a bit limited and in Swedish only, but worth a peek for the lowdown on the team's latest struggle to gain promotion.

A livelier, fan-run alternative resides at: www.dsv.su.se/~jonas-we/.

Big business – but the Råsunda seems soulless

Eat, drink, sleep…

Bars and cafés

There is no genuine tradition of bars or pubs in Stockholm, and the huge taxation on alcohol makes a night out here one of the most expensive in Europe. A pint will set you back anything from 30kr to 50kr. In the Eighties, mock English and Irish Pubs sprang up – even if your natural inclination is to avoid such places, you have little choice.

Södermalm is the liveliest part of town; get off at Medborgarplatsen on the green metro line and there are bars in just about all directions.

Lackebiten, Götgatan 9. A long, narrow bar with a full menu, live music at weekends. Bohemian and Afro-Caribbean crowd. Green tube to Skanstull.

Melody, Kungsträdgården. Daytime café and restaurant, night-time two dance floors and a meeting-point for the techno scene. Two minutes' walk from Kungsträdgården tube.

O'Leary's, Götgatan 11. American-style sports bar and restaurant. Sky Sports and TV always on for big European nights. Green tube to Medborgarplatsen.

Oliver Twist Pub, Repslagargatan 6. Over-the-top 'English Pub', cluttered with Britannia tack, brown sauce on the bar, and pints of bitter. Green tube to Medborgarplatsen.

Ottos O'Slag, 7 Upplandsgatan. A straightforward whisky and beer bar, next door to the more upmarket **Ottos Skafferi**. Carlsberg and Berlin's Jever beer on draught. A five-minute walk from T-Centralen.

Tre Backar, Tegnérgatan 12–14. Cellar with live music and a cheap bar upstairs. Open 'til midnight. Green tube to Rådmansgatan.

Restaurants

Eating out is expensive. A main meal will cost upwards of 80kr, and three courses with a couple of drinks will top 300kr. As elsewhere in Sweden, the cheapest way to fill up is to take advantage of a lunchtime special. For around 50kr, you'll get a main meal, salad, bread, juice and unlimited amounts of coffee.

Anders LimpBar, Barnhusgatan 14, on the corner of Vasagatan. Salad bar owned by the former AIK, Arsenal and Everton winger. Team shirts and photos from USA '94 hang on the walls, above the counter which serves an acceptable 50kr lunch deal. Limp means 'loaf' in Swedish and when he got a break from the Goodison reserves, the man himself sometimes served up the salad. Five-minute walk from T-Centralen.

Café Pierrot, Götgatan 78. Södermalm is attracting a young, arty set and this is where they meet. Full international menu, tea and alcoholic coffee specialities. Green tube to Skanstull.

Restaurant Pelé, Upplandsgatan 18. Opened in 1970, as a tribute to the man who dazzled Stockholm in '58. Italian owners keep the theme low-key with just one portrait behind the bar. For the final of USA '94, they had to watch Roby Baggio's penalty miss surrounded by 400 Brazilians. As well as having a big-screen TV (used sparingly), the Pelé also offers tango classes. Reasonably priced Italian, Swedish and Brazilian dishes, outstanding yellow-and-green Pelé T-shirts for 85kr. Visa accepted. Near T-Centralen.

Slingerbulte, Stora Nygatan 24. A reasonably priced traditional Swedish restaurant, with a set lunch for 60kr. In the old town (Gamla Stan), ten minutes' walk from T-Centralen.

Accommodation
Finding somewhere to stay in Stockholm isn't normally a problem, but it almost certainly won't be cheap.

Hotellcentralen (☎08/240 880) is a booking agency at the Central station which charges a fee for its services. For private rooms contact **Hotelljänst** (☎08/104 457), who can normally find something for 300–400kr a night.

Anno 1647, Mariagrand 3 (☎08/644 0480). Around 300kr per person, close to the old town.

City Back Packers, Barnhusgatan 16 (☎08/206 920). New, clean youth hostel with kitchen, sauna, cable TV and laundry facilities. Six- or eight-bed rooms for 140–180kr per person. Five minutes from Cityterminalen – turn left up Vasagatan.

Lord Nelson, Västerånggatan 22 (☎08/232 390). A beautiful, upmarket hotel in the heart of the old town. Prices vary according to season, and you should book in advance.

Pensionat Oden, Odengatan 38 (☎08/612 4349). Around 200kr per person per night in this small, family-run pension. Book in advance. In Norrmalm, fifteen minutes' walk from Cityterminalen. Turn left up Vasagatan and continue straight ahead on Upplandsgatan until you reach Odengatan. Or take a taxi.

Lennart Johansson – the ex-AIK boss credited with the commercialisation of European football

Gothenburg

⚽ IFK 557　⚽ Örgryte 559　⚽ GAIS 559

Fans in Gothenburg never tire of telling you that their city is the football capital of Sweden. In contrast to Stockholm, football grounds fit into the environment here, and the locals follow the game with passion and commitment.

As the industrial centre of Sweden in the late nineteenth century, Gothenburg naturally became the first city to take to football, and the early Swedish competitions were exclusively for Gothenburg clubs. Even when the Gothenburg-based Swedish FA allowed Stockholm clubs to compete, the local sides, in particular

Örgryte IS and GAIS, dominated. Sweden's first international (an 11–3 win over the Norwegians in July 1908) took place at Gothenburg's Valhalla stadium.

After World War II, the city's grip on the game weakened. GAIS won their last title in 1954 and Örgryte had to wait until 1985 for their fourteenth championship. But the failures of the big two allowed IFK Gothenburg to emerge in the Eighties as a new force, not only in the city but in the country as a whole, and in Europe.

All three of Gothenburg's main clubs, IFK, Örgryte and GAIS, play at the old

Gothenburg essentials

Arriving at the **airport**, you can take a thirty-minute bus ride to the city centre. It costs 60kr and leaves every fifteen minutes.

If you are travelling by **ferry**, Scandinavian Seaways trips from England come in at Skandiahamn – from where there's a forty-minute shuttle bus into the centre costing 35kr. Arriving from Denmark, you will dock at one of three ports nearer the city. Bus #86 and tram #3 pick up at all of them and drop off in the city.

Nya Ullevi – setting for big European games

Trains arrive at Central station and most domestic **buses** arrive at either Nils Ericssonplatsen or Heden, both of which are centrally located.

City transport consists of trams and buses, and each journey costs 7kr, regardless of the number of times you hop from one route to another – buy tickets at the kiosks adjacent to major stops. The **Value Card** is a transport smart card available at *Tid Punkten* ticket offices, offering reduced-rate travel between 9am and 3pm. It costs 100kr or 50kr, and is swiped on entry – press '2' for a city journey and press 'BYTE' if you plan to continue the journey on another bus or tram. Another alternative, available from the city's two tourist offices, is the **Gothenburg Card**, which offers a range of free and discounted museums, tours and ferries as well as free public transport and a ferry trip to nearby Fredrikshavn. A 24-hour card costs 125kr, a 48-hour one 210kr.

The main **tourist office** is by the canal on Kongsportplatsen 2 (June–Aug daily 9am–8pm; Sept–May Mon–Fri 9am–5pm, Sat & Sun 10am–2pm), with a smaller office at the Nordstan shopping centre, adjacent to the Central train station.

The central **taxi** booking number is ☎031/65 00 00.

All together now – IFK have been celebrating almost continuously for more than a decade

Ullevi stadium (Gamla Ullevi). Next door is the new Ullevi (Nya Ullevi), built for the 1958 World Cup finals. The Nya Ullevi has hosted several internationals, was a venue for Euro '92 and is where IFK play their big European games.

The thrilling fields

 IFK Gothenburg

Gamla Ullevi stadium, Ullevigatan
Capacity 18,000
Colours Blue-and-white striped shirts, blue shorts
League champions 1908, 1910, 1918, 1935, 1942, 1969, 1982–84, 1987, 1990–91, 1993–96
Cup winners 1979, 1982, 1983, 1992
UEFA Cup winners 1982, 1987

While the national team had been consistent performers, Swedish club sides were notoriously weak in European competition – that is, until IFK Gothenburg came along.

The man responsible for turning IFK from just another Swedish part-time outfit into a respected force in European football was Sven-Göran Eriksson. He took over the reins in 1979, the year Malmö FF confirmed their status as the country's top club side by reaching the final of the European Cup. In his first season he led the side to a domestic cup win, but it was in 1982 that IFK made their big breakthrough.

After defeating Hamburg 1–0 at the Ullevi in the first leg of the UEFA Cup final, the 'blåvit' ('blue-and-whites') hammered the Germans 3–0 away, with a classic display of counter-attacking football. It was the first time a Swedish side had won anything in Europe. Shortly after the victory, Eriksson joined Benfica, but IFK continued to progress under Gunder Bengtsson and Björn Westerberg.

In 1986 they made the semi-finals of the European Cup, where they lost on penalties to Barcelona. The disappointment didn't last long. In 1987, IFK won the UEFA Cup for the second time, with a victory over Dundee United.

In three Champions' League campaigns during the Nineties, IFK have claimed the scalps of Manchester United, FC Porto and AC Milan among others Their success has seen supporters' clubs being set up outside Gothenburg, and the blue-and-white shirt can now be seen in towns and villages all over Sweden.

Although IFK still have players who study or have some part-time work, they are edging closer to becoming the first full-time professional club in Sweden. Cash from the Champions' League has allowed the club to take more players on a full-time, professional basis, and IFK have even bought back some Swedish players from abroad, such as Stefan Pettersson from Ajax and Stefan Lindqvist from Xamax Neuchâtel. But the club remains incapable of keeping its younger talent. Following the victory over Milan in 1996, winger Jesper Blomqvist swapped shirts permanently.

IFK enjoy the perfect setup of playing their league games at their traditional home – the tight little Gamla Ullevi – while moving European ties next door to the Nya Ullevi. Atmosphere is maintained for league games while the demand for tickets is met for big nights. The fans are happy but so, crucially, is the bank manager.

Getting a ticket
You can buy tickets at Gamla Ullevi and at the *Bengans* record store in the Central train station (Mon–Fri 10am–6pm; Sat 10am–2pm). Prices for league matches are: standing 60kr for adult over 16, 40kr for children; seats 80kr. At Champions' League matches prices are higher – you could pay anything between 150kr and 300kr for a space in the all-seated Nya Ullevi.

Here we go!
Both stadiums are a well-signposted five-minute walk from the Central station.

Swift half
The most popular meeting place for fans is the **supporters' club building** on Friggagatan 8. There's a souvenir shop here as well as a bar.

Publications
The two local papers, *Goteborgs-Posten* and *Goteborgs-Tidningen*, have good coverage of all the Gothenburg clubs. Both are dailies and cost 7kr. *Änglatjöt* ('Angel Chat') is an IFK fanzine that's been going for seven years, and is considered one of the best of its kind in Sweden. However, it does have a new rival, *Rena Rama Blåvit* ('pure blue-and-white').

Ultra culture
IFK's supporters' club is named *Änglarna* ('The Angels'). The group has around 3500 members. IFK have had problems with hooligans and, following a series of unsavoury incidents, were forced to play their 1996 Champions' League qualifier against Ferencváros in Norrköping.

Uneven – the Gothenburg derby between IFK and ÖIS

Club shop

You'll find the best one in the headquarters of the Angels, **Supporterklubben
Änglarna**, Hotellplatsen 2. It's open
Mon–Fri 10am–3pm, with late opening until
6pm on Thursdays. For European games
there are stalls at the stadium which may
be cheaper. At the Gamla Ullevi, there is
a club shop open on matchdays inside the
main stand.

In the net

'Where Angels Dare' is the name of a
remarkable site maintained by IFK fan Magnus Andersson. Lovingly researched,
meticulously updated and with English
translations throughout, this is one of the
finest one-man club sites in Europe, at:
www.mstud.chalmers.se/~md1lazio/IFK.html.

Groundhopping

While IFK have revitalised football in
Gothenburg, the local clubs which dominated the early days of the Swedish league
are struggling, seldom playing to crowds of
more than a couple of thousand unless, of
course, the opponents are IFK…

Örgryte IS

Gamla Ullevi, see IFK above
Colours All red with blue trim
League champions 1896–99, 1902, 1904–07,
1909, 1913, 1926, 1928, 1985

ÖIS have won just one title since their prewar glory days. When they won the
championship in 1985, it was the first time
the team had finished in the top three since
the Sixties. But there weren't many around
to celebrate. The fan base has shrunk and
the club failed to build on their title win –
the best players were snapped up by
wealthier teams and the side fell into the
first-division south in 1991. They returned
to the *Allsvenskan* in 1993 but lasted just

one season. In 1995, a promising young
side won the first-division south title but
has struggled in the premier, avoiding the
1996 relegation play-offs by just one point.

If you want to help the faithful drown
their sorrows, the **White Corner** bar,
Vasagatan 43b, is a five-minute walk from
the Ullevi. It was a favourite haunt for IFK
fans until a recent change of ownership.

GAIS

Gamla Ullevi, see IFK above
Colours Green-and-black striped shirts, white
shorts
League champions 1919, 1922, 1931, 1954
Cup winners 1942

If you thought Örgryte were struggling…
Gothenburg's other prewar giant, Göte-
borg Atlet & Idrottsälskap, have won
nothing at all since 1954. After spending
much of the Eighties in the first division
they returned to the top in 1987, and two
years later finished third in the league,
above IFK. But the 'Mackerels' went back
down in 1992 and in 1996 were relegated
to the regional league.

These days they play to an average
crowd of around 1500, a fair proportion
of whom seem to end up at the **White
Corner** bar (see Örgryte, above) after the
final whistle.

Eat, drink, sleep…

Bars and clubs

Like Stockholm, Gothenburg is a costly city
in which to spend a night out. If you're feeling flush, the Avenyn and its surrounding
streets are crowded with bars, cafés and
restaurants. Gothenburg also has an abundance of attractive old coffee houses,
tucked away all over the city.

Auld Dubliner, Ostra Hamnagatan. There are
several Irish bars in town but this is the oldest,

having been established in 1870. Five minutes' walk from Central train station.

Café Lyckam, Vasagatan 5c. A seventy-year-old cafe which has remained virtually unchanged in both its appearance and its down-to-earth clientèle. In a side street off Avenyn, ten minutes' stroll from the train station.

Junggrens Café, Kungsportsavenyn 37. The 'Youth Café', and for generations the meeting point for Gothenburgers starting their night out. Five minutes from the train station.

Nivl, Avenyn 9. In the daytime, a café serving decent lunch deals. At night the three floors are opened up, with a trio of bars and a disco on Thursday, Friday and Saturday nights.

O'Leary's, Ostra Hamnagaten 37. American-style bar with Tex-Mex kitchen and sport on TV. Opposite the *Auld Dubliner*.

Paddingtons, St Pauligatan 4. English pub with a large expat clientèle glued to the Sky TV, and the occasional Swedish Liverpool fan. From the train station, take bus #34 or tram #1, #3 or #6 to the Retbergsplatsen.

Restaurants

You may be able to eat slightly more cheaply in Gothenburg than in Stockholm – but not much. As ever, lunchtime set menus are your best chance of tucking into local specialities such as smoked meats and fresh herring at an affordable price.

Brasserie Ferdinand, Drottnninggaten 41. No photos of Les, unfortunately, but more than 120 different beers and a wide menu of Scandinavian and international cuisine. By the train station.

Bruggeriet, Kungsportavenyn 3. Traditional Swedish nosh with a huge choice of draught and bottled beers.

Froken Olssens Kafe, Ostra Latmgaten 14. Famed for its open sandwiches and its cakes – a good spot for a cold lunch. Five minutes from the train station.

Gyellene Prag, Sveagaten 25. Students hang out here for the cheap Czech food and fine draught Budweiser. From the Central train station, take any of trams #1, #2, #3, #4 or #9 to Linne.

Accommodation

The main **tourist office** offers the Gothenburg Package, which includes a hotel, breakfast and the Gothenburg Card for between 400kr and 600kr, depending on the hotel. A cheaper alternative is to ask them to find you a **private room** – expect to pay around 200kr per person, including their commission.

Aveny Turist, Södravägen 2 (☎031/20 52 86). Rooms for 200–300kr per head in the centre of town.

City Hotel, Lorensbergsgatan 6 (☎031/18 00 25). Bang next to the Avenyn and ideal for a short stagger home from the nightlife action. Between 250kr and 350kr.

Hotel Riverton, St Badhusgatan 26 (☎031/10 12 00). Upmarket hotel with a great view over the harbour. Prices upwards of 600kr.

Nordengarden, Stockholmsgatan 16 (☎031/19 66 31). Centrally located, private youth hostel with beds for 130–160kr.

Switzerland

"The organising committee, in its wisdom, allocated the 1954 World Cup to Switzerland, where the locals appear to be more interested in climbing up and down their mountains, explaining why their clocks and watches are so much better than any others in the world, or generally catering for their annual influx of tourists."

So wrote the normally reserved Tom Finney in *Finney On Football*. He may have fallen back on old stereotypes but his point is nonetheless a telling one. A country which appears to have everything it needs for a thriving football scene seems curiously uninterested in the continent's most ardently followed professional sport.

On paper, it all looks great. There is no shortage of money available – Switzerland's stable economy is the envy of Europe and there are plenty of potential corporate sponsors for the game. A country sandwiched between a number of soccer hotbeds and made up of three of the continent's top footballing ethnic groups – Germans, Italians and French – should produce top-class players. The national team should be able to marry the discipline of the Germans with the tactical awareness of the Italians and the flair of the French. Yet somehow, it just doesn't happen.

Perhaps it is the very factors listed above which explain the rather dull character of the country's football. No wars, no revolutions, no economic hardship to escape from – here football is not an outlet for frustrated passions as it is in so many countries, but simply one pastime among many others. The multi-ethnic state, rather than creating a delicious mix of playing and supporting styles, encourages fans in Zürich to tune into SAT1 to watch Borussia Dortmund rather than follow a local side, while down in the Italian-speaking region of

Affluent – cigars are *de rigueur* for Swiss fans

Ticino, supporters nip across the border to Turin to watch Juventus.

Yet despite the absence of a popular football culture, Switzerland is, officially at least, the home of the game. FIFA, world football's governing body, are up in the hills overlooking their bank account in Zürich, while their European equivalents UEFA are on the shores of Lake Geneva in the town of Nyon. It's not just the stability of the Swiss franc that persuaded these bodies to set up home in the confederation – Switzerland took an early and active rôle in the organisation of the game on the continent and was one of the seven founding members of FIFA.

According to the historians, the first organised games of association football in continental Europe took place in Switzerland in the 1850s, between teams of English and Swiss students. FC St Gallen were founded in 1879 and seven years later the country's most successful and best-known team, Grasshopper Club, were formed in Zürich. Indeed most of the teams currently in the top flight of Swiss football were formed before the turn of the century and a national championship, played between the winners of three regional leagues, began in 1897, at a time when many European countries were still learning the rules from visiting English engineers.

After getting plenty of experience in international competition in the form of *ad hoc* friendlies – mostly against neighbouring Austria, Italy and Germany – from 1905, the Swiss won a soccer silver at the 1924 Paris Olympics; they lost out in the final to a strong Uruguay side after beating Czechoslovakia, Italy and Sweden. But they failed to build on this promising start in international football and in the following years suffered heavy defeats to Austria, Holland and Germany. The Swiss also took part in all six of the International Cup competitions between 1928 and 1938, finishing last in each of them. Swiss club sides had a similar lack of success in the Mitropa Cup.

After Austria had given them several lessons on the field, the Swiss FA decided to turn to an Austrian to coach their national team. In 1937, Karl Rappan took the reins for the first of four spells in charge which were to span four eventful decades. Rappan's approach was pragmatic – if the Swiss were to compete on the international stage, they would have to do so through strength of numbers in defence.

With its use of a sweeper and wingers who tracked back to defend, Rappan's so-called *verrou* ('Bolt') system was twenty years ahead of its time. The formation laid the groundwork for *catenaccio* and other sweeper systems, and also introduced the concept of the counter-attack. Up until the Bolt, most football tactics were concerned with the line-up of the attacking players; Rappan brought tactics to defensive and midfield play.

Rappan was not just a shrewd tactician, he was a great motivator, imbuing a side that had suffered a decade of defeats with new-found confidence. At the 1938 World Cup, Switzerland reached the quarter-finals

We'll be back – the Swiss national side bid a typically dignified farewell from Euro '96

Basics

Citizens of many EU countries require only an identity card for entry into Switzerland, but Britons require a **full passport**, as do Americans, Canadians, Australians and New Zealanders.

The Swiss currency is the **Swiss Franc** (Sfr), divided into 100 centimes (c), the latter referred to as *Rappen* in some German-speaking areas. There are coins for 5c, 10c, 20c, 50c and Sfr1, Sfr2 and Sfr5, along with notes for Sfr5, Sfr10, Sfr20, Sfr50, Sfr100, Sfr500 and Sfr1000. Banks are generally open Mon–Fri 8.30am–4.30pm. Credit-card cash machines are widespread. Exchange rates tend to be best in banks but you'll also find exchange offices in major train stations and at post offices. The current rate is around Sfr2.25 to £1.

Public telephones are easy to find and accept 10c, 20c, 50c, Sfr1 and Sfr5 coins as well as phone cards, which are available at post offices and newsstands for Sfr10 and Sfr20. International calls can be made from almost all street phones – dial 00 and then the country code. From outside the country, the code for Switzerland is 41 – add 1 for Zürich.

Switzerland has a superb **public transport** system – fast, integrated, clean and environmentally friendly. The state train company, SBB/CFF, covers all the main intercity routes while private firms run mountain railways to smaller, rural destinations, and buses pick up the slack in the most remote areas. Fares are calculated per kilometre – a 100km journey costs Sfr30.

The **Swiss Pass**, available at all train stations, offers four-day, eight-day and fifteen-day options at Sfr200, Sfr250 and Sfr290 respectively. In addition to state railways, the Pass entitles you to travel free on lake steamers, most postbuses and bus/tram networks in major cities. A cheaper option, and more sensible if you'll be doing only a limited amount of travelling, is the **Half Fare Card**. This costs Sfr85, is valid for a month and gives a fifty percent discount on all trains, buses and lake ferries.Tourist information centres (*Verkehrsbüro* or *Office du Tourisme*) are often located close to stations.

Aside from their **wonderful chocolate**, the Swiss produce little in the way of *haute cuisine*. The staple diet in German-speaking areas is *Rösti*, basically a load of grated, fried potatoes covered in cheese or other toppings, while francophone areas are keen on *fondue*. Swiss **beer** and **wine** are both better than their international reputations might suggest, but neither is cheap.

with a 4–2 win over Germany, before losing 2–0 to Hungary.

Postwar Swiss football was given the ideal chance to make an impression when the country was awarded the 1954 World Cup finals. Stadia across the land were upgraded and two wins over Italy earned the hosts a quarter-final spot. Up against their old rivals the Austrians, the Swiss took a three-goal lead but eventually lost a bizarre game 7–5.

They would qualify for all the World Cups until 1966 only to make little impact, and after '66 it would be 28 years before they returned to the finals. The Seventies and Eighties were a grim time for Swiss football, brightened only by a modest improvement in the form shown by the nation's clubs in European competition. FC Zürich repeated their 1959 run to the semi-finals of the European Cup when they reached the same stage in 1977. A year later their city rivals Grasshoppers reached the last four of the UEFA Cup.

But again it took a foreign influence to put some pride back into Swiss football. In 1989, former West German international Uli Stielike took over as national-team coach and, although he failed to take his team to either Italia '90 or Euro '92, he laid the foundations for the best postwar Swiss side, which reached the peak of its powers when Roy Hodgson took over from Stielike in 1991.

Hodgson, a former lower-division player in England, had enjoyed a successful spell as a coach in Sweden before taking charge of Swiss side Neuchâtel Xamax. Although unknown in his homeland he was respected in Switzerland and, after his appointment as national-team coach, he was to become a hero as crucial victories over Scotland and Italy earned the Swiss a place at USA '94.

The side included several players based in the German *Bundesliga*. Alain Sutter, the ponytailed midfield creator; Italian-born anchorman Ciriaco Sforza; and the formidable front pairing of Stéphane Chapuisat and Adrian Knup all brought their major-league experience to bear on a team that had previously lacked the conviction to turn its potential into achievement.

In the States, the Swiss survived a tough opener by drawing against the hosts, then mounted a stunning 4–1 win over Romania before bowing out in the second round to an effervescent Spain.

Hodgson guided the same squad past Sweden and Hungary and on to Euro '96, but he was to miss out on a homecoming. Having accepted a coaching post at Internazionale, the Englishman felt he could combine his rôles at club and international levels. The Swiss FA thought otherwise, dismissed Hodgson, and replaced him with Artur Jorge, who immediately set about trying to turn a settled squad and strategy upside-down.

In England, drawn in a tough group with the hosts, Scotland and Holland, the Swiss finished bottom after scoring only once – from the penalty spot – in three matches.

Jorge's post-tournament sacking and the appointment of the more sympathetic Rolf Fringer should ensure that not all Hodgson's good work is undone, while at club level the performances of Grasshoppers in the Champions League have given the domestic game some unaccustomed international attention. Even so, a poorly functioning league system, low crowds and the ongoing exodus of the nation's best players continue to leave Swiss fans looking enviously across their borders.

Essential vocabulary

French
Hello *Bonjour*
Goodbye *Au revoir*
Yes *Oui*
No *Non*
Two beers, please *Deux demis, s'il vous plaît*
Thank you *Merci*
Men's *Hommes*
Women's *Dames*
Where is the stadium? *Où est le stade?*
What is the score? *Où en sommes-nous?*
Referee *L'arbitre*
Offside *Hors jeu*

German
Hello *Guten Tag*
Goodbye *Auf wiedersehen*
Yes *Ja*
No *Nein*
Two beers, please *Zwei Bier, bitte*
Thank you *Danke*
Men's *Herren*
Women's *Damen*
Where is the stadium? *Wo ist das Stadion?*
What's the score? *Wie steht's?*
Referee *Schreidsrichter*
Offside *Abseits*

Match practice

A visit to a Swiss league game is a relaxing experience. Turning up two minutes before kick-off? Don't worry. You can still choose the best seat in the ground and, once ensconced there, munch on a sausage or casually sip a beer. You may well see local fans getting worked up about what's going on before them, but they are never abusive – a frustrated stamp of the feet or smack of hand on thigh is all the aggression you'll see. Swiss sports fans, it seems, save their energy for whooping and ringing cowbells on the piste.

The Swiss campaign runs from mid-July to early June the following year, finishing a

Roi Roy – English coach Hodgson shook the Swiss game out of its traditional apathy

month earlier if the Swiss national side is involved in the World Cup or European Championship finals. There is a lengthy winter break from early December to late February, when the Swiss can concentrate on their favourite sports: ice-hockey and skiing. There are indoor tournaments in January, and 'warm-up' friendlies for the spring season start in early February.

Matches are either played on Saturday (kick-off times vary from mid-afternoon to early evening) or Sunday afternoons (at around 2.30pm). There are a handful of midweek rounds spread throughout the season. Although games traditionally take place simultaneously, this is starting to change as television begins to play a bigger rôle, prompting the staggering of fixtures over the course of a weekend.

The league

In the autumn half of the season, twelve teams compete in what's known as National League A, playing each other twice. The top eight sides at Christmas then have their points totals halved and play each other twice again in the second half of the season for the title and UEFA Cup places. This championship group is known as the *Meisterrunde*. Meanwhile, the bottom four sides from the pre-Christmas NLA are 'relegated' to spend the spring season playing-off against the top four sides 'promoted' from the twelve-team NLB; all pre-Christmas points are annulled, and the top four teams at the end of the campaign have the privilege of rejoining the NLA the following season.

Although this league structure means there is an exciting relegation dogfight in December, the title race only becomes interesting in spring, and demotion to the post-Christmas *Promotionsrunde* sounds the death-knell of any NLA team's season.

Every year the Swiss FA considers scrapping this heavily criticised league structure, which has been in place for a decade now. Mid-ranking clubs complain that they must permanently live with the threat of relegation, while teams involved in Europe mutter darkly about having to play too many games. The latter seems a weak point – Swiss sides play a not unreasonable 36 league games a year and rarely make it beyond the second round in Europe anyway. Still, the debate continues and the possibility of change in the near future cannot not be ruled out.

Up for the cup

The Swiss Cup final is a one-off affair, always played in June at the ramshackle national stadium, the Wankdorf in Berne. From season 1997/98, NLA clubs will only join in at the last-32 stage, a round later than previously, as a concession to complaints about the allegedly crowded fixture list. Ties are all single matches, which go to extra time at the end of ninety minutes, then penalties if the teams are still level.

No-one gets too excited about the cup until the final itself; it's not uncommon, even up to the quarter-final stage, to see ties on tiny provincial grounds where fans are standing behind a rope with their dogs on leads, while in the background, 9-year-old boys play a game of their own.

The back page

Few Swiss players complain about being hassled for autographs in the shopping centre, their anonymity a consequence of football's low-key media coverage. A weekly newspaper, *Sport* (Mondays, Sfr3.50), has a big football section, including some international coverage; it's worth picking up, if only to check kick-off times.

There are no Swiss football magazines save for an annual season preview title,

Kick-off (Sfr10); with its glossy team portraits, squad info and interviews with coaches, it bears a striking resemblance to the pre-season *Sonderheft* produced by the German magazine *Kicker*, which also sells well in Switzerland.

The Zürich daily papers *Tages Anzeiger* and *Neue Züricher Zeitung* both have decent sports sections.

Action replay

As elsewhere, the relationship between Swiss soccer and television is in a state of flux. In February 1997, the Swiss FA sold the rights to domestic league and cup games to a Swiss-German joint venture which plans to broadcast games on the German channel SAT1. The deal runs from season 1997/98 until 2001. The idea is that the Swiss state channel, DRS, will continue to show highlights of domestic games, while SAT1 will show some live games and matches involving the Swiss national side, broadcasting to Switzerland via satellite.

However, it seems likely that the DRS highlights show *Sportpanorama* (Sundays, 6.30pm) will remain in some form. The programme's top pundit is the former West German star Günther Netzer, who is amiable enough but dull and uncompromisingly neutral – which is probably why the Swiss like him.

Half-time

Football is treated as a family day out in Switzerland, and one consequence of this is that there's plenty of quality food available. Most clubs have a restaurant and more modest *Bufe* facilities both inside and outside the stadium. Sausages and beer prevail but some clubs, such as Grasshoppers,

Problem area – Zürich's Letzigrund offers a uniquely obscured view

make a special effort to

offer alternatives. In French-speaking areas you'll find *pomme frites* with mayonnaise.

Ultra culture

You might see the odd ultra-style banner proclaiming the presence of some 'Blue Boys' gang or other, but those behind it will most likely be enthusiastic youngsters whose parents expect they will soon grow out of it. Friendly, multi-lingual Swiss fans pride themselves on their sporting behaviour and this is definitely one country where you can feel safe wherever you are sitting.

Terrace chants are quickly picked up as they often consist of no more than the club's name followed by lots of la-la-la-ing. Don't be surprised to hear the odd song in English. At Zürich's Hardturm stadium, opposing fans have been heard to sing, in perfect English: "Can you see the Hoppers hop?" But, typically, the chant fades out before the "I can't see a... thing" refrain.

In the net

Switzerland's national FA, the SFV, has an official website at: www.football.ch/. You'll find a detailed history of the association and news on all levels of the national team, including youth and women's football. Choose between French and German language. For the latest results and a stats archive, try Reinhard Kahle's site at: www.marwin.ch/sport/fb/ch/index.e.html. This is regularly updated, with an English option and masses of good links. More stats are on offer at Ken Butler's extensive European soccer site, one page of which takes you into a Swiss football prediction league: www.sfu.ca/~kbutler/swisspl.html.

Zürich

Grasshoppers 567
FC Zürich 570

Switzerland's largest, most prosperous and most cosmopolitan city is also the best place to get a taste of the local football. The town's two long-established clubs present a contrast between contemporary glamour and fading tradition, while Zürich itself is perhaps the only city in the country to possess a strong football culture, albeit an often well-concealed one.

The Zürich derby between Grasshoppers and FCZ drags out the passive support twice a year (more if both clubs feature in the *Meisterrunde*, as they did in 1997) and is one of the few occasions when there is any real needle on show – though there's no history of trouble between the two sets of supporters.

Surprisingly, the Swiss national team rarely deign to appear here. Locals, however, are proud of the fact that in eight matches played at Zürich's Hardturm since 1967, the men in red have maintained a hundred percent record.

The thrilling fields

Grasshoppers

Hardturm stadium, Hardturmstrasse 321
Capacity 22,000 (all-seated)
Colours Blue-and-white halved shirts, white shorts
League champions 1900–01, 1905, 1921, 1927–28, 1931, 1937, 1939, 1942–43, 1945, 1952, 1956, 1971, 1978, 1982–84, 1990–91, 1995–96
Cup winners 1926, 1932, 1934, 1937–38, 1940–43, 1946, 1952, 1956, 1983, 1988–90, 1994

If one team are capable of making the leap from sleepy, Swiss semi-professionalism to the European soccer élite, then Grasshopper Club of Zürich are that team. Grasshoppers are the most popular club in the city and the most unpopular in the rest of the country, where they are seen

Zürich essentials

Zürich's **airport** is 10km outside the city at **Kloten**. The fastest and cheapest way into town is to take one of the many trains that leave regularly to a range of destinations, many of them stopping *en route* at Zürich Hauptbahnhof, right in the centre of the city.

The Hauptbahnhof boasts a large underground shopping centre complete with reasonably priced restaurants, cafés and bars. Just outside on the right is the excellent **tourist information point** at Bahnhofplatz 15 (open Mon–Fri 8.30am–7.30pm, Sat–Sun 8.30am–8.30pm), which sells maps and offers a hotel booking service.

The Hauptbahnhof is also the central point for the city's ultra-efficient **urban tramway network**. Tickets should be purchased in advance from machines at the platforms. A single journey (*Kurzstecke*) costs Sfr3.20. Unless you really are just making one journey, a day pass (*Tageskarte*) is a bargain at Sfr6.80. The city's outer suburbs are linked by a high-speed **S-Bahn** service. Both trams and S-Bahn run until around midnight, after which your only option is a taxi – expensive at Sfr3 per kilometre, plus a standing charge of Sfr6.

A **listings magazine**, *Züritip*, comes free with the *Tages Anzeiger* newspaper on Fridays and can be found in many bars. The tourist information office issues a quarterly listings magazine, *Zürich Next*, which is one of the better of its type. *Toaster* is a monthly listings and entertainment magazine, particularly strong on the club scene.

as the epitome of Zürich's bourgeois wealth. Known locally by their initials, GC, they are the most successful club in Swiss history with 24 league titles and 18 cup wins to their credit. They have also been the only Swiss club to make a lasting impression in Europe. Their recent appearances in the Champions' League surprised many – although never looking likely to get near the final, the team impressed with their organisation and occasionally attractive football. Honours at home are taken for granted but exciting European nights against top-class opposition are a relatively new (and eagerly awaited) phenomenon at the Hardturm.

Formed by English students in 1886, GC won the first Swiss championship final twelve years later and have been a near-constant presence in the top rank ever since. Most of the key players in prewar Swiss national sides were Grasshoppers', among them the Abegglen brothers, Max and André, who became the top two Swiss international scorers of all time with 62 goals between them. At European level the

club competed regularly in the tough Mitropa Cup competition, peaking with a quarter-final appearance in 1937.

After picking up Swiss titles at will in the early postwar period, GC hit a dry patch, failing to win a single domestic honour between 1957 and 1970. The suffering was made worse by the fact that across the city, FC Zürich were enjoying a revival.

A championship win in 1970 restored the faith of the fans, but it wasn't until 1978 that a superb UEFA Cup run laid the foundations for the revitalisation of the club. Inter Bratislava and Dynamo Tblisi were defeated to set up a quarter-final with Eintracht Frankfurt, at which Switzerland's traditional footballing inferiority complex *vis à vis* the Germans was swept aside, GC winning on away goals. In the semi-final they beat Bastia of France 3–2 in Zürich, but a 1–0 defeat in Corsica cost them a place in the final.

Four titles and three cup wins then followed in the Eighties, and the club's domination of the Swiss game has stretched almost uninterrupted into the current decade. Grasshoppers' position was greatly enhanced by Champions' League qualification in 1995 and 1996, which brought Ajax and Real Madrid – as well as considerable amounts of cash – to the Hardturm. Today no other Swiss club can match GC's organisation and commercial clout. Many Swiss internationals still play abroad, but those that don't play at Grasshoppers.

The Hardturm has been gradually upgraded into an all-seater stadium but has lost none of its character, which remains essentially that of a classic, English close-to-the pitch ground. It would be pushing it to say that big-time football has arrived in Switzerland, but Grasshoppers have set the standard for others to follow.

Getting a ticket

Crowds for domestic games rarely climb above 10,000 and tickets can be bought at kiosks outside the entrances. European games are often sold out well in advance, however, so check ahead for availability with the club's ticket office (☎01/272 3370). Adult prices range from Sfr15 to Sfr40 for domestic games, with Sfr20 buying you an excellent view from the east stand (*Ost Tribüne*) overlooking the corner flag at the home end.

Note that ticket prices can rise by up to a hundred percent for European games, when the club goes out of its way to offer fans some regional cuisine appropriate to the visiting side. The paella for Real Madrid in 1996 was a great success, but a year later Scots fans came to the Hardturm to find the local caterers obviously short of haggis and neeps, and were confronted instead with a 'Rangers Stew' strongly reminiscent of a British school dinner of the mid-Seventies.

Here we go!

The ground is a ten-minute ride on tram #4 from the Hauptbahnhof, direction

No Swiss miss – Viorel Moldovan puts the blue-and-white halves ahead against Auxerre

Werdhölzli. Get off at the **Sportplatz Hardturm** stop.

Swift half

There are plenty of stalls both inside and outside the stadium. The **GC Café** under the north stand is usually closed off on matchdays as a press area. If you prefer a real bar, the **Hürlimann**, by the tram stop on Hardturmstrasse, is a popular meeting point and comes into its own for the rare occasions when there is no alcohol inside the ground.

Publications

GCZ Magazin is the unimaginatively titled but well-designed matchday programme costing Sfr2.

In the net

Grasshoppers have a surprisingly limited presence on the Web. In the absence of any extensive one-club site, official or otherwise, the best online bet is Matthias Neeracher's match-report service at: err.ethz.ch/~neeri/soccer.html. Matthias files his reports in English on a regular basis and, by comparison with the arrogant trumpeting of many single-club sites, his comments can be disarmingly honest. He also runs an electronic Swiss soccer mailing list, accessible from the same page.

 FC Zürich

Letzigrund stadium, Herdenstrasse 47
Capacity 27,000 (11,000 seated)
Colours Blue-and-white striped shirts, blue shorts
League champions 1902, 1924, 1963, 1966, 1968, 1974–76, 1981
Cup winners 1966, 1970, 1972, 1973, 1976

If Grasshoppers are the most untypical Swiss club – organised, affluent and making an impression in Europe – then across the city you can get a taste of what the rest of Swiss football is like. Expectations are low at FC Zürich, but the team have not always played second-fiddle to their neighbours and are proud of their working-class roots.

They were formed in 1896 out of a merger of three local clubs, FC Turicum, FC Excelsior and FC Viktoria. The aim was to unite in order to challenge the dominance of Grasshoppers, but that challenge has been sustained only once – during the Sixties when FCZ won three league titles including a double in 1966.

In 1964 the team reached the semifinals of the European Cup, where they were hammered 8–1 on aggregate by Real Madrid. They made it to that stage again in 1977, going out 6–1 on aggregate to Liverpool. Jakob Kuhn, capped 63 times by his country, was a member of both those semi-final squads, one of a tiny band of top-class players who have stayed loyal to the club throughout their careers.

The last time FCZ won anything was in 1981, but the club's centenary in 1996 provoked a surge in interest, a friendly match with Juventus filling the Letzigrund and the acquisition of Tomas Brolin on-loan from Leeds indicating a growing ambition at the club.

The Letzigrund is actually a municipal athletics stadium, with a radical design in which the roof slopes down and away from the pitch to a point behind each goal, hindering the view from what is usually one of the most popular gathering areas for fans. Plans are afoot to redesign the roof and make the stadium all-seated.

Getting a ticket

You'll pay Sfr30 for a seat in either of the main stands, Sfr15 for a place on those strange terraces. The view from the latter is actually not too bad if you stand well back, and the atmosphere there is much better than in the stands. Unless it's very cold, most people actually sit down on the terraces, and you can expect to be tutted at, or even have beer sprayed at you, if you insist on standing.

Tickets are readily available at the stadium immediately before the game at the stadium, and for the occasional big match, they can be bought in advance here, too.

Here we go!

On matchdays there are **special trams** from the Hauptbahnhof to the Letzigrund. Otherwise you can take tram #6, #7, #11 or #13 up the Bahnhofstrasse from Hauptbahnhof as far as Paradeplatz, then change onto a #2 (direction Farbhof), getting off at Letzigraben. The stadium is on your right. Its fifteen minutes' journey from the centre.

Swift half

On the corner of Herdenstrasse and Baslerstrasse, by the main entrance to the stadium, is the **Ziz Zac Bar**, which serves draught Löwenbräu and has wooden tables outside in warm weather.

Publications

They must have agonised for an eternity trying to come up with an original title for FCZ's match programme, and finally threw caution to the wind – the result is *Magazin*, a low-budget, low-interest production costing Sfr2.

Ultra culture

Despite the obstruction, the area behind the goal is the place where FCZ's younger supporters gather. When they get bored they are fond of throwing flares onto the athletics track, prompting a steward wearing an industrial glove to run and pick it up before snuffing it out in his bucket. The poor old bloke struggles as the fans throw more flares behind his back, and everyone guffaws as he is still too busy with the first flare to get to the next one in time. And that's about as raucous as it gets.

In the net

In contrast to Grasshoppers, FCZ have been quick to back an official website. It's nicely put together, regularly updated and contains a detailed history as well as the usual match-report archive, stats areas and picture gallery. The text is German only but it's worth having a peek at: www.fcz.ch/.

Italian influence – FCZ's Giuseppe Mazzarelli

Eat, drink, sleep...

Bars and clubs

A night out in Zürich can be one of the most expensive in Europe. It was once one of the more boring as well, but in recent years the variety of bars and clubs has improved enormously. In particular, guest DJs from all over Europe have invigorated the club scene, shaking the city out of its previously sleepy existence.

The old town on the north bank of the River Limmat is the best for drinking and eating, with the cobbled, pedestrianised Niederdorfstrasse offering a fair sprinkling of bars and restaurants. It is here that visiting fans from elsewhere in Europe will generally be found several hours before kick-off, psyching themselves up for the encounter ahead by getting angry about the price and quality of Swiss beer – although once you've come to terms with the likely size of the bill, it doesn't taste too bad.

Café Odeon, Limmatquai 2. Lenin reportedly stopped for a pint here on his train journey from Moscow to Islington. Sadly, he didn't take the idea of the grand old coffeehouse back to Soviet Russia with him. The *Odeon* outlasted Lenin's state and remains an attractive riverside hang-out for poets and artists, with one area for coffee and another for draught Kronenbourg.

Linth-Escher, 23 Linthescher Gasse. Opposite the Hauptbahnhof and ideal for a pre-match drink, this place is actually busy throughout the evening and is one of the few bars in the station area where you don't feel out of place if you don't work in a bank. Daily menu with fair prices, in an honest, pubby atmosphere.

Room for one more up top – any seat will do at the Zürich derby

Magic Factory, Wagistrasse 7. Home to the best techno nights in Zürich when Phuture Rhythm gather the top local DJs together with international guests. Two rooms with separate sounds; check listings to see what's on. Bus #31 along Badenstrasse to Wagistrasse.

Nelson Pub, Schützengasse. Sadly not a tribute to the former English second-division side now struggling in the North West Counties League. Rather, this is an expat hangout, worth visiting for Sky Sports shown on a big screen. Avoid the

Guinness, though. Just off the Bahnhofstrasse and within walking distance of the Hauptbahnhof.

Rote Fabrik, Seestrasse 395. Live music venue with an adjoining café bar that serves food. The international acts performing here bridge the full musical spectrum, with rock, jazz, blues, pop and indie. Check listings to see who's in town.

Wüste Cocktail Bar, Oberdorfstrasse 7. Jazz-funk and mellow house sounds for a pre-party crowd at weekends. Frozen vodkas are the house speciality. A tad pretentious, but worth a look if you're tired of beer and sausages.

Restaurants

As befits the city's commercial status, food in Zürich has an international flavour, with French and Italian dishes jostling for attention alongside traditional Swiss specialities such as *Rösti*. Eating out in an upmarket place, however, may be an experience your credit-card company will not forgive you for. Better to eat in a pub or beer-hall, or have your main meal at lunchtime – look out for a *Mittagsmenü*, a set lunch for between Sfr15 and Sfr20, on offer in many central restaurants.

Bar Bistro Heugumper, Waaggasse 4. *Heugumper* is German for Grasshopper and this place is owned by the club. Upstairs is for officials only; downstairs is a bistro open to the public. Apart from the green grasshopper on the wall outside, there is no football theme to this rather expensive eaterie, and you're more likely to find bankers here than kids in blue-and-white halves. In the centre of town, just off the Bahn-hofstrasse, opposite the Paradeplatz.

Commercio, Muhlerbachstrasse 2. One of the advantages of eating out in Switzerland is that Italian and French restaurants can't get away with

Corridors of power – FIFA and UEFA

Many places claim to be the home of football, but the most important decisions on the future of the game are taken in Switzerland.

FIFA, football's world governing body, is based in the suburbs of Zürich. Since its foundation in 1904, the organisation has grown in importance. Initially its membership consisted of the FAs of Belgium, France, Holland, Denmark, Spain, Sweden and Switzerland. Today 191 nations are affiliated to an association which takes responsibility for, among many other things, organising the World Cup and the football tournament of the Olympic Games.

Until the foundation of FIFA, the undisputed 'controller' of the game was

Flag day – UEFA has revolutionised the marketing of football

the **Football Association** in England, and the FA maintains a rôle in the administration and regulation of the game worldwide. The **International Football Board**, responsible for the laws of the game, has a permanent British majority, and for almost twenty years the FIFA presidency was held by an Englishman, Sir Stanley Rous.

Since Rous' departure from the scene in 1974, the Brazilian João Havelange has been in charge. Under his guidance, FIFA has become increasingly business-oriented as the licensee for lucrative **World Cup sponsorship** deals – although Havelange himself has been criticised for running the organisation as if it were his own personal fiefdom.

FIFA's European equivalent, **UEFA**, is based in Nyon, close to Lake Geneva. It was formed in 1954, and its establishment triggered the beginning of the major continental competitions. The European Cup was first played for in 1958, and two years later the European Championship was held for the first time, as the European Nations' Cup – all under UEFA's auspices.

Like FIFA, UEFA has become a major business broker as well as a sports administrator. Since his appointment in 1990, UEFA president Lennart Johansson has overseen the gradual transformation of the European Cup into the **Champions' League** – complete with central sponsorship, TV rights auctions and the marketing of the competition as a corporate brand.

For both organisations, Switzerland has been a home of enduring appeal. At the turn of the century FIFA needed to be in **the heart of Europe**, the home of the game, while UEFA had to find a base at the height of the Cold War, when **Swiss neutrality** was a key attribute.

In recent years Switzerland's economy has been the most potent reason for staying put. The Swiss franc is **UEFA's official currency**, and the Swiss banking system has been adept at handling complex international business transactions, while remaining politically discreet.

Neither headquarters is currently **open to the public**, but both FIFA and UEFA plan to open museums before the millennium.

Jailbreak at the Hardturm – a Grasshopper escapes its cage

Rösti Bar, Hauptbahnhof. Rarely does a train station restaurant offer high-quality, wholesome food at a reasonable price – this one does. Prices are fair at Sfr7 for a basic *Rösti* with onions, cheese and bacon, and you can't get more central than this.

Accommodation

Many of Zürich's hotels are geared towards the business community, with prices to match. But the sheer size of the city makes it possible to track down a reasonably priced room, and it needn't be too far from the nightlife action, either.

Hotel Hirschen, Niederdorfstrasse 13 (☎01/251 4242). Reception is open round the clock at this centrally located hotel. Smart rooms housed within a centuries-old building, with or without private shower. From around Sfr60 for a single room. In the old town.

Hotel Italia, Zeughausstrasse 61 (☎01/241 0555). Rundown but friendly hotel with single rooms for Sfr65, doubles for Sfr85. Your shower is in the hall. A little west of the city centre, beyond the River Sihl.

poor imitations. This is a decent, moderately priced Italian. Centrally located.

Rheinfelder Bierhalle, Niederdorfstrasse 76. A typical Swiss-German beer hall, with an easygoing atmosphere, a minimum of frills and decent food available all day. The cheapest *Mittagsmenü* is tempting at only Sfr12.50. If the place looks a little on the full side, there are plenty of alternatives in this street and the adjacent Limmatquai in Zürich's old town.

Marthahaus, Zähringerstrasse 36 (☎01/251 4550). If you're desperate and sure you don't mind sleeping in a dormitory bed, this place is for you – a privately run hostel, well-located in the heart of the old town. For as little as Sfr50 per person per night.

Pension St Josef, Hirschengraben 64 (☎01/251 2757). Convivial little place, between the old town and the university. Around Sfr60.

Turkey

You don't need to look hard to find football in Turkey. The taxi driver will ask you your team before the meter has started running, the hotel receptionist will tell you which TV channels are showing games that night on handing over the key to your room. What makes Turkey different from other emerging football-loving nations is that its passion is almost exclusively for the domestic game. Despite the fact that this nation of around 60 million has a poor record in international football, and regardless of Turkish clubs' failure to win anything in Europe, there is minimal interest in the goings-on in Italy or England. The attention is focused firmly on local competition.

It is this enormous popular interest, bountifully supported by local businesses and media, that has pushed Turkey out of the ranks of the minnows and into a position of international respectability. The national side's qualification for Euro '96 and impressive runs in Europe by Fenerbahçe and Galatasaray have made it easy to forget that, in the early Eighties, the Turks were twice hammered 8–0 by England.

The three main clubs, Galatasaray, Fenerbahçe and Beşiktaş, were all founded at the turn of the century in Istanbul and have dominated the honours ever since. Initially, however, the game received a hostile reception from the last of the Ottoman empire's rulers, Sultan Abdülhamid. The sultan, sensing the loss of both empire and power, was suspicious of any foreign-influenced organisation and banned all clubs playing the 'British' game of football.

No coincidence, then, that the 'big three' all sprang up in areas of the city with large Christian and Jewish populations and famous foreign schools; non-Turkish citizens were exempted from the sultan's clampdown and local Turks took advantage

Backs against the wall – the Turks at Euro '96

of this by sneaking into expatriate sides. By the time the sultans had lost their power and the Turkish republic was established by Mustafa Kemal Atatürk (a Fenerbahçe fan) in 1923, local football had become organised with a thriving Istanbul league and, from 1937, a system of play-offs between Istanbul sides and those from the regions. It wasn't until 1959, though, that a fully professional national league was instituted.

The national team had begun playing friendlies almost as soon as the republic was formed, and its encouraging early form, with wins over a string of Baltic and Balkan opponents, suggested a nation picking up the game quickly. Turkey qualified for the 1950 World Cup finals by beating Syria

7–0, then withdrew at the last minute. They actually turned up in 1954 but were knocked out at the group stage, after losing twice to the eventual winners, West Germany.

There then followed a long decline in which the Turks failed to qualify for any major tournament until Euro '96. The only player of any note to emerge before the Seventies was Lefter Kücükandonyadis, an ethnic Greek who played for Fenerbahçe in the Fifties and scored 21 goals in 46 appearances for the national team.

Hakan Sükür – Turkish goalscoring legend

On the domestic club scene, the emergence of Trabzonspor, founded in 1967 and winners of a first title just nine years later, provided a long overdue challenge to Istanbul's dominance. The two sides from the Turkish capital Ankara, MKE Ankaragücü and Gençlerbirlıt, have still mustered only three cup wins between them. Altay of İzmir's two cup wins and a run to the semifinals of the 1969 UEFA Cup have been the only other performances of note from the Asian part of the country, even though it represents some 97 percent of Turkey's land mass.

In a bid to boost performance at the European level, an increasing number of foreign coaches and players have been brought into the Turkish game. Initially most of the players came from Yugoslavia and other parts of Eastern Europe, but coaches were imported from across the continent, many of them staying in their jobs for only short spells before quitting after rows with the clubs' famously impatient presidents.

The most successful foreign coaches were Englishmen Brian Birch and Gordon Milne. Birch, a former Busby Babe who débuted for Manchester United at the age of 17 but failed to establish himself at Old Trafford, led Galatasaray to three league titles and a cup win in the early Seventies. Two decades later, former Liverpool star Milne took Beşiktaş to three titles before leaving – of his own volition, unusually – for the Japanese J-League. (He has since returned to Turkey to coach Bursaspor.)

Yet it was a Turkish-born coach, Fatih Terim, who finally ended the national team's absence from élite competitions when he coaxed a young side past much-fancied Sweden and Hungary and onto Euro '96. With the standard of Turkish football on an upward curve and

Basics

In addition to a full **passport**, UK and Irish citizens require a **visa** for entry into Turkey. This is valid for a stay of up to three months and can be obtained at passport control for £10, but visa queues can be long, so allow time for a delay on entering the country. Visitors of most other nationalities do not require a visa, but check with your local embassy before departure.

The Turkish currency is the **lira**, indicated as TL. With **inflation** running at around seventy percent annually, prices fluctuate wildly from month to month; we've given rough sterling equivalents throughout this chapter. The exchange rate is currently 200,000TL to £1. Get rid of your spare lira before leaving, and don't bother buying any before you depart – you'll get a better rate in Turkey.

The best rates can be found at **Döviz exchange offices** located all over Istanbul. Banks (usually open 8.30am–noon and 1.30–5pm) are slow and charge varying levels of commission. Cash machines accepting Visa and Mastercard are widespread, and credit cards can also be used in many shops in the centre of Istanbul.

Public telephones are concentrated around squares, transport terminals and post offices. Buy tokens from the stall near the phones, or phonecards in units of 30, 50 and 100 – the latter are more practical for international calls. For an international line out of Turkey, dial 00 followed by the country code. For provincial numbers dial 0, then the local code. The code for the European side of Istanbul is 212, for the Asian side 216.

Turkey's **train network** is pretty skeletal so the best way to travel around the country is by **bus**. If you have visions of being squeezed into an overcrowded jalopy which will break down in the middle of a mountain pass, think again – long-distance coaches boast air-conditioning, chilled drinks and, in summer, free splashes of cologne from the conductor. Buy tickets from any of the dozens of **travel agencies** in central Istanbul, many of which have English-speaking staff – they'll tell you which of the city's several **suburban bus stations** your service departs from.

---

entrepreneurial cash pouring into the game, it can't be long before a Turkish club makes it to the very top of the European game.

Essential vocabulary

Hello *Merhába*
Goodbye *Haşan kal*
Yes *Evet*
No *Hayir*
Two beers, please *Iki bira lütfen*
Thank you *Teşekkürler*
Men's *Erkek*
Women's *Kadin*
Where is the stadium? *Stadyum nerede?*
What's the score? *Kaç kaç?*
Referee *Hakem*
Offside *Ofsayd*

Match practice

Forget your normal matchday routine. There is no tradition of drinking in a bar before the game in Turkey, and to arrive an hour before kick-off for a major match is cutting it fine. For the big derby games in Istanbul, particularly the Galatasaray–Fenerbahçe clash, fans begin to gather in the morning to discuss the prospects for the game. By the afternoon the area around the stadium will be buzzing with fans gathering to eat from *büfes* and talk tactics.

Most fans enter the stadium at least two hours before kick-off. An hour before kick-off the music starts – Turkish pop stars such as Rafet El Roman and Tarkan record football versions of their big hits, and the whole stadium sings and dances along for the full hour as the tracks are played over the PA.

When the teams come out to warm up, they go through an elaborate ritual with the fans. The supporters shout out the name of each player and the word *buraya* –

"come here!" The player, always known by his first name, then runs to the fans and punches the air three times before blowing a kiss to the stands.

The most popular stars may have to do this several times before kick-off. Few players have ever refused to partake in this act of mutual appreciation, and the *buraya* is one of the first things explained to foreign players on arrival at a Turkish club.

The Turkish season runs from the middle of September to the end of December, then takes a three-week break in January. The second half of the season runs from the end of January until the end of May.

League games are played over the weekend and kick-off times vary. There is often a game on Friday evening, kicking off at 7pm. Saturday and Sunday games kick off at 1.30pm during autumn and winter, at 5pm or 7pm in spring and summer.

Live TV matches usually kick off at 7pm, as do midweek cup games and, barring TV interference, international games.

The league

The *Türkiye Futbol Liga* consists of an eighteen-team first division (*1.Liga*) with each side meeting home and away once. The second tier consits of five regional leagues of twelve clubs, who play each other home and away before the winter break. Following the break, the top two teams from each of the regional leagues form a ten-team *Play Off Liga*, from which the top two are promoted at the end of the season.

In order to ensure that those who did not make the play-off group still have something to play for from January, the team with the best record in the five regional leagues also goes up – though not until participating in yet another play-off mini-league after the end of the regular season. The bottom three from the top flight are automatically relegated. The third tier consists of eight regional divisions.

Up for the cup

Qualification rounds for regional league sides begin in mid-July, but the first round proper of the *Türkiye Kupa* is in November, and even then, first-division sides are not included. The bottom ten sides from the previous season join in the second round, with the top eight waiting until the third round. Until the quarter-finals games are decided on the night with extra-time and penalties. From then on games are two-legged – including the final itself.

Tickets

Big derby matches *always* sell out, so buy a ticket in advance from the stadium. Even if a game has been designated as sold out, club officials may manage to rustle up a handful of tickets if you tell them you have travelled from afar to watch their team. If you still have no joy, there'll be touts operating around the stadium from breakfast time on matchdays – expect to pay anything from double to ten times face value.

Ticket prices vary according to the status of the match. For a normal league game at a small club such as İstanbulspor, you'll pay just over £1. Count on five times that for a big city derby, at which your ticket will be no guarantee of swift entry into the stadium. Queues are chaotic and disorganised, and you should watch out for pickpockets in the crush.

For lesser games you can pay at the turnstile but you should still queue up for entrance at least half an hour before kick-off and try to bring change with you – those with the exact amount are often allowed to go to the front of the queue.

At the ground, the seated area will be indicated as *oturulacak yer*, while standing will be shown as *ayakta duralacak yer*. The terracing behind the goal is the *kale arkasi*.

Half-time

At big games you won't want to leave your seat at half-time and there is little reason to. The Turks don't like any distraction from their football and that includes eating and drinking. At smaller grounds, a wandering salesman may offer tiny, potent cups of tea (*çay*) or cartons of fruit juice (*meyva suyu*). Your best bet is to fill-up before the game from *büfes* or from street vendors selling *kebap* or spiced meatballs (*köfte*). You won't find beer or kebabs inside any ground.

Action replay

The subscription satellite channel Cine 5 has the rights for live Turkish league games, which they show on Saturday and/or Sunday evenings at 7pm. Sister company Show TV, which is non-subscription based, shows the game either 'as live' or as extended highlights immediately after the final whistle has blown. It also shows a goals round-up after each game.

NTV is a new channel which shows highlights packages from the major European leagues and has the rights to national-team games. Star TV, owned by İstanbulspor president Cem Uzan, has the rights for the Champions' League and the Turkish second divison – there is a highlights package from play-off group games on Mondays at midnight.

HBB shows live Spanish games and highlights, while Kanel D also has foreign games along with other bits and pieces – though their main attraction is İlker Yasin, former no. I commentator for Cine 5 who switched allegiance after a contract dispute; his vivid and highly opinionated commentaries make him the nation's favourite voice of football.

Football pops up all the time on Turkish TV, with players appearing on cabaret shows and lengthy reports on evening news programmes. Don't miss *Televole* (Show TV, Mondays, 9pm) – sixty minutes of football comedy and sketches, plus a showcase for pop musicians to première 'football' mixes.

The back page

You won't go short of football info in Turkey, and carrying one of the three daily sports papers under your arm has the added value of keeping Istanbul's tourist-

Shout it out – football is no longer a male-only pursuit

baiting street traders off your back.

Fanatik, Fotomac and *Spor* all cost around 7p and are similar in design and content – broadsheet size, tabloid style. They are packed with large colour photos, soundbite quotes and snippets of gossip. All have two or three columnists dedicated to each club, who provide the talking points for your first cup of tea.

The best of the three is the newest, *Fanatik*; little more than two years old, it devotes two pages each to Fenerbahçe and Galatasaray and a page each to Trabzonspor and Beşiktaş.

Fanatik also has the best football TV commercial in Europe: as a doctor is inspecting a row of baby boys in a hospital, he removes their nappies to find the first has a red-and-yellow striped (Galatasaray) penis, the second yellow-and-blue (Fenerbahçe) and the third claret-and-blue (Trab-zonspor); he then lets out a scream as he uncovers a penis with no colours at all...

On the magazine front, the weekly *Spor & Spor* (Fridays) is filled with posters and 'at home with Hakan' features.

As an antidote to all this gloss, the major daily papers have sport on their back page, where you'll find fewer photos and more analytical writing.

Ultra culture

Ever since Manchester United's players and fans reported on the cauldron they faced in Istanbul when they were knocked out of the European Cup by Galatasaray in the early Nineties, Turkish stadia have gained a reputation as being among the most intimidating soccer venues in Europe.

The relationship between players and fans is close – as demonstrated by the *buraya* – and the supporters see themselves not as passive spectators but as an active component in the whole event. Flags, smoke bombs and flares are accepted as being part of the atmosphere, but violence is not and the heavily armed (and often heavy-handed) police aren't there for show. Trouble is rarely pre-arranged along the lines of West European ultra clashes, but the Turks can be poor losers – team buses are frequently attacked and after a 1997 derby, a Fenerbahçe player was stabbed in the street by Galatasaray fans. It is not unknown for fans to attack their own players after a particularly dismal performance.

Another worrying factor is the celebratory firing of guns – two people died during street festivities after Turkey beat Hungary to qualify for Euro '96. Away from the Fener–Gala clash, however, trouble is rare and the headlines are made by more bizarre incidents, such as that involving a drunken Fenerbahçe fan who, following a defeat by Beşiktaş in 1997, beat up his wife before jumping to his death from a fifth-floor window.

In the net

There is no generic Turkish football web site, and those interested in an overall update may be better off checking out one of the individual club sites listed below, since these almost always contain links to other teams. Hasan Tezcan's stats archive at: www.algonet.se/~tezcan/tfa/ is strong on historical information but can't be relied upon to provide latest scores.

Spectacular setting – whichever way you look at it, the İnönü is a graceful arena

Istanbul

Turkey's official capital may be Ankara, deep into Asia, but the nation's soccer city is Istanbul – a 24-hour, seven-day-a-week football madhouse. The traditional gold and leather merchants of the famed Grand Bazaar are today flanked by stalls dedicated to soccer souvenirs, and you'll see kids kicking a ball wherever they can find more than ten square metres of free space.

The thrilling fields

 Beşiktaş

İnönü Stadi, Kadirgalar Caddesi
Capacity 45,000
Colours Black-and-white striped shirts, white shorts
League champions 1960, 1966–67, 1982, 1986, 1990–92, 1995
Cup winners 1975, 1989–90, 1994

Try as they may, Beşiktaş Jimnastik Kulübü can never escape from being the third club in Istanbul. The club has a fine stadium, a good support base and a decent domestic record, particularly in recent years. Yet games between Beşiktaş and the 'big two' never have quite the same needle or significance as the Fener–Gala derby itself.

Pelé described the İnönü Stadi as "one of the most beautiful football grounds in the world". It's not the architecture that provokes such awe, but the stadium's setting. Nestled at the foot of the hills that lead up from the Bosphorus, it is surrounded by those rarest of commodities in Istanbul – grass and trees. From the east stand you can see the straits and just make out the roof of the Dolmabahçe palace on the shoreline.

The club's regal surroundings are a legacy of its first major benefactor,

Osman Pasha, a member of Sultan Abdülhamid's government when the club was formed in 1903. The team earned their first nickname The Car Men from those early days when the Pasha provided his players with cars in which to travel to and from matches.

Today they're the Black Eagles and their best moments have come in the Nineties under imported coaches Gordon Milne and Christoph Daum. The former led the club to three titles, bringing over a certain Les Ferdinand, then struggling in QPR's reserve team, to boost his strikeforce.

Since then the Beşiktaş line has been successfully led by the likes of German international Stefan Kuntz and Nigeria's former Everton striker Daniel Amokachi. Yet despite the domestic plaudits the team have consistently failed to impress in Europe, their best run coming in 1996 when they reached the third round of the UEFA Cup.

Here we go!
Buses #30b, #71 and #76 make the short journey between Taksim and the Bosphorus suburb of Beşiktaş and all go past the stadium – you won't miss your stop.

Swift half
There is no bar anywhere near the stadium, save for the pricey **Hotel Bosphorus** on the slopes above. So sink one at Taksim or in Beşiktaş itself, which has an abundance of pleasant cafés.

Club shop
Souvenir stands spring up around the ground on matchdays. Otherwise, take your pick along any of Istanbul's main shopping streets.

In the net
A suitably puffed-up eagle sits proudly atop the Beşiktaş homepage at: www.bjk.com/.

Istanbul essentials

Istanbul's Atatürk **airport** has two terminals, one for international (*dişhatlari*) and one for domestic (*içhatlari*) flights. Buses make the kilometre journey between the two every half hour and then continue into the city. The bus journey costs £1.30 and ends at Taksim square, the city's commercial centre. Given the level of traffic congestion in Istanbul, the journey can take as long as an hour and a half.

Airport insecurity – Istanbul greets United, 1994

A **taxi** into the centre of the city could set you back as much as £10. A cheaper option is to take a cab to the nearest train station, Yesilköy, and thence a train to central **Sirkeci station**, which has bus connections to most areas of the European part of the city. **International trains** from the rest of Europe also terminate at Sirkeci.

Istanbul is split down the middle by the Bosphorus strait, which divides the European and Asian parts of the city. Most of the tourist sites, nightlife, hotels and all football stadia (except Fenerbahçe's) are on the European side.

Getting around the city is a cheap but frustrating exercise. There are two kinds of **buses**. The orange ones are privately run; pay the young lad at the little cabin on entry. For a ride on a publicly run bus, buy a ticket at the *bilet* kiosk in terminals. Tickets on both types cost around 25p for a journey within the central area, but state your destination when purchasing the ticket as some trips require two tickets. All buses display their route on the front of the vehicle.

There is one central **tram line** which runs from the long-haul bus terminal of Topkapı down to the old city in Sultanahmet, ending by the Bosphorus at Eminönü. Cross the Galata bridge from here and you'll find the *Tünel*, Istanbul's underground funicular railway, which will haul you up to the city's single pedestrianised shopping street, İstiklâl Caddesi, which runs on to Taksim.

Taxis are yellow and usually cheap – just make sure the driver has the meter on. An alternative to cabbing it is the *Dolmuş*, a kind of communal taxi which follows a set route displayed on the front of the vehicle. Pay the driver on entry; prices vary but are lower than for normal taxis. In the past a *Dolmuş* was likely to be an American limousine from the Fifties or Sixties; today they are mostly modern minibuses.

You can cross the Bosphorus by bus, but the fastest and most attractive journey is by **ferry-boat**, either from the main terminal at Eminönü, adjacent to Sirkeci station, or from Beşiktaş. Buy a token (*jeton*) for 25p at the entrance to the Beşiktaş service; pay the same amount to the onboard collector on other routes. The main terminal on the other side of the water is at Kadıköy – ferries terminating there often call at Haydarpaşa **train station**, for rail services to Asia, along the way.

Street maps available in Istanbul have little detail so try to buy one before you go. You'll find **tourist offices** on Divanyolu Caddesi near the Hippodrome (daily 9am–5pm, ☎212/522 4903), by the *Hilton Hotel* on Cumhüriyet Caddesi and, best of all, at Meşrutiyet Cad 57 (Mon–Fri 9am–5pm, ☎212/527 0051).

This is one of the best one-club sites anywhere in Europe, with an amazing stats archive, match reports from a range of Turkish media, stills and animation from *Fanatik*, QuickTime action movies in a 'Beşiktaş TV' area, an interactive chat zone and much more besides.

Much of the content is in Turkish but all the key signposting is in English, too. What makes the site all the more remarkable – and gives it a rootsy edge missing from so many comprehensive one-club sites – is that it receives no backing from the club whatsoever.

Fenerbahçe

Fenerbahçe Stadyum, Fener Caddesi, Kadıköy
Capacity 30,000
Colours Yellow-and-blue striped shirts, white shorts
League champions 1959, 1961, 1964–65, 1968, 1970, 1974–75, 1978, 1983, 1985, 1996
Cup winners 1968, 1974, 1979, 1983

While Galatasaray are probably the best-known club outside of Turkey, Fenerbahçe Spor Kulübü are the most popular within the country. The club claim to have 25 million supporters, and while that might be stretching it, there is no denying the strength of support for 'Fener' in the provinces as well as in their heartland: the Kadıköy district of Istanbul, on the Asian side of the Bosphorus.

The Canaries were the third team to be formed in Istanbul, out of the ranks of a French college, St Joseph's. The team competed in the Istanbul league but were overshadowed for much of that period by Galatasaray and Beşiktaş, despite winning 9 of the 34 championships prior to the setting up of a national league. The team's popularity was earned away from competitive football, in a

series of memorable friendly matches. With Turkey in chaos during the Balkan Wars, World War I and subsequent war with Greece, Fenerbahçe played on, taking on representatives of various enemies and occupiers in a series of exhibition games, the most famous of which came in 1923 when a British Army XI were humbled 2–1.

Since the setting up of the national league, Fener have been regular contenders. After a lean spell in the early Nineties, they have risen back to the top under the guidance of club president Ali Şen. A charismatic figure with fingers in many pies, Ali Şen is the Bernard Tapie of Turkish football – although he did his spell of porridge while Tapie was still playing for his school team in France.

Now in his second stint as president, Ali Şen was elected on a simple promise – to bring the championship to Fenerbahçe for the first time since 1989. He achieved that in 1996, albeit not without some controversy; the president loves to play the press and his promise to take referees under his 'protection' caused uproar on the other side of the Bosphorus. In Kad-

Physical – Beşiktaş' Ertugrul Saglam takes another knock

Canaries in heaven – Fenerbahçe celebrate their historic but flukey win at Old Trafford, 1996

ıköy, meanwhile, he is treated like royalty. Fenerbahçe's domestic success has not been transferred to European competition. Nonetheless, visitors from Manchester will be constantly reminded of victories over City in 1968/69 and United in 1996, the latter during Fener's first appearance in the Champions' League.

The potency of Bosnian striker Elvir Bolic, scorer of the only goal of the game at Old Trafford, illustrates an astuteness at the cheaper end of the transfer market which should stand the club in good stead in the short run, while an influx of new cash from a re-constituted board of directors – all but the president resigned in early 1997 – may allow Fener to compete for bigger international names in the quest for yet greater glory.

Here we go!

Take a boat to Kadıköy harbour from Eminönü on the European side of the Bosphorus. Then follow the main road up the hill to the stadium, or take a £1.50 taxi if there's a hot sun out.

Swift half

The **Köşe Burger**, opposite the club shop, is where the big-match discussions start over excellent hamburgers and cooled cans of Tuborg.

Club shop

The **Fenerbahçe Shop** underneath the main stand is surprisingly spartan but does offer an Atatürk badge in club colours. Next door is a better-stocked **Adidas shop** offering the full range of canary-coloured sportswear. Both are open daily 10.30am–5.30pm, later on matchdays.

In the net

Fenerbahçe were the first Turkish club to back an official homepage – all elaborate graphics, JavaScript errors and impenetrable Turkish text at: www.fenerbahce.org. Less heavy-handed with the gimmicks (and therefore quicker to access) is Bülent Ünal's 'Forza Fenerbahçe' site at: www.mis-souri.edu/~c655788/. Another unofficial homepage is maintained by Erman Civelek at: eden-backend.rutgers.edu/~civelek/. Stats are the strong point here, but there is some English content coupled with the usual Turkish-language news, match-report archive and wide choice of links.

Galatasaray

Ali Sami Yen Stadyum, Bükükdere Caddesi, Mecidiyeköy
Capacity 33,000
Colours All yellow with red trim
League champions 1962–63, 1969, 1971–73, 1987–88, 1993–94, 1997
Cup winners 1963–66, 1973, 1976, 1982, 1985, 1991, 1993, 1996

Like their rivals, Galatasaray Spor Kulübü were formed from the efforts of a student team. After an early tour to Switzerland, the soccer-playing pupils of Galatasaray high school brought a Swiss football song, *Jim, Bom, Bom*, back with them. The song has stayed with the team to this day and earned them their nickname, *Cim Bom*.

Gala's Ali Sami Yen stadium is cramped into the Mecidiyeköy district, where tower blocks dominate the skyline and an inner-city motorway flies overhead, bringing extra noise and pollution to one of Istanbul's least attractive suburbs. Happily, the club's influence spreads far beyond their ground. This is the largest sports club in Turkey, with nearly 10,000 members participating in a wide range of pursuits. The club also own several businesses and one of the islands in the Bosphorus, complete with swimming pool, harbour, restaurant, disco and casino.

The Lions, as they are also commonly known, were the first Turkish team to play abroad when, during the Balkan Wars, they travelled to Transylvania to play Kalosvár (now Cluj-Napoca). In the modern era the team have been regular participants in

European club competition, but only in recent years have they had any results to show for their endeavours.

In 1989 Gala had the best European run of any Turkish side, reaching the semi-final of the Champions' Cup, defeating Rapid Vienna, Xamax Neuchâtel of Switzerland and AS Monaco before losing to Steaua Bucharest. In 1992 they reached the quarter-finals of the Cup-Winners' Cup, and the following year they pulled off a major upset in knocking out Manchester United (after a thrilling 3–3 draw at Old Trafford and a tense, goalless stalemate in Istanbul) to qualify for the Champions' League. They made it to the League again in 1994/95 when, although they failed to make it out of the group stage, they beat Barcelona at home and again held United to a draw in Istanbul.

Galatasaray has also been the club to have produced the three major stars of modern Turkish football. In the Seventies, Metin Oktay bagged 608 league and cup goals for his club and was first-choice striker for the national team (he was tragically killed in a car accident in 1995), while in the Eighties Tanju Çolak (see p.590) was the player whose pin-up was on every young Turkish boy's bedroom wall.

The current hero at the Ali Sami Yen is Hakan Sükür, whose goals enabled Turkey to reach Euro '96. Hakan became the first Turkish player to move to a major European club when he joined Torino in 1995. He stayed only a few months, homesickness and domestic problems leading to a swift return to the Lions' Den, where he quickly resumed his rampant goalscoring.

European adventures or not, Galatasaray's support demands nothing more than victory over Fenerbahçe. When that was achieved in the Turkish cup final of 1996, Gala's Scottish coach Graeme Souness planted a red-and-yellow flag on the Fenerbahçe field, provoking rioting in the stands. Though it received swift condemnation from Gala officials, the act made Souness a hero in Mecidiyeköy. Then again, as Souness discovered when Fenerbahçe pipped his side to the title and he was fired, derby glory lasts only as long as the next game.

In 1996/97, former Turkish national-team coach Fatih Terim arrived at Gala and immediately set about constructing a title-winning side, adding the guile of Romanian midfielder Gheorghe Hagi to the goal-poaching of Hakan. It proved a combination no other Turkish side could live with.

Success on a plate – Hagi delivers another Gala pass

Here we go!

Any bus to Mecidiyeköy – from Taksim take #50 or #59a. The stadium is five minutes' walk from the bus station.

Swift half

The **Altin Fici**, next to the Shell petrol station opposite the ground, requires a sprint across a busy road running under the motorway. It's worth putting your life in the hands of Turkish drivers for, with real spit, sawdust and draught Efes beer. There are a number of **restaurants** nearby.

Club shop

There are several booths around the perimeter of the stadium which are open on matchdays. During the week, any sports shop or street market will sell Gala gear.

Club museum

The Galatasaray high school, halfway along İstiklâl Caddesi, has a small museum open only on Wednesday afternoons. The curator speaks English and will gladly tell you the story in full.

In the net

The official Gala homepage resides at: www.galatasaray.net. There's an excellent history, comprehensive stats, info on the club's other sports sections and even a couple of roaring lions to bid you welcome, but the content is in Turkish only. An unofficial site is run by Özer Aydogar at: www.geocities.com/Colosseum/3878/. Here you'll find a full English-language links section and a news archive in Turkish. Pick of the bunch, though, is another unofficial site run by Hasan Tezcan of the archive mentioned on p.580. It's stats-based but there is some English content alongside the extensive Turkish news, player interviews and video clips. Head for: www.cimbom.org/football/.

Groundhopping

Two of the city's lesser lights, Sariyer and Zeytinburnuspor, were relgated in 1996/97, but a trip out to one of these smaller grounds can tell you more about the state of Turkish league football than the highly charged 'event' atmosphere of a major derby. Take your pick...

İstanbulspor

İnönü Stadi, as Beşiktaş above
Colours Yellow-and-black shirts, white shorts

Since their return to the first division in 1995, İstanbulspor have abandoned their Bayrampaşa stadium to groundshare with Beşiktaş. The move might make sense for games against the big Istanbul clubs, but for encounters with minor provincial sides the İnönü feels empty with barely 4000 souls turning up to watch.

After decades of popping up and down between first and second divisions, İstanbulspor now have the financial backing to mount a serious challenge to the domination of the big three. Their president, Cem Uzan, who has among his interests Star TV and south coast club Adanaspor, is talking big but, as yet, the team haven't translated his optimism into trophies.

The club's biggest star was Seventies striker Cemil Turan, who notched up 19 goals in 44 appearances for the national team, including a hat-trick against Bulgaria in the 1973 Balkan Cup. Alas, like most of İstanbulspor's talent he was snapped up by one of the bigger clubs (in his case Fenerbahçe), a trend Cem Uzan has pledged to halt.

The club have also been dabbling in the international transfer market, with mixed success. Dutchmen Peter van Vossen and John van den Brom lasted only slightly longer than their former coach at Ajax, Leo Beenhakker, sacked by Uzan four months into his contract in 1995.

Sariyer

Yusuf Ziya Önis Stadi, Eski Sular Yolü 42, Sariyer
Capacity 12,000
Colours Blue-and-white shirts, white shorts

Despite never having finished in the top three or made it as far as the cup final, Sariyer Gençlik Kulübü have been a pretty constant mid-table presence in Turkey's top flight. A trip to their scruffy ground, with a playing surface your local pub team would bitch about, is a refreshing escape from the madness of the city.

An hour's bus ride up the Bosphorus, Sariyer is a quiet fishing town with a number of excellent seafood restaurants. It offers an easily accessible taste of the Turkish countryside and its mediocre football. To get there, take bus #25b from Beşiktaş, or #40 or #40s from Taksim to the end stop. The ground is a five-minute walk straight up from the bus station.

The **Stadiyum Kirathanesi**, on the right as you approach the entrance to the ground, does not serve alcohol in deference to the mosque up the road. An alternative is the **Baba Necmi** on Eski Sular Yolü, a small restaurant/bar serving draught Efes.

Zeytinburnu

Zeytinburnu Stadyumu, Zubeyde Hanim Caddesi 1, Zeytinburnu
Capacity 10,000
Colours All white with blue trim

If someone were to write a 'rags to riches' novel about a Turkish footballer, the 'rags' period would be set here. Surrounded by tower blocks and wasteland in one of Istanbul's poorest districts, the Zeytinburnu stadium looks like a half-finished provincial Albanian ground. Huge chunks of concrete terracing are relieved only by a small stand on the halfway line. The directors' box is surrounded by a barbed-wire fence — given that the team have never won a thing, one

Flying Dutchman – Peter van Vossen flees İstanbulspor

over the place, catering for all tastes. The local *bira* is **Efes Pilsen**, which is surprisingly good and has an almost 100 percent monopoly. The traditional watering hole is a *meyhane* where beer and raki – a powerful aniseed-flavoured spirit – are accompanied by plates of salad or cold snacks (*mezes*). A *birahane* is much the same thing.

Western-style bars and clubs can be found in Taksim and along the Bosphorus. In summer, discos and nightclubs pop up spontaneously, mostly along the European side of the Bosphorus – ask around for info as there are no listings magazines.

suspects it is not there to protect board members from being mobbed by jubilant fans.

Which is not say there isn't plenty of footballing activity here – the backstreets and patches of scrubland around the ground play host to scores of games any day of the week. Maybe the scouts would be better off looking there.

To reach this wilderness, take the tram from Eminönü to Zeytinburnu – the ground is a ten-minute walk from the tram stop. The **Stad Büfe**, on the corner of the nearby park and the entrance to the ground, sells cold cans of beer. Behind the main stand is the **Stad Birahanesi**, a seedy, smoky cellar bar where the mood is usually heavy with talk of relegation.

Eat, drink, sleep...

Bars and clubs
Forget all the nonsense about the rise of Islamic fundamentalism – Istanbul is a fine night out. There are bars and restaurants all

Café Marti, Caşap Gurler Cad 10. Kadıköy isn't noted for its nightlife but, despite its location and scruffy interior, Café Marti is an ideal place for watching a game on TV. Two screens stand at either end of the room and the working-class clientèle provide the expert analysis while downing cheap Efes. Ferryboat to Kadıköy – the bar is on the waterfront.

Madrid Bar, İpek Sok 16. Unusually for a bar popular with the expat community, this is cheap and nearly always packed. An ideal place for getting the inside track on Istanbul football and nightlife. Friendly staff and half a litre of Efes for 50p. Bus to Taksim (İpek Sok runs parallel to İstiklâl Cad).

Memo's, Salhane Sok 10/2. Dress up and dust off your credit cards – this is where the emerging business class of Istanbul goes to drink and dance away the sales bonus. Strict door policy and often long queues, but once you're in, the beautiful views of the Bosphorus – and beautiful clientèle – make the wait worthwhile. In Ortaköy, the city's nightclubbing epicentre, with other bar/club options all around. Any bus to Ortaköy from Taksim.

Sefahathane, Atlas Han 209 (just off İstiklâl Cad). Next door to the *Atlas* cinema, in a small courtyard, Sefahathane is a tiny, trendy bar with a range of foreign bottled beers and spirits. Fine sound system playing jazz-funk, slightly yuppie crowd. Bus to Taksim.

Şamdansa, Türkbostan Sok 22. Disco and bar which spills out onto the gardens in warm weather. The sounds are a mix of techno, Turkish pop and rock. Open 'til dawn. Bus to Yeniköy.

Restaurants

Turkish food has far more going for it than the admittedly **ubiquitous kebab**. *Güveç*, a casserole of meat and vegetables, and *tas kebap*, a traditional stew, are both good alternatives if you become bored with the range of spiced and grilled meats.

Along the Bosphorus there is no shortage of fine fish (*balik*) on offer and in summer salads are excellent, as are soups (*çorba*). Turkish sweets and cakes are outstanding.

Borsa, Taksim Cad 4. Just off Taksim square, this is part of a popular chain of Turkish fast-food joints. As well as burgers and fries, there are good kebabs and more wholesome dishes including

soups and stews. Hardly *haute cuisine* but the place is constantly packed out with a young crowd. Draught Efes, of course, and a smaller, less smoky branch on İstiklâl Cad. Bus to Taksim.

Haci Baba, İstiklâl Cad 49. One of the more expensive restaurants in the area, but it's worth forking out £20 for three courses of excellent Turkish cuisine and outstanding service. Bus to Taksim.

Olimpiyat, Neşet Ömer Sok 8a. Smart restaurant owned by former Fenerbahçe and Turkish national-team player Ahmet Erol. The walls are covered with black-and-white blowups of Fener and Olympic action. In the back there is a *Toto* (football pools) room with a fine collection of portraits. Full Turkish menu, licensed bar. Ferryboat to Kadıköy, restaurant opposite harbour.

Rejans, Emir Nevruz Sok 17. If you're going to splash out, this is the place to do it. The most famous restaurant in Istanbul, famously staffed by Russian emigrés and situated in the old diplomatic quarter, also has a more informal bar serving food in the cellar. Bus to Taksim.

Follow in Eric's footsteps along the Bosphorus – but be sure to get to the game two hours early

Super Restaurant, Bekar Sok (just off İstiklâl Cad). Super indeed. A fine budget option with a variety of kebabs and *mezes*. A filling meal won't set you back more than a couple of quid and there is plenty of cheap beer on draught. A popular meeting place for clubbers and also for those attracted by the 'hostess bar' in the basement; the 'hotel' on the upper floor requires no further explanation. Bus to Taksim.

Accommodation

There is plenty of reasonably priced accommodation in Istanbul and during the football season you should have no problem finding a room. The hotels around Taksim are the most expensive but there are good options all over the city. In high summer, many of the smaller places fill up and booking in advance – or at the reservation office at the airport – is worthwhile.

Gezi Hotel, Mete Cad 42 (☎212/251 7430). Right next to Taksim square and close to the main shopping and nightlife venues. The terrace restaurant looks out over the busy streets, and the rooms are clean and comfortable. From around £30 per night. Bus to Taksim.

Otel Deniz, Kaşap Gurler Cad 2 (☎216/414 5234). Right on the front in Kadıköy, just five minutes' walk from the regular ferries travelling across to the European side and a fifteen-minute stroll to the Fenerbahçe stadium. Clean, en-suite rooms with TV for around £15 a head. The staff will talk football on request. Ferry to Kadıköy.

Ugur Pansiyon, Kaşap Osman Sok 2 (☎212/516 0138). Also advertised as 'Bobby's Place', this is a straightforward, cheap option in old Istanbul. The roof terrace bar has a fine view of the Sea of Marmara. Bus to Atmeydani.

Yeni Saray Oteli, Selmanipak Cad, Çeşme Sok 33 (☎216/337 0777). You get a great view of the Bosphorus from this family-run hotel with a restaurant, bar and terrace café. Around £30 a night. Ferry to Üsküdar on the Asian side.

From the 'Golden Boot' to a prison cell...

In the Eighties, **Tanju Çolak** was Turkey's goalscoring pin-up. Having begun his career with Samsunspor, he made his name during the second half of the decade with **Galatasaray**, winning the 'Golden Boot' award as **Europe's top goalscorer** in 1987/88. A Bosphorus version of the English 'fancy-dan', he nurtured a wayward, playboy image while scoring a string of vital goals, such as those against East Germany which almost resulted in Turkey qualifying for Italia '90.

In 1991, a number of foreign clubs approached him; he turned them all down but then shocked the Gala faithful

Dammit! Tanju Çolak forgets his car keys

by signing for **Fenerbahçe**. He scored 27 goals in 23 games for Fener in 1992/93, but that summer he was dismissed by the club for what they called 'disciplinary reasons'.

In fact, Tanju had been **arrested** for his part in a car-smuggling ring, stealing Mercedes-Benzes from Germany, changing their identity and re-selling them in Turkey. After being found guilty and sentenced to 22 months in prison, he **skipped bail** and fled to the former Yugoslav republic of Macedonia where, in a rare display of Balkan co-operation, he was **extradited back to Turkey** to begin his stretch of porridge...

Yugoslavia

'You have arrived too late," one Partizan Belgrade fan said. Standing in a crowd of 800 in a stadium capable of holding sixty times that, it is easy to understand his bitterness. Nowhere has football fallen from greatness so rapidly and so painfully as in the rump Yugoslavia.

In 1990 the country seemed on the brink of becoming one of the giants of the European game. The national side had been desperately unlucky to bow out of Italia '90 at the quarter-final stage, losing a shoot-out after their ten men had played all the football against an ultra-defensive Argentina in Florence. At club level, Red Star Belgrade were assembling a bold young side capable of some of the finest counter-attacking the continent had seen in years. As Red Star

Serb skipper – Japan-based playmaker Dragan Stojković

glided effortlessly to a 1991 European Cup win over Marseille, the national side embarked on a similarly impressive run toward the Euro '92 finals in Sweden.

Then came war. The heart of the old Yugoslav federation was being torn apart by Europe's most brutal conflict since 1945, and football – like so many aspects of normal life – would never be the same again.

After some vacillating, UEFA decided it could not defy the logic of United Nations sanctions and at the last minute banned Yugoslavia from Euro '92. They were replaced by Denmark, whom the Slavs had already eliminated at the qualifying stage, and who went on to win the entire competition.

Yet, even had the war-torn country been allowed to send a team to Sweden, that team would have been shorn of much of their attacking talent. Of the 24 goals the Slavs scored in their Euro '92 qualifying

games, 19 came from Croats, Slovenes, Bosnians or Macedonians – all of whom had withdrawn from the national side by the time of the finals, their nationalities now those of independent states. Croatian and Slovenian clubs had pulled out of the Yugoslav league at the end of the 1990/91 season, the Bosnians and Macedonians a year later.

While independent Croatia, Slovenia and Macedonia all took part in the qualifiers for the 1996 European Championship, the ban on the Yugoslav national team was to last throughout the qualifying competitions for USA '94 and Euro '96, and clubs from what was left of the old federal league were barred from European competition until 1995/96.

Today's Yugoslav league comprises teams from Serbia and the tiny republic of Montenegro. Of the giants of the old six-state league, only the Belgrade rivals, Red

Star and Partizan, remain, with provincial opposition – of a sort – coming from Vojvodina Novi Sad and the biggest Montenegrin side, Budućnost Podgorica.

Faced with a dramatically lower standard of football, falling crowds and pitifully low salaries, the stars of Serbian soccer have left in droves. Today more than a thousand Yugoslav players are plying their trade in leagues around the world, along with scores of coaches whose tactical awareness bears testimony to the success of the old federation's national coaching programme.

Historically, socialist Yugoslavia's football mirrored the country's political development. In the years immediately after World War II the game was reorganised along classic Communist lines, 1945 seeing the formation of an army side, Partizan, and a police team, Red Star, as well as the two major Croatian clubs, Dinamo Zagreb and Hajduk Split. While the Belgrade duo were learning to hate each other, the national team strutted their stuff in the tournament 'amateur' socialist countries focused so much attention on – the Olympics. After a remarkable series of silver medals in 1948,

1952 and 1956, Yugoslavia defeated Denmark to win gold at the 1960 Games in Rome. In the same year they finished as runners-up in the first-ever European Championship, then called the Nations' Cup, losing to the Soviet Union in the final.

During the Sixties and Seventies, Yugoslav club sides featured seven times in the finals of European club competitions, and with big domestic clashes regularly attracting 60,000-plus crowds, pressure began to build for clubs to be freed from their Soviet-style structure. Professionalism was gradually introduced in the Seventies, and by the early Eighties clubs had been given the right to run their own affairs, many developing commercial interests around their stadia, effectively turning their land into miniature business parks.

Yugoslavia's liberal (for a Communist country) travel policy allowed players to move abroad to Western clubs from the mid-Sixties, a development which intensified in the Eighties without having much detrimental effect on the domestic game. The most recent, sanctions-inspired exodus has been far more damaging, but now that those same sanctions have been lifted,

History lesson – Serbs, Croats, Slovenes and Bosnians line up together for Yugoslavia at Italia '90

Yugoslav clubs are free to call in the millions of dollars they are due for all those transfers. Money won't bring back the glory days overnight, but it should enable Yugoslav football to start the long, slow climb back to the summit it so nearly scaled before the bloodshed began.

Essential vocabulary

Hello *Zdravo*
Goodbye *Do vidjenja*
Yes *Da*
No *Ne*
Two beers, please *Dva piva, molim*
Thank you *Hvala*
Men's *Muški*
Women's *Žanski*
Where is the stadium? *Gde je stadion?*
What's the score? *Koji je rezultat?*
Referee *Sudija*
Offside *Ofsajd*

Match practice

The crowds may have been driven away by the lack of competition, turning out in numbers only for the big Belgrade derby, but the standard of football in Yugoslavia remains surprisingly high for a country which has effectively lost two generations of star players.

Serbian fans initially found it difficult to get used to supporting their national team again. When the side returned to action against Uruguay in March 1995, sections of the crowd booed the old Yugoslav national anthem, and after Savo Milošević had bagged the only goal of the game in front of the Red Star fans, he turned away from them and ran to celebrate in front of his own Partizan supporters.

With the Partizan and Red Star stadia less than a mile apart, there is no territorial basis to the teams' support. Indeed, every town and village in Serbia has neighbours who support one or other of the big two.

The league season begins at the end of July and breaks for winter between early December and mid-February. The spring season runs until mid-May, slightly later if there is no major international tournament in the summer.

Matches are generally held on Saturdays in the countryside, while the overload of Belgrade teams in the top flight has seen the introduction of staggered fixtures in the capital, with games on Friday and Sunday evenings as well as Saturday. In late spring and early autumn games tend to kick off at 5pm; in the colder months they can start anytime between 1pm and 3pm.

The league

Following the break-up of the old federal league in 1992, a two-tier first division with two groups of ten and a complex end-of-season play-off system was introduced. For the 1996/97 season a twelve-team élite 'A' division was formed, with each team playing each other three times in the campaign. After the usual home and away games, the venue of the third match is determined according to league position, with the top six sides having home advantage in six of the eleven remaining games. At the end of the season the bottom two of 'A' division are replaced by the top two from 'B' division, the third-placed team in 'B' playing off with the tenth-placed side from 'A'.

Below the two first divisions there is a two-tier second division organised along identical lines, comprising semi-professional and amateur clubs. Below that are the republican leagues, the name being a hangover from prewar days when this level was made up of national divisions for the six federal states. Today it consists of four Serbian leagues, one league in Montenegro, and a Belgrade league known as the *Zona*.

Up for the cup

With more than 2000 teams involved, the Yugoslav cup kicks off almost as soon as the previous season has ended, although the big boys don't get involved until the regular season has begun. The format for the early stages of the competition is one-legged ties, with extra time and penalties. The semi-finals are two-legged affairs, as is the final.

Tickets

Tickets (*kartya*) are bought at the stadium and cost 10–20 dinars for standing (*ska-janje*) and 20–40 for seated (*sedenje*) areas. Prices may vary according to the status of the match.

Half-time

Yugoslavia's footballing delicacy is the sunflower seed (*semenke* or *sunje*), toasted black until it resembles a rabbit dung pellet. Outside the stadium, before and especially after the game, fans fill up on a *pljeskavica* – the superior, Serbian version of the hamburger – always freshly grilled and costing around 5 dinars. *Čevapčići*, shish kebab pieces, make an excellent hot sandwich, usually served with salad.

Beer can be bought in any stadium restaurant but is not allowed in the stands or on the terraces.

Action replay

As they did with most embargoed products, the Serbs found a way around international sanctions to get their fix of televised international football. In fact, for as long as the sanctions went on, Serb fans had access to more free European footie TV than anyone else on the continent, as satellite broadcasts from the major European sports channels were pirated and shown by anyone with access to a VCR and a transmitter. Total chaos ensued, with scores of small, private channels offering international football on an *ad hoc* basis.

The state channel TV1 has the rights for Yugoslav domestic football. Live games are broadcast on Friday and Sunday evenings, with a highlights package on Saturdays at 9pm. The Belgrade channel Studio B offers weekend action from the local city league on Fridays or Saturdays, and has a

Basics

To enter Yugoslavia, virtually all require a **visa**. Regulations and cost vary depending on your nationality. As well as paying £20 for the visa, UK citizens currently have to produce a **letter of invitation** from a Yugoslav citizen or organisation. All of this could well change in the near future, so you should consult your Yugoslav embassy.

The Yugoslav currency, the **dinar**, has been pegged to the German mark in an attempt to halt hyper-inflation. The current rate is about four dinars to the mark. You can change money at all banks and hotels, and at Belgrade's main train station and airport. The **black market** offers a significantly better deal and the safest way to change 'black' is at your hotel reception.

Take **plenty of cash**, preferably Deutschmarks, as credit cards are accepted only at the top international hotels. Banks will not give cash against Visa or any other card. Ignore the stickers in shops promising Visa service – these are left over from the pre-sanctions days.

Making an **international call** from Belgrade, let alone the Serbian countryside, is a difficult process. Street phones, which are all coin-operated (minimum 1 dinar), will not allow international calls. You can make such a call from a hotel, but at a high rate. In Belgrade, your best bet is to head for the **post offices** at Takovska 2 or Zmaj Jovina 17. Dial 00, wait for the tone, then dial the country code. The international code for dialling Yugoslavia from outside the country is 381, after which the code for Belgrade is 11, Novi Sad 21, and Podgorica 81.

For travelling out of Belgrade and into the countryside, **trains** leave from Belgrade's Centar train station, while international and domestic bus services leave from the coach station in **Novi Beograd**, Belgrade's new town. However, travelling across the country is difficult and many areas – particularly those adjacent to the Bosnian and Croatian borders, and the ethnic Albanian region of Kosovo – should probably be avoided altogether.

Propaganda war – Red Star's *Delije* ultras get the Serbian flag on European TV, Bari, 1991

daily evening show, *SOS* – an abbreviation for 'Everything About Sport' – which shows goals and highlights, usually around 7pm.

Private channels, such as Palma and Pink, still show foreign matches from the Italian, Spanish and English leagues, whenever they can lay their hands on a tape.

The back page

Yugoslavia had a thriving sports media prior to the war, but many of the magazines, including the popular weekly *Fudball*, have vanished from the newsstands. The daily sports paper is *Sportski Journal* (6 dinars). A technicolour nightmare hardly lending itself to an early morning read, it nonetheless offers authoritative coverage of the domestic game along with international results and news. *Tempo* is an amusing, gossipy sports and lifestyle glossy, published weekly.

Ultra culture

Anyone who saw a game between a Serb club and a Croatian one in the Eighties would have had a taste of what was to come. For while the politicians maintained the Tito-era slogans of brotherhood and unity, on a Saturday afternoon the old hatreds spilled out – and the fixture that aroused the most hatred and violence was Dinamo Zagreb versus Red Star Belgrade.

Today, few opposition fans bother to make the trip to Belgrade, and Red Star's travelling support has vanished. While this is good news for those who like their football hooligan-free, it also means many matches lack atmosphere; only the Belgrade derby and internationals create any.

In the net

There is no Yugoslav-run generic website, but over in the States, Phil Davies hosts the Yugoslav Football Homepage at www.geocities.com/Colosseum/Field/4880/. This is basically just a stats archive, but it contains info on the national team as well as domestic results, and is very efficiently maintained.

Belgrade

Red Star 596   Partizan 599   OFK 601
Radnicki 602   Zemun 602   Cukaricki 602

Like the rest of the country, the Yugoslav capital is slowly getting back to normal after years of international sanctions and the stresses and strains of being on a quasi-war footing. It's a weird and curious city, if rarely a very attractive one. The grounds may be run-down and local enthusiasm muted, but dig a little deeper and you'll still find evidence of Belgrade's long tradition for cool and cultivated football.

The thrilling fields

 Red Star

Stadion Crvena Zvezda, Ljutice Bogdana 1a
Capacity 97,000
Colours Red-and-white striped shirts, red shorts
League champions 1951, 1953, 1956–57, 1959–60, 1964, 1968–70, 1973, 1977, 1980–81, 1984, 1988, 1990–91, 1995
Cup winners 1948–50, 1958–59, 1964, 1968, 1970–71, 1982, 1985, 1990, 1993, 1995–97
European Cup winners 1991

Created by the Communists, Red Star (*Crvena Zvezda* in Serbian) are the club most closely associated with the nationalist regime of Slobodan Milošević. The greatest moment in the club's history, their 1991 European Cup triumph, coincided with the explosion of Serb nationalism and the intoxicating mixture of football glory and war has left its mark on the club. Today even the club's general manager, Vladimir Cvetković, finds time to be the Serbian Minister of Sport, fulfilling both rôles from his office in the stadium complex. Businessmen, *mafiosi*, bureaucrats and Socialist Party politicians all know it pays to be seen at Red Star.

The Communists liked to portray Red Star as the team of the Belgrade workers

and, unlike so many clubs created by such totalitarian régimes, this one successfully established itself as a genuine 'people's team'. When they were formed in 1945, officially as the team of Belgrade university, Red Star took over the site of the popular prewar club Jugoslavija. The stadium was completely redeveloped in the early Sixties into a modern, covered bowl, complete with athletics track. With a vast capacity (the record crowd stands at 96,070 for a Cup-Winners' Cup semi-final against Ferencváros in 1975) and a sizzling atmosphere, the fans nicknamed their ground *Marakana*.

Crvena Zvezda have been a major force in Yugoslav football ever since the Fifties. Inside-right Rajko Mitić, skipper of the successful national team throughout that decade, was the linchpin of the side which lifted the club's first title in 1951, along with long-serving international 'keeper Vladimir Beara. Between 1956 and 1960 Red Star won four titles in five seasons, with left-winger Bora Kostić the fans' favourite, establishing a tradition of wing play which was for many years the hallmark of both Red Star and Yugoslav football. In 1956/57, Kostić and co took part in their first European Cup campaign, which saw them play Manchester United on the eve of the Munich air disaster. They fought through to the semi-final before losing 1–0 to Fiorentina.

By the Sixties Red Star had set up an impressive youth structure, with a soccer academy coaching kids as young as five and an enormous network of scouts operating all over Yugoslavia. One of the first stars to come shining off this production line was Dragan Dzajić, who took Kostic's no. 11 shirt in both club and national colours. Dzajić was the star of the side that won the Yugoslav double in both 1968 and 1969, and his subsequent move to French club Bastia established the trend of Red Star players finishing their careers abroad.

Red Star enjoyed good runs in European competition in the early Seventies under coach Miljan Miljanić, but it was just as Yugoslavia was crumbling that the club's greatest moment beckoned. With a team crammed with talent, such as playmaker Robert Prosinečki, Montenegrin striker Dejan Savićević and midfielder Siniša Mihajlović, they annihilated Rangers and Dynamo Dresden before a last-minute own-goal gave them a 4–3 aggregate win over Bayern Munich in the semi-finals.

In the final they met Marseille in Bari. Marseille had former Red Star hero Dragan Stojković, who surprisingly only made the bench – everyone in Belgrade was convinced he just couldn't face playing against Red Star. The match itself, between two sides capable of breathtaking football, was a dull affair, Red Star winning a shoot-out they later admitted to having played for. It was a sad and inappropriate way for the club to reach their goal.

In the face of impending ethnic conflict, the class of '91 disintegrated. Savićević,

Mihajlović, utility man Vladimir Jugović and the spectacular Macedonian goal-poacher, Darko Pančev, all went to Italy. Prosinečki was sold to Real Madrid and, despite being half-Serbian, went on to captain Croatia. By the time Red Star were knocked out of the following year's Champions' League by Sampdoria, not one of the European Cup-winning side remained.

Yet the club they left behind continued to attract the best talent in what was left of Yugoslavia, and three domestic titles since the federation's break-up have confirmed Red Star's status as no. 1 in Serbia. Getting back to the top in Europe will take a little more time.

Here we go!
Ride bus #42 from Bulevar JNA for 25 minutes, getting off at Ljutice Bogdana.

Swift half
If time is on your side, get off bus #42 a stop earlier at Trg Oslobodjenja, where there are a number of grills and bars. **Pronto Pizzeria** serves good Italian food as well as the usual Serbian meaty snacks.

Red Star, Crvena Zvezda, *Marakana* – no matter what you call it, the stadium is a mighty sight

It also has a good range of foreign beers. Next door is a decent but unnamed traditional Serbian bar. Just by the bus stop is the **Avala** – the Red Star restaurant where ex-players and influential fans chew the fat.

After the game, visit **Caffè Roma Belgrano** on Bore Stankovića, right next to the national library. The bar is owned by Red Star and AS Roma fan Dejan, who has filled his tiny, shiny bar with memorabilia from both clubs – real espresso and cappuccino on the menu, Red Star club song on the tannoy.

Face of today – Red Star striker Dragan Vulević

Publications

Programmes are produced only for European club games and international matches. They are usually dual-language and cost around 10 dinars.

Club shop

Underneath the west stand, next to the supermarket, is the **Red Star Boutique** (Mon–Fri 9am–5pm, matchdays 9am 'til kick-off). Prepare yourself. As well as the usual scarves and hats you can buy ex-Red Star hooligan chief and suspected war criminal Arkan's official wedding video, his popstar bride Ćeca's *Greatest Hits* and 'I Am a Serbian' T-shirts emblazoned with a roaring tiger, symbol of Serb aggression. Do yourself a favour – choose the 'Best in the World '91' scarf instead.

Ultra culture

In the Eighties, Red Star's ultras had a well-earned reputation as one of the best-organised and potentially violent units in European football. For home games, they would meet at nine in the morning to drink at the Zeleni Venac marketplace, marching *en masse* from there through the city and up to the *Marakana*. The journey would take around an hour, perhaps a tad longer for those smashing windows or engaging in running battles with police.

Today Red Star's *Delije* ('strong boys') would scarcely rate a mention in a European hooliganism survey, their organisation weakened by war and the welter of unappealing fixtures served up by Serb-only football. If you see trouble, it's most likely coming from the *Dieselistas*, so-called because of their fondness for the Diesel designer jeanswear label, who gather at the south end of the stadium.

In the net

Red Star Belgrade are the only Yugoslav club to host an official website, at: www.beograd.com/redstar/. The homepage is a multimedia extravaganza of moving graphics, icons and downloadable songs, guaranteed to test both your computer's memory and your patience. Beneath the gimmicks, there is surprisingly little in the way of solid info. More informative is the unofficial site hosted by Radovan Stojanović at: ourworld.compuserve.com/home-pages/delija/homepage.htm. You'll find pictures of fans, latest results, a brief history of the club and more pictures of fans.

Partizan

Stadion Partizan, Humska 1
Capacity 50,000
Colours Black-and-white striped shirts, white shorts
League champions 1947, 1949, 1961–3, 1965, 1976, 1978, 1983, 1986–7, 1993–4, 1996–97
Cup winners 1947, 1952, 1954, 1957, 1989, 1992, 1994

Tito's *partizans* were the Communist guerrillas who liberated Yugoslavia from Fascism in World War II. Glorified in street names,

youth groups and theatres throughout the former Yugoslav federation, they were soon to have Belgrade's army team named after them, too. It was no surprise that they swiftly established themselves as one of the country's leading clubs.

Their ground, first known as the Stadion JNA (Yugoslav National Army Stadium) was built on the hillside above Red Star's *Marakana*. It is a more modest, open affair than its neighbour. Politicians might need roofs and VIP lounges; soldiers can stand in the rain.

In their early years Partizan enjoyed the usual Communist army privilege of being able to commandeer the best local talent. Two years after their formation they had lifted their first double, and the Partizan side of the Fifties provided several of the national Olympic team, including two footballing legends, Stjepan Bobek and Milan Galić. In the mid-Fifties, the club were run by an army general named Franjo Tudjman, who as president of Croatia would lead his

Belgrade essentials

Belgrade's **airport**, 18km from the city centre, is regularly served by international flights from all major European capitals. A shuttle bus leaves half-an-hour after every flight and costs 15 dinars. It calls at the central bus station in Belgrade's new town, Novi Beograd, before terminating at the Hotel Slavia in Belgrade proper.

A better bet, if you have accommodation pre-booked, is the **private minibus** (25 dinars) which will take you to your hotel or any address in Belgrade. Taxis from the airport are expensive and best avoided.

In the city, **public transport** consists of buses, trolleybuses and trams. A one-day ticket (*Dnevna Bus Kartya*) costs 15 dinars and is valid on all services. Buy tickets from kiosks and tobacconists. Public transport runs between 4am and 11.30pm, after which night trams run every 30–60 minutes. Note there is no central 'hub' for Belgrade's tram or bus network.

Taxi drivers will try to rip you off, but those bearing the logo *Beo-taxi* have earned a reasonable reputation – call ☎011/443 443 to book.

The main **tourist information centre** is in the underpass at Terazije (open daily 8am–8pm, ☎011/635 343 or 635 622). There are also offices at the central train station (daily 7am–9pm, ☎011/646 240) and at the airport (daily 7am–10pm, ☎011/602 326).

Street maps of the city can be purchased at tourist information, bookshops and kiosks, for around 11 dinars. Although these will use Latin type, most street signs are in the **Cyrillic alphabet**.

Belgrade has no real **listings magazine** for nightlife but *Beorama* (10 dinars) is a monthly cultural guide. The tourist office gives out the occasional programme of events in English.

country in the war against the Serb-dominated Yugoslav National Army forty years later. While Tudjman's football background gave plenty of ammunition to Belgrade's political satirists during the war, his lasting legacy was to change the club's colours from red-and-blue to the now famous black-and-white stripes.

When Tito rejected the Soviet road in the Fifties, the generals lost their grip on the club and Partizan had to compete with everyone else. In 1963 the club became officially independent from the army, although a firm link remained until the late Eighties. The gradual weakening of army influence increased the club's willingness to welcome an Albanian, a Bosnian or a Slovene into their ranks – in contrast to Red Star's aggressive pro-Serb stance. The result was the creation of a support base outside of Serbia which remains today, albeit to a lesser extent.

Despite regular success at home, Partizan have a poor record in Europe. Their best performance came more than thirty years ago, when they reached the 1966 European Cup final before losing 2–1 to the immortal Real Madrid. Defeat marked the end of an era of domestic domination; between 1966 and 1975 Partizan failed to win a single trophy, and even their status as Belgrade's 'other club' seemed in danger, as twice in the early Seventies OFK finished above them in the league.

The rot wasn't stopped until the mid-Eighties, as Partizan twice pipped Red Star to the title on the last day of the season in 1986 and 1987. Those campaigns, with their huge crowds, brave challenges from Velež Mostar and FK Sarajevo and Croat successes in the cup, saw the multi-ethnic Yugoslav championship at its best.

By contrast, Partizan's successive title wins in 1996 and 1997 have done little

Getting his cards – if he can keep his mouth shut, Niša Saveljić will be Partizan's next big export

more than confirm their position as the only effective challengers to Red Star. The lack of real competition outside of the old enemy has driven many fans away from home matches. The club has survived on the sale of talents such as Predrag Mijatović, Savo Milošević and Saša Ćurčić to the West. But the Partizan spirit is dying.

Here we go!

Take bus #42 from Bulevar JNA, get off at Trg Oslobodjenja, then walk up Dr Milutina Ivkovića for ten minutes to the ground.

Swift half

As with Red Star games, fans tend to gather at Trg Oslobodjenja for a pre-match beer and bite. The **Restoran Partizan**, inside the stadium, is an upmarket affair with a full menu.

Club shop

There is no official shop, but you'll find stands outside the ground on matchdays.

Ultra culture

Partizan's fans are the *Grobari* – 'Gravediggers' – and while their rivalry with the *Delije* of Red Star remains as tense and potentially explosive as ever, this lot can boast nothing like the troublemaking tradition of their neighbours. Few now actually turn up for home matches, and even fewer carry their shovels to away games – not even those played just across town at minor Belgrade clubs.

In the net

Zoran Stojanović's original Partizan site is only sporadically available at www.ica.net. A recent alternative, with the advantage of actually being run from Belgrade itself, has been set up by Vladan Cosić at: www.beograd.com/vlaja/fcparti.htm. Like the Red Star sites it's great on graphics but less forthcoming when it comes to providing information. An eccentric gathering of European club links embraces, for some reason, Ajax, Milan, Beitar Jerusalem and Crystal Palace among others.

Groundhopping

Such is Belgrade's domination over the Yugoslav game that at any given time there will be at least seven or eight clubs in either 'A' or 'B' divisions of the top flight. Matches at any of these grounds lack atmosphere but you'll be pleasantly surprised by the standard of football – these clubs may be struggling but the Serbian language, it seems, has no equivalent of 'hit-and-hope'.

OFK

Omladinski stadion, Mije Kovačevića 10
Capacity 25,000
Colours All white with blue trim
League champions 1931, 1933, 1935–36, 1939
Cup winners 1953, 1958, 1962, 1966

Along with Radnički, Omladinski Futbal Klub are the great survivors from Belgrade's prewar football scene. Founded in 1911 as BSK, they won the league five times in the Thirties. Their only successes since then have been in the cup, but in 1963 OFK beat Napoli in the quarter-finals of the European Cup-Winners' Cup before losing out to Spurs in the semis.

In the late Sixties OFK fielded a front-line of The Three S's – Joska Skoblar, Paja Samaudžje and current national-team coach Slobodan Santrac. It was during this era that the team's cavalier style earned them the nickname 'Romantics'. OFK have always attracted a following of bohemian and intellectual fans, alienated by the militarism of Partizan and nationalism of Red Star. But the romance has little chance of flourishing so long as OFK continue to sell their best players to the two Belgrade giants.

Today the Omladinski stadium, which once resembled an amphitheatre, is a sad, crumbling, graffiti-blighted mess. To reach it, take bus #27A from Bulevar Revolucije to **Partizanski Put**, getting off just by the huge Partizan cemetery – about a twenty-minute ride. Enjoy a meal before the game

Slobodan Santrac – OFK's most famous son

at the **Restoran OFK** behind the main stand, and a post-match beer in the **OFK Caffe Beostar** next door. And don't miss the *Kladionica* – the last surviving stadium bookmakers in Belgrade – on the corner of the west and south stands.

Radnički

Stadion Radnički, Tosin Bunar 190, Novi Beograd
Capacity 4000
Colours Red-and-white shirts, blue shorts

Red Star may have the name and the connections, but Radnički are the original Belgrade communist club. Their name means 'Workers' and their badge, dating from 1920 when the Communist Party set up the club, bears a glorious *Crvena Zvezda* – a symbol which was then one of change rather than of the status quo.

After World War II the team spent most of their time in the Yugoslav second

division, and have barely improved their position since the disintegration of the old federal republic. Radnički's finest hour was a 5–3 defeat by Partizan in the 1957 cup final, but hope, as they say, springs eternal.

Take a fifteen-minute ride on bus #82 from Novi Beograd bus station to **Studentska**. The stadium is tucked in a hillside, where **Restoran Radnički** serves up roast pork off the spit.

FK Zemun

Gradski stadion, Ugrinovacka 80, Zemun
Capacity 15,000
Colours Green-and-blue striped shirts, blue shorts

The fishing town of Zemun, on the Novi Beograd side of the river Sava, is a taste of traditional Serbian country life and a popular weekend escape, offering a relaxed contrast to the city centre. Its football team FK Zemun are enjoying their return to the first division, and even got a taste of European action in the 1996 Intertoto Cup. As factory team Galenika they spent most of the Fifties and Sixties battling to stay in the top drawer, finally succumbing to relegation in 1967.

Crowds rarely touch a thousand but the ground is worth visiting for the **Zemun Café** next to the main entrance, with its classic black-and-white blow-ups of Sixties stars like Milijaš Milan. Take bus #84 from Gavrila Principa across the river, getting off at **Dobrovoljacka** – the journey takes half an hour.

Ćukarički

Ćukarički stadion, Beogradski Bataljona 25
Capacity 8000
Colours White shirts, black shorts

Ćukarički is where the Belgrade *nouveau riche* are building their new houses. The club sponsors, property company Stankolm, are doing much of the selling, and with their profits have taken this local club from the Belgrade league up to the first division, though how long they can stay up remains to be seen. The **Restoran Ćukarički**, to the right of the car park, seems to attract more punters than the team.

Take bus #23, #37 or #58 from Kneza Milosa to **Beogradski Bataljona**, getting off by the McDonald's. Prepare yourself for a hike up the steep hill to the ground – this team aren't nicknamed 'The Highlanders' for nothing.

Eat, drink, sleep...

Bars and clubs

The once vibrant, cosmopolitan Belgrade social scene was hit hard by war and sanctions. But since the embargo was lifted the city has started to warm up, albeit in a somewhat haphazard way. Cafés, bars and clubs are popping up – and closing down – all the time. However, anything called 'nightclub' is best avoided unless you like the idea of checking in your Makrov pistol

The ultimate hooligan

With the wind of war blowing, everyone in Yugoslavia knew something was going to happen in 1991. The Eighties had seen ethnic-based football hooliganism on the rise, and the tensions between **Serbia** and **Croatia**, in particular, had spilled out onto the terraces long before the first shots were fired.

The **violent riot** that took place when Dinamo played Red Star in Zagreb in 1991 is seen by many as the starting point of open hostilities. The Croats claimed that the mostly Serbian police in Zagreb stood by as Red Star fans piled into the Dinamo section of the ground. Dinamo midfielder **Zvonimir Boban** intervened and got a taste of Serbian law and order for his trouble.

The game has become one of the many Yugoslav war myths, and the truth about what really happened has been lost among the rival boasts of heroism. One man who has certainly never been shy to boast of his rôle in the day's events was the then-leader of the Red Star ultras, Zeljko Ražnjatović, better known by his nickname **Arkan**. He was arrested at the game and, while there were to be no more matches between Red Star and Dinamo, Arkan and his boys from the terraces were to return to Croatia, this time in battle fatigues and carrying guns rather than baseball bats.

Arkan became leader of 'The Tigers', a group of assorted volunteers and ex-convicts who carried out the first wave of ethnic cleansing in Croatia – many of them were the same hooligans he had led to confrontation at the Dinamo stadium.

You might have thought that a major European football club would be slightly embarrassed to have an alleged war criminal as leader of its ultras. Not a bit of it. Walk into the VIP bar at Red Star's stadium and you'll find a picture of Arkan alongside those of the 1991 European Cup-winning side. Indeed, returning from the fighting in Croatia in the autumn of 1991, Arkan was given pride of place as the club celebrated its Intercontinental Cup win over Colo-Colo, and his presence helped to turn the party into a Serb nationalist rally. After the team had paraded their silverware, Arkan ran to the home end holding his own 'trophy' – a street sign from a cleansed Croat village.

Today, Arkan has swapped the terraces for the boardroom and become a powerful figure in the Belgrade underworld. Bring up his name in conversation and the topic will be swiftly changed. What is known is that he has a patisserie shop and his own political party, both located opposite the *Marakana* car park. Unable to find a way into the powerful leadership at Red Star, however, he is believed to be supporting minor Belgrade outfit Obilić, although as with most things concerning Arkan's activities this cannot be confirmed...and you don't want to ask him.

with your macintosh. The best parties are usually out-of-town and unadvertised, although you may get some info from one of the student clubs. For late-night drinking and dining, head for the boat bars on the Novi Beograd side of the Sava, next to the two main bridges, Most bratsvo i jedinstvo and Stari savski most. The **local beer** tends to be weak but draught Bip and Jelen are passable. A pint will cost 7–12 dinars. Expect to pay twice that for imported Heineken or Kaiser. Serbian **plum brandy**, *Slivovitz*, is the traditional chaser, best served warm. All bars listed are in the centre of the city.

Bitef Club, Drinčičeva ul 1, on corner of Bajloui market square. Crowded, fun disco with expensive beer and pumping sound system. Partizan fans on the door.

Caffe Club Panta Rei, Tadeuša Koskuškog 63. Live jazz and rock club, with a bar offering everything you thought Belgrade wouldn't have. Live music at weekends. Open 9pm–2am.

Dom omladine, Makedonska 22. 'The Youth Club' has jazz and posing midweek, an all-or-nothing disco at the weekend.

Irish Pub, Kneza Miloša 14–16. A fair effort, with the Irish 'theme' kept to a minimum and two floors full of students and intellectuals. Kilkenny and Guinness on draught.

Restoran snezana, Knez Mihajlova 50. Bang in the middle of the main pedestrian shopping street. At night the terrace is a perfect spot for watching young Belgrade while downing 7-dinar Jelen beer. Fine sandwiches plus a full menu.

Restaurants

During the war, eating out in Belgrade became so **expensive** it went out of fashion. Even today, a decent meal with drinks for two will cost 100 dinars. Surprisingly, the restaurants inside the main hotels are reasonably priced. Though the nationalists wouldn't admit it, Serbian food displays a distinct Turkish influence and basically consists of variations of grilled meat.

Dva Bela Goluba, 29 Novembra ul. Considered *the* Serbian restaurant, worth the expense. The mixed grill is a monster meat feast.

Franchet d'Esperey, Bulevar JNA 18a. Busy, authentic, affordable Italian close to the *Marakana*.

Gradska Caffe, Trg Republike. Excellent pizza, coffee and cakes. Ideal for an *al fresco* lunch.

Grčka Kraljica, Knez Mihajlova 51. The Serbs love Greek food and this is the best place for char-grilled Hellenic standards.

Restoran Medera, Bulevar revolucije 43. Famed for its football clientèle, this is where Dejan Savičević and Savo Milošević go to catch up on the gossip and meet their agents. Pricey Serbian menu.

Accommodation

Rooms are not cheap in Belgrade, a city whose hotels were built for the capital of a much bigger and wealthier country than Yugoslavia is today. A mid-range hotel will charge DM80 a night, in cash and in Deutschmarks please. Smaller hotels will take dinars, but the rate charged is often higher than if paid in hard currency. Ask tourist information about **private rooms**.

Centar, Trg bratstva i jedinstva (π011/644 055). Good value, but with just 43 rooms available, it's worth booking in advance.

Hotel Park, Njegoševa 4 (π011/334 723). Fair-priced three-star place in the centre of town. A bar next door has constant footie on the box.

Hyatt Regency, Milentija Popovića 5, Novi Beograd (π011/222 234). Luxury international five-star hotel, with swimming pool and an outstanding kitchen.

Studentski Dom, Trg bratstva i jedinstva 1a. Large youth hostel with 450 rooms including doubles and singles.

Stay in touch with us!

ROUGH*NEWS* is Rough Guides' free newsletter. In three issues a year we give you news, travel issues, music reviews, readers' letters and the latest dispatches from authors on the road.

direct orders from

Amsterdam	1-85828-218-7	UK£8.99	US$14.95	CAN$19.99
Andalucia	1-85828-219-5	9.99	16.95	22.99
Australia	1-85828-220-9	13.99	21.95	29.99
Bali	1-85828-134-2	8.99	14.95	19.99
Barcelona	1-85828-221-7	8.99	14.95	19.99
Berlin	1-85828-129-6	8.99	14.95	19.99
Belgium & Luxembourg	1-85828-222-5	10.99	17.95	23.99
Brazil	1-85828-102-4	9.99	15.95	19.99
Britain	1-85828-208-X	12.99	19.95	25.99
Brittany & Normandy	1-85828-224-1	9.99	16.95	22.99
Bulgaria	1-85828-183-0	9.99	16.95	22.99
California	1-85828-181-4	10.99	16.95	22.99
Canada	1-85828-130-X	10.99	14.95	19.99
China	1-85828-225-X	15.99	24.95	32.99
Corfu	1-85828-226-8	8.99	14.95	19.99
Corsica	1-85828-227-6	9.99	16.95	22.99
Costa Rica	1-85828-136-9	9.99	15.95	21.99
Crete	1-85828-132-6	8.99	14.95	18.99
Cyprus	1-85828-182-2	9.99	16.95	22.99
Czech & Slovak Republics	1-85828-121-0	9.99	16.95	22.99
Egypt	1-85828-188-1	10.99	17.95	23.99
Europe	1-85828-159-8	14.99	19.95	25.99
England	1-85828-160-1	10.99	17.95	23.99
First Time Europe	1-85828-270-5	7.99	9.95	12.99
Florida	1-85828-184-4	10.99	16.95	22.99
France	1-85828-228-4	12.99	19.95	25.99
Germany	1-85828-128-8	11.99	17.95	23.99
Goa	1-85828-275-6	8.99	14.95	19.99
Greece	1-85828-131-8	9.99	16.95	20.99
Greek Islands	1-85828-163-6	8.99	14.95	19.99
Guatemala	1-85828-189-X	10.99	16.95	22.99
Hawaii: Big Island	1-85828-158-X	8.99	12.95	16.99
Hawaii	1-85828-206-3	10.99	16.95	22.99
Holland	1-85828-229-2	10.99	17.95	23.99
Hong Kong	1-85828-187-3	8.99	14.95	19.99
Hungary	1-85828-123-7	8.99	14.95	19.99
India	1-85828-200-4	14.99	23.95	31.99
Ireland	1-85828-179-2	10.99	17.95	23.99
Italy	1-85828-167-9	12.99	19.95	25.99
Jamaica	1-85828-230-6	9.99	16.95	22.99
Kenya	1-85828-192-X	11.99	18.95	24.99
London	1-85828-231-4	9.99	15.95	21.99
Mallorca & Menorca	1-85828-165-2	8.99	14.95	19.99
Malaysia, Singapore & Brunei	1-85828-232-2	11.99	18.95	24.99
Mexico	1-85828-044-3	10.99	16.95	22.99
Morocco	1-85828-040-0	9.99	16.95	21.99
Moscow	1-85828-118-0	8.99	14.95	19.99
Nepal	1-85828-190-3	10.99	17.95	23.99
New York	1-85828-171-7	9.99	15.95	21.99
Norway	1-85828-234-9	10.99	17.95	23.99
Pacific Northwest	1-85828-092-3	9.99	14.95	19.99

In the UK, Rough Guides are available from all good bookstores, but can be obtained from Penguin by contacting: Penguin Direct, Penguin Books Ltd, Bath Road, Harmondsworth, West Drayton, Middlesex UB7 0DA; or telephone the credit line on 0181-899 4036 (9am–5pm) and ask for Penguin Direct. Visa and Access accepted. Delivery will normally be within 14 working days. Penguin Direct ordering facilities are only available in the UK and the USA. The availability and published prices quoted are correct at the time of going to press but are subject to alteration without prior notice.

around the world

Paris	1-85828-235-7	8.99	14.95	19.99
Poland	1-85828-168-7	10.99	17.95	23.99
Portugal	1-85828-180-6	9.99	16.95	22.99
Prague	1-85828-122-9	8.99	14.95	19.99
Provence	1-85828-127-X	9.99	16.95	22.99
Pyrenees	1-85828-093-1	8.99	15.95	19.99
Rhodes & the Dodecanese	1-85828-120-2	8.99	14.95	19.99
Romania	1-85828-097-4	9.99	15.95	21.99
San Francisco	1-85828-185-7	8.99	14.95	19.99
Scandinavia	1-85828-236-5	12.99	20.95	27.99
Scotland	1-85828-166-0	9.99	16.95	22.99
Sicily	1-85828-178-4	9.99	16.95	22.99
Singapore	1-85828-135-0	8.99	14.95	19.99
Soutwest USA	1-85828-239-X	10.99	16.95	22.99
Spain	1-85828-240-3	11.99	18.95	24.99
St Petersburg	1-85828-133-4	8.99	14.95	19.99
Sweden	1-85828-241-1	10.99	17.95	23.99
Thailand	1-85828-140-7	10.99	17.95	24.99
Tunisia	1-85828-139-3	10.99	17.95	24.99
Turkey	1-85828-242-X	12.99	19.95	25.99
Tuscany & Umbria	1-85828-243-8	10.99	17.95	23.99
USA	1-85828-161-X	14.99	19.95	25.99
Venice	1-85828-170-9	8.99	14.95	19.99
Vietnam	1-85828-191-1	9.99	15.95	21.99
Wales	1-85828-245-4	10.99	17.95	23.99
Washington DC	1-85828-246-2	8.99	14.95	19.99
West Africa	1-85828-101-6	15.99	24.95	34.99
More Women Travel	1-85828-098-2	10.99	16.95	22.99
Zimbabwe & Botswana	1-85828-186-5	11.99	18.95	24.99

Phrasebooks

Czech	1-85828-148-2	3.50	5.00	7.00
French	1-85828-144-X	3.50	5.00	7.00
German	1-85828-146-6	3.50	5.00	7.00
Greek	1-85828-145-8	3.50	5.00	7.00
Italian	1-85828-143-1	3.50	5.00	7.00
Mexican	1-85828-176-8	3.50	5.00	7.00
Portuguese	1-85828-175-X	3.50	5.00	7.00
Polish	1-85828-174-1	3.50	5.00	7.00
Spanish	1-85828-147-4	3.50	5.00	7.00
Thai	1-85828-177-6	3.50	5.00	7.00
Turkish	1-85828-173-3	3.50	5.00	7.00
Vietnamese	1-85828-172-5	3.50	5.00	7.00

Reference

Classical Music	1-85828-113-X	12.99	19.95	25.99
Internet	1-85828-198-9	5.00	8.00	10.00
Jazz	1-85828-137-7	16.99	24.95	34.99
Opera	1-85828-138-5	16.99	24.95	34.99
Reggae	1-85828-247-0	12.99	19.95	25.99
Rock	1-85828-201-2	17.99	26.95	35.00
World Music	1-85828-017-6	16.99	22.95	29.99

In the USA, or for international orders, charge your order by Master Card or Visa (US$15.00 minimum order): call 1-800-253-6476; or send orders, with complete name, address and zip code, and list price, plus $2.00 shipping and handling per order to: Consumer Sales, Penguin USA, PO Box 999 – Dept #17109, Bergenfield, NJ 07621. No COD. Prepay foreign orders by international money order, a cheque drawn on a US bank, or US currency. No postage stamps are accepted. All orders are subject to stock availability at the time they are processed. Refunds will be made for books not available at that time. Please allow a minimum of four weeks for delivery.

Good Vibrations!

ROUGH GUIDES ON THE WEB

Visit our websites www.roughguides.com and www.hotwired.com/rough for news about the latest books, online travel guides and updates, and the full text of our Rough Guide to Rock – all 1058 entries!

AT GOOD BOOKSHOPS · DISTRIBUTED BY PENGUIN

Losing the European Cup Final to Red Star Belgrade was bad enough

But trying to get a copy of Football Europe in Burnley can be murder

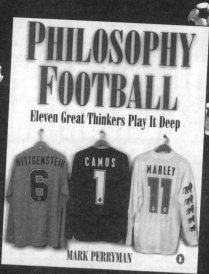

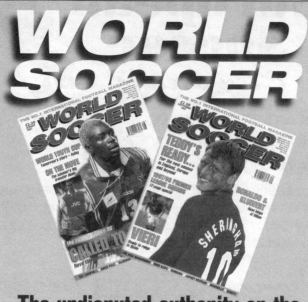